# Global Home Business Directory

---

*Official Publication of the Network Marketing and Direct Selling Industries*

---

**Marketing Solutions, Inc.**

**HC 6, Box 58A**

**Aitkin, MN 56431**

Printed in the United States

I

# The Global Home Based Business Directory® Is Proudly

**Supplier Member**

# MADE IN THE USA

**MLMIA**
Multi Level
Marketing Industry
Association
**USA Corporate Support Member**

---

## Published by Marketing Solutions, Inc.

## Disclaimer

Marketing Solutions, Inc. has attempted to make this directory as accurate as possible. There may be mistakes of content and typography; however, the publisher makes no guarantees, warranties, or representations of any kind. This directory is designed as an all-encompassing sourcebook for the network marketing and direct selling industry. The reader is urged to investigate and verify information and its applicability under any particular situation or circumstance.

The publisher assumes no liability or responsibility to anyone with respect to contracts, negotiations or agreements that may result from information in this directory, or for any loss or damage caused or alleged to have been caused directly or indirectly by such information. If legal advice or expert assistance is required, the services of a competent professional should be contacted.

ISBN - 0-9650208-3-5

# Get in on the ground floor with Eventus!

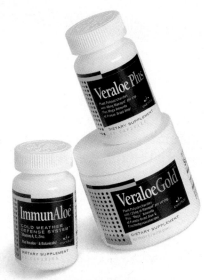

Unbelievable ground-floor earnings opportunity backed by 18 years of stability await those who join Eventus International as we are launching the most exciting network marketing opportunity of the new millennium! Eventus blasts you into the booming $12 billion a year nutraceutical market with the world's most advanced total wellness products, the best pay plan in existence and cutting-edge e-commerce technology. Enjoy a lucrative, flexible, home-based career, with more time for the better things in life like travel and golf. How much you earn and when you work is up to you. With Eventus, your success is unlimited!

If you're serious about your financial future, join the thousands of individuals who are living their dreams with Eventus.

## Real Nutrition Real Results

Eventus innovation leads the multi-billion dollar nutraceutical revolution with patented technologies, advanced ingredients and next-generation formulas that deliver real nutrition at the cellular level, building total health and wellness. Revolutionary Eventus products include: **Heritage Gold Formulas**™, the first and only line of nutraceuticals uniquely customized by a person's heritage. **Veraloe Plus**™ and **Veraloe Gold**™, daily all-natural immune stimulators.

## Immediate and residual income.

The Eventus compensation plan offers higher commissions and overrides, and more bonuses than other network marketing plans. Earn immediate income, build long-term prosperity with lucrative sustainable downlines and receive multiple paychecks every month. Eventus has the stability of founding company BeautiControl,® one of the world's most successful direct sales wellness companies with 18 years in the business.

## Competitive e-commerce support!

From virtual offices to personalized Distributor web pages to electronic ordering and sponsoring, you are on-line and ready to do business in the 21st century.

*Richard Howard, president of Eventus*

*"Eventus offers what virtually no other network marketing opportunity can: a golden, ground-floor opportunity backed by founding company BeautiControl, an international direct sales firm with 18 years in business."*

## Team Eventus

Some of the world's greatest sports legends choose Eventus products to enhance total health and wellness.

- **Nolan Ryan,** National Baseball Hall of Fame inductee with unprecedented 27-year major league pitching career.

# eventus
International

Contact Eventus now at **1-800-943-8085** or www.eventusonline.com for a free information package.

# Publisher's Note

The opinions, recommendations, claims and accuracy appearing within this publication are those of the writers and authors themselves and are in no manner to be construed as statements, positions or endorsements by Marketing Solutions, Inc., publishers of the Global Home Based Business Directory.

# We're Independent

For the record, the Global Home Based Business Directory is published and owned in its entirety by Marketing Solutions, Inc., a Minnesota corporation. None of the shareholders of the corporation has any affiliation, relationship or vested interest in any network marketing or direct selling company. Conversely, no advertisers or network marketing/direct selling company, their employees or representatives possess any ownership or investment in Marketing Solutions, Inc. Only in this manner are we able to serve all companies in a fair, objective, uncompromising and unbiased fashion.

# Editorial Privilege

All companies profiled in this directory were granted total control over the content of their messages. All statements and claims were published as received. Editing and proofreading were limited to reduction of word count and grammar editing to conform to our page format. We also assume no responsibility for typographical errors once the final company copy has been submitted and prepared for printing.

Marketing Solutions, Inc. shall be held harmless by any statements, opinions and claims expressed herein by advertisers or network marketing/direct selling companies.

# It's a beautiful life!

## Flexibility, excellent earning opportunities, unlimited rewards with **BeautiControl**®!

*A rewarding new life awaits you at BeautiControl. As one of the most successful home-based skin care and beauty businesses for 18 years, BeautiControl has helped thousands of people achieve their financial dreams with groundbreaking products, a simple success plan and lucrative earning opportunities!*

## Groundbreaking products!

Developed by leading scientists in our Research Institute, BeautiControl's cutting-edge products literally sell themselves! Our revolutionary Regeneration Gold® and Cell Block-C™ skin duo actually helps repair dangerous precancerous skin cell damage while generating fresh, new skin cells, and prevents future damage with antioxidant vitamin C free-radical fighters and daily SPF 20.

BeautiControl also offers advanced skin care, color-coded cosmetics, nutritional supplements, therapeutic bath and body treatments and special problem solvers.

## Incredible income, fast!

With BeautiControl's exclusive Fast Track Star Bonus Plan, you can earn incredible income, fast. There's no waiting! Earn lucrative direct commissions and bonuses, and multiple monthly paychecks. BeautiControl provides everything you need to succeed, including professional training and our easy step-by-step Planner for success.

## A fun, flexible lifestyle!

Choose the hours that are best for you and enjoy more time for yourself and your family. How much you earn and when you work is up to you!

## With BeautiControl, you can:

▶ Work from home

▶ Set your own hours: full or part-time

▶ Earn immediate income and lucrative direct commissions

▶ Earn diamond jewelry, spectacular vacations and a company car for a job well done

▶ Have fun meeting new friends and helping others

▶ Grow personally and professionally

## Getting started is simple!

*Call a BeautiControl Consultant in your area, call 1-800-BEAUTI-1 or visit www.beauticontrol.com*

BEAUTICONTROL®
THE WORLD'S PREMIER SKIN CARE AND IMAGE COMPANY®

# Global Home Based Business Directory®

Volume Two - 2000 Edition
Printed in the U.S.A.
A publication of Marketing Solutions, Inc.
HC 6, Box 58A, Aitkin, MN 56431
Editorial Office:
R.R. 2, Box 183, McGregor, MN 55760
E-mail: global@mlecmn.net
Web site: www.ghbbd.com
Fax-on-Demand: (512) 505-6850
Phone: (800) 496-0277
Fax: (218) 927-4613

Publisher – **Jerry Hoffman**
Associate Publisher – **Jeffrey S. Hoffman**
Editor – **Michael A. Hoffman**
Associate Editor – **Bud Meier**
Marketing Director – **Vernard Soper**
Production Director – **Susana Valdez**
Circulation Director – **Marguerite Chapman**
Public Relations Director – **Richard Foster**
Fulfillment Director – **Richard Draughon**
Cover Design – **Larry Ruppert**
Creative Design – **Jeff Scott**

**Darleen J. Hoffman** – President

**Contributing Writers:** Peter McGugan, Jerry York, Carrol Leclerc, Scott Morris, Leighton Kaonohi, Freya Manfred, Frank Clancy, Bernie Herlihy, Warren Wechsler, Arlene Weintraub, Mike Spataro, Adrian Miller, Jeffrey Dobkin, William J. McDonald, David M. Anderson, Dan Jensen, David H. Sandler, Leonard W. Clements, Joyce Barrie, Herschell Gordon Lewis, Jay Rifenbary, Keith Petersen, James Law, Robert Van Reypen, Alan Rothman, Tomina Edmark, Erik Van Alstine, Matt Allen, Edie Jeffers, Jesse Hardman, Paul Lambert, Lloyd Langdon, Sherri Mead, Ridgely Goldsborough, Carol Wheeler, Karen Hube, Scott DeGarmo, Carmen Valdez

**Legal Contibutors:** Gerald P. Nerha, D. Jack Smith, Jr.

# Our New Look

Of the many changes we implemented in this, our second edition of a publication designed and edited to serve the network marketing industry, two stand at the head of the class. First and foremost is our name change from the International Network Marketing Directory to Global Home Based Business Directory. Obviously, the latter title better defines our objectives and in the process allows us a broader reach -- home-based business. However, not for a moment have we abandoned our primary function; that is to publish a directory that will serve as the official standard bearer in print for the network marketing industry. On that score, we feel confident our mission has been accomplished, which brings us to the second most significant change that indelibly validates our commitment to the network marketing industry. We have selected 100 of the premier companies in the land for placement in this edition. Each company selected has been awarded an unedited full page profile to tell their personal story to our millions of readers and subscribers. We could well have published 200 -- 300, or more. In the interest of credibility, however, we limited our selection to only those companies that have maintained a standard of excellence throughout the years, or, in several cases, a handful of unknowns our panel felt were odds on favorites to succeed. Finally, please note our front cover statement: "Official Publication of the Network Marketing and Direct Selling Industries." Network marketing and direct selling? Indeed! The decision to include many of the time honored direct selling companies proved a natural and fitting extension of our editorial format. After all, most of the network marketing companies profiled are members of the Direct Selling Association, the official body of the direct selling industry. What better showcase to dramatically increase name recognition throughout the planet than the largest distributed publication ever produced for either industry? Once reviewed, we feel confident you will share our conclusion we have remained faithful to our pledge all the while playing a catalytical role in the ascendancy of network marketing and the home-based business industry at large around the globe.

**Jeffrey Hoffman, Associate Publisher**

# Opportunity has its rewards

*A business plan built for two... we love it!*

**The opportunity to build your own business can be rewarding in different ways to different people.**

You set the goals, go your own pace, schedule your own time, and determine what you want in return. You can market as many, or as few, product lines as you choose — from personal care products to popular brand-name catalog merchandise. More than 3 million entrepreneurs in some 80 countries and territories have found this business opportunity made possible only through Amway is worth a closer look. See for yourself. Perhaps *you* can discover the rewards you've been seeking.

## Amway®

**The Business Opportunity Company™**

If you'd like to know more, call for a free brochure at **1-800-544-7167** or visit our website at **www.amway.com**   © 1998 Amway Corporation
In Canada call **1-800-922-6929**.

# Cover Illustration

Our exquisite cover design was illustrated by Larry Ruppert, a graduate of Layton School of Art in Milwaukee, WI. He served as a graphic designer for Schmidt Publishing Company before being drafted in 1960. Returning in 1971, Ruppert performed as an artist/illustrator for a Madison, WI advertising agency before moving on as a studio artist in 1974 for Severson Art & Design and later for Art Directions.

Leaving the United States to travel abroad in 1980, Ruppert returned and free-lanced in the Milwaukee and Chicago area before relocating in Minneapolis where he joined Spectrum Studio in 1994. Ruppert resides with his wife of 20 years Annabel, in the Twin Cities suburb of Minnetonka. Spectrum Studio, Inc., has represented the finest commercial artists in the Upper Midwest for more than a quarter century; offering a broad variety of talent to satisfy the most discriminating demands of clients including advertising agencies, design firms and corporations. For further information contact Renae Lefebvre or Matt Krieger at the appropriate address listed below.

Spectrum Studio, Inc., 1503 Washington Avenue South, Minneapolis, MN 55454. Phone: (800) 500-1394 or (612) 332-2361, E-mail: sstudio@earthlink.net, Web site: www.spectrumstudio.net

# Oxyfresh Worldwide, Inc.
## THE ETHICAL DIFFERENCE

Oxyfresh is **uniquely** committed to doing business in a way that honors **you,** your family, and those to whom you offer our products and business **opportunity.** We do business the right way, and the fact that we have been **successfully** doing so since 1984 means a lot to our **people.** *What could it mean to you?*

"Listening, partnershipping, building relationships, financial freedom, value-based selling, vision, self-motivation, and leadership development—these are the unique characteristics of Oxyfresh Worldwide, Inc.—the qualities that make this company great. I joined Oxyfresh 12 years ago as a single parent and a practicing dental hygienist with no retirement or pension plan. My part-time business allowed me to retire before I was 50 with a six-figure annual income. I truly live a life of choice thanks to Oxyfresh. To me, that means being able to do what I want, when I want, with whom I choose! It's a **good** thing!"

—Sharon Ludders

"Oxyfresh is a company unlike any other. Integrity, honoring one's values, and commitment to one's success are qualities some companies only wish to have. These are the qualities that Oxyfresh operates by. That's why we chose Oxyfresh to be the source of our present and future income and the source of our family's security. Not only is our family living a comfortable life thanks to our Oxyfresh business, but we are living the life we choose. It's a lifestyle some only dream of, but one that can be had by any who choose to pursue it."

—Tom & Corinne Ventullo

"Oxyfresh Worldwide, Inc. has allowed us to live a lifestyle of **choice.** We chose Oxyfresh because integrity and dedication are the trademarks of President and CEO Richard Brooke. We wanted the best products, the best leadership, and the best compensation plan. In Oxyfresh we have it all. We retired from our dental practice after 37 years. Our new

profession and passion in life is Oxyfresh. We are truly having fun helping others achieve their goals. We have a very comfortable lifestyle, enjoying our sports cars and traveling the world. Come join Oxyfresh and achieve your dreams."

—Don & Mary Lou Vollmer

**To find out for yourself what makes Oxyfresh so unique, call 1-800-223-7374.**

# Publisher's Page

## Validated Credibility

*Jerry Hoffman*

It was measurably short of a miracle, albeit a major achievement nonetheless to research, select and publish in this issue, a master list of the top 100 network marketing and direct selling companies throughout the North American Continent. The rigid criteria we employed is a testament to our commitment to showcase only those companies so richly deserving of international exposure. To that end, we feel our mission to unveil for the very first time, the pioneer's, legend's and the companies responsible for the sustenance, growth and even existence of both industry's, has been accomplished. Indeed, a significant milestone that validates our pledge to publish a definitive listing that will create instant credibility from our millions of readers throughout the globe.

Lest the entries be the sole opinion of our staff, we enlisted a panel of industry experts to assist us in our selection process. While many were obvious choices; Amway, Avon, Tupperware, West Bend, Shaklee, Nature's Sunshine, Excel Communications and Herbalife to name but a few, several newer arrivals were included as odds on favorites to succeed. Six time honored firms named for inclusion are conspicuous by their absence due largely to their inability to meet copy deadline constraints.

For the countless thousands of industry representatives who have been searching for a "legitimate" directory free from special interests, politics, favors and other encumbrances and the millions seeking to start their very own home based business, we proudly present the definitive answer — the Global Home Based Business Directory.

*Bob Hall*

### Bob Hall — Role Model

In our all too invasive "what's in it for me" culture, Bob Hall, professional network marketing company executive for Integris International, is a rare study and survivor of a treasured bygone era when people instinctively helped people for no reason, simply because it was the standard of the times — the thing to do. Somebody needed a helping hand, they reached out without hesitation; never pausing and wondering aloud if there was a "payback" at the other end. A simple "thanks" was all the "payback" necessary for providing assistance, advice, recommendations and the giving of time and effort.

Listen to Jim Anderson, network marketing distributor, consultant, marketing director, company owner, business associate and long-time friend of Hall: "Bob Hall is the most unselfish and talented 'people person' I have ever met," Anderson delivered. "From a professional perspective, he is consistently focused on winning 'as a team,' and is the consummate player/coach. His continual up-beat, mentoring style of encouragement help to create and foster an ongoing 'laughter in the locker room' atmosphere in the day-to-day environment." Anderson continued.

I, as well, have experienced Hall's "give and give more" philosophy over the past year. We were in the process of changing the name of our publication from an ambiguous and cumbersome International Network Marketing Directory to a defined, in phase and targeted Global Home Based Business Directory when I was first introduced to Bob Hall. The purpose for his call was simply to inquire about our publication and whether or not he could help in any way. The call proved the launching of a seamless affiliation that would continue and point the way for many positive changes in our "new look" publication. He was always there; recommending, suggesting, encouraging, reaching out and giving of himself for the sole purpose of helping — without pretense, recognition, applause or monetary gain. Anderson was on the mark when he said Hall is in "a class by himself," and the network marketing industry is the prime benefactor of his association.

# CONFESSIONS

The Hottest Training Course in MLM History

## of a Network Marketing Millionaire

*Dale Calvert, 15 year MLM Veteran*

# How would YOU like to develop a network marketing organization of 61,307 distributors and over 80Million $$$ in sales??

# YOU CAN!!

*That is what I have done in only 4 short years . I am ready to share with you step-by-step, method-by-method how I did it, so YOU can do it too!*

**These Secrets have been closely guarded for the past decade.** They have only been revealed to my Inner Circle Leadership Team. For a *limited time*, they are available to you, but only if **YOU ACT NOW!**

**This information has created millions of dollars in income for myself and my Inner Circle Leadership Team.**

## WHY SO MANY MLM PROFESSIONALS CONSIDER THE CONFESSIONS VIDEOS TO BE THE BEST INVESTMENT THEY HAVE EVER MADE:

"Dale Calvert is a network marketing genius. Forget everything you think you know. I feel that old timers in the
industry, like myself, benefit from this training as much as rookies. I have been full time in the industry for 25 years and top producer with two companies. Dale has shared with me more workable ideas and made me more money than all my other mentors combined. His Confessions training will do the same for you. I hope old pros are smart enough to realize you need it." **Anna Watts, IN**

"My distributors used to drop out quicker than we could replace them. Since I started teaching Dale's methods to my downline for **"keeping them in,"** I now have one of the strongest retention rates in the company. We have also enjoyed a $300,000 annual income. To be quite honest, I hope you don't order the Confessions training. Your frustrated downlines have been quitting to join me for the past couple of years. I don't know if I like the fact that you are about to learn how to start **"keeping them in."** **Kenny Jeanette, KY, 9 years in MLM**

## DON'T WAIT! CALL NOW!!

24-Hour Recorded Testimony Line  888-644-3940      24 Hour FAX-ON-DEMAND  502-868-6650
CODE# IMD-01
WWW.MLMHELP.COM

# Global Home Based Business Directory®

## Volume 2, 2000 Edition

12

26

96

30

54

138

4

# CONTENTS

## FEATURE ARTICLES

**Network Marketing Grows Up**————————————————————4
*Have cartoon friends and comic book heroes progressed more than this maligned and misunderstood industry?*

**Do The Products/Services Have "Intrinsic Value?"**————8
*Companies and their independent representatives operate in a seeming minefield of laws. Time to take a closer look at regulations and interpretations.*

**Forever Living's Rex Maughan – Ahead of the Class**———12
*A humanitarian of the first order strives to bring health and prosperity to millions.*

**What Do You Do Without Cash Or Credit? – Barter!**———18
*It worked a hundred years ago and still can play a role in your business success today.*

**Primer Of The Industry's Buzz Words**————————————21
*Read, learn, memorize and communicate on the same level as the experts.*

**JoAnn Krause Expands On An Already Storied Career**———26
*Hall of Famer JoAnn Krause is looking for a company with the balanced combination of financial resources and "sizzle" products.*

**Targeting The 50 Plus Generation**————————————————30
*An increasingly aging America is an economic force too powerful to ignore.*

**What's Wrong With This Letter**————————————————————33
*A competent letter does a journeyman job. A highly effective letter does a Meistersinger job.*

**No Excuse! I'm Doing It**————————————————————————36
*As Ben Franklin once said: "He who is good at making excuses is seldom good at anything else."*

**Are You A Sloppy Listener?**————————————————————40
*We can speak only 135 to 175 words per minute, but we can absorb 400 to 500 during the same period.*

**The 10 Worst Mistakes In Direct Mail**————————————42
*The headline is the single most important of any ad or promotion. On the basis of one line, the reader instantly makes the decision to continue - or not continue - to read.*

**Five Steps To International Success**————————————————44
*You cannot control or influence the uncontrollable elements, but you can and must adapt to achieve a successful business outcome in the foreign marketplace.*

**Bankruptcy: Myths And Truths**————————————————————50
*The reality is that bankruptcy is increasingly accepted as a fact of American life. It is used, and sometimes abused as well as serving as a financial tool or negotiating strategy.*

**Expert Advice On List Selection**————————————————————52
*You say that selecting a list for telemarketing purposes is like rolling the dice? Not if you're armed with the facts.*

**Doing It...Sabrina's Wei**------------------------------------------54
*Package beauty, brains and an unquenchable desire for success and enter-Sabrina Wei.*

114

**In Search Of Top Caliber Talent**------------------------------------60
*An in-person meeting dramatically increases your chances of making the right choice.*

**The Joy Of Coaching**-----------------------------------------------62
*While coaching finds little favor in the corporate marketplace, it is the very lifeblood of network marketers.*

**Multi-Level Or Pyramid?**-------------------------------------------66
*The answer lies in the "smell test," a proven formula perfected by one of the nation's foremost industry attorneys.*

**Are You Smart About Money?**---------------------------------------71
*Eight questions will determine your financial IQ.*

142

CANADA

**Exclusive Interview With Paul Zane Pilzer**------------------------74
*Network marketing at its root is all about building people, not about building businesses.*

**Communications Is Everything**-------------------------------------78
*By communicating more effectively with potential buyers, you cut through the rhetoric and posturing that often takes place between prospect and seller.*

**Compensation Breakage**--------------------------------------------81
*Breakage can be a strong competitive advantage if used correctly and for the right reasons.*

**The Extinction Of Excellence?**-------------------------------------84
*Endangered certainly, but there's a movement back to the more difficult but successful formula of network marketing.*

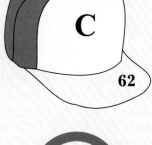
62

**Dale Calvert's Ascendancy To The Top**----------------------------88
*Everything's coming up roses for the number one ranked distributor of New Image, but reaching the top is another story.*

178

**Techniques To Yield Positive Responses**--------------------------92
*While closing is an integral part of any sales call, it should not be the primary focus.*

**Doris Wood... "Den Mother To The World"**-----------------------96
*She has invested more than 40 years of her life to network marketing, and continues unabated to helping others achieve their dreams.*

**Preface From "Heart To Heart"**------------------------------------106
*The real power of network marketing.*

36

**Portion Control**---------------------------------------------------108
*Thinking about manufacturing offshore? Consider the cost of quotas first.*

**Just Don't Do It!**-------------------------------------------------110
*Here's 20 valuable tips on how to effectively manage your business day – and personal life.*

218

**Ultimate Selling Tips To Move Any Product Or Service**------119
*Selling is a highly learnable skill. Here's expert advice from sales trainer and motivational speaker Pam Lontos.*

**No Hope In Dope**-------------------------------------------------122
*Leighton Kaonohi's crusade against drugs, tobacco and alcohol in our nation's schools is an uphill battle at the least, but he moves ahead undeterred.*

222

236

158

250

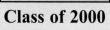

Class of 2000

256

**Executive Challenges In Our New Millennium————130**
*One thing is certain. Those refusing or unable to adapt to rapid change will be earmarked for extinction.*

**Facts And Myths Of Network Marketing————————134**
*The author serves up his "ABC Technique."*

**The Doctor Is Out – And In – Network Marketing————138**
*Abandoning a thriving medical practice is a risk few practitioners would make. Not so for Dr. Matt Silver who found the winning RX with FreeLife International.*

**Canada————————————————————————142**
*The network marketing industry continues to thrive and expand while its lifestyle remains unparalleled.*

**Pyramid, Ponzi & Investment Schemes————————151**
*A must read for everybody about to enter the home-based business market.*

**Welcome To The New World Of Network Marketing————166**
*Companies must adopt a more aggressive marketing philosophy to compete in an ever-crowded and savvy marketplace.*

**Net Relations————————————————————172**
*In our new world of communications, companies must exploit the unlimited marketing muscle of the on-line world.*

**Portrait Of Courage————————————————178**
*Enviro-Tech's unassailable Dian Hodge motivates others while meeting head on the challenge of a radical mastectomy.*

**The Legacy Of Geri Cvitanovich-Dubie————————181**
*Nearly 20 years ago she became the very first Herbalife distributor. Today, her indominable spirit and unquenchable will to succeed has earned her the title of "Queen of Herbalife."*

**Success Yourself————————————————————194**
*There are fundamental and powerful resources available to make your dreams come true that are already within your grasp and simply need to be awakened.*

**How To Succeed Big In Network Marketing————————200**
*Just when you felt you've heard and read it all, here comes another formula on how to push the success button. Would you believe a refreshing perspective could make it happen?*

**Here's To The Lady!————————————————————204**
*Meet Renata Lee...singer, model, actress, mountain climber and network marketer extraordinaire.*

**Getting Your Press Release Into Print————————209**
*Press releases can be both simple and complex instruments to write. Simple because they can take almost any form and have a chance to be published, and complex because every elements adds to or detracts from your chances of getting it in print.*

**The Passion Of J.F. Robert Bolduc————————————214**
*Matol's tenacious, no-nonsense leader sets sail to establish Matol as a potent force around the globe.*

**Robin Stroll Finds A Rewarding Life In Children's Books—216**
*Who says you can't rekindle the creative fulfillment and happiness you achieved as a child? At age 50, Robin has turned back the clock.*

**Make The Feds Your Next Customer————————————218**
*Ninety percent of all purchases made by the U.S. Government are less than $25,000. Can your company ignore this best kept secret?*

**The Arrival Of Beverly Sassoon**--------------------222
*The personification of beauty and success, Beverly is positioning her powerful brand name in the right places – network marketing - -to capitalize on the next chapter in contemporary retailing and global e-commerce.*

**Strategic Alliances Builds Competitive Advantages**--------227
*American corporations have begun turning to outsourcing as a way of unburdening themselves from tasks in which they lack expertise.*

**Deciphering Network Marketing's Secret Language**--------229
*A veteran writer and author unmasks the con games and the dialogue they employ to reel in the uninformed and impressionable.*

**Direct Sales & The Internet; A Perfect Marriage**--------234
*Home-based companies choosing to take full advantage of the opportunities offered via the Internet will have a competitive advantage in the short and long-term.*

**Bruce Jenner Seeks Olympic Gold For Entrepreneurs**--------236
*Nearly a quarter century has passed since his decathlon victory at the 1976 Olympics in Montreal. At long last, the one-time world's greatest athlete has found a home with Longevity Network.*

**Growing Global**--------------------------------242
*Beyond the North American boundaries, a home-based tidal wave is in full swing.*

**Principles Of A Successful Compensation Plan**--------246
*While there are many factors that contribute to the success or failure of direct selling companies, the compensation plan is at the head of the list.*

# DEPARTMENTS

**Publisher's Page**--------------------------------X
*An unexpected friendship*

**Pin This Up!**--------------------------------158
*People, places, events, discoveries, forecasts.*

**Top Award Honors**--------------------------------250
Hall of Fame: *Only those whose invaluable contributions to the success of the network marketing and direct selling industries are enshrined.* Women of Distinction: *From a field of 50 outstanding candidates, we have selected nine role models for our millennium celebration.* Men of Distinction: *Financial success alone will not validate a ticket to this elite group of super achievers.*

**The Top 100**--------------------------------280
*Here they are; never before published full page profiles on 100 of the very best network marketing and direct selling companies gracing the North American Continent.*

**Consumer Information Center**--------------------------------378
*The most comprehensive and diversified consumer information listings ever offered under one cover. From housing, women's rights and charitable organizations to retirement, SBA microloans and wildlife services, this one-stop source will eliminate once and for all, the frustration of locating those impossible to find clubs, associations and programs.*

**Advertising Index**--------------------------------483
*An alphabetized and page number listing of all advertisers in this edition.*

# Attention Readers!

*"If it ain't broke....BREAK It!"* is the advice of Robert J. Kriegel in his best selling book published by Warner Business Press.

Said Kreigel in his forward: Visionary business leaders know that the path to obsolescence is paved with good plans gone bad. They know that you can't get to the top while you're looking at the bottom line. And they know that what you need to make it in this unpredictable market is a double dose of "Break-It Thinking."

Randomly published throughout the editorial section of this directory are excerpts that debunks the myth of conventional wisdom and challenges you to tamper with success in a changing business world. All passages are denoted by the symbol at right.

**Robert J. Kriegel**, Ph.D., is the co-author of *"The C Zone: Peak Performance Under Pressure"* and co-author of the New York Times best-seller *"Inner Skiing."* A former all-American athlete and pioneer in the field of performance psychology, Kriegel has been the mental coach for many Olympic and professional athletes and has been called by *U.S. News and World Report*, "One of the leading authorities in the field of human performance." The *New York Times* said his work "created a revolution in performance practices." He has also been a marketing and advertising executive with a major New York advertising agency, has taught at Stanford University's Executive Management Program, and is a commentator on "Marketplace" on National Public Radio.

A former member of the California Governor's Council and a national spokesman for Bristol-Meyers Squibb, Kriegel currently gives speeches and programs for major corporations and associations around the world. He lives and works in Muir Beach, California.

**Louis Patler, Ph.D.**, is president of the B.I.T. Group, an international training and consulting company based in Marin County, California, that brings "Break-It!" thinking technologies to corporations, associations and governments. Dr. Patler, award-winning author, speaker, and former editor of the *American Trend Report,* lives with his family in Mill Valley, California.

*If it aint broke... BREAK IT! is available in most bookstores throughout the United States.*

# E-commerce: The Way Of The Future

**Global Resource Network**

We represent a tremendous opportunity that has just started on the Internet...
The first 3-Dimensional, Interactive, Virtual Reality Internet Mall.
Over a thousand categories of goods, open 24 hours a day, worldwide!

In 1998, $50 billion dollars was spent on the Internet, it is predicited to reach an amazing $1.2 Trillion by 2002.

"The unique compensation plan is a blankblan of light combining the high commission of direct sales, the best of network marketing and leadership in the advancing technology of the new millennium!" *GLOBAL IMPACT*

- Mission is to spread wealth
- Grand opening launch, now!
- New 3D, high-tech, server-based, Internet high speed software, with 360 degree viewing, and zooming.
- Discounts on everything you buy!
- Millions of customers going on-line every day
- Cyberspace is the future of marketing
- Interactive Auctions, diverse merchandise

- Registering allows you to participate in the 7 rewarding ways the Compensation Plan pays our, based on sales at the 3D Mall.
- Each representative receives a VIP discount access code to shop with or refer others to the mall
- Commission up to 30% of cost of goods sold.
- NO SALES TAX–NO PERSONAL VOLUME
- Easy, Fun, Gound Floor Opportunity
- Profit sharing plan creates

**E-mail: Globalresource@email.com -- Call today toll free: (808) 395-8034**

# E-Commerce will exceed $1.2 Trillion by 2002!
## Be a part of their global expansion!

*Have you ever wished you had invested in the ground floor opportunity of the next up-and-coming Internet company?*

### E-COMMERCE IS <u>THE</u> BUSINESS OPPORTUNITY OF THE NEW MILLENNIUM

Where would you be now if you had bought into Microsoft or IBM at their inception? The projections from hundreds of expert sources tell us that **E-COMMERCE** will revolutionize the trade and commerce industry worldwide. Global Resource Network is an association of independent consultants working with AHM, the exclusive marketing arm for the first **3-Dimensional** Mall scheduled to launch within days of this article going to print.

The popularity of the PC and the Internet have given business owners the ability to have the same impact as large corporations have had with millions spent on media campaigns. The Internet has leveled the playing field. This allows a global presence for those with the foresight to become positioned with the leaders in this new technology. The Internet is one of the most powerful marketing tools on the planet. Projections from hundreds of sources are all pointing to the Internet and e-commerce as a wave we all should want to catch. Savvy financial advisors are pointing to the growth of Internet stocks as a prime investment for the next decade. Will you be positioned to reap the rewards? We believe that we can assist you to connect with the leaders in this field! To set up your own internet business, and marketing operation, to success fully navigate the WORLDWIDE WEB with power success.

The 15 million dollar commerce business has gone-on-line and there are opportunities available to the independent entrepreneur to have multi-million dollar exposure, income, marketing, strategies and fantastic position for those who act now. This arena, and trillions that will be spent in the next couple of years on the Internet, represents the largest shift in business in the history of mankind.

Do you have the foresight to be involved? Will your present vision bring you the just rewards for your efforts? We are here to assist you and combine our strategic alliances with the advanced technology that will ensure your success.

---

*Imagine...* **having the impact to reach millions**

- Be part of our marketing team for the first 3-D mall on the Internet
- Reap the rewards of a very generous compensation plan
- Use the natural momentum of e-commerce to catapult your income via cyberspace
- Strategic marketing experts will help you navigate with lead generation programs
- Be part of an advertising media that is doubling every 100 days - Tech Report

### Why you want to be in this industry:

- This business is just beginning - you're in at the start
- The 37 million people who currently surf the web daily could be your customers
- The 3D mall is a unique environment selling virtually every product on the planet

**CALL TOLL FREE: (808) 395-8034 – E-mail: globalresource@email.com**

# matol

## WE MADE HISTORY, THEN WE WROTE THE BOOK!

It only takes a moment to discover a lifetime of opportunity.

*Matol Moments* is a book with many stories. From one man's personal vision, to the treasured memories of the countless people that shared in a dream, "Matol Moments" is a journey of discovery - and the journey has just begun.

This corporate biography is not just a detailed account of one company's achievements, it is a celebration of the people who made it happen.

MATOL *Moments*
A CELEBRATION OF MATOL PEOPLE
by
J.F. Robert Bolduc
with the collaboration of
Marie fabiola Bolduc

*"Join me in reliving the history of Matol in our new book, "Matol Moments". From the first seed planted by Karl Jurak in 1922, up to the present day - Matol Moments is truly a celebration, not only of the past, but of the limitless future."*

**J.F. Robert Bolduc**
Co-founder, Chairman & CEO

www.matol.com

# Network Marketing Grows *Up*

**Leonard W. Clements**

**Network Marketing** has endured perhaps the longest childhood mankind has ever known. Even our old cartoon friends and comic book heroes seem to have progressed further than this often maligned, and greatly misunderstood industry. While Mickey Mouse was discovering true love, and Superboy was becoming Superman, network marketing putted right through five decades with the same image: that of a "pyramid" of pushy friends and neighbors selling soaps and shoe polish door-to-door.

## A lot can happen in 50 years

Amazingly enough, most folks still seem to perceive network marketing in much the same way even today, despite the fact that one would have to travel back at least two decades to have the above description even begin to apply. Network marketing, or multi-level marketing as it has been called through most of its history has, in fact, evolved significantly over the years.

## A Century of Progress

Bona fide pyramid and Ponzi schemes did exist throughout the early part of this century, the most prominent of which was one operated by Carlo Ponzi himself. Ponzi offered a $1,500 return on a $1,000 investment, the difference being made up by the next investor. Ponzi made millions, until the pool of gullible prospects dried up. He died a penniless ex-con.

Pyramid schemes, which are actually quite different in structure than a Ponzi scheme, allowed individuals to invest money into a system where you were then rewarded based on the number of others you persuaded to invest as well. Although technically this scheme never paid out more than it took in, many of those who got in early reaped monumental rewards, in lieu of the late-comers who lost their entire investment.

In the Fall of 1945, Carl Rehnborg, founder of a medium size nutritional supplement company called Nutrilite Corporation (previously known as California Vitamins in the 30s), had an idea. Why not utilize the same method of compensation but apply a genuine value in return for the investment? Rather than simply reward for recruiting, their sales people would be rewarded based on the movement of a legitimate product. Little did Rehnborg know that this would one day, some 35 years later, become the defining criteria for a legitimate, legal network marketing operation.

The next major player to enter the network marketing arena was Shaklee Corporation in 1956, soon followed by Neo-Life in 1958. In 1959, two successful Nutrilite distributors decided to embark on their own network marketing venture. They called it American Way, which was quickly shortened to Amway. Despite the fact that Amway is generally known as the "grandfather" of multi-level marketing, both Shaklee and Neo-Life have seniority and still exist to this day (as does Nutrilite Corporation, a subsidiary of Amway).

In the 60s, the baby boomers began to leave the nest and homemakers across the country found a great way to spend their new-found spare time--selling soaps, cosmetics and plastic bowls to their friends and neighbors. The "home party" style of selling was all the rage. The 70s, what many consider to be the "dark age" of network marketing, saw a proliferation of money games, chain letters, and the resurgence of blatant pyramid schemes. The infamous airplane game was launched (the epitome of an illegal pyramid), along with many other quasi-legal plans. A shadowy fog was cast over the network marketing arena and the lines of ethics and legality became severely blurred. In 1975, the Federal Trade Commission initiated an action against a network marketing company that began the laborious and expensive task of once and for all delineating between legal network marketing operations and illegal pyramid schemes. The battle lasted more than four years and needless to say, the network marketing company emerged victoriously.

Armed with a legitimizing body of law, a dramatically increasing cost of living, and a plethora of high-tech promotional tools, the network marketing industry flourished at an unprecedented rate in the 80s.

During this decade, the number of participating distributors rose from 1.4 million to more than 6.5 million. The number of legitimate, U.S.-based network marketing opportunities increased tenfold and have expanded into more than 60 foreign countries. Major mainstream corporations began to discover the power of having an army of marketers behind them, all utilizing the most effective, least expensive advertising method available--word of mouth. Rexall, Watkins, Colgate-

Palmolive, Gillette, MCI, US Sprint, and even IBM, to an extent, have all utilized network marketing either directly or through subsidiaries.

Although the soaps, shoe polish and plastic bowls are still available, well over 10,000 additional products are now network marketed as well. Nearly every market niche imaginable is now addressed by network marketing companies. The door-to-door method of sales all but vanished some ten years ago. Not only is there rarely anyone home to answer the bell (mom and dad are both at work now), but the prospect of entering a stranger's property during the evening hours is no longer a viable sales option for all but the most courageous. In fact, many network marketing companies forbid door-to-door sales of their products for this very reason. Times have changed--and so has network marketing.

**A Guilt by Association**

Today, on the verge of its 50th anniversary as an industry, network marketing still suffers greatly from a guilt-by-association. Many uninformed state and federal regulators still harbor a grudge against any business operation which they perceive to create a pyramidal hierarchy. In fact, network marketing "downlines" do not form a pyramid, but rather a diamond shaped hierarchy. The typical corporate structure, however, does form a pyramid, as does the government and branches of the military. Perhaps the greatest irony of all is that network marketing is the only form of business that does not form a pyramid!

The greatest challenge of all in erasing the stigma that surrounds network marketing involves a biased and unsympathetic media. Beyond the increasing glut of sensationalistic, tabloid-style information sources, and the simple fact that "bad news sells," network marketing has also suffered from an additional bias exclusively its own. The survival of most mainstream media is based on advertising dollars, and network marketing is an industry that rarely, if ever, advertises in the mainstream media. Those few reputable media sources, such as the one you are holding in your hands, who present a "balanced" presentation of network marketing should be commended for their fairness and objectivity.

*As this maligned and misunderstood industry continues to grow morally, improve professionally, and expand geometrically, the next half-century of network marketing promises to be a masterpiece.*

To this day, stories of garages full of unsold products, unfulfilled promises of overnight riches, and deceptive or heavy-handed recruiting practices abound. This was, in fact, a legitimate complaint against network marketing as late as 1992. During that year, a network marketing company was the subject of a severe media beating due primarily to regulatory scrutiny on both the state and federal level relating to the aforementioned sales and recruiting practices. The company in question was by no means the most guilty of the lot, but they were by far the most visible due to their unprecedented growth rate at the time. The result was a much more clearly defined set of rules and guidelines relating to product and income claims, as well as sales and recruiting practices. Today, that model is followed by numerous honest, ethical and professionally run network marketing companies. In fact, "front loading" and "stock piling" of products are considered quite taboo, and the old ultra-hyped, get-rich-quick "opportunity presentation" is missing from all but the most desperate of distributor organizations. Such practices are policed by numerous "watchdog" organizations within the industry itself, various state and federal regulatory agencies, as well as the legal departments within the majority of network marketing companies themselves. Those few that continue the "old school" style of multi-level seem to get all the attention--thus maintaining the negative perception.

The prejudice that exists toward network marketing is continually reinforced by those who try their hand at the business and fail. The network marketing arena is packed with scapegoats. It is interesting to note that those who fail in their attempt at a sales career in any other industry are usually considered to be poor sales people. Those who try and fail at network marketing are almost always considered victims. The truth is, no legitimate network marketing company requires a product purchase of any amount to be distributed for their company. Not one. Any purchase, whether it is for personal consumption or to stock inventory for resale, is entirely voluntary. Furthermore, generous refund policies have been installed in most every legitimate network marketing program. As in any sales position, higher financial rewards are paid to those who meet higher quotas. Unfortunately, many folks simply don't want to wait for a customer base to naturally form over time, so they "buy into" a high paying position by meeting the required quota out of their own pocket. Again, a totally voluntary, and usually very poor business decision likely based on emotion rather than good common sense.

The fact is, network marketing indeed offers prospective entrepreneurs one of the lowest financial risk factors of any form of self-employment available. As with any legitimate business venture, reliable full-time incomes may involve several months of hard work, perhaps even at an initial loss. But an up-front investment of only a few hundred dollars does provide a very real opportunity to earn a few hundred dollars back each month in residual income, perhaps for life. Many conservative network marketers build their business only to the point of earning $200 to $300 per month. That same, small additional income will provide a comfortable, secure retirement for most if properly invested--an agenda championed by many wise network marketers today.

Granted, the opportunity for great wealth in network marketing is commensurate to winning the lottery, but it is commonplace today to find comfortable livings or supplemental incomes being earned by those who take the business seriously.

## Carving Out a Living

Network marketing has been likened to a sharp, sturdy chisel; a tool which one may use to carve out a comfortable living for themselves and their families, or perhaps simply a secure retirement. A tool that is many times sold as a magic wand--simply wave it over your head and great riches will fall from the sky. A tool that, if ignored, will do nothing, and if abused, could destroy. But a tool that, if properly cared for, ethically used, and responsibly shared, may very well provide every American living today with a genuine opportunity to live their entrepreneurial dream. A dream that is borne of a desire for control--for freedom--and the peace of mind that the needs of ourselves and our loved ones are met.

This chisel we now call network marketing has been in the development stage for an over 50 years. It has evolved to the point of near perfection in its design. Tomorrow's challenges will fall on those sculptors of today to continue in their efforts to become skillful, responsible mentors; to instill in their proteges a strong sense of morality, commitment, ethics and integrity. All vital traits that must be practiced by not only the chisel maker, but by the one's whose hands will hold it.

As this maligned and misunderstood industry continues to grow morally, improve professionally, and expand geometrically, the next half-century of network marketing promises to be a masterpiece!

*Leonard Clements has concentrated his full-time efforts over the last eight years on researching and analyzing all aspects of network marketing. He is a professional speaker and trainer, and currently conducts Inside Network Marketing seminars throughout the U.S., Canada and Mexico. He is also the publisher of the "MarketWave Alert" letter, an MLM analysis and watchdog newsletter. Mr. Clements is the host of "Inside Network Marketing," a weekly live call-in radio show on KSCL 1080, and he is the author of the controversial book, "Inside Network Marketing," an objective, no-holds-barred, insider's look at the MLM industry. He is also the author of the best-selling cassette tape, "Case Closed! The whole Truth About Network Marketing," which has been labeled "the best" generic recruiting tape by six MLM company presidents.*

*Mr. Clements has been involved in the MLM industry for 19 years and is a successful distributor for a prominent MLM program (which is never mentioned in either the book or the cassette tape).*

*To receive additional information about MarketWave and it's products, please call (800) 688-4766, or write to MarketWave, 7342 North Ivanhoe Avenue, Fresno, CA 93722.*■

# The GHBBD is cleaning up the industry

## *It's a big undertaking and we are requesting your help. Together, we can make a difference in the industry*

If for any reason you believe there is a company or individual associated with the network marketing/direct selling industry or home based business at large that you feel is operating illegally in the United States, or Canada, fill in the form below and the GHBBD Watch Force will conduct a thorough investigation and publish our findings in our 2001 edition of the GHBBD. Your name and comments will remain strictly confidential. Send comments to: Marketing Solutions, Inc., HC 6, Box 58A, Aitkin, MN 56431. Or fax to: (218) 927-4613

# GHBBD WATCH FORCE

Name of Person(s) or Company(s) in Question_____

Address_____

City/State/Zip_____

Phone/Fax_____

Comments_____

_____

_____

_____

# Do The Products/Services Have "Intrinsic Value"

**Gerald P. Nehra**

Companies and their independent representatives operate in a seeming minefield of laws, regulations, and interpretations of those laws and regulations. A hot topic of discussion and attention is the question of "retailing." I suggest you test the company you are considering, or the company whose program you are working, against these ideas, some of which are brand new.

Begin by examining two severe interpretations of "retailing." First, the North Carolina Office of Attorney General has negotiated settlements with MLM companies attacked as pyramids in their state. North Carolina, in these settlements, has required 70 percent of the sales of the MLM company to be to persons outside of the program. Second, the Omnitrition case, of which much has been written, says,

in its strictest interpretation, that sales to your own independent representatives' are not "retail" sales, and therefore, commissions cannot be paid on them. Fortunately, not even the California Attorney General Office (the Omnitrition decision is from a Federal Appeals Court sitting in California) has interpreted that language very strictly. The California Attorney General Office has acknowledged that reasonable amounts of purchases by independent representatives are commissionable

> **"Intrinsic value" means the purchaser wants or needs the items and is willing to buy them without the added incentive of an income opportunity.**

in their settlement negotiations with AuQuest, settled after the Omnitrition decision.

What is going on here? What is all the fuss? Pyramids and endless chains are illegal in the U.S. You cannot "pay to play." Simply stated: No company offering you an income opportunity with multi-level compensation can charge you anything to join. Additionally, you are not required to purchase products or services. And last but not least, you cannot be charged for the right to recruit others. Such a "charge" is prohibited as an illegal "headhunting fee."

In my view, the only legal basis a

regulator can have to challenge commissions on independent representative consumption is to characterize product purchases as "headhunting" or "paying to play." Another version of the same problem is the specific requirement in many laws that the company's plan be "primarily" about moving products and services to consumers, rather than about recruiting more "participants." But that issue brings us back to the same place. If the purchases are linked to recruiting, rather than to traditional marketplace supply and demand, then the purchases will be deemed disguised "headhunting" fees.

Nothing I have written above is new. The traditional methods of dealing with these concerns are the "ten customer rule, 90 percent buy back protection, and the 70 percent rule," derived from the 1979 Amway decision. These protections and techniques all have their good points. Yes, some regulators view them as inadequate, or subject to manipulation, going so far as requiring company verification of the representative submissions.

The following is a new and I believe, complementary idea, and applicable to companies whose structures allow them to identify what sales/purchases are for intrinsic value. "Intrinsic value" means the purchaser wants or needs the items and is willing to buy them without the added incentive of an income opportunity. Case in point: If the surrounding facts support the position that the goods are being purchased for their intrinsic value, then the purchases are not being made "to play the game." The facts must counter the regulatory accusation that, but for the income opportunity, no one would buy the products. I also propose (remember, I said these are new ideas) that the status of the purchaser (specifically, a total outside consumer or some form of independent representative) should make no difference. I will expand this by looking at various types of purchases:

## 1. The Traditional Retail Customer

A person totally unconnected to the company offering the income opportunity, and usually unknown to the company, because he/she purchased from the independent representative. There should be no question that the sales to such persons are for intrinsic value.

## 2. The Customer "Direct Fulfilled" by the Company

The company knows this person because the company has a distribution system that provides direct shipping to end-users. The independent representative tells the company to ship, or the customer calls the company, identifies the independent representative who told them about the company for sales credit purposes, and places an order. The company deals with each order as it occurs and maintains no separate file of customers. It treats the order as if placed directly by the independent representative, but with a different ship-to address. There should be no question that sales to such persons are for intrinsic value.

## 3. The Preferred Customer

Many companies encourage their independent representatives to connect preferred customers directly

to the company. Sometimes application forms are used, and identification of pin numbers are issued. Customers order directly. These persons, however, do not sign an independent representative application, and do not have an income opportunity. There should be no question that sales to such persons are for intrinsic value.

## 4. The Independent Representative Without a Right to Sponsor

Some companies offer a separate delineated single level income opportunity. None of the purchases of these people can possibly be deemed "to play the game of an endless recruiting chain," because these persons do not have the right to recruit other independent representatives. These sales are for their intrinsic value, or for resale to customers, and there can be no argument made that the sales are disguised headhunting fees, since the person cannot recruit other income opportunity seekers.

## 5. The Independent Representative Who "Signs up" to Buy Wholesale

This is very new thinking, and not yet tested with regulators. I am writing to argue that the right to sponsor others in the independent representative agreement is an "offer" of a multi-level income opportunity, which is accepted when--and only

when--the act of sponsoring occurs. A person signing up to purchase at the independent representative price, and choosing not to sponsor, cannot be purchasing "to play the game," since, again, no recruiting of income opportunity seekers has occurred.

## 6. The Non-sponsoring Independent Representative

This is also very new thinking, and not yet tested with regulators. I am willing to argue, and if unable to convince a regulator, to the appropriate judge (with good facts), that purchases by a non-sponsoring independent representative cannot possibly be a disguised headhunting fee, or a "payment to play." The reason is based on simple logic--the independent representative has (for the moment, at least) declined the company's offer to "participate" (a word with legal significance) in the multi-level portion of the income opportunity. No argument can be made that the purchase is to qualify

> *I am willing to argue, and if unable to convince a regulator, to the appropriate judge (with good facts), that purchases by a non-sponsoring independent representative cannot possibly be a disguised headhunting fee, or a "payment to play."*

for downline bonuses, or for the right to recruit, since recruiting of additional participants has occurred.

## 7. The Sponsoring Independent Representative

In many companies that have low monthly business volume requirements to qualify for bonuses on the business volume of downlines, the following occurs: The independent representative consistently orders in excess of the minimum needed to qualify for all available downline bonuses. First, the amount above the minimum needed to qualify is not "to play the game," since only the minimum is needed. A second and optional argument can be made that all of the order is for intrinsic value, since one ordering solely to "participate" would just order the minimum. This may be more aggressive than necessary, but is worth noting.

### Conclusion

Many companies are structured to have available, at the corporation, statistics supporting the above purchases for intrinsic value. It's of public record that I represented one of the companies settling with North Carolina. Their facts did not warrant to fight in court. The company has since closed. If a company has "good facts," which I define as over half of their sales "for intrinsic value," I will fight for them in any state, including North Carolina. I believe retail sales defined in this manner (which is one approach, and not the only approach) directly address conduct that the anti-pyramid and endless chain laws seek to regulate. That regulated and prohibited conduct is the sale of products and services that no one will buy for their intrinsic value, but will only buy to participate in and further an illegal endless chain. When such circumstances surround such sales, the sales become disguised headhunting fees, specifically prohibited by the laws of most states. Would you buy your company's products, absent the income opportunity? Would anyone? The answer needs to be "yes." If a company's sales are "primarily for intrinsic value," I believe the company can withstand legal scrutiny.

*Gerald P. Nehra is an MLM Specialist Private Practice Attorney. He is one of only a few attorneys nationwide whose practice is devoted exclusively to direct selling and multi-level marketing issues. His 28 years of legal experience includes nine years at Amway Corporation, where he was Director of the Legal Division. He can be reached at 1710 Beach Street, Muskegon, MI 49441, Phone: (616) 755-3800, Fax: (616) 755-4700, E-mail: MLMAtty@aol.com. You are invited to visit his web site at: http://www.mimatty.com.* ■

## Workaholism

"If someone tells me they are working ninety-hour weeks" says GE CEO Jack Welch, "I say you're doing something terribly wrong. I go skiing on the weekend, I go out with my buddies on Friday and party. You've got to do the same or you've got a bad deal. Put down a list of the twenty things you are doing that make you work ninety hours, and ten of them have to be nonsense..."

Echoing Welch, former Time Warner Co-Chairman Dick Munro says, "I'm dead against workaholics. Working like that causes you to lose enthusiasm and vitality and inhibits creativity." To confirm this, Munro said that throughout his long career at Time Inc., starting as a college graduate, he very rarely took a train home later than 6:00 P.M.

# I.D.E.A. Concepts™

# TV infomercials . . . direct mail . . . best-selling books . . . Welcome to directNET Marketing!

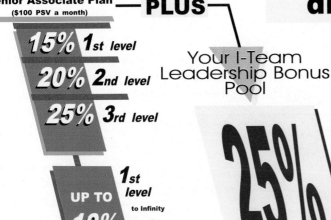

**Senior Associate Plan**
($100 PSV a month) — **PLUS**

**15%** *1st level*
**20%** *2nd level*
**25%** *3rd level*

UP TO **10%** *1st level to Infinity*
Infinity

Your I-Team Leadership Bonus Pool

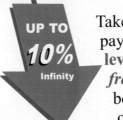

**25%**

UP TO **10%** Infinity

## Get Your Share Of Tens Of Thousands Of Leads!

It's the most incredible customer-generation program the network marketing industry has ever seen. It's **directNET**--the marriage of the booming **direct** response industry and **NET**work Marketing. And it's exclusively available through I.D.E.A. Concepts, acclaimed by *MLM Insider* magazine as one of the "Top Ten Companies of 1998."

Imagine customers from TV infomercials, direct mail campaigns, and endorsements in hot new books becoming *your customers*. They can be--when you join I.D.E.A. Concepts.

Take a look at the company's regular pay plan--**60% on the first three levels.** Analyze the benefits of the *free customers* placed in your bonus pool. And, most important of all, check out the company's innovative wellness and personal care products.

Then you'll want to be part of a pioneering, business-building phenomenon. *Call today!*

## Five Ways To Learn More:

▶ **Contact Bob Bodie, an Independent I.D.E.A. Concepts Representative, at: 1-888-921-6566, or 1-303-978-0891**

▶ **Listen to a brief hotline message at 1-800-552-4332 (IDEA)**

▶ **Visit the corporate website: http://www.ideaconcepts.com**

▶ **Call Fax-On-Demand: 1-521-505-6808**

▶ **E-mail: rjbodie@earthlinks.net**

*His giving, sharing and humanitarian acts are legendary. These, and his insatiable drive to bring health and prosperity to millions around the globe places...*

## Forever Living's Rex Maughan

# Ahead of the Class

**Freya Manfred**

Listen to the refreshingly direct and altruistic words of Mr. Rex Maughan, one of the most successful network marketing people in the world and the founder of Forever Living Products, a growing billion-dollar empire: "I'm proud of our company and our distributors are our best marketers and I want to help them help themselves. I also like to instill the idea that they can, in turn, help their communities. I want people to know that I'm not doing what I do for fame or money. I, too, want to help others." Since Forever Living Products has over five million distributors with companies in the United States and in sixty-five foreign countries, Maughan has obviously lived up to his words, providing healthful living as well as savings accounts for the well-being of a global community!

*Rex Maughan*
*Helping others help*
*themselves around*
*the world*

Maughan has a deep and powerful sense of the reason why he became involved in the network marketing business. "When I got out of college I was working two or three jobs just to get by, and I wasn't able to enjoy my family and all the other good things in life. I know what that's like. That's why we, at Forever Living Products, try to help people reach any goal or dream they can conceive of, and we want to do that all over the world." Under Maughan's guidance, Forever Living Products recently celebrated their 20th anniversary in Scottsdale, Arizona, with a new international headquarters, where they added five new countries to their global "family." Though they experienced a $43 million dollar jump in sales in 1997 and a total of $1.255 billion for the year, Maughan says, "We don't have to be the biggest. We just want to be the best."

While Maughan points out that "twenty years is an exceptionally good record for network marketing," this remarkably creative salesman who genuinely cares about his customers plans to fly his network marketing company even higher in the future.

He explains that the logo for Forever Living Products is a seagull, which is modeled after the main character in the book, Jonathan Livingston Seagull, by Richard Bach. "*Jonathan always wanted to fly higher, faster, and see farther,*" says Maughan. "He did not wish to be an ordinary seagull. That is what we wanted to do and plan to continue doing with this company--helping others develop their own businesses and themselves."

Maughan is a native of Soda Springs, Idaho, where he learned honesty, team work, and the value of hard work on his family's ranch. "My father was a rancher and a farmer and my parents had a great work ethic. When I was a child we worked very hard after school, on weekends, and even all summer." The ranch was located in a climate which has a short growing season. "If the crops were planted late it was especially vital in the fall to get them in as fast as possible and then go next door to neighboring ranches and help them bring their crops in before the snow arrived. I learned at a young age to stress team work." Therefore, when Maughan decided he wanted to be successful in life, team work and helping others were a natural part of his goal. "Every place I've worked I've known that if you work as a team, everyone is happier."

After graduating from Soda Springs High School, Maughan attended Arizona State University, simultaneously working a number of jobs, including doing printing for a blood bank and maintaining a line of "kiddie rides" in stores. After college he worked with a national CPA firm and a real estate development company, before establishing himself in the Del Webb Corporation where he worked for thirteen years and served as vice president in charge of realty, management and recreational resorts. Throughout his life he has continued to invest in real estate, including marinas and resorts, because he feels "very comfortable" with this type of business. "Others sometimes ask me, 'Why resorts?' and I like to say that

I'm in the resort business because if I'm going to work hard I want to work in fun places!" He is also the largest manufacturer of houseboats in the United States, and uses them in his various marinas.

Though highly successful in real estate, Maughan dreamed of expanding worldwide to reach people of all income levels and backgrounds, and this vision eventually led to the business of network marketing. "In real estate you can only work on one thing at a time, but in network marketing you can train many people at the same time to duplicate yourself so that everyone can have solid financial remuneration at the end of the month." Maughan first heard about network marketing when a friend told him about a company selling diet products.

***Maughan standing beside his treasured antique Ford, bearing of course, his company's name and logo***

"I wasn't interested in dieting myself, but I went to the meetings and saw all of these books and testimonials of how people lost weight and how it changed their lives. I also listened to what some of these products had done for others in network marketing, and I realized you can recruit and train and help others to build a meaningful, successful business. I saw vividly how a team can do so much more than working single-handedly. So I got 'the vision' real fast—it is such a great way to help others."

Carefully studying the potential of the network marketing business, Maughan decided it suited his aspirations perfectly because he could focus on compensation for all involved. Looking at the existing marketing plans, he decided there was a better way to involve other people at all levels, so he developed his own marketing plan based on the idea that the "finest programs are those which help people earn financial freedom and develop others into millionaires." He established a balanced distribution of compensation making it realistic for everyone from corporate presidents to beginners to make a comfortable living without bearing an unreasonable workload, "so people could actually work where and when they want, make a good living, and have time to enjoy their families and other personal interests."

After Maughan developed the right marketing plan, he began looking for products in which to give people better health. He set his sights on a previously untapped resource: Aloe Vera. Thanks to careful research, he met a team of doctors who had invested a better part of two decades developing the stabilization of the plant, which supplies significant amounts of minerals, amino acids, and vitamins, including B-12, a vitamin typically found only in animal products. Maughan knew his Aloe Vera products would not only provide customers with dietary supplements and other healthy substances, the B-12 component would also offer vegetarians a unique vitamin source. "You can make all the money in the world, but if you don't have health you won't enjoy it," he says.

Two years later, in 1980, Maughan purchased his own Aloe Vera plantations, ensuring that Forever Living Products would have a reliable source of its prized product. A year later, Maughan purchased his supplier—and the company has grown steadily ever since. Today it is the largest grower and manufacturer of Aloe Vera products in the world, boasting more than 5,000 acres of Aloe Vera plantations in Texas, Mexico, and the Dominican Republic. The second largest line at Forever Living Products is from the apiary, bee pollen, royal jelly, natural bee honey, and bee propolis (which doctors say is a natural antibiotic developed from sap which bees collect and use to protect the hive). Many other products from the company, including ginseng, gingko, fish oils, and Forever Kids Multivitamins, are intended to promote healthy living. "I don't introduce a product unless I know it will help others to have better health," says Maughan. "It's just wonderful to see so many people feeling better and living healthier lives."

Forever Living Products has operations in Japan, Taiwan, Philippines, Great Britain, Mexico, Malaysia, Hong Kong, Poland, Argentina, Germany, and fifty-five other countries. This year it is establishing new offices in Africa, India, and Scandinavia, among others. In the United States it has been named by *Arthur Andersen's ranking of top businesses* as the number one privately held company in Arizona for the past three years. But true to Maughan's belief that "the more money you have, the greater responsibility you have to become

*Even the ubiquitous Maughan needs a break -- seen here at one of his ranches enjoying a moment in the sun on horesback*

a good citizen and help other organizations and people." Forever Living Products contributes to the global community in many distinctive ways. Maughan loves national parks and he spent seventeen years as the Chairman of the National Park Hospitality Association, fostering preservation of our natural resources in conjunction with better facilities and services for the visitors. In Samoa, Maughan donated money to build a school for 250 students and simultaneously managed to persuade the Samoans to stop a timbering project and set aside 30,000 acres of low level rain forest as a National Park. He also put two and a half million dollars into the restoration of the 1890 house of writer, Robert Louis Stevenson, which is now open every day as a museum. "Samoan is my second language, and the Chiefs there conferred upon me the High Chief title of Tilafaiga," says Maughan.

Maughan is proud that Forever Living Products tries to buy for their offices the "nicest, oldest, best buildings in each country and restore them so they can be productive and also enhance the community in which they stand." Their oldest building, Longbridge Manor, is in the United Kingdom; Maughan recently learned that friars lived in this manor back in 1043. In Parramatta, a suburb of Sydney, the company has restored a building called Willow Grove, built in 1886, situated next to a twelve story high rise which "makes our office look like a garden of Eden." They have done more restoration work on a 200-year-old castle in the Czech Republic and on a large mansion in downtown Rio. Three years ago they were able to buy the Trovato Mansion in Capetown, South Africa, built in 1897 on five acres, with a garden, planting 150 aloe plants so all the flower and botanical people can come in to see them as well as the rest of the community. "This sort of restoration maintains the historical integrity of a community and is also great for them economically," says Maughan. "We are presently in the process of rebuilding the home of American author, Zane Grey, according to the original plans, which we purchased. And my high school class has established a Soda Springs Historical Museum back in Idaho to beautify the town and promote tourism."

Maughan's amazing success has allowed this husband and father of three to enjoy his own life away from work, but his employees have reaped impressive benefits as well. "We're unique in that we pay more bonuses to our distributors than any other company, and we also offer more incentives to our distributors too," he says.

Income is based on sales, but a variety of efforts are rewarded with bonuses such as cars, boats, houses, and even airplanes. The company provides a profit-sharing program, free international trips, visits to manufacturing plants and plantations in Texas and vacations to Las Vegas and Grand Canyon, among others.

Maughan's two sons and his daughter work in the business with him, and their latest product is named Sonya Color Collection after his daughter. "My children are distributors in the company and they are our greatest promoters," he says. "We try to teach that you can be a family business, people helping each other. Both sexes can be involved, because some people relate better to women and some relate better to men."

*Maughan positioned in front of only a handful of the nation's 65 flags where Forever Living owns aloe vera plantations*

Although Maughan says his hobbies are visiting his ranches

and seeing the baby calves grow up, restoring homes, establishing museums, visiting antique bookstores to purchase books, and owning and maintaining Southfork Ranch in Dallas (where the TV series DALLAS was filmed), his main hobby is "helping others obtain better health by using our products to change their lifestyles as well as helping them get what they want in life." Maughan's conversation is salted with health-oriented slogans. He says he encourages people to "Die young at a very old age," and to "add life to your years while you add years to your life."

He says, wisely: "I don't look back, because I'm not going that way. I look to the future because that's where I'm spending the rest of my life. I never wanted to sell or bail out or turn back. The saddest days of my life are when I think about how many people I haven't been able to help. Everyone has a health problem and everyone can use more money, and that is what I am working on."

What can anyone say to this astonishing goal, except "Thank you, and bravo, Rex Maughan!" ■

*Thanks to Maughan, Forever Living is the largest grower and manufacturer of aloe vera in the world*

16

# IMPORTANT MESSAGE
# FOR OUR READERS

## Visit our Online version of the Global Home Based Business Directory at: *ghbbd.com*

Keep abreast of all the latest and exciting news and opportunities about the fastest growing industry in the world. Contents include company updates, new products and services, real life feature articles on leading distributors and representatives, consumer information center, selling tips to move any product or service, choosing the best home-based business for you, Hall of Fame inductees, celebrity profiles, news, views, facts and anecdotes. View *The Bulletin Board*, the worlds first online newsletter serving the Direct Selling and Network Marketing industry.

If you are a victim of downsizing, searching for that rewarding part-time position, seeking a career change, looking to take back control of your life–all in the comfort, safety, privacy and convenience of your own home, look no further–rush to our web site and choose that "just right" company for you to start your very own home-based business.

In 1975, only 2.5 million Americans worked from their homes. In 1997, 40 million Americans, or 38 percent of our nation's work force, worked from businesses out of their homes or as telecommuters for corporations. Indeed, the $200 billion home-based business revolution is in full swing.

The Global Home Based Business Directory, the official publication of the Network Marketing and Direct Selling industries is now playing at

# What do you do without cash or credit?
# *Barter*

*Joyce E. Barrie*

**WHAT IS BARTER? Barter** is simply the exchange of goods or services for trade rather than for cash. The one-on-one concept of barter is a trade between two people of what they wish to offer each other without using cash as the medium of exchange. Sophisticated, computerized barter companies allows you trade your products and services with other clients through a nationwide network.

The acceptance of barter as a highly profitable way of doing business is most evident by the fact that barter now accounts for almost $700 billion in world commerce. There are some very respectable barter companies whose purpose is to bring together business and professional people who are willing to exchange the products and services they sell for products and services they need to operate and expand their business, without the availability of cash. Barter organizations make this possible through their vast networking capability.

**HOW DOES BARTER WORK?** On the one-on-one level, it's as simple as you telling me you would like to do my taxes this year in exchange for a professional consulting session with me. If we both agree on this exchange of services, we have bartered. If you and I pay cash to each other for our respective services (even if the dollar value is identical) it is not considered a barter situation.

On a more sophisticated level, if you want to acquire some product(s) or service(s), and you don't have a cash flow and/or you have no idea of which company will barter with you, you can simplify the process by joining a professional barter organization. The barter company operates as a clearing house for the goods and services of its members. You can join a national barter organization by paying a one-time membership fee of $495, then it's $6 a month in barter and 10% cash for any purchase. There is no transaction charge on the sell side. The annual renewal fee is $60 cash and $90 on trade. Other barter companies have similar sign-up fees, yet may charge you 5% cash for any purchase and 5% cash for any sale. These fees are small compared to the tremendous leverage you have in purchasing power.

**WHY BARTER?** *First and foremost:* You significantly increase your purchasing power and conserve cash by making purchases using the barter system instead of cash. *Second:* Additional business. The barter community will bypass the cash competition to barter with you. This might even generate referrals that pay you in cash. *Third:* Increase your cash intake. You barter advertising, brochures, print and direct mail to bring new cash customers your way.

**WHO BARTERS?** Countries, corporations, retailers, business owners and individuals are involved in this cashless exchange of goods and services. Thirty-five percent of the world trade is done by barter. Britain trades aircraft for Arabian oil.

Corporations use barter to obtain office equipment. Retailers use barter to exchange their merchandise for what they need from the barter network. Individuals exchange their respective services with each other. For example, I would be willing to barter professional seminars for a color computer scanner, telemarketers, graphic artists, professional organizers, a great dentist, book agent, computer teacher, fitness trainer, professional meeting rooms, a private office and/or loft space for scheduled classes. I would also be willing to barter my services for a matchmaker.

*How about you?* If you are in advertising, have a retail store or restaurant, have computer and/or fax machines, supply printing services, you are a prime candidate for the barter network. Unfortunately, not everyone is accepted as a member. Honorable barter companies are committed to the success of their members. They will decline your application if they already have enough members offering what you wish to offer.

*If you would like more information on bartering or would like to join a barter organization, contact me,* ***Joyce E. Barrie***, *President, Joymarc Enterprises, Inc., (212) 759-5556.* ∎

*Those who apply themselves too closely to little things often become incapable of great things.*

**Francois, Duc de la Rochefoucauld, Sentences and Moral Maxims, 1665, maxim 41**

# Breakage, Leg, Stacking, Roll-Up?
# Primer of the Industry's Buzz Words

*Dan Jensen*

## ACCUMULATED GROUP VOLUME

A distributor's group volume from the day he or she becomes a distributor to present. This value does not clear or reset each commission period; it continues to grow.

## ACCUMULATED PERSONAL VOLUME

A distributor's personal volume from the day he or she becomes a distributor to present. This value doesn't clear or reset each commission period; it continues to grow.

## ACTIVE

Only *active* distributors may have earnings. A distributor is considered *active* when they have at least Personal Volume and/or Group Volume. Some plans impose other requirements as well.

## BACK END

A term used to describe the portion of a Step-Level/ Breakaway plan which pays commissions to breakaway distributors (also see *Front End* ).

## BONUS VOLUME

The Qualifying Volume from the sales order that will be the volume credited for a sale. It is added to the Personal Volume of the purchasing distributor, his Group Volume, and the Group Volume of upline distributors according to the plan. This volume may optionally be different from the volume on which the commissions are paid (see *Commissionable Volume*).

## BREAKAGE

Many distributors are either unqualified or ineligible to receive some or all types of commission each month. When these unpaid commissions are retained by the company, they are called *Breakage. Breakage* also happens when an order is placed by a distributor who is close to the top of the genealogy such as a distributor sponsored directly by the company or an *orphan*. In these cases, some or all of the commissions that would normally be paid to an *upline* are retained by the company because there are few, if any, distributors in the purchasers upline. Please note that commissions are always paid *upline*. When the upline is small or nonexistent, the company retains the unpaid commissions, causing *Breakage.*

## BREAKAWAY

When distributors are promoted to a certain title, they "break away" from their sponsors and are thereafter called "Breakaway" distributors. Their group volume is no longer included in their sponsor's group volume. Breakaways are entitled to additional compensation, usually called a Generation Override. Breakaway positions are usually considered sales leaders.

## COMMISSIONS

An amount paid to a distributor on his or her direct and downline Commissionable Volume. It usually comprises Commissionable Volume within their group. Some plans call all forms of payment to distributors a "commission."

## COMMISSIONABLE VOLUME

The assigned value of each purchased product on which commissions are paid. It is the currency of the country in which the order was placed (though the eventual commission check may be issued in yet a different currency). Sales aids usually have no *Commissionable Value*. Commissionable products have a Commissionable Value which does not have to equal the price paid for the product.

## COMPRESSION

Used to describe the impact on a genealogy when a distributor is terminated.

## DISTRIBUTOR

A person or entity in the genealogy with a class of "D" (distributor) is a distributor. Anyone who is given credit for a purchase or can receive commissions must be in the genealogy. All distributors must sign a distributor agreement to avoid being considered employees of the corporation. Some companies allow two or more people to join together as a single distributor entity. This is also called *distributorship.*

## DOWNLINE

The distributors personally sponsored by a distributor, as well as all the distributors they sponsor, etc. Example: You sponsor Jim, who sponsors Mary, who sponsors Ted. All these distributors are in your downline.

## ENROLLING SPONSOR

The sponsor who recruits a new distributor or customer. This person may be different from the sponsor assigned to a new recruit in some compensation plans such as Matrix or Binary. It may also be different if the enrolling sponsor of a distributor is terminated. In this case, the distributor is placed directly under the sponsor of the terminated distributor.

## EXEMPTIONS

Distributors may be permanently or temporarily exempted from meeting certain requirements for qualification. These should be clearly defined but not published. Distributors should not expect to be exempted when they fail to meet their qualifications even when they have an excuse. Reality requires this capability, however, to deal with corporate mistakes and other exceptions.

## FRONT END

A term used to describe the portion of a Step-Level/ Breakaway plan which pays commissions to non-breakaway distributors.

## GENEALOGY

The sales organization of a company or distributor. It is also called a downline.

## GENERATION

The relationship between an Upline Breakaway and a Downline Breakaway, not including non-breakaways. The first Breakaway in any leg is a First Generation Breakaway. Generations are counted based on this period's fully qualified title.

## GENERATION OVERRIDE

The commissions paid to upline generations based on Group Volume. Note that this is only paid to Breakaways.

## GROUP

Includes all downline distributors not including any other breakaway distributor or the groups of any other breakaways.

## GROUP COUNT

The count of distributors in a group not including one's own self. Also called group size.

## GROUP VOLUME

The total of all Personal Volume sold by a group for a commission period. This includes one's own Personal Volume.

## INACTIVE

Each commission period that a distributor is not *active,* he is considered *inactive.*

## LEG

Each personally sponsored distributor and all his or her downline. Also, called *Line of Sponsorship.* If a distributor recruits five other distributors, placing them on his first level, each recruit comprises a *Leg* of a sponsor. *Leg* is also used to signify a single chain of distributors where "A" sponsors "B" who sponsors "C" who sponsors "D," etc. Together, they are often referred to as a *Leg.*

## LEVEL

The position a distributor has in a downline relative to an upline distributor. Distributors personally sponsored are *level one* to the sponsor. Those distributors sponsored by level one distributors are *level two,* relative to the original distributor.

## LEVEL OVERRIDE

The commissions are paid to upline distributors based on relative position in the genealogy. Note this is only paid to qualified levels. This type of commission is usually paid only in Uni-level compensation plans, not Step Level/Breakaway plans.

## ORPHAN

When a new distributor joins a company, a distributor application form is completed and sent to the company. On the application, the new distributor's sponsor name and account number is noted so the company can link the new distributor to their sponsor. Occasionally, the sponsoring distributor noted on the application is either incorrect or nonexistent making it impossible to correctly link a new distributor to an existing sponsor. In such cases, the new distributor is called an *orphan.* Procedurally, most companies have a distributor in their genealogy called "Orphan Account" to which all orphans are temporarily linked until their correct sponsor can be resolved. Commissions paid on the purchases of these orphans are usually retained by the company as *breakage* because there is no upline. Resolving orphan-sponsor linkages quickly is a high priority with most companies to avoid problems caused by not paying commissions to the correct upline.

## PAID-AS TITLE

The title a distributor is qualified for in each commission period. This title is not necessarily the distributor's permanent, official title. The Paid-As Title may change with each commission run but the Title doesn't. The Paid-As Title will never be greater than the permanent title.

## PERSONAL VOLUME

The value of commissionable products purchased in a commission period is called Personal Volume or PV. It is based on the sum of each purchased product's *Qualifying Volume.* It is credited to one and only one purchasing distributor in a commission period. It represents the total value of commissionable product purchased. It is usually included in the distributor's

Group Volume. When retail customers buy directly from the company, the *Qualifying Volume* of their order is usually included in the Personal Volume (and Group Volume) of their sponsoring distributor.

## QUALIFYING VOLUME

The value of a commissionable product which is applied toward distributor qualifications in the compensation plan. This value is added to both Personal Volume and Group Volume when purchased. It is different than Commissionable Volume. Commissionable products have a Qualifying Volume that does not have to equal the price paid for the product.

## QUALIFIED

In most plans, a distributor is "qualified" if they can receive *Generation Overrides.*

## QUALIFIED LEVEL

Some Uni-level plans which pay commissions based on *levels* instead of rank or title pay based on *Qualified Levels*. In those plans, a *Qualified Level* is represented by cache *qualified* distributors in a single *Leg* or single chain of distributors. Inactive distributors are not counted as *Qualified Levels* in these plans.

## RECRUIT

A distributor who is recruited by another distributor to participate in the compensation plan or business.

## RETAIL VOLUME

The total retail value of commissionable products is called Retail Volume. Retail Volume is seldom used by compensation plans. Most plans rely on wholesale values to determine qualifying and Commissionable Volumes used in their compensation plan.

## ROLL-UP

If a commission payment cannot be paid to a distributor due to that distributor being inactive, unqualified, or not eligible in a given period, the payment will "roll up" to the next qualified, active and eligible distributor upline. In most plans, the volume does not roll up with the payment which would result in increasing the Group Volume of upline distributors based on the poor performance of their downline. The practice of volume roll-up is not recommended while the practice of commission or override roll-up is recommended.

## SPONSOR

The distributor immediately upline of a distributor. It is *usually* the person who originally recruited the distributor but may be different if the sponsor has inherited one or more people through *Compression* due to the termination of previously sponsored distributors. It may also be different in plans that automatically place new recruits in certain spots or positions based on plan rules such as in Matrix or Binary plans. In these plans it is common for the sponsor to be different from the original *Enrolling Sponsor.*

## STACKING

A usually undesirable technique used by distributors to manipulate the compensation plan. Stacking occurs when a distributor recruits other distributors, placing them in a single Downline, Leg or chain instead of directly under the recruiting distributor.

## UNENCUMBERED GROUP VOLUME

To avoid the Group Volume of one distributor inadvertently promoting his sponsor (and his sponsor, etc., which is often called Stacking), some plans require Group Volume used for advancement to Breakaway position to be derived from sources other than new breakaway distributors. These other sources are most often other legs within the Group which are not being advanced to Breakaway positions. The Group Volume derived from these other sources is considered *Unencumbered Volume*. This distinguishes it from the Group Volume used by a downline distributor that breaks away. Some plans allow a portion of the Group Volume of a distributor achieving Breakaway status to be included in the unencumbered Group Volume of his sponsor. For example, a plan might allow excess or unused Group Volume of a downline distributor who is achieving Breakaway to be included in his sponsor's Unencumbered Group Volume. The purpose of this is to avoid distributors manipulating the intent of the compensation plan by funneling all their volume into one downline distributor, causing an entire Leg to be advanced to Breakaway status.

## UPLINE

A distributor's sponsor, along with his or her sponsor, etc. All distributors in the genealogy above a distributor are referred to as his or her upline. For example, if A sponsors B who sponsors C who sponsors D, then the upline of D consists of A, B and C.

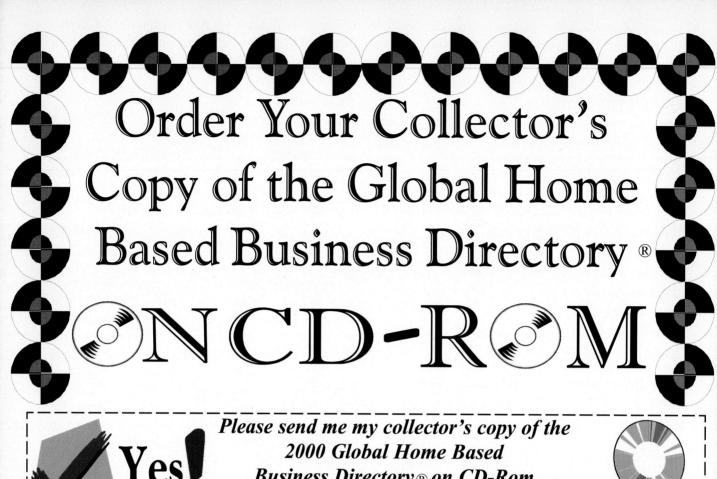

# Order Your Collector's Copy of the Global Home Based Business Directory ®

# ⦿N CD-R⦿M

**Yes!**

*Please send me my collector's copy of the 2000 Global Home Based Business Directory® on CD-Rom*

**Special Charter Offering -- ~~$29.95~~ Now Just $24.95**

Add $6.00 Shipping & Handling (Minnesota Residents add 6.5% sales tax)

PAYMENT   VISA ⦿   MASTERCARD ⦿   CHECK ⦿   MONEY ORDER⦿

Credit Card #_____ Exp. Date_____

Name_____

Address_____

City/State/Zip_____

Signature_____

**Marketing Solutions, Inc.**
**HC 6, Box 58A**
**Aitkin, MN 56431**
**Phone: (218) 927-3369, Fax: (218) 927-4613**

(all sales final)

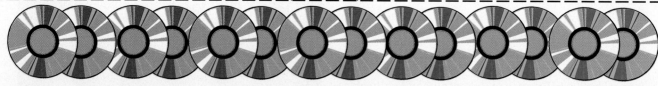

# HOW MUCH IS INFINITY?

FINALLY THERE'S
A COMPANY THAT
ALLOWS YOU
TO EARN WHAT
YOU DESERVE.

## NO CAPS
## NO LIMITS

NO WAY

OF BEING

CUT OFF

BY YOUR

LEADERS

OF YOUR

ORGANIZATION

*Introducing Leading Minds international*

an all-new company that's full of pleasant surprises. That's because Leading Minds International has been created for distributors, by distributors. We know how to make your business sizzle, because we've been there. Everything about Leading Minds International is done to help you succeed. From a stable corporate office, to a powerful value-based product line with impact and sizzle, to a compensation plan that doesn't hold you back. And most importantly, you won't be just another corporate stepping stone, but an important partner for success. We invite you to join with us in the launch of this revolutionary new way to build and run a network marketing company. Find out more about Leading Minds International and our expansion opportunities by calling today.

# 1-888-275-4LMI

LEADING *minds*
INTERNATIONAL
An Environment for Forward Thinking People

# Hall of Famer...

## *JoAnn Krause Expands on Another Winning Chapter in an Already Storied Career*

*Frank Clancy*

The Southern California home of JoAnn and Larry Krause once belonged to baseball superstar Barry Bonds, so it seems appropriate to describe her recent experiences in network marketing with a term borrowed from the sport pages. When the company with which she was affiliated went out of business in June 1996, Krause became a free agent. And, as Bonds himself had been a few years earlier, JoAnn Krause became a highly desirable free agent.

Though deluged with recruiting pitches, Krause took more than a year to sort through her myriad options, and as of this writing had not made a final choice. "You've got to have the right combination of financial resources and the 'sizzle' product," she explained. "Lot's of companies have one or the other; not many have both."

Newcomers and network marketing veterans alike can learn both from how JoAnn Krause has succeeded in the past and how she's planning her future.

Krause, a member of the International Network Marketing Directory's first Hall of Fame, was raised in Menasha, Wisconsin, the oldest of eight children in the Karasek family. They lived in a big, beautiful old parsonage. A solid middle-class family, her father worked as a high school biology teacher. The Karaseks valued hard work. And they valued the ability to sell products they were proud of. To earn Christmas money, Krause and her younger siblings made glittery wooden N-O-E-L's in the high school woodshop, then sold them door to door. "We learned to accept rejection," Krause recalls. "We also learned that if we had something we really valued and felt

*JoAnn Krause--The right combination of financial resources and sizzle products*

proud of, it was good to share with other people. My parents really taught us to sell at a young age. If it was something that was good, selling was very honorable."

Krause got her first job at age 15, as an "Avon Lady," the

> *"We always look for products that will enable people to get great results quickly. Then it's easy to share the products with others."*

youngest in the country. With little training, she did well. Years later, selling seems to come as naturally to Krause as breathing; she hardly thinks of what she does as selling. "We always look for products that will enable people to get great results quickly," she explains. "Then it's easy to share the products with others. It's like going to a great movie or a restaurant and telling your friends about it. We look for products that propel people," she says. "When I can take people who are not networkers and teach them what I've learned, I get real excited. I'm good at it, I think, because I like it so much. To me it's the easiest way of doing business. You're simply sharing those things that you have a passion for. If you're just doing it to make money it's a terrible business. If you find a product you have a passion for, it's much easier to sell."

Whether describing a product or talking on the phone to a potential distributor, Krause avoids the hard-sell approach. "The process is quite simple and personal," she explains. "What you're actually trying to do is find out what a person's needs and wants are. You're trying to find out where that person is in life, and whether your product or company is a good fit for him or her. If it works, great. If it doesn't, that's all right too. I hate to see people pressured. There have been times when people have approached me to sell something, and they are genuine, and they've left me a bridge back to them after I turned them down. And you know what? At times I've walked across that bridge," Krause reasoned.

Like many people involved in the industry, Krause stumbled accidently upon network marketing . When she was in her mid-twenties and the mother of two children-- her younger child, Wendy, was an infant, a friend invited her to a party where a line of custom-fitted bras were being sold. Fitted properly, the bras were far more comfortable--and healthier--than what women could buy in stores. Krause liked them so much that she started sending friends to parties. Before long, she was referring so many that she was asked to join the company. Eventually she became an assistant to the company vice president, in charge of motivational training nationwide. Though the company had a rudimentary compensation plan, she was hooked on network marketing. While Krause was managing a large Nutri System, she was introduced to a nutritional product that she realized could impact the lives of many people. Even though Krause was earning a respectable income as a manager, soon the loss of doubling her income potential and more freedom time propelled her into network marketing again. She and Larry quickly learned the plan and helped develop the required numbers of leaders to reach the top. The Krauses look back at the growth and schooling they learned while in this company; even though there were internal circumstances within the company that caused them to move on at that time, they still use the product. From there, Krause was introduced

*Jared and Stacey Krause*

to a weight management product. Because of her past experience in this field it was a natural fit for her. It was a system in front of a trend that she knew would sweep America. Here she earned in one month more than most people total in one year. Her time in the industry was paying off.

▶

She switched in the fall of 1994 to a start-up company with a hot new product--electronic cards that, when purchased in advance, enabled consumers to save a substantial amount of money when making telephone calls away from home. "When we first started selling prepaid phone cards," Krause remembers, "nobody knew about

> *"During times of prosperity, plan for adversity. I always tell people to be good givers, invest wisely and save."*

them." That was also Krause's first real involvement in marketing a product that wasn't directly related to health. "It was," she says, "a paradigm shift." No longer could the customer's health be the source of her passion. What she quickly realized was that helping a customer to save money was itself a gift. And she saw the financial independence had a profound effect on the emotional well-being of her distributors. "I also saw for the first time that people who were successful and did so well, that it changed their lives."

The downfall of that phone card company, and Krause's ability to land on her feet--with the financial resources to devote more than a year to scouting new opportunities, drove home something she had long told distributors in her downline: "During times of prosperity, plan for adversity. I always tell people to be good givers, invest wisely and save," Krause says. In truth, JoAnn and Larry Krause did more than land on their feet. They have thrived.

The Krauses live in Murrieta, California, an hour north and inland from San Diego, in a gated community built around a golf course designed by Jack Nicklaus. (Larry golfs, but JoAnn does not;

she's going to learn). Larry, once a manager at a utility company, accepted an early retirement offer, an easy decision to make, in some respects, since the Krause's income from network marketing was double his salary. In their free agency, they spend a good bit of time with their three grown children and grandchildren (the youngest an infant), who live in California and Oklahoma. Indeed, Krause considers time with family--and the closeness time brings, to be one of network marketing's greatest gifts.

Larry's retirement has given them even more freedom. "I always used to think that to be able to buy a one-way ticket and go on a trip--to go away and decide later when to come back--would be the ultimate expression of freedom," he said. "I haven't done that yet, but I will someday." Asked to name a destination, JoAnn mentions two widely divergent places: Hawaii and Israel. But the trip will more than likely have to wait. With her enthusiasm, experience and skills, JoAnn Krause isn't likely to remain a network marketing "free agent" for long. And, while she's done several stints in traditional businesses, she fully expects to join another network marketing venture. "We are definitely believers in the industry," she says.

Here are some of the questions Krause asks about every potential company:

*Scott and Stacey Krause*

❋ Does the company have a "sizzle" product or products? By definition, few companies if any, can be selling similar merchandise--and are not available in stores. Not long ago, prepaid phone cards were precisely this type of product. But the business, Krause believes, was partly a victim of its own success. Before long, anyone and everyone began selling phone cards. "We always choose a company that is ahead of trends and has consumable products that are unique," Krause explains.

❋ Does the company have the necessary financial backing? "In the past, you could start a network marketing company on a shoestring," Krause says. "We have a lot of success stories in the industry that started that way. Today, you need at least $3 million to assure a successful launch of your business. You can't start out on a shoestring and expect to make it like you could as recently as ten years ago."

✳ Do they have the staff and technical equipment to support distributors? Advanced communication systems, including 24-hour voice mail, fax-on-demand, internet communications and a web site, have become essential tools in the industry. At one company, Krause recalls, she could leave a single phone message and send it to all of her key leaders by hitting one button. That saved time-- and gave her more time to be with her family.

✳ Who's running the company? Do the people in charge have the background to keep a business running once it's successful? Again, Krause uses the phone card company as an example. "It was so successful that it was overwhelming to a young company," she says. Of course, in evaluating potential companies, Krause has a tremendous advantage over newcomers. After 30 years in the industry she knows a whole lot of people.

✳ Will your sponsor support you? Can you trust him / her? "You better respect the person who's telling you about the opportunity," Krause says. "He/she had better be a person of integrity, someone you can trust. If not, wait for someone you can...It's critical that the person you connect with will be a good sponsor and take care of you."

All of which would only lead JoAnn Krause to the biggest question of all: Which "team" would this free agent choose?■

 ## False "Truths"

It seems natural for us to focus on the negative, to the exclusion of the positive. But because we have not factored in positive experiences, our assessment isn't accurate. Dwelling on past failures or mistakes offers us a skewed and unrealistically negative account of our abilities. To make matters worse, we then take this to the next level, from performance to self-image. We focus on the putt we missed and begin to think of ourselves as a lousy putter. We dwell on the one question we muffed in the meeting and conclude that we are a poor presenter. We then "carry" this attitude the next time we are faced with a similar situation. And the "lousy putter" tries too hard and blows another...

These unrealistically negative views quickly become vicious cycles, reinforcing feelings of inadequacy about ourselves and affecting our self-esteem. Remembering only the errors, we begin to doubt our ability to handle the job.

Balance the losses with the wins and you get an accurate view of your ability and of how well or poorly you *really* did in a situation. If you are like most people you'll find that you are doing much better than you thought and that, in fact, you aren't giving yourself credit for being as good as you are.

# Targeting 50+ -- Mining The Wealth Of An Established Generation

*Direct marketing's new opportunities will follow the path of an aging America. The demographics, psychographics and economics of today's 50+ market, particularly men and women now age 50-60, are far too powerful to ignore.*

By shattering the myths of aging, direct marketers are putting together profitable new strategies for success. For example, the age of 50 has often evoked the image of someone turning gray and turning off to life due to both a dwindling spirit and dwindling finances. After all, an American's life expectancy at the turn of the 20th century was only 47 years. Yet as we are in the 21st century, American life expectancy has soared to 80, according to the National Academy on Aging.

Marketers have long coveted the considerable discretionary dollars possessed by teens and twenty somethings. We have also targeted the family-oriented needs of adults in the 30s and 40s. The demographics and economics of today's 50+ market, particularly men and women now age 50 to 60, are far too powerful to ignore. Consider these four key factors:

**1.** Fifty and older is becoming the dominant demographic in America. Between 1995 and 2010, the 50+ population will grow by an astonishing 41 percent. Between 1990 and 1998 alone, the demographic segment of Americans from age 50 to 59 grew from 21.8 million to 27.6 million (U.S. Bureau of the Census). That's an increase of almost 5 million people in this age group, or 27 percent. And right behind them are 40.3 million of their younger brothers and sisters age 40 to 49, an increase of 27.7 percent from 1990.

**2.** Fifty isn't old anymore. Sheer numbers alone are impressive, but marketers have even more reasons to value graying Americans. If you saw Mick Jagger perform during the Rolling Stones' last U.S. tour, you know that 50+ has a whole new image. And by the way, who do you think attended the Stones concerts? Audiences included hordes of men and women 50+ who make up the leading edge of the Baby Boomers and their immediate predecessors. Many brought their adult or teen kids (and in some cases, grandchildren) along to show them that this graying generation can still rock'n roll. Marketers of everything from health and beauty products to fitness equipment to clothing will find exciting new opportunities in this demographic if they rethink what it means to be 50.

**3.** Fifty doesn't mean down-scaling life. Improved medicine and more positive attitudes regarding health and health care have provided Americas age 50 to 60 with far better health than previous generations. Moreover, their older brothers and sisters aged 60 to 70 also enjoy improved health and longer life expectancies. As a result, seniors are, and will increasingly become more able to enjoy active lifestyles. We will see a greater demand for golf courses and all the equipment, clothing, and teaching aids that accompany them, plus senior softball leagues, tennis facilities, and educational programs and all the products and services that support them. Men and women 50+ will travel more, too. And they'll travel in many different ways. Some will go to resorts and take luxury cruises. Many will choose bicycle tours through the American West, vacations their parents would never have considered as either appropriate or practical.

**4.** Fifty represents unprecedented wealth. Yes, poverty will always affect some aging Americans. Others will just get by. But remember that the American economy has returned to world preeminence in the 90s, and the 50+ demographic will reap many of the rewards.

While downsizing has wounded many Americans in their 50s and 60s, our robust economy has enhanced the cash flow and estates of millions more. Men and women 50+ have poured massive amounts of money into mutual funds for investment and retirement, as have their younger counterparts who will soon be turning 50 year after year. And while these Americans often face the problem of supporting aged parents, millions of 50+ Americans are already beginning to inherit sizable estates from parents who achieved considerable financial success during the post World War II era. What's more, the run-up of housing prices over the past 25 years, plus higher limits on the profits of home sales, will create additional wealth.

In spite of government and media concerns, much of the current generation from 0 to 60 and the cohort behind them will see Social Security as playing only a secondary role in retirement planing; icing on the cake if you will. This could not be said of most of their parents. Direct marketers of financial services will find themselves helping a growing population of new, affluent retirees not simply to survive but to support unprecedented levels of consumption.

## The myth of homogeneity
It may appear from what I've already written that everyone in the 50+ demographic is the same. But gray hair is likely the only factor that unifies those in their second half-century. We must consider the variety of life stages and diverse attitudes that form varied segments in the mature market. They include:

### Leading-edge Boomers (50-60):
Americans just preceding the Boomers into their 50s +, the first Boomers reaching the half-century mark, as has President Clinton, are active working people at the peak of their careers and earning power. Even with college expenses they enjoy considerable spending power. Their incomes may dip with retirement, but they will also see children graduate and mortgages get paid off.

### Pre-Retirees (50-60):
These men and women are shifting their thinking towards life after careers and are actively planning investment strategies and real estate purchases for new primary homes and/or vacation homes to pave the way. Their assets will increase impressively between now and retirement.

### Early Retirees (50-60):
While members of the previous group are planning to leave their careers behind, these folks have already done so. Some are financially independent. Others are cashing in on early retirement or employer benefit packages spurred by down-sizing and are creating new careers, full or part-time, to augment retirement income. At the same time, many people in these two groups are devoting considerable time to community organizations and politics, traveling widely, or combining these activities with work or consulting as they restructure their lives.

### Young Elders (60-70):
True, this group is slowing down a bit, but having jettisoned most responsibilities and expenses, people in their 60s are increasingly taking advantage of good health to pursue hobbies and travel. Many continue to work part-time to stay active as well as maintain substantial levels of disposable income. Most also enjoy doting on grandchildren with gifts and recreational travel.

### Active Elders (70-80):
Here's the real surprise in American demographics. People are not only living longer, they're generally living better. It's amazing how many people into their 80s are not only filling cruise ships but traveling at home and abroad with groups like Elderhostel. Understanding their mortality, they're also often highly focused on making their children's and grandchildren's lives easier through cash gifts, trusts, and purchases of expensive items ranging from toys to furniture, vacations, and even automobiles.

### Sunset Elders (80-95+):
Spending wanes as elders face declining health and activity levels, but don't be fooled. In their final years, these oldest Americans often shift their purchasing patterns to providing for their children, grandchildren, and even great grandchildren. We also recognize that this segment has needs that can be reached through their 50+ children who frequently become caretaker/consumers for their parents. They take over such tasks providing guidance and even bill paying for purchases ranging from clothing and appliances to home health-care items and services. As you can see, the above demographic segments often overlap. And the health, lifestyles and financial positions of people within the same demographic segment may vary greatly. Take cruise travel, for example. You must create different strategies to reach 60-year-olds who are working and want shorter cruises and those who are retired and have time for longer cruises. Many men and women in this age group will restrict cruising to luxury ships. A growing number will want to sail on smaller vessels with more adventurous or environmentally oriented itineraries. Marketers or financial services to 70-year-olds will find some young and active elder more concerned with maximizing their income while others wish to conserve and grow their estates for their children and grandchildren.

## Factoring changing life experiences
Over the years, the behaviors of specific cohorts has changed significantly. For example, Americans who turned 50 in 1960 or 1970, and who grew to adulthood during

the Depression, generally revered thrift and often passed up major expenditures, even with money in the banks. Boomers now 50 grew when jobs were plentiful, careers were secure, and lifestyles reflected a prosperous America. They became an I-expect-to-have-it-now generation. They survived the 1960s and 1970s, became money-conscious in the 1980s, and have seen their investments soar in the 1990s. They spend money with a confidence their parents never had and will continue to do so. And unlike their parents today who generally don't understand technology, they freely respond to direct mail, catalogs, and infomercials by telephone and electronic commerce via the Internet.

Defining a specific target groups expectations, lifestyles, psychological profiles, and hot buttons makes all the difference. Given the diversity of the 50+ market that takes effort. But given the sheer numbers of people and dollars, this effort can pay off handsomely.

*__Bernie Herlihy__, who is over 50, is president of the Herlihy Marketing Group in Oakland, Ca. He can by reached by telephone at (510) 839-3620, Fax: (510) 839-4739, E-mail: bernie@herlihy.com.*■

# Cutting And Chopping

When the going gets tough, cut your losses! Cut budgets, cut costs, cut overhead, cut R&D, cut inventory. Cut, cut, cut. From Apple to Zenith, very few companies were exempt from the cut-and-chop mind set of the eighties.

As a result of this, euphemisms like "downsizing" and "restructuring" crept into the vocabulary of American business. As providence would have it, what if you picked up the morning paper and saw the following headlines on the front of the business page:

Raychem Will Trim Workforce by 900 - Layoffs Part Of Restructuring Effort

Big Hospital Supplier To Lay Off 6,400

New England Bank To Ax 5,600 Jobs

While it seems reasonable to get "leaner and meaner" in more competitive, fast-changing times, remember, you pay a high price for cutting costs. Despite all the layoffs of the past decade, despite increased automation and just-in-time inventory systems, U.S. productivity crept up by a scant 1.2% a year on average in the eighties. That's virtually no improvement from the seventies.

You want further evidence? Think about this: More than half the 1,468 restructed companies surveyed by the Society for Human Resource Management reported that employee productivity either stayed the same or deteriorated after layoffs.

If you want employees to love the customer and provide great service, to really make quality job one, want them to be more productive, assume more responsibility, take more risks, and make faster decisions, be wary of the lean-and-mean approach. Seventy four percent of managers at downsized companies said their workers had lower morale and distrusted management.

The cut-and-chop mentality creates an environment that cuts quality, innovation, and motivation as well. Performance is replaced by conformity, innovation by maintenance of the status quo. Spirit and morale plummet. People are scared and constantly look over their shoulders. The motivation is to keep a job, not to keep improving; to play not to lose, rather than to play to win. As a result, though you may have cut your costs, you've often cut your lifeline as well.

Bell & Howell, buffeted by takeover skirmishes and rumors of layoffs, became aware that the resulting "nervousness and gloom cost money." Rumors were spreading faster than voice mail. Their sales reps reportedly spent as much time on the phone, seeking updates of the rumors, as they did in the field selling. Studying sales performance during this period, B&H determined that at least 11 percent of profits (millions of dollars) were lost to the "lean-and-mean blues" of their *retained* employees.

# What's Wrong with This Letter?

*Herschell Gordon Lewis*

A sales letter doesn't have to be terrible to be worthy of improvement. Most business owners know how to write a competent letter. If they didn't, they probably had one heck of a time trying to get their businesses up and running. But "competent" isn't synonymous with "highly effective." A competent letter does a journeyman job. A highly effective letter does a Meistersinger job.

Take a look at the letter below that we have chosen for analysis (the names have been changed to protect the guilty). Nothing much seems awry, does it? But let's carry that sample letter into a rhetorical laboratory, where we can dissect it. Ah! We see a flaw here and a foible there. How could we have missed all those imperfections at first glance?

Is the opening too gushy? You bet it is, because it rings phony. Should paragraphs be indented? You bet they should, because every readership study says indented paragraphs are easier to read. Do we have a couple of grammar glitches and punctuation lapses? Well, yeah. Is the closing treacly and punchless? Sort of.

We give this letter a B minus. It's a

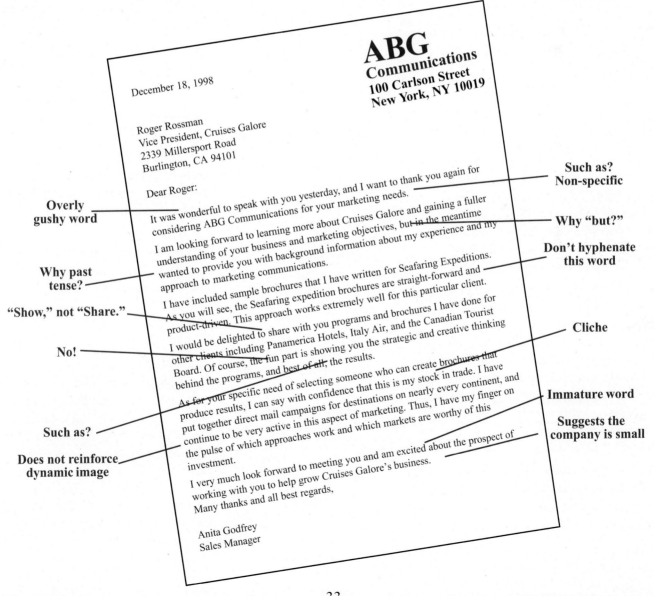

33

passing grade, but it's a lower grade than a business owner should score.

## Watch Your Words

A couple of compliments about the one-sentence first paragraph:

First, it is one sentence. Score one for the writer, for readability. Second, it has "you" twice, plus "your." Another point for targeting.

> *A competent letter does a journeyman job. A highly effective letter does a Meistersinger job.*

But let's deduct at least a point for "It was wonderful to speak with you yesterday." Come on, it wasn't wonderful. It may have been enlightening. It may have been gracious of the guy. It may have been pleasant. But wonderful? Don't writhe in pseudo-ecstasy because a prospect agreed to take your phone call. That turns you into a toady.

Then there's that nondescript word "needs." I propose that you never again in a sales letter use the word "needs" as a noun. Why? Because you always have a more specific term at hand (why not "to handle your marketing program"?), and an absolute rule of forceful communication is:
*Specific outsell generalizations.*

## Minor Questions About Usage

The second and third paragraphs provide background the writer obviously couldn't provide in a phone call. **Three minor points:**

1 Replace the word "but" in the second paragraph. "But" is a stopper, often misused. What might the writer have written instead? In my opinion, nothing. Put a period or semicolon after "objectives" and add "I" between "meantime" and "wanted."

2 "Wanted" absolutely, positively should be changed to "want." Why put this in the past tense? Customers deal in the right now.

3 What is that hyphen doing in "straightforward"? Of course the spell checker didn't catch it, because both "straight" and "forward" are legitimate words. But the writer should have caught it.

## "Share With You?"
## "The Fun Part?"

We have two separate problems in the fourth paragraph. "Share with you" is more personal than showing samples warrants. It also has a mildly pejorative overtone, with the "sharer" subliminally positioning herself above the "share." And did you catch "Of course, the fun part is...?" That's far too giddy, too teenage-like, too ingenue-ish to have any place in a business letter.

Understand, please: Enthusiasm is a potent sales weapon. But (note the use of "but" for this purpose) when enthusiasm is sophomoric, there goes image.

## Good Penultimate Paragraph

The next-to-last paragraph shows confidence and ability. There is no usage problem with "need" in this instance. One might mount a mild attack on "...this is my stock in trade" as cliche, as well as the vagueness of

the word "results" (a more specific phrase such as "increase sales" or a brief example of what the writer has done for other clients would have been better).

The one glaring drop-off in this paragraph is the word "continue." If that criticism puzzles you, consider that when someone tells you she "continues to be very active," the implication somehow is that she's nearing the end of her career.

The last sentence of this paragraph is excellent.

## Here We Go Again

Two "let's not" imperatives about the final paragraph:

1 Let's not be overly frilly. "Excited" is on the madcap side. "Enthusiastic" is a better way of one professional communicating with another.

2 When a prospective supplier suggests she's going to "help grow" a client's business, it implies that the business is now small. "Help enhance" is safer.

## Conclusion

See how much damage we can inflict on what at first glance seems to be a well-written letter? In fact, it is a well-written letter; it just isn't as spectacular as it might have been if the writer had read it through the eyes of the recipient.

*Herschell Gordon Lewis is chairman of Communicomp, a direct marketing advertising agency in Plantation, Florida. He is the author of "Selling on the Net" and "Sales Letters that Sizzle" (NTC Publishing Group, Lincolnwood, Illinois) and "Silver Linings" (Bonus Books, Chicago), a book about selling to the mature market.* ∎

**po-ten-tial (pə-ten′shəl) *n*. The inherent capacity for growth, development or coming into being.**

"*Transforming Human Potential into Purposeful Lives*"

# No Excuse! I'm Doing It

*Jay Rifenbary*

## What's an excuse?

Did anyone ever give you an excuse for not coming to a opportunity meeting or showing the marketing plan? Was the person ever you? The dictionary defines an excuse as a lie, a ruse or a cover up! And as Ben Franklin once said, "He who is good at making excuses is seldom good at anything else."

## Why does great success elude most people?

Most people don't live the lives they really want because of limitations they place on themselves--often in the form of self-imposed burdens called excuses! The reason for this is fear, which always lies at the heart of excuse making. Excuses produce negative thinking, depression, narrow mental horizons, and an ingrained "habit of failure."

Leaning heavily on excuses can cause problems ranging from resentment and anger, to partial or total failure. The crutch of excuses keeps people from growing, from developing their skills, maximizing their dreams and goals, and living the life they want.

One of the world's richest men, J. Paul Getty, had a plaque in his office which employees could easily read. It said, "Find a way to make one." He didn't tolerate excuses, and you will get greater results when you don't either.

Most people sabotage or "short circuit" their own success simply by making or accepting excuses. Ironically, they don't even realize they're doing it because it probably becomes an innocent, subconscious habit. Excuses are a "hidden" road block to truly great success. They need to be totally eliminated before you can succeed the way you really want to. If someone keeps making excuses, their progress will slow and they'll probably get "stuck" in a rut. I first learned about the "No Excuse!" way of life when I was a cadet at the United States Military Academy at West Point. It was one of four phrases you could say in response to an upperclassman's questions or comments. Yes Sir!, No Sir!, No Excuse Sir!, and Sir, I do not understand! Excuses simply were not tolerated. You took responsibility. It's a basic statement that leaves nowhere to hide. It played a vital role in my decisions as a thinker. It means to "clean the slate, get over it and get on with it." For those who want greater success, there's no time for unproductive excuse making.

Fundamental to the philosophy is that people need the dignity of satisfying work to make their own and others' lives better, as in network marketing. Whenever we combine labor and love with self responsibility, true success follows. That's the foundation of the "No Excuse!" philosophy. It can guide you to work smart at your business and create a life you love living.

*Guard against drudgery and discouragement in everything you do. To be effective at this, realize that your networking business contributes to your well-being, as well as that of others. And remember, anything you let get in the way of applying yourself to your goals is only an excuse!*

The "No Excuse!" approach to life is for people who grow and accept that success and failure are simply outcomes of their own behavior! Failure is just a stepping stone, a lesson to prepare you to achieve what you want. Many people see success only in the lives of others, which can cause them to develop an apathetic and defeating attitude. But it's difficult to recognize your own success if you are caught in a web of negative thinking. "No Excuse!" means you accept responsibility, throw out negative thinking, and no longer allow others to control your potential for happiness and success. "No Excuse!" supports your efforts to identify, work toward, and achieve your dreams and goals. The "No Excuse!" philosophy is meant to challenge you to explore your thoughts, feelings and perceptions, so you can realize wisdom, goodness and strength. You can then give more of your energies to serve others while building your business. It's important to let go of the need for approval while you begin traveling the road to fulfillment. The real or imagined expectations of others simply don't matter. If you still have a job, you may need to align some of your personal expectations with that of your boss. Just be careful your actions are in line with your value system.

## You're the decision maker in your own life

When I made my first parachute jump as a student at Airborne School in Fort Benning, Georgia, my parachute

36

lines tangled as I exited the airplane. As a result, my parachute canopy was also tangled and could not fill with air. I was falling to the ground, rather than floating gently. If I had hesitated for even an instant--to make an excuse, it would have fatally distracted me from the enormity of my predicament. I would not have been able to react quickly enough to save my life.

You too have the power to choose. Your accumulated choices structure the life you lead. Acknowledging you have choices is a first step toward accepting responsibility. Choosing to exercise your personal power by making changes, like choosing to build a network marketing business, is a challenge and joy in and of itself. It's also your responsibility to allow and encourage others to make decisions as well. When you use your power to do something in your best interest, like network marketing, it's also in the best interest of others. It's a win-win situation.

*Remember, your results depend on your choices and actions. Your actions, based on clear self-awareness accompanied by self-responsibility, can create turning points in your life.*

When you live a "No Excuse!" life, you will never again allow yourself to be "pushed by circumstances" or other people's desires that aren't in your best opportunity and responsibility to make a decision. You will accept responsibility for the actions you take that contribute to your failures and successes. You will not blame anyone else for your failures, nor take all the credit for your successes. But, you'll always be aware of the part you played in both. You will rejoice in your successes and view your failures as learning experiences. When you live a "No Excuse!" life, you will be drawn toward your dreams.

Maybe you're not sure what you want out of life. You might be reluctant to admit it. That's fine, many people have been "beat up" and "put down" so many times that they've given up on their dreams. If that is you, I

suggest energizing and challenging yourself to do whatever it takes to "snap-out-of-it." You can do it! The time is now! The missing link may simply be that no one ever shared with you how exhilarating it is to assume responsibility for your own life, dreams and goals.

*To be more successful it's likely you're going to need to make some changes. If you want change in your life, you need to initiate that change. After all, doing the same thing and expecting a different result could be considered a form of insanity! If you're waiting for life to change, guess what? It waits. You need to make it happen.*

## Be the hero in your own life

Were you taught that "life is a struggle?" This perception causes a lot of unhappiness. To "struggle" implies you are in a negative no win state. This dim view of life acts as a self-fulfilling prophecy and leads to negative results. It's an attitude of defeat. This is not to say life isn't challenging. Without challenges your life would be boring; you would experience little, if any personal growth. Challenges test you and help you stretch to new levels of achievement. As you incorporate the "No Excuse!" philosophy into your life and business, you'll find doing it without a struggle mentally is more effective, not to mention easier and more fun. Strive for the excitement and joy self-responsibility brings when you accomplish a goal. If you are reluctant to leave the comfort zone of hiding in shadowy fears, fine! It's your decision when to step out. It's a wonderful feeling when you understand and accept that outcomes depend on actions. This is the "cause-and-effect" principle. Even if you choose to stay in the shadows of your fears, and you accept responsibility for it, you have reached a level of awareness that most people will never know.

You can be a hero in your own life story. Whether or not this is apparent to anyone else is irrelevant. It's only important that you have reached this fundamental realization, essential for any meaningful accomplishment.

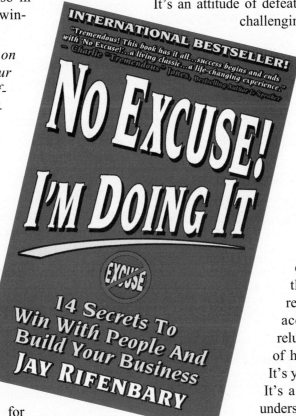

INTERNATIONAL BESTSELLER!

"Tremendous! This book has it all...success begins and ends with 'No Excuse!'...a living classic...a life-changing experience." — Charlie "Tremendous" Jones, Bestselling Author & Speaker

# NO EXCUSE! I'M DOING IT

EXCUSE

14 Secrets To Win With People And Build Your Business

JAY RIFENBARY

Although your decision making process can be influenced by others and the environment, it is ultimately your decision to act or not. The actions you take largely determine how you live your life, and whether or not you make your dreams come true.

## How good are you at making excuses?

The following list of questions will help open your eyes to the excuse making that may exist in your own life today. Read them out loud so you can hear your own voice. This will make it easier to be truthful with yourself.

▪▶ Do I use the words can't or couldn't, when actually won't or wouldn't is the truth?

▪▶ Do I procrastinate and not do what I need to because after all, I'm only human?

▪▶ Do I avoid meeting new people because I'm in my office all day, or I live in a small town?

▪▶ Do I accept defeat, convinced that nice guys finish last?

▪▶ Do I excuse myself from blame for a wrong doing because I was only doing what I was told?

▪▶ Do I fail to make phone calls because I lost the number?

▪▶ Do I smoke or overeat because I simply can't help myself?

▪▶ Do I fail to show the plan because I can't find anyone that would be interested?

▪▶ Do I blame my business stagnation on my upline or the economy?

▪▶ Do I neglect setting goals because I can't find the time?

▪▶ Do I say, I don't have time to avoid taking action to become more successful in my life and in business?

▪▶ Do I say, I don't have the money, when it's not true?

▪▶ Do I say, It's in the mail, when it's not?

▪▶ Do I say, I'd do it, but, when I'm about to offer an excuse?

▪▶ Do I make excuses instead of doing whatever it takes to give myself the life I want?

If you answered these questions honestly and, like many people, said yes to some of them, you are well on your way to eliminating excuses from your life and on the road to living a life of self-responsibility.

What are some of the decisions you are preparing to make this week, month or year? Which will have the most impact on your personal life and in your business? Are those decisions personal, financial, educational, family or spiritual? Are you willing to make the decisions necessary and take action to move forward? Are you willing to accept responsibility for the outcomes of those decisions? Be courageous. Write a list of decisions you'll soon be making that will impact your life and the lives of people around you. This heightens your awareness of the excuses you may have frequently used to either avoid facing decisions or taking responsibility for the results.

## How to keep excuses in check

We all live largely by behavior patterns and habits. They are practical solutions to our need to have ready responses to everyday situations. They are necessary and, for the most part, serve us well. In certain circumstances, however, our logic can falter. We may fall back on excuses to explain a failure or justify a fault.

### Keep these things in mind:

▪▶ Initially, the challenges of "No Excuse!" are just that--challenges. Relinquishing excuses requires effort.

▪▶ What's true for you is true for me. We all face problems that have a certain degree of similarity. We all need reasons to live, people to love, work to do, and joy to share. We all have sorrow and disappointment to bear.

▪▶ We're all better off when we're on the path of self-responsibility and action. Most of us are immobilized by the habits of blaming and excuse making, to one degree or another.

Will you grow rich with "No Excuse!" living? Yes. "Rich" may or may not include more money. That depends on you. "No Excuse!" living will:

▪▶ Enrich your own life and others you come in contact with.

▪▶ Give you the elements to create the success you want for yourself, your family and your business.

▪▶ Begin with a self-responsible act; accept that time is what you're born with, and your life is what you make it.

## Take charge of your life--you can do it!

Create your life based on your own dreams and goals, not those of others. We all have the ability to accept or reject who we are and what we're doing. Think about it. How often do people try to mold themselves to someone else's expectations to please them? If we do, we will probably suffer in silence or denial, the tragedy of not accepting ourselves and what we choose to do--like not following our dreams by building a networking business. Owning your life means having the courage to face up to such truths. It means risking, and maybe even taking relationships to the edge to accept yourself. That's OK. Just be yourself. The bonus is, you're likely to generate more respect from others. If your parents, siblings or friends don't approve of what you're doing, that's their choice. You may have noticed that the less you seek recognition from others the more you are at peace with yourself. To a point, it's appropriate to seek advice from or model your behavior after a few select people whom you respect; people whose lives are worthy of emulating, such as leaders in the business. It is also human nature to desire acceptance from others, but don't do it at the expense of your values. Focus only on those people who have your best interest at heart, whose value system is admirable to you, and who love and support you. By getting in the business, you've probably already examined your life and decided to head in a new direction. You weren't receiving the outcomes you desired, and saw the business as the way to get them.

Practicing "No Excuse!" principles will enhance your feelings of self-worth, self-love, and self-esteem. You'll also have an opportunity to learn to let go of people you may be using as protection from the fear of rejection. You'll learn how to create new relationships and live life on your own terms. As you let go of beloved people who don't support you, and stop hiding behind them, you and they will experience a freedom to love each other beyond anything you've ever known. You will experience life more fully when you realize that you determine your future. With "No Excuse!" thinking, you no longer blame events or other people for your shortcomings, failures or timidity in taking action. You have the opportunity to lay the foundations of a future of living your life to the fullest.

You may want to ask the questions that anyone on a new path might ask: Am I ready for this? Am I responsible enough? Am I capable of dealing with success? Am I capable of dealing with failure? Am I prepared to accept the impact my new found self-responsibility will have on my family and friends? Am I willing to take responsibility for my actions when things don't go my way? Am I willing to stop weaving an intricate tale of "inescapable" coincidences to tell the world how everything conspired against me? Am I willing to say "No Excuse!?"

**There's "No Excuse!" not to live your dream**
The greatest thing I have learned so far in life is to accept responsibility for my own life. Realize we are where we are today, because this is probably where we chose to be several years ago. If you're not where you want to be, it's time to move on. It's the "No Excuse!" thing to do.

I hope you embrace the "No Excuse!" lifestyle, practice self-responsibility, and take charge of your family, yourself, and your business. Follow the dreams in your heart and become the best you can be. You'll be more successful with your business when you treat it as a "No Excuse!" experience. When the going gets tough, just say, No Excuse! It can help you achieve your goals, build your business, become free, and live your dreams.

I dare you to get started living a "No Excuse!" life right now. Call your upline and say "No Excuse! - I'm Doing It" You'll both be excited. Go for it. You can do it. There's "No Excuse!"

*Jay Rifenbary is a professional speaker, consultant, trainer, and founder of the Rifenbary Training and Development Center. He is a graduate of West Point, was a qualified Airborne/Ranger and Military Commander, and sales and management executive. He's sought after as a speaker and author on success, motivation, leadership, communication, team building, and family and interpersonal relationships. To order "No Excuse -- I'm Doing It," call: (800) 724-0845, or fax your request to: (518) 587-6417.* ■

# Are You a Sloppy Listener?

## *You may be missing out and messing up if you're not paying attention*

*Arlene Weintraub*

I recently completed an assignment for my boss, who turned around and told me I was missing a key element. This is not the first time something like this has happened. I know I'm not deaf, but I can't figure out why I keep getting it wrong when she gives me directions.

Chances are your hearing is fine-- you're just not listening as carefully as you should be. Many professionals don't realize that listening is as important a career skill as any other. "Good listeners make fewer mistakes. They do the job right the first time," says Tony Alessandra, Ph.D., author of *Charisma: Seven Keys to developing the Magnetism That Leads to Success* (Warner Books). Good listening draws people to you, enabling you to form stronger alliances with your clients.

So what exactly is good listening? "It's the ability to take in the sounds and sights around you and ferret out what's important," says Kristin Anderson, a trainer who teaches communication skills through her Minneapolis-based company. Here are some ways to help you tune in:

### Minimize distractions

If you find your attention lagging, the problem could be your surroundings.

An easy solution is to insist that business discussions take place in a quiet place. "Give yourself permission to create the best possible listening environment," Anderson suggests. "Never hold a meeting at a time when you might be distracted by other responsibilities."

### Write it down

We can speak only 135 to 175 words per minute, but we can listen at the rate of 400 to 500 words a minute, notes Alessandra. The ability to make the most of that leftover time, which experts call the "speed gap," often separates a good listener from a bad one. Bad listeners daydream or think about how they are going to react before they've heard the entire message. A better strategy is to jot down the crucial points, says Alessandra. This will not only help you record the assignment accurately, but will assure the one speaking that you're not leaving it to memory. Another tip: Note questions in the lefthand margin. That way you can spot them easily when it's your turn to speak.

### Keep your emotions in check

People often miss key points because they're too busy reacting to something other than what's being said. You may feel distracted, for example, because the one that is speaking talks in an unusually loud tone of voice. Or you may have a co-worker who, much to your chargrin, occasionally calls you by a name that throws you off course. Learn to control your gut reaction to them. This way you'll make sure you are concentrating on the content of the message, not the delivery of it.

### Engage your whole body

Listening with more than your ears helps you to stay focused and reassures the speaker you're on track. Carolyn Coakley, co-author of the textbook, *Listening* (McGraw Hill), suggests making regular eye contact, leaning forward slightly and nodding your head every once in a while to demonstrate attentiveness.

Finally, sprinkle in a few brief vocal cues, such as "uh-huh" or "I see." "If you don't give these cues, the speaker might wonder if you're staying with him/her throughout the conversation," Anderson says. By demonstrating that you're a good listener, you'll increase the speakers confidence in you and enhance your relationship with him/her.

*Arlene Weintraub is an associate editor at "P.O.V. magazine" in New York City.* ∎

## Excel in a Changing World

In order to excel in a changing world you must build on your strengths. Don't try to be good at lots of things; be great at one.

If you strive to be well-rounded, you will probably end up flat.

# Multi Tech

## Putting the Power of a Virtual Office to Work for Your Home-Based Business

- PROFESSIONAL SALES PRESENTATION
- 24 HOUR ANSWERING
- DATABASE MANAGEMENT OF VOICEMAIL
- NO BUSY SIGNALS
- FAX & VOICE BROADCAST
- EMAIL NOTIFICATION
- ONE BUTTON CALL RETURN
- MESSAGE NOTIFICATION
- PERSONAL GENEALOGY
- CONTACT MANAGER
- CALL SCREENING
- FAX ON DEMAND
- ON LINE WEB MANAGER

## It's revolutionizing the network marketing industry.

The most powerful tool ever created for the network marketer can be fully customized to fit the needs of your business or opportunity. Sales presentations, voicemail, fax on demand, web managers, broadcasts and contact managers all in one package – MultiTech combines the power of the Internet with the ease of the telephone. MultiTech gives you new freedom in your business. Listen to your messages and graph your advertising results from any Internet connection. Put MultiTech to work for you and discover just how far your business can go.

**Another tool to fast track your business by VHS Direct**

**Contact:** Communications Division

## 800-597-2640

VHS DIRECT, INC., DEPT. 777
5814 W. Pico Blvd. Los Angeles, CA 90019
Tel: 323 937-0915 Fax: 323 937-0917

# The 10 Worst Mistakes in Direct Mail

*Jeffrey Dobkin*

I made all these mistakes, so you don't have to! Yes, I made plenty more, too. You can learn from my mistakes and increase your chances of success. It's just as easy to succeed as anything else, so follow these few simple guidelines of exactly what not to do. Don't worry, you'll find many other mistakes to make on your own, but at least you won't have to make these.

## 1 Not knowing your audience

All writing should be to a specific targeted group that you research until you know it intimately. Aim for your readers' personal hot spots, in a writing style and level with which they are comfortable. Learn how the group feels, acts, what your audience likes or hates. Then, craft your writing in style and content specifically to your readership.

## 2 Mailing to the wrong list

This is probably the most common and most fatal error made in mailings. Spend as much time on researching your list as you do on the creative aspects of writing and layout, and on the research about your products, pricing, and offer. Unless the people on your mailing list have a desire or need for your product (or service), they're going to be tough to convince, and probably impossible to sell. Offering Buick mufflers to Chevy owners just won't work, no matter how great the copy or price.

## 3 Not writing to clear objectives

Nothing muddies good writing like not having a specific goal. Make sure you know where you're going with each piece you write, then stay focused. Write your objective first, in the upper right-hand corner of your page, and refer to it often. Stay on target. My objectives are usually to have people call, write, or send in the business reply card. Ninety-nine percent of the time it's for a free brochure or booklet, offered so we can send a more qualified prospect a harder hitting package.

## 4 Price before offer

> *The headline is the single most important element of your ad. Solely on the basis of this one line, your reader makes the decision to continue--or not to continue--to read.*

"Only $49.95!" No matter what you're selling, a price has no meaning until readers know what they're getting. Make sure you tell them about your product first. If your number one sales point is your product's low price, you may introduce the price early on in the same sentence.

## 5 Price before benefits

"Just $89.95!" may sound like a great price to you for a stereo, but if you present it first--before showing exactly how great the radio is, most readers will go right past your ad, or toss your brochure out before they even see your product or offer. You need to tell readers what makes your price so great, in terms of benefits to the reader.

## 6 Wrong price point

There are thousands of theories on how to price your product correctly. Funny, each formula gives you a different answer. My formula is correct, and it works with every product, every time: Let the market set the price. You do this by testing each price point you feel will work, and seeing which one brings in not only the most orders, but the most overall profit. That's your price; simple isn't it? This is the only way I know of to set the correct price for maximum profit in direct marketing. The only way.

## 7 Inadequate testing

There's no reason to lose big money in direct mail. Everything is testable, and you should test small mailings until one is clearly a winner. Then ramp up slowly. Next time mail to a slightly larger test group. If that works, test mail still larger mailings. Until you know you're absolutely going to be profitable, stick with smaller test mailings, so you'll never lose a large amount of money. How will you know you'll be successful? As long as you mail the same package to the exact same list, your results should be the same.

►

42

### 8 Wrong objective to your marketing price

Asking for the sale instead of selling the call can be a fatal mistake. The objective of a small or classified ad for any product more than $10 is to get the prospect to call or write in. Unless you're sending a long, hard-selling direct mail piece (or have a full-page direct selling ad) your objective again should be to make the reader call for additional information or your free informational booklet. Generally, you do not ask for the sale in an ad or short letter; you ask for a call. Offer the product, show the benefits, and sell the call hard. This is the secret of success in direct marketing.

### 9 Wrong headline

The headline is the single most important element of your ad. Solely on the basis of this one line, your reader makes the decision to continue--or not to continue--to read. Use the Jeff Dobkin 100 to 1 Rule to create both the headline of your ad or press release and the teaser line on your envelope: Write 100 headlines, then pick the best one. Take several days for this task. If you can figure out a quicker and better way, please let me know.

### 10 Not telling your readers exactly what you want them to do

You should tell your readers several times exactly what you want them to do. Be specific. Let readers know exactly what action you want them to take; tell them again and again. I wrote a sales letter for a printer and actually asked a dozen times for readers to call! Excessive? After mailing it, the printer had to hire two more people to answer the phones. If I can smoothly weave "please call" into the copy this many times, you can ask for the call at least three or four times without being obnoxious.

*Jeffrey Dobkin is the author of "Uncommon Marketing Techniques," and "How To Market A Product For Under $500." He is also a speaker, a direct mail copywriter, and a marketing consultant. To contact him, call (610) 642-1000, or fax (619) 642-6832.* ∎

## A Lawyer Who Broke The Law

Gary Friedman, the youngest partner in an East Coast law firm, loved the drama of the courtroom and was very good at it. Well known throughout the area, he was clearly a rising star with a promising future. But Friedman felt increasingly cramped by the traditional combative and adversarial legal tactics in which no one ever really seemed to win. He also noticed that his euphoria after a win was very transitory. In fact, in these all-or-nothing verdicts he wasn't even feeling so good about winning anymore.

Following his values, Friedman decided that he couldn't do what was "right" for him and for his clients within the confines of lawyering as he knew it. He began to wonder if there couldn't be an alternative. As a result of much soul searching, Friedman started a practice in "mediation" law. Rather than having a combative, alienating environment in which each party was pitted against the other in a bitter battle, Friedman worked with *both* parties, helping them to reach an agreement based on fairness rather than greed. In mediation, the power is with both parties' arriving at a *mutually agreed-upon decision,* a far cry from the traditional setting in which a judge makes the decision and the parties often don't see, much less talk to, each other. The lawyer/mediator's role was to help *both* parties create solutions that worked for both sides, to bring people together, not separate them.

Today, Friedman's groundbreaking work is widely known and respected. In addition to his successful mediation center in the San Francisco area, he teaches at the Stanford Law School and conducts training programs in mediation for lawyers and judges throughout the United States and Europe. Following his values resulted in Friedman making it possible for more humane lawyering and litigation. Having the courage to question the rules of a very old game, Friedman created a new one that was guided by the values of fairness and provided value for everyone.

# Five Steps to International $uccess

*William J. McDonald*

The global economy is here! More and more direct marketers are investigating business opportunities outside the United States. While companies that never ventured abroad until recently are now seeking more receptive foreign markets, those with existing foreign operations realize they must be even more competitive to succeed against other international operators. For the firm venturing into selling their products for the first time and for one already experienced with such activities, the requirement is a thorough and complete commitment to its foreign venture.

The movement beyond your domestic borders accounts for the complexity and diversity found in international marketing operations. Nevertheless, direct marketing concepts, processes, and principles all apply. The goal is still to make a profit by promoting, pricing, and distributing products for which there is a demand. The problems you face in reaching that profit goal come from the uniqueness of foreign operations and the variety of strategies and tactics necessary to cope with operating in other countries. However, it's not about different concepts of marketing for those environments within which your plans are implemented.

Differences in infrastructure, technology, competitive dynamics, legal and government restrictions, customer preferences, culture, and any number of other uncontrollable elements can, and frequently do, affect profits from your international activities. Those differences also create uncertainty because they must be coped with in designing your marketing program.

You cannot control or influence the uncontrollable elements, but instead, you must adapt to achieve a successful business outcome. In that sense, the controllable elements of your marketing decisions must be accommodated to the frequently unique uncontrollable elements of a foreign marketplace.

The uncertainty of different foreign business environments creates the need for a close study of the operating environment within each new country. Different solutions to fundamentally identical marketing tasks are often necessary because of those unique environmental conditions. A strategy that is successful in one country can be rendered worthless in another by differences in political climate, stages of economic development, or culture.

For example, adding the new elements of long distance, language, customs, and tariffs to the normal complexities of fulfillment is forbidding. The fulfillment steps most likely to be affected by offshore marketing are response mechanisms, order entry, data processing, payment processing and shipping. When designing the order form, you must view the ordering process from the vantage point of foreign nationals. Data entry problems are a critical factor often overlooked by marketers new to international activities. Finding economical ways to ship printed matter is of particular importance because distribution of catalogs and other promotional materials can be costly.

## Five Steps to Going International

Following five basic steps will help you get your international venture off to a smooth, orderly, and successful start. The steps for going international are illustrated by stories and experiences of others.

## Assess Your International Potential

Because international growth requires an extension of your firm's resources, you must first focus on assessing your international potential. This should give you a picture of the trends in your industry, your domestic position in that industry, the effects that international activity may have on your current operations, the status of your resources, and an estimate of your domestic and international sales potential. In general, you should not get into international markets unless you have a secure base of operations in the United States.

Next, find out about candidate countries by using market research. It's easy to ruin an otherwise well-conceived plan by making fundamental cultural, partnering or resource allocation mistakes. It's far better to put the time into research at the beginning rather than find out when it's too late that you didn't do enough homework.

In addition to target market demographics, your research should help characterize each candidate country's cultural context and political climate. Research can also reveal the level of support available, including print shops, list services, telemarketing, postal and shipping, computer services, and what U.S. marketers now operate in each country.

The multi-country and multi-cultural nature of international business makes gathering information more complicated and expensive than when done for only one country. The data that is abundantly available in most industrialized counties is often not available in developing countries. General economic statistics such as gross national product, inflation, and interest rates that are important to any country analysis are hard to find for regions of Asia, Africa, and Latin America.

Considerable difficulties can be encountered comparing research about various countries because units of measurement and group classifications differ among those countries. For example, the definition of "urban" varies substantially from country to country, depending on relative population density. In Japan, for example, urban is defined as an area with 50,000 inhabitants and in India it includes all places with 5,000 inhabitants or more.

Because governments and private organizations generate large amounts of data, there are a variety of such data sources, ranging from those that provide general economic data to that focusing on specific products. The principal external secondary data sources are the U.S. government, the governments of other countries, international agencies, trade and business associations, and some large data service organizations. For example, the U.S. Bureau of Census issues World Population, which contains worldwide demographic data; Foreign Trade Highlights, published

by the Department of Commerce, provides basic data on U.S. merchandise trade and major trading partners and regions; Background Notes, prepared by the Department of State, present a survey of a country's people, geography, economy, and foreign policy; and Export Information System Data Reports, available from the U.S. Small Business Administration, contains a list of the 25 largest importing markets and the 10 best markets for U.S. exporters.

### Get Expert Advise and Counseling
Once you have assessed your international potential and made a decision to commit time and resources, the next step is to get expert advice and counseling.

Many groups in the private sector and government provide guidance to companies planning to go international. Industry trade associations are also very useful, as are private consulting firms and the business departments of some of the major universities.

If you are entirely new to international marketing, call the U.S. government's Trade Information Center, toll-free, at (800) USA-TRADE, (800) 872-8723. If you are further along, contact the nearest district office of the Commerce Department's International Trade Administration. State governments are another source of assistance.

### Select Your Countries
After reviewing your research and digesting the advice, the next decision is about which country or countries to enter. You need to prioritize information about each country's environment, including economic strength, political stability, regulatory environment, tax policy,

infrastructure development, population size, and cultural factors to reflect influences on the candidate countries. For example, the economy of a country is generally considered critical to most businesses and is normally ranked high in importance. Equally critical are political factors, particularly government regulations. Others are more dependent on which product you market. For example, the technological stage of a country plays a more influential role for computers than for cosmetics.

European countries are frequently attractive candidates because they are more industrialized and stable than most of the rest of the world. However, while those countries tend to get good rankings, they are very competitive markets. Although they have high sales potential, it may already be tapped by many competitors.

Where this is not the case, like with China and India, it can mean a large investment of time and capital. For some companies, this is the right approach because they have the resources to invest and need the large populations to make their strategies work.

Another approach is to enter several countries simultaneously, focusing on target markets common to all countries. This avoids the risks associated with a "single market at a time" effort. By targeting multinational segments, you reach individuals from a variety of countries who all share a common interest. The benefits of this approach are relatively low cost, minimal investment, and lower risk.

Several U.S. companies--Lands' End, Viking, Paper Direct, QVC, AOL and CompuServe, among others, have entered the German market with success. Lands' End relied on German language consumer response lists for the bulk of its launch. Copy-heavy direct response print ads in newspapers and direct response TV commercials were also used to generate requests for catalogs. Viking opened operations in the United Kingdom, Ireland, France, Belgium, and the Netherlands, before making the decision to enter Germany late in 1994. Although they knew that Germany had the greatest potential and significant number of obstacles, it was concerned over the regulations related to privacy, data protection, and marketing promotion.

In selecting among countries, you should pay attention to local purchasing power. Expect to price your goods according to the market. You may also need to reposition your product to appeal to specific income classes or redesign your product to make it more affordable, including cheaper versions and repackaging in smaller sizes.

A country's infrastructure of essential services such as transportation, communications, utilities, and banking, has a tremendous impact on your ability to conduct business. For example, shipping goods overnight, using telemarketing, or reaching large audiences efficiently, can pose major problems in developing countries. Because computer technology might also not be advanced, the establishment and maintenance of databases may be difficult.

Neiman-Marcus Direct hopes to skim the cream of Mexico's consumers by mail. The fact that the average household receives only 10.1 pieces of mail a year should leave plenty of space in Mexican mailboxes, if there were enough mailboxes. A dearth of mailboxes is only one of the problems Neiman-Marcus Direct faced in mailing its international catalog to Mexico. Among the others: A scarcity of Mexican lists, a postal service infamous for corruption and slow delivery speed, longer address lengths, no demonstrated consumer propensity to shop through mail, and no established Mexican catalog industry.

Despite those obstacles, Neiman-Marcus Direct sent Mexico 100,000 copies of an abridged Spanish version of its American catalog. Prices were listed in pesos and included all tariffs and duties. Orders went into a bilingual telemarketing center in Dallas. The results were good enough for Neiman-Marcus Direct to keep processing. Catalogs are now mailed out four to six times a year.

## Develop an International Strategy

In developing an international strategy, write a business plan that lists short and long-term goals, the competitive niche you're seeking, and how you're going to position your offering. In general, a successful strategy identifies and manages your objectives, both immediate and long range; specifies tactics you will use; scheduled activities and deadlines that reflect your objectives and tactics; and allocates resources among those activities. The marketing plan should cover a two to five year period, depending on what you are selling, the strength of competitors, conditions in the target countries, and other factors. Keep your strategy flexible because often it is only after entering a country that you realize that your way of doing business needs modification. Successful campaigns are those in which plans can be changed to exploit unique local conditions.

Set Realistic Sales Goals--
Don't underestimate the local competition. Local companies can be highly sophisticated operations. More importantly, they know their country and understand how their culture operates and reacts.

Most manufacturing firms begin their global expansion as exporters and only later switch to another mode for serving a foreign market. Exporting has the advantage of avoiding the costs of establishing manufacturing operations in a country, which are often substantial. By manufacturing the product in a centralized location and exporting it to overseas markets, you may be able to realize economies of scale. However, this has drawbacks, including whether shipping from the U.S. misses the location economies of moving production elsewhere. Exporting may result in high transport costs that make it uneconomical, particularly for bulk products. Exporting problems sometimes arise from delegating your marketing in countries where you do business to a local agent who does a less than adequate job.

L.L. Bean and Lands' End, two of the largest U.S. catalogers operating in Japan, followed very different strategies. L.L. Bean's strategy has been to develop the market completely from offshore, and it has been very successful in that approach. It mails into Japan from the U.S., receives orders in the U.S., and fulfills orders in the United States. Its only concession to a local presence is several customer service desks in Tokyo, which it contracts to a third party. Full page advertisements are placed in local newspapers (in the Japanese language) offering a free catalog. English language catalogs contain Japanese language instructions and order forms. By managing its business in Japan from offshore, L.L. Bean enjoys a significant reduction in its mailing costs. Lands' End has taken a completely different route by establishing itself offshore as a Japanese company. It offers an English language catalog with U.S.

dollar pricing and a Japanese language catalog with prices in yen.

Joint ventures are also a popular mode for entering a new country. With this arrangement, each party holds a percentage of ownership and contributes a team of managers who share operating control. Some firms seek a majority share and thus tighter control. Joint ventures enable you to benefit from a local partner's knowledge of a country's competitive conditions, culture, language, and politics. In many countries, political considerations make joint ventures the only feasible entry mode. On the negative side, joint ventures are associated with potential loss of control over subsidiaries.

Eddie Bauer Japan has a joint venture with Otto-Sumisho, Inc. to develop Eddie Bauer stores and distribute catalogs in Japan. Eddie Bauer Japan's first major effort was a 16 page Eddie Bauer sportswear insert in the "For You" catalog in the summer 1994. The following year, they mailed four Japanese language catalogs.

In a wholly owned subsidiary, you own 100 percent of the new subsidiary in a foreign country. You can either set up a completely new operation in that country or acquire an established firm and use it as a springboard. With a wholly owned subsidiary you can maintain tight supervision over operations in the country, and you benefit directly from the experience gained from operating in the market. On the other hand, a wholly owned subsidiary is generally the most costly method for serving a foreign market because you must bear the full costs and risks of setting up operations. You must also bear all the risks associated with learning to do business in a whole new culture.

When pricing your product for sale in a country, pay attention to the relationship of the dollar to the foreign currency, concentrating on its purchasing power and the price levels. If you're unique, you may be able to command a higher price.

By pricing products in yen, pounds or deitsche marks, you risk losing profits due to currency fluctuations. But, you can reduce or protect your exposure to swings in exchange rates with a money management technique called "hedging." It's a risk management tool that helps you protect your overseas profits by locking into an exchange rate. If you get the right rate at the right time, you may even gain on the exchange. But, a mistimed contract can result in losses. However, a practical solution price selection is to "pad" your product price by adding five percent (or more) to your product's

> *When pricing your product for sale in a country, pay attention to the relationship of the dollar to the foreign currency, concentrating on its purchasing power and the price levels.*

price to accommodate fluctuations in currency exchange rates.

The most important barrier to your international plan may be culture. Whether adapting an existing package or developing an entirely new creative one, you need to be sensitive to a country's tastes, customs, taboos, and habits. For example, the product and audience in the target region should determine whether to translate into a local language.

In going overseas, companies such as Gateway and Dell had to entice customers to a new selling approach because people were accustomed to buying from a store or dealer. Dell tripped up and Gateway was slow to get going, but aggressive moves by both companies caused competitors much discomfort.

### Select Your Media

After investigating and selecting foreign countries for your product, the last step in an international venture is to select a one or more marketing media. However, first, there is the decision to market products directly or, alternatively, to utilize the services of an intermediary. You should make it on the basis of your firm size, the nature of your products, your previous export experience and expertise, and business conditions.

List costs can vary considerably from country to country. To get the best discounts, seek out a recommended broker in that country, or find a good broker in your own country who is prepared to negotiate lower rates for international lists.

Because mailing lists in Russia are so unreliable, the Hearst publishing empire decided to forgo direct mail altogether in the launch of Cosmopolitan magazine. Instead, it counted on newsstand sales to distribute the first issues to potential readers, hoping for large pass-along rates, and for readers to return one of almost a dozen reply cards bound or blown into every issue.

In the U.S., magazine launches are usually accompanied by mail drops to potential subscribers, often from lists of existing subscribers to other magazines. That approach was not feasible in a country where the mail is notoriously unreliable and where, until recently, ordinary Russians subscribed to publications by filling out a form at their local post office. Often, Russian publications had no idea who their subscribers were and went by post office numbers when measuring circulation.

Internationally, postal reliability and rates limit mail order offerings, including catalogs. However, where the postal systems work well, they can be too expensive for mass marketing. For example, Japan has an excellent postal service, with reliable and fast deliveries, but the costs can be prohibitive. The lone exception to the usually inadequate national postal systems in Third World countries is Brazil, where there is overnight delivery of first-class letters 86 percent of the time.

Door-to-door selling is popular in Asia because they tend to put as much importance on who they are buying from as on what they are buying. For the same reason, telemarketing is not widespread in Asia, although it is growing.

Fulfillment poses such a challenge to international marketing, perhaps because there is no one right method. Garnet Hill, a consumer apparel cataloger, fulfills orders to customers in 15 to 20 other countries from its centralized facility in Franconia, NH. A centralized facility is usually less costly for a cataloger, providing it can find a fast, economical way to ship. It sends an average of 15 to 20 packages a day to Japan. Paper Direct, a leading direct marketer of preprinted papers and supplies for the laser and desktop publishing industry, takes a centralized approach to world market fulfillment. It offers more than 3,000 items through two separate catalogs to customers in 35 countries.

## Summary

Going international first requires that you asses your international potential to get a picture of your industry trends, your domestic position in your industry, the effects exporting may have on your current operations, the status of your resources, and any anticipated sales potential. The next step is to get expert advice and counseling. After reviewing your research and expert advice, select a country or countries in which to sell. You need to prioritize information about a country's environment, including economic strength, political stability, regulatory environment, tax policy, infrastructure development, population size, and cultural factors to reflect their influences on the countries you are considering.

Develop a written business plan that lists short and long-term goals, the competitive niche you're seeking, and how you are going to position your offering. A successful international marketing strategy identifies your objectives; specifies tactics you will use; schedules activities and deadlines that reflect your objectives and tactics; and allocates your resources.

*William J. McDonald is the general manager of New Thinking: An International Marketing Services Agency (http://www. newthinking. com). He is the author of two books: "Direct Marketing; An Integrated Approach," published by McGraw-Hill and "Cases in Strategic Marketing Management," published by Prentice-Hall. Dr. McDonald holds a Ph.D. and Masters degree from the University of Chicago and a Masters of Management from Northwestern University. He can be reached at 555 University Avenue, Suite 275, Sacramento, CA 95825, by phone at (916) 488-3139, and on the Internet at wjm@newthinking.com.* ∎

# Doing Something You'd Do For Nothing

With interviews of over 500 top performers, it was discovered that the most common ingredient for success was that people love what they are doing. Their work brings them not only satisfaction but considerable joy. Doing something you love brings joy, passion, and excitement into your life. It gives you more vitality and makes you *want* to get up in the morning.

"I enjoy (my work) so much," says Tony Tiano, president of KQED-TV, "it doesn't ever seem to be work. I'm surprised every time I get a paycheck!" Tiano is reflecting what I hear whenever I talk to a top performer: making your business a pleasure is necessary.

"You can be born with $100 million," observes David Brown, producer of *Jaws, The Sting,* and *The Verdict,* "but unless you find something you really enjoy, money is of no consequence. I always did something I would do for nothing."

SETTING GOALS... NOW *THAT'S* A CLASSIC!

# Opportunity has its rewards

**The opportunity to build your own business can be rewarding in different ways to different people.**

You set the goals, go your own pace, schedule your own time, and determine what you want in return. You can market as many, or as few, product lines as you choose — from personal care products to popular brand-name catalog merchandise. More than 3 million entrepreneurs in some 80 countries and territories have found this business opportunity made possible only through Amway is worth a closer look. See for yourself. Perhaps *you* can discover the rewards you've been seeking.

**The Business Opportunity Company**™

If you'd like to know more, call for a free brochure at **1-800-544-7167** or visit our website at **www.amway.com**    © 1998 Amway Corporation
In Canada call **1-800-922-6929**.

# Bankruptcy: Myths and Truths

*David M. Anderson*

In my view, the bankruptcy law is proof that attorneys actually do have a sense of humor. I realized this in law school when I discovered the basic operation of bankruptcy law: "You mean there's a law that lets you tear up all your bills? Is this really legal?

Previously, I was under the impression that "bankrupt people" would be taken away to some remote prison, haplessly banished forever.

The reality is that, at least among attorneys and business people, bankruptcy is increasingly accepted as a fact of American economic life. It is used, and sometimes abused, in many situations as a financial tool or negotiation strategy.

Although my law practice is almost exclusively in the area of business law and commercial litigation (bankruptcy is a separate specialty), the pervasive nature of bankruptcy law and practice means that all business people will likely be dealing with bankruptcy issues at some time during their careers, possibly as debtors, preferably as creditors.

BANKRUPTCY LAW

In this article, I would like to generally discuss some important bankruptcy issues and problems for business people, and offer some self-defence techniques which will let you laugh (ok, at least smile) when someone who owes you money files bankruptcy.

## Liquidation vs. Reorganization

The procedure most people think of when bankruptcy comes up is the Chapter 7, or **liquidation** bankruptcy. This process is commenced by the debtor, but may also be commenced by creditors. It results in the sale of liquidation of the assets of the debtor. This means the debtor is left with nothing at the end of the process, right? Wrong. The law allows what many people, especially creditors, feel are extremely generous exemptions which allow the debtor to retain a homestead and motor vehicle (up to a certain value), and many household goods and other property. The exemptions may be claimed under federal or state law. Not surprisingly, most debtors choose the exemptions which allow them to retain the most property.

Under **reorganization** bankruptcy, Chapter 11 (corporate) or Chapter 13 (individual), a plan is proposed by the debtor which allows for a portion, usually 10% to 50%, of the debts to be repaid over a period of time. Again, exemptions are allowed and certain debts such as secured real estate are placed in a priority position. However, if the plan payments are not made as agreed, the court or creditors will likely petition to convert the proceedings to a liquidation bankruptcy.

## Stay and Discharge

**Stay** and **discharge** are two crucial concepts in bankruptcy. Once a petition in bankruptcy has been filed, the **automatic stay** goes into effect. This is one of the most important concepts in bankruptcy. Essentially, it is akin to a police officer shouting: "FREEZE!"

The automatic stay prohibits all creditors, their attorneys or collection agencies from taking any action against seeking permission from the bankruptcy court. Severe penalties may be imposed on a creditor who knowingly violates the automatic stay.

The ultimate goal of the debtor in bankruptcy is the discharge of his/her debts. This is accomplished following the distribution of assets if a liquidation bankruptcy or the successful completion of the plan if a reorganization bankruptcy.

Certain debts are, in most circumstances, not dischargeable, such as taxes and student loans. In addition, if the debt was incurred by means of fraud or by use of materially misleading financial statements, a creditor can petition to obtain an exception to the discharge. Bankruptcy judges, however, will scrutinize such claims by creditors and the creditor has the burden of proof in establishing such fraud or dishonesty of the debtor.

## Pre-Bankruptcy Self-Defense Techniques

There are a number of methods to increase the likelihood that your debt will get paid, even if your debtor files bankruptcy.

▶

First, just as the three most important things in real estate are location, location, location, the three most important things as a creditor in bankruptcy court are security, security, security! The tools that will put you in a priority position in bankruptcy court are mortgages, security agreements, UCC-1 filing statements (for equipment accounts receivable and other assets) and mechanics liens. These tools, if properly drafted and filed with the appropriate agency or office, will ensure that you will at least get the value of the security in the bankruptcy proceedings.

Second, if your debtor is a corporation or limited liability company (LLC), with either no credit history or poor credit history, you need to secure personal guaranties from the principals or others whose credit you have thoroughly checked.

Finally, and this one, believe it or not, is not as obvious as it sounds: File the Proof of Claim Form!

If you are listed by the debtor as a creditor, you will be

> *The reality is that, at least among attorneys and business people, bankruptcy is increasingly accepted as a fact of American economic life. It is used, and sometimes abused, in many situations as a financial tool or negotiating strategy.*

sent the notice of filing the bankruptcy case, and in most instances, instructions for filing a proof of claim form which accompanies the notice. An incredible number of creditors see the notice from the bankruptcy court and don't bother to send in the form, believing that the likelihood of payment is remote. If you don't file the form, you can't collect any money available.

## Alternatives to Bankruptcy

Good bankruptcy attorneys will explore the available alternatives to bankruptcy, since regardless of the increase of bankruptcy filings, there remains a negative stigma and it will adversely impact credit for up to 10 years. Here are a few options for debtors to explore:

### Private Reorganization

Essentially, this procedure, in lieu of bankruptcy, involves the debtor's attorney or representative contacting each creditor or the primary substantial creditors and proposing the payment of a percentage of the debt owed, either in an immediate lump sum or in a series of payments, with the understanding that if the proposal is not accepted by the creditor, the alternative is bankruptcy. Most creditors will be open to this alternative, especially if they are convinced that they will obtain more money sooner than in bankruptcy court.

### Asset Protection Strategy

This requires considerable ongoing planning and forethought, but essentially involves arrangement of one's financial affairs in a manner which renders and individual or business financially "bullet proof." In other words, through corporations, LLCs and through a combination on insurance, gifts and establishment of trusts, one becomes impervious to creditors' threats and lawsuits. Bankruptcy law is essentially viewed as a protection strategy. If an individual or business has no available assets, it needs no protection.

### Be Proactive

Many bankruptcy actions could be avoided by establishing and maintaining a sound business plan and first action to seek help before reaching a crisis stage. Prevention and planning can help you avoid problems which might necessitate bankruptcy down the line.

*David M. Anderson, is a business and Internet law attorney with 18 years experience representing small and medium-sized businesses. He can be reached at Anderson Law Office, 701 Fourth Avenue South, Suite 500, Minneapolis, MN 55415. Phone: (612) 337-9504. E-mail: dma@visi.com.* ■

## Polish The Stone, Don't Reshape It

Everyone has been on the receiving end of the Conventional Wisdom that warns us to shore up our game and improve our weaknesses. But plugging up holes in your game can be a very frustrating and time consuming activity. It also, as every Break-It Thinker knows, distracts you from honing and perfecting your strengths, from polishing the stone.

# Expert Advice On List Selection

*Keith Petersen*

*These basic questions and answers will help provide you with a solid understanding of telemarketing lists.*

**Q What are my list choices?**

Lists come in all shapes and sizes. Some may have only a few names, others may have millions. Some are compiled, others are response. Some have business names, others have consumer names. More important, some allow telemarketing, unfortunately many don't.

**Q Where do I go to find lists to rent?**

Most direct marketers use the services of list brokers. List brokers have intimate knowledge of what lists are on the market and which lists have worked for similar offers. They will listen to what your needs are and put together a list recommendation. This is a free service and usually includes list titles, quantities and costs. List brokers often have areas of expertise that can provide the extra boost to make your project a success. They get a 20 percent discount from the list owner/manager and charge you the published rate.

If you want to go it alone, you can get a copy of the SRDS book of lists. Each list on the market will be shown along with the list sizes, selections available and costs. Each listing will also have the name of the list manager responsible for marketing the list who will help you with your order. If your business is a telemarketing service agency, you may be able to get the 20 percent broker discount if you ask and can prove you are reselling (renting) the list for an end user.

**Q What does a list cost?**

How long is a piece of string? Compiled files (which use the phone book as a basis) can start around $35 to $45 per thousand with phone numbers and go up as you add geographic or demographic selections. Response files (subscribers, members, buyers and responders) start around $55 per thousand and can go up to $200 per thousand or more. Each list owner has their own perceived value of their files and sets their price accordingly.

**Q What's the story on renting for telemarketing purposes?**

Many lists do not allow telemarketing. Most magazine current subscriber lists cannot be telemarketed; however, expired subscribers can usually be called.

The balance of response files may or may not allow telemarketing--you will have to speak with the list manager to find out. Even if telemarketing the list is accepted, many list owners require a script prior to final approval.

If you select a compiled file, you will generally not need approval for telemarketing unless you request information on children. Again, in this case, you may be required to obtain script approval.

One last hurdle. Some lists may approve telemarketing, but not have telephone numbers. Then you will need to have a good data processing service bureau append phone numbers to the list.

**Q What is phone appending and what results can I expect?**

Phone appending, simply put, matches phone number with a name and address and adds that phone number to the record. Expect to find just over 50 percent phone numbers for the files you submit. You will not get unlisted or brand new phone numbers. Prices for this service start around .06 cents for each record found and move down with higher quantities.

**Q Any secrets of the pros I can use?**

Here are some points to focus on:

**(1)** Don't be afraid to ask someone to use their list. The best lists may be those that are not on the market.

**(2)** Consider companies with similar clients. It never hurts to ask, and the cost may be much lower than similar lists on the market.

**(3)** Target even the best lists using geographic and demographic selections. Use ages, incomes, home values or ZIP codes to help narrow your list to those most likely to respond.

**(4)** Run your list against the DMA Do Not Call list, and the Florida and Oregon, Do Not Call list. These folks are not likely responders anyway and you do your reps and company a favor by staying away from possible litigation.

**(5)** Consider other suppression files to remove unlikely responders. The Polk Choicemail product, available at many data processing service agencies, and bad credit suppression files can help eliminate nonresponders and improve your conversion rates. Again, work a deal so as not to pay for these bad records.

**(6)** Negotiate with list owners/managers. Make sure to only pay for net names used. If the list does not have phone numbers, set it up so you pay only for those records to which you later append a phone. Get discounts for large list orders. If you are renting multiple lists, pay each list owner only for unique records. Any merge/purge processor can provide you a report showing the net records used from each list.

**(7)** Last but not least, be sure, as in all you do, to carefully code and track the performance of each list. Future projects and continued success require careful tracking of all results. Knowing what works and what doesn't is the key to long-term success.

So there you have a quick, basic guide to list rental. Choosing the proper list when asked can be the most important part of making a telemarketing or mailing campaign successful. In the end, your best plan of action may be to develop a good relationship with someone knowledgeable about lists. You'll be glad you did.

*We strongly encourage you to submit any questions concerning telemarketing list selection to: Q&A, One Technology Plaza, Norwalk, CT 06854. If you would like your questions answered specifically by* **Mr. Peterson**, *please address your envelope to his attention.* ∎

## Keep Your Dreams Alive

Once you have found your dream or rekindled one you thought was gone forever, the real work is *keeping the dream alive.* One way to accomplish this is to have reminders of it all around you. These will help you remember why you are doing what you are doing, rekindle your fire, and rejuvenate your spirit. Remembering your dreams will put your everyday activities into a larger perspective.

A regional sales manager for Hewlett-Packard had a dream of having H-P dethrone IBM in his area, with himself at the helm. The problem was, as he looked out his office window, he faced a large building with the letters IMB on it.

So, to keep reminding himself of his dream, he took a picture of the IBM building, sent it to an art studio, and had the "IBM" airbrushed away and "H-P" put in its place. He enlarged the photo to poster size and put it on his wall. On the new "H-P building" he outlined the penthouse with yellow pen and wrote "my office." Every day it graphically reminded him of where he wanted to go and what his dream was.

There are small reminders in every walk of life:
The salesman who kept a picture of his dream car, an old reconditioned Corvette, at the top of his sample case, so it was the first thing he saw whenever he opened it.
The schoolteacher who began collecting maps of bike routes across the country to serve as a daily reminder of her dream of cycling from coast to coast.
Arnold Schwarzenegger, seven-time Mr. Universe, who would go into the corner of the gym every hour and visualize himself winning the Mr. Universe contest again.

All these reminders help to keep dreams alive. They add kindling to the fire in our hearts every day. They keep us moving forward and give us more vitality.

Jesse Jackson's son said it eloquently in nominating his father at the 1988 Democratic Convention: *"The shame in life is not to fail to reach your dream, but to fail to have a dream to reach."*

# Doing It...Sabrina's Wei

**One Of Network Marketing's Brightest Stars Sets Sail On Her Greatest Challenge**

Her friends call her a genious, others a savvy unstoppable force. With these credentials, starting her own company comes as no surprise for the Vancouver-bred beauty

*James Law*

I t's a beautiful autumn day in Vancouver, Canada. The leaves are falling and the air is crisp. The sun is shinning off the snow-capped mountains. Sitting in the lobby lounge of the Pan Pacific Hotel, we watch the sea planes take off along the waters of Burrard Inlet. Anyone who has ever spent time in this city is aware of these magical moments. There's a special feeling that flows through a persons body when they leave here. However, I have an added bonus: I'm sitting with Sabrina Wei, whom I've known for years, and at times, felt I have taken for granted. When I examine what her contribution has been to my life, it's difficult to deny her impact. At 5'8" with long, jet-black hair and model perfect features, the casual observer might see her as a Vancouver socialite who spends most of her time shopping without a care in the world. However, once she begins to speak, it's nearly impossible to ignore the substance behind the exterior.

Sabrina was born and raised in Vancouver, Canada, to nurturing parents of Chinese descent. She garnered academic honors throughout high school and college, culminating her education at the top of the Dean's honor list, and presided as president of two collegiate business and investment societies.

At age 17, Sabrina was the youngest person ever hired by what is now the prestigious CPA firm of Deloitte & Touche. While working toward the position of Senior Auditor, she also specialized in finance and investments, additionally learning the fundamentals on how to build a company, starting from the ground floor. She learned what it takes to

**With mom at her side, Sabrina bags a trophy at an International Heritage award banquet**
*(in October, 1998, the company folded)*

run a company in a responsible manner, enabling it to remain a long term, viable entity.

When Sabrina was 20-years-old, life took on a dramatic change. One weekend, while working at the office, she noticed the partners of the firm were also working. This was when she realized that the senior partners were always bringing in new clients and servicing the existing ones. Did they ever have the time and freedom everyone longs for? With the writing on the wall, she saw what a 40-year

plan was for most people was turning into a 45 to 50-year plan for her. Was this what she wanted? Certainly not! With that in mind, Sabrina kept an open mind about life and opportunities. She was definitely prepared on the day someone introduced her to network marketing.

Sabrina often traveled with her parents from Vancouver to Seattle. On one particular occasion, her parents wanted her to meet with friends to share an "opportunity." Little did Sabrina realize at the time what an important

*Sabrina (center) takes a break from the rigors of everyday life to enjoy an outing with friends*

turning point that trip would become. Given her accounting background, Sabrina viewed the opportunity as entrepreneurial. She immediately realized all the benefits of network marketing and was amazed that this concept had never before been introduced to her. Then again, who would have thought that she, of all people, would be interested in network marketing. Sabrina uses this example that you can't forecast who will or will not join this industry. In comparison with traditional business, she also recognized the pitfalls and risks had either been drastically reduced or eliminated through network marketing. After reassuring her parents of the advantages of a career change from accounting, she was soon helping Nu Skin enter the Canadian market. Within one year, Sabrina had climbed the ranks to Diamond Executive, the first person ever to hold this title in Canada. Nonetheless, she moved on —joining Images International (now Neways) where she soon became a regional vice president and helped

launch the company's entry in the Hong Kong market.

Why would a successful networker earning a six-figure income leave an industry that had changed her life? When asked this question, there is a look of disappointment that comes over Sabrina as she answers. "As time passed, I became concerned about the hefty quotas that were assigned and onerous for the part-time person. I felt as though I were selling a dream — a dream most people couldn't accomplish; only a few at the top." She always felt that compensation should be geared more towards the success of an average person; the part-timer or beginner. "If they, of all people, can find success on a consistent basis, it reduces or eliminates attrition, the greatest problem in network marketing,"

Leaving the network marketing industry, Sabrina spent the next five years building a successful investment consulting business in the Orient. However, upon her return to

Vancouver, she was working on a project when an event happened that would change her life. She and I were introduced to each other by a mutual friend. At the time, I had my own computer consulting business that took care of today's financial needs, but not the tomorrow's. Sabrina saw my potential that evidently escaped me. She felt I would be perfect for network marketing; especially given the fact she had watched the industry's growth and improve into something she was confident in recommending. Though skeptical, Sabrina went on to explain the benefits and why I would prove the ideal candidate. Finally, I agreed to take a closer look. It was then that Sabrina began searching. The research and scope of her examination brought out aspects of the business that I myself would never have thought of. It was far more than what she had learned while in accounting. There was the insight of what it would take to have an opportunity favorable for the common person, plus an understanding of the ethical

*Candace (left) and Anna (right) join Sabrina at the Miss America contest*

responsibility to accept nothing less than having every element in place before moving forward. At this point, I decided to jump in -- only if Sabrina was there to support me.

Sabrina put her investment consulting business on hold and jumped back into network marketing. The research paid off. In just three years with International Heritage, Inc., I went from being broke with no assets and bad credit, to living a lifestyle most only dream of. However, Sabrina is more pleased with my self-development than my monetary status. And humble as she is, does not feel I owe her anything. She recognizes the fact I was the one who did the work. Still, when I take the stage for a training session and look out into the audience, there sits Sabrina, grinning from ear to ear. I also know she's brimming with pride because of my accomplishments. As an individual who initially abhorred even the thought of public speaking, I went on to earn

Top Trainer award two years running. All the credit goes to Sabrina and her faith in me to be the very best. She impacted my life and others in a very positive vein; not only financial, but personally as well.

While with International Heritage, Sabrina seized the opportunity to excel. She was an original board of directors member, a top income earner and a member of the Executive Council of the President's Advisory Board -- the volume of her organization accounted for approximately 40 to 50 percent of the company's overall business. You might say that lightning struck twice in Sabrina's life, bringing her to the top in both companies. This time, however, she not only brought others along, but myself as well. This made the journey much more satisfying for both of us.

How many times have we all heard that nothing in life is for certain -- other than death and taxes. Even with all

the research conducted in the early stages, no one could predict if International Heritage would survive. It definitely cut the odds in our favor. International Heritage achieved phenomenal success, earning $200 million in sales with its more than 200,000 representatives. However, in October 1998, due to unforeseen circumstances, IHI turned the key in its door for the final time. For Sabrina, this was an emotional time as she had built friendships with so many others. In the blink of an eye, it was all taken from her. Even though there was no clear choice for anyone, it was interesting to observe the various paths other pursued after IHI.

I can still remember the morning Sabrina called me to weigh our respective options. We had been

*A winsome Sabrina at her graduation ceremony from Simon Fraser University*

*'Whatever it takes, we want to be able to provide the best customer service, and to accomplish that, we have to do everything well. There is no margin for error'*

helping others start a new company. Suddenly, we had our doubts about the direction in which that company would go. We both received attractive offers from other companies that included a host of tempting amenities. Was this a reason to sign on with another company? Absolutely not! Sabrina had a definitive set of criteria in mind before moving forward with any company. Everywhere she looked, there was that certain something missing. Finally, the answer -- starting your own network marketing company! Gathering a core of leadership and utilizing all her knowledge, Sabrina proceeded down a path of no return. Leading Minds International, Inc. was now born. Pre-launch was December 1998, followed by the official door opening ceremonies in January 1999.

The entire premise of Leading Minds is founded on the statement, "Give me a place to stand and I can move the world." Currently, there are plans for four distinct product lines: An age defiance group of high impact personal care, plus nutritional products targeted towards feeling and looking better, technology products that are related to telecommunications, virtual office, cell phones and Internet products. Additionally, there are fine collectibles from around the world. Finally, the company will provide financial services, including taxation and asset protection services for retail representatives and employees. Sabrina feels strongly about providing products people want and can value, whether or not there is an opportunity attached.

Recently, I asked Sabrina why Leading Minds should be any different than another start-up venture within the network marketing industry. She stated, "There's has been a very strong trend recently towards

*Sabrina engages in donkey polo between mind storming sessions*

outsourcing specific functions, rather than becoming experts and making mistakes along the way. If we are not able to be the best at something, that's exactly what we've done. Whatever it takes, we want to be able to provide the best customer service, and to do that, we have to do everything well or hire the best to do it for us. To be successful, you shouldn't necessarily work harder, you should work smarter." This theme has been prevalent in all she has accomplished thus far in her professional life. "Whatever you want to do, look for a mentor in that field. Look for successful people, seek out the experts and don't go it alone. Always be open to new ideas and other ways of thinking," Sabrina recommends.

What does Sabrina hope to accomplish with LMI? It's pretty obvious she has never done anything half-way. She plans to set new standards for a start-up venture in this industry, and work together with other companies to raise professionalism, giving the industry a better image. On the personal side, she hopes to provide people with more freedom of time and money.

Sabrina is passionate about the business. She applauds its ability to change lives for the better and provide an equal opportunity for all, regardless of age, gender, race, finances, skills or experience. Sabrina feels a strong belief in helping others overcome personal and self-imposed limitations.

As one who has been touched by Sabrina's own personal philosophies, I am a living testimonial that she does not expect much. Her belief in the industry and what it can do for others is not a dream; it's reality.

There is an intensity emanating from Sabrina to others that simply cannot be ignored. The path she is now on with Leading Minds is one that was inevitable. To quote an old saying: "Genius does what it must and talent does what it can." For myself, I'm buying the coffee today. I think I owe her at least that much. ■

**Robert Van Reypen**

We have all heard the old time tested adage: "A person is judged by the company he keeps." Today, another one exists: "A company is known by the people it attracts and keeps."

In order for a company to attract top caliber talent, it is imperative to have a meaningful Mission Statement, high quality products, financial stability, ethical policies and procedure, and last but not least, strong management. Once a company finds top caliber talent, it should provide the following: competent financial management and excellent customer service. Encouragement and recognition for key managers, plus the fulfillment of its commitment to the chosen candidate must also be implemented. No company has ever failed because a key player was "over qualified." However, by hiring the top talent is not an unconditional guarantee of a happy, long-term relationship. There are other factors to consider. The company has an obligation to create and maintain an environment that is conducive to working together as a team. To draw the maximum from a key player, that person should feel needed and very much appreciated. Unfortunately, in many instances this is not the case.

*Customers who cut corners in hiring competent talent is akin to shooting ones self in the foot. The company will limp along while the aggressive "go-getters" willing to pay a professional fee for finding them a quality position, will move onward to financial prosperity and industry recognition.*

capable of doing in the future, what his/her goals are and the job expectations. It also gives the candidate the opportunity to determine if the company and position will provide a long-term, mutually satisfying relationship. Both parties must possess a certain chemistry between them when making a final decision. The recruiter in charge of hiring should always keep in mind that a candidate will be able to fit nicely within the company structure and work well with others.

Another aspect to consider is value received from professional executive recruitment assistance. This depends upon the relationship between client company and recruiter.

# In Search of Top Caliber Talent

There must be complete trust and mutual commitment. The recruiter's task is to

Customers who cut corners in hiring competent talent is akin to shooting ones self in the foot. The company will limp along while the aggressive "go-getters" willing to pay a professional fee for finding them a quality position, will move onward to financial prosperity and industry recognition. Therefore, an honest, straightforward interview is a must in setting the stage for a meaningful and mutual evaluation.

A resume or "track record" is historical. Using a resume as the sole piece of information to judge a candidate without the benefit of a face-to-face meeting has been a hinderance for many companies, and not necessarily the best choice. Because of this oversight, too often a top caliber candidate who possesses a strong potential to contribute is passed up. An in-person meeting consisting of frank and open discussion between both parties is beneficial. This tells the company what the candidate is

seek a qualified candidate in accordance with the agreed upon position profile. It is the client's obligation to respect the recruiter's judgement in presenting the candidate, recognizing that his/her professional reputation is an effective contribution to the strength of a client's key management team. Additionally, the recruiter must receive prompt payment from its client for the agreed upon price. Unfortunately, there have been situations wherein the recruiter has fulfilled his/her commitment, only to have the client company attempt to dispute or delay payment of a fee. However, I choose to think these companies are in the minority, even though they do cast a cloud over the industry.

Remember the face-to-face meetings and the camaraderie that should always exist between the parties in question. And one final reminder: Hire the best. You'll be glad you did. ∎

When It comes to
Financial Freedom
and Nutritional Science

ENOUGH SAID!!!

www.integriscorp.com or call 1-800-550-7558

# The Joy of Coaching

*Peter McGugan*

As the century turns, network marketing soars high among the fastest growing sector of a booming U.S. economy; and with good reason. As long as people hunger for hope, self-esteem, independence and upward mobility, home is where the heart and business will flourish. Sixty four percent of the U.S. population will be working full or part-time from home in 2004.

The rocket fuel for this trend is a cutthroat corporate culture.

## When mother corporations became mutha corporations.

Early in the century, corporations promised and delivered life-long relationships and secured pensions, until 1980s business school grads discovered they could boost profits and stocks by liposuctioning management. It was cancer to loyalty.

Grooming someone else for achievement and excellence is fool hardy in any corporation that right-sizes by escorting employees off the property with armed guards. In corporate America, coaching someone to do your job is often the beginning of your end. Coaching is the antithesis of most corporate cultures.

Corporate America does not speak the language of relationships or foster individual achievements while network marketers speak of little else.

## *When fueled by passion we become fluent in the language of the heart.*

According to a national survey gauging the changing values of America, what we now hunger for from a career is professional development that is appreciated and financially rewarded. Network marketing feeds the hungers of Americans. These hotel meeting room camps for corporate refugees draw us to an open doors, skys-the-limit entrepreneurial adventure that promises you'll be trained, motivated and celebrated each step of the way!

"Our chief want in life is someone who will make us do what we can." Emerson

The cutthroat culture of corporate America is network marketing's rocket fuel. It delivers people to the door. Once they are there we must remember, it's all about relationships. What keeps people engaged and performing is effective coaching.

## Coaching 101

Imagine these words being given to you by someone you've coached.

> *The cutthroat culture of corporate America is network marketing's rocket fuel. It delivers people to the door.*

"How do I say thank you for the gift of hope, the foundation of skills and the realization of my dreams? You've changed my life and the futures of my children. They will grow up better and stronger because of you. Words cannot describe the difference you've guided me to make in our lives."

This is the competitive advantage and primary product of network marketing. SKUs are merely tools for the true products; hope, relationships and feelings.

Coaching has a simple premise. The talent (student) asks the coach "How do I do that?" The coach asks themself, "What is the most respectful, motivating and effective way I can contribute to their competence?" The answer is effective coaching.

## The Essence of Coaching

▮▶ Saying something familiar enough to be understood yet distinct enough to foster change.

▮▶ Mapping out a linear performance/learning process that efficiently leads to the desired destination.

▮▶ Emphasizing individual strengths, advantages and passion.

▮▶ Celebrating a personal style as it evolves.

▮▶ Eclipsing the risk and pain of changing with motivations to achieve.

▶

▮► Projecting and planning celebrations for achievement.

The coach's role is to keep each achievement a clean win; to not allow guilt, self-sabotage or conflicts to delay achievement. There must be no regrets or conflicts involved in the win. To change we question old beliefs, jettison tired assumptions and refresh our identity and skills, all while maintaining well-being, family community and personal values.

## Interpretations Create Behavior

Events, communication or incentives do not determine behavior. It is the interpretation or baggage we bring to an experience that determine our actions.

When the past you've had works against the future you want, a coach invites you to try on new thoughts -- to build on the action oriented feelings.

## Four Strategies

**1.** Seeing old issues a new way by asking "what is the lesson to be learned from my past and used for my future?" Once you've learned the lesson the past has to teach you to move forward.

**2.** Eclipse fears doubts with desire. People change their behavior for one reason: to move from a place of pain to get to a place of lesser pain. Make lists of all the benefits of growing verses the benefits of staying the same, and your desire to accomplish can be three times more powerful than your reasons to not accomplish.

**3.** Eliminate the losses of gains. Often achieving in one area of life creates loss in another area. We might sabotage success because relationships with friends or relatives may suffer. We can see success as distancing until we find ways to enhance our relationships with it.

**4.** Building skills eclipses resistance. With right abilities, resources, enthusiasm and know-how, anybody can do anything!

A coach helps people create new interpretations and find better ways of performing. Together you eliminate obstacles to achieving and create a clearly winning path to the talents' desired prize.

## When to Coach

▮► During a progress review.

▮► When there is a loss momentum or focus.

▮► When asked for help.

▮► When growth or change require new skills.

Coaching fails when the destination or process the coach has in mind doesn't excite the talent. We invest effort for the reward we hunger for.

Coaching doesn't work when giant steps are placed in front of us. We need things to be understandable and doable from the place we are today. When ability and expectation are not close enough to one another, a leap of faith can result in injuries. Think in terms of a series of baby steps.

Coaches are handicapped as soon as they're in it for the money rather than the shared achievements.

Achievements won't happen when the talent isn't sure why they're doing it. Hopes shift and change. Dreams are misty things and the closer we get, the less appealing some look. Fresh new reasons must replace tired old ones and the new cause must be enthusiastically supported with photos, journaling and tangible evidence. We've got to see the destination and build our desire to be there.

> *Coaching doesn't work when giant steps are placed in front of us. We need things to be understandable and doable from the place we are today.*

Coaching works best when a talent is reaching for their personal goal.

Photographs and journals keep your eyes on the prize and the goals are aligned with a greater purpose than just our own desires. When others win because of our victory the winning is complete.

## Removing Resistance

We resist success because we are attached to or defending something. Invite your talent to go deep into their resistance feelings, to get images, sounds or feelings about the core of it. Then negotiate the elimination of the fear of loss by creating healthy, positive options that eclipse the risk.

### A Coaching Dialogue

 You seem to be stuck at your present level. Is it a plateau you can't get yourself off?
**Talent:** Yes. For a year now.

 Let's find out why this place seems safer than growing. Let's understand what you are defending. Is that O.K. with you?

**Talent:** Yes

 What is your next professional goal?

**Talent:** To become a director.

**C:** How does the idea of becoming a director, of changing your position in the company feel when you think about it? Close your eyes and imagine being a director.

**Talent:** It feels good.

**C:** Do you have any discomfort with being a director? Any resistance to the title of director?

**Talent:** No.

**C:** What else would this change mean for you?

**Talent:** More income.

**C:** Think about having that increased income. How does that feel?

**Talent:** Good...and not good.

**C:** Where do the "not good" feelings come from?

**Talent:** I'm not sure.

**C:** What names would you give the not good feeling.

**Talent:** Fear...loneliness...anger.

**C:** Imagine holding the cash and walking through different aspects of your life.

**Talent:** I don't want to take it home.

**C:** Why?

**Talent:** I'm worried about my family and my time with them. With my husband. The children are O.K.; they like the money.

**C:** What about him?

**Talent:** It wouldn't be good for him...to see it.

**C:** Why?

**Talent:** It's too much. It's more than he would...more than would be good.

**C:** Would you be earning more than he does?

**Talent:** I think so. More than he would like.

**C:** O.K. Now change the scene in your mind. He is proud and happy to see you holding the cash. What has happened that made him happy?

I'm happy too! I donated part of the money.

**Talent:** Is that all it took?

**C:** I went to him and asked permission to grow my business and he said "Of course. Grow!" Ahh. I feel better. I don't think I need to stop myself anymore.

By allowing her to understand the real cause of her self sabotage you've coached her through a performance block and created a clear win. She is able to donate to a good cause and keep her relationships intact.

## A coach frees us to take action

Proper coaching equips people to be a long-term performer who can self-correct and self-motivate. It isn't about dependance.

It teaches us to find resources in ourselves, our relationships, our organization and communities that allow us to continuously improve. We become our own coach as we go on to coach others.

It is always both the coach and the talent that are engaged in a learning process.

*California's Association Executives have named **Peter McGugan** their speaker of the year twice and meeting planners have rated him among the top ten professional speakers in America.*

*He is a strategic growth coach, best-selling author, psychologist and trend tracker. His articles have appeared in more than 30 national magazines and he's been featured on many national talk shows. His first book "Beating Burnout," became an instant best-seller and his new book "When Something Changes Everything," is a moment to moment guide for managing change and reinvention. As a strategic growth coach, Peter keeps the crown on king-of-the-hill corporations. Informative, entertaining and motivating, his keynote presentations "Beating Burnout," "Trend Tracking: What's Hot, What's Not & What's Next," "The Joy of Coaching," and "Business is from Mars, Customers are from Venus: How to grow your business strategically" are invariably the best attended and highest rated events at national and international conventions.*

*He can be reached at (760) 320-8888.* ■

# HOMEBusiness Journal

Nation's Leading Home Business Expert

Lindsay Frucci

## How To Stir Up A Winning Home Business

## MLM Success
### Encouraging News From The Front Line

## 25 Tips For Working At Home

NO PUDGE!

RASPBERRY

JUST ADD YOGURT
ALL NATURAL
NET WT. 15.7 OZ • 598g

# Multi-Level or Pyramid?

*D. Jack Smith, Jr.*

An unlawful pyramid is a people gathering scheme in which to obtain personal financial gain.

A legal multi-level marketing company is one in which all sales materials, literature, oral presentations and every feature of its efforts evince a sincere desire to merchandise legitimate goods and services to the public.

This is the "alpha" and "omega" of multi-level marketing in two short paragraphs. It is a simple common sense statement which, when understood, should clearly convey to a beginner the difference in these two entities. Further, it is the "bottom line" and summation of all the rules, regulations, statutes, interpretations and case decisions that have been brought to focus on this question.

In dealing with my first multi-level marketing client, I was given the best piece of advice of my career by an attorney general in charge of consumer protection to the effect that if a sales organization walks like, talks like, looks like, feels like, and smells like, a network marketing company, it probably is a legal multi-level marketing company. On the other hand, if the 'glamour, pizzazz and romance' in its materials is primarily on the recruitment aspect, it is probably a pyramid scheme.

Every one of my corporate clients and all who have heard me speak on multi-level marketing topics for the last seventeen years knows that it is no secret what state gave me this advice.

I have always referred to it as the best piece of advice I have been given and called it the "Oregon Smell Test."

In addition to the first two sentences above, this "smell test" really does tell 95% of the story.

*A trend encouraged by the Direct Selling Association and adopted as a law by an increasing number of states requires that a company offer a 90% buy-back provision to guard against "loading."*

In this complicated society of ours, however, virtually nothing is permitted to remain at its simplest. So, regrettably, there is more to the story.

A number of other questions must be asked if we are to focus on this question microscopically as many do, and more important, as many regulatory authorities do.

First, is this company involved in moving a "real" product to the public at reasonable prices or is there no product at all, or merely a sham product to give the color of legitimacy to otherwise pure recruitment efforts?

An unlawful enterprise will have no emphasis on retail selling of goods and services and worse, can be identified in some cases by language in the materials to the effect that "no selling is involved."

An unlawful enterprise can many times be identified because there is no emphasis on work or business building and the "atmosphere" surrounding its materials and efforts very often will be stated and implied that all one has to do is "get two, who get two, who get two, and we'll all get rich."

Previously, all that was required was a genuine emphasis on retail sales.

At this writing, a controversial court in a case involving the Omnitrition Company used language to arbitrarily indicate that 70% of a company's products must come to rest in the hands of members of the public not involved in the sales force in order to be legal. This is unfortunate but must be noted at this time.

This "rule" has never been the law

and the rapidity with which the state legislatures are moving to correct this impression indicates that this unrealistic and arbitrary approach will not be with us for long. Nevertheless, some regulatory agencies have seized upon this language as if it did declare a new universal "rule," and for now, 70% should at least be a goal in a company's efforts to move legitimate products to non-involved ultimate consumers or the public at large.

An unlawful enterprise can sometimes be detected when its compensation, rewards and promotions are not based solely on product sales volume.

Pyramid schemes are characterized by **(1)** rewards for the mere act of recruiting known as "head-hunting" fees and/or **(2)** large charges or cash investments to be a distributor or **(3)** heavy required product purchases to be a distributor which practice has been known traditionally as "loading."

A trend encouraged by the Direct Selling Association and adopted as law by an increasing number of states requires that a company offer a 90% buy-back provision to guard against "loading." All regulatory agencies are comforted when they see such a provision in a company's sales materials and anyone attempting to determine the sincerity and validity of a company should at least look for this as one of the clear indicators of legality.

Lawful multi-level marketing companies also offer training and support and require some bona fide marketing, supervisory or product handling function in order to participate. This is necessary in building any real business enterprise.

Pyramid schemes can further be detected by outlandish claims of all kinds, not expressly limited to exaggerated earnings claims. The old saying: Anything that seems too good to be true, probably is too good to be true, and is never more apropos than in this area. Common sense will go a long way towards protecting anyone who is examining a purported multi-level marketing company.

Some other clues are representations that the company activities have been "approved" by the Attorney General's offices or Better Business Bureaus. Attorney General's offices never "approve" or certify any MLM company because of the continuing possibility of future violations.

Further, unlawful enterprises often have a feature requiring payments from one distributor to another and not all dealings with the company itself.

It is also a fact of life that those promotions even mentioning the word "offshore" in its materials, which in itself is illegal, will be given the utmost scrutiny by all United States regulatory authorities. I have had the state of Wyoming refuse to accept a multi-level marketing company for its required multi-level registration solely on the grounds that its references to offshore activities raised too large a cloud of suspicion. Whether this is justified or not, anyone considering doing business with a company involved in offshore activities should be aware that the company is inviting regulatory challenges which might jeopardize the prospect's future income and chances for long-term permanent success.

Multi-level marketing companies involve eight different bodies of jurisprudence, each of which has various differences among fifty states in the United States.

The fact that we must pay attention to four hundred possible different bodies of law compels any prospect to determine whether or not the enterprise has had the benefit of specialized multi-level marketing legal counsel. Simply put, if the company has not sought this specialized legal knowledge its activities are sooner or later doomed. The fact that its flaws have been unrecognized and not challenged for a period of time is no assurance of safety. Eventually "the shoe will drop."

Multi-level marketing involves first and foremost the law of fraud. This sounds like a lawyers word but it is, in reality, any form of dishonesty such as stealing, lying, cheating, obtaining money by trickery, deceit, misrepresentation or exaggeration. Properly, all regulatory authorities will assault any appearance of fraud

> *Multi-level marketing involves first and foremost the law of fraud. This sounds like a lawyers word but it is, in reality, any form of dishonesty such as stealing, lying, cheating, obtaining money by trickery, deceit, misrepresentation or exaggeration.*

with all the resources at their disposal. This is the biggest and worst crime that a company can commit or permit by failing to control the statements and activities of all those with which it is affiliated, including its distributors whose enthusiasm occasionally leads them to rewrite otherwise legal company literature.

In addition to fraud, multi-level marketing criss-crosses pyramid laws, lottery laws, securities laws, franchise laws, business opportunity statutes, buyers club laws, and referral sales acts in addition to the possibility of touching other consumer protection statutes, although these latter are primarily directed at prohibiting specific acts of fraud.

Thus it can be seen, that while the beginning first two paragraphs of this article are clear and true, this is a complicated field of jurisprudence in which appearances can be just as important as the reality, and the way things are said are just as important as their intended meaning.

From a beginning forty years ago of no developed case law because there was no multi-level marketing industry to regulate, and no statutes on the books at all except those dealing with the old-fashioned "empty" pyramid or hollow recruitment schemes, this industry has rapidly developed to the point where it is universally recognized in the United States and at least its basic principles and governing rules which have been discussed in this article are commonly accepted and understood by industry participants and regulatory agencies alike.

There are still many vagaries and ambiguities in this newly developing body of law and its finer points are not yet settled. It seems that there is one or two new "fads" in regulatory enforcement each year.

Nevertheless, this industry has come from nothing to one of the most vibrant, dynamic and unique methods of moving goods and services and, therefore, benefits, to the public as has ever been envisioned or created.

All of us can be extremely proud to have been involved in this developing frontier. It is incumbent on each of us to so conduct ourselves that the respect and acceptance of our industry continues to grow as we furnish people's needs and luxuries throughout this entire world.

*D. Jack Smith Jr. is the senior attorney in The Law Firm of D. Jack Smith, an association, Clark Tower, 5100 Poplar Avenue, Suite 2700, Memphis, Tennessee 38137, (901) 685-7299.*

*He is a member of the Tennessee and Washington, D.C. Bars.*

*A graduate of Vanderbilt University and Harvard Law School, Mr. Smith practices exclusively in the areas of multi-level marketing and direct selling law and litigation.*

*Mr. Smith is a frequent speaker, panelist and author on MLM and Direct Selling topics, having published articles in this area for seventeen years.*

*He is the author of "United States Multi-Level Marketing Law — A Survey," which is in its third edition.*

*He is a former General Counsel and Board Member of the National Association of Multi-Level Marketing Companies, a member of the Lawyer's Council of the Direct Selling Association, and an attorney for and board member of the Multi-Level Marketing International Association which named him "Attorney of the Year" in 1989.*

*His practice includes the U.S. and Canadian companies and those desirous of doing business in the United Kingdom and the European Union.* ∎

*The only hope for the human race is for the rate of population increase to continue to exceed that of bureaucratic growth.*

**Athur H. Robinson,**
**Albany Times**
**Union, July 6, 1975**

# ARE YOU SMART ABOUT MONEY?

## Test your financial IQ

*Karen Hube*

How savvy are you about managing your finances? Do you know the best way to make your money grow? Here are eight questions that cover basic areas of personal finance. Tally up your score and see where you stand when it comes to matters of the pocketbook.

**1. What kind of return should I expect on my Long-term stock investments?**
a) 5.7 percent
b) 10.9 percent
c) 12 percent
d) 18.4 percent

**2. If my investment earns an average annual 10.9 percent return, how long will it take to double my money?**
a) 2 years
b) 7 years
c) 12 years
d) 17 years

**3. My most important savings goal should be?**
a) My child's college tuition
b) A house down payment
c) My family's summer vacation
d) Retirement

**4. Which debt should I pay off before I invest money in stocks or a mutual fund?**

a) Mortgage
b) Home equity loan
c) Credit card balance
d) College loan

**5. What difference would it make if the interest on my 30 year $150,000 fixed mortgage is 8 percent vs. 9 percent?**
a) $106 a month/$381,160 for 30 years
b) $47 a month/$16,920 for 30 years
c) $81 a month/$29,160 for 30 years
d) $74 a month/$26,640 for 30 years

**6. How much disability insurance should I have?**
a) 60 percent of annual income
b) Half of what I make
c) Enough to replace my full income
d) One third of my earnings

**7. The reason to look for a mutual fund with no-load and below average fees is?**
a) Sales charges and fees can significantly erode returns
b) Up-front costs will be lower
c) No-load funds are managed better
d) No-load funds are less volitile

**8. Which investment vehicle will make money grow the fastest?**
a) Mutual fund
b) Tax-deferred annuity
c) IRA
d) 401(k) plan

**ANSWERS**

**1: b** These days, while in the midst of one of the longest bull markets in history, investors are disappointed if a stock posts anything shy of a 20 percent return. Here's a little dose of reality: The S&P 500's average annual return since 1926 is 10.9 percent. "I have clients come in expecting to make 20 percent a year on their money," says financial adviser Michael Kabarec of Palatine, Illinois. "Eventually this bull market is going to end and investors will be forced to come out of the clouds." Still, a 10.9 percent return is nothing to scoff at. Long-term government bonds, by comparison, have returned about half that--an average 5.1 percent over the same period of time, and these days a one year certificate of deposit yields about 5.2 percent.

**2: b** Whether you put $100 or $100,000 in an investment growing an average 10.9 percent a year, it will double in just seven years. And here's the better news: Thanks to the beauty of compounding returns, the more your money grows, the faster it will multiply. Still assuming a 10.9 percent annual return, your money will triple in 11 years and quadruple in 14 years.

**3: d** The great risk of retirement, which could last 30 years or more, is that you could outlive your assets. "You must make retirement savings a priority while you're young," says David Bugen, a financial planner in Chatham, New Jersey. "Otherwise you may not be able to quit working."

▶

In retirement, your only sources of income will be Social Security, a possible pension (although fewer and fewer companies offer them today) and your own savings.

Sending your youngster to college should be a top priority, but there are plenty of college funding options available if you come up short. One example: a subsidized or unsubsidized Stafford Loan for a student loan, guaranteed by the federal government. Subsidized loans are need-based aid; if your child qualifies, the loan is interest free. An unsubsidized loan must be repaid with interest, but rates currently at 8.25 percent are low. Or, if you want to assume the debt instead of or in addition to your child, there are PLUS loans (8.72 percent interest) for parents. Contact the financial aid office of your child's school for information and applications, or call the Federal Student Aid Information Center: (800) 433-3243.

**4: c** If you carry a balance on your credit card, chances are you pay more in interest (average: 17 percent) than you could hope to earn on an average stock investment. That means any gains you get from your investment will be wiped out by the interest paid on your plastic, which is why experts say you should pay off credit cards first.

What about college loans and mortgages? As long as you're investing in stocks, you shouldn't have to worry about the interest on college loans (currently below 9 percent) or mortgages (now a tax-deductible 7.30 percent on a 30 year mortgage) wiping out your earnings. In addition, it takes most people years to pay off their mortgage, so no matter what the interest rate, don't let that debt stop you from investing.

**5: a** Even a single percentage point can make an enormous difference in how much you'll pay over the life of your mortgage. That's why it's extremely important to consider refinancing if rates drop, or to hunt down the best rate for a new mortgage. Start by asking your realtor if he or she knows of firms that publish mortgage data on lenders in your area. One option: HSH Associates of Butler, New Jersey, publishes loan terms offered by up to 80 lenders in most states every week: (800) 873-2837.

**6: a** According to the Department of Labor, only 40 percent of all workers in medium-to-large-size companies receive long-term disability insurance from their employers. Whether or not your company provides it, however,

> *According to the Department of Labor, only 40 percent of all workers in medium-to-large-size companies receive long-term disability insurance from their employers.*

it's important to have. You are three times as likely to become disabled as you are to die before age 65, points out Denise Leish, a financial planner at Money Plans in Silver Spring, Maryland. "It's hard enough being disabled without worrying about losing your house," she stated.

When considering coverage, be sure you get a policy that provides at least 60 percent of current income, usually considered enough since certain costs (such as commuting and clothing) go down if you're disabled. Also, insurance companies won't sell policies large enough to replace 100 percent of income, since

they reason it ruins your incentive to work.

If your company doesn't provide disability insurance or you would like more than 60 percent coverage (you can usually buy supplemental insurance that will replace another 20 percent of income if your employer paid the initial 60 percent), call around for the best rates.

**7: a** When you decide to invest in a mutual fund, you have a choice between load funds, which are purchased through a broker for a sales charge, and no-load funds, available directly from fund companies such as T. Rowe Price. Here's what a difference buying a no-load fund with low fees can make: If you had invested $5,000 in a no-load with below average expenses of 1 percent and an average return of 10 percent, after 20 years you would have $31,849. But if you had put the same amount in a load fund with an average sales charge of 1.7 percent and above average expenses of 1.75 percent, after 20 years you would have $24,486.

**8: d** You simply can't beat the tax break that you get with the typical 401(k) plan or equivalent 403(b) plan. As you undoubtedly know, a 401(k) lets you invest pretax dollars that grow on a tax-deferred basis. In addition, employers usually pitch in 50 cents for every dollar you invest up to 6 percent.

While a tax-deferred annuity and IRA will give you tax advantages, there's no company match to help build your nest egg.

What about mutual funds? Let's say you invest 10 percent of your salary in a 401(k) plan with a 50 percent match each year, beginning at age 23. Let's also assume your average annual salary over the span of your career is $60,000, and you earn an average 10

> *Even a single percentage point can make an enormous difference in how much you'll pay over the life of your mortgage. That's why it's extremely important to consider refinancing if rates drop, or to hunt down the best rate for a new mortgage.*

percent annual return on your savings. At that rate, you'd have $4.8 million in your 401(k) by the age of 65. But if you had put the same amount (minus, of course, the company match and tax-deferred growth of your earnings) into a mutual fund that returned 10 percent a year, you'd have $2.1 million by the time you retire. The numbers speak for themselves.

**YOUR SCORE**

**7 to 8 correct:** Congratulations! you clearly understand the basics of managing your money. To stay on top of your finances, be sure to set aside at least a couple of hours each month to review all aspects of your family's money matters and make any adjustments needed to stay on target for meeting goals.

**4 to 6 correct:** Not bad, but you have some blind spots when it comes to finance. Take a look at your incorrect answers and brush up on those areas you're weak in.

**0 to 3 correct:** Chances are you haven't had the time or inclination to pay close attention to the best ways of managing your money. Consider hiring a financial planner who can help you get on track with every aspect of your finances, from insurance and investing to budgeting and taxes.■

## Dreams Come In All Sizes And Shapes

Your dream doesn't have to revolutionize an industry, win the Olympics, or make a million dollars. It doesn't even have to be about business or something that makes a buck.

Dreams can be general or abstract, such as wanting to make a difference in people's lives, own your own business, be renowned for your work, or have a loving relationship. Tony Tiano, president of KQED-TV, the San Francisco public television station, says his vision is "elusive, like an abstract painting far off in the distance. I can just barely see it. It's something I want. It moves me."

In other instances your dream can be more specific - like John Naber's dream of winning the gold medal, or a dream of becoming president of the corporation you work for, or writing a novel. Our dreams come in all shapes and sizes. The key is to have a dream that inspires us to go beyond our limits. Dreams ignite a fire in us and give us "genius and magic." Consider some of the following varied dreams:

Peter Brown, a housecleaner, dreams of opening his own restaurant.

Catherine Partman, mother of five, dreams of starting a business, writing a book, and producing a videotape to educate expectant mothers and new parents.

Tim and Tina Frederick, financial analysts, dream of opening a bed and breakfast in Northern California.

Trish McCall dreams of spending a year in Italy with her family.

Charlene Modena, a teacher, dreams of living on the sales of her art.

Having a dream - whether it is personal or professional, big or small, realistic or crazy - and *pursuing* it, adds meaning to your life. It gives your everyday activities a larger sense of purpose. And when your dream is shared by those you work or live with, it's doubly exciting.

Myrtle Harris, a senior citizen, dreams of speaking to seniors groups around the country about all the resources available to them. Taking advantage of one such resource (discounted airfares), she fulfilled one of her dreams, to go to the Kentucky Derby. As she says, "just getting there was a thrill. My horse didn't win, but I did!"

# Exclusive Interview With Paul Zane Pilzer

**Best-Selling Author of** *'Unlimited Wealth' – 'Other People's Money' – 'God Wants You To Be Rich'*

*Alan Rothman*

I was very excited at the opportunity to have done an interview with Paul Pilzer. More important, he is very supportive of the future for home-based business in general and network marketing as a specifically viable method of doing business.

Pilzer is the author of three best-selling books, Unlimited Wealth, Other People's Money, and God Wants You To Be Rich: The Theology of Economics. He received his MBA from Wharton, became Citibank's youngest vice president, and served as economic adviser to Presidents Reagan and Bush. He is the founder and publisher of Zane Publishing, Inc., a leading international CD-ROM educational publisher. He has also served as an adjunct professor at New York University. He shared some exciting concepts as to how and why everyone can enjoy material and spiritual wealth in our abundant world working from home. Do not pass go without reading this article.

## The power of a single thought

During our discussion, Pilzer referenced the economic model put together by a 21-year-old British college student in 1931. The student attempted to answer the following question: "Why, in a free-enterprise economy, would a worker voluntarily submit to direction by a corporation instead of selling his own output or service directly to customers in the market?" The student was Ronald H. Case, the 1991 winner of the Nobel Prize for economics. The paper explained that the corporation exists because of its ability to reduce the transaction costs between individuals. To explain this concept, Pilzer uses the example of a manager that wants to hire a typist. The manager would have high transactional costs in finding the typist, testing the level of skill, negotiating the price for the service that would far exceed the effort for delegating the service of typing of the letter. On the other hand, the typist would trade off his or her independence and higher per diem pay for a guaranteed time and place to work. The manager would hire only the labor or service that was needed. The costs to a corporation for benefits (i.e. health care and retirement) and other items not

*Pilzer feels innovative individuals finding better ways to distribute already existing products or services are making the greatest wealth in America.*

directly compensated for performance are identified as inefficiency costs. The greatest reason that inefficiency costs have risen dramatically for the corporation is its relative ineffectiveness in comparison to the individual entrepreneur in implementing technological change.

## Take this test before you are fired or downsized!

In my discussion, Pilzer indicated that people who worked for a large corporation needed to be realistic in the assessment of their job assignment. **First** analyze the work you perform each day from the standpoint of its contribution to your employer. **Second**, what is the actual function that you do, how does it fit into the total objective of your company, and **most important**, how does the company profit from what you do? From making this assessment you will be able to determine the level of the inefficiency costs to the corporation and what actions they may take with your position. People start to think of the company as their society. The fact that a person has been with an employer for twenty years has no relevance to an economic model. The pay should be based on the value of the service you are providing. In the future, Pilzer feels that American business will become smaller and more specialized. It will become common place to leave your corporation and be re-hired as an outside contractor or supplier, and in many cases assist in the survival of your former employer.

## Where is the gold mine?

Pilzer feels innovative individuals finding better ways to distribute already existing products or services are making the greatest wealth in America. In the future, he feels creative individuals who find better ways to deliver affordable, quality health care products and services will make some of the largest money. There is a merger developing of economics and happiness, according to Pilzer. People are looking for ways to get more value out of the existing wealth that we have. In short, the improvement of the quality of life rather than the physical quantity of the things we have. We are moving away from just obtaining material things. Developing the relationship with the spouse and children, friends and business associates becomes the center piece model. People want a better lifestyle. You do not want to eat just because you are hungry, but desire to obtain a unique dining experience. Since many of our hours will be spent working, we are challenged to find how we can better enhance this working experience. For many of us there is nothing better than working from home, because we want to interact with our family and friends throughout the day. Paul feels that home-based business was the original role model for our society going back thousands of years. People lived and worked on the family farm. The theories and formulas of Ronald H. Case developed in 1931, are equally valid today. Pilzer suggests most big companies should not exist and the majority of people should work from home. Technology and communication are becoming so cost-effective it is spearheading this direction. With fax machines, telecommunications and the Internet, we can work at many locations and one of those locations can be the home.

The transaction costs of dealing around the nation are presently insignificant. In many cases long distance charges are lower than the cost for local calls. This wave of working at home is nothing more than a return to what we used to do. The economic unit of productivity is the individual mind with a personal computer connected to the Internet or a phone line.

*When you buy something, you want to have a good experience. Your ultimate experience is going to come from dealing with people that are going to improve the quality of your life.*

When Paul graduated from Wharton in 1976, he was determined to work for a city bank with an IBM 370-mainframe computer. The mainframe computer became the building block for the Fortune 500 company. Twenty years later, personal computers are used as that model, and people can do that from home. Paul explored the type of work done from home. Manufacturing activity is less than 15% of the economy. Another 20% work in food service. The majority today works in some type of service sector.

### The role for Pilzer

The main role he plays is to act as a teacher. He states, "Learn new things and teach it to your students, being on the cutting edge of your field, which means always be searching for new information." He has been teaching finance at New York University for 19 years consecutively and never missed a class. His dedication was so intense that when he had projects in Moscow, he would hop on a plane on Sunday to arrive for class on Monday, and back on a plane to return to Moscow on Tuesday. N.Y.U. recently agreed to make Pilzer a "dead professor," an offer he could not refuse. The Dean indicated that normally celebrity instructors who author popular books are recognized by the school for their worth after they are dead. The school then realizes their material should have been used in the classroom setting instead of the standard curriculum. The school decided to treat Paul as a dead professor now, so he could teach his class based on his own material. Paul conducted his first class in 1997, entitled: The Economics of Abundance, Unlimited Wealth and God Wants You To Be Rich: The Theology of Economics. These are used as the two textbooks for the class. It was his most exciting class since he first taught finance in 1979. In the class he not only throws out his established views, but also what he thinks to be true but cannot yet prove it. Paul stated, "I am always excited by the new, rather than what I did yesterday." Paul was excited as he described how he gets to bounce new ideas off his students and jointly evolve and refine those thoughts. What these young kids think and do is the cutting edge of our society.

### The secret formula to success

Start looking at what businesses do in companies you have worked for or operations with which you are familiar. Usually you will have been a supplier or customer. Analyze that work and determine what components of that work can be done by individuals working at home. Because of changes in technology, you can re-tool that environment and be more competitive than the large corporation. Find out what the corporate market does, and figure out a way to be economically viable and competitive. The next wave of software is going to be GroupWare, where you can log on the Internet and be connected with 10 or more people and work on the same project; almost like a group of people in a conference all using the same blackboard to organize a group meeting with each individual using a different color. We are here to evoke a response from people. The corporate environment does lend itself to allow people to elect others they would prefer to spend time with. Paul feels that network marketing will be a strong model for future growth. In network marketing you choose whom you wish to spend time with. You choose the people with the values that you want to share with yourself and your family. The relationship we build with people is the only thing that really matters. Think of the person that hired or promoted you, or the people that complemented you on some of your work projects. Being able to touch people and give them their chance in life is very important. Network marketing at its root is all about building people, not about building businesses. The essence of it is taking the individual and helping him or her develop their skills and actualize their potential. With that comes life-long friendships. Network marketing comes with the end result that most people want from a corporate job. When people are successful in a corporate job, what do they want? Time with their family; better relationships with their children, and time freedom. Network marketing often comes from day one with the end result that people seek from a 30 year corporate position.

## Conclusion

People want to go high-touch, the positives of the past in our minds. When you buy something, you want to have a good experience. Your ultimate experience is going to come from dealing with people that are going to improve the quality of your life. Paul loves to assemble information and help teach it to someone else. Paul states, "Teaching and learning is the foundation of my life."

*Alan Rothman (arothman@fea.net) is an author, columnist, speaker, and consultant to the network marketing and communications industry. For info, call (949) 362-9233 or leave a message at (800) 593-9234. Author of "Power Networking," "LocalNet," and "Secrets of the MLM Millionaires." Visit http://www.hgionline.com/pages/whatsnew.htm. Read Alan's weekly column, "Secrets of Success" on AOL under keyword MLM or Network Marketing. See our cover stories in various publications at your local bookstore. Order your copy of "Power Networking: Why Enrich is for Everyone!" $19.95+$3 for S&H. For a report on "Secret Methods for a Six-figure Income," send your request and $5 to Rothman, 24401 Caswell Ct., Laguna Niguel, CA 926677. Coming soon! A nationally syndicated radio show with access to major markets for exposure. Write for free details to be part of the campaign. If you can't dazzle them with talent, astonish them with perseverance.* ■

# Biomune--The First Name in System Support...

- **Over $20 million in Research & Developement**
- **Original formula used in practice for nearly 20 years**
- **Patented Processing**
- **Proprietary**
- **Clinical studied by renowned Viro-Immunologist Jesse A. Stoff, M.D.**
- **Matol Biomune OSF™ Plus honored at International Congress on Homeopathy and Alternative Medicine in June 98**

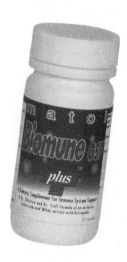

High concentrations of specific transfer factors, contained in the extract of colostrum and whey, in conjuction with the herb astragalus, makes Biomune OSF™ Plus a synergistically unique supplement ideal for immune system support

## The Best Defense is a Good Offense

The immune system is an army of cells and organs that defend the body against attack. Enemies of the immune system include bacteria, viruses, parasites, germs, and various other microscopic invaders. These invaders penetrate the body's natural shields, such as the skin, and make their way towards their target destination. Your immune system, the first and last line of defense, produces highly specialized cells such as lymphocytes to counter the threat. Included among these lymphocytes are natural killer (NK) cells, whose mission is to seek and destroy any "harmful" invaders that penetrate the body's initial defense positions. This is especially important because low or absent NK cell activity is associated with virtually all human disease.

Pollution, stress, the escalating rate of infectious disease, and the ability of bacteria and viruses to thrive, despite the use of antibiotics, are just a few of the factors that affect the efficiency of your immune system.

## A Unique Synergistic Combination

To combat the increasing risks, the creators of Matol Biomune OSF™ Plus have successfully developed a unique dietary supplement using two key ingredients: an exclusive extract of colostrum and whey; and astragalus. Produced by a patented, pre-calving process, the exclusive extract of bovine colostrum and whey is extracted using a proprietary process which produces a collection of very small molecules that contain a "transfer factor." The colostrum/whey extract is obtained from a select herd of cows in which no antibiotics or artificial substances of any kind are fed to the animals. These immune factors have been clinically shown to increase natural killer (NK) cell activity.

The other ingredient, Astragalus, is a traditional Chinese herb used for centuries because of its known abilities to stimulate the immune system. The herb has been used for many viral infections such as the common cold or flu. When combined with the enriched bovine colostrum and whey extract, the outcome is a unique synergistic combination that has ushered in the new generation of immune system support.

*"When I came to know these doctors, my immune function was severely compromised with a blood test showing my NK cell activity at only 17. Within months my health was again vital and my NK cell activity is now 130!" –Sylvia Waiwaiole*

## Because no one is immune to disease

*Call or write me today: Sylvia M. Waiwaiole, Matol Australasia Corporation Ltd. 644 Keolu Drive, Kailua, Hawaii 96734, Phone: (808) 261-5324, Toll Free: (888) 280-4603, PIN# 4681, Fax: (808) 263-4156, E-mail: waiole@pixi.com, Web site: www.matol.com/dist/sylviaw*

# Communication is Everything!

*David H. Sandler*

> *Most sales calls are flabby encounters that end on an unclear note. Here's how to trim the fat by improving your communications with prospects.*

# For

most sales reps, this scenario must have a familiar ring to it: On a call to a new prospect, the two of you begin to feint and parry in search of a competitive advantage. The dialogue meanders, miscommunications stall a connection and the meeting drags on longer than necessary. Before you know it, you're out the door without a clear understanding of whether you should pursue the sale or cut and move on to the next customer.

The fact is, it doesn't have to be that way. You can avoid such time-sapping sales calls by putting a concept called "up-front contracting" to use. With this approach to sales presentations, you form a series of verbal agreements with prospects about the purpose of the meeting itself and the results both sides are seeking. By communicating more effectively with potential buyers, you cut through the misunderstandings,

rhetoric and posturing that often takes place between prospect and seller.

As a result, up-front contracting facilitates the process of qualifying prospects. You'll better determine that they have a problem your product or service can solve, can pay for the solution and have the authority to make a purchasing decision. It also allows you to trim the fat from a sales call without interfering with a potentially good relationship.

While some salespeople naturally employ the principles of up-front contracting in their presentations, many others do not. Most sales calls are flabby encounters, characterized by wishy-washy communications between the two parties. That's a real problem for salespeople at small and midsize levels, who work against time. Leaner margins, a narrower revenue stream and a "grow or

die" motto mean that these reps have less time to play games with potential customers.

## Reality Checks

Up-front contracting can be used throughout the sales process, in a variety of ways to improve the quality of communications with a potential buyer. On your next sales call, try using the concept to accomplish these objectives:

## Lay Out an Agenda

Like any type of meeting, a sales call will be most productive when you establish a framework for it. By clarifying the purpose of the call and mapping out the points to be covered, you'll make the most efficient use of the time allotted to you and gain greater control of the sales process.

A clear statement about the purpose of the call will help set the agenda. For example, you might inform the prospect that you will use the time to ask questions about his or her business, and to answer questions about your products or services. The sales call is less likely to veer off course when the buyer knows that both sides will have a chance to gain concrete information.

To further develop the agenda, simply ask the customer for input on his or her needs. One possibility: "I've been in sales for a long time and I have many clients. I've found that there are no accidents, and I believe there is a reason for us being together. What motivated you to invite me to your office?" A more specific approach is to ask prospects to list the items they want to address during the meeting, or to share the five biggest problems they have in your area of expertise.

That way, you can tailor your presentation to fit their needs.

## Set a Time Frame for the Call and Fend off Interruptions

It's only natural to begin the bonding process with a prospect by engaging in some casual conversation. But you've probably been on calls where you discuss everything but business and then the prospect says, "Okay, what are you selling? I only have 10 minutes left."

With the principles of up-front contracting, you can avoid this common mistake by asking the prospect how much time he or she has set aside for the meeting. It doesn't hurt to say directly that you consider both parties' time to be valuable and that you want to make sure not a minute is wasted.

Similarly, you can minimize the potential for interruptions which may allow the prospect to take control of the sales process. A typical scenario: The meeting is running smoothly, the prospect is talking about his or her needs and then the phone rings. Perhaps due to anxiety, to provide an escape hatch or to diminish your power as a salesperson, the prospect takes the call and tunes you out. But the buyer may lose his or her train of thought and you'll have a tough time refocusing the meeting.

A comment such as the following will help prevent this problem: "I don't know whether this has happened to you, but I've participated in meetings which have been interrupted by telephone calls and people walking in an out. This can be distracting. Can we

*By far, the most widespread obstacle is a discussion of money. Many salespeople consider any talk of price and payment terms to be a deal killer, so they put it off until the very end. But with that approach, you'll have to end the presentation with your worst fear staring you in the face.*

make sure this won't happen during our meeting?"

## Determine When to Cut Your Losses

Too many sales calls move forward on uncertain terms. Neither party commits to taking further action or-- and here's the tricky part--agrees that there is no basis for a relationship at that time. But under the tenets of up-front contracting, the sooner you acknowledge a mismatch between the prospect's needs and your offerings, the better.

Not surprisingly, some salespeople avoid up-front contracting for this very reason. They simply don't want to hear that the relationship will not work, so they stick to the conventional sales pattern no matter what. Do the dog-and-pony show, counter any stalls and objections, go for the close and never back off.

The simple fact is, there's no point to wasting valuable time on low-potential prospects. Either side should be able to say "no" if there is not a fit, and a statement such as the following will get that point across: "As we ask and answer each other's

questions, we may decide there isn't a fit between what you need and the product or service that I provide. If we reach that point, are you comfortable with telling me so?"

Then, make sure you give the prospect the chance to say "yes" as well. One example: "On the other hand, if you see that my product or service makes sense to you we can decide to move forward to the next step. Okay?"

## Deal With Your Biggest Fears Up-Front

Most salespeople dislike at least one aspect of the selling process. Some fear asking the questions needed to identify the prospect as a decision maker (Mr. Customer, are you able to make the decision to purchase my service today?). Others uncomfortable with the process of probing into the prospect's needs (Ms. Customer, can we talk in more detail about your payroll system?).

By far, the most widespread obstacle is a discussion of money. Many salespeople consider any talk of price and payment terms to be a deal killer, so they put it off until the very end. But with that approach, you'll have to end the presentation with your worst fear staring you in the face. It makes more sense to address the issue at the start of the meeting, and thus create a verbal contract with buyer that he or she can pay for your product.

As an example, you could say the following: "Before I begin talking about my product or service, let me tell you what my concern is. My concern is that when I get to the end of my presentation, you're going to like what you see and hear, but I'm going to have difficulty asking you for money. So that I can give your problem my full attention, are you okay dealing with the money at the beginning of the presentation?"

**End the Call**
**With a Clear Result**

Have you ever left a meeting thinking you had the sale in the bag, only to find out later that you didn't? This usually occurs because the rep allows the prospect to end the call on an unclear note. For example: "Well, Sam, based on what you told me so far, it certainly looks good. I don't see any reason in the long run why you won't get the order, assuming things work out."

Up-front contracting helps you cut through such smoke and arrive at a concise agreement as to what will happen next in the relationship. Either you and the prospect will move ahead if you're on a one-call close--with the buyer placing a small initial order, for instance, or you'll be invited back for another meeting if necessary.

To achieve either result, you must be explicit and certain in your communications: "I believe I have a clear understanding about what we are trying to accomplish. To prevent any misunderstanding later on, would you please tell me what happened today so I can make sure we're in sync?" If the prospect doesn't say what you expect, you can provide a clearer description of the outcome you're seeking.

When you come right down to it, up-front contracting helps you to communicate more effectively throughout the sales process. You won't hold long, rambling meetings with prospects who don't have a need for your offerings and the funds and authority to buy. Equally important, you won't leave things hanging up in the air with those who do.

*Sandler Sales Institute is an international sales & sales management consulting firm with 170 offices in North America. For a free paperback edition of "Why Salespeople Fail (and what to do about it)," call (800) 638-5686, or E-mail us at info@ sandler.com.*■

# Out Of The Mouths Of Babes Came...

Specialists overthink, looking for sophisticated solutions to what are often simple problems. At a lunch break with several top executives of a major new resort, the general manager said that everything was working great, with one exception: their new "state-of-the-art" outdoor cafeteria wasn't making money. "People are spending considerably less on food than we projected, and for the life of me I don't understand it. Our research shows that customers think the food is great, the service terrific, and the scenery sensational." He had hired several restaurant consultants and had covered all the bases. "We've tried everything - changed managers, suppliers, themes, interior colors, menus, seating arrangements - everything. And we still can't turn a profit."

At this point I got in line for lunch. I grabbed a salad, sandwich and juice and was trying to make some room on my tray for dessert. At that same moment I watched a little boy in front of me try to squeeze a dish of ice cream onto his tray, knocking his sandwich to the floor. "I told you not to take so much," his dad yelled. And the light bulb flashed! I went back to our lunch group and told them what I had just witnessed. "Look, I'm no expert, but have you ever considered buying bigger trays! I think that kid wouldn't have dropped his food, his dad would of had a better day, I'd have dessert, and we all would have spent more money...if we had bigger trays!"

Out came the firehoses. "That tray is the industry standard, we're getting them at a great price, they're just the right size for our dishwashing machines." All very rational. Exactly what you'd expect them to say. However, the general manager took me literally. "Let's try it," he said, "we've tried everything else." Within three months the bigger trays (and the bigger dishwashing machine), produced a $1.50 increase per person, per meal. That represented almost one-half million dollars in increased revenue annually, approximately 50 times the cost of the change - and the restaurant went back into the black for the first time. Seeing the situation as a beginner, I was able to come up with an *obvious* solution to what had been considered a complex, even mysterious problem.

# Compensation Break*age*

## Why and How?

*Dan Jensen*

Breakage is defined as the commissions left unpaid each month compared with the theoretical maximum of the plan. If a compensation plan pays a maximum of 45% but the actual payout is 35% each month, then the breakage would be 10%. On the surface, one might suggest that breakage is unfair, unethical, or at the very least, misleading, considering a plan that represents itself as paying 45% but actually pays 35%. Upon further study, however, a plan that uses breakage wisely will reward the producers much more generously than one without breakage. It allows a company that can only afford 35% for commissions expense to pay perhaps 45% or more to the distributors doing the greatest amount of work. Breakage can be a strong competitive advantage if used correctly and for the right reasons.

## Objectives for breakage in a plan

Every piece of a good compensation plan has a specific purpose or desired result. With breakage, we want to:

**1.** Keep the total commission expense at or below a target maximum. If we can only afford to pay 30% with breakage we can often afford a plan which can pay out up to 35% to 40% (or more) to the productive distributors.

**2.** Reward specific behaviors which are most desired by the company such as recruiting, retailing, building managers and leaders, and retention.

**3.** Reward those who exceed minimum levels of performance more than those who don't.

**4.** Avoid rewarding distributors who fail to perform consistently.

## The benefits of properly using breakage

Breakage is applied by imposing reasonable rules to qualify for commissions. If a distributor fails to perform at a desired level, the commission that he or she would otherwise receive is retained by the company. For example, if a distributor failed to meet his or her $100 minimum personal volume requirement, the company might keep their commissions instead of paying them to another distributor. This allows the company to pay more to other distributors who are meeting or exceeding the desired level of production. In essence, the company withholds commissions for lack of performance and increases the compensation of those performing well. The advantages are obvious:

**1.** Distributors who meet or exceed expectations are rewarded more generously using commission dollars that would have been kept by distributors who are performing less.

**2.** The company's financial stability would allow them to pay more than they could otherwise afford expanding the capacity of the plan to provide incentives for desired behavior. The company gets more of what it wants (desired behavior) and the performing distributor gets more of what he wants-- compensation and recognition. Breakage can be a win-win deal for both company and distributor.

There are many ways to implement breakage and the methods may vary according to the type of plan used.

## Example #1

Bob, a breakaway manager, fails to meet his minimum $100 personal purchase for the month. He would have received a 24% commission of $200 on his group volume, rather than paying it to his upline. Bob's $200 is retained by the company. The company determines that 1% of total payout is retained from unqualified managers like Bob each month. The company decides to place 1% into a bonus pool paid to every distributor who sponsors at least three people in the month. For each new recruit, the participants in the bonus pool receive one share of the pool. The company happily discovers that redirecting the commissions into the pool has resulted in a 10% increase in recruiting and a 4% increase in sales volume for the fiscal year from those new recruits. Equally important, over $100,000 has been paid to those distributors recruiting three or more people in a month making many happy and committed distributors.

▶

## Example #2

After a recent compensation plan change, the plan calls for a 4% 1st generation bonus to managers who achieve $100 in personal volume and $1,000 in group volume. If a manager achieves $2,000 in group volume, the commission is increased to 7%. When the 4% is paid instead of the 7%, the company retains the difference as breakage. The company has determined that about 25% of their managers achieve the $2,000 GV level, so they pay out the 7% 1st generation bonus about 25% of the time. The total 1st generation bonus paid is around 5%. In their old plan, the company paid out a 5% first generation bonus if the manager achieved $1,000 GV. In their new plan (4% to 7%), they pay out the same commission but have found a 50% increase in managers achieving $2,000 GV each month. They can afford to pay 7% to the higher producers out of the 1% obtained by lowering the original 5% to 4%.

> *Breakage is applied by imposing reasonable rules to qualify for commissions. If a distributor fails to perform at a desired level, the commission that he or she would otherwise receive is retained by the company.*

## Strategies for the wise use of breakage

**1.** Don't set performance thresholds (GV, PV, etc.) too low. Breakage is only available when there is a gap between poor performance and desired performance. If you need to set low levels of performance, offer graduated compensation opportunities for those who are willing to work harder. Low performance requirements produce low performance.

**2.** Redirect the breakage into new incentives when possible. Increasing the 5th generation bonus from 5% to 6% may make a few leaders happier, but they may not do anything different to obtain larger checks for doing the same old things (no wonder they are happier). Putting another 1%, however, into a new 6th generation bonus (assuming the old plan paid only five generations) which is contingent on adding another three personally sponsored breakaway leaders will stimulate leaders to recruit and build more front line breakaways than before.

**3.** If your plan uses titles or ranks like stair-step breakaway plans do, then always use paid as titles. Let distributors keep the highest title they achieve, but always pay them as the title they actually qualify for each month. To continue paying them based on performance that occurred months ago is wasting incentive dollars which could be applied to the better producers. It also reduces breakage opportunities.

**4.** For group volume incentives (front end stair-step), consider rewarding the breakaway manager based on his actual group volume instead of his title. For example, if a plan calls for a breakaway manager receiving a maximum of 25% on his group, consider adding a minimum volume level to receive the full 25%. If he falls below the minimum, then he would earn less, perhaps much less than 25%. The difference between actual and maximum would be retained as breakage and added to other incentives in the plan.

**5.** Never roll up volume from an unqualified breakaway to his upline. Rolling up commissions (called *commission*) is often desired, but avoid rolling up volume which would add to the group *volume* of upline managers. This results in creating phantom qualification volume for upline managers not related to any real performance and often rewards the poor performer who receives a nice check and wonders what he did to earn it. The net effect is to eliminate breakage and waste your incentive dollar.

**6.** Distinguish between *active* and *qualified* when qualification levels are defined. *Active* usually refers to personal performance often measured in Personal Volume (PV). *Qualified* often goes beyond *active* adding group volume or sponsoring requirements. Breakage rules can be defined differently for *an active* and *qualified distributor*. For example, the company might keep as breakage some commissions for *unqualified* distributors who fail to meet their group volume requirements, but roll up commissions (no breakage) for those distributors who are not *active*.

**7.** Grandfathering: A common technique when a company changes their compensation plan is to **grandfather** existing leaders and distributors into former (often lower) levels of performance requirements to "soften the blow" of the new plan. While this may be essential to winning their support for a much needed plan change, it is often unwise to offer these special arrangements for long periods of time. Wise companies often make grandfathering a temporary or transitionary arrangement. Grandfathering often reduces the breakage the company would otherwise receive due to poor performance. The net effect is that the producers are compensated less while the poor producers are compensated more.

## Other sources of breakage

1. Shallow company downlines: Companies that sponsor wide and new start-up operations find a "windfall" in the commissions left unpaid because there is no upline to pay them to. Be careful, however, because as the downline grows and matures, this short-term windfall diminishes.

2. High end titles and ranks: Many companies implement plans where the top end ranks or titles are achieved so rarely that few, if any, collect the corresponding commission benefits. These unpaid commissions provide breakage until more and more leaders achieve these higher titles and collect the commission benefits.

## Finding breakage
## opportunities in your plan

To determine where your breakage opportunities are,

## Follow these steps:

1. Write down each type of commission your plan

pays and what its maximum payout could be. For example, if your plan pays out five generations in the "back end" of 5%, then your maximum generation bonuses total 25%. Try to identify each individual type of commission such as 1st generation, 2nd generation, group volume bonus, etc.

2. Determine how much each type of commission actually pays out.

3. Subtract the actual payout from the maximum for each commission type. The difference is your breakage. Once you know where you already have breakage, you can also spot areas where you don't. Look at these areas and determine if you want to have more breakage and modify the plan accordingly.

## Conclusion

Breakage can be a significant competitive advantage if you use it wisely, and a terrific tool to reward the producing distributors more than you could otherwise afford. All plans have some breakage opportunities which can be tapped to make the plan an even more powerful motivator. As in most things, moderation is more prudent than extremes when applying the principles of breakage to your own plan. ∎

# The Extinction of Excellence?

*Leonard W. Clements*

*A man sees an ad offering a wealth building business opportunity. It instructs him to call an 800 number to hear a "powerful, life-changing message." He listens. He is then instructed to pull down some basic information from a fax-on-demand. He does. Within the documents he receives is a distributor application. He signs up. He places the same ad. Others call. Others access the fax-on-demand. Others join.*

*A woman receives a cassette tape in the mail titled "Wealth Secrets." She listens. The secret?* Just mail out tapes like this one. There's a phone number to call on the tape case and a distributor pin number. She calls the number. She orders some cassette tapes and mails them. Others call in to enroll, providing her pin number. Others order cassette tapes.

You hand a friend an "opportunity video." He watches it. It closes by offering him an opportunity to purchase a $20 "Money Making Info Pak." He does (eliminating the need for you to inventory or mail promotional material). He joins--and buys 100 videos to hand to his friends.

Simple, duplicatable, turn key, phenomenal systems, aren't they?

Yes--in theory.

No--in reality!

For most folks, network marketing is a career choice. It's a way out of the rat race. It's an endeavor that will, hopefully, earn them a comfortable living. One that will pay the mortgage, feed their family, and provide a secure retirement. Most people take choosing how to create a livelihood pretty seriously. They really put some thought (if not four or more years of study) into what they are going to do for a living the rest of their lives. Apparently, many people are willing to base this decision on a two page faxed document or a 20 minute cassette tape message.

As upline sponsors, do we really want them to? Really? I mean, how serious can a person be taking this business who spent 20 minutes to evaluate it and $20 to join it? Think about it. What is the greatest allure to systems like these? Isn't it the simplicity? The alleged effortlessness? The ease? Don't systems like these

> *For most folks, network marketing is a career choice. It's a way out of the rat race. It's an endeavor that will, hopefully, earn them a comfortable living.*

basically say, "If you think this business might be too hard, here's a system for you." It suggests that the "Wave 3 Technologies" will do the work for you. The system will build your downline, rather than you. So, who would systems like these attract? Well, most likely those who feel they can't do it on their own, or don't want to work very hard! It's kind of like improving the GPA on report cards by separating all the C and D students into one class, then grading everyone on a curve --as used to improving their study skills and helping them learn more. Or a better analogy might be that it's like moving the pitchers mound further away from the batter to make the ball easier to hit, rather than teaching the batter how to be a "heavy hitter." Yes these systems might help the distributor put up some impressive numbers, recruitment wise, but not the numbers that really count--like, amount of dollars on the check! I have a system that will allow everyone to recruit 100 distributors an hour! I'm serious. All you have to do is walk up to every person you see, gently tap them on the right shoulder and say "I declare you a distributor!" That's it. Totally duplicatable, requires no expensive sales aids, easy to teach, and will create genealogy that will stretch from Fresno to Miami. But, of course, no income whatsoever. And many of these systems we have today are not that far from this!

Most of these systems do provide at least some sales volume and income. But how much and for how long? Are these participants in your opportunity really getting involved to pursue a long-term, career changing business opportunity? Do you really think they are joining because they have a great loyalty toward the product? Or, are they buying into the system? Is the method of building

84

the "product" they are really buying? So what do you think these people do if, or when, that product stops performing, or never performs for them? They throw it away! They have no real vested interest, at least emotionally if not financially, in the business. They likely have little or no affinity towards the real products--it was just stuff they had to buy to make the system work.

A few years ago, it's arguable exactly when, this product focused, merit based industry metamorphosized into a big, giant recruiting contest. Today, almost every "system" is designed to simply slam people into the business. The introduction of all this "Wave-3 Technology" back in the 80s was supposed to help us communicate with people--not communicate for us. We've abused this technology. We've let it spoil us. We are soft and lazy (as a group--there are exceptions, of course).

Rather than lowering the bar, how about if we all get back to train people to jump higher? Rather than bringing the business down to meet the mediocre, why don't we bring the mediocre up to the level of excellence that is required to succeed in this business? One way we might accomplish this is to stop creating systems that are based on what we wish people would do, or what we think they should do, and start developing more systems based on what they will do. This age old concept of "Find a need and fill it and the world will beat a path to your door" is, at least semantically, quite flawed. We, as a society, don't buy "needs," we buy wants. We "need" to eat low fat foods--we want bacon double cheeseburgers. We "need" to exercise more--we want to just take a pill that will create the same results. How many of us "need" to see moving pictures projected on a screen, or ingest carbonated sugar water? No one. Yet, the motion picture and soft drink industries are two of the largest on Earth. Why? Because it fulfills a major *want*, not a need.

Sure it would be wonderful if all your new recruits could afford to distribute $20 "prequalifying" or "prospecting" packages. It would be great if all those prospects would actually read the book you send them or thoroughly study the product and comp plan material, watch the video, and listen to all the audio cassettes. Life would be grand if, by the time you followed up with them on the phone they were fully informed, objectionless, and ready to dive right in. Or, better yet, if all this could be accomplished without even making the follow up call! It would be MLM Utopia! A land where the whole world *wants* to hear about your opportunity, is *excited* about attending your next opportunity meeting, and fully cooperated with the entire recruiting process. Am I exaggerating? Have you listened to any presentation on any "system" that does not describe a perfect world scenario where you ask your friend if he or she has time to listen to an "exciting, life changing message" and your friend says, "Sure, Bob, sounds great. What's the number?" Or, have you ever heard anyone describe the "referral" prospecting technique where you ask a friend if they "know anyone who would be interested in making an extra $5 to $10 thousand a month" and the friend actually believes you're *not* really asking them? All the time, right?-- and it's pure fantasy!

So, you've got this great, automatic, turn-key, duplicatable system. Great. Now, where do you get the leads to run through it? Who sells the prospect on *why* they should listen to the 800 number or cassette tape? Who answers their detailed questions about the compensation plan or products? Who addresses their concerns or objections? Who motivates them once they're in? Who teaches them, if they do join, how to do all of these things and how to teach it to others? This is direct sales, which does not lend itself to the cookie cutter approach of franchising (although many "system" proponents will rationalize their approach by citing the success of the franchising industry). Two of the most fundamental, basic aspects of sales, at least in every *other* direct sales related business, is describing *benefits* as opposed to *features*, and discovering what your

> *This age old concept of "Find a need and fill it and the world will beat a path to your door" is, at least semantically, quite flawed. We, as a society, don't buy "need," we buy wants. We "need" to eat low fat foods--we want bacon double cheeseburgers. We "need" to exercise more--we want to just take a pill that will create the same results.*

prospect *wants*, and tailoring the "pitch" to match. In other words, don't tell them what your product does, tell them what they are going to get out of it. How is it going to improve their life? How can you do that without first discovering what aspect of their life needs improving? Very few people teach this benefits focused approach in network marketing, yet it's an extremely acquirable skill that you wouldn't last even one day without in *any* other sales position!

These "systems" take a blind, shotgun approach. There is absolutely no customization of the "pitch" to match the wants of the prospect. They all just assume it's money. It's not, ever. If all we wanted was money, then why do we quickly exchange it for something else the moment we get it? What they want is the *something else!* And the "system" has not the slightest clue what it is! Furthermore, the system is one of dozens, selling an MLM program that's one of hundreds. So your fax-on-demand spits out a page that exclaims, in big bold print, that your comp plan has a "Matching Bonus!" Or, your product contains "HGH precursors!" So what? What does that mean to me, the prospect? How do these things benefit me, and how will they provide me with a marketing advantage if I choose to be a distributor? What's more, federal and state regulatory agencies have us all on a short leash when it comes to describing the can and can't say? Does it protect you and your company from regulatory action? How could it? There's only so much you can cover in a five minute recording or a five page fax.

This is a 53-year-old business. There's really nothing new or revolutionary about it. Everything's been tried, and what you see today are just variations of what's already been done in the past. If we want to discover what works, all we have to do is look back over the last half century and see what has worked, then do that! Take a look at the most prolific, wealth generating era of network marketing, from about 1982 to 1992. Most of the obscenely richest distributors today (we're talking six digits monthly) originally made their fortunes back then, and they simply maintained it through the rest of the 90s. Many have lost most or all of it since then. Compare the number of mega-earners from back then to those that have appeared within the last six years. It's a small fraction. There are a myriad of theories to explain this phenomenon, but one certainly must be the advent of the "simple, turn-key, duplicatable system" and the turning away from tried and true methods of building. Things like, oh, talking to people!

Fortunately, there appears to be the very beginnings of a migration back to the more difficult but successful form of network marketing (yes, excellence in network marketing isn't extinct, just endangered). Even a few of the most die-hard "system" guys are now converting over. Even perhaps the biggest advocate of machine made downlines (you know, the guy with the bag on his head?) I hear is now promoting a more personal, product focused approach (and good for him). And I didn't just use the term "guys" generically. MLM's women, in general, still seem to have no problem with making prolonged human contact. It seems to be only the guys who desire an alternative form of communication (as any John Gray book would attest).

Never in the history of network marketing has someone built a large, lasting, big income producing downline using any type of simple, automatic system (name one!). Now, make a list of all those who have achieved lasting success and you have a list of people who are *professional, hard working, excellent network marketers!* Or, a few who got lucky and enrolled one or two *professional, hard working, excellent network marketers!* You'll also have a list of people who, at one time, were NOT *professional, excellent network marketers!* Professionalism and excellence IS duplicatable! Although it might require some, God forbid, *hard work.*

But as the last 53 years of MLM, and the last six million years of human existence, has taught us...work works!

*Leonard Clements has concentrated his full time efforts over the last eight years on researching and analyzing all aspects of network marketing. He is a professional speaker and trainer, and currently conducts Inside Network Marketing seminars throughout the U.S., Canada and Mexico. He is also the publisher of the "MarketWave Alert" letter, an MLM analysis and watchdog newsletter. Mr. Clements is the host of "Inside Network Marketing," a weekly live call-in radio show on KSCL 1080, and he is the author of the controversial book, "Inside Network Marketing," an objective, no-holds-barred, insider's look at the MLM industry. He is also the author of the best-selling cassette tape, "Case Closed! The whole Truth About Network Marketing," which has been labeled "the best" generic recruiting tape by six MLM company presidents.*
*To receive additional information about MarketWave and it's products, please call (800) 688-4766, or write to MarketWave, 7342 North Ivanhoe Avenue, Fresno, CA 93722.*■

# Roadblocks, Reversals, Rejections, Fail to Stop...
# Dale Calvert's Ascendancy To The Top

*Dale Calvert*

**Carmen Valdez**

For years, Dale Calvert had a constant reminder of his future goals. The wall of his make-shift office featured a photo of large, stately homes in the Mallard Point sub-division. At the time, he and his family were living in a 600 sq. ft. house; Calvert knew a lakeside Mallard Point home was exactly what they wanted.

"I used to drive out there at night in my old beat-up Chevette," Calvert recalls. "I would pull up to the gate but couldn't get in because it's a gated community. In my mind, I would visualize that one day we would be living there. That alone was a driving motivation for me."

Today, Calvert and his family have realized their dream. They live in a 4,000 sq. ft. home at Mallard Point; however, they have decided to move to even larger quarters and are building a 15,000 sq. ft. home on a 103 acre horse farm in central Kentucky where they will be able to hold huge company barbecues. How can they afford such a lifestyle? Calvert is the #1 distributor of New Image International, serving as director of marketing. In just a few years, his life has been totally transformed.

Founded in January, 1994 by Ron Frederic, New Image began with 84 associates. During its first year, it had $3.8 million in sales. By January 1995, there were 1,000 associates attending the national conference and $16 million in sales. Two years later, in January 1997, there were 3,000 associates attending the national conference and $25 million in sales. In 1998, 5,000 associates attended the national conference and there was $35 million in sales. Indeed, New Image is growing at a rapid rate. Eighty percent of the company's business encompasses five states.

In the past, Calvert had worked with two other network marketing companies and, for a period of time, he marketed a specialized health insurance product to people who are self-employed. But Calvert believes New Image is a different type of company; it's associates are able to sell the products – weight loss, health and nutritional items – directly to customers, making it possible for them to earn money before they sponsor others. Although the top producers all make six figure incomes, someone who spends only a few hours a week sharing products may earn a few hundred dollars a month.

"Their mothers, brothers, aunts, uncles and everybody they work with want to lose weight," Calvert says. "I lost 16 pounds when I first started taking the products, and everyone I knew wanted to try them. It happens for everyone else that way too."

Another unique feature about New Image is its training policy. "Most companies have no common method of teaching," Calvert said. "All their distributors use their own methods to train other distributors. It creates confusion. People don't know who to follow. We unified our organization and separated ourselves from the masses. All of our people are doing the same thing and using the same training programs. I always tell people that you need to have one system and stick with it. Don't let your people run around like chickens with their heads cut off."

New Image associates care about their fellow associates and about building relationships, which Calvert maintains is the essence of network marketing. "We have been able to give people the freedom to do what they want to do," Calvert said. "This is really about having freedom, potential and building better lives for our associates and their families."

Just a few short years ago, Calvert was desperate. Business reversals had left him deeply in debt. His credit cards had reached their maximum limits and it seemed as though he were spiraling into an endless pit. However, because he never stopped believing his situation would improve, his belief came true.

Calvert, his wife, Stephanie, and their three daughters are about to move into their new home, consisting of five bedrooms, seven and one-half baths, home theater, game room, outdoor pool and two offices. What forces could possibly explain this extraordinary financial reversal? To Calvert, now 38-years-old, the answer is simple: New Image International.

"For me, it has never been about money," says Calvert. "It's the freedom and ability to help others realize their untapped potential. I think most people die with their music still in them. However, because I consider myself an average person, it has enabled me to bring out the best in average people. New Image has corrected the two major problems within the network marketing industry. Usually, a person starting out can't make any money. We have eliminated that with our awesome retail opportunity. You don't have to sponsor a sole to make money. And finally, all New Image people are trained in the same methods. That unity creates a strength and power."

"I started to look at my other options when I was employed at IBM. I could have become a technician or maybe a department manager, but I couldn't see spending 40 years building a dream for someone else. I felt like I was in prison every day," Calvert said.

It was at this point when he decided there was a need for his own business. When one of his friends shared some tapes from a network marketing company, the decision had been made. Calvert decided he would become a distributor. At age 22, he was working during the day at IBM and networking with Stephanie evenings and weekends.

"We had a tremendous start, and in 1985, four years after we started network marketing, we went full-time. Both of us were in the One Percent Club, President's Club and drove a bonus car. We knew we had to do well and worked extremely hard. If it didn't work, I would be back at IBM where I was miserable," Calvert said.

"A businessman once told me there were only three ways for the average person to become wealthy in this country: You can inherit it or marry into it; your money can work for you through investments, or you can duplicate yourself through the efforts of other people," he stated. The first two were out of the question.

Early in 1986, the Calverts won an award for developing the most new supervisors within their company. However, by October of 1986, three of their key distributors had left the state.

"At that point we had two children and our income was cut in half," Calvert says. Naturally, his main concern was to support his family. Finally, in 1987, he began marketing the specialized health insurance product.

"We got back on our feet. I was Rookie of the Year for the Great Lakes area and Agent of the Year for the state of Kentucky. Then, in early 1988, I was moved to a management position. This is when we sold our network marketing distributorship. I started recruiting and training sales people, and would only hire those with fire in their eyes. My district, the state of Kentucky, was third in the nation - behind New York and California," Calvert recalled.

Despite what he thought to be a financial reversal from his lean years, at the end of 1988 Calvert was squeezed out of his job. The two managers above him decided that if he wasn't in the loop, they would make more money. "They would get my commissions," he stated. "That's when I got back into network marketing," Calvert says. The business he entered, which sold water and air filtration systems, took off quickly. "During our first 90 days, we made about $25,000. By the end of the first year, we paid off all our debts." Finally, Calverts luck was headed in the right direction.

Ron Frederic approached him, asking if he would help implement a marketing program for New Image. "I told

> *"For me, it has never been about money," says Calvert. "It's the freedom and ability to help others realize their untapped potential. I think most people die with their music still in them. However, because I consider myself an average person, it has enabled me to bring out the best in average people...*

him I wasn't interested in changing companies, but I would put together a training program for him. During this time, my wife had complications from surgery and I was home helping out for about three months. I went on Ron's weight loss products and lost 16 pounds. When friends saw that I had lost weight, they asked for the product. Then their friends started asking for the product. One morning I woke up a 5 a.m. in a cold sweat, thinking all my life I had products that people needed but didn't want. This was the first time I had a product that people want," Calvert said.

From the eighty four people who attended New Image's first national conference, sixteen were part of the Founders Club. "These were people who followed me from the other company, which has since been doing poorly. They gave up everything they had to start with me from ground zero and they are still with us; all making a six figure annual income. With

> *"...All of our people are doing the same thing and using the same training programs. I always tell people that you need to have one system and stick with it. Don't let your people run around like chickens with their heads cut off."*

New Image, I saw the chance to take everything I had learned from mistakes I made with other companies and built a solid company that would more than feed our grandchildren," Calvert said.

Calvert predicts that in the future, New Image will become known as the company that returned network marketing to its roots.

"Where else can you put in three to five years and create total, passive six figure yearly incomes for the rest of your life," Calvert says. "I have been able to help people all over the country do just that. This business is about building relationships with people and bringing out the best in them. That is our mission."

*Dale Calvert has chronicled his story on a tape entitled "The power of a dream." For more information, check his web page at www.DaleCalvert.com.* ■

## Pointing The Finger

Blaming occurs when a mistake is so obvious it can't be denied, so you try the "next-best" thing: pointing a finger at someone else, you say "It's not my fault!" The boss blames the staff, marketing blames research and development, the teacher blames the student. The blamer tries to put everyone else on the hook.

Consider the golfer who tensed up and overcompensated and hit a drive into the rough, a natural mistake that could be corrected next time. But instead, he blames the course's narrow fairways, the architect for designing it that way, the wind, other people's loud voices, and his caddy. He is willing to blame anything rather than admit an error. Sounds familiar, doesn't it? We do it all the time. We blame the client for not buying, the boss for not listening, the audience for not clapping, the baby for not eating.

A partner in an East Coast investment group, talking about a client of his who had fallen on hard times, said it was tough to find the real problem. "They were all too busy pointing the finger. They were blaming the boss, the customers, new laws, unions, or a new competitor. Anything but themselves. And as a result, they never got to the heart of the problem."

Turnaround specialist Timothy Finley said about a company he bought that he found the president "pointed the finger of blame at the sales manager for the lack of profitability, and the sales manager pointed the finger of blame at the president." Looking at the facts objectively, Finley discovered that both had made mistakes. But according to him each was so busy passing the buck that there was "too much blaming and not much learning."

# Opportunity has its rewards

**The opportunity to build your own business can be rewarding in different ways to different people.**

You set the goals, go your own pace, schedule your own time, and determine what you want in return. You can market as many, or as few, product lines as you choose — from personal care products to popular brand-name catalog merchandise. More than 3 million entrepreneurs in some 80 countries and territories have found this business opportunity made possible only through Amway is worth a closer look. See for yourself. Perhaps *you* can discover the rewards you've been seeking.

**The Business Opportunity Company**™

If you'd like to know more, call for a free brochure at **1-800-544-7167** or visit our website at **www.amway.com**    © 1998 Amway Corporation
In Canada call **1-800-922-6929**.

# Techniques to Yield Positive Responses

*Adrian Miller*

*Just about everybody involved in selling has been trained in the art of closing. Most sales training books, manuals, tapes and workshops include discussions of closing techniques such as assumptive, alternative choice and "why not." In fact, the motto "close or lose" has been the battle cry in many organizations. But while closing is an integral part of any sales call, it should not be the main focus.*

Unfortunately, some reps may close too early in their calls because they have become too strongly focused on closing. By doing so too early, they run the risk of alienating their prospects and losing other closing opportunities.

Professional business reps can avoid these pitfalls by honing their closing skills. They can learn the techniques that will enable them to close at appropriate points during their sales calls, thus increasing their call effectiveness and positive response.

## Precall Planning

The sales process starts even before calls are made. Plainly stated, more sales are made when you have a well-conceived plan of attack than when you "wing it."

Does this sound pretty simplistic? Then consider the many times you have received a call during which the rep meandered from one topic to another, never quite getting to the point of the call. Furthermore, keep in mind the need to choose your words and plan your communications with great care because the telephone does not afford the luxury of body language, visual aids and eye contact.

## Tried-and-True Techniques

Once you have planned your sales path, you can use some tried-and-true techniques to generate more sales from your calling efforts. Used properly and regularly, these techniques should yield an increase in positive response.

## Explaining the Benefits of Your Product or Service

Don't overlook the need to explain. Too often, reps assume their prospects are fully informed and educated on the benefits of what they are selling. As a result, they concentrate solely on explaining features, without going the extra step to fill in the answer to the age-old question asked by each and every prospect. "What's in it for me?"

Without helping prospects to see the benefits, you are counting on them to do the work for themselves, which is not conducive to making sales.

The simplest method to help prospects see the benefits of your product or service is to use the following "transition phrases" in your presentation:

♦ "Allowing you to."

♦ "Providing you with."

♦ "Enabling you with."

♦ "Therefore, you will be able to."

Include strong benefits statements and explanations in your presentations and you'll be certain to increase your positive results.

## Ask the Right Questions

If you ask enough questions and if you ask the correct ones, your prospects will tell you how they need and want to be sold. Many reps are afraid to ask questions because they think they may not be able to handle the prospects' responses. In fact, that might be true, especially if they have not taken enough time to prepare for their calls by knowing how they will respond to questions and objections.

Open-ended questions, positioned properly, can provide you with a wealth of information that will help you to stress the benefits that are important to all of your prospects' situations.

## Develop Strong Rebuttals

Most sales are made on objections. Let's face it, if you call prospects and they were willing and ready to buy the very second you called them, chances are they were planning to make those purchases even if you hadn't reached out to them. It's a perfect example of being in the right place at the right time.

But since you can't count on much for the majority of your success, you must be prepared to persuasively and successfully overcome objections raised by your prospects. Once again, reflect on the calls you may have received. Have you ever raised an objection, only to have the rep virtually ignore it and move on to another point? Did that make you want to buy the product?

►

The best way to overcome objections and ensure yourself more sales is to follow these four steps:

### Acknowledge the Objection
If you don't take the time to make certain prospects know you have heard their concerns, they are going to feel you are ignoring them and are not interested in their thoughts.

### Mention That you Have Heard or Dealt with This Objection Before
This is how you establish credibility (sort of like "been there, done that!").

### Provide Benefits-Oriented Responses to Objections
It is critical to include benefits. By rasing objections, prospects are blatantly asking you for more information and asking you to show them how your products or services will benefit them.

### Close on Each Objection
This is the most critical step in overcoming objections. If you don't close on each and every objection raised by your prospects, they are not certain what they should be doing in the call.

### Why Closing is Important
Closing relieves prospects of uncertainty. It is a call to action. If you do not close, your prospects will not know what to do. In most cases, they will terminate the call in a manner that is unacceptable to you, i.e., stall on the decision, ask if you can call back or request literature.

Perhaps the most important fact to remember about closing is that you will probably have to do it more than once on each call. If fact, a typical sales call might require you to close two or three times before you are able to provide the prospect with enough information and benefits to lead him or her to buy.

Once you have pre-planned your coherent, well-focused presentation, remember that you need to:

**Develop a strategy for explaining the benefits of your product or service fully and clearly.**

**Ask the questions during the sales calls that will elicit answers that reveal your prospects' special needs.**

**Provide strong and sharply focused rebuttals for their objections.**

**Close as often as needed during the call to make the sale.**

*Adrian Miller is president of Adrian Miller Direct Marketing, a telemarketing consulting firm based in Port Washington, New York.* ■

## The "Alice's Restaurant" Bank

"Banks today face perhaps the biggest challenge because they were regulated for so long, they have no entrepreneurial legacy," Jack Wilborn, consultant to many banks and partner at Arthur Andersen & Co. recently said. "Consequently, banking's ranks are filled with conservative, Type B personalities, people who wait for the customers to come to them. This was acceptable in the old days, but in this era of deregulation, when the competition is fierce, it is a strategy that no longer works. Banks need to be more innovative and creative than ever, while avoiding the irresponsible practices of many S&Ls. But that's easier said than done, he explains."

"The problem with banks is people who think we have to do things the way we always have," says Casey Mackensie, executive vice president of First Nationwide Bank. Seeking to attract the volume and traffic found at discount stores, she got the mountain to come to Mohammed. Mackensie was instrumental in opening First Nationwide branches in 164 K Mart stores.

Bank One's branch near Columbus, Ohio, is a financial center that as *Fortune* magazine reported, "resembles Alice's Restaurant: you can get anything you want." Laid out like a shopping mall, complete with the inevitable rock music and neon signs, it has been designed by the company that does K Mart, WalMart, and Sears stores. To reach the teller's window located along the back wall, customers walk past minishops selling everything from real estate and travel services to discount stock brokering. The bank is a roaring success. After just two years in operation, it has more than 9,000 accounts and a whopping 35 percent share of local deposits.

# How to build your dream network marketing business

# Doris Wood...
# 'Den Mother to the World'

*Frank Clancy*

In Doris Wood's official biography, which can be found, among other places, on the MLMIA web site, mlmia.com, you'll find listed her vast experience as a

explain, she'll conclude that it's both true and not true—it's a number chosen to provoke the reader, and perhaps to plant a seed in the occasional one who, like her, might

*Doris Wood the "original" den mother to the MLM industry*

distributor, owner, speaker, writer and consultant to the network marketing industry. However, her proudest accomplishments are her children and grandchildren, high achievers all. She then refers to nine (children) by adoption.

Nine adopted children? It's a number that begs—nay, demands—explanation. And if you ask Doris Wood to

be inclined to take in strays. Wood did not formally adopt nine kids, but more than nine have lived in her home during their teenage years and came to know her as a surrogate mother.

"When my children were in high school," Wood explains, "they had many friends who either had problems at home

*The den mother is a grandmother -- and a proud one at that, seen here with (from left), Peggy Sue, Taylor and Kim*

or couldn't make their grades. There was some problem someplace. My children asked me if their friends could come and live with us. Their "real" parents agreed and they moved in. This happened throughout high school and college."

After her children had finished college, Wood adds, "I missed having so many people around. It was then that I began to invite other young people who did not have all the advantages in life and who would like a mentor to spend six months or a year living with me." Wood considers them her adopted children. They call her the den mother to the world. It's as good a description of Doris Wood as you'll find. And it's as relevant to her professional life as it is to her personal life. Few people in the network marketing industry have as much experience as this white-haired matriarch who lives in Irvine, California, and looks like both Dolly Parton and Mary Kay. (When they make a movie of my life, she jokes, Dolly Parton could play my part and when they make one about Mary Kay, I'll play hers.) And, she still takes in many people who find the MLM couch quite comfortable. Nor will you find many people who are as visible. Wood, the Executive Director and President Emeritus of the Multi-Level Marketing International Association (MLMIA), is

one of the most often quoted experts in the entire industry. Equally important, few people in the industry have helped to nurture as many successful individuals, companies and institutions.

Doris Wood entered the network marketing industry when it was truly in its infancy. The year was 1957. She was married, had two children, and wanted to return to work. Her background was in journalism.

Wood's family had just moved to a new area of St. Louis when a neighbor invited her to attend a party. It wasn't, however, a strictly social event—someone was going to be displaying jewelry. "I didn't want to go," Wood recalls. "In fact, I was adamant about not going. But I went…I guess I wanted to meet some of my neighbors. The party changed my life. I don't remember knowing that you could earn money by doing things like that," Wood says. "The lady did the demonstration and sold the jewelry, but she never approached me about selling jewelry. I didn't go to sleep that night at all. The next morning I called her (Texene Long) and told her I wanted to be interviewed by her manager. I had no idea what the industry was about."

Ignorant though she might once have been, Wood was immediately successful. "I took to it like a duck to water, because I had always been a people person." She remembers, "I'd say what I was doing, and other people wanted to do it too." For eight years, Wood sold costume jewelry at parties. In 1964, she was one of the first distributors in the nation to do a million dollars in sales. That would equate to about $10 million today.

It was at that time, in many respects, a very different business in a very different industry. Wood had all of 160 distributors in her downline. The most expensive item in the line—a three-piece set that included a broach, bracelet and earnings, cost only $5.95 each. "People really concentrated more on the selling of the product than they did the recruiting of other people." Wood didn't think so much about residual income; it was right-now income that she was more interested in.

In 1972, she and her family moved to California. Having succeeded as a distributor and working at corporate level for several years, in 1976 Wood decided to try a different side of network marketing. She and three partners founded a company called AloEssence Cosmetics, which, as its name implies, sold beauty products. Although AloEssence began with only $170,000 worth of capital, it grew quickly, to the point where it had 50,000 distributors across the United State and Canada. Wood stayed with the company for three years. "It was the first time I had owned a network marketing company," Wood recalls, "and I made a mistake…I had three partners, all married men. As I recall, none of them had ever had anything to do with skin care and none of them certainly had ever applied lipstick. And, I didn't get my agreements in writing."

Several years later, as she tells the story, a man named David Gufstofson initially invited her to his home to discuss working for him as a consultant. She arrived in a newly purchased, sparkling white, silk suit. At the door, she was greeted by Gufstofson and two young, highly enthusiastic —soaking wet —German Shepherds. "They shook and jumped all over me. Gufstofson then ushered me into the living room and sat me down on the couch that was covered with dog hair. I never did wear that suit again."

One of Wood's first questions was, "Why me? I told him, I don't know anything about computers. Why do you want me to be involved?" And he said, "Doris, you teach me about people and I'll teach you about computers, I want to do this."

Despite its inauspicious beginnings, Wood's relationship with Gufstofson thrived. However, the company did not. Commodore started selling their computers at K Mart for $50 less than they were purchasing them for and the company never really had a chance. However, David went on to write a great motivational book and became a great

*A family affair. Doris with (from left), son Duayne, daughter Kim and son Doug*

*Doris with her counterpart, Carrol Leclerc, president of the Canadien MLMIA (Multi-Level Media Industry Association)*

public speaker and Doris learned how to use computers… including desktop publishing.

"David and I had a chance to talk recently," Doris told us "and we agreed that Commodore might still be in business today, and possibly a leader in their field had they kept their commitment to their dealers, particularly the one with the sales concept of selling computers MLM. However, they went for one big sale and a short-lived success trying for the blue light special."

When that didn't work out, Wood knew she should return to her love of helping people by being a consultant to the industry.

It is the tremendous breadth of her experience in network marketing, Wood believes, that makes her such a good consultant. "Whatever problems a client faces, I've been there and done that." As a consultant, Wood operates under the umbrella of The Wood International Group or T.W.I.G. She's worked for clients companies in Switzerland, Australia, South America, South Africa and Asia, as well as the United States. In each case, she has scrupulously avoided becoming directly involved in those companies to avoid any conflicts of interest. "My belief is that a consultant should never be a part of the (client)

company. You need to know which hat you're supposed to wear. I believe you can't be a good consultant for one company if you're a distributor for them or another."

What Wood has become involved in—deeply involved, is the Multi-Level Marketing International Association (MLMIA), based in Newport Beach, California, which is also known as the Association for Network Marketing. As Co-founder, President (now President Emeritus) and Executive Director of the MLMIA, Wood has, more than any other single person, been responsible for building the organization into a powerful force both inside and outside the network marketing industry. It is, in a real sense, another of Wood's many adopted children.

Here's how she explains the rationale for developing the MLMIA into an organization that represents everyone in the network marketing industry. The corporate, the support, and the distributors are all part of the industry, each with a different specialty, each of them with some of the same needs and some with very different needs. She knows, she's done them all. She compares it to the American Medical Association, which represents physicians regardless of specialty—whether they are cardiologists or surgeons, pediatricians or specialists in treating the elderly.

99

Given her 40 years or so of experience in the network marketing industry, Doris Wood has a unique and valuable perspective on how it's changed—and on what it takes to be successful in network marketing. That perspective is more than personal. Wood is the author of *We've Only Just Begun: A History of Network Marketing*, written in 1994.

Some of the differences between the past and present are glaringly obvious. Not long ago, for example, there were only a relative handful of network marketing companies that exclusively sold a narrow range of products and no services. Very few men worked in the industry. Though technically independent, distributors had to report every week to their managers; they had to attend regular meetings, and had to give detailed reports showing the number of people they'd spoken to about the business, how much product they'd sold, and how many people they'd recruited. The industry itself carried a stigma that made it more difficult to recruit others. There was no such thing as a heavy hitter and distributors seldom moved from one company to another.

But many other changes, in Wood's opinion, are deceptive. "I sometimes have to remind people that we did have telephones," she says, with a hint of laughter in her voice. "However, the only reason to make a long distance phone call was because somebody died, had a baby or got married. There was no other reason to make a long distance call. This meant we did all of our recruiting locally. There wasn't any long distance sponsoring. When I was selling costume jewelry, we did a million dollars of business and the people were within a 30 mile radius of our office. We didn't have fax machines, we didn't have three way calls, and we didn't have the Internet. What we had was our two feet and the gumption to go out and do it."

Wood is definitely not opposed to technology and change. However, she does believe that technology too often distracts distributors and others in the industry from their proper focus: on people. "All of those technological innovations are really good if you use them as tools," Wood says, "but if you use them as a crutch, and you think you don't have to go out and see people, they are not good things. In other words, the more things change, the more they remain the same."

Some forty years ago, Wood took to the industry, in her words, like a duck to water because she instinctively knew that success in network marketing depended on a distributor's ability to communicate with, get along with and help other people. Wood mothered her downline no less than the stream of adopted children who shared her home. Though she's older now than she was (of course), Wood has no plans to retire soon. Age, she insists, is a state of mind. But don't call her the grandmother of the network marketing industry. That's a special word reserved for the several children of her children. Besides, she's extremely busy.

There is still the MLMIA to run, although she and the board keep looking for the administrator who loves and understands the industry who would like to give back. There are several partially written books to complete, her personal web site, MLMradio, and dreams of a foundation that would document the industry's history. Indeed, Wood remains as dedicated to the network marketing industry as she was decades ago; as she was when she started the MLMIA.

Why such dedication to an industry, particularly one that has not made her, unlike many of its other leaders, wealthy? "Network marketing gave me an opportunity for tremendous personal growth, enabling me to travel both domestically and international, that I don't believe I would ever have done otherwise. I've been to many, many countries as a spokesperson for the industry. Most important of all are the people I have met. I think it's wonderful that some of the people I truly care about are making a million dollars a year. But I knew them and they were special to me when they weren't making a dime, " Wood recalls.

Here Wood pauses for several moments to reflect on what she's said. One of her most endearing traits is her ability to laugh at her own expense, whether it's the memory of a dog-worn, white silk suit or her own relative honesty. "I don't know why I work so hard for the industry. Sometimes I think I need my head examined and then I get a letter or a call from someone that I've met along the way who thanks me for being there and I know why I'll continue until the last breath." Den Mothers are always there to guide and love. ■

# Get in on the
# ground floor
# with Eventus!

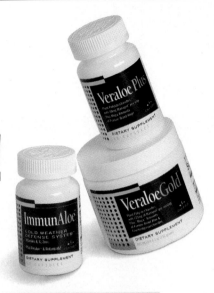

Unbelievable ground-floor earnings opportunity backed by 18 years of stablility await those who join Eventus International as we are launching the most exciting network marketing opportunity of the new millennium! Eventus blasts you into the booming $12 billion a year nutraceutical market with the world's most advanced total wellness products, the best pay plan in existence and cutting-edge e-commerce technology. Enjoy a lucrative, flexible, home-based career, with more time for the better things in life like travel and golf. How much you earn and when you work is up to you. With Eventus, your success is unlimited!

If you're serious about your financial future, join the thousands of individuals who are living their dreams with Eventus.

## Real Nutrition
## Real Results

Eventus innovation leads the multi-billion dollar nutraceutical revolution with patented technologies, advanced ingredients and next-generation formulas that deliver real nutrition at the cellular level, building total health and wellness. Revolutionary Eventus products include: **Heritage Gold Formulas™**, the first and only line of nutraceuticals uniquely customized by a person's heritage. **Veraloe Plus™** and **Veraloe Gold™**, daily all-natural immune stimulators.

## Immediate and residual income.

The Eventus compensation plan offers higher commissions and overrides, and more bonuses than other network marketing plans. Earn immediate income, build long-term prosperity with lucrative sustainable downlines and receive multiple paychecks every month. Eventus has the stability of founding company BeautiControl,® one of the world's most successful direct sales wellness companies with 18 years in the business.

## Competitive e-commerce support!

From virtual offices to personalized Distributor web pages to electronic ordering and sponsoring, you are on-line and ready to do business in the 21st century.

*Richard Howard, president of Eventus*

*"Eventus offers what virtually no other network marketing opportunity can: a golden, ground-floor opportunity backed by founding company BeautiControl, an international direct sales firm with 18 years in business."*

## Team Eventus

Some of the world's greatest sports legends choose Eventus products to enhance total health and wellness.

- **Nolan Ryan,** National Baseball Hall of Fame inductee with unprecedented 27-year major league pitching career.

## eventus
International

Contact Eventus now at **1-800-943-8085** or www.eventusonline.com for a free information package.

# Pre-Paid Legal

# Preventive Health Care Provider of the Legal World

*Harland in a relaxing moment with wife Shirley*

**P**re-Paid Legal Services, Inc. was founded on the premise that "necessity is the mother of invention."

It was 1969 when Harland Stonecipher, founder and president of Pre-Paid Legal Services, Inc., was involved in a car accident. At the time, he was employed as a school teacher. Although he had insurance to cover his medical costs and car repair, plus life insurance to help his wife if he had died, he was totally unprepared for the legal costs. Stonecipher learned the hard way that legal services, while necessary, are well beyond most people's budgets. The experience left him wondering how quality legal help could be made more affordable and accessible. It occurred to him that a legal "insurance" program could be the answer. Members would pay an affordable monthly fee guaranteeing them access to help when they needed it. Stonecipher set his sights on just such a program, and in 1972 he launched Pre-Paid Legal Services.

At the onset, growth was slow. Law firms were reluctant to take part at first, preferring to generate their own business and fees. Stonecipher persevered and the company grew, slowly but steadily, in its first ten years. In 1983, he expanded the concept into the network marketing arena, and Pre-Paid Legal Services began to enjoy a far more rapid growth. However, in 1986 financial problems forced the company to pull back. This reversal didn't stop Stonecipher from moving forward with his vision, and by 1994 the company began experiencing explosive growth. Since then, Pre-Paid Legal Services has been a strong and steady provider of legal help.

What accounts for its longevity and survival, even in rough times? Stonecipher attributes his success to a high level of credibility and market awareness. As his company has expanded, he's received favorable attention from such respected sources as *Forbes*, *Fortune*, and *Money* magazines. The strength of the company, its financial soundness (it currently carries no debt and has considerable cash reserves), and steady growth have all led to it becoming one of the fastest

> *What accounts for its longevity and survival, even in rough times? Stonecipher attributes his success to a high level of credibility and market awareness.*

growing companies on the New York Stock Exchange. Pre-Paid Legal is recognized as a reputable, stable business.

Stonecipher's company is somewhat unique in the world of network marketing in that there are a large number of associates selling only the product; no recruiting for new members. He believes this product-driven approach is what has brought the company to its successful status. "The question you have to ask is, will people buy this product?" He says: "There's no point in setting up a marketing plan if there's no legitimate product to market."

When it comes to representation, does he look only for people with legal backgrounds to represent his product? Not at all. He looks for people from all walks of life. A firm belief in the value of the service being marketed is absolutely necessary. They can take that belief and sell only the product, or they can work with the product and recruit new members, whichever they feel most comfortable doing. At the same time, they have a unique opportunity to build their own business. Most people have the ability to own and run a business, but the opportunities are limited. "McDonald's is a good franchise," Stonecipher says, "however, you have to invest several hundred thousands of dollars up front." Pre-Paid Legal Services can put someone in business for approximately $250. The long-term residuals are another benefit; he still has earnings coming in from contracts drawn up in 1973.

As important as growth is, Stonecipher is more concerned about taking care of the consumers. He feels strongly that if growth isn't controlled, they won't be able to provide the quality of service they're known for. The

> *"Americans are supposed to be guaranteed equal justice under the law, but that often means it's just as equal as you can pay."*

American Bar Association estimated that 52% of Americans have a legal problem of one kind or another. Unfortunately, they don't have the means to hire the necessary help. Stonecipher views his company as being the preventive health care of the legal world. "We're a private company helping solve a public issue," he says. "Americans are supposed to be guaranteed equal justice under the law, but that often means it's just as equal as you can pay."

If the top 10% of wage earners in America can afford a lawyer and the bottom 10% have access to a public defender, that leaves a whopping 80% unprotected and unprepared for legal problems. That's Stonecipher's market, and he says they've barely scratched the surface. For an average monthly fee of $16, access to high quality legal services are available. "Many people out there have never set up their will," he says. "These are covered in our service. Having a lawyer draw one up would easily cost as much as a full year's enrollment. It pays for itself." As for some early

criticism that such a legal service would encourage lawsuits, the opposite has proven the case. By addressing a problem early on, the chances of settling it amicably are much greater. "On the other hand," Stonecipher says, "you see the same situation over and over again. Someone has a small legal problem, but can't afford a lawyer. So they put off doing anything about it and end up in a lawsuit, which could probably have been prevented if they'd had access to a lawyer immediately."

The company's stability and reputation can be demonstrated by its welcome into the corporate world. Many companies have brought Pre-Paid Legal Services in as an added employee benefit. Stonecipher has a group of salespeople who are trained and certified to work only in the area of employee benefits. This has proven to be a highly successful way of reaching the 80% factor of people who may need legal help.

From an accident in 1969 to a company that has spread to nearly all of the 50 states and is now about to expand into Canada, Pre-Paid Legal is the perfect example of a vision made into reality. Stonecipher is proud of his company, its success and its credibility. But life is not all work. He lives in Ada, Oklahoma, with his wife, Shirley. They have two grown sons and three grandchildren, ("I just had one over for a sleepover last night!") He owns his own airplane, and he and Shirley enjoy traveling together to meetings around the country.

*If you think you can, you can.*
*And if you think you*
*can't, you're right.*

**Mary Kay Ash,**
**New York Times,**
**Oct. 20, 1985**

# Get the most out of your home based business,

# With The Business Plan We Have Written For You.

At Matol Botanical International Ltd., we believe in the value and benefits of a home based business.

During the past 14 years we have paid out over $560 million to our Distributors and we plan to push that total over a $1 billion in the next six years. Our compensation plan delivers what the other ones promise. We have a proven system that will work for you, just like it has for so many others.

Your Matol business plan features the tools, systems and most importantly, the access to our information services that you need to succeed immediately. Specifically, you have our TOLL-FREE telephone and fax services at your disposal when you need them. They include a blue chip customer service department, a 24 hour-a-day INFO-LINE with weekly conference calls, powerful testimonials, and Fax-on-Demand / Fax Flash. Best of all, these services are available at no extra cost.

You also receive full color Matol Journals, monthly newsletters and updates, not to mention a corporate presence on the internet. All of which are designed, with you in mind, to be effective sales aids and marketing tools.

Our plan is geared to keep you well informed, motivated and able to make a positive impression on everyone you meet.
We provide year-round, first class events and top notch regional business meetings so you and your prospects can always be involved.

Our major programs feature information and training sessions on our family of award winning products, along with recognition and development seminars making our business plan truly complete.

As a Serious Nutrition Company with a Healthy Attitude, we are well established with our flagship - Km®, putting us at the forefront of turn key opportunities.

There has never been a better time to start your home based business with us, since we have just launched an exclusive new product line featuring a proprietary, patented process which we believe will make history.

## Call 1-800-363-3890 for your FREE information and get started today!
### Your timing is perfect.

www.matol.com

BOTANICAL INTERNATIONAL LTD.

# Preface From 'Heart To Heart'-
## *The Real Power Of Network Marketing*

*Scott DeGarmo & Louis Tartaglia, M.D.*

They come from all walks of life. Before entering the network marketing industry, they were doctors, lawyers, nurses, military officers, housewives, students, ministers, entrepreneurs, executives, farmers, laborers, schoolteachers, athletes, policemen, clerks, computer technicians, welfare mothers, pilots, and college professors. Today, they hold the following truths about network marketing to be self-evident:

❤It's an exciting, energizing, uplifting way of life. You're in constant contact with positive people who are your friends, mentors, and coaches. They help you undergo empowering personal transformations that remove the obstacles to your success.

❤It's a new form of entrepreneurship open to all. You don't need bank funding to get started. You don't need to call on hundreds of investors or raise millions of dollars. You can use your own money from your piggy bank to launch your own dream and there's no limit to how big that dream can be.

❤Sophisticated business experts endorse the *heart to heart* method of selling. Financial analysts, corporate executives, marketing consultants and even medical doctors have found that the personal testimonials used in network marketing are the most effective way to spread the word and distribute products.

❤You can create the lifestyle you want. Rather than becoming a tool of the business, you shape your work to the way you and your family want to live. You can travel, move abroad or live in multiple locations. You can make the choice to live a life that's emotionally fulfilling. You're surrounded by people who genuinely want you to succeed. Network marketing fosters true cooperation. Colleagues are profoundly motivated to help one another, both because they are bound in close relationships and

> *Much of the criticism of network marketing is baseless in fact. Press coverage of the industry is inaccurate, misleading, and incomplete. Network marketing companies are radically different from traditional businesses, and are notoriously misunderstood by the media.*

because their success depends on mutual support

❤Many people never find happiness or fulfillment working for a corporation. Sadly, too many unjustly blame themselves, as if their unsuitability for corporate life were a personal failure. They spend their years trying to adjust, or to find the perfect job. Yet many of these same individuals may well find enormous satisfaction working in a home-based

business. As a 25-year-old woman said after getting a taste of being a wage earner: "It would be a waste of my life to live that way. You only get one chance to go through this life."

❤Competition is not the way. Traditional organizations will always be rife with internal competition. We often try to hide this fact from ourselves and then feel shocked or betrayed when it becomes obvious what game is really being played. Workers and managers compete among themselves for pay, status, recognition, advancement and job security. Network marketing by contrast, is structured in such a way as to render all of the above pointless.

❤There's room for everyone. Being disabled, disadvantaged, handicapped, ill, unemployable, or saddled with past failures are no bar to prospering in network marketing. Some of the most successful network marketers in the field suffer from chronic ailments and terminal illnesses. Top distributors include single mothers who have never been in the workforce, people whose health problems prevent them from holding a steady job, plus all sorts of workers who were fired, downsized, or were helpless as their businesses went under.

❤Your mind is opened to unlimited possibilities. Ingrained skepticism often leaves people incapable of imagining themselves wealthy. Such was the case of a former journalist. After seeing dozens of examples of network marketers who had achieved what he thought impossible, he overcame his self-imposed limitations and became a millionaire.

♥Personal growth equals business success. You have access to a limitless supply of personal growth with a network marketing company. When nurtured and tended to in the proper fashion, a business can undergo an astonishing explosion of growth. It's the best way to introduce a product and achieve rapid market penetration, as many fortunate distributors have found.

♥Much of the criticism of network marketing is baseless in fact. Press coverage of the industry is inaccurate, misleading, and incomplete. Network marketing companies are radically different from traditional businesses, and are notoriously misunderstood by the media.

♥People find close friendships, emotional support -- even romance and marriage. Meeting someone aboard a cruise ship, then falling in love and getting married at a wedding in front of hundreds of people in your organization may seem too fortuitous to merit examination. But in fact it happens more often than one may imagine.

♥You are part of a new wave of home-based businesses. Ever since the beginning of the Industrial Revolution, work has been taking men and women out of their homes and shaping their lives -- always with the battle cries of Centralize, Mechanize, and Standardize.

Corporations have dictated when we worked, where we lived, and the income we earned. Akin to a slave to the company store. Now, for the first time since we began streaming into the factories some 200 years ago, the trend is reversing. In 1975, a mere 2.5 million Americans worked from their homes. In 1997, more than 40 million Americans operated part or full time businesses out of their private residences. Without a doubt, the revolution to take back control of our own lives from the privacy, comfort and safety of our homes is in full swing and will only continue as we realize that happiness and financial security can be found beyond the traditional corporate culture.

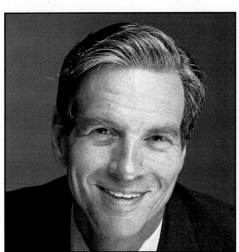

*Scott DeGarmo is an internationally recognized expert on management and entrepreneurship. As the first mainstream business editor to cover network marketing, he is credited with putting the industry on the map of the publishing world.*

*During his 14 years as Editor-in-Chief & Publisher of "Success" magazine, Scott became known to millions of entrepreneurs and network marketers.*

*Under his leadership, Success grew from a small, little-known publication without a single page of national advertising to a publication of award-winning renown and readership of 1.6 million before selling his interest in 1997.*

*In his publishing career, Scott also has launched a successful weekly newspaper, a science magazine and the national publication, "Working at Home," which he conceived and served as editor-in-chief & publisher. Earlier in his career, he was the editor of "Family Weekly" magazine, which he built to a circulation of 13 million. Scott also reported for the Washington Star and served as newsman for United Press International.*

*Since selling his interest in Success in 1997, Scott has been writing and speaking on topics ranging from venture capital to marketing. He frequently appears on cable and network television and has had multiple appearances on such programs as the "Today" and "Oprah Winfrey" shows.*

*His current book, "Heart to Heart: The Real Power of Network Marketing," is written with psychiatrist Louis Tartaglia. It is packed with useful, inspiring, and often amazing information on the subject of home-based business. To order on the web, reach amazon.com and search by title or author, Heart to Heart, The Real Power of Network Marketing, by Scott DeGarmo.*

*Scott lives in New York City with his wife, Barbara, an editor. They enjoy traveling and outdoor activites.* ∎

# Portion Control
## Thinking about manufacturing offshore?
## Consider the cost of quotas first

*Tomima Edmark*

You can't pick up a newspaper today without reading about one company or another making the decision to manufacture its products offshore. Pricing in the marketplace has become a kind of bidding war, and many businesses are finding that to compete, they must shop for foreign manufacturing alternatives. If you decide you want to manufacture your product offshore, you have to factor in the cost of an import quota.

The idea of placing quotas on the amount of goods that can be imported into the United States is not new. In 1792, Alexander Hamilton sponsored legislation to institute import quotas that served to protect infant American industries and allow them to mature rather than face defeat by imports. Since then, some type of quota has always existed in this country. Today, the vast majority of import quotas are found in the textile and apparel industries, although quotas on other import items, such as tuna, cheese and some type of watches, also exist.

There are several types of import quotas, including the following:

### Global quotas

A global quota designates the total amount of a specified product that can be imported in one year. For instance, there could be a global quota of 100 million baseball caps that will be allowed into the United States during any given year.

That global quota is then broken down, and specific quantities are assigned to individual countries in the form of absolute quotas.

### Absolute quotas

These are assigned to an import product from a specific country for a particular quantity. For example, the U.S. Customs Service could establish an absolute quota in which only 10 million pairs of cotton pants from India are allowed to cross U.S. borders in a given year. Any Indian cotton pants over that number would be refused entry by U.S. Customs.

### Tariff-rate quotas

Products assigned this type of quota have no quantity cap. However, similar to the U.S. tax system, the more you bring in, the higher a tariff you'll pay on the goods.

### Seasonal quotas

These are usually assigned to food items and correspond with the growing seasons. For example, when strawberries are in season, a quota on imported strawberries may be assigned to prevent a glut, which would cause price erosion in the U.S. market.

So how are these quotas determined? This is where it gets dicey. In general, quotas seem to be more a reflection of political intervention and lobbying than of market forces.

Officially, two government agencies are involved in the establishment of quotas: the office of the U.S. Trade Representative (USTR) and the Committee for the Implementation of Textile Agreements, which is made up of representatives from the departments of State, Commerce, Labor, Treasury and Agriculture. Quotas are generally negotiated for each country at one time to last for several years.

Currently, the United States has negotiated absolute quotas with 47 countries. Once a quota is assigned to a country, the U.S. government doesn't get involved in the process by which the country drives up its quotas. As a result, there's great opportunity for corruption and favoritism in exporting countries. Some countries hold quota auctions, where quotas go to the highest bidders. Others allocate their quotas to specific factories. And, as you can probably guess, the friends and family of those in power are often awarded large portions of certain countries' quotas.

Like it or not, as an entrepreneur trying to import a product you've manufactured offshore that has an assigned quota, you're now a pawn in this game and must pay to play.

### HOW IT WORKS

Lets walk through a practical example of how you'd go about importing an item that has a quota assigned to it. Let's assume you've designed a cardigan sweater, only to find it will be too expensive to make locally. Market research has discovered that similar cardigan sweaters have been imported from India and the cost to manufacture them there is significantly lower than what your local company charges. However,

India has an assigned quota on these sweaters. So what's your first step?

The first thing you should do is find a buying agent, a representative who lives in the exporting country and has a relationship with various factories in that country. He or she also has the know-how to procure quota visas for your goods. The agent will contact the different factories to find the one best suited to make your sweaters at the most reasonable price and with the level of quality you specify. In return, the agent takes a percentage of the cost of your goods. Finding a good buying agent can be a long, drawn-out process, but a good place to start is the U.S. embassy or consulate for the country in which you intend to manufacture your product.

Before a quota visa can be purchased for your sweaters, you have to decide on the quantity of sweaters and the number of shipments to be made per year. Say you plan to import two shipments of 5,000 cardigan sweaters for a total of 10,000. Armed with the information, the buying agent will now acquire two quota visas issued by the government of India for 5,000 sweaters each. Because a quota visa must accompany each shipment accepted by U.S. Customs, two quota visas must be procured.

Keep in mind that once a quota visa is arranged, it's usually final. If you change your mind at the last minute and want to increase the quantity of each shipment to 5,500 sweaters but have already purchased quota visas for 5,000, you're probably out of luck.

The price for quota visas fluctuates constantly--the higher the demand for one, the more expensive it will be. In general, visa costs tend to go up toward the end of the year when their availability becomes more scarce due to the increase in demand for products during the U.S. holiday season.

To help with the receipt of your sweater shipments into the United States, you'll also need a customs broker. These brokers live in the United States and know how to handle the mountains of paperwork (including the quota visas) that accompany imported shipments. A customs broker is an expert at avoiding those "gotchas" (like missing or incorrect paperwork) that can keep your shipment held up in U.S. Customs indefinitely. Since the customs broker receives all paperwork prior to the receipt of a shipment, he or she can check to make sure your quota visas are legitimate, which will save you time and hassles. You can get a list of licensed customs brokers from your local U.S. Customs office.

The sweater example illustrates the importance of finding reliable and honest buying agents and customs brokers. Jack Wasserman, an international trade lawyer and senior partner with Wasserman, Schneider, Babb & Reed in New York City, offers examples of just a few of the potential problems that could throw a monkey wrench into your shipment, some of which can be avoided by hiring a reputable agent or broker:

(1) The factory is late with your production.

(2) The raw materials have the incorrect fiber content.

(3) The manufacturing quality is poor.

(4) The country's entire quota is used up by the time your shipment is ready. (A quota visa can't be purchased until the product has been manufactured).

(5) The visa is deficient; for instance, it's issued for the wrong category of a particular product.

(6) The classification of your merchandise is wrong. (For example, U.S. Customs finds your cotton sweater line to be a wool sweater line).

(7) U.S. Customs questions the country of origin.

Wasserman advises checking references before hiring a buying agent and then creating a written agreement to guard against potential problems. Also, don't pay him or her in advance; reliable agents won't request this. And when paying an agent with a letter of credit, make sure it's written carefully so payment isn't made before you have a chance to review the production situation.

**EASING UP**

There is some good news on the horizon regarding quotas. In January 1995, the World Trade Organization (WTO) agreed to eliminate all textile and apparel quotas among its members by July 1, 2005. This has put pressure on nonmember countries, such as China, to comply with WTO requirements so their quotas will be lifted as well.

NAFTA has also had a positive impact on quotas. Since its signing, products made with North American fabric and assembled in Canada and Mexico are free of quota restrictions. It's important to remember, however, that the elimination of quotas doesn't mean you won't have to pay customs duties. The United States still has power to levy duties on any imported goods.

If you'd like more information on quotas, you can log on to the following Web sites: www.USTR.gov and www.customs.ustreas.gov.

*Tomima Edmark is the inventor of the TopsyTail and several other products and is author of the "American Dream Fact Pack," ($49.95), available by calling (800) 558-6779. Questions regarding inventions and patents may be sent to "Bright Ideas," Entrepreneur, 2392 Morse Ave., Irvine, CA 92614.* ■

# Just Don't Do It

*Carol Wheeler*

**T**hey say we all have the same 24 hours every day. And I am convinced they're right, at least technically. So why is it that some people are able to wring all 86,400 seconds out of those hours and the rest of us just manage to... oh, dictate a few letters, start four projects and (maybe) come close to finishing one, go through the papers in our in-box (half of which we did nothing with yesterday), answer 12 phone calls and return eight (usually missing the person we're calling), attend two meetings and grab a quick lunch, leaving us, on average, with four tasks left over for the next day?

It's not as if we've relaxed all day. Not at all. We've been hard at work. We feel harried and frazzled and convinced we'll never catch up. At least that's the way it is in most offices I'm familiar with, except for those lucky few colleagues who sail through the tasks of the day and leave the rest of us in their wake, staring open-mouthed at the clean desks they leave behind. Have these people made a life work of time management (if so, how do they find the time?) Or is it a quality one is born with, like blue eyes or a musical gift? I write this standing up. Don't laugh. It's a beginning. I found this particular tip on page 93 of *Manage Your Time, Your Work, Yourself,* by Merril E. Douglass and Donna N. Douglass. Well, actually I took that idea of standing up when you open your mail one step further. But it works. Standing up prevents my usual lolling and twirling around in my desk chair waiting for inspiration. If I'm standing, I might just as well keep typing, which is what I find myself doing, and at a faster rate than usual. Besides, Hemingway used to write standing up, and it's almost like getting exercise while you work (for exercises to do at your desk, see *Time-Management for Executives* by Lauren R. Januz and Susan K. Jones). I may be onto something here. Of course you're aware of the science (or is it an art?) of time management. How could you not be? Its evangelists and their publications, seminars and tapes are everywhere. And yet most of us are still behind at an all too-rapid pace. In a way, there's almost too much expertise available. The problem with all this material is that we simply don't have time for it.

As it happens, time, or at least the question of which organizer to use to try to catch hold of it has been a concern (not an obsession, certainly not) of mine for years. I do in fact have some expertise in the subject since I personally possess one of the largest, most complete collections of date books in the Western world. I am also a graduate of "Time Management for the Year 2000," an all-day seminar given by the makers of a now-defunct organizer system I once admired. So it seems natural that I have been called upon to share my own favorite time-management tips (bolstered by the wealth of information in several popular guides on the subject) in the interest of helping you get a grip.

**1. The to-do list** is, to me, the simplest, most essential and most liberating rule of all. Make a detailed one every morning or, even better, the night before. Include absolutely every little thing you need to do, thus freeing your mind "for more creative pursuits," says Alan Lakein, time guru extraordinaire, in *How to Get Control of Your Time and Your Life* (one million books in print). Have a pad and pencil by your bed for recording the many tasks that race through your mind as you try to drift off to sleep. But by all means, don't leave it at that. Follow up with rule number...

**2. Prioritize.** "Pick up dress at cleaners" may be on the same list as "Prepare presentation for board" but it doesn't have the same urgency (unless it's the dress you're going to wear for the presentation). Lakein and others suggest labeling each item A, B, or C in order of importance. Knowing the order in which you can actually perform your tasks, both big and small, is a great help.

**3. Write scripts for phone calls.** Except for the most basic of calls, write down what you want to say before you pick up the receiver. Sound too studied? I thought so at first, but I've found that whenever a delicate or diplomatic phone call is in the offing, committing the right words to paper beforehand helps me get to the point faster and saves anxiety. It also helps me avoid mere socializing.

**4. Avoid scraps of paper.** It's time to admit that you are simply too old for scrawls on backs of envelopes.

**5. Buy an organizer/planner,** (do I have to tell?) and use it. In *The Ten Natural Laws of Successful Time and Life Management*, Hyrum W. Smith (and he should know, as CEO of Franklin Quest, the organization that makes a best-selling planner) offers some planner tips that sound like wisdom to me: (1) Take your daily planner with you everywhere (even on vacation). What if you're lying on the beach, Smith asks, and you come up with a brilliant idea? You rush back to your room, dust off your planner and commit your epiphany to its pages. Then you return to the sand, kick back and forget it. You can do that because whatever it was that was screaming in your mind has now been transferred to your planner. (2) Use only one calendar. Smith says it's a "monumental mistake" to let someone else, like your secretary, take over your calendar. Instead, meet with him/her at the beginning of the month to see what openings there are that he/she can schedule for you. Then draw a line through those times in your planner, reminding you not to schedule them until you check with him/her. (3) Commit to planning every day. Maybe you don't have to do that on vacation, but (unfortunately) that is a minor exception.

**6. Learn how to read periodicals** the short way--otherwise whole days can be eaten up just by *Forbes, Fortune and Business Week.* The table of contents is there for a reason; use it, no matter how seductive the cover looks. Anything that doesn't speak to you isn't worth digging for. Either

look at the appropriate pieces immediately or mark them for you to copy.

**7. Always allow twice as** much time for a new project as you think it might take--especially when you hear yourself thinking, "Oh, yeah, this will be a cinch."

**8. Discourage impromptu visitors.** Amusing as it is, socializing can make it impossible for you to complete your work, thus causing unbearable stress and mind-numbing anxiety. Here's how to tactfully chase away interlopers: (1) Stand up when people come into your home office. Not only will you be celebrated for your exquisite politeness, you'll also discourage lengthy interruptions. (2) Remove any number of guest chairs beyond one from your office That way you won't have two visitors at once, chatting with each other while you're at your desk trying to get some work done. (3) Put your visitors to work. Alec Mackenzier, management consultant and author of the *Time Trap*, tells of a man who kept a folder marked "visitors" in which he put small, boring tasks that he didn't have time for. When an uninvited guest arrived, the man would say, "I have some work to finish up here. While you're waiting, would you mind adding up this column of figures?" Not surprisingly, the man reported a sharp decrease of drop-ins.

**9. If all else fails, lower your standards.** That's the way to force yourself to get started on the toughest projects. Otherwise, whole days can disappear while you roll through the easy tasks and you still haven't started that long-range report that you're not exactly sure how to approach. It begins to sap your strength. So just start--you'll soon find you're doing a splendid job.

**10. Take time to smell the flowers.** Or eat a long, luxurious lunch, get a massage, have a facial. Soak in a bubble bath or prowl some antique shops. Much as you'd like to believe otherwise, you cannot use every minute of your life to advance your career, tend to your family or achieve other laudable goals. You must take time for yourself regularly or suffer the burnouts, bad temper and stress injuries at the very least.

**11. Remember that perfectionism** and procrastination go hand in hand. For all you procrastinators out there, consider this deathless line from a great editor: "Done is better than perfect." I find this almost painfully difficult, but in fact it is not necessary to rewrite ordinary, everyday memos four times. If there's an error, correct it with pen and route the memo immediately. Then you can go on to conceptualize the next major project for your department.

**12. Get up early.** Morally, I am opposed to this one, but it does work. Getting up one hour early for a whole year creates ten extra work weeks! (Excuse me, but on that note, I think I'll go back to bed).

**13. If you must procrastinate** (many of us have that need), do it strategically. How many times have you perused and re-perused an ambiguous letter or complicated request, wondering how to answer it, whether to respond, where to file it, then finally made the agonizing decision to put it in one folder rather than another and then never heard another word about it (luckily, because you immediately forgot where you filed it?) If there's any chance that a relatively unimportant task may never have to be done (and often, this is indeed the case), try setting it aside in some special place, far away from the action. More than likely, you'll never hear another word about it.

**14. Don't forget to allow for the unexpected.** It's the unpredictable events that are almost always guaranteed to intervene when you've promised to finish a rush job faster than anyone has a right to expect.

**15. Learn some stock responses** to "Got a minute?" That's the innocent little question that can use up much of your day and leave you with little time to accomplish the pressing tasks that are at the top of your to-do list. Try, "Actually I'm really jammed" or "If it's really quick, what can I do for you?" Followed by "Why don't you take that up with Joe" or "Why don't you decide what you think should be done and see me in the morning?" (These are all solutions suggested in *The Time Trap*). Rehearse these responses; they'll roll off your tongue the next time someone barges into your office.

**16. Learn to say NO** (in various ways to various people, but politely and firmly). If you're caught off guard by a request, say, "Can I get back to you on that?"

**17. Create your own ideal day.** Everyone is different, says Alec Mackenzie in *The Time Trap,* but your own preference will serve as a template for your daily plan and determine when to schedule the toughest tasks. My ideal day, for instance, would be to schedule the conceptual work for the morning, when I'm as fresh as I'll ever get. Don't forget to include time for contemplation, too.

**18. As silly as it sounds,** ask yourself, often, "Is this the best use of my time right now?" That's what Alan Lakein suggests in *How to Get Control of Your Time and Your Life*. Maybe the thought of constantly repeating one phrase to yourself sounds weirdly cultish, but I can assure you it does become second nature. Just before you make an unnecessary phone call, for instance, or pick up the magazine you don't have time to read, the question can help you deflect that time waster and work wonders on your schedule.

**19. Take a deep breath** and set aside a chuck of time to actually read, cover to cover, a book of value to you.

**20. Return to these rules** and your favorite time-management guides whenever you begin to get that frazzled feeling. It's all too easy to fall back into bad habits under the crush of work.∎

# Ordinary People, Extraordinary Dreams

This country was (and is) built on dreams of ordinary people who, by following their dreams, accomplished extraordinary things. In the 1930s, for example, A.G. Giannini, although very bright, left school at 14 to take care of his two younger brothers on a small family farm. Later he got a job working for a bank and had a dream about starting one of his own that would serve "the little guy." He believed that on the strength of many little guys, a national bank could be built. By having the courage to make then unheard-of loans for automobiles and appliances, his dream was realized by the time of his death in 1949. The bank he founded is called Bank of America.

Or consider Pete Seibert's story. A ski instructor and former ski trooper in World War II, since the age of 12 Seibert had wanted nothing more in his life than to start a ski area. One day, after an exhausting seven-hour climb in deep snow, he reached the summit of a mountain in the Gore Range in Colorado. Staring down at the vast bowls below and at the stunning peaks beyond, Seibert said to himself it was "as good as any mountain I've seen."

Compared to the hard work that followed, the seven-hour trek was like a leisurely stroll. Seibert had to climb mountains of red tape, meet the U.S. Forest Service's stiff leasing requirements, and raise large amounts of capital "from frugal friends and suspicious strangers" in order to buy land from ranchers and build a village. "Everybody else thought we were crazy," says Seibert, "but we thought we could do any damn thing we pleased."...Seibert's dream is now a reality called Vail.

Use these handy postpaid cards to start your very own home-based business now !

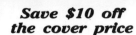

**BUSINESS REPLY MAIL**
FIRST-CLASS MAIL PERMIT NO. 2 AITKIN, MN

POSTAGE WILL BE PAID BY ADDRESSEE

MARKETING  SOLUTIONS
HC  6  BOX  58A
AITKIN  MN  56431-9901

**Use these handy postpaid cards to start your very own home-based business now !**

---

**BUSINESS REPLY MAIL**
FIRST-CLASS MAIL PERMIT NO. 2 AITKIN, MN

POSTAGE WILL BE PAID BY ADDRESSEE

MARKETING  SOLUTIONS
HC  6  BOX  58A
AITKIN  MN  56431-9901

---

**BUSINESS REPLY MAIL**
FIRST-CLASS MAIL PERMIT NO. 2 AITKIN, MN

POSTAGE WILL BE PAID BY ADDRESSEE

MARKETING  SOLUTIONS
HC  6  BOX  58A
AITKIN  MN  56431-9901

# Now YOU can cash in on
# E-COMMERCE!

Never before has there been a phenomenon depicted on the front covers of magazines like Time, Fortune and Money, and on major newspapers each and every day!

It is the future. It is the Internet. It is electronic commerce.

Forrester Research increased its estimates on Internet commerce to $3.2 trillion by the year 2003. In other words, e-commerce will be growing by 30,000% in the next 5 years!

Shopping and buying on the Internet is the **TIDAL WAVE** of the future that is here today! If you want to ca$h in on this opportunity, just give us a call.

# PriceNet*USA*.com

# 310-782-1458

# How Living Deep in the Amazon Created a Breakthrough Network Marketing Tool

*Brian Alan Didier*

Gaellen and Michael Quinn were living 1,000 miles up the Amazon River working as unpaid volunteers with a social and economic development project when it hit them. They were searching. They needed answers. There had to be a way to make the poor people of the world wealthier. They wanted to discover the secret.

Once owners and operators of a multi-million dollar computer mail order company, they published a 64-page catalog and ran full page advertisements in computer magazines. The Quinns had started their very successful business at home with a $60 mail order advertisement, but they sold it to work for free deep in the Brazilian Amazon and it changed their lives.

While less than 10% of Brazil's 160 million people are middle class and above, the vast majority are poor beyond most Americans' ability to imagine. Tens of millions live in shanties made of wooden slats or in mud huts on monthly incomes of $35 or less. Incredibly, even the poorest of the poor are optimistic, hard working and generous-hearted.

"No one understood why we sold our company. We worked hard to build it, and the money and challenges

*Macaws are common in the Amazon. Although it is illegal, hundreds of species of rare birds, monkeys, and other animals are offered for sale everywhere. Once a man offered to sell the Quinns a magnificent cobalt blue Macaw for $35. In the U.S. this rare bird sells for $15,000. Macaws in captivity are known to live 70 or more years.*

were pouring in, but we wanted our children to see that the world wasn't all like southern California," Michael explained. "We wanted them to know first-hand that we are all connected as human beings on this planet.

"We had always wanted our family to have the experience of living overseas. At the time, one of our daughters was in 8th grade and the other was in her first year of high school. It was only a matter of time before they would be off to college. If we didn't make the move to live overseas then, it was likely that we would never go together," said Gaellen.

### Amazon-style personal development

Michael Quinn was the co-director of a rural polytechnic school in the jungle and an orphanage for street children in the nearby city of Manaus. So the Quinns had a rare first hand glimpse into a world they had never known.

It was one of those "character building" experiences. The Amazon is hot and humid all the time. You're always wet -- either because you're sweating so much, or because you just got caught in a torrential rain. Leprosy, yellow fever and rabies are common. Power outages are routine. Inflation was averaging 30% or higher per month.

"It was about as different an environment as you could go to," Gaellen remembers, "We were fish out of water. It makes you see everything with new eyes as you flop around gasping for air and trying to figure out how things work."

Living side-by-side with the outcast and forgotten members of society, the Quinns found that the humblest of people with little or no formal education can do incredible things, and change their own lives, if they learn a step-by-step system to do it. Again, the Quinns wondered how they could help more people succeed and prosper as they had.

### Making people wealthy around the world

Their question was answered when they returned to the United States. That's when they learned about network marketing, and saw that a way already existed that could be an instrument to make people wealthier around the world.

After thoroughly studying the industry, they decided to use their managerial and organizational skills to do everything possible to make sure network marketing companies succeeded in helping their distributors take a share in what Michael calls "the largely unrecognized potential for the greatest redistribution of wealth in history."

While they were astonished to learn how simple it was to succeed at network marketing, because so much of the hard work of building a business was already done for them by the distributor's company, the Quinns' were also shocked to see how many people fail at this business. They were also surprised to hear people in the industry

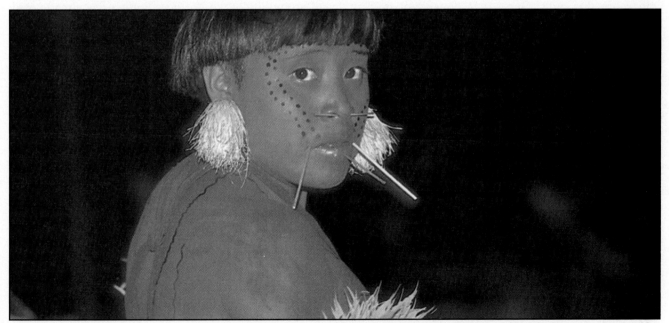

*Huge regions of the Amazon are still being explored. While the Quinns lived there a new tribe was found that had never had contact with Brazilians or anyone else. A 600 mile long river covered by a dense forest was also discovered. The Amazon stretches over an area about two thirds the size of the continental United States.*

say, "that's just the way the industry is." They felt it was like saying if 95% of elementary school children fail, it's because "that's just the way elementary school is." On the contrary, their experience in the Amazon taught them that almost anyone can learn to systematically take action and succeed with the help of a simple, well thought-out self-training tool.

To support the entire direct sales industry, Michael and Gaellen Quinn created the *Network Action Business Builder* to help network marketers automatically develop essential time and business management success skills overnight. "We are determined to see this industry reach its potential, and to do our part to back up every company that wants to redistribute wealth through personal and individual initiative," Michael said.

The *Network Action Business Builder* is now used by distributors in more than 45 network marketing and direct sales companies. A recent comprehensive customer survey has revealed that the Business Builder moves distributors from lower levels of activity to dramatically higher levels of productive activity in the success critical areas of prospecting, follow up, sales, recruiting and coaching.

### Detailed survey proves it works

"We knew it would work from the start because top distributors were saying things like, 'How on earth did you figure this out?' One MLM consultant told us, 'You've done a great service for the entire industry.' Jay Abraham, who is world famous as a marketing wizard, calls it a 'template for action,' and has optioned it to have a custom version made for sales professional worldwide. Scott DeGarmo, former long time editor and publisher of *Success* magazine, endorses it saying, "It's clear a tremendous amount of intellectual capital has been poured into the *Business Builder*.'"

"Recently," Michael added, "we surveyed people to determine their level of activity before they started using the *Business Builder* and what happened to their productivity while they are using it. Survey respondees reported eye-popping jumps in productivity. For example, before using the *Business Builder*, nearly 92% of respondees were not recruiting or were recruiting at the very lowest level of activity."

"This confirms that low productivity is just about what the industry has come to expect. But the really exciting thing is that the survey proves that while using the *Business Builder* nearly half of all the people in the lowest activity category moved into a higher activity category. There was an astonishing 1662% increase in the number of people recruiting 3 to 5 people per month, and a doubling of people who recruit 6 to 15 people per month. That's what an effective system can do! We also saw amazing gains in prospecting and follow up activity, in sales and in coaching."

"What's more," Gaellen said, "95% of survey respondees reported that the *Business Builder* makes the business easier to do; 87.5% said this tool helps them to continue going forward in spite of difficulties and setbacks; and 80% told us the *Business Builder* increases their self-confidence in the day to day 'doing' of their network marketing business."

### Dedication and service helps new and experienced distributors

It took the Quinns two years of intense full time effort, consultation and reflection to develop the *Business Builder* as a tool to help this industry succeed. "We have the solution and can turn the tide, but many companies are busy chasing new distributors instead of maximizing the great ones they have now who are already begging them, 'Hey, teach me how to make this work!' The really lucky thing for us is that in the Amazon we learned to be patient," Michael said.

"The tremendous effort we have put into the development and promotion of the *Business Builder* has already paid off because it has been proven to produce the results it was designed to accomplish. We can prove that both highly experienced and new distributors are doing their work with less stress and getting immediate results."

For more information about the *Network Action Business Builder* and how it can help you dramatically increase productivity, or on what to see and do in the Brazilian Amazon, call Michael or Gaellen Quinn **(800) 870-8034**. Or, to learn more about the *Business Builder*, visit their company website at www.networkaction.com.

Brian Alan Didier, a former high school teacher, is now a full time distributor with AdvoCare. Mr. Didier uses the Network Action Business Builder. He lives in Taylor, Texas, and says, "As a teacher I know the importance of methodology. What they've done is awesome. It's simple and it works. It has helped me with my follow up immensely and really makes it easier to do this business. I always know exactly what I have to do next everyday." You can contact Brian at **(888) 546-8899**.

# It's a beautiful life!

## Flexibility, excellent earning opportunities, unlimited rewards with **BeautiControl**®.!

*A rewarding new life awaits you at BeautiControl. As one of the most successful home-based skin care and beauty businesses for 18 years, BeautiControl has helped thousands of people achieve their financial dreams with groundbreaking products, a simple success plan and lucrative earning opportunities!*

### Groundbreaking products!

Developed by leading scientists in our Research Institute, BeautiControl's cutting-edge products literally sell themselves! Our revolutionary Regeneration Gold® and Cell Block-C™ skin duo actually helps repair dangerous precancerous skin cell damage while generating fresh, new skin cells, and prevents future damage with antioxidant vitamin C free-radical fighters and daily SPF 20.

BeautiControl also offers advanced skin care, color-coded cosmetics, nutritional supplements, therapeutic bath and body treatments and special problem solvers.

### Incredible income, fast!

With BeautiControl's exclusive Fast Track Star Bonus Plan, you can earn incredible income, fast. There's no waiting! Earn lucrative direct commissions and bonuses, and multiple monthly paychecks. BeautiControl provides everything you need to succeed, including professional training and our easy step-by-step Planner for success.

### A fun, flexible lifestyle!

Choose the hours that are best for you and enjoy more time for yourself and your family. How much you earn and when you work is up to you!

▶ Earn immediate income and lucrative direct commissions

▶ Earn diamond jewelry, spectacular vacations and a company car for a job well done

▶ Have fun meeting new friends and helping others

▶ Grow personally and professionally

### Getting started is simple!

*Call a BeautiControl Consultant in your area, call 1-800-BEAUTI-1 or visit www.beauticontrol.com*

### With BeautiControl, you can:

▶ Work from home

▶ Set your own hours: full or part-time

## BEAUTICONTROL®
THE WORLD'S PREMIER SKIN CARE AND IMAGE COMPANY®

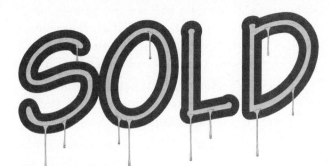

# SOLD

# The Ultimate Selling Tips to Move Any Product or Service

*Alan Rothman*

**Take heed:** If you're oblivious to your customers' needs, your sales pitch could fall on deaf ears.

Pumping up profits. Keeping the numbers up. If you've been in business for any length of time, you know how important sales are to keeping your business afloat and making it thrive. But if you're like many business owners, you also know how tough it can be to get customers to say that final "yes."

Sales trainer and motivational speaker Pam Lontos is no stranger to this challenge. She had some 20 years of sales experience before starting Lontos Sales and Motivation Inc. in Orlando, Florida, in 1981. A year earlier, Lontos had increased sales 500 percent as vice president of Disney's Shamrock Broadcasting.

How did Lontos go from salesperson to superstar? She started by adopting one of the tenets she uses today to help non-confrontational types and other salespeople excel. "Salespeople aren't born; they're trained."

In this interview for AOL readers, Lontos reveals some of her inside secrets to help your business' sales skyrocket to new heights.

**Rothman**: How important is the skill of selling in business today?

**Pam Lontos**: In today's competitive market, selling is the name of the game. The biggest mistake you can make is thinking you are not in sales. You are always selling. It is vital if you own a business because your money is coming from your customers. And if you don't know how to sell, you aren't going to make any money.

Regardless of how inexperienced you

> *Giving facts when you talk is not selling; it's telling. It will not build the right type of relationship you need to clinch the sale.*

are in pitching your products, ideas or services, selling is a highly learnable skill. The best part is that you can not only learn it, but you can also enjoy doing it.

**Rothman**: Why do so many people have a tough time selling?

**Lontos**: Many people think of themselves as creative people, not as salespeople. They don't want to use sales techniques that might be perceived as too pushy or direct.

To succeed in business, you need to know what questions to ask your customers. People come to you because they want the benefit of your expertise. People fear making the wrong decision; they want to buy from someone they perceive as an expert they can trust.

**Rothman**: Is it best to recite facts about your product or service to your prospects?

**Lontos**: Giving facts when you talk is not selling; it's telling. It will not build the right type of relationship you need to clinch the sale.

You must have passion for what you do; however, talent and passion must be fine-tuned by taking care of your customers' needs. You must build a rapport with your customers by finding out their needs. You want them to buy from you and refer all their friends as well.

**Rothman**: One of the messages you teach is that salespeople aren't born, they're trained. What do you mean by that?

**Lontos**: Salespeople are not cut out of one mold. Some people are quiet; others are outgoing and enthusiastic. There are many different types of personalities. However, everyone has the ability to develop the habits needed to be a good salesperson. These skills include knowing how to listen, when to be assertive and when to empathize.

**Step one** in selling your product or service is to develop trust and build emotional rapport through a common bond. **Step two** is to ask questions and get the prospect to say he or she wants what you have. **Step three** is to handle objections promptly. **Step four** is to explain the benefit of what is in it for the prospect. **Step five** is to close the sale. If you haven't been able to close the sale, **step six** is to go back to the start of the circle of emotional rapport and questioning.

**Rothman**: What is the number one fear of every salesperson?

**Lontos**: Without a doubt, it's rejection. If you never ask for the sale, you'll never hear the word "no." That's why you have to believe in what you're selling.

When I sold health-club memberships, it was for a club where I had lost 50 pounds. I believed in that program, and I never minded asking for the sale. If I let a prospect go without closing the sale, I felt I was doing him or her a disservice. It's important to have the mind-set that if a customer walks out without buying your product or service, his or her life is not going to be as good. When you believe that, you'll do everything possible to get that customer to buy from you.

**Rothman**: What is the number one reason prospects say no?

**Lontos**: The main reason people don't buy is fear of making the wrong decision. They'll go with the person who takes away that fear. People may say no five or six times before they say yes because they have said yes too quickly in the past.

**Rothman**: When you go out in the field with salespeople, what common mistakes do you observe?

**Lontos**: Talking instead of listening and failing to build rapport and trust before they start selling.

The salesperson will go in and just start talking about his or her product or service without describing any benefit or determining why it's important to that particular person. They won't ask questions to find out what a person needs. Then, if the person says "I'll think about it," they stop at that point and get ready to leave, and that's just when they should jump in and start really selling.

**Rothman**: How can business owners reprogram their minds for success?

**Lontos**: Constantly see things in a positive light. When something adverse happens, you need to understand it's just temporary. Take 10 minutes each day, close your eyes, and feel yourself in a situation that is a positive reflection of what you want to happen.

> *The strongest human need is to be appreciated. Learn to ask questions of the prospect and listen to the answers. You must do your research and determine how you can help the client or prospect.*

**Rothman**: How important is it to remain positive?

**Lontos**: It is essential that you remain positive. You must have the attitude that you will never give up. Even if six customers in a row don't buy from you, or if you don't have a sale for three days, you can't let it get you down. You must try new techniques.

Find out what everyone else is doing, and do something different. If you're like everyone else, you won't stand out. You must give extra customer service to get people to come to you. Walt Disney went through two or three bankruptcies before he became successful. When

people believe in themselves so much, they will have persistence and stick with it. Be positive no matter how bad things appear.

**Rothman**: What are some inside secrets to help Rothmans become super salespeople?

**Lontos**: The strongest human need is to be appreciated. Learn to ask questions of the prospect and listen to the answers. You must do your research and determine how you can help the client or prospect.

First, write down the six most common objections your customers typically raise. These are the reasons prospects don't want to buy now. Then, write down how you will counter these objections. It's important to practice so your comments are natural and flow smoothly. If you can't come up with the correct answers yourself, read books or listen to tapes on the subject of sales.

**Rothman**: Based on your experience in the field, are there other tips you offer business people to put them over the top?

**Lontos**: No matter how much business is coming in, never stop marketing. It's also very important to trust your intuition and to hire employees or consultants, not because you like them but because they can do the job.

Take the time to help others. Many good things have come into my life by taking this approach.

**Rothman**: How do you build trust with a client?

**Lontos**: Always find something you like about the client. Think and feel "I like you and I think you are terrific" while you are talking to the client. In your conversations, show you care about your clients and their businesses. It's important to find a common bond between you.

**Rothman**: Can you give us some sample questions that might help close the sale?

**Lontos**: You can take control by asking strong questions like, "What is your main concern?" or "Is there something you haven't told me?"

People will gravitate toward you if they feel you are helping them and that you care. Always talk about benefits and end results. Discuss what they want. You must personalize your approach so you show you care about your clients and about solving their problems.

*Pam Lontos*

**Rothman**: Can you give us an example?

**Lontos**: I recently gave a seminar for cake designers. These people not only wanted customers to buy cakes from their bakery, but also to order the bigger cake, the nicer icing and the fancier decorations. I told them to think about not just selling a cake but selling memories. Think how happy

their customers will be 10 or 15 years from now when looking back with their children at wedding pictures. Seeing themselves cutting the cake is a memory they will cherish forever.

Another type of person may be more interested in impressing his or her friends. One may be more interested in the taste of the cake. Therefore, qualifying questions will help you discover what they really want, and if you listen, you'll obtain the answer. You will not only make the sale but also satisfy them and make them happy.

**Rothman**: Once you've been properly trained in sales, is it a skill that will stay with you?

**Lontos**: It's like riding a bike -- you don't forget. If you get back out there and start doing it, it comes back to you. I learned how to sell, and I learned how to be motivated. I'm not saying I didn't have setbacks. I'm not saying I don't have ups and downs. I feel down like everybody else, but now I know how to bring myself out of it.

### Contact Sources

*Lontos Sales and Motivation Inc., PO Box 617553, Orlando, FL 32861, (407) 299-6128*

*Alan Rothman is an author, columnist, speaker, and consultant to the network marketing and communications industry. For info, call (714) 362-9233 or leave a message at (800) 593-9234. Author of "Power Networking," "LocalNet," and "Secrets of the MLM Millionaires." Visit http://www.hgionline.com, Look at What's New? E-mail him at arothman@fea.net.*∎

# No Hope In Dope

**Leighton Kaonohi**
**No Hope In Dope™ Program**

One of the main functions of law enforcement is to prevent crime through intervention and/or preventive education.

To achieve this goal, Officer Kaonohi developed two programs using the approach of emotionally charged education and interaction to prevent crime.

With the first program, Officer Honolulu targets elementary school children. No Hope In Dope focuses on intermediate and high school students. Both were reviewed by the United States Office of Substance Abuse and Prevention and were found to be scientifically accurate and in conformance with public health principles and policies. The organization also found the programs to be very appropriate for its intended audience.

**Officer Honolulu™**
**Safety Program**

Officer Honolulu was created to address the problem of crime against children. The program employs innovative learning strategies that are understood by young children and can be easily utilized by them in emergency situations.

The story. . . Officer Honolulu was a legendary Hawaii police officer who worked on the island of Oahu in the late 1800s. He held a special bond with children, teaching them how to be safe, and was always ready to lend a hand to anyone in need. His broad smile and wholehearted laugh were his calling card. After years of community service, Officer Honolulu, confident he had done all he could to make Hawaii a safer place for children, vanished without a trace, but vowed to return should the children fall prey to danger and evil.

Well, the day has finally come. Officer Honolulu has returned, bringing with him an important message about safety and drug awareness for the children of Hawaii.

The character of Officer Honolulu is played by Officer Kaonohi himself! Dressed in the traditional uniform of a police officer in Hawaii during early 1900s, and sporting shiny brass buttons and a keystone cop hat, Officer Honolulu delivers messages of safety and crime prevention through song, dance and games. An atmosphere of fun is created which makes children receptive to the messages. A coloring book also is part of the program and is used in follow-up lessons.

In 1989, United States Senator Daniel Inouye invited Officer Honolulu to visit two schools in Washington, D.C. It was no surprise that the program was a big success.

**No Hope In Dope™**

Officer Kaonohi's deep concern about the growing drug

Just Say NO!

122

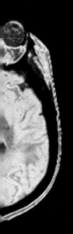
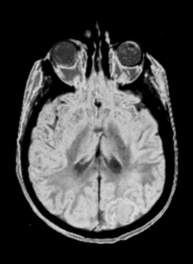
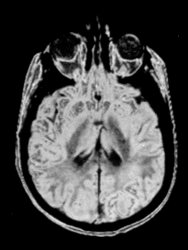
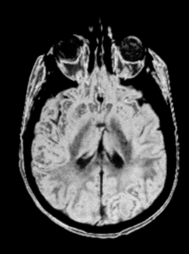
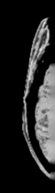

# ARE YOU A LEADING MIND?

This world is full of all types of people. But right now, we're only interested in leading minds—people who have the rare gifts of being forward thinkers and natural leaders.

We want you to join with us in building a new kind of company. A company created for distributors, by distributors. A company that gives you a stable corporate foundation to build upon. And most importantly, a company that doesn't view you as a stepping stone, but as an important partner for success.

Introducing Leading Minds International, an all-new company devoted to helping you succeed.

We've put together a powerful product line that spans from our scientifically developed "Age Defiance" personal care products to advanced telecommunications, virtual office, and financial services. These are products that deliver results as they have been carefully developed in conjunction with leading professionals. And our services are joint-ventures with some of the most well-known Fortune 500 companies in America.

We invite you to join with us in the launch of this revolutionary new network marketing venture. It's the way you'd build and run your own company. Find out more about Leading Minds International by calling 1-888-275-4LMI today.

LEADING *minds*
INTERNATIONAL
*An Environment for Forward Thinking People*

## Join In the Launch With Leading Minds!
Call Today 1-888-275-4LMI or visit us at www.leadingminds.net

problem in schools prompted him to develop an anti-drug program for intermediate and high school students. No Hope In Dope dispels the misconceptions about drugs and alcohol and seeks to prevent its use.

Preventing the use of illegal drugs and misuse of over-the-counter drugs including alcohol and tobacco, are the primary goals of this program. The first step in doing this is to dispel the misconceptions about alcohol, tobacco and other mind-altering drugs by instilling an emotional appendage to existing drug education proven to be effective. The program attempts to bring anti-drug messages down to a personal level, showing students how drug use affects their lives, their homes, schools and communities.

Next, taking into consideration the physical, intellectual, social and emotional facets of personal development, the program employs a community-based approach. The students families, their peers, school administrators, teachers, counselors, community leaders and business people are called upon to offer their support. All those involved help enforce the anti-drug messages, encourage constructive behavior and serve as positive role models.

### Proof Positive

Since the programs' inception in 1988, Officer Honolulu and No Hope In Dope have received national and local recognition, reaching more than 500,000 students statewide.

The data collected strongly indicates that the No Hope In Dope program has been well received by students and school personnel, and has delivered a strong and informative anti-drug message.

The exchange of productive dialogue between the No Hope In Dope presenters, students, teachers and parents has been unrestrained because saving lives has become more important than sparing the emotional pain often experienced in truthful encounters. The program has offered hope and opportunity.

On many occasions, school counselors have reported that several students with serious drug and/or family problems found the courage to ask for help as a direct result of their contact with the No Hope In Dope programs.

Teachers and counselors also have benefited from the programs. With training and support provided by the No Hope In Dope staff, they can more easily identify students with drug problems and assist them and their families along the road to recovery. One example of the powerful impact the program can have is seen in a case recently documented by the media.

A student who participated in the No Hope In Dope program confronted her mother and asked her to stop using drugs and seek help. When her mother refused, the student found the courage and confidence to turn her mother over to the authorities. This parent served seven years at the Oahu Community Correctional Center, for the possession and sale of harmful drugs. During the last three years of this mothers prison term she was a speaker in the No Hope In Dope program, spreading anti-drug messages to students. In 1997, this mother died from the AIDS virus, proving once again that there is No Hope In Dope.

This is an example of the program's success in breaking the cycle of drug use in the home, an important area to reach when educating youth and the community on drug use. With the continued support and dedication by members of the community, Hawaii's youth will have the courage and confidence to continue the fight against drugs for generations to come.

Police Officer Leighton Kaonohi's unique and original program has unveiled a simple, yet explosive ideology that young people all over Hawaii have adopted as their motto: "The key for you and me is staying drug free, Cuz There's No Hope In Dope."™

## NO HOPE IN DOPE
## AN ANALYSIS OF THE PSYCHO-SOCIAL PRINCIPLES WHICH CHARACTERIZE THIS PROGRAM

### F. Ross Woolley, Ph.D.

This article examines some of the fundamental characteristics of the No Hope In Dope and its associated programs, from the standpoint of current theories and research in human behavior. Because of the large number of interventions that are currently being used in an effort to address the epidemic use of psychoactive drugs, both licit and illicit, it is impossible to explore differences between approaches individually. It is the position of the author that, although there are common elements shared by many of the interventions, No Hope In Dope (NHID) differs so significantly from any other program, identifying it as "unique" and without peer.

NHID and its companion activities, including the Officer Honolulu program for elementary school age children, are first and foremost preventive in their approach. A recital of the facts regarding the extraordinary costs and lack of success in rehabilitating chronic users of psychoactive drugs is beyond the scope of this paper. The following aphorism attributed to the Sages of the Yellow Emperor of China over three millennia ago is as appropriate today as it was then: Treating the disease once it has begun, is like digging a well after you have become thirsty, or forging your weapons after you have already engaged in battle.

NHID is different from other programs in many critical and fundamental aspects. Although it is educational, conveying new information is not its apparent focus, rather it reinforces information that is generally already known and places it in a context that is usable to the audience. It is often assumed that youth are ignorant regarding the risks of drug use; however, with adequate information they will be sufficiently armed to make rational and correct decisions. The fallacy of this notion is well documented. Research regarding risk-taking among adolescents is replete with examples which show that information alone is a minimal deterrent to engaging in high risk behavior. It should be pointed out the risk-taking is not limited to young people; however, they are particularly vulnerable. It has been said that "In personal decision making . . . individuals diverge from rationality in a number of important ways. For one, they have a foreshortened time perspective. They value immediate gratifications more than they value those that are far in the future." An example of such irrational behavior can be seen in a study conducted in Philadelphia approximately one month following the announcement of Magic Johnson, the star NBA player for the Los Angeles Lakers, that he had become infected with HIV and would undoubtedly develop AIDS. Among those studied, men over 25 reported a sharp decline in unprotected sex as a result of the announcement. Conversely, those under 25 actually indicated an increase in high risk behavior. There is little doubt that these young men knew that AIDS is a fatal disease; however, they had seen an apparently healthy man tell the world that he was infected, and in the face of his personal tragedy he was going to go on with life,

*Treating the disease once it has begun, is like digging a well after you have become thirsty, or forging your weapons after you have already engaged in battle.*

including continuing to play professional basketball.

That which is demonstrated by the above incident is a manifestation of what is called the availability heuristic. The NHID program does not let the problem of the availability heuristic overwhelm the importance of the message by exposing the audience to individuals who have been rehabilitated. In order to counter the notion that one may engage in illegal high risk behavior and emerge unscathed, the role models selected from prison populations who are brought to the program are individuals who are still incarcerated, representing the norm of the convicted drug-related felon. These individuals do not present an image of normalcy, freedom of action, or contentment with their lot in life. To the contrary, they represent a "high probability" example which serves to revise the availability heuristic. Consistent with the model presented above, the NHID activity differs from other approaches in that it has not yielded to the need that many organizers feel to maintain a "politically correct" position. The likelihood of failure has been commented on when political and social interest become the driving force.

It's been said that, "If a person believes we are mere pawns of fate, he or she is apt to take chances." A central message of NHID is that we have significant control over our individual behaviors. A certain level of risk-taking is unavoidable in life, but only those which have a positive outcome are worth taking.

One of the most significant departures for the NHID program from traditional interventions is the coupling of the behaviors which lead to peer support and cohesiveness. Indeed, NHID when fully implemented involves not only the target audience, young people, but also the entire community. Adjunct programs include the Families Against Drugs (FAD) and a NHID Parade to which the entire community is invited. The use of drugs leads social isolation and alienation. NHID is the antithesis of social isolation.

In reality, what NHID is doing is providing an opportunity for people to experience friendship among peers and filial emotions where they are often lacking in the home environment. The importance of such emotions is often

> *"If a person believes we are mere pawns of fate, he or she is apt to take chances."*
> *A central message of NHID is that we have significant control over our individual behaviors. A certain level of risk-taking is unavoidable in life, but only those which have a positive outcome are worth taking.*

discounted by the lay public. Perhaps the most dramatic demonstration of the importance of friendship and social support resulted from the now classic study conducted by Berkman and Syme. The results of this sentinel study showed that people who had strong social support networks that were based on trust, love and commitment, actually lived longer than others. The most important findings were that deaths from all causes were lower among those who had such support and that the results persisted across all ages, races, economic strata and educational levels.

What NHID is doing is laying the foundation for social support that is protective against harmful behaviors. Since the Berkman and Syme study was published there have been conservatively, an additional 100 replications of their findings.

Clearly, one of the major differences between NHID and other programs is this intensive participation with the student audience and their community. By definition this approach is more difficult, time consuming, costly, and requires a level of commitment on the part of the program staff that goes well beyond monetary compensation. As one looks at cost-effectiveness, however, an inexpensive program that doesn't work is infinitely more expensive than its counterpart which has a greater initial cost but produces significant positive results.

The cost factor and staff commitment raise yet another important difference between NHID and other programs. Flay has stated: "Population and individual strategies may also support each other by mutual reinforcement. For educational strategies to be most effective on a population-wide basis, they need to be sustained in frequency and intensity and be free from conflicting messages." The potential for introducing conflicting messages in a substance abuse program is very high. Although it has received some attention from the press, the issue of alcohol and tobacco as "gateway" drugs has been one that is difficult for many people to acknowledge. There is, however,

substantial evidence that alcohol and tobacco are risk factors for other substance abuse. These two factors (sending mixed messages and tobacco and alcohol as gateway drugs) are a critical factor in examining the nature of the NHID activity. If, indeed, the staff are communicating that the use of addictive psychoactive substances is inappropriate, then the use of such substances would indeed be sending a mixed message. There is no question that it is perfectly legal for any member of the NHID staff, all of whom are over 21 years of age, to use alcohol or tobacco products. However, as a matter of personal commitment, none of them use these substances. In other words, even though the audience might not be aware of their choice to abstain from the use of these substances, they are taking the statement of Flay (cited above) literally, so that there are no mixed messages.

There is considerable evidence that many of the factors that lead to substance use may have a biological basis. Various markers for such behaviors have been identified among those who engage in impulsive, unsocialized sensation seeking. There are, based on Zuckerman's research neurochemical markers including: norepinephrine, serotonin and dopamine which are associated with sensation seeking behavior. These same substances are, of course, metabolites or derivatives of many of the substances that are used by abusers. Consequently, it is clear that individuals who are using those psychoactive drugs that contain or metabolize into these compounds are likely to engage in behaviors that place them at high risk. Although there has been no research associated with the NHID program, it is not illogical to assume that individuals who may have a genetic/biological propensity to high risk behavior who become involved in the program may find less risky outlets for their sensation seeking tendencies. Thus, a side effect of the program may well be to prevent inappropriate behavior among a group of individuals who are not substance users, but are prone to the same problems.

No Hope In Dope was not developed based on the data from empirical research on behavior, rather it is the product of a dedicated law enforcement professional who used his experience, common sense, and a strong moral commitment, and then assembled a group who shared common beliefs and experiences. As with any successful program, a careful analysis of its components can be

▶

# JOURNEY TO
# HEALTH & WEALTH

*A*t Sunrider®, we recognize that being healthy is a lifelong process, a lifestyle. For that reason, our diverse range of products is designed for all ages, and to be consumed and enjoyed throughout our lives. It provides us with the passage through which we journey towards health.

Sunrider® believes that we can achieve health not only by eating and drinking healthy, but through the use of other everyday products as well.

That's why aside from our best-selling foods and beverages, we feature SunSmile®, a line of super-concentrated household and personal care products that are made of natural and herbal ingredients.

Our Kandesn® line of beauty care and cosmetic products is made of unique formulations of the best ingredients that nature can provide to insure that health and beauty go hand in hand.

Best of all, with Sunrider's incomparable compensation programs, not only will you continue your lifelong journey towards health and beauty, you can also be handsomely rewarded along the way.

With Sunrider's truly unique features—owner expertise, Sunrider® owned state-of-the-art manufacturing facilities, business opportunities in more than 27 countries, an outstanding marketing plan, and exclusively formulated products which combine the best of eastern and western cultures—the Sunrider® journey to health and wealth is definitely worth taking!

**SUNRIDER®**

SUNRIDER® INTERNATIONAL • 1625 ABALONE AVENUE • TORRANCE, CA 90501 USA • (310) 781-3808
WWW.SUNRIDER.COM

> *There is considerable evidence that many of the factors that lead to substance use may have a biological basis. Various markers for such behaviors have been identified among those who engage in impulsive, unsocialized sensation seeking.*

validated by the work of credible researchers. There is little doubt that the program is unique, not because the concepts are new, rather it brings solid principles together in a way that maximizes their potential for success.

A final comment regarding NHID and its commitment to integrity is important. Morality is a subject that often divides and is carefully avoided. The reality is that most of the programs that have attempted to accomplish what has been done by NHID have tried to do so in a "morally neutral" environment. Moral judgment is as important to the success of this program as any single element and probably all of them combined. We cannot ignore the importance of teaching and setting in its rightful place the issue of morality. Hudgins and Prentice identified the issue clearly in their research and summarized it by stating: "Nondelinquent adolescents used higher stages of moral judgment than did delinquent adolescents." The NHID program is based on sound moral principles which have been eroded in our society.

## AWARDS RECEIVED BY LEIGHTON KAONOHI, SR.

### 1989
Ten Who Made A Difference-Honolulu Star Bulletin

### 1990
HPD Police Parent of the Year

George Washington Medal of Honor
Presented by: Freedom Foundation

KITV-4 Hanahou Award

F.B.I. Community Service Award
Presented by: William Sessions, Director of the F.B.I.

Kava Bowl Award: Presented by the Samoan community for his dedication to the Samoan youth

### 1991
Outstanding Service and Innovative Projects
Proclamation by Mayor Frank Fasi

Award for Excellence in Community Service
Brigham Young University, Hawaii Campus

### 1992
NFL Pro-Bowl Magazine Recognition
Honored during NFL Pro-Bowl halftime

National Police Officer of the Year
Honorable Mention

International Association of Chiefs of Police and Parade Magazine

### 1993
Police Service Commendation
New York Police Department

### 1994
Police Hero Award: Presented by President Bill Clinton

Community Service Commendation
State Senate of Hawaii

### Officer Leighton Kaonohi, Sr.

Officer Leighton Kaonohi, founder of the No Hope In Dope and Officer Honolulu programs, was born in Honolulu, Hawaii. He was raised in a community that is known for its violence, murders, and the sale of drugs. The one thing that Leighton strongly believes that kept him from a life of crime, was the love and great example his mother and father set for him. He was the youngest of five children, in a home that was not rich in money, but overflowing with a love for God, and each other.

While attending Waimanalo Elementary and Intermediate school, three of his classmates died from drugs, two committed suicide and one was murdered. The visual impact of those senseless deaths had a profound influence on his life. Little did he know, that some day he would be inspired to create a program that would touch thousands of lives and change his personal direction.

In 1988, after serving eight years with the Honolulu Police Department, Leighton had reached a crossroads in his life. He questioned the value of the work that he was doing. He could see young people and their families being destroyed because of drugs and the effects it had on those who used them. He was no longer content to just arrest people for selling and using. Leighton discussed the pain he was feeling with his wife Beatrice and expressed his desire to leave the police department and do something else which would allow him to be a part of the solution and not just picking up the pieces. A few weeks later, Leighton began receiving dreams that were so vivid he could remember everything he saw and heard. April 6, 1988, Leighton started the No Hope In Dope Program, which has become the life mission of this simple, humble servant of God.

For the past 19 years, Officer Kaonohi has been an outstanding community leader and volunteer, coaching youth athletics, fulfilling a term as president for the Waimanalo Jaycees, serving on the Waimanalo Neighborhood Board and acting as an advisor to the Boy Scouts of America. He is an active member in his church, and has held many leadership positions. He presently serves as Ward Assistant Clerk with the Kaneohe II Ward.

Over the span of his career, Officer Kaonohi has developed a unique style of getting things done. His sincere desire to make the community a safer place for our youth is evident in his tireless efforts. He has been visible in the community promoting the police department and his peers in a positive light, and has played a major role in bridging the gap between the community and law enforcement officials. He is an officer who symbolizes the aloha spirit, and is respected by his peers.

**Sergeant (ret) Eldean Kukahiko**
**Honolulu Police Department**
"I have worked with Officer Kaonohi for more than eight years. There are those whose commitment to society is measured by financial and personal gain. Officer Kaonohi is not such a person. Without hesitation, I can honestly say I have never met another man as caring, honest, loyal and dedicated. His standards for life are above reproach--he walks his talk. Children all over Hawaii look to him as a role model. Community leaders, government officials, school administrators, church leaders, local celebrities and his peers respect him highly.

A police officer for 19 years, he has an unblemished record. His work has made a significant impact on countless individuals. Numerous letters from those involved in his programs have expressed their thanks and gratitude. These programs have touched the lives of over 250,000 children and young adults nationwide. With continued support from the community and local and national government agencies, Officer Kaonohi and the No Hope In Dope programs can continue to

*The one thing that Leighton strongly believes that kept him from a life of crime, was the love and great example his mother and father set for him.*

make a difference. Officer Kaonohi has received many awards for his work with the Officer Honolulu and No Hope In Dope programs, but has never lost sight of the team effort which has led to the programs success. 'Together we can make a difference' and 'It must be us and we and never I and me' are two phrases constantly spoken by Officer Kaonohi. He believes that the driving force behind the program is a loving and caring team of individuals dedicated to our youth and fighting the war on drugs."

*Leighton K. Kaonohi, Sr. can be reached at his E-mail address: no.hope.in.dope.@iname.com, Web site: www.nohopeindope.com.* No Hope In Dope™ is a U.S. International service and trademark. Any use of this mark is prohibited.■

*Officer Leighton Kaonohi, Sr. in uniform*

# Executive Challenges In Our New Millennium

## Embracing Change With Resources That Promote Greatness

*Erik Van Alstine*

> *If your business is going to make it in our new millennium, you must retain and cultivate innovative, motivated people. This is by far the greatest challenge business executives will face in our new millennium.*

If the next one hundred years is anything like the last, we're in for some major changes. One hundred years ago man got around mostly by horse, was just beginning to understand electricity, and couldn't imagine the possibility of manned flight. There was no concept of the moving picture, the telephone, much less the computer. We've come a long way in a short time.

Then, like now, changing times provide opportunities to capitalize upon or to miss. In 1903, the president of Michigan Savings Bank advised Henry Ford's lawyer not to invest in the Ford Motor Company because "The horse is here to stay, but the automobile is only a novelty...a fad." In 1899, the British scientist, William Thompson said, "Radio has no future. Heavier-than-air flying machines are impossible. X-rays will prove to be a hoax." As for the submarine, even science fiction writer H. G. Wells, said he couldn't imagine such a vessel "doing anything but suffocating its crew and floundering at sea."

So what will the next one hundred years bring? Certainly many good things and many challenges as well. Futurist Alvin Toffler divides history into three gigantic waves of change. The First Wave--the Agricultural Age, spanned thousands of years. The Second Wave--the Industrial Age, from mid 1600s to now, is playing itself out after 300 years of dominance. The Third Wave--the Information Age-began in the 1950s, and is just getting started.

As communication and transportation technology further develops, the world will continue to shrink. Up to 90 percent of the world's languages may disappear in the next century as information technology creates a global culture. English is already the overwhelmingly dominant language in areas such as business and science.

The top 10 technologies with the greatest potential for business profits in the coming decade are: 1) genetic mapping, 2) super materials, 3) high-density energy sources, 4) digital high definition television, 5) miniaturization technologies, 6) smart manufacturing, 7) anti-aging products and services, 8) medical treatments, 9) hybrid-fuel vehicles and 10) entertainment.

As the century progresses, technological change will continue to accelerate, and the pace of life will quicken as well. And in the 21st century, job security will be finally seen for what it is--a 20th century ideal. People and businesses will experience more difficulties making their forecasts and, faced with new realities, will have to reinvent themselves or languish. Whole industries will become obsolete, while entirely different industries will emerge. As Dickens said, the 21st century will be "the best of times and the worst of times." The best of times for some. The worst of times for others.

Those who are uncomfortable with change will find it difficult to cope with the new millennium. They'll be like the bitter old man who said "I've seen a lot of changes in my lifetime, and I'm against every one of 'em." But if you have a sense of adventure, this is the most exciting time in history to be alive. Let me share with you some of the challenges I believe we'll be faced with in the next one hundred years, and some practical ways to meet them.

## Challenge Number 1: Managing and Interpreting Information

If executives are going to serve their customers well, they're going to have to know their customers well. This requires gathering and interpreting information about customers and the business environment in general.

In addition to general customer information, there's the more specific customer information that you gather from them as they do business with you. Do you know your customers well? Are you continually getting feedback, and making sure that key people in your organization know that information? What are the specific buying habits of your own customers? How can you use this information to serve them better?

To meet these challenges, business leaders of the next millennium will need a heart full of wisdom more than a head full of facts. They will have to focus on the underlying principles that never change, because the rules and circumstances will always be

to properly understand and interpret the facts that are in place, they're confident in the midst of chaos and as a result, less likely to be intimidated.

## Challenge Number 2: Staying Focused

The "good" can be the mortal enemy of the "best" in our lives. And since there is so much "good" out there, it's a lot easier to get distracted.

Options are clamoring for our attention at every turn. The average American sees hundreds of advertisements per day. Pagers, fax machines, e-mail, cell phones, junk mail, meetings and that ringing phone will keep clamoring for a large chunk

*People and businesses will experience more difficulties making their forecasts and, faced with new realities, will have to reinvent themselves or languish. Whole industries will become obsolete, while entirely different industries will emerge.*

But wading through the available information is a challenge itself. Every few years, the amount of published information on the planet doubles. Add to that our increasing ability to access knowledge, and you've got a recipe for information overload.

There's a huge amount of information out there about your customers already. But finding it, sorting it, and applying it to your business is going to become more and more challenging. Every day, people are gathering information about consumers, whether from grocery store scanners, ATM machines, magazine subscriptions, television viewing habits, Internet surfing, credit card purchases, or the drawing for a Hawaiian vacation that you entered at the mall.

changing. They will have to set up systems that allow them to cut through irrelevant information and zero in on information most vital to the success of their business.

Business leaders must be information system-oriented. They're going to have to be more system-oriented than fact-oriented. And these systems must be developed to function in the background, not getting in the way of doing business in the most flexible and effective ways.

Those who are rule-oriented, or lean toward bureaucratic management will find themselves more and more frustrated, and constantly behind the times. Yet, those who are principle-centered can maintain their moorings even when confronted with the flurry of information. Because their ability

of our time.

Opportunities will abound, increasing your options, and intensifying your need to make right choices. Now more than ever, you and your company must clarify a sense of purpose. When we connect with a clear, compelling purpose, we can focus and prioritize, and our lives come into balance. Clear purpose enables us to shed unnecessary information, to eliminate unnecessary options, and simplify our lives. It enables us to say no to second best in order to say yes to the highest priorities.

So how do you discover your life purpose? Taking a personality test is a good start, helping you clarify your gifts and strengths. You can figure yours out with the Keirsey Character Sorter. Just log on to http://

www.keirsey.com, take a short multiple question test online, and they'll process the results instantly. There's also an interesting section that compares your personality type with that of some famous people. I've done this with my staff and found it to be very confirming and enlightening.

The process of developing a personal and corporate mission statement can get you a long way toward connecting with your unique purpose. In developing my own, and that of my company, I've used two resources: *The Seven Habits of Highly Effective People* by Stephen Covey, and *The Path* by Laurie Beth Jones. Of the two, I prefer *The Path* because of its simplicity. But each takes a unique approach, so I recommend each of them for greatest clarification.

Once you and your company leaders clarify their personality types and define personal and corporate mission statements, you'll be able to stay focused, giving you a strategic advantage over competitors and a better handle on organizational priorities.

## Challenge Number 3: Cultivating Great People

If your business is going to make it in the next millennium, you must retain and cultivate innovative, motivated people. This is by far the greatest challenge business executives will face in the next millennium.

The most important resource on planet earth are productive, creative and innovative people. In his book *The Ultimate Resource*, Julian Simon argues that our natural resources will never run out because of the constant innovations that continually define what a resource even is. When a shortage drives a resource's prices up, these higher prices represent a profit opportunity that leads inventors and businesspeople to seek new ways to satisfy the shortages. Many fail, a few succeed, and "the final result is that we end up better off than if the shortage problems had never arisen."

Back in the late 1800s and early 1900s, gasoline was a worthless derivative in the refining process. Refiners let it run into the rivers, because kerosene was what they were really after. Kerosene was used as lamp oil to heat and light American homes. Gasoline had no beneficial use, and couldn't even be defined as a "resource." But with the internal combustion engine's invention by Nikolaus Otto in 1877, gasoline became valuable. Today the kerosene derivative of crude oil is practically useless, and gasoline is the major "resource" we seek in refining crude oil.

Quality people are the real key to business success. Andrew Carnegie, one of the richest men of the industrial age, wrote his own epitaph, revealing the secret of his success: "Here lies one who knew how to get around men more clever than himself." Charles Schwab, one of Carnegie's "clever" men, stated, "I consider my ability to arouse enthusiasm among men the greatest asset I possess."

It boils down to this: Great companies require great people. People are the "ultimate resource." So how do you attract and retain great people? Long-term, the best way is to build them from the ground up. When you focus on developing people, you engender loyalty. You cultivate a commitment to the team and the vision that great hiring practices can never compensate for.

Building requires tools. It also requires hard work. You cannot build a house without a saw and hammer, and you cannot build great people without some good resources. Then, once you have the tools, you must put them to work consistently. Herbert Spencer stated that "The great aim of education is not knowledge but action." Business leaders must find educational tools and resources that will move their people to action and will equip staff members with relevant knowledge that will help them make progress in their lives and careers.

Incite (http://www.incite.net) is a resource for business leaders who want to develop the potential of their people. This exciting new life-education and motivational resource aims to inspire and promote greatness in people through the consistent, long-term use of motivational and educational tools. Incite offers hundreds of books, audio and videotapes, and workshops from categories like leadership, biography, inspiration, family, worldview and personal development.

By getting involved in Incite, you and your staff can invest in your company's most valuable resource-- your people. Cultivating great people is indeed the most important task of the next millennium, and Incite can help you prepare for the challenge.

*Erik Van Alstine, chief executive officer of the Tacoma, Wash.-based integrated communication company Signature Media, is the founder of Incite, the leading provider of resources that promote greatness in people and organizations. To learn more about this life education and motivational resource, call (253) 620-2400, or visit our website at www.Incite.net.* ∎

**trans-form (trăns-fôrm′) *v*.** To change markedly the form, or character of, especially for the better.

*"Transforming Human Potential into Purposeful Lives"*

### The Challenge:

To transform field leadership by developing personal and corporate efficacy, the belief in one's ability to set and reach goals as well as perform at a higher level commensurate with potential.

### The Solution:

The "Investment in Excellence" seminar developed by The Pacific Institute; education that has earned the acclaim of the world's psychological associations and higher learning institutions for providing measurable transformations in self and collective efficacy within people and organizations.

# FACTS AND MYTHS OF NETWORK MARKETING
# The 'ABC Technique'

*Len Clements*

you ever try to pour hot coffee into a thermos with the lid still on? Could you put a video cassette into your VCR if it already had a cartridge in it? Of course not. Unfortunately, the way that most people prospect for multi-level partners makes about as much sense.

For many years, we've all been taught to call up our friends and try to get them to come to an opportunity meeting, or at least read some information or watch a video about a multi-level marketing opportunity. To do anything different would be going against the number one commandment of our industry. In other words, "Thou shalt not try to reinvent the wheel." I'm certainly not about to suggest otherwise. However, I do believe there are very effective ways of making the wheel roll a little smoother and a little faster.

First and foremost, we must remember that when you propose your opportunity, you are offering a business opportunity; a chance at being a true entrepreneur. Secondly, you are proposing your prospect become involved with multi-level marketing. In other words, you have at least one, and probably two major challenges here; challenges you must overcome before you can even think about proposing your specific opportunity. Challenges that, nine times out of ten, is the main reason why your prospect won't even look at your opportunity.

Surveys indicate that about 85% of all working Americans would like to own their own business, if they could. In other words, if all obstacles were removed, they would prefer to be their own boss rather than work for someone else. This amounts to over 160 million people! These are your prospects. When they are asked, they usually come up with these four reasons why they don't want to start a business:

*It takes too much money*. I don't have thousands of dollars to invest in a business. *It takes too much time*. I don't want to work 80 hours a week to get my business going. *Too risky*. More than 80% of all businesses fail in the first two years. *I don't know how*. I've never taken any business courses. I don't know anything about taxes, accounting, marketing, etc.

I can assure you, if your prospects are not currently operating their own business, they have considered the possibility at some time in their lives. They have also determined all the reasons why they can't (probably all four reasons). Therefore, before you even start to offer your multi-level opportunity, you might want to dispel, at least slightly, these beliefs about why they can't go into business for themselves.

Let's say you are having lunch with your friends and you casually mention the fact you are thinking about starting your own business. Then you ask if they have ever considered it. Sure, they have considered it at some time or another.

Well, why didn't you, you ask. They will inevitably respond with one or more of the previous four reasons.

Now comes the fun part. You ask them if they would ever consider going into business for themselves if the total start-up costs were less than $500, and the income potential was higher than the earnings of some CEOs of fortune 500 companies; the total time investment could be as little as 10 to 20 hours a week; they could continue to work in their present job until the income from their business was sufficient to earn them at least an equal income with very little risk, and best of all, there were numerous consultants available to them who are experts at running this business, who would train and advise them personally for an unlimited number of hours, for the life of their business, absolutely free! Not only that, but there is another company that will take care of all your research and development, shipping, payroll, sales taxes, legal problems, etc. And this company will do this for them every month, for the life of their business, for around $20.00 a year.

Of course, your friends won't believe any of this. Ask them if they would consider it if all this were true. Most likely they'll say something like, "well, sure, but there's got to be a catch." Is this not an exact description of your basic multi-level business opportunity? Is any of this even an exaggeration? No. You've just completed step "A" of the "ABC" technique.

Now, for the first time during this conversation, you will suggest that this type of business involves "network" or "multi-level" marketing. But don't get into your specific opportunity yet. There may be a major hurdle yet to overcome. You still have step "B" to take care of.

▶

There are basically three types of people you are going to come across during your recruiting efforts. First, the cynic or skeptic. They believe multi-level marketing companies are all scams, get-rich-quick schemes, illegal pyramids, involve door-to-door and home party sales, etc. One person I know even referred to them as "cults." For whatever reason, these people have a low opinion of multi-level marketing in general. The second types are those that don't know anything about multi-level marketing, perhaps only that it's something like a pyramid, or that they've at least heard of Amway or Mary Kay. The third are people who were originally in the second group who heard about someone who made a lot of money doing multi-level marketing. By the way, if you find someone in this group, skip step "B." This step is presenting the multi-level marketing concept as a viable, honest form of business. This usually involves explaining what multi-level marketing is not, not what it is.

Step "B" could be an entire column unto itself. Basically, you may want to mention that there are several million people in the U.S. that are pursuing this form of business. Also,

> *The real trick to successful recruiting in any multi-level marketing organization is not convincing someone who has looked at your opportunity to get involved with you; it's getting them to just look at the opportunity.*

throw out names like Rexall, MCI and US Sprint, which all involve multi-level marketing as a means of obtaining new customers. Briefly explain the obvious difference between an illegal pyramid and a legitimate multi-level company. Include favorable articles about the multi-level marketing industry in general. You may want to lead in with a generic video or audio cassette that serves to only legitimize the industry, not promote any particular opportunity. Whatever you can do to give the industry more credibility, do it now.

Once these first two "preparation" steps are completed, you should then hand your prospect the video or literature about your opportunity. Challenge them to find the catch. Tell them you can't, even though you also thought it was too good to be true. Instead of trying to get them to find out what all the good things there are about your program, encourage them to find all the bad things! Challenge them to debunk it. Someone would be much more likely to watch a video if it were for the purpose of justifying their negative beliefs, than to contradict them. It's human nature.

The bottom line is this. The real trick to successful recruiting in any multi-level marketing organization is not convincing someone who has looked at your opportunity to get involved with you; it's getting them to just look at the opportunity. Don't you agree? Once someone seriously looks at a good multi-level opportunity, it's very hard to not be at least a little intrigued.

Unfortunately, nine out of ten won't seriously look. Actually, I'd guess five out of ten won't look at all! You've got to get them to just look. If you have a good opportunity, the rest will take care of itself.

A good analogy here would be the thermos and the VCR. Like the thermos, you must open your prospects mind before you can pour anything into it. And like the VCR, there may already be something in there you may have to remove first. To borrow an analogy from Anthony Robbins (Robbins Research), it's as if your beliefs have legs like a chair. Only these legs are usually solid steel instead of wood. Believe me, people's beliefs as to why they can't go into business for themselves, and sometimes what they believe multi-level marketing to be, are solid beliefs. If you don't do something to at least weaken those legs before you come in with your new belief, forget it. It will bounce right off.

I'm certainly not suggesting that this "ABC" technique is going to knock down those legs (although it could). If you can at least instill some doubt in the mind of your prospect, some spark of interest, or at least pessimistic curiosity, you've made a major gain.

For the last 50 or so years, in almost every multi-level marketing organization, we've all been taught to go straight to step "C." Contact your prospect and propose your multi-level business opportunity. "Multi-level marketing" and "business" may be scary propositions, and needlessly so. Steps "A" and "B" are designed to reduce or eliminate this stigma, enabling you to bring more prospects to step "C." Get them to look! ∎

# GENERIC TELE-CONFERENCING SCHOOL

## for
## Home Based Businesses
## and
## Network Marketing Distributors

## Start Reducing Attrition TODAY!

Our 4, 8 and 12 week courses are priced right to teach your distributors how to be more successful in their home-based business (any business or network marketing company). Our private classes are one hour long, strictly generic and conducted over the telephone.

### Subjects include:

- **How you can save up to $5,000 or more per year on your taxes** by starting your home-based business

- **Powerful telephone techniques** that teach you the secret to recruiting many new distributors

- **Postcards** turnkey marketing systems to generate leads, recruit and build your organization

- **And much more**

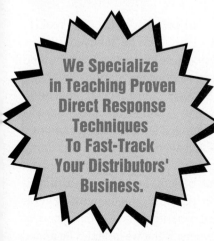

We Specialize in Teaching Proven Direct Response Techniques To Fast-Track Your Distributors' Business.

## Learn The Secrets Of Being Successful From The Comfort Of Your Home!

Home-based business owner attending class over the phone.

Many of our classes are supported by millions of dollars in media, promoting our lead generating programs to help distributors become more successful in whatever network marketing company they work with.

### Company benefits

- You profit by sending your distributors to our school
- We help you reduce attrition
- New profit center
- Can be private labeled for your company

## Another Tool to Fast Track Your Business by VHS Direct.

*Secrets To...*
As Seen On T.V.!
CREATING WEALTH FROM HOME

**Contact:** Training Division

## 800-665-0286

VHS DIRECT, INC., DEPT. 777
5814 W. Pico Blvd. Los Angeles, CA 90019
Tel: 323 937-0915 Fax: 323 937-0917
© 1999 VHS Direct All Rights Reserved.

# The Doctor Is Out - And In - Network Marketing

**W**hy would a board-certified physician with an established practice choose to leave it all behind to work with a fledgling network marketing company?

## FREEDOM!

Dr. Matthew Silver of Columbia, Maryland, retired from his medical practice in December, 1996, to work full-time with FreeLife International. He started with the company in April, 1995, only two months after its creation. When he retired from his practice a year and a half later, he had replaced his medical income entirely from FreeLife. A year after that, he was earning over twice what the average family practice physician brings home. He attained the position of Corporate Director in less than two and a half years with FreeLife.

The income derived from FreeLife was an important factor, and equally so, was the freedom that came with it. A family practice physician can be on call at all hours of the day and night, with unforeseen emergencies erupting at any time. There was also the nagging dissatisfaction that came from treating illnesses he strongly believed could have been prevented with the right information and nutritional supplements. When Dr. Silver left the practice, he gained control of his time and his life. "I do what I want, when I want," he says. "I'm very busy, but I don't mind working hard for residual income. FreeLife gives you the opportunity to live as you wish."

Dr. Silver had been involved in the network marketing industry for 17 years prior to his joining FreeLife. While he'd experienced success with other organizations promoting nutritional supplements, he felt that FreeLife not only met but exceeded his expectations and aspirations. Before joining them, he did a due diligence study, checking the fledgling company's financial backing, integrity of the company's leaders and the marketing plan, all of which impressed him greatly.

Most importantly, he felt that FreeLife offered products he believed in. As a physician, he'd spent years promoting the concept of prevention. Believing in the adage, "an ounce of prevention is worth a pound of cure," he was discouraged at how little technology and managed health care was doing to prevent illness. In accordance with these beliefs, he had been affiliated on a part-time basis with several nutritional supplement companies over the years. But it wasn't until he joined

*Dr. Matt Silver*

FreeeLife that he felt he'd found a company whose products and mission were completely in sync with his philosophy.

"Network marketing lives or dies on the strength of the product," he says. He feels that companies with consumable products have the greatest likelihood of longevity, and also points to exclusivity and uniqueness as qualities that will make or break the network marketing effort. FreeLife met his requirements on all of these lines.

Dr. Silver speaks very highly of Dr. Earl Mindell, author of *The Vitamin Bible*, which has more than nine million copies in circulation in over 30 languages. Dr. Mindell believes in nutrition as a means of prevention and has a 15-year exclusive contract with FreeLife to serve as their spokesperson and product development expert. FreeLife also has an exclusive contract with Linda Chae, the world's leading expert in organic skin care. A third contract with Eurovita International of Denmark, provides them with exclusive U.S. marketing rights to that company's nutriceuticals, which Dr. Silver describes as representing the latest advancement in the field of nutrition.

Finding that FreeLife offered everything he wanted in a network marketing company, Dr. Silver threw himself wholeheartedly into the business and has been tremendously successful by anyone's standards. In just two years of full-time activity with FreeLife, he has over 20,000 people in his organization with an annual group volume in excess of $2 million. Additionally, Dr. Silver has served on FreeLife's prestigious Executive Leadership Council on multiple occasions and has been a member of the President's Team as well.

As young as FreeLife is, the company has twice been featured in *Success*

magazine and is the youngest company to ever appear on the cover. FreeLife is also a member of the Direct Selling Association and was voted "Best Company of the Year" three years in a row (1995-1997) by *MLM Insider*, as well as being voted "Company of the Year" by *Profit Now* magazine in 1996 and 1998.

Dr. Silver is FreeLife's lead physician distributor; however, he is quick to point out that you don't have to have a medical background to succeed with

**Silver in uniform**

FreeLife. "I have a proven track record of creating network marketing leaders and helping anyone, regardless of professional background or prior network marketing experience, attain a high level of success in this business."

To Dr. Silver, detail product understanding is not nearly as important as being STD: Successful, Teachable, and Dissatisfied, because those factors largely determine the strength of motivation to succeed. He feels it's not enough to be the first two; it's necessary to be dissatisfied with your current station in life. Whether it's a matter of not feeling that your potential has been met to the fullest

or feeling that you are a slave to your job with no control over your whole life, this dissatisfaction provides a major component to a person's motivation to join the ranks of network marketers.

Dissatisfaction is also seen by increasing numbers of consumers who are seeking alternative approaches through vitamins, herbs and other supplements. Recent articles in *Time* magazine and other prominent publications have vividly reported the health benefits of these alternative approaches to health. "This is not a fad, but a revolution," says Dr. Silver. "We're moving into an arena where people are taking responsibility for themselves and their health." People are becoming more and more interested in the area of preventive health. Dr. Silver quotes Dr. Mindell as saying his goal is to close half the hospitals in the country by providing the means to prevent illness from occurring.

This is where Dr. Silver's career is bridging two areas. With expertise in both camps, he feels he can impact upon the health of potentially hundreds of thousands, by leveraging his time through the FreeLife program. Throughout his career, he has also been a health educator and continues that role at FreeLife. By sharing his in-depth medical perspectives with FreeLife's sales force, he increases their knowledge, and this in turn contributes to the impact they are able to make with their customers.

Dr. Silver stresses that medical knowledge is not the most important factor in working with FreeLife. "Enthusiasm and motivation are equally important," he says, "because ignorance on fire can be more valuable than knowledge on ice. Anyone with enough enthusiasm can learn what they need to succeed here."

▶

Sharing his knowledge with other FreeLife members and customers is a part of his career that he truly enjoys. He prides himself in servicing people, and part of that service is introducing them to the FreeLife opportunity. "You can sell a product you believe in, and you can live a highly

possibility of earning a four-figure monthly salary within just a few months, and a five-figure monthly income after only two to three years is not unusual. The bottom line is that with FreeLife, optimum health and prosperity are both a matter of choice.

With FreeLife, Dr. Silver feels he's

Another key feature to the success of any network marketing company is taking advantage of market awareness and market exposure. Dr. Silver feels that the recent announcement of the impending release of Dr. Mindell's Vitamin Bible for the 21st century will create a massive new serge of interest by the baby boomer generation in FreeLife's products and opportunity.

**Dr. Silver proudly leaning against his Mercedes-Benz**

If ever there was a time to get involved with FreeLife, a true company with destiny, this is it. One of his favorite sayings is "Carpe diem," which means, "seize the day!"

Dr. Silver's enthusiasm spreads to his personal life as well. Married to a human resource professional, he is the father of two adult children. In his spare time--which is one of the luxuries of his new life-- he is also very active.

prosperous life. With FreeLife, you have products that you truly can promote and believe in, and thereby become highly successful." He feels it's very important to share the opportunity for the "good life" with others. In doing so, he has attracted large numbers of other health care workers as well as entrepreneurs and corporate professionals who are looking to either supplement their present incomes or develop alternative careers.

"Health is your greatest wealth," he says, "and wealth is a supplement to enjoy health." Good health allows people to pursue their financial goals; reaching those goals allows them to enjoy their lives to the fullest. "With FreeLife, the average person has the

found the ideal way to enhance the health of the average person through sharing information and products that promote wellness, and providing financial security to those in the network. He feels that network marketing is "the embodiment of the best ideals of the free enterprise system" and "the best chance for the average person to obtain true financial independence."

In addition to their cutting edge products, Dr. Silver is proud of FreeLife's technological support, which includes fax-on-demand, a corporate web site, Internet lead generation, voicemail training and support systems, and teleconferencing. Providing its sales force with the tools to succeed is one of the company's foremost attributes.

He's a long-distance runner, who also enjoys racquetball and cycling. Flying lessons are a current passion, as he loves to travel. Above all, he loves the teaching and presentations on behalf of FreeLife, and helping others become successful.

*To receive a free FreeLife Business Opportunity Pack or for more details, contact **Dr. Silver** directly:*

*Home Office: (800) 484-7809, security code, 5043 or (410) 964-1842, Voice mail: (888) 261-4455, Fax: (410) 740-5414, E-mail: DoctorSilver@webtv.net, Address: PO Box 2226, Columbia, MD 21045.∎*

# CANADA

## Marketing  Lifestyle Environment
### *The Network Marketing Environment in Canada Continues to Thrive and Expand in 1999*

*Carrol Leclerc*

**Deregulation** of the Canada **Telecommunications** Industry opened up the channels for multi-national corporations to link Canadian consumers to affordable global communication products and services and therein connected the average household to global shopping and multiple MLM/direct seller business opportunities. Today, one out of every two households recognize and/ or purchase products and services from direct sales/MLM operations or participate in network marketing programs.

## International Marketing:

International marketing representatives traditionally limited their retail customer base and sponsoring activities to local regions or North American jurisdictions.  Thanks to the developments in communications via Internet e-commerce and telecommunication technology, a representative can place daily calls or engage in ongoing communications with customers in Japan, the Philippines, Taipei or U.K. for the near identical cost of a Canadian postage stamp.  It is no surprise the network industry is evolving at a rapid pace.

## Entrepreneurship:

**Network marketing** has come of age in a global community supporting millions of network marketers in the International and National arenas. The core fundamental philosophy to participate in a MLM business is based on non-discrimination of race, language, gender or cultural background requirements. No discrimination is necessary other than legal age requirements and regulatory compliance requirements in the country and jurisdiction of the transaction.  The self-employed entrepreneur's sales achievements are the rewarding factor for promotion to higher earnings in the compensation programs. The driving force of entrepreneurship or independent self-employment is attributed to unlimited earning potential.

## Quality of Life:

Canada, as a whole, is known for its quality of life.  According to the United Nations Human Development Index, Canada has the highest quality of life of any nation.

The United Nations report on 160 countries name Canada the best place in the world to live. Survey indicators used education, life span, purchasing power, social and economic development, focusing advantages of clean environment, low crime rate, affordable homes, and easily accessed leisure activities enhance Canadian overall well-being.

Perhaps Canada's diverse multi-cultural populations sets a global example, or perhaps the stringent Canadian MLM operating regulations in Canada extends the message that Canadian marketers are protected by consumer regulations.  Regardless of the reasons, new multi-national companies continue to enter Canada's marketplace, while new Canadian owned operations strive to establish their business at home, looking to the U.S., Asia and European countries for market expansions.  The trend is to establish ground floor stability in Canada, then expand to International markets for global market revenues.

## Canadian Regulatory Compliances:

Despite Canada's weaker currency, higher unemployment and stringent regulatory compliance regulations that govern operations, network marketing and direct selling still flourishes.

Due to Canadian multi-cultural population and their close alliance to European and Pacific Rim countries, the financial challenges experienced by other countries created a rippling effect on the Canadian traditional business.  This rescissionary effect has not hampered MLM sales activities or the overall industry's growth. MLMers experience an opposite effect as economic downsizing affects the traditional sectors, and consumers look to network marketing sales opportunities to supplement, replace or enhance their income. ▶

## Industry Growth:

Canada hosts approximately 450 MLM direct seller companies with approximately two thirds of these operating companies originating from the U.S.A., and one third originate in Canada, representing over 4,680,000 independent marketers or home-based business owners.

**Sixty percent of the population of Canada is geographically located within 100 miles of the Canada/U.S. border**. Cross border marketing is a way of life for networkers. U.S. networkers migrate into Canada and most U.S. marketers have contacts and associates in Canada. Marketers can earn two pay cheques; one from their Canadian sales activities and one from the U.S. sales achievements.

Independent marketers prefer a seamless marketing and compensation program where they can sponsor and sell products and services in the U.S. and Canada in a near identical manner, particularly with the explosive growth of telecommunications and Web Internet companies sponsoring and selling product to global markets. Seamless marketing can be accomplished if the corporation has set up appropriate structuring. However, if the corporation has not completed or complied with the Canadian regulatory requirements to sell or sponsor a Canadian resident, the Independent Representative and company may be reprimanded and/or subject to legal consequences.

## CANADIAN FEDERAL COMPLIANCES:

Under the Canadian Federal Government, Industry Canada's Competitions Bureau administers the Competition Act, which is the primary regulatory component of the marketplace framework that governs all business activity in Canada. Amendments to the Act were introduced in April 1992 and in February 1999. The primary regulations contain measures directed against deceptive practices to MLM and pyramid selling schemes included, but not limited to the following key regulations:

**(1)** There can be no fee to register as an independent marketing participant

**(2)** There is no mandatory purchase requirement as a condition to participate in the plan

**(3)** No compensation is paid for the mere act of recruiting or sponsoring other participants

**(4)** No inventory loading or large amounts of products can be sold to a recruit in unrealistic amounts

**(5)** Failure to provide participants with the right to return product on reasonable commercial terms

Canadian participants in a plan are required to disclose the average annual earnings of a typical participant in the program at each sponsoring presentation. Average annual earning disclosure amounts are pre-approved by the corporation under the Competition Bureau guidelines.

## Advisory Opinion:

The Competition Bureau will provide review services of a company's compensation plan and marketing materials. This review is referred to as an Advisory Opinion Letter. The cost of Advisory Opinion is $500 to $25,000, depending upon the complexity of the program and the time and/or number of amendments and follow-up review procedures that may be required to achieve compliance and ultimately a positive advisory opinion letter.

## Telemarketing Regulations:

In February 1999, Bill C-20 received final approval enacting numerous amendments to the Competitions Act, including revision and regulations on telemarketing activities, labeling, merger notification and misleading advertising.

Although direct sales and MLM activities may not directly entail telemarketing, many companies and/or their participants use telemarketing and infomercial promotions, including telemarketing activities which may entail misleading or advertising statements that fall under the Bill C-20 amendments.

**Summary of Amendments – Bill C-20**
**This enactment modernizes the *Competition Act* to respond to a changing business and enforcement environment, by increasing flexibility in the administration of the Act and efficiency in its enforcement. The enactment includes:**

**(a)** New provisions to strengthen the enforcement action that can be taken against deceptive telemarketing solicitations

**(b)** Creates a non-criminal adjudicative mechanism with an improved range of remedies to deal with misleading advertising and deceptive marketing practices

**(c)** Revises the treatment of claims made about regular selling prices to provide greater flexibility and clarity

**(d)** Permits judicial authorization for interceptions of private communications in relation to conspiracy, bid-rigging and receptive telemarketing

**(e)** Modifies the administration of the merger notification process

**(f)** Broadens the authority for the making of prohibitive orders to include prescriptive terms, as a means of promoting compliance and avoiding prosecution for less serious infractions

(g)   Formalizes existing responsibilities in relation to the administration and enforcement of certain labeling statutes

## Provincial and Territorial Industry Regulations:

The ten provinces and two territories within Canada (excluding Nunavut) administer their own unique and individual regulations for direct sellers and MLM operations including consumer protection disclosures and retail sales requirements.   Federal and Provincial compliance regulations apply to all participants including e-commerce transactions, Internet programs, corporate activities and printed marketing materials and the individual marketers who sponsor others into a program or sell products and services.

In most provincial jurisdictions the regulations include registration, licensing, plus posting of a security bond as a condition of licensing.  Other considerations entail the cost of products sold to provincial consumers and the number of independent marketers registered in the province.  Provincial municipalities may require the independent marketers to hold a municipal  license and/ or carry a personal I.D. card  issued from the MLM company they are registered with prior to commencing sponsoring or sales activities.

## CANADA'S HISTORICAL EVENT:

Canada celebrated a historical event on April 1, 1999 with the official inauguration of a new territory known as **Nunavut,** pronounced nun-a-vut, Inuktitut word meaning "Our Land."

This territory joins Canada's ten provinces and two territories, being the 13th independent Canadian jurisdiction.  The Nunavut Territory is carved from the Arctic Circle and the eastern half of Northwest Territories negotiated in the 1992 to 1998 Inuvit land claims agreements.  The new territory encompasses 20% of Canada's landmass or 1,900,000 square kilometers spanning three time zones representing an area twice the size of the province of Ontario.  The population of this remote region is estimated at 25,000 with an average income of $11,000 annually.                    ▶

# CANADIAN POPULATION STATISTICS
## Provincial and Territorial Population and
## Described by Ethnic Origins

|  | Total Population | British (1) Isles only | French only (2) | Minority Population | Minority % of Total Population |
|---|---|---|---|---|---|
| Canada | 28,538,125 | 4,873,970 | 2,696,270 | 3,197,480 | 11.2 |
| Newfoundland | 547,160 | 315,795 | 7,050 | 3,815 | 0.7 |
| Prince Edward Is. | 132,855 | 56,825 | 8,495 | 1,520 | 1.1 |
| Nova Scotia | 899,970 | 296,850 | 38,450 | 31,320 | 3.5 |
| New Brunswick | 729,630 | 182,395 | 123,840 | 7,995 | 1.1 |
| Quebec | 7,045,080 | 214,125 | 2,064,985 | 433.985 | 6.2 |
| Ontario | 10,642,790 | 2,250,705 | 303,820 | 1,682,045 | 15.8 |
| Manitoba | 1,100,295 | 173,030 | 33.575 | 77,355 | 7.0 |
| Saskatchewan | 976,615 | 139,835 | 18,740 | 26,945 | 2.8 |
| Alberta | 2,669,195 | 440,445 | 47,575 | 269,280 | 10.1 |
| British Columbia | 3,689,755 | 792,615 | 48,120 | 660,545 | 17.9 |
| Yukon Territory | 30,650 | 5,230 | 700 | 1,000 | 3.3 |
| Northwest Territories | 64,125 | 6,090 | 915 | 1,670 | 2.6 |

1996 Report – Statistics Canada

# The Best Defense

## ...is a Good Offense

The immune system is an army of cells and organs that defend the body against attack. These enemies include bacteria, viruses, parasites, germs, and various other microscopic invaders. They penetrate the body's natural shields, like the skin. Your immune system, the first and last line of defense, produces highly specialized cells such as lymphocytes to counter these threats. Included among these lymphocytes are natural killer (NK) cells, whose mission is to seek out and destroy any "harmful" invaders that penetrate the body's initial defense positions. This is especially important because low or absent NK cell activity is associated with virtually all human disease. Pollution, stress, the escalating rate of infectious disease, and the ability of bacteria and viruses to thrive, despite the use of antibiotics, are just a few of the factors that can affect the efficiency of your immune system.

### matol

## Biomune OSF ™

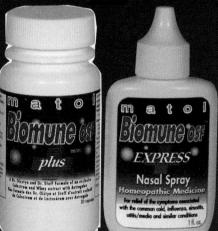

## BIOMUNE OSF™ Plus

- Over $20 million in Research & Development
- Original formula used in practice for nearly 20 years
- Patented Processing
- Proprietary
- Clinically studied by renowned Viro-Immunologist Dr. Jesse A. Stoff
- Honored at the First International Congress on Homeopathy and Alternative Medicine in June '98.

## BIOMUNE OSF™ EXPRESS

As a homeopathic medicine, this nasal spray is effective for relief of the symptoms often associated with

- the common cold
- influenza
- sinusitis
- sore throats
- earaches
- tonsillitis
- laryngitis

and similar conditions which may be bacterial, viral or a combination of both.

With infectious disease being the #1 cause of illness in North America, just imagine the incredible opportunity in these bottles!

**For more information, call 1-800-363-3890, access our Fax-On-Demand at 1-800-363-6286 (doc.#001) or visit our web site at www.matol.com**

## Visible Minority:

Profile breakdown on Ontario and British Columbia contained half of Canada's total population. They accounted for almost three-quarters of the visible minority population. The 1996 Census showed that about three out of ten individuals identified as a visible minority were born in Canada and the rest were immigrants.

The proportion of visible minorities varied considerably from less than 1% of the population of Newfoundland to highs of 18% in British Columbia, and 16% in Ontario. The proportion was below the national average of 11% in all of the other provinces and territories. Almost half of the South Asian and Black population of Canada lived in Toronto, along with about two-fifths of Canada's Chinese, Koreans and Filipinos.

British Columbia's immigrant population grew by nearly 25% between 1991 and 1996, the fastest rate of growth among all provinces and territories. The greatest impact of this trend was felt in the Vancouver census metropolitan area. New immigrants accounted for over a third of the population. Asian-born immigrants accounted for 44% of the immigrants in B.C., outnumbering European-born immigrants who accounted for 40%. Considering the high percentage of Asian-born immigrants in the province, it comes as no surprise that over a quarter of a million British Columbians reported Chinese as their single mother tongue. Family structure also showed changes. Of all family structures in B.C., the lone-parent family was the fastest growing between 1991 and 1996, increasing by nearly 30%. Growth was also strong among common-law couple families which increased by 22.6% since 1991. More than three-quarters (75.9%) of all B.C. families were headed by a married couple.

The tremendous increase in population brings with it important changes to the ethnic, cultural and linguistic make-up of Canada. New trends in immigration, language and family structure undoubtedly have a significant impact on MLM and direct sales business activities and the development of independent marketers networks.

Statistics revealed British Columbia is the most rapidly changing province in Canada, leading the country in population. In fact, B.C. is the only province that has grown at a faster rate than the national average in every Census since Confederation.

## MLM CORPORATE OFFICE – WESTERN CANADA

The Vancouver lower mainland municipalities have attracted international, national and corporate offices and distribution centres for a large percentage of Canadian MLM/direct seller companies. This favoured location is due primarily to cross border flow of MLM activities to and from U.S. marketers in Utah, Arizona and California who experience similar lifestyles, multi-cultural heritage. Marketing trends flow into Eastern Canada's popular locations for corporate offices in Toronto or metropolitan areas and the Montreal region in Quebec.

## B.C. TAX -- PERSONAL & BUSINESS

Highlights of tax cuts effect on January 1, 1999, as well as tax reductions and rate freezes since 1995

- The provincial personal income tax rate decreased by 2 percent to 49.5 percent of basic federal tax on January 1, 1999. Since 1995, the personal income tax rate has been reduced by 6 percent.

- The top marginal income tax rate decreased to 52.7 percent on January 1, 1999 and will be 49.9 percent on January 1, 2001.

- Small business tax rate was reduced on January 1, 1999 and possibly again in year 2000. With these cuts, the tax rate will have been reduced by 20 percent since 1995

- Corporation capital tax threshold increased to $2.5 million in paid-up capital on January 1, 1999, resulting in tax savings of $20 million.

- By 2001, 90 percent of businesses will not pay corporation capital tax.

*Note: The comparison of overall taxes includes: provincial child tax benefits, property tax, medical services plan premiums and provincial payroll taxes, retail sales tax, fuel tax and provincial income tax. All taxes except property taxes, have been calculated using rates in effect for January 1, 1999.*

The 1999 tax cuts mean B.C. families continue to pay among the lowest provincial tax bills in the country.

## Visible Minority Population in Vancouver, Mostly Asian:

In 1996, British Columbia had the second largest visible minority population after Ontario. There were 661,000 persons in British Columbia who were members of a visible minority group. These individuals accounted for 18% of British Columbia's total population, the highest proportion of any province. A total of 565,000 individuals in Vancouver identified themselves as members of a visible minority, 18% of the Canadian total, compared with just under half of the province's total population.

Vancouver has experienced high levels of Asian immigration in recent years. Asians comprised about nine out of ten members of Vancouver's minority population. Chinese formed the largest group in Vancouver, accounting for half of the total. South Asians were the second largest group, forming one-fifth of the visible minority population in Vancouver.

Vancouver was also home to the largest community of Japanese in Canada, as well as the second highest numbers of Chinese, South Asians, Filipinos and Koreans. Overall, 32% of the Chinese and Japanese in Canada lived in Vancouver, as did 26% of Koreans.

Quebec's visible minority population in 1996 was 434,000, the third largest total after Ontario and British Columbia. They represented 6% of Quebec's population. A total of 401,000 individuals identified themselves as members of a visible minority in Montreal in 1996, representing 92% of the province's visible minority population. In contrast, Montreal had less than half (47%) of the total population of Quebec. Montreal had sizeable communities among several visible minority groups. Blacks were Montreal's largest such group, accounting for 30% of the visible minority population. Arab/West Asians, who represented 18% of Montreal's visible minority population, constituted its second largest Latin American and South Asian communities. About 26% of Latin Americans and 22% of Southeast Asians lived in Montreal.

## Cross Country Marketing:

Multi-national and International MLM direct seller corporations have strategically located corporate head offices and International Distribution Centres in Vancouver and lower mainland locations to capitalize on the flow of cross border marketing activities of MLMers.

Products and services and MLM business opportunities flow into Canada from U.S. markets primarily from Washington, Arizona, Utah and California regions. Canadian sales and marketing flow from Canada into the U.S., due to lifestyles, multi-cultural and marketing environments, which are similar in Western U.S. and Western Canada. Additionally, British Columbia hosts a large Asian indigent population offering direct ties into the Asian Pacific Rim markets.

## MULTIPLE INTELLIGENCE
## NEW LEARNING STYLES:

Do you believe we are a reflection of our children or are the children a reflection of their parents? Most parents will be the first to acknowledge we often learn from our children, and recognize the process of learning never stops.

New learning techniques being implemented in the classroom can be beneficial when applied to MLM network training programs, bridging a greater understanding of adult learning and behaviourial patterns regardless of age, cultural background, language barriers or lifestyles. Network marketers who recognize their individual learning styles often discover a greater confidence level that can enhance communication abilities within family circles, social interactions and undoubtedly contribute to building an independent MLM business. Recognizing the multiple intelligence style within your MLM organizations can be a powerful asset in recognizing your leadership qualities.

## Everyone Uses Multiple Intelligence:

Have you ever wondered why some people immediately absorb a video or web site training program? Why is it that 90% of independent representatives do not read the corporate training manual and experience problems completing basic product order forms? Yet, the same individual has a great memory for everyone's name and personal details. They can recall "word for word" presentation from large noisy group seminar events. Why is it that some networkers cannot sit still for a 30 minute business briefing? However, they captivate an audience, maintain total focus for a two hour presentation of mathematical variations of a compensation program. Learning styles are unique to each individual.

Encouraging independent representatives to recognize and expand their multiple intelligence skills will strengthen your team and validate their individual abilities. Confidence builds commitment, commitment builds team synergy.

## Multiple Intelligence Indicators:
### Spatial-Visual intelligence:
Picture smart people like visualization, 3-D construction and idea sketching. They often see clear visual images when they close their eyes and have vivid dreams.

### Verbal-Linguistic intelligence:
(word smart) people like storytelling, tape-recording one's words. Books are very important to them.

### Logical-Mathematical intelligence:
Number smart people like classifications, categorization and science thinking. Their minds search for patterns, regularities or logical sequences.

### Interpersonal intelligence:
People smart persons like co-operative groups and board games. They like group sports and pastimes, rather than solitary ones.

▶

**Bodily-Kinesthetic intelligence:**
Body smart people like competitive and cooperative games plus hands-on thinking. They find it difficult to sit still for long periods.

**Musical-Rhythmic intelligence:**
Music smart people like mood music, rhythms, songs, taps, and chants. After hearing a piece of music once or twice they sing it accurately.

**Naturalist intelligence:**

Nature smart people like to spend time outdoors and notice patterns in nature.

**Interpersonal intelligence:**
Self smart people like self-paced instruction, goal-setting sessions. Don't mind spending some time alone.

(ref: BbyJ21099.NOW publication)

# THANKS TO YOU... THE MESSAGE IS SPREADING

*From the Desk of Carrol Leclerc, Founder, President and Volunteer - MLMIA*

## "What MLM Company Should I Join?"

*The word is out! MLM is the sought-after legitimate business opportunity avidly pursued by consumers. It is not a question of "Is it MLM?." The question is "Which MLM Company should I join?"*

The Multi Level Marketing International Association, Canada, is dedicated to representing the MLM Industry by providing a source of pertinent information, building better relationships between industry participants and those who impact direct sales/MLM business by providing educational opportunities, benefits of member support to help perpetuate this rapidly growing billion dollar industry. The Association is a non-profit organization with dedicated professional officers and directors who donate their time and expertise. MLMIA Canada published a Hot Line Inquiry Phone Number (604) 421-1880 for generic inquiries and members. Information Line is still answered by the old fashioned way (by a real person, not a machine).

Volunteering time to the Multi Level Marketing International Association has been an "eye opener.' Many callers just want to confirm if MLMIA is real. Forty two percent of all calls are consumer inquiries pertaining to due diligence on MLM companies. New representatives most often call within the first ten days of joining and/or before making a decision to participate. The most often asked question is "What MLM company should I join?"

Although the Canadian Association office will not provide any individual endorsement if the company is a member company, the information given to callers is generic due to the Association's protocol. This information source is often the only source available to consumer.

In mid 1998, the temperament of calls began to show a pattern with more and more calls requesting directions to MLM operations. This change confirms MLM companies and their marketers are presenting a positive industry image by presenting their products and business opportunities in a favourable, legitimate manner operating within Canadian compliance guidelines. Many companies have implemented internal policing policies to stay alert to industry practices and adhere to new regulatory requirements. They are effectively spreading the MLM word. In 1999, consumers seldom ask, "Is MLM legal?' "Is it a pyramid?"

The Industry has experienced many challenges over the past fifty plus years, continually gathering support and acceptance primarily due to the power and the spirit that is imbedded in self development of independent entrepreneurship, plus the army of dedicated individuals who perpetuate the independent marketer philosophy, despite challenges and set backs. Their dedication prevails.

Thank you on behalf of the MLMIA Canada. Our thanks go to the truth teller, the marketer and MLM companies who are spreading "the news" of their business and opportunity in a True and Ethical Manner" without hype or inflated earning claims.

**Thank you from our volunteer staff, Board of Directors and Committee Members across Canada.**

▶

# Opportunity has its rewards

**The opportunity to build your own business can be rewarding in different ways to different people.**

You set the goals, go your own pace, schedule your own time, and determine what you want in return. You can market as many, or as few, product lines as you choose — from personal care products to popular brand-name catalog merchandise. More than 3 million entrepreneurs in some 80 countries and territories have found this business opportunity made possible only through Amway is worth a closer look. See for yourself. Perhaps *you* can discover the rewards you've been seeking.

**The Business Opportunity Company**™

If you'd like to know more, call for a free brochure at **1-800-544-7167** or visit our website at **www.amway.com**     © 1998 Amway Corporation
In Canada call **1-800-922-6929**.

*Carrol Leclerc* is the founder of CLC Management Inc., a Canadian business consulting company that provides MLM/Networking services to clients in eight countries. A prominent MLM Executive Business Consultant, she has worked with numerous MLM companies to establish marketing criteria for Canada. She started as a distributor, winning awards for sales and recruiting, and soon rose to the top. From senior management positions in numerous high profile MLM companies, to chairman of the board, Carrol has performed at every level of the MLM Industry including expert witness testimony for Law Enforcement Agencies. Her ability to assess a company's marketing strategy, evaluate bottom line corporate profits and structuring of new start-up companies, to defining distributor needs have created a high demand for her expertise.

Carrol has written numerous articles and reviews for national and international publications and is a sought- after speaker. Her appearances on radio and television have been applauded by thousands.

Through twenty years of experience, Carrol has recognized the international need to inform consumers and corporate entities of the complexities of MLM regulatory compliancies. Drawing on her resources, she prepared a unique informative volume, "The MLM Compendium of the Canadian Regulatory Compliance." The book is an indispensable tool for all serious MLM companies, either operating in Canada or contemplating Canadian operations.

Carrol is the Founder and President of the MLMIA Cda, a non-profit association mandated to provide support to direct sellers and the MLM industry.■

## The Beginners Mind-Set

"It used to be, the bigger the nerd you were, the better the researcher," says Francois P. Van Remoortere, president of W.R. Grace & Co.'s research division. "That's changed now," he says. "Some of the best advice comes from people who know the least about a specific operation."

This isn't to belittle experience, information, or expertise. But the key to keeping ahead of change is to learn to *think like a beginner.* With a beginner's mind you will be more open to what is emerging and better equipped to anticipate change. The beginner isn't attached to old ways of doing and seeing things and won't spend a great deal of time "beating a dead horse" or accumulating sacred cows. Looking at the world with a fresh eye and open mind, the beginner will see things that the expert will miss.

Thinking like a beginner is a state of curiosity where you see situations anew, not letting old information and the "benefits" of experience cloud your judgement. Experience, after all, took place in the past, and the thinking, strategies, and information that worked in the past are often outdated and obsolete.

As a renowned maverick, the French architect and designer Phillipe Starck, has demonstrated, new eyes accompany the perpetual beginner. He says simply, "I am an amnesiac. This is why I always arrive fresh at a problem.

# Pyramid, Ponzi & Investment Schemes
## Is One Hiding Behind Your MLM Progam?

*Leonard Clements*

*Pyramid, Ponzi and investment schemes* disguised as legitimate MLM programs continue to flood the U.S. market. But unlike their predecessors, they're hiding their true nature better than ever. Many quasi-pyramids and money games today are taking great advantage of the ignorance of most people as to what constitutes an illegal pyramid. Please understand, I do not use the term "ignorance" in a derogatory manner. The term comes from the word "ignore" and many of us are simply ignoring a few basic, simple facts that make up a composite of a typical pyramid or other scheme. Also, understand that I am not an attorney, an attorney general, or a postal inspector; however, I know what questions they ask--and so should you! As I describe the legal definitions of these various kinds of schemes, I'm going to use plain English. For example, where the proper legal language might refer to the payment of "consideration," that being anything from gold dust to chickens, I'm going to assume that it's safe to just say money. If you want all the verbose legalese, call a lawyer.

Let's start with the old classic--the Pyramid Scheme. By definition a Pyramid Scheme is one where there is some kind of direct financial reward for the act of recruiting another person into the scheme. A blatant pyramid scheme would involve no product at all. You simply pay cash to play, hoping you recruit enough people to cash out for several times what you originally invested.

The roots of most pyramid MLM law is founded on the Amway vs FTC decision in 1979. Perhaps the single most defining characteristic of a legal network marketing company vs an illegal pyramid scheme came from these hearings. Essentially, the question was asked, "Can the last person in still make money?"

Obviously, the last person in a pyramid scheme will never make a dime. But if you were the very last person to ever sign up as a distributor

> *A blatant pyramid scheme would involve no product at all. You simply pay cash to play, hoping you recruit enough people to cash out for several times what you originally invested.*

for Amway, or any number of other legal MLM operations, could you still make money? Of course. By buying the product at wholesale and selling it at retail. The last person in, with no recruiting, can still make money.

If you were the last person to sign up in your MLM program, could you expect to be able to mark up the product or service and resell it to an end user? That is, someone who only wants the product or service? Are you and your downline distributors buying the products because you genuinely want them, or are most of the distributors making token purchases simply to satisfy a quota in the compensation plan? Having real products of value to an end user is a key element of a legal MLM enterprise.

Having said that, one of the most common, and least accurate questions you can ask in determining if something's a pyramid scheme is simply asking, "Is there a product?" Almost every pyramid out there today has thrown in some kind of token product knowing you'll ask that question. Some extremists will go so far as to tell us that the "service" they provide in exchange for your fee is their administration of the intake and outgo of cash. Some will claim you are paying to have your name added to a mailing list. Of course, the typical chain letter leads you to believe you are paying for the report of some kind. However, there are literally dozens of schemes out there that are not as obvious. Some offer what appears to be an abundance of bona fide, tangible products. But again, the focus should be on value and motive.

One of the best examples I can recall was a program called The Ultimate Money Machine. For $300 you were to receive such items as luggage, a 35mm camera, and a seminar on

▶

cassette tape valued at, of course, hundreds of dollars. The camera was cheap and had a value of less than $10, and the luggage you unrolled from a tube. Total cost to the company for all of these products was less than twenty dollars!

A program called Euro-Round required a $100 payment in exchange for nothing. Later, to "make the program legal," they added a little book.

Schemes like Investor's International, Common Wealth, Global Prosperity, Delphin, and its various other incarnations, would have you buy some literature and a few cassette tapes, with a material cost of around ten to twenty dollars, for usually about $1,250. Their rationalization is

certificate is purchased, even if it is never redeemed. The result? Nothing but paper, most of it cash, being exchanged. There is a great deal of recent legal precedent in this area. The upline should never be paid out of any kind of downpayment, layaway, voucher purchase, or any other similar transaction that does not involve an immediate acquisition of a product or service of value. In other words, no one should get paid until an actual product gets shipped.

As to "motive," again, are you and others buying the product because you want that product or can sell that product, or are you buying it because you have to make money? For example, if a company pays commissions on sales aides or

know the answer. Just ask yourself this question: "Would anyone realistically ever purchase this product or service without participating in the income opportunity?" Thousands of people purchase products from such companies as Nu Skin, Watkins, Herbalife and Amway every day without becoming distributors. They just want the product. This is true for most of the MLM companies out there.

How exciting is that big ad you just saw that boasted "NO SELLING!" Consider it a big red flag.

Let's discuss Ponzi Schemes. First of all, a Ponzi is not the same as a pyramid, although Ponzis are often referred to as a pyramid. In a pyramid scheme, you pay in X, the pyramid promoters keep, let's say, 20% of X and use the other 80% to pay all those who "cash out." Not unlike legitimate MLM operations, a distributor can earn far in excess of what they personally paid in, but the MLM company itself never pays out much more than 40 to 50% of every wholesale dollar that comes in.

*Ask yourself this question about the progam you are evaluating: "If all recruiting stopped today, would this company still be able to pay monthly commissions in the months ahead?"*

that "Information is priceless!" Okay, let's reluctantly give them that. But such schemes usually withhold a larger and larger portion of your income to qualify you in subsequent stages, or cycles, and these funds are allegedly for the purchase of a live seminar on some Caribbean island. At the top stage you might end up paying as much as $100,000 for a seven day seminar in Belieze. It better be catered.

A few companies today still offer product vouchers or certificates that can be spent on items out of a catalog or from various local merchants. They are only offering the funds to purchase these products. There is usually a commission paid once the

distributor training, which several are doing as of this writing, this creates a legal vulnerability. You can't mark up a product brochure, distributor manual or distributor training course, and resell it to someone who's not a distributor. Obviously, you would never have purchased any of these items if you weren't a distributor yourself. These are sources of income that can only be derived from recruiting because recruits are the only ones that would ever purchase them.

So don't just ask if there is a product involved. Question whether the product is even close to being worth the overall price paid. You don't have to be an economics genius to

In a Ponzi scheme, you pay X to the promoter who promises that you will receive a certain specific return, say 2X (twice your investment) back in a few days. The promoter accomplishes this by finding another person who will buy into the same promise, then uses the second person's investment to pay off the first's.

As an example, let's use Carlo Ponzi himself. Back in the early 1920s, Ponzi offered a $1,500 return on a $1,000 investment. When person A paid him $1,000, he then hustled person B to believe the same pitch and invest another $1,000, then took $500 from Bs money to add to As original investment, and paid A back his $1,500! Of course, a modest "service charge" was retained by Ponzi. With only $500 of Bs investment still in hand, Ponzi now needed to find person C so he'd have another $1,000 to add to the $500 he already had, and then pay person B his promised $1,500. Now, he had to find yet two more persons to have the funds to pay off person C, and so on.

Even though Ponzi accumulated millions, he died a penniless ex-con. Ask yourself this question about the program you are evaluating: "If all recruiting stopped today, would this company still be able to pay monthly commissions in the months ahead?" Although there may be no pyramidal hierarchy involved, a Ponzi Scheme does involve the need for a never ending flow of new participants making the initial investment. This also falls, once again, on the value of the products. If not one new person is ever again enrolled as a distributor, could sales volume realistically continue to move through the organization?

But there's more to consider. Let's say a company has great products that people love and would continue to purchase even if they didn't make money. However, for every wholesale dollar they pay to the company, the company pays $1.05 back to the distributor force in commissions and bonuses. In other words, their compensation plan has a 105% payout! Technically, if they really did pay out more than 100%, this would be a Ponzi Scheme. The company must sell one more product to be able to cover the compensation for the previous sales, otherwise, they would be 5 cents short. And there are a number of MLM deals today that claim to have such exorbitant payouts. In reality, they most likely do not. Probably not even close. For example, one MLM program claims a 112% payout, but the percentage is based on the point value of each product (called BV, or Bonus Value), not on the actual dollar amount--and the BVs average about 68% of wholesale dollars. Another company promotes a 109% payout, but usually forgets to mention their 75% BV ratio, and the fact that the 60% they pay on the first two levels (15% and 45% respectively) is only on the first $300 purchased by each distributor during the month. They pay 5% on all the volume over that. Yet another company claims a payout that actually exceeds 200%! The catch is, they pay a higher percentage on those you personally sponsor, and the payout they display in their ads is

"Investment" Schemes. The three regulatory agencies we need to be concerned with the most, from an MLM opportunity standpoint, are the Federal Trade Commission (FTC), Food & Drug Administration (FDA), and the often under considered Securities & Exchange Commission (SEC). From a personal, independent contractor standpoint, you have the IRS to worry about as well. But that's another article. You'll likely never have to contend with either the FBI or FCC--unless, of course, that "sense of well being" you get from your herbal product is derived from a South American poppy, or you enroll Howard Stern as a distributor.

Getting back to the SEC... "Securities" are basically things you

> *I'm curious as to why these companies would want to even create the illusion that they are paying out more than 100%. Why would they even want to pretend they are a Ponzi Scheme?*

based on the absurd scenario that every single person in your downline is personally sponsored.

So, just because someone says they pay out more than they take in (over 100%), doesn't necessarily mean they are running a Ponzi Scheme. There's very likely a catch. Still, considering state and federal regulator's penchant for taking on a guilty until proven innocent attitude (they attack first and ask questions later). I'm curious as to why these companies would want to even create the illusion that they are paying out more than 100%. Why would they even want to pretend they are a Ponzi Scheme?

Last, but not least, let's discuss

invest money in, such as stocks, bonds, mutual funds, commodities, etc. You have to register the securities you sell with the SEC and you have to have a license to sell them. Skip either step and you might be going away for a while.

In 1946, as part of the SEC vs. W.J. Howey Co. decision, the Supreme Court defined an investment contract as one where "the scheme involves an investment in a common enterprise with profits to come solely from the efforts of others." (The word "scheme" is used here and throughout this paragraph, in a basic, non-derogatory sense). There are three things to consider: First, is there money being paid into the scheme (an investment?) Second, are there other people paying money into the same scheme (a common enterprise?) Note that, so far, every MLM operation appears to meet the first two criteria. But the third test is where we depart, or should depart, from a security. Is the money you

legal action against such schemes because they have a 100% failure rate all on there own! In fact, when the SEC gets involved it's usually due to a pyramid scheme allegation and, a pyramid scheme could also be considered an unregistered security!

*Personally, I believe we, as adults, should be allowed to do whatever we want with our own money as long as there is full disclosure and we are made aware of all the risks involved. We're spending the half our government allows us to keep. It's our money!*

make from the scheme derived solely from the efforts of others? I don't know about you, but I work my tail off about 50 hours a week building and managing my downline! Sure, your time investment ideally forms a bell shaped curve (part-time, full-time, eventually back to part-time), but there should always be a mandatory effort on your part to build, manage and support your organization.

This, of course, does not bode well for schemes (I'm using the negative connotation now) where you pay a "downline building service" to build your downline. It appears to be undebatable that all three aspects of the "Howey Test" apply to such a deal. You pay money to the same promoter, such as others with their promise to do all the work for you while sitting back and cashing the checks. There has not been a lot of

In closing, I want to make it clear that this article is not necessarily based on the author's opinion of the way it should be. Much of this discussion is based on years of precedent, not just my layman's interpretation of the law. For the record, I am a Libertarian. Personally, I believe we, as adults, should be allowed to do whatever we want with our own money as long as there is full disclosure and we are made aware of all the risks involved. We're spending the half our government allows us to keep. It's our money! In fact, I'll go so far as to say I personally feel pyramid schemes should be legal. Not providing full disclosure about the risks and not being truthful about potential benefits should be against the law. If all this information is provided, then we should have the right to be stupid with our own money. Having said that, rules are rules. Until someone

changes them, we've got to play by them. My soap box is cracking. I'll step down now.

*Leonard Clements has concentrated his full time efforts over the last eight years on researching and analyzing all aspects of network marketing. He is a professional speaker and trainer, and currently conducts Inside Network Marketing seminars throughout the U.S., Canada and Mexico. He is also the publisher of the "MarketWave Alert" letter, an MLM analysis and watchdog newsletter. Mr. Clements is the host of "Inside Network Marketing," a weekly live call-in radio show on KSCL 1080, and he is the author of the controversial book, "Inside Network Marketing," an objective, no-holds-barred, insider's look at the MLM industry. He is also the author of the best-selling cassette tape, "Case Closed! The whole Truth About Network Marketing," which has been labeled "the best" generic recruiting tape by six MLM company presidents.*

*Mr. Clements has been involved in the MLM industry for 19 years and is a successful distributor for a prominent MLM program (which is never mentioned in either the book or the cassette tape).*

*To receive additional information about MarketWave and it's products, please call (800) 688-4766, or write to MarketWave, 7342 North Ivanhoe Avenue, Fresno, CA 93722. ∎*

# What would you pay to get a new distributor?

# GENERIC NETWORK MARKETING RECRUITING TAPE

Alan Rothman, radio talk show host and syndicated industry columnist.

**60 minute radio talk show format with well-known guests, makes an ideal hand-out. Works for <u>any</u> distributor in <u>any</u> Network Marketing Company.**

- Relevant subject matter discussed by the host and guest
- Expert testimonials
- Interaction between call-ins
- This tape lends greater credibility to your organization
- A customized tape, with distributors' own phone number given out by the host enhances your distributors' successful image

## Benefits:

- Encourages potential distributors to contact the person who gave them the tape
- Phone number given out 6-8 times during the show
- Promotes positive industry image
- Tape is customized for company or its distributors

## Powerful Interviews And Testimonials That Convey A Positive Industry Image And Help You Build Your Organization

### • First Of A Series •

**Call Now For Your Free Sample Tape**
**323-937-0915**

Alan Rothman hosting the show, "Secrets To Creating Wealth From Home".

## Alan Rothman is a Syndicated Columnist for:

- Entrepreneur Magazine
- Spare Time Magazine
- Home Business Journal
- Success Magazine
- Inspire Magazine
- Advantage Networker
- His column also appears weekly on America Online website (Secrets of MLM).

## His Guest and Celebrity Interviews Include:

- GENERAL COLIN POWELL
- BILL GATES
- BRIAN TRACY
- ZIG ZIGLAR
- PAM LONTOS
- DR. LAURA SCHLESSINGER
- STEPHEN CANNELL
- JAY LENO
- PETER LOWE
- EDDIE ALBERT

## Another Tool to Fast Track Your Business by VHS Direct.

*Secrets To...*

As Seen On T.V.!
**CREATING WEALTH FROM HOME**

**Contact:** Radio Talk Show Division
# 800-665-0286

**VHS DIRECT, INC., DEPT. 777**
5814 W. Pico Blvd. Los Angeles, CA 90019
Tel: 323 937-0915 Fax: 323 937-0917
© 1999 VHS Direct All Rights Reserved.

*People are always blaming their circumstances for what they are. I don't believe in circumstances. The people who get on in this world are the people who get up and look for the circumstances they want, and if they can't find them, they make them.*

**George Bernard Shaw, Mrs. Warren's Profession, 1893, Act ll**

Still the #1 Selling Video for Network Marketing

Over 200,000 Satisfied Customers

$9.95
per copy
or as low as
$3.95
per copy

For details call 1-888-484-7826 or visit our website.

www.ItsAboutTime.net

*"It's About Time" is distributed by the i.V Group. Please reference #300.*

# PIN THIS UP

## Workplace of the Future

Looking forward to the next 100 years? The future wave favors people who take care of people, people who work with computers and people who take care of those computers. The new millennium will shift the world economy from one balanced on workers' backs to one balanced on workers' minds. But don't expect change overnight. As the shift becomes more prevalent toward home business, plan on a 50 hour work week or more if you fall in this category. Former Labor Secretary Robert Reich, now writing a book called "The Work of the Future," says that the proliferation of alternative workplaces will continue as more people work from home, share "virtual teams" and lease desks instead of maintaining a corporate office. Such concepts as "corporate hotels," where people from various companies set up temporary shop, will become more prevalent.

## SHAKLEE'S PHILOSOPHY LIVES ON AROUND THE WORLD

Dr. Forrest C. Shaklee, Sr. came out of the heart of America, born in 1894 on a farm in Carlisle, Iowa. He gave America his heart, his mind and a philosophy that still inspires the lives of millions. Through his philosophy, his life and the company he founded, he changed lives, health and the fortunes of people throughout the world.

## A CHANCE MEETING

Amway's co-founders, Rich Devos and Jay Van Andel met when both were sudents at Grand Rapids Christian School in Michigan. While it was a business arrangement that brought the pair together; DeVos paid Van Andel a quarter each week for rides to and from school. Early on, they agreed to start a company of their own. In 1959, they founded Amway. The rest is history! In 1998, Amway generated sales of more than $7 billion.

## HOMEMAKERS REJOICE

Homemaker's Idea Company President Madolyn Johnson, said she founded her company so other women could have the choice of gaining the flexibility and extra income of their own business while raising a family. "The value of family and the belief that the home is the core of family life have created a common company focus," she said. "Everything revolves around the home...our products are designed for the home, sold in the home, by homemakers to other homemakers. Through our products and our people, we are making a difference and raising the level of dignity in the word 'homemaker,'" she reasoned.

## IN THE BEGINNING

Ever wonder how The West Bend Company got its start? In 1911, seven men formed the West Bend Aluminum Company to produce aluminum pie plates, ladles and cups. Their first manufacturing facility was an old button factory located on the west bend of Milwaukee River. By 1920, the company developed the "waterless cooker," making West Bend a household word. Today, the company not only is a leader in stainless steel cookware but also a top ranked small electrical appliance manufacturer.

## IT'S ALL IN THE NAME

Your company has the capacity to be a powerful, nationally recognized brand represented by a family of products. And distributors can exploit that power on the local level. By establishing your corporate "brand," connecting your distributors to it with integrated selling and marketing tools, and providing strong distributor communications and public relations from the corporate and at the local level, you can tap into your full marketing potential.

A brand name can be a powerful thing. Even though direct selling is built upon a principal of independence, distributor success can increase exponentially when he or she is supported by a consistent corporate vision portrayed by the image of the company and its products. That connection -- if it's strong -- will represent quality and trustworthiness to distributors, their prospects and customers. Matt Allen, Signature Media.

## AROUND THE WORLD

Rex Maughan, founder of Forever Living Products, a growing billion dollar world empire, focuses his thoughts and energy on bolstering healthy lifestyles and savings accounts alike. "My goal is to help people in every country around the world to have better health and more money and time to enjoy it," Maughan said. He's well on his way. Now in its 20th year, the Scottsdale, Arizona-based company, named the number one privately held business in Arizona the past three years by Arthur Anderson's rankings, boasts five million distributors in 65 countries.

## NO ROCKING CHAIR FOR DORIS WOOD

By 1996, Doris Wood, founder of the Multi-Level Marketing Industry Association (MLMIA), completed her fourth decade of service on behalf of the network marketing industry. Starting as a distributor, Doris moved on as director of training and vice president of sales for several companies, owned two MLM firms and served as speaker, writer and consultant on six continents. The lady has touched all the bases and one would conclude is ready for the rocking chair or planing a well deserved trip around the world.

Hold on! Like one of the books she authored, *"We've Only Just Begun,"* Doris continues to motor at full speed. What is her motivation to continue the good fight? Let Doris tell it like it is: "Although I've never been adverse to money, it wasn't what motivated me," she explains. "It's the people," she exclaims! "Helping, guiding and watching people be able to put their children through college or purchasing their homes. Seeing people have the freedom to become whatever they want to be. And I want to complete my mission, which is to strengthen and help network marketing grow around the world." Throw away the rocking chair and tear up the travel itinerary!

## FOR HEAVEN'S SAKE!

Celebrated business consultant Sandi Donaldson-Shenoha has launched a newsletter called "Heaven's Downline," designed to "inform the nucleus of Christians so considerable in our industry." Sandi says that effective consulting consists of strengthening mutual trust between companies and their distributors. "People in the office may not understand the ups and downs of life in the field and trenches, while distributors must appreciate the complexity of the corporation," she points out. Thus her bottom line: "A skilled business consultant is a master troubleshooter; one who not only spots weaknesses, but also roots out causes and expedites the return of sound corporate health. Corrections are like remodeling a house," she continues, "you need additions, upgrades, rearrangements, sometimes even removals and re-starts that save companies thousands of dollars."

## STOP HIDING!

Julius Yardley, consultant to business leaders the world over, recently completed a six month study on chief executives of the network marketing industry and came away with cogent advice for industry leaders: "Come out of hiding and communicate with those who have something important to suggest, contibute or recommend," Yardley admonishes. "This industry is in a class by itself. They have built in 'fortress mentality' -- one might call it paranoia. Why all the secrecy? It baffles me! I placed two calls to each of 10 companies and only one contacted bothered to display the common courtesy of a return. Wake up guys; especially those with failing marks in public relations."

## MCDONALD ADDS TO TROPHY CASE

RACHAeL International's President and Chairman of the Board, Gary McDonald has not only led companies to success, but also the Direct selling Industry. One of the founders and executive vice presidents of Tupperware, he was also instrumental in bringing the entire DSA into the limelight of positive public recognition. McDonald was twice chairman of the board of the DSA, bringing about the "Code of Ethics" for the industry. He was the youngest ever to receive the DSA's highest honor -- induction into its Hall of Fame. This honor has been accorded to less than 50 people in the nearly 100 years of existence of the association. McDonald can now add another laurel to his trophy case, he is one of nine honorees inducted into the Hall of Fame in this edition of the Global Home Based Business Directory.

## FASTEST GROWING OCCUPATIONS

In the following order, futurists have completed their list of the fastest growing occupations in our new millennium: (1) Desktop publishing (2) Computer support specialists (3) Database administrators (4) Personal and home care aids (5) Occupational therapy assistants and aids (6) Physical and corrective therapy assistants (7) Home health aids (8) Human service workers. Take a close look. The aging of America is at hand.

## CLEAN LIVING PAYS OFF

Vern Soper, a principal with Marketing Solutions, Inc., publishers of the book you are reading, credits bowling, deer hunting, long walks, lifting weights and a possitive attitude for a life that has spanned 94 years. "If you can get out of bed in the morning and walk to the breakfast table, you have no right to complain," Soper was quoted as saying. "My only concern now is how I'm going to spend the next half of my life," the transplanted Idaho native mused.

## WHAT IS YOGA

As the instructors arewont to repeat, yoga is not an exercise. The goal of this 4,000-year-old discipline is to heal. It goes about doing this by putting the body through a series of intense anaerobic postures. These can be quite taxing, but they're not designed to pummel the body the way, say, training for a marathon does. Most of the postures require strength and balance with a meiative focus that calms the nerves. Balance, relaxation, reduction of pain in the spine or the joints--such things yoga is assuredly capable of delivering. True believers are also convinced that a good yoga session has a beneficial effect on every organ, from the spleen to the liver.

File Edit Special

## AVON LEADS THE WAY

Avon has more women in management positions (86%) than any other Fortune 500 company. Seventeen of the company's 54 officers (32%) are women and six sit on the board of directors. Women in top executive positions at Avon include Andrea Jung, president and chief operation officer and Susan Kropf, president, Avon North America.

Indeed, since 1885, 34 years before winning the right to vote, women have sold Avon products across the United States. Avon's Women of Enterprise Awards program, created in 1987 in conjunction with the Small Business Administration, annually recognizes six women entrepreneurs for extraordinary business success.

Opportunity has its rewards

*A business plan built for two... we love it!*

**The opportunity to build your own business can be rewarding in different ways to different people.**

You set the goals, go your own pace, schedule your own time, and determine what you want in return. You can market as many, or as few, product lines as you choose — from personal care products to popular brand-name catalog merchandise. More than 3 million entrepreneurs in some 80 countries and territories have found this business opportunity made possible only through Amway is worth a closer look. See for yourself. Perhaps *you* can discover the rewards you've been seeking.

**The Business Opportunity Company**™

If you'd like to know more, call for a free brochure at **1-800-544-7167** or visit our website at **www.amway.com**     © 1998 Amway Corporation
In Canada call **1-800-922-6929**.

# REACH MILLIONS OF READERS

## FREE Publicity        FREE Publicity

### FOR ALL

### NETWORK MARKETING AND DIRECT SELLING COMPANIES

### SEND US YOUR

PRESS RELEASES, NEWS ARTICLES, NEW PRODUCT ANNOUNCEMENTS, SPECIAL EVENTS, CONFERENCES, CHANGE OF ADDRESS, AND ALL OTHER PUBLIC INFORMATION YOU WANT PUBLISHED IN THE

# THE GLOBAL HOME BASED BUSINESS DIRECTORY

Please Send Correspondence to:

Marketing Solutions, Inc., 27442 Burgstaler Road, Aitkin, MN 56431
Attention: Publicity Department

---

# Check Us Out!

Visit Our Web Site: ghbbd.com for ordering information and current news about our Global Home Based Business Directory and the many web sites and newstand locations where our directory can be purchased. For volume discount orders or personalized promotion projects, please call (800) 496-0277.

## Several Web Sites Where Our GHBBD Can Be Purchased

amazon.com

barnesandnoble.com

borders.com

2 millionbooks.com

booksnow.com

chapters.ca

buy.com

BookLand

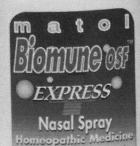

# This Page Has
# No Business In
# This Directory
## It Belongs In TheMail
## Don't Delay!
## Start Your Future Today

# Two ways to turn the lights on

## PRESENTATIONS ON:
Future Trends for Home Business
Grow Your Business Strategically!
How to be Nice and Assertive
How to Live with Your Business
The Skills of Change Masters
The Joy of Coaching
Beating Burnout

Peter McGugan is on the advisory board of two fast growth companies and his client list includes Monsanto, Southwest Airlines, Marriott, Kodak and Creative Memories. He's a direct selling veteran, best-selling author, psychologist, trend tracker and strategic growth coach. Meeting planners have rated him among the top ten professional speakers in America. His articles have appeared in more than 30 national magazines and he's been featured on many national talk shows.

## For Solutions call (760) 320-8888
## www.petermcgugan.com

# Network Marketing Companies Must Use a Strong Marketing Strategy to Ensure Success of Promotional Tactics

*Matt Allen*

appears to be the most expedient "answer" to the marketing "problem." A new video, a new product, expansion into a new market, even looking at a public offering are on the list of "marketing answers" and a means for quick infusion of capital. All of these "solutions" can end up costing far more than they profit the company.

It's time for the industry to move past the arbitrary "trial and error" method of testing marketing ideas. It's time for comprehensive marketing strategy.

Direct sellers have achieved success by taking business strategies from the corporate world and making them their own, while leaving behind the hindrances of the time-for-money equation. Developing a comprehensive marketing strategy a corporate method that is well worth adopting.

It used to be that a direct sales company started with an idea, some strong products and dynamic people to build the business and sell product. Although this remains a critical portion of the equation, an increasingly competitive environment, regulation issues and distributor retention are leaving direct selling companies seeking methods to distinguish themselves from the pack.

MLMs have depended upon distributors to set the tone for their businesses. With products and compensation plan in hand, the image of the company has by default been shaped by those business builders, for better or worse. If those first key distributors had sales expertise and marketing know-how and the company had solid products and a good compensation plan, the business probably fared well. Without this balance they are likely among those fabled network marketing failures statistics.

MLMs that have survived and prospered often find themselves searching for the latest marketing technique or business expansion opportunity. When seeking solutions, MLMs are quick to apply whatever

Ever notice how you remember a clever line in a commercial, or a certain logo? When you hear the same words and see the same image consistently, it makes an impact. You remember it. In the consumer's mind this consistency adds up to the difference between McDonald's and say, Mac's Drive Inn. When you need to eat quickly, one is a known and trusted source, and the other is not worth the risk. That difference in image is the product of a carefully designed, well managed, thoughtfully implemented corporate marketing

▶

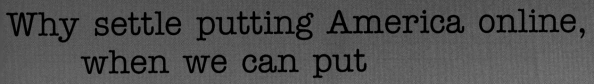

strategy. The strategy leads the targeted consumer to top-of-the-mind awareness of the brand. The results of the strategy in action provide a certain feel or personality. In short, a clear market positioning of the company and/or its products or services.

But have no fear. You don't need millions of dollars to spend on advertising frequency to achieve impact and build trust with your potential distributors and customers. In fact, more so than the corporate giants with colossal ad budgets, MLMs need to get the most mileage out of every dollar they spend on any marketing effort. Beginning with the plan helps to give you that maximum mileage. A comprehensive marketing strategy supported by the correct marketing mix for your company and its products requires careful research, thoughtful planning and strategic implementation. When a company commits to this level of planning, it will achieve a marketing mix that will result in a clear and consistent corporate image and distinction for its products in the marketplace.

This process, determining what position you want to achieve in the marketplace and how you will get there, is committing to a journey that will lead to success. Without this road map, not only will you waste valuable time and money taking detours to ineffective "answers" to your marketing challenges, but you will also increase frustration among your team and cause confusion and poor morale to develop among your distributors, because they won't know where you're headed either.

Many times companies begin with what they think is a solution, only to find that the tactic didn't work. It didn't achieve the desired result. Don't blame it on the thing. Blame it on starting with a tactic and not with

a plan. *Your tactics must have proper foundation in a plan to truly meet the marketing challenge.*

Although each one needs to have foundation in a well-developed strategy to leverage for success, that strategy *may* lead to consideration of some of the following tactics:

## It's All In The Name

Your company has the capacity to be a powerful, nationally recognized brand represented by a family of products. And distributors can exploit that power on the local level. By establishing your corporate "brand," connecting your distributors to it with integrated selling and marketing tools, and providing strong distributor communications and public relations from the corporate and at the local level, you can tap into your full marketing potential.

A brand name can be a powerful thing. Even though direct selling is built upon a principal of independence, distributor success can increase exponentially when he or she is supported by a consistent corporate vision portrayed by the image of the company and its products. That connection, if it's strong, will represent quality and trustworthiness to distributors, their prospects and customers.

## Logo Development And Package Design Help You Introduce Yourself

We all know that first impressions are important. Your business logo and the design of your product labeling are an introduction; a handshake and hello to your many audiences: prospects, customers, investors, corporate and civic neighbors, and even regulators. What image are you conveying in that handshake? Is it a firm and intriguing welcome, or the dreaded wet fish?

## Corporate Messages Articulated With Consistency

Whether promoting individual products or communicating your value to prospective investors, corporate messages can be a potent tool. Your collateral material: product catalogs, the company background piece, even annual reports and other presentations of your business are critical messages to be communicated with consistency.

## Distributor Selling Tools--It's Your Image Coming And Going

Distributor Business Builder Kits are oftentimes the new recruit's first comprehensive look at your company, or their last. What are you communicating about the value of your business? The potential of the opportunity? The uniqueness of your products? High quality distributor tools can train, educate and increase the effectiveness of your entire team.

Distributors have relationships with approximately 200 people. These are the people in their sphere of influence. For them to be most influential with their contacts, they need tools that help them present the products clearly and professionally, in a non-confrontational manner.

Many companies provide distributors with only one prospecting tool. This can actually limit distributor performance because their prospects, like all of us, know that people make decisions based on timing in their lives. A "no" today may be a "yes" next month if a new set of information is presented in a compelling way. With an array of prospecting tools presented through a variety of media, you can make sure that you're connecting with the widest audience. You give your distributors choices of the tools that will work best for them and their prospects. With a set of tools that is presented over time, each tool can highlight one of the many great benefits of joining your company.

Of course there are options beyond one more brochure. It's important to acknowledge that the printed page is not always the best way to communicate. Conveying your message with the latest computer and film technology, or pocket size audios, can help your distributors connect with their prospects when time is of the essence.

## Exploit The Power Of The Implied Third-Party With Public Relations

An implied third-party endorsement of your company or its products by the news or trade media is an achievement that can tremendously enhance the results of your marketing efforts. With public relations, you can help exploit the huge marketing potential of this often overlooked communications discipline.

PR is not as simple as "putting a positive spin on it" or "taking cover." It's about skillfully controlling and managing the delivery of your carefully shaped message. Through proactive public relations, you can build relationships with key members of the media, deliver stories that interest them and generate "great ink" for your company.

## New Media Services-- Technology That Works

In today's competitive market, it's essential for a company to tap the resources of technology. A company can use the strengths of the Internet, CD-ROM technology, and corporate Intranets to strengthen its position and unity.

Also, it is generally accepted that on-line commerce has become a necessity for market leaders and should be a vital part of any marketing strategy.

## Get The Word Out With Advertising

Yes, direct selling is a word-of-mouth business. But what words and whose mouth? You can help strengthen your corporate identity and message through a strategic advertising program which supports that strong corporate image. Putting your ads in the right place is critical. When your message is in the right place, you reinforce it with those who need to hear it, because it really doesn't matter how clear your message is if the wrong people hear it.

## Image Really Is Everything--Handle It With Care

Your image is made up of all the things that represent you, from how your distributors present your business and the tools they use to do it, to the form the new recruit uses to join up. It's also what is or isn't being said about you in the consumer and trade media. It's your logo and packaging. It's everything with your name in it or on it. It's your brand.

Is your image clear and consistent or muddled and confused? Chances are if it's not a product of a well-designed, strategically implemented marketing plan, it's the latter.

People like to be associated with a company that has a good image. If your image is an accurate reflection of what your company is all about, communicating the vision, the benefits, the possibilities powerfully, it will actually help you target and keep the most likely candidates for

business builders that will take you to the next level of success. The image you create and set at the corporate level will position your company with your various audiences--your distributors, your employees, your investors and your corporate and government neighbors. Does your corporate position help your organization link to success, or are there always some missing connections?

You can maximize the return on important business building investments with help from marketing and communication professionals. Thoughtful planning and skillful implementation will provide long-term returns by helping to leverage your distributors for maximum results.

Signature Media Services can lead you to marketing solutions that will work for your distributors today, and will truly help your company link to success for the next level of your business growth.

*Matt Allen has over 15 years experience in sales and marketing and has consulted with many of the fastest growing companies in the industry. He is director of MLM sales for Signature Media Services, Inc., a marketing and communications firm specializing in meeting the unique needs of the direct selling industry with success-driven solutions. Services include comprehensive creative and marketing strategy, professional distributor tools, training and personal development, web site and CD-ROM development and public relations. You can reach Allen at (800) 587-6528, ext. 157.* ■

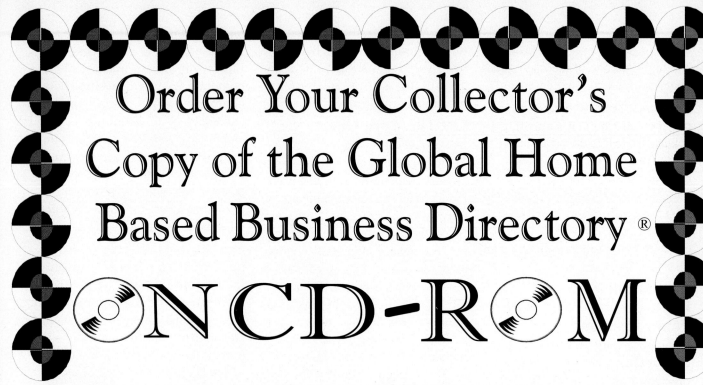

# Order Your Collector's Copy of the Global Home Based Business Directory ®
## ON CD-ROM

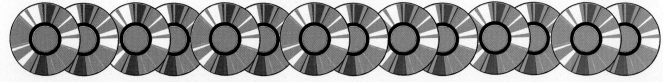

# Net Relations: A Fusion of Direct Marketing and Public Relations

*Mike Spataro*

Today, a company cannot afford to ignore the Web as an integral component of its business. The Web is quickly joining broadcast and print media as an indispensable media platform for delivering marketing messages to target audiences.

The rapid growth of the Web has led to a new marketing communications discipline referred to as "Net Relations" the intersection of traditional marketing, public relations and the Internet. Net Relations is a new set of communications skills and services that capitalize on the global reach, instantaneous communications and functionality of the Web to reach target audiences. As a result, companies have to understand this new area of communications to exploit the tremendous marketing muscle of the on-line world.

Net Relations has blurred the line between marketing and public relations by offering companies a new suite of interactive services to reach targeted buyers. New Web savvy marketers are using on-line events and promotions, live chat, multimedia product announcements, Web site advertising, on-line media and a host of other new marketing and public relations services to help grow their businesses. The best companies now realize that the Web is an essential part of their marketing mix.

Net Relations is a fusion of marketing and public relations. It combines direct marketing and public relations to deliver messages directly to the audience as well as using on-line writers to reach audiences by delivering information directly to them or by attracting them to Web sites where that information resides.

## Internet Growth

The Web is the most dynamic communications platform to come along since the invention of television. Now accessed by over 100 million worldwide, it's no wonder that a new industry is evolving to address this huge and growing new generation of Web surfers.

Driven by declining prices for PCs, greater use of the Internet and accelerating adoption of on-line commerce by every size company, the Internet posted incredible gains in 1998 in terms of consumer usage, on-line advertising and electronic commerce. The Web is nearing mass market status, according to many who follow the industry.

## Business on the Internet

Net Relations can be extremely important in helping draw target audiences to the information, products and services on a company's or an organization's Web site. Today, more and more companies have Web sites, and it is estimated more than 40 million pages of information are now up on the Web. Sites are being used in a variety of ways, including presenting important information about a company and its products; direct selling of goods and services and as a delivery channel for software and information products. To cut through the clutter, companies need help in raising on-line attention and awareness of their products and services.

Some forward thinking companies have already built on-line marketing departments. Cisco, a leader in e-commerce, has Internet sales in excess of $1 billion. On-line stock trading by small investors is one of the hottest growth markets, as well as Internet telephony. Everywhere you turn the Web is revolutionizing business. The public relations disciplines are not immune to these changes and are being heavily impacted by this electronic revolution.

## Media Relations Changing

There is an increasing number of people who click onto the Web to get their daily news and information. This trend has been at the expense of traditional news media. The latest media statistics show a 13 percent decline in TV viewing over the past two years.

Readership of weekly news magazines is down 8 percent and newspapers have lost 5 percent of their audience.

Net Relations uses the Web to deliver marketing or branding

messages to a focused audience. This can be accomplished by communicating with the growing contingent of journalists who write the news, features and reviews that appear on news delivery sites. Net Relations can also help a company communicate directly with its customers by delivering information directly to them or by attracting them to Web sites where that information resides.

## What Should a Company Do?

A few years ago, companies didn't even have to consider how to include the Web in their marketing strategy. Today, it is the fastest growing component of the industry. Virtually every smart company is demanding an Internet strategy. As in any new opportunity, there is a great deal of confusion about how companies should use the Internet to further their marketing and public relations goals. These are the six critical steps companies must take toward implementing an effective Net Relations program:
(1) Learn the language of the Web
(2) Research your target audiences on the Web
(3) Understand the services available
(4) Create a focused plan
(5) Hire Web savvy professionals
(6) Prepare for the future

## Learn the Language of the Web

Net Relations incorporates many aspects that use the language of traditional direct marketing and public relations. However, there are technological components for which there's a new language that people have to learn. Search engines, user groups, meta tags, banners, key words, streaming video, applets, hyperlinks, spiders, intelligent agents, live chat, list servers. The list goes on and on.

The importance of knowing the language of the Web cannot be underestimated. Every day another company is offering another Web marketing service. Unless a Web marketing professional is able to efficiently analyze and evaluate all of the services that are coming in what seems like an endless barrage, it will be impossible to lend the type of focus that is necessary for success in your Internet marketing effort. The only way to sort out the wheat from the chaff is by knowing the language of the Web.

Learning the new Web technology language does not mean you have to become a Web geek to master how to take advantage of the strengths of the Internet. The vastness of the Web often confuses companies from a marketing standpoint, but if you don't use it to your competitive advantage, be prepared, because your competition surely is or will very soon.

## Research Target Audiences

Like any good media relations plan, you have to target editors who are most interested in the company's business strategy, management and product lines. All editors are responsive to news that they think their audience will want to read. What separates on-line journalism from traditional print media is immediacy and unlimited space. Most Web publishers operate their sites like on-line wire services; their print editions may be published weekly or monthly, but on-line are updated several times a day. That means more stories and more opportunities for coverage. And, with the Web, global communications takes on a new definition. Your message is instaneously communicated throughout the world.

The Web is fragmenting and segmenting so much that there are now places where you could represent your client or your company and completely bypass the media, going directly to places reaching audiences. Extensive analysis must be conducted to determine how a company's Web site is ranked and categorized in major search engines and Web directories. One of the many challenges is to enhance the ranking of your Web site on these well visited search engines and directories.

## Understand the Services Available

Net Relations services can run the gamut from simple e-mail pitches to on-line editors, to executing a global on-line event, promotion or contest. Savvy business executives are conducting on-line interactive chat with the press or directly with customers bypassing the media. Feeding competitive information from the Web into an organization or helping a company establish strong partnership links to other Web sites as a way to increase traffic to their sites are also elements of a strong Net Relations program.

Some companies are already conducting interactive product demos and giving on-line corporate and product presentations on their Web sites. A fully interactive virtual press room for editors and customers to visit is vastly superior to putting up a laundry list of boring press releases.

It is extremely important to understand the amount of traffic that your Web site is attracting. Marketing professionals must plan, establish, and manage effective corporate presence on the Internet. Marketing professionals must research and prioritize the keys that are important to their sites success. They must know where their competitors are ranked in the search engines and make strategic changes to keep their own pages highly visible. Their Web site must be listed with the top search engines that are capable of driving traffic to a site. It is a common mistake to blindly carpet bomb the Internet and its more than 300 search engines in hopes that something good will come of this. Focus is extremely important and effective strategy for improving search engine rankings.

### Create a Focused Plan

Every company needs a customized Internet strategy, but be prepared to change it on the fly. The Web is literally changing on a weekly basis. One company may need on-line media relations while another needs advice on how to set up a crisis communications plan on the Web and still another wants to find out what people on-line are saying about the newest products. Net Relations is not a substitute for good traditional networking and public relations, but it is a critical component to your current overall marketing plan.

A Net Relations strategy that is right for one company may not be right for another. It all depends on the overall marketing and business goal. If a company needs to encourage downloads of its new software product, it needs to emphasize getting that specific message out to the target audiences who would want to try the product. This could involve a comprehensive change in core messaging if the previous communications were emphasizing brand awareness. Fortunately, it is easy to shift Internet messaging on the fly to accommodate new campaigns and business imperatives.

### Hire Web Savvy Marketers

Companies are beginning to hire people who have Internet skills. Recent college graduates who have been using the Web for years are sometimes the best qualified to fill some of these new roles. Web savvy employees are in high demand, both in corporate public relations and marketing, and in consumer and high-tech agencies.

The Internet has reached clear viability as a marketing medium and more professionals are choosing to specialize in the field of Web marketing. However, there is still a tendency for marketers to use the techniques that worked for them in the past and to avoid anything that is new and untested. The new breed of Internet marketer must be encouraged to try things, even at the risk of making mistakes. This is the only way that a company can keep up with the incredible pace of change of the Internet. When it comes to Internet marketing, every company must be a learning organization.

### Prepare for the Future

Even though the Web is the most dynamic communications platform to come along since the invention of television, its current stage of development can be compared to where black and white TV was 50 years ago. The Web is in its infancy. Advancing computer power will only bring greater and greater functionality to the Internet. Now is the time to think of a Web site as a fully functional communications platform in which to conduct all types of strategic and tactical communications.

Webcasting will lead to multicasting as bandwidth improves and the Web becomes a multimedia wonderland. In a very short period of time, virtually every news site will look like a wire service, daily newspaper, TV and radio station all rolled into one as multimedia services improve. This will require all of us to find even more new ways to do our jobs as the role of Net Relations continues to reshape public relations.

*Mike Spataro is vice president, Net Relations at Miller/Shandwick Technologies. He heads up a dedicated team that delivers Internet PR strategies for clients from London to North America to Singapore. He can be reached at (617) 351-4147 or at msataro@miller.shandwick.com.* ■

## Lessons Of Aikido

You can't control the unexpected, but you can control your *response* to it. Practitioners of Aikido, a form of martial arts, know that they may get thrown if they resist an attacking force. So they learn to blend *with* the force and use an attacker's energy for their own advantage.

By analogy, if you resist the unexpected by sticking to the original plan, you will be "thrown" and your progress impeded. Being flexible enough to shift your direction so that you move *with* this change, rather than against it, will give you more energy and power. When you go with the flow of change, the unexpected becomes your ally, not your adversary.

# Shaklee Leader Loses Six Year Battle With Cancer

**TRIBUTE**

Dr. James H. Whittam

Shaklee President & CEO

1949-1999

Dr. James H. Whittam, president and CEO of the San Francisco-based Shaklee Corporation, died April 15, 1999, at Stanford University Hospital after a long and heroic battle with cancer. He was 49.

Both a scientist and business leader, Dr. Whittam played key roles in the operations of the domestic and international Shaklee marketing operations as well as science and technology functions. Dr. Whittam spearheaded the establishment of Yamanouchi Shaklee Pharma (YSPharma, Inc.) in 1997. Located at Stanford Research Park, YSPharma, Inc. is dedicated to the development of novel drug delivery technologies, representing the pharmaceutical division of Shaklee Corporation. His professional experience also included top management research and development positions at Proctor & Gamble, Vidal Sassoon and the Gillette Company. Successfully operating in the academic, scientific and business worlds, he was unique in the industry as the only scientist to head a major direct-selling company.

"Dr. Whittam will be remembered as an outstanding executive, an accomplished scientist and, above all, a caring person," commented Dr. Earl Cheir, Chairman of the Board of Shaklee Corporation and Dean Emeritius of Haas Business School at the University of California, Berkeley.

Born in Queens, New York, in 1949, Whittam was graduated magna cum laude from New York City College in 1972 with a bachelor's degree in chemical engineering. He taught chemistry at City University of New York (CUNY) while earning his Ph.D. there in chemistry and biochemistry in 1975. CUNY honored Dr. Whittam with the Curtman and Myton Pantzer Awards. He then went on to receive an MBA degree from Boston University of Management in 1977.

A Bay Area resident for over 20 years, Dr. Whittam served on various community boards, including the UCSF Foundation's Science Committee. He was a member of numerous professional and scientific organizations and has had his works published in scientific and trade journals. An avid runner and athlete, Dr. Whittam competed in both the Boston and New York marathons as well as numerous local races. He served as a member of the U.S. Ski Team Sports Medicine Council and as nutritional consultant to the U.S. Ski Team for eight years. Along with William L. Haskell, Ph.D., of Stanford University and the American College of Sports Medicine, he initiated one of the first academic conferences on "Nutritional Determinants in Athletic Performance."

*Competing in marathons was only one of Jim's many passions. His celebrated life came to an end when he succumbed to lung cancer on April 15, at the age of 49, leaving behind a wife, two sons and a daughter.*

Dr. Whittam is survived by his wife Sibylle, daughter Lauren, and sons Christopher and Alexandre of Hillsborough, Calif., as well as his mother, Barbara Whittam, sisters Denise Whittam, and Barbara Schechter, and brother Dennis Whittam, all from the New York area.

The family asked that contributions in his memory be made to the James H. Whittam Charitable Fund, care of Peninsula Community Foundation, 1700 South El Camino Real, Suite 300, San Mateo, California 94402.

*The great pleasure in life*
*is doing what people*
*say you cannot do.*

**Walter Bagehot, quoted by Peter Potter,**
**All About Success,**
**1988, "Challenge"**

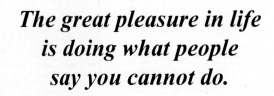

# BILL & ELAINE NUGENT'S
# PROGRAMS FOR SUCCESS

Bill & Elaine Nugent are the authors of **12 Proven Strategies & Tactics Used By The 'Secret Society' of Top MLMers** and the training cassette: "Network Marketing: Top Secrets Revealed!" Bill & Elaine Nugent's Programs For Success was featured as the "Success Story" for the March 1998 issue of **Network Marketing Connection**.

## PRESENTING THE IDEAL NETWORK MARKETING COMPANY

- We are Independent Distributors for a dynamic 3 year old company that has recently obtained the U.S. marketing rights to an amazing new natural herbal extract.. This product promotes joint health so well that after its introduction in Australia it got over 30,000 unsolicited testimonials from people thrilled with its benefits! It's also one of the few natural products backed by double-blind, placebo controlled clinical studies.
- The company has exclusive rights to market this product in the United States (contract was signed November 3, 1997). No other company will ever sell it. No "me too's"!
- The product is considerably more effective than its nearest natural rival product (glucosamine) and has no side effects like its pharmocological rivals. The active ingredient is extracted using a technological process that's virtually impossible to duplicate. The bottom line is it's NOT DUPLICATABLE and has NO COMPETITION! It's like having a patent on Vitamin C!!!
- In addition to the new product, the company has a whole line of highly effective nutritional supplements developed by Dr. Earl Mindell, author of *The Vitamin Bible* and a host of other up-to-the-minute books on nutrition.
- The product line also includes Linda Chae's skin care products. These are the world's first and foremost line of organic skin care products.
- The compensation plan is generous and balanced.
- Products are value priced. These products are the best values in the industry when compared milligram for milligram. We love to do price comparisons!
- In this company you have outstanding products that outshine the competition - backed by world renowned researchers and outstanding company management. It's the closest thing we've found to the ideal network marketing company!

We project that our company and its new product will soon be household names all across America. Will you have your distributorship up and running when this happens? Come join us and let's do it together! For a FREE VIDEO & info pack leave your name, address and phone number at **1-888-572-3671.** Also check out our Fax-on-Demand at **1-888-291-8520, Extension #001** and visit our web page at http://members.aol.com/b1e1nugent. You can E-mail us at b1e1nugent@aol.com (the number "1" and not the letter "L" follows the b and the e) or you can write to us at P.O. Box 1316, New Rochelle, NY 10802-1316.

## TRAINING AND SUPPORT

- We offer a wide array of training and support programs for **all types** of serious networkers.
- We are in direct partnership with the man that the September 1997 issue of *Success* magazine said "has arguably made more millionaires than any one network marketer in the world."
- Are you a sales type? We'll teach you how to be successful with one-on-one personal recruiting methods, recruiting over the phone, three ways etc.
- Are you a bookworm? We'll teach you how to build a huge organization through the mail and other mass marketing techniques.
- Do you like to work with health professionals? We'll train you how to recruit rheumatologists, chiropractors, nutritionists and other health professionals. We anticipate that thousands of health practitioners will be joining our organization soon. The question is: how many of them will be in your organization? The time to act is now! (To get our free info pack see above)

## HOW TO OBTAIN OUR MANUAL & CASSETTE

To obtain our manual **12 Proven Strategies & Tactics Used By The 'Secret Society' Of Top MLMers** and the cassette tape "Network Marketing: Top Secrets Revealed!" send $19.95 plus $3.50 for shipping and handling (Total $23.45. New York State residents please add appropriate sales tax) by cashier's check or money order payable to Bill & Elaine Nugent, P.O. Box 1316, Dept. INMD, New Rochelle, NY 10802-1316. We use Priority Mail. (To obtain the cassette tape only just send $2.00 cash or money order.) Or call our 24 hour, 7 day order line at **1-888-217-6493.** We accept MC, Visa, Discover, AmEx (Your credit card statement will show a charge from the Research Institute, New Rochelle, NY).

*"And God said, Behold, I have given you every herb bearing seed, which is upon the face of all the earth, and every tree, in which is the fruit of a tree yielding seed; to you it shall be for meat."*
*Genesis 1:29*

# Portrait of Courage
## Enviro-Tech's Dian Hodge Motivates Others While Overcoming Personal Odds

*Edie Jeffers*

According to Dian Hodge, network marketing is about overcoming obstacles. "It's not only about goal setting and achievement, but about finding a person's needs and satisfying them," says the Vice President of Personal Care for Enviro-Tech International (ETI). "I believe in encouraging people where they are. If their goal is to be able to buy a new sofa, sit down on that sofa and go no further, I'm happy to help them do that. If a person wants to pay off all of their debt and never have to work for someone else again, I'm also happy to help them do that." Dian believes it all boils down to a personal decision: "Whenever I'm speaking, I always say, 'The difference between I can and I can't is an apostrophe T.'"

Even when challenged with recent life-threatening circumstances, Dian held to this belief.

Her understanding of the power of self-confidence began at a young age. When she was seven-years-old, one of Dian's chores was to help her mother hang the sheets on the clothesline. "When I grow up, I'm going to have someone else do this for me," she told her mother. Perhaps without knowing it, she set an important goal for herself.

At age 15, young Dian already stood nearly six feet tall and was the subject of much adolescent teasing. "The boys used to make fun of me. They called me 'giraffe,'" says the Chattanooga, Tennessee native.

But the final joke was, as they say, on them.

### From Behind the Counter to The Runway

While working behind the counter of the hometown ice cream parlor, the teenager was asked to be in a TV commercial for the store, Kay's Kastle. After getting a little airtime under her belt, more doors began to open for Dian. A local department store saw the commercial and wanted her to model for them. "Then the boys who used to make fun of me and were much shorter tried to get dates with me!" she mused.

Dian became a runway model, and made $15 for a few hours of work. "This was big money back then." Within a few years, her modeling would take her around the country on tours for department stores. "I did trunk shows throughout the United States." Stops along the way included New York, Dallas, Tampa and later, London, with a career that spanned nearly 42 years.

▶

*Dian Hodge--An unstoppable force*

And it was a memorable career. Recently, while visiting the YMCA in Tampa, Dian was spotted by a woman who was the former fashion coordinator at Ivy's department store in that city. "That was 18 years ago!" she says excitedly. "She remembered working with me when I used to live there. We're going to stay in touch."

## From Modeling to Innovating

While still active as a model, Dian moved to Dallas and became a personal care consultant for a major skin care and cosmetics company. She completed her lengthy tenure assisting the international division with recruiting and training for its newly established Great Britain operation. After serving another leading cosmetic and skin care company as its vice president of sales and marketing, Dian founded her own skin care and fragrance company.

A move to Las Vegas brought Dian to the doorsteps of many of the globe's largest hotels. She began to knock on those doors often, and eventually landed several accounts to develop proprietary fragrances. "'*We Make Scents*' was our motto," says the owner of the now inactive Fortray International. She also developed skin care lines for boutiques and dress shops.

"My hotel customers would often ask me what my signature fragrance was, and I thought, 'My goodness, I better create one.' And I did!" In an attractive black, white and gold box with an exotic, yet alluring scent, the fragrance *Dian* was chosen to be featured for sale when QVC did a live broadcast from The Rio Hotel in June of 1997. This special formulation was based upon the aroma of many culinary delights. "To help television viewers imagine the fragrance, I arranged a basket with chocolate chip cookies, white chocolate truffles, mandarin oranges, jasmine, nutmeg and lilac," she says. This visualization tool, along with many energetic endorsements from members of the live audience, helped to move 800 bottles in six minutes on the shop-at-home network.

## Enviro-Tech International Seeks to Cater to Female Distributors

One of the people watching QVC that day was Patricia Dominguez, newly appointed chief executive officer of Enviro-Tech International. She was hard at work looking for ways to increase the number of female distributors in the company's 70 percent male distributor force. In search of someone who could build a skin care line, she had learned from a consultant that "one of the best in the industry was right there in her backyard," Dian relays. "With my own company a success, I wasn't looking to go to work for a network marketing company. But I hit it off with Patti and agreed to come on board as a consultant."

Dian continued to serve her own clients part-time while she went to work developing the products that would help Enviro-Tech build its female distributor base. The initial days with the Las Vegas-based company were exciting times for the veteran motivational speaker. The company's male distributors had long had success marketing Dri Wash 'n Guard, Enviro-Tech's line of waterless car and home care products. Yet, in a selling program typically built upon the involvement of couples, the wives were generally left on the sidelines. To develop a skin care line that would capture ETI's captive female audience was another challenge that enticed Dian. "Women are such good networkers because we talk more. We're always telling other women about a better restaurant, a better store, a better product. Through network marketing, we're able to help women change their lives by affecting their appearance, feeling better about themselves *and* increasing their income," she says.

## The Challenge of a Lifetime

With Dian, her biggest challenge was just around the corner. "A week after I began to work for Enviro-Tech, I went for a mammogram and found out I had breast cancer. Within a week's time I had a radical mastectomy, and learned that chemotherapy would be necessary." Dian told no colleagues, family or friends of the diagnosis. "I didn't want anyone to know until it was over."

At the urging of her oncologist, she did call upon a member of a support group before her first chemotherapy treatment. "She told me I needed to go ahead and shave my head because I was going to lose all my hair, quit my job because I was going to be sick and wouldn't be able to work, and that I needed to just plan to stay home until the chemo was over." Dian made it clear that she wasn't going to take this lying…or sitting down. "I told her that I had just taken a consulting position with a major company, and I was going to be traveling around the country promoting my new skin care line. I just didn't have time to stay home and be sick! And if I did lose my hair, they made perfectly wonderful wigs now-a-days."

Dian preferred to obtain her support from continuing her work with Enviro-Tech, developing and promoting INVE'™, the company's new skin care line for women, which was introduced in July of 1998.

"When something life threatening or earth shattering happens to you, what do you do?" Dian asks. "You have to go on. You don't give up. That's what I was encouraging others to do when I was out on the road promoting these new products." Exhorting others was clearly a cathartic experience for this survivor. "Sometimes I would take chemo, get on the red eye and go give a talk the next day. When I was on stage motivating other people to overcome their obstacles, I was also motivating myself. When I encouraged them to take a step toward their dreams, I was also reminding myself to overcome my challenges."

Dian continued with chemotherapy, and she continued to motivate others. "The products are about making people feel better about themselves, at whatever stage they are in life."

**A Unique Opportunity for INVE'™ Product Research**
The chemotherapy also offered Dian an unusual opportunity for product research. "When going through chemo you're skin gets very dry. I saw women with dry skin, cracks around their lips, just very dry all over." However, Dian was able to think about developing a solution for people going through such circumstances. "I took what I observed into consideration during the product development stage for *INVE' Age Defense, INVE' Vitamin E stick* and *INVE' Body Silk*. I was gaining an understanding of the unique needs of women experiencing chemotherapy, and at the right time, I would be able to bring this new understanding to the marketing program for the products. Because I only use Sweet Almond oil in the products, they are also helpful for women with sensitive skin. The rare oil is mild and won't clog pores. It's a clear and very light oil," she says.

The INVE' line is suitable for any woman who wants a simple and effective skin care regimen. "Our skin care regimen works together to care for your skin in a fast, easy and gentle way. With INVE' being safe for the most sensitive, your skin appears softer, more subtle, more vibrant and younger looking." Dian asserts that healthy skin leads to a healthy attitude. "Many women want to feel better about themselves. It's a proven fact, the better you feel about yourself, the more successful you become. Everybody looks at your face, not your hands, or your feet. By having a good skin care regimen, you gain more confidence that you do indeed look your best. INVE' makes your skin feel wonderful." Economically priced, INVE' matches the quality of department store brands and includes steps for cleansing, exfoliating, toning, rejuvenating, moisturizing and protecting the skin.

Dian's cancer is in remission, which she says is largely because of her own positive attitude. Her doctor agrees. "My oncologist told me that the reason I did so well was because of my positive attitude and that I did stay busy. Working with ETI and developing the INVE' line helped me to focus on helping other women. Maybe I could help other women who had cancer, or some other difficulty. If you encourage others to overcome their obstacles, then you yourself overcome your obstacles. If you focus on motivating other people, you don't have time to feel sorry for yourself. After all, life is what you make it."

It wasn't until Dian had completed chemotherapy, six months after her initial diagnosis, that she told her now close friend, Patti. "After the chemo was over, Patti asked me to come on with ETI full-time. I finally confided in her, 'I didn't tell you before, but I've had breast cancer, and I've been going through chemo for the last six months,'" Dian relays. "Needless to say she was shocked, and needless to say, I accepted the position of vice president of personal care! The next day she and Chairman and Founder, Rod Yanke, sent me a huge bouquet of flowers with a card saying how much they admired me and what I had done. The flowers practically filled the room, and it made me feel so special for having walked through this personal challenge."

> *A firm believer in acknowledging achievements, small or large, Dian is building Enviro-Tech's recognition programs to award distributors for their outstanding accomplishments in recruitment and sales.*

**Dian Leads the Way as Enviro-Tech Recognizes Important Achievements**
A firm believer in acknowledging achievements, small or large, Dian is building Enviro-Tech's recognition programs to award distributors for their outstanding accomplishments in recruitment and sales. While she passes out rings, watches and even trips to hard-working distributors, corporate colleagues enjoy her cheerful greetings, encouragement, and even an occasional hug. A young employee gave Dian a report she was quite anxious to receive late one day. As she embraced him, she said, "Thank you so much!" Just out of her earshot, he said, "I love it when I get hugs for doing my job."

To Dian Hodge, developing products that help people feel better about themselves, then motivating and recognizing them for achieving their goals is like one big hug for doing her job. "It's not really a job when you would do it for free." ∎

# Paradise and Personal Prosperity...
# The Legacy of Geri Cvitanovich-Dubie

**G**eri Cvitanovich-Dubie is a true example of the American dream! She ranks in a unique category as a network marketing history maker. A legend in her beloved company and adored by hundreds of thousands in her Herbalife family, she has taught the secrets of multi-level marketing success to countless aspiring entrepreneurs. Her lifestyle in Hawaii is akin to the wealthy; however, she remains a warm enthusiastic model of the best success story of the working woman.

*Geri with husband Daniel on the grounds of their palatial estate in Hawaii*

Geri's story includes the heritage of her family's journey from Europe to the land of promise and a new beginning...America. The impact of her family's struggles and a life that taught the rewards of a strong work ethic instilled the character that Geri manifests today in her amazing success with Herbalife.

Geri's maternal grandmother Michalowski married when she was 17-years-old. A few years later, her husband left for America in search of making a better living. The plan was for his wife to later follow. In 1914, she was one of the fortunate to go aboard the last boat out of Poland before the outbreak of World War 1. While in America, the couple lived in the Polish community of New York City. Both labored under adverse conditions, one of which neither spoke English.

Grandfather Cvitanovich also yearned to pursue the American dream and to escape the war. Leaving his wife and two sons behind, he left Yugoslavia for America. When he had saved enough money, he sent for his wife, but his sons were left in the care of an aunt. To help the family out financially, Geri's father joined the Merchant Marines at the young age of 14. Unfortunately, her grandfather died of pneumonia without ever seeing his sons again. The family then pooled whatever money they had to send the boys to America. Anthony, Geri's father, was soon drafted and once again found himself in Europe. Grandmother Cvitanovich was now alone in America with no husband or sons. Always in the back of her mind was the frightening thought that the American dream would be lost forever if Geri's father were to be killed in the war. Fortunately, he survived being wounded and returned to America. Shortly after, Geri's parents were wed.

From stories handed down, letters received from abroad, and trips she took to visit family while in high school, Geri quickly learned that although they were lower middle class, they were rich compared to their relatives overseas. A very strong work ethic was instilled in her and her twin brother. Both began working

*"All your dreams can come true"*
Geri Cvitanovich-Dubie

when they were just ten years old. They sold lemonade, raked leaves and mowed lawns; anything that would provide extra money for their family. Everybody chipped in and the children felt proud of their contributions. Geri's father worked as a commercial fisherman, and between the fresh fish he caught and the vegetables they grew, the family ate well. Geri learned from her family that although money is important, it does not bring true happiness. She was very inspired at a young age to earn money so that she would be secure, and also felt a calling to teaching.

In addition to attending school and doing whatever extra work she could find, Geri excelled in sports. She became an avid cyclist and placed fourth in the National Trials, which qualified her to compete in the 1974 World Trial Games. Her performance would have qualified her for the Olympics if cycling had been recognized as an Olympic sport during that year. She eventually quit competitive cycling because of the physical risk. Her father once commented to her, "Too bad you don't put that energy into getting a job."

Geri worked very hard to earn enough money to put herself through college. She majored in physical education with a minor in dance. While in college, she discovered alternative medicine and the healing benefits of herbs, and that they could actually increase her health and athletic performance; not to mention the fact she was blessed with a healthy, strong body. Learning about alternative diets and the value of exercise and herbs became a hobby for her.

***A backdrop of frolicking Dolphins form an idylic setting for Geri nestled against a palm tree***

183 ▶

*Geri accommodates a horde of autograph seekers at an Herbalife rally*

Geri's success as a dancer provided the opportunity to be the youngest person to ever teach at the local junior college and at a federal prison. In every job she had, Geri noticed that everyone seemed to be depressed about work and no one seemed to be excelling. She felt her employers were paying her barely enough to keep her from quitting, so she was inspired only to work hard enough to keep from getting fired.

> **While in college, she discovered alternative medicine and the healing benefits of herbs, and that they could actually increase her health and athletic performance; not to mention the fact she was blessed with a healthy, strong body.**

While in college, Geri took a speech class, which she flunked because she stuttered so badly from stage fright. Already insecure about her lack of marketable skills, this experience convinced her she had none of the requirements to succeed in business. After six years of schooling, Geri expected to find success as a teacher. Unfortunately, that wasn't the case. Dangerous neighborhoods and overcrowded schools made her feel she was controlling behavior rather than educating. She felt physically threatened, both by the unruly students and quality of the physical environment. Many of the people in the neighborhood were sick and there were an unusually high number of children with disease. The paint on her car began to peel because of the poor air quality. Although she had always enjoyed excellent health, by the time Geri started her Herbalife business she was exhibiting signs of illness, was approximately 20 pounds overweight and feeling tired.

As a teacher she was earning only $800 a month and discovered, to her dismay, that when she worked as a grocery checker in college, she earned more money than she did as a teacher! To make ends meet Geri taught school during the day while working nights and weekends at the local grocery store. Tired and disillusioned, she wanted more from life and realized that the security and prosperity she was looking for couldn't be found working for someone else in the traditional job market. She was consumed by fear and kept asking herself, "What if I got sick?" "What if I got fired?" "What if I get divorced and end up a single mother like my girlfriends?" She felt she walked a tightrope between survival and financial failure. During this difficult time, her upbringing gave her courage because she knew she was living in a country where she could prosper if she held on to her dreams and was willing to work hard and learn. Geri answered ad after ad, searching for just the right business that could lift her out of this life of misery. Many of the business ads she responded to didn't sound legitimate or stable, or she wasn't qualified. Always an optimist, she told her best friend at the grocery store that when she found the right business opportunity, she would share it with her and they would both be rich!

**"Prisoner? Are you tied to a desk? Do you hate punching a clock?"** So read the ad that changed the life of Geri Cvitanovich-Dubie forever. She felt this ad described her lifestyle which had become a virtual prison.

The year was 1980 and Mark Hughes, an energetic 23-year-old with a dream to bring better nutrition and free enterprise to the world, had placed the ad. At age 18, Mark suffered a tragic personal loss when his mother took an improper combination of prescription weight loss medication that resulted in an overdose and death. Determined to make a difference, he set out on his own to create a healthy and safe alternative to this type of dangerous dieting. His program was based on the concept of nourishing the body rather than depriving it. Utilizing natural herbal remedies and the very unique concept of cellular nutrition, which enables the body to utilize nutrients on a cellular level, he developed a program to lose weight while improving a person's overall well-being. This innovation, in conjunction with an ingeniously lucrative marketing plan, paved the way for the great success to come. Herbalife was born!

The first Herbalife business opportunity meeting that Geri attended was held in a garage-sized room in dire need of a paint job. A very youthful Mark Hughes stood at the front of the room with a flipchart which read "Welcome To My

*(from left) Geri, Herbalife Founder Mark Hughes, his wife, Darcy, and Geri's husband Daniel*

185

Family." During the presentation of his dream and marketing plan, Geri noticed that the guests were leaving one by one. She thought they were going to the restroom, but after a while it was evident they were not coming back and that she was the only person remaining. The sole audience member, Geri listened to Mark intently when he said, "For your life to change you have to change, and if

Mark Hughes. "Mark gave me a feeling of instant trust and I felt that somebody cared about me more than any business or educational institution ever had. The enthusiasm and joy he exuded were definitely lacking in my previous job experiences. I knew then that he was somebody special and that this business would work. He had been selling products out of the trunk of his car, but

*Geri on one of her globetrotting tours in Africa on a charity mission*

you change yourself, everything else will change for you. You don't have to change what's outside, all you've got to change is what's inside. To have more, you simply have to become more." Seeing the enormous potential, Geri recognized Mark's vision and signed on right away. She realized that in her present state, working two jobs to make ends meet, she had nothing to lose and everything to gain.

In a recent interview Geri recalled her initial meeting with

he knew that the research he had done was based on very sound principles of nutrition. The products he developed would help people all over the world improve their health, and could also provide them with financial security. His dream was not just to be wealthy, but to help people."

Mark Hughes has helped several others accomplish their goals, achieve certain wealth, and experience greater joy and satisfaction in their lives. He has become very familiar with people's dreams and has helped them solve their problems. The best thing Mark gave Geri was the benefit of his philosophy, the foundations of which are living successfully, how to be wealthy and how to be happy.

Mark Hughes' ideas worked for Geri and she is now a woman of fame and fortune, and will always be grateful for meeting Mark. Geri feels there is no mystery to the income she earns. The marketplace pays a lot for products that will make a person look and feel better, and it pays an enormous amount to provide stable careers in today's unstable worldwide economy.

Similar to Geri stumbling upon the ad in the paper, Mark, almost by accident was introduced to network marketing. He was working at a clothing store earning approximately $1,000 a month. A customer asked if he would like to earn an extra $300 per month selling a diet drink called "Slender Now." In just eight months he became the top distributor, escalating his earnings to $8,000 a month. Despite Mark's success, the company went bankrupt. He joined another company, rising to the rank of top distributor.

> *...Geri recalled her initial meeting with Mark Hughes. "Mark gave me a feeling of instant trust and I felt that somebody cared about me more than any business or educational institution ever had..."*

However, they, too, went bankrupt and once again Mark found himself unemployed and in need of an income. Inspired to start his own company, he contacted an herbal manufacturer and renowned herbalists from China and began research to create his own product line. With a loan of only $30,000, Mark's vision was on its way to fruition.

Geri remembers that in the beginning there were no real sales tools available to Mark's distributors. About a year later a simple idea turned into a fantastic way to attract customers. Mark created a button that read, "LOSE WEIGHT NOW -- ASK ME HOW." Immediately, people

*Former President Gerald Ford happily meets up with Geri at a golf course in Palm Springs*

187

*The "Queen" pauses from her non-stop schedule to the delight of a lucky photographer*

The company that began from the trunk of Mark Hughes' car and made $2 million dollars its first year, is now publicly held and had escalated to over $1.5 billion in sales in 1998! The products are being distributed in 43 countries around the world and the numbers are growing. Expectations are that this year will surpass $2 billion in sales volume.

During the first five months, Geri promoted Herbalife part-time between her two jobs. When she went full-time she worked seven days a week, fifteen hours a day for seven months straight. Although this was a hectic pace, Geri says, "It really didn't seem like work." Her main job as a distributor was to contact at least twenty people a day, ten about the products and ten more about the opportunity. "What I lacked in skills I made up for in the number of people I talked to and eventually increased my skills," Geri said.

In the beginning there wasn't much in the way of an income, but Geri believed in Mark's dream. She was ready to do whatever it took to sell these products and build a business. Geri feels her greatest asset was that she was "teachable" and willing to do whatever Mark told her in order to reach her goal. He told her, "To earn an above average income you have to do above average things." He told Geri that she had two choices: She could work out her problems of insecurity in the business world, or she could continue to be a victim of her lack of skills. She chose to improve her skills and learn to speak to people, in spite of her terrible experience in college. She already had a strong work ethic, but with Mark's tutelage she learned to overcome her shyness, to fake courage when she was frightened, and to talk about the future with confidence and certainty. She learned to project where she wanted to be with her voice, her image, and her style. She learned to "walk the walk" and eventually the marketplace reflected this success back to her. Geri told others, "You can do it! I'm doing it" She took great inspiration from the Nobel Prize Winner, Roger Sperry, who said, "What we think, causes things to happen," Geri began to use this philosophy in all areas of her life, and learned that she had the power to manifest her own destiny.

began approaching him. Finding customers was easy; after all, there are at least 72 million people in this country alone and more worldwide trying to lose weight. Herbalife presented an opportunity for anybody with the right enthusiasm and desire.

Geri suggests to everyone reading this article to join the small percentage of disciplined people and discover what your best truly is. She says, "Our lives are affected by two major things: One is price; the other is promise. It's not easy to pay the price if you can't see the promise. Therefore, do what it takes to discover what you truly want. Once you have seen and felt that ideal future, that promise and achievement, you will be ready and able to pay the price."

> *Geri feels her greatest asset was that she was "teachable" and willing to do whatever Mark told her in order to reach her goal.*

Another inspiration to Geri has been her mentor, Mr. Jim Rohn, an acclaimed and revered philosophical teacher who conducts motivational seminars around the world. Jim told her, "With consistent discipline applied to every area of your life, you will discover untold miracles and uncover possibilities and opportunities."

"When I became a millionaire," Geri said, "I discovered that the money was not all that important. What became important and the powerful question was, 'What am I becoming?' It's not what you acquire, it's what you become along the way that makes you valuable. The key to setting goals is to set the ones that will make you a better person when you achieve them."

In just six weeks with Herbalife, Geri lost 16 pounds, rid her body of cellulite, and had more energy than ever before. She found she could eat anything she wanted with her now very different metabolism. Her body became healthy. She felt and looked great! All she had to do was tell her story to everybody! By the second month her hard work paid off and she received her very first royalty check for 97 cents! She was elated. The next month her check for $6.94 was a 500 percent increase over the prior month. She thought, "I'm going to be rich!" To this day she keeps a copy of this check framed in her office. Mark was also excited and told her to share her enthusiasm about the monetary increase with everyone she knew. When others saw her results and spirited enthusiasm, they were drawn to her and the products.

Most people would snicker at a 97 cent paycheck, but not Geri, who has now multiplied that into the millions. No longer having to put in long hours, she is enjoying a life that most people only dream of.

Geri found and developed people everywhere she went. After five months of introducing many of her co-workers to the opportunity, she was able to quit teaching and grocery checking. Today, her downline has hundreds of thousands of distributors, and the royalties and residual income have surpassed her wildest dreams. "It's wonderful to know that if I stopped working and took several years off, the Herbalife business would continue to provide an incredible income and would support my family in a wonderful lifestyle, allowing us to do as we please. When you have financial freedom, many of life's pressures disappear because you know that you are in charge of your life," Geri stated. ▶

*A massive throng fills the rafters at an Herbalife annual convention*

189

**Having your slice of the world, best depicts this scene with Geri and husband, Daniel**

Nearly six years ago Geri moved to Hawaii where she lives in a stunning waterfront estate. The property has a breathtaking 180-degree view of one of the most beautiful beaches in the world. From her patio, she can see humpback whales breaching, gorgeous sunrises, and majestic islands that are just a kayak's ride away. The open-air home covers 7,000 square feet with a separate guesthouse and is decorated in an eclectic style with artwork and artifacts she and her husband have collected during their travels to exotic places, including Bali and Africa. The "island feeling" of the home is accentuated with Koa walls (an indigenous wood which is now quite rare) and a

*After five months of introducing many of her co-workers to the opportunity, she was able to quit teaching and grocery checking. Today, her downline has hundreds of thousands of distributors, and the royalties and residual income have surpassed her wildest dreams.*

lush tropical garden complete with a waterfall spilling into the fish pond.

Geri met her husband, Daniel, at a seminar on naturopathic medicine. There was an instant bond between them because of their interest in alternative medicine, spiritual growth and charity work. They became fast friends and worked together for various charity organizations. It was during this time that Geri and Daniel fell in love. She refers to Daniel as her "twin flame." Geri was not looking for a partner, but felt there was a void in her life that only true love could fill. She found her perfect match in Daniel, and they continue to work together on many projects, including various charities such as the Herbalife Family Foundation, Make-A-Wish Foundation, the American Cancer Society and several local shelters.

Daniel has achieved great success as a naturopathic doctor and a consultant for the movie and television industry. Currently, he is collaborating with the Millennium Television Network (MTN), which starts broadcasting on December 31, 1999. MTN will air live coverage of millennium events around the globe. This production team has produced events such as Live Aid, the Academy Awards and the Olympics. This broadcast will be the single largest live interactive communication ever created, launching the Year 2000. With his media savvy, Daniel has also helped Geri improve her television presence and speeches when she tours around the world on behalf of Herbalife.

Geri's success story has made her a living legend. Often she is referred to as the "Queen of Herbalife." She has appeared in numerous videos and is a public speaker at seminars all over the world. Geri will be featured in a book entitled, *The Global Power of Network Marketing,* by David Roller (Prentice Hall). Last year she was the topic of an article in *Success* magazine's "Working At Home" edition. Additionally, *Woman's World* magazine recently contacted her pertaining to an interview for a feature story.

"Through some of the proceeds from the sales of our products and the contributions of Mark and other distributors," Geri says, "it is very rewarding to see people being helped around the world." Herbalife is a major contributor to the D.A.R.E. Foundation, for example, which is how their own daughter learned to say "no" to drugs in school. In addition, Mark and Prince Ranier of Monaco, are currently building another orphanage with the proceeds of the foundation.

There is an old saying, "Give a man a fish and you feed his family for a day; teach the man how to fish and you'll feed his family for a lifetime." Geri says, "If you love

*The spectacular view from within Geri and Daniel's estate of the Pacific Ocean dramatizes the unique serentity of their corner of the world*

all people as if they were your own family and offer them an opportunity, you will change lives and they in turn will help others. We really do have the power to make this world a better place. You can't believe how willing people will be to help you if they know you are willing to help yourself."

Geri looks forward with great excitement to the many changes the upcoming millennium will bring to the world. She sees herself as an important part of this new age.

In addition to Herbalife being an excellent weight loss and nutritional supplement, distributors and customers are purchasing it as a possible survival food. The Y2K computer problem could bring food distribution to a standstill for a while. Some Herbalife products could definitely provide a nutritionally complete food source with a long shelf life, in addition to being very easy to store and prepare.

▶

191

Geri maintains that the old ways of earning money are changing and people are realizing that a home-based business, together with today's technology, offer freedom for more time with your family, time for your spirit, and financial independence.

"I believe there are no coincidences. If you're reading this article, it's not a coincidence. You have the power to make a choice for yourself. Go for it! No matter how big your dream, it really can be yours. This year can represent a quantum leap in its fulfillment. Remember the old saying, 'If it's to be, it's up to me.' Believe in your dream."

Geri believes that to be on the cutting edge, you need an edge to cut with. She says, "That edge is your belief in yourself, sharp and ready to go. All glory comes from daring to begin. Who knows, if you aim at the sun, you may hit a star."

One of her favorite quotes is: "Like the proverbial pebble drops into a still pond, the shift of consciousness we make in our personal lives sends out tiny but important waves that will ripple over the surface of the world." Geri continues: "Herbalife has given me a moment in time when I, as one person, have a chance to help other people in the world by providing proper nutrition, free enterprise and financial security. It's given me a chance to make a difference and connect with people, so I know what it's like to be human. Day after day we discover our own lives because we never know what we'll find. Every discovery is another gift we give ourselves. Dreams are the soul's pantry; we must keep it well stocked and our soul will never hunger. Most people seem to be interested in turning their dreams into reality. And there are those, like Mark Hughes, who turn reality into dreams. He once told me, 'You must be the change that you wish to see in the world.'"

*Geri can be reached at: 305 Hanani Street, Suite 122, Kailua, HI 96734, Phone: (800) 715-SLIM, Fax: (808) 263-5707, Fax-on-Demand: (800) 628-9404, E-mail: success@hawaii.rr.com, Web site: www.ihbn.com, access code: BL1200.* ∎

## Fear Frightens Even The Best Of Us

Even the greatest performers are afraid before going out onto the stage, the court, or to the conference table. Helen Hayes says she used to go "stone-deaf" on opening nights. Ann Miller would get dizzy and nauseated. Dame Margot Fonteyn has said she felt so much fear before dancing *Swan Lake* in Moscow that she felt clumsy, awkward, and nearly immobilized. Gloria Steinem recounted that the idea of speaking to a group, much less a big audience, was enough to make her heart pound and her mouth go dry. Even Winston Churchill used to say he felt as though there was a block of ice in his stomach every time he was to address Parliament.

In our culture, the tendency - especially for men - is not to acknowledge fear. Being afraid is not "macho." Yet many peak performers have readily admitted to "stage fright." Bill Russell, one of basketballs greatest players ever, used to throw up before most games. Edwin Moses, Olympic gold medalist and former world-record holder in the 400 meter hurdles, who went *years* without a defeat, says that each time he races, "It feels like I'm being led to my execution."

Fear is a common experience even with the "swashbuckler" types who always look cool. Dennis Eckersley, the Oakland A's All-Star relief pitcher, generally considered one of the best closers in baseball, says that every time he goes out to the mound in the late innings, when the ball game is in the balance, he is scared. "At the All-Star game, I sat down with Jeff Reardon (of the Twins). He's been a great closer for years, and he always looks so cool out there.

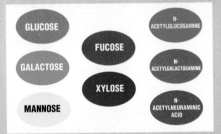

# Success Yourself!

## A Three-Step Formula for Total Fulfillment

*Warren Wechsler*

Have you ever wondered why some people achieve great things even when they are blessed with few special skills or lucky breaks? Have you ever asked why some people with an excess of talent and contacts never realize their true potential? Have you ever felt that you were too old, too young, too poor, too sick, too tired or just too unlucky to realize the successes that every fiber in your mind, heart and soul desires?

There are fundamental and powerful resources available to you to make your dreams come true that are already within your grasp and simply need to be awakened. Passed down from generation to generation, from the greatest philosophers and teachers in the history of humankind, these truths are at your fingertips. Whether studying the great teachings of the Bible, the lives of the grandest entrepreneurs, or the history of the world's most successful people, the same themes appear over and over again. Yet in today's times, many of us have succumbed to the idea of the day. We have given away our own power to excel. We've lost our way. We've gone from people who make things happen to people who let things happen--or worse yet, people who say, "What the heck happened?" We've been mesmerized by the latest fads and outright lunacies, from quality circles to self-empowerment, from ropes courses to right sizing, from Homer Simpson to the Dilbert Principle (whatever that is).

There is a way to create your own success, a way to "Success Yourself," a three-step, easy-to-follow formula for total fulfillment. It works for business people and sales people, for homemakers and students, for husbands and wives, and for parents and children. And it begins with an understanding of one definition of success.

"Success is the process of defining our dreams as tangible goals, detailing the plans that will make them achievable, and then taking action consistently to reach our goals while enjoying our experiences."

Understanding and leveraging the above definition is the way to "Success Yourself." It has the three-step formula embedded in it. In order to attain the personal and professional achievement that is everyone's destiny and birthright, start with a goal, detail a plan and then launch by action.

### Step One--The Goal

Many people have some idea of what they want to accomplish in their lives, but very few ever take the time to transform their ideas into concrete goals. Few of us have ever been taught how to do this. We take all these different courses in school on the business, social and physical sciences, but when it comes to planning our careers, and business or private lives, hardly any of us has ever been trained to work out our life's goals.

There are four attributes to successfully define a dream as a goal. First, the goal must be *personal*. It is difficult to succeed in pursuing someone else's goal. Managers try to set goals for their employees, parents try to set goals for their children, and coaches for their athletes, but unless the individual is passionate about the goal and buys into it personally, chances are it will not be accomplished. We'll fall off the track, or sabotage our own efforts, or have to be constantly reminded of what needs to be done. This is counterproductive and will not allow us to "enjoy our experiences."

The second attribute of a goal is that it must be *specific*. It is not enough to want to be "richer," or "successful," or "happy." We all want those things, but those statements are too vague.

When I say specific, I mean time-oriented, measurable and with a firm deadline. To put it another way, "who will do what, by when?"

The third attribute of a goal is that it must be *realistic*. I don't mean that we should set our sights low. I firmly believe in setting high, challenging goals that stretch my limits. When people say that they'll lose thirty pounds by their best friend's wedding, or live in this big beautiful house, or pay off all their debts by the end of the month, you know they are bound to fall short of their goals. They have set themselves up for failure by setting their expectations too high. In addition to being realistic, however, goals need to be challenging. If we make our goals so easy that their attainment is effortless,

194 ▶

the benefits are likely to be short-lived and empty. Our goals need to be realistic and also challenging. We need to expend a substantial amount of effort into a goal to find its attainment rewarding.

The fourth attribute of a goal is that is must be *written*. Many people succeed in making their goals personal, realistic and specific without putting them down in writing. Yet, until we put pen to paper, our goals are just dreams. A Chinese proverb says that the palest ink is better than the best memory. Writing down our goals provides the reference point we need in order to stay focused on our priorities. We can visualize our goal, put together the appropriate plan to accomplish it, and then unlock the power to act upon it.

## Step Two--The Plan

Once we have a clearly defined goal, the plan becomes our road map. The plan is what we utilize in order to accomplish our goals. It is our monitoring and feedback system. It allows us to keep track of our time and control the events in our lives. Another way of looking at this is to say that detailing our plan enables us to do the right thing at the right time.

In order to have an effective plan, we must understand the concept of non-discretionary time. Appointments, with ourselves and others, are times in our lives where we know we're going to be committed for a certain amount of time and during that time, we won't be able to work on anything else. Scheduled activities drive our unscheduled activities. Imagine wanting to exercise in order to lose weight, and making an appointment with yourself from 3:00 to 4:00 p.m. to participate in an aerobics class at a workout studio. If somebody said to you, "Hey, can we get together between 3:00 and 4:00 p.m. at the coffee shop to talk about this week-end's plans?" You would say "No, I'm sorry. I have an appointment." This example demonstrates the power of creating non-discretionary time. It allows us to bring an incredible amount of control into our plan by making commitment to scheduling the activities of our plan.

There are five elements to an effective plan. The first element is to *create a list of activities*. This breaking down of our goal into activities enhances the road map which will guide us to our destination. It shows us what needs to be done, how far away we are from attaining the goal, what resources we'll need, what commitment we'll need to make, and how much energy we'll need to guarantee success. Many people, once they see how long the list of activities can become, will find that either their goal needs to be adjusted because of a lack of time to commit to it, or other commitments need to be changed so that the goal can be achieved.

The second element to an effective plan is to make sure that *each activity is small enough*, based on how much time and resources we are able to commit to the goal. Many people create activity lists that really are additional goals masquerading as a list of activities. This makes people procrastinate, or worse yet, give up, because they feel that the task at hand is insurmountable.

When I wrote my first book, *The Six Steps to Excellence in Selling*, I found that understanding how small to make my individual activities on my list was a major success factor in moving from idea to publication in five months.

The third element of an effective plan is to *prioritize* our list of activities.

People who do not prioritize experience what I call the "whiplash effect." What happens is that they start looking from the top of the list to the bottom, trying to find something they can do quickly or very easily. The head snapping to and fro as it moves up and down the list causes the "whiplash."

Some activities are more important to us than others, and we need a system of ranking to identify what to work on first, second, third, etc. The way we will prioritize our activities first is by using alphabetical letters. The most vital activities on our list we'll call "A" priorities. "A" means the activity is vital, critical and urgent to our success. The next level of importance is the "B" activities, or those things that we consider important, yet not as vital, critical and urgent to our success; not necessarily as important as our vital activities, but nonetheless, important to us. "C" stands for activities that are somewhat important to us. We would probably achieve our goal without them, and they would either be "icing on the cake," or would make our achievement that much better if they were accomplished.

When we've completed prioritizing our activities into A, B and C, we will most likely find that we have more than one A, B and C. So it's important to apply the "theory of 1-2-3," which is to go back through our list and then prioritize the As, Bs and Cs, starting with the As, in terms of how vital, critical and urgent to our success they are. We will then have a list that shows A1, A2, A3, B1, B2, B3, and so on.

The fourth element of an effective plan is to *set deadlines to begin*. Many people set deadlines to complete a task or activity, yet very few schedule deadlines to begin. The saying, "Well begun is half done," is true. Set deadlines to begin the activities. You'll find that the act of deciding to begin will give you momentum you need.

Closely related to deadlines is the fifth element of an effective plan. It's called *tracking*. Getting to the point where we've completed an item on our to-do list, and can put a check mark next to it, gives us a sense of accomplishment. We can say to ourselves "yes, I've finished that!" It's the small step along the journey and shows us in a concrete manner that we're making progress towards our goal.

### Step Three--Action

Another Chinese proverb, "A journey of ten thousand miles begins with the first step," shows us once again the most important factor in "Success Yourself," which is to take action. Think about the slogans you remember from sports and business. "Go for it!" "Just do it!" "Go get 'em!" "Ready, aim, fire!" "Ready, set, go!" From my own experience and that of thousands of people I've worked with, I've found that a goal is a great start, an excellent plan builds confidence and creates enthusiasm, yet a willingness and commitment to take action is what separates those who make their

dreams come true from those who are still dreaming.

The one and only element of effective action is to have a daily strategy meeting with yourself. Many of us don't really do much advance planning each day. When I give my live seminars, I ask the question, "How many people spend between zero and five minutes a day planning what they are going to do?" And usually about half the hands in the room go up. There are 1440 minutes in a day and when we spend less than ten minutes a day planning (less than 1%), it should be no surprise that we don't accomplish our goals in life. What I am suggesting, therefore, is that we have a meeting of fifteen to twenty minutes with ourselves every day. I mean in private, by ourselves, before the hustle and bustle of the day sets in. Many people do this prioritizing and planning the night before, some people do it early in the morning. Read your goal, look at your plan, and then select one activity to act on during the day. Ask yourself these four questions as you read over your goal and plan.

**1.** Is it vital I work on this goal today?

**2.** What plan item needs to be scheduled into my day so that I can accomplish this goal?

**3.** What will be the benefits that will accrue to me when I do accomplish this goal?

**4.** What will the consequences be for me if I do not complete this goal or this plan item?

Are you ready to take the challenge to "Success Yourself?" It's as easy as 1-2-3. Goal--Plan--Action. It's up to you to take the first step. You have in front of you a powerful, simple and effective technique to achieve anything you want in life. Whether what you desire is financial, spiritual, business, personal or physical, using the three-step formula for total fulfillment will bring you "Success Yourself!"

*Warren Wechsler, founder and president of Total Selling Systems, works with salespeople and business owners who want to increase their sales and incomes. Warren's best-selling book, "The Six Steps to Excellence in Selling," was selected as the best sales book of the year by the Los Angeles Times. Warren is an adjunct professor at the University of St. Thomas Management Center in Minneapolis. Contact Warren at (888) 778-7335.* ■

## Break The Mold And Break It Again

Everything around you is in a chronic state of flux. A Hewlett-Packard senior manager, who was also an engineer, not so jokingly gave me a key bit of his wisdom: "If your product is successful, it's already outdated."

Keep looking at new technology, new materials, new delivery systems, new information. Keep checking with the customer. Keep your eye on the competition. Keep changing to meet the changes in the world around you. Like the surfers do, keep looking "outside" to see what's coming on the horizon. If you don't, the next wave will leave you flailing in the backwash.

*Success is simply a matter of luck.*
*Ask any failure.*

**Earl Wilson, quoted by**
**Peter Potter, All**
**About Success,**
**1988, "Luck"**

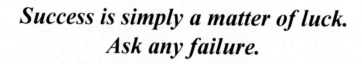

# When was the last time someone
# PAID YOU TO
# LOSE WEIGHT??

## DO YOU HAVE TWO MINUTES TO LEARN HOW TO:

**Dramatically Improve Your Health**

**Lose Weight Safely & Feel Great At The Same Time!**

**Make Money**

**Increase Energy**

**All Natural**

**Dr. Recommended**

**100% Guaranteed**

Before

After

Before

"I'm so happy to have found a healthy system my whole family can use. Together we've lost 135 pounds! We are enjoying better health than ever before and I can't believe I am making money doing this!
-Lois D.

CALL US NOW!
24-hr toll-free info line: 1-800-715-SLIM (7546)
www.ihbn.com (access code: WP1200)

# How to Succeed BIG in Network Marketing

*Scott Morris*

The knowledge of "how to succeed" in network marketing brings us to the reason why this article was written. It is designed for you, to give you an important understanding of what you need to make an "informed" decision.

## Criteria For Choosing The Right Network Marketing Company

Consider the following. You are one of the best network marketers on earth. A dedicated professional many times over. But now you're out of work! How could that possibly happen? Your network marketing company closed its doors, despite your herculean effort. It happens all the time. Why? Network marketing companies have the same failure rate as all other businesses, meaning the largest percent fail.

Your first important hurdle is in choosing a company. Use this following checklist to help you evaluate companies. Your chosen company should have:

- **Products that will have a lasting competitive edge**
- **A management team with a proven record of success**
- **A highly motivational pay plan**
- **A strong financial base--be rock solid or debt free**
- **Strong sales aids--like brochures, booklets, and cassettes that really help to sell the product and the company**
- **Ongoing support and training--to enhance your skills while keeping your motivation high**

The most important decision you'll ever make in network marketing is selecting the right company. If these key points are found lacking, that particular company has a severe handicap in a very competitive marketplace. Once you've actually selected a company, you are ready for the second most important thing that you'll need to do:

## Develop A Business Plan

If you want to do well in your own business, it is essential to develop a proper business plan. Consider the following:

- **What is your primary motive for succeeding?**
- **How much time will you devote to succeeding?**
- **How much money are you prepared to invest?**
- **When will you work your business?**
- **Where will you work your business?**
- **How will you receive proper training?**
- **How will you find good prospects?**
- **How will you approach them?**
- **How will you train others to succeed?**
- **What are your realistic income goals? 1 year, 2 years, and 5 years from now?**
- **Are you prepared to stay the course?**
- **Do you find satisfaction helping others?**

These questions are fundamental considerations for constructing a practical and effective business plan. With a business plan you are forced to decide on how important your long-range goals are, and then make specific plans in writing, to utilize both your time and resources to achieve your dreams.

## Getting Your Business Started

Everything we've discussed so far has been preliminary to actually starting your business. Let's discuss what you need to do to get your business started.

You can organize your home-based business in just one day. However, becoming organized is a very simple proposition. It means:

- **Having a place to store it**
- **Having a place to record it**

In order to get yourself organized, buy yourself file folders, have a drawer to put them in, buy a date book to record appointments, take notes, and maintain a sheet of frequently called phone numbers.

## The Products And The Compensation Plan

What two things will influence people when they're listening to you?

- **How effective the products are**
- **How appealing the compensation plan is**

It is important that you become an expert in both. Within this industry we often hear the phrase, "You must be a product of the product." This means to use all the products often enough to be able to tell people firsthand how effective they are. Your testimonial is the most important "persuader" you'll ever possess.

An important thing to remember is that the products and comp plan are the two most interesting things to your prospect. How much you believe in them will determine your ability to influence someone else.

▶

# Running on Empty?

# Fuel up at www.incite.net

Success in business requires more than a great idea. You've got to stay motivated, overcome rejection, develop your relational and communication skills, and stick with it.

We know you want to make your life count. That's why we developed Incite – a life-education resource on the Internet that aims to inspire and promote greatness in people.

Incite offers hundreds of workshops, books, audio and videotapes from categories such as leadership, biography, family, inspiration, worldview and personal development. In addition, you can subscribe free to "Daily Spark — Life Lessons from the World's Greatest Teachers," and get the boost you need to stick with it day in and day out.

Whether you're traveling across town, or traveling through life, you don't want to run out of fuel. Incite is a reservoir of resources you can tap week after week, month after month, that can help you down the road toward greatness.

**Resources to Fuel Your Fire**

## Become An Electronic Rebel

The electronic revolution is well underway! The modern network marketer is familiar with all of the following tools:

**Cell phones - 3-way calling - Conference calls - E-mail - Answering machines - Voice mail - Fax machines - Fax-on-Demand - Computer chat rooms - Electronic bulletin boards - Desktop publishing - Business software - Videos - Cassettes - Call forwarding, etc.**

You may choose not to utilize some of these tools; however, the most successful people in the industry use nearly all of them. Remember, as your own boss you control your business decisions.

## Duplication And The Marketing Plan!

Two other important issues:

- **Duplicating Your Success**
- **Developing A Marketing Plan**

We'll address duplicating your success first. In order to have an organization that keeps growing, you must pass along a great deal of information. Passing on the knowledge of how to succeed is called "duplication." You'll often hear the following phrase in the industry, "Duplication is your key to success."

The best way to pass on this important information is to use a standardized format because it saves training time. Many people put their information on paper, or even cassette tape, and then pass it on.

While we're on the subject of communicating to your organization, it's worth mentioning that you must communicate often. Every opportunity to communicate something new is also an opportunity to motivate others. Once someone joins your program your role changes from "persuader" to "trainer" and "motivator." The "heavy hitters" in the network marketing industry are excellent trainers and motivators.

## The All-Important Marketing Plan

Some people refer to the "compensation plan" as the "marketing plan." For our purposes the marketing plan is how you're going to solicit prospects. It's what gets the phone ringing off the hook!

To get the phone to ring, you need to get the word out that you're in business.

The best way to get the word out about your business is through:

- **Personal Contacts**
- **Advertising**

We will cover both. First however, once you've decided on what promotional materials will best promote your products and opportunity, you'll need to decide on a plan for approaching prospects. The questions that you'll first need to ask yourself are:

- **Who will you approach, and why?**
- **How will you approach them, and what will you say?**
- **When will you approach them?**
- **How often will you approach them?**

It's important to give thought to these questions even if you can't have all the answers immediately.

## Personal Contacts

Personal contacts will be comprised of people that you will contact yourself. It is a simple task to construct a list of 100 people that you'll want to approach. The list would include relatives, friends, neighbors, acquaintances and business contacts. It's worthwhile to utilize the yellow pages or the phone book to identify prospects as well.

Get the prospect to "open up" and talk to you. Ask "open-end" and provocative questions. The more they talk, the better! Your opening words often determine how well you'll be received for the course of the conversation.

## Advertising Your Business

Henry Ford once said that if he had a nickel to spend on a shoelace business, he'd spend a "penny on shoelaces," and "4 cents to advertise it!" That advice served Henry Ford well and it can do the same for you!

## The BIG Secret

When I first started in network marketing I went to several personal contacts and didn't do very well. I even gave away free products and still couldn't generate much interest. The product worked well, but I just didn't have a very receptive audience. I felt like quitting!

Then I mailed postcards to people who were looking for a home-based business. The mailing generated 147 leads in just six weeks. From that time on I've been dedicated to sharing what a great opportunity network marketing is for the average person.

You must advertise your way to success if you want to succeed big. That's the secret! I've met many millionaires in network marketing, and all of them have a slightly different approach. However, they all share something in common as well. They advertise.

Think of it this way. If your phone rang 25 times each week bringing you 25 new people, anxious for information on your products or opportunity, wouldn't it be hard to fail in your business? Now imagine, all of your key people advertising too! That's how people build massive organizations in network marketing.

Where should you advertise to find good prospects?"

- **Network marketing magazines**
- **Business opportunity magazines**
- **Network marketing web sites**
- **Card decks for business opportunity seekers**
- **Mailing lists for business opportunity seekers**
- **Mailing lists for business opportunity buyers**
- **Mailing lists targeting product users**
- **Newspaper classifieds:**
*Business Opportunity* **section**
- **Magazine classifieds targeting product users**
- **Pre-qualified lead programs**
- **Fax blasting**
- **Local envelope coupon stuffers**
- **Local bulletin boards**
- **Doorknobbing (locally)**
- **Stack materials in high traffic areas**
**such as businesses, offices, and waiting areas**
- **Local direct mail**
- **Computer chat rooms, bulletin boards,**
**and e-mail, if permitted**
- **Through self-promotion; fliers, bumper stickers,**
**signs, business cards, etc.**

Always test your advertising in a small way before committing to a large investment. Advertising is an "investment" strategy not a crap shoot! Expect to refine your advertising. You may receive better results by changing something in the ad or running it in another vehicle. The largest companies in the world are constantly fine-tuning their advertising.

## Now That You Can Get The Phone Ringing

How will you handle all the responses? If a customer wants more information and contacts you firsthand, that's a one-step response process. If they are to call a recorded message, or pull up a fax-on-demand before contacting you, that's a two-step process. What's the best approach? The rule of thumb here is that if time permits, talk to everyone first. If you are overwhelmed with leads, you should use the two-step to pre-qualify those that you should spend your time with.

A rotating voice mail box allows you to share advertising with one phone number for a group of people, and have the leads automatically dispensed equally. You may then split the advertising cost between everyone. This is referred to as co-op advertising, and is an effective way to generate many leads for people in your organization.

Prospects are very important and you'll spend your money just to get a chance to present your story. Respond immediately to them because they are often looking elsewhere at the same time, and the first one to respond to them often creates a first impression advantage.

## Closing Thoughts

The world is overcrowded with people that want success "the easy way." They spend time dreaming, and thinking, but are unwilling to pay the price and make the sacrifices that it takes to turn their dreams into reality. I learned long ago you'll encounter these people while you're doing your network marketing business. You can waste time with people that want you to do all the work for them. Find someone that has the spark to succeed. Spend your time finding and developing this kind of person and you will succeed.

*Scott Morris is a network marketing trainer and a consultant to the industry. He is a well-known author and speaker. He has made several cassette tapes on how to successfully build a network marketing business from home, and how to advertise effectively for it. You may contact him at P.O. Box 5267, Dept. 1, Lansing, IL 60438.* ■

# Here's to the Lady!

## Meet Renata Lee... Singer, Model, Actress, Mountain Climber, Real Estate Entrepreneur and Network Marketer Extraordinaire

*Freya Manfred*

*Renata Lee*

Add high energy, a resolute drive to succeed, a deep love of adventure and independence and a strong sense of honesty and integrity to an ability to lead others, and meet Renata Lee, a woman with a long list of incredible credentials who has been working full-time in the network marketing industry for 11 years.

Lee, a native of Southern California, was raised in the Los Angeles area and spent her childhood summers in Montana, climbing mountains with her father, a schoolteacher who later became a track and cross country coach. When she was seven, Lee's parents divorced, and during the school year she lived with her mother, who has been a nurse for over twenty-three years, seeing her father on weekends and school vacations. "I was very fortunate as a kid because I got to spend an equal amount of time with both parents," she says. "Both of my parents were very concerned about my well being!" With her father she developed the "adventurous and exploratory" sides of herself, because he "has always been a pioneer out of his time, setting records for mountain climbing which still have not been beaten. He explored everything, and quite often he took me with him!" Meanwhile, life with her mother was also a growing experience, because of "her great zest for life and a wonderful sense of humor. She's one of those people who is always the 'life of the party.'" Lee also spent a lot of time with her grandparents, especially her grandmothers, and says she enjoyed being an only child because she was able to "develop a real sense of independence."

Lee was born "a giver" and "a sharer," traits which her parents fully encouraged. She says she was also "skinny, scrawny, and very shy about just being me." She felt so overcome by shyness that in the tenth grade she was uncomfortable speaking to anyone for the first half of the year, except on stage, where she starred in the school play. "I was always very comfortable on stage," she says. During that year she vowed she would come out of her shyness, and developed her own personal exercise in which she practiced focusing on other people instead of herself. "I realized that a lot of people probably felt the same way I did. At that moment I understood the power of personal growth and started feeling better about myself. However, it was getting into network marketing later on that really accelerated that part of my personal growth by leaps and bounds."

Lee says she has "a country side and a city side," but was "never a nine to five individual" because "I've always been intrigued by so many areas of life." Always an overachiever in high school, and thinking she might want to become a doctor, she took German for three years because a great deal of medical research is written in German. She also set her sights on the entertainment industry, and became very involved in drama, which she had also done in summer stock theater as a child.

In college Lee took aeronautics and flying lessons, though she'd never been in a plane. Later she worked as a security guard and then as a dispatcher for a major police department. She took classes in real estate law, sold real estate, and aspired to get her broker's licence; however, she decided to move on to the entertainment field because she realized that "in real estate you are only as good as the last house you've sold. Selling homes didn't truly meet my entrepreneurial dream."

After receiving a scholarship at the Performing Arts Cooperative in Hollywood, Lee worked as a singer, a model and an actress, doing commercials and film work and co-starring in three original musicals. "I've always been very driven," she says. "I don't know where the energy comes from." She managed the Mortgage Trading and Finance Department of Security Pacific Merchant Bank sixty hours a week while simultaneously singing and dancing in a production of "Pepper Street," the longest running musical in Los Angeles, where she "fell into" the network marketing business. "One of the gals in the show was sharing nutritional supplements with the cast and working in a networking company and I saw that an above average income could be made which might permit me to further pursue my entertainment career."

Lee jumped in with both feet and became so immersed in and intrigued by network marketing she never looked back. She worked with nutritional products for her first seven years in the industry, becoming a regional seminar manager, putting together and coordinating meetings for groups in excess of 1,500 people, and corporate training, reaching the top in all three companies she worked with. "I realized the power and impact of a residual income," she says. "I saw that others had success as well as time for themselves and their families. They could keep their own schedule and pursue other areas of life with zest and curiosity. In fact, I was so excited about the network marketing business I decided to go out and save all the other starving actors I'd met in Hollywood, so they could share in my wonderful future.

*A beaming Renata (right) serving as Maid of Honor at half-sister Sheri's wedding*

205

*Renata and father, Roly, at cookout in Montana*

people in her organization while also working as the first female corporate trainer brought on by that company. True to her high energy profile, there were times when over 1,100 people a week were coming into her organization while she was simultaneously traveling the country and doing corporate trainings. "My phone rang every thirty seconds for eighteen months. It was a remarkable experience! Obviously, one cannot build a network marketing business all alone. Without a team of people all believing in their product and working toward one common goal, 'leaders' such as myself cannot be successful. I have been blessed to have attracted other fabulous team builders who have become incredible leaders." Her resilience and ability to survive difficult periods was revealed when the president of that telecommunication company suddenly announced one day on a leadership call, "We just took the company behind the barn and shot it." The company had simply grown too fast.

After taking over a month to travel and recuperate, Lee began consulting for a brand new start-up company. Her role was to fill a fundamental need in the network marketing industry, that of a liaison between corporate and field marketing people. She was brought on to act as a "voice" for both sectors, because she understands what it takes to build a network marketing organization and what it takes to support it.

However, over a three month period I came to see that the mentality of most of these actors was not what was needed. I became successful when I realized that working with individuals who were more comfortable with success than I was really proved to be the key."

"When I first got involved in networking I had no clue how it even worked," Lee says. "I saw a vehicle to become successful, and I saw other people doing well and I thought, 'Well, why not me?' However, while I was getting started I fell on my face and ran into brick walls more times than I can tell you. I came very close to quitting many times. But even at that I still managed to make over $4,000 a month in my first year in the business. Why? Because I did not quit."

"A lot of people think they can learn to do network marketing from reading about it in a book," Lee says. "Well, I'm here to tell you that the only way to learn it is to do it. The only way to it is through it. You must be willing to stray out of your comfort zone, and if you develop some persistence, tenacity, and a good measure of patience, you can start developing a business you never thought possible." She says the long-term rewards for her in the network marketing industry have been extraordinary, financially and in every other way. "I am a totally different individual today growth wise, and I have developed long-term relationships that will be with me forever because of the time I have spent in this industry."

In her eighth year in the industry Lee segued into a telecommunication company and had over 42,000

*With mother, Patricia, on vacation in Oregon*

"How to merge corporate and the field into one voice — now that is the big question!" Lee says. "Sometimes corporate competes with its own field, and vice versa. People can waste precious time questioning each other within the same company. Corporate individuals who haven't been in the field, quite often have no idea of what it takes to build a business and distributors usually have no understanding of what it takes to run a network marketing company, and yet both are attempting to produce the same results - to build a strong, successful organization. This lack of communication usually creates major gaps between the two. It is one of the greatest dichotomies of the industry and brings down many otherwise terrific companies."

As passionate as she feels about the industry, Lee, who has also been featured in an infomercial on the home-based business industry, does not believe network marketing is for everyone. She gives the following simple advice:

**1.** If you don't like people, don't even think about doing network marketing, no matter how much money you believe you're going to make. This is a people business!

**2.** If you don't like the telephone, don't even think about doing network marketing. This is a relationship business and you have to follow up, follow through, and spend time on the phone developing those relationships.

**3.** If you are not into personal growth, don't even think about doing network marketing. If you are, however, you will start to discover amazing things about yourself and grow in ways you never thought possible. Network marketing brings you face-to-face with yourself.

Renata Lee lives in Orange County, California, with Bob Newnam, "the love of my life," whom she met during her first network marketing experience. They have been together for ten years, and she says, "He's my Rock of Gibralter and support

> *"A lot of people think they can learn to do network marketing from reading about it in a book," Lee says. "Well, I'm here to tell you that the only way to learn it is to do it."*

system. He adds such balance to my life."

Although Lee is thankful for the financial rewards she has realized through the years in network marketing, her devotion to the industries future is unchallenged. "It is most important to me that the network marketing industry be entirely legitimate," she says. With her typical life-enhancing sense of humor, she concludes: "Plus, where else can you go to work in your bathrobe every day?"

***Renata Lee*** *can be reached via fax at (714) 775-0116.*∎

***Renata with the love of her life, Bob Newnam***

# Getting Your Press Release into Print

*Jeffrey Dobkin*

> ***The press release selection process is simple, fast, and brutal--and very unforgiving of mistakes or poor work.***

I seldom recommend an ad campaign until a press release has tested the media and has proven we can get a qualified response from the target audience. We don't always get in with our press releases, but we always try.

On the flip side: For industrial marketing, an ad is the logical conclusion to a successful press release campaign. A client should be willing to take out an ad schedule after a successful press campaign shows that the media and the market can be profitable.

Press releases can be both simple and complex instruments to write. Simple because they can take almost any form and still be published. Complex because every element adds to or detracts from your chances of being published. Additionally, releases can be so general that they serve very little of the marketing function (i.e., they produce no inquiries, no prospects, and no sales), or they can be written to draw the maximum response from the best-qualified prospects. Which would you like to have published?

A press release is a one, or two page write-up of your product or service in a "news" style of writing. It's sent to magazines and newspapers, usually with a black and white photo. The magazine sets the type, and when the release appears in print it looks like an article the publication wrote. It's always published for free. Everyone likes new products, even magazine editors, and they know their readers do, too.

The chance of having your release published depends on the quality of your release and the publication. Industrial magazines are easier to get published in because their circulations are smaller, their audience is more focused, and less publicity material is aimed at them. They are also more "market friendly"--what's good for the market they serve is good for most of their readers.

It's much harder to get releases published in consumer publications. It's like shaking hands with the Pope --you can do it, but usually not without a great deal of trouble and expense. The numbers tell you why. Industrial publication circulation figures are usually 5,000 to 30,000, the latter being a fairly big industrial magazine circulation. They are almost always under 100,000. In consumer publications, circulation of 100,000 is small when you are shooting for the general interest magazine like *Newsweek* or *House Beautiful*. *Targeted* market publications like *Runners World* or *Field & Stream* can be lower, but either way, the number of releases they get is quite staggering.

First, let's make sure your release is strongly considered for publishing, then we'll make sure it's written effectively to generate the maximum response. Then we'll look at the (shhh) secret process.

## Keys to an Effective Release

The closer you can come to the accepted standard for writing press releases, the greater your chances of

> ***It's much harder to get releases published in consumer publications. It's like shaking hands with the Pope--you can do it, but usually not without a great deal of trouble and expense.***

being published. Why? (1) The standard format makes it easier for editors to read, scan, and edit. (2) It lets editors know that you know what you are doing and that your organization will be a responsible firm when dealing with their readers. (3) Well presented releases add credibility to your offer, and editors will feel that their readers will receive a good product. Any editor in his or her right mind would never accept a release from a firm whose marketing material is poorly formatted or is full of typographical errors, knowing their product is probably like that, too. (4) Most editors get so many releases that they can afford to be choosy, and they are. With good reasons: It's their neck on the line when the release is published. A poor selection of editorial write-ups can get the editor (or publisher) calls from disgruntled subscribers.

## Parts of the Release

The top of the release is called the header. It is separate from the body copy and contains a release material. Make sure it contains a release date.

*Editors cut releases from the bottom, so keep all the important stuff at the top. The editor knows anything cut from the bottom of a correctly structured release won't be missed.*

For example, "For Release August 2000." If your news can run anytime, say "For Immediate Release" in large bold print. Send a release two to four months prior to the publication date of the magazine or one to two weeks prior to the publication date of the newspaper in which you'd like it to appear. The header also contains a line stating, "For Additional Information Contact:" followed by your name, company, and phone number. After that, give editors a kill date--state "Kill Date" and the date after which you no longer want your release to run. If it's OK anytime, state "No Kill Date." The header presents information about the background of the release to the editor at a glance.

## Writing the Perfect Release: The Biggest-Benefit Headline, and the Benefit-First Release

As with all the ads I write, I write the objective of the release first. Since I can't sell the call as hard as in an ad, my marketing objective in

a press release is usually to generate the maximum number of inquiries and orders from qualified prospects.

Start with a great headline. Write the headline with as much thought and care as you would write a headline for an ad. Capture the major portion of your market at a glance. An easy way to do this is to start the release with a headline that offers your biggest benefit. The formula for an effective release headline is NEW PRODUCT OFFERS BENEFIT, BENEFIT, BENEFIT.

Just like when you create an ad, the headline of your release will determine how many people will read the rest of the release. So offer benefits, benefits, benefits. And you'll get response, response, response. An example: "New lightweight tennis racquet offers easier swing, faster ball speed, and is less tiring." When this is your headline, every tennis player will read it and continue reading the rest of the release.

Editors cut releases from the bottom, so keep all the important stuff at the top. The editor knows anything cut from the bottom of a correctly structured release won't be missed. So continue the benefit of the headline into the first few lines of your body copy. "A new lightweight tennis racquet that won't tire you out when you play has just been introduced by

the Racqueteers. It offers more accurate ball placement, better control, and is easier on the elbow than heavyweight racquets."

See how many benefits are crammed into the first two lines? And chances are 98 percent are in the first two sentences. In the Benefit-First type of release, the most important information is found at the top of the story. Benefits presented in the first two sentences won't be cut. Nice formula, eh? Continue writing the body of your release in an inverted pyramid style, with the most important information at the very top of the story. Whatever style of writing you select for your pitch, make it sound like it's "news." If it sounds too much like an ad, or if the body of the release is written with too much sell, it will take too much time for an editor to rewrite; so it won't get rewritten, it'll get tossed out.

Double-space the body copy of the release, leaving big margins. Anything you can do to make the editor's job easier and faster gets your release closer to being published.

At the very end of the body copy of the release, write "For Additional Information Contact:" and then your company name, address, and phone number. After your street address, put the word "Dept.-" with an underscore line after it. The magazine editors will insert their publication's initials in this block when they publish your release, so when you get inquiries, you'll know from which publication they came.

Try to confine your release to one page, with the body copy double-spaced, and don't use very small type to cram more in. If your release runs more than one page, don't break a paragraph in the middle--end the first page at the end of the last full paragraph, then type "MORE" at the bottom of the page so editors will know to look for another page. If there isn't one, they'll know it's missing.

## Start the Next Page With a Fresh Paragraph.

Releases end with the number sign typed three times (###) or three asterisks(***); either set of marks signals the end of the release. Busy editors appreciate use of these symbols.

If you are writing a release to be published in a particular magazine, read some of the other releases in the magazine and copy the magazine's particular style of writing. Write directly to the audience of the magazine. When you send your release, mention the name of the column in which you'd like it to appear. Editors are impressed by people who take the time to know their magazine and direct their energies specifically to it. To even further increase your chances of being published, include a personalized letter to the editor with your release.

If it's a photo release, include a crisp black - white 5" x 7" or 8" x 10" glossy finish photo, unfolded, so note: the envelope size you'll need for mailing photo releases is larger than a standard number 10. If there is a crease or fold in the photo, it won't be usable since the crease will show up when printed.

The correct way to identify a photo-- and your release photos should always be identified--is to take a shipping label or file folder label, write the product name and your company name and phone number on it, then stick it on the back of the photo.

If you write directly on the back of the photo, chances are the pen or pencil will push into the emulsion side of the photo (front) and scar the photo, making it unusable. Editors know this

scar will show up if the photo is printed, so it won't be.

If it's not obvious which end of your product is up, write "TOP" in very small letters in the top white photo margin. If an editor doesn't know which side is up, he won't guess -he'll simply toss it out and use another firm's release (not separately). Photos are never returned, so don't ask. If you need it, have a duplicate made before sending it.

## The Editorial Selection Process -Part Deux: You are the Editor

> *If you are writing a release to be published in a particular magazine, read some of the other releases in the magazine and copy the magazine's particular style of writing. Write directly to the audience of the magazine.*

Let's take a look at a press release from the other side of the desk. You are the editor.

It was unusually cold and damp when you awoke this morning, but the building super doesn't put the heat on till October 1. Too bad you ran out of coffee over the weekend. Through bleary eyes you shower and dress and get into your car still groggy and tired. As you drive to work, it starts raining hard. You can't remember ever seeing such a heavy volume of cars on the expressway, even for a Monday.

Even though you left 15 minutes early, you arrive at 10:15, an hour and fifteen minutes late. There are nine phone messages written in various hieroglyphics on scraps of paper on your desk. You can decipher only four of them. There are 12 voice

mails, including one from the publisher asking you to come into his office when you get in to prepare for a 9:30 meeting with the magazine's largest advertiser.

Sitting at your desk, you look at the imposing volume of press releases. Three days are left till the closing of your gala Back-to-School issue. In a stack to your immediate right are about 80 releases. In a stack to your left, there are four unfinished stories and three uneaten slices of Friday's pizza in a box from Luigi's. Everything except the pizza is marked for your "Immediate Attention" for the upcoming issue. This backlog of work happens every single month around the closing date.

So how do you, the editor, pick out releases? First, you look through them and throw out all the ones that don't give you double-spaces. This cuts the pile by about a third. It gets rid of the novices. (Now you understand why your releases should be double-spaced).

As the editor, you also trash all the releases that don't look good-- smudges, typos, fingerprints, poor photo copies--figuring if the release doesn't look good, or if the photo isn't crisp, the literature your readers will receive, if any, will be of the same quality. This may reflect poorly on your magazine, so you throw them out. (This brings us to Lesson 2:

Submit neat, clean-appearing releases, double-spaced, with good sharp, in-focus photos).

Now you go back through the pile of about 40 releases, knowing you have room for about eight in this issue. Each month some people write with a ball point pen on the back of their photo exactly what the photo is, the release information, or their own version of *War and Peace.* So you check for writing on the back of the photos--you won't be able to print these without the writing showing through, and you toss them out, too. You see this mistake every month. Some people never learn.

The pictures with no identifying information on them could get imposed incorrectly in the production department, so you throw them out, too! Well, that was easy. If it were earlier in the month, you could now take a break. You'd go for a nice lunch, or for a beer. But since things always back up around the closing dates, you have to keep working. You start eyeing the pizza carefully. Is that a mushroom, or did it just move?

The acceptable product releases are now reviewed for newness, freshness, and newsworthiness and evaluated for proximity to your editorial style. Is there a good industry match? Will it be of interest to your readers? Does it look like a good product to introduce? Is it designed well? Are your readers going to be happy or disappointed if and when they get the literature, or if they order the product? If everything clicks, the release advances to the next level.

With about 20 releases surviving, and no other possible way out, you read them. The ones needing the least amount of rewriting make your job easier, and that slims the pile down to about 15 high-quality releases. But this month you have room for only eight.

**The Secret Process**
So you, the wild-eyed editor now with eight cups of coffee under your belt at just 11:30, go to the top of the stairs and throw all the remaining releases up in the air directly over your head. The eight that land on the top few stairs get in, and the rest that floated downward are trashed or saved for the next month's consideration. And that's why they call it editorial, because they don't all get in, and marketers like yourself have to submit to this "part handpicked" and "part random" selection process that dictates what runs and what doesn't.

What I mean by this is, there is a great element of risk that your release won't run, no matter what you do. At the last moment you can get bumped for any reason, or no reason at all. You have to accept this as part of the mystique of the press release, as opposed to an ad for which you purchase space and which absolutely does run.

What are your chances of being published? For a new consumer product release, 5 percent. In an industry trade Journal, 20 percent. If you are known to the industry or your product is industry specific, perhaps 40 percent. If you call the magazine and speak to the editor personally, the chances of your release being published may be as high as 80 percent or 90 percent, from just the one phone call. But the release still must be formatted and written correctly.

Keep your releases as close to the standard format as possible; it shows you know what you are doing, the product is probably good, and readers will be happy with you, as well as with the magazine, for giving your product and firm editorial support. It's up to gravity and the luck of the float to get your release into print.

*Jeffrey Dobkin is the author of "Uncommon Marketing Techniques," and "How to Market a Product For Under $500." He is also a speaker, a direct mail copywriter, and a marketing consultant. To contact him, call (610) 642-1000 or fax (610) 642-6832.* ∎

## Necessary Evil

A University of Massachusetts study reports the Conventional Wisdom that work is increasingly seen as a *"necessary evil."* It pays the bills, buys the toys, and in theory enables us to have financial security now and/or later. It doesn't matter if you enjoy your work, since work is expected to be hard, perhaps even unpleasant. The idea of intrinsic pleasure in your work, of enjoyment on the job, or not having a dramatic separation between business and pleasure, is alien to most of the American work force. John Madden puts it succinctly, "As soon as people hear you say 'business,' they know you're not talking about fun."

# Use Our Incredible Marketing Services and
# SKYROCKET YOUR INCOME
## To Over $100,000+ *This Year!*

## Utilize Our Marketing Services & Give Your Opportunity A Super Boost!

WE HAVE IT ALL ..... our One Stop Marketing company will generate qualify leads for you at below wholesale prices. Whether you want to advertise in magazines or card decks.....we'll give you a wide range of choices to choose from.

In addition, we also have incredible responsive mailing lists that you can use to direct mail your opportunity to. WE ARE THE ACTUAL LIST OWNER AND NOT BROKERS! Compare us and you'll find our leads will always make you more money!

Looking to generate more leads? If you or your organization are ready for mountains of leads, then Card Deck Advertising is your choice. But don't overpaid for them, instead give us a call and we'll save you a bundle (in fact, we can save you over 50%!). How can we do this? Since we are representatives of many deck publishers out there, we are able to secure wholesale volume prices and therefore, pass the savings along to you! Let us become your one stop shopping store for all your promotional needs.

Our leads are the best! They come with phone numbers or without. Past customers have had responses range anywhere from 1% - 18%! Because we generate our own names, we have full control of who our customers are. This control is what gives you quality - **and our is the best in this industry**. The money you make from our leads will be well worth your investment.

Our Magazine, ADvantage Networker, targets people who are looking to start their own homebased business. They range from novices to pro's in the industry. We direct mail this magazine for highest responses (23,000+) and past advertisers have gotten responses as high as 5%!! Very low ad rates allows anybody to promote their business at maximum savings!

## Call our Fax On Demand at 703-904-9888 Ext. 998.
## Or Call Toll Free 1-888-846-7256 for more info.

LeadMaster 29 John Street #PBM 130 New York, NY 10038

# The Passion of J.F. Robert Bolduc

*Frank Clancy*

Had a prudent investor analyzed the business plan for Matol Botanical International Ltd. when the company was founded in the fall of 1984--that is, if Matol would of had a formal business plan-- he would almost certainly have said the company had no chance to succeed. Matol had virtually no capital, its founders had no experience in the network marketing industry, and there was only one product to sell: A dark brown liquid that even its most ardent devotee, Matol Chairman, J.F. Robert Bolduc, delicately describes as an "acquired" taste.

**What Matol did have was a story to tell. A story, passion and purpose.**

The story belonged to Karl Jurak. A native of Austria and an amateur botanist, Jurak had developed the previously unnamed elixir, which was made from 13 plants and herbs, in 1982, after a near disastrous loss of strength while climbing a mountain. For more than 60 years, he'd brewed the herbal concoction himself and given it to relatives and friends.

The passion belonged to Bolduc. A Quebec native whose family had immigrated from France in 1652, Bolduc was introduced to the dark-brown potion by Jarak's son, Anthony, in 1982. It was, he remembers, "not unlike falling in love. I was convinced that product was meant for me to do something with."

The sense of purpose came when Bolduc, who was then working as a marketing analyst, read a magazine article about network marketing. "It was like an electrical charge went through the room," he recalls. "I had been using the preparation, and I made a direct connection. I saw that there, on that piece of paper was a way for me to take that preparation and bring it to life; make it into a going concern."

Story, passion and purpose all came together when Bolduc and Anthony Jurak formed Matol, with Karl Jurak's blessing in 1984. Since they knew virtually nothing about network marketing, for six months Bolduc and Anthony Jurak attended every direct sales meeting they could find; Avon, Shaklee, Amway and Mary Kay. They introduced the newly named botanical formulation to the world on Bolduc's 34th birthday, October 22, 1984, at the Westin Four Seasons Hotel in downtown Montreal.

Of 132 people who said they'd attend that meeting, four showed up. Characteristic of his outlook on life, Bolduc doesn't focus on the 128 people who failed to show up for that meeting. All four guests signed on as distributors.

After just two months, Bolduc quit his regular job to become Matol's first full-time employee, (he was paid $.10 Canadian for every bottle of Matol sold). Matol expanded to the United States in 1986, selling its first trademark elixir there under the name "km." The first day the company sold a million dollars worth of Matol was in February 1989.

Matol introduced its second product, a fiber supplement known as FibreSonic, in 1991. That same year, Bolduc attended an advanced management training program at the Harvard School of Business. "I could see rapidly the day we were going to be a billion-dollar corporation," Bolduc says of his decision to attend the grueling program. "I had never run a billion-dollar company, nor had anyone else at Matol. I saw two choices: Get a hired gun to run the company or get myself back in the saddle and improve my education," he explains.

A few years later, as Bolduc puts it, "fame and fortune caught up to the company." He and his partners became mired in a bitter legal dispute over who would control Matol's future. For more than two years, business ground to a halt.

▶

214

By early 1997, Bolduc had emerged victorious. He proceeded to bring Matol back from near death. Now he sees even the company's darkest hours as one of its biggest strengths.

**That leader is of course, Robert Bolduc**

Bolduc is a man of paradoxes. A self-described gladiator and poet--professor of both a fierce temperament and a pronounced tendency to see the world through rose colored lenses, Bolduc had succeeded in large part by steering Matol back to its roots. Today the company has as strong a corporate culture as you'll find in the network marketing industry, as strong as you'll find in any industry.

Though no longer a one-product company, as of the middle of 1998, Matol offered just 12 products, including a skin care lotion, vitamins, and meal replacement shakes. Among its newer products are one dietary supplement designed to boost the immune system and another designed to prevent cancer.

Matol plans to introduce more products. "But we only need products that live up to our standards," Bolduc says. "We're not going to put out products just because other people are selling them. We believe you put out products when they are ready, and your people are ready."

A commitment to ethics and science are at the core of Bolduc's approach to business. "For me, ethics is not about being perfect, it's about understanding that if you honor a commitment, honor your word, you're setting standards that everyone in the organization can relate to, that everyone can follow. This whole industry is built on truth and trust. If you don't have truth and trust, you can never have a successful organization," he states.

For a nutritional company like Matol, Bolduc says, "science is integrity. Today we have the means and the resources to work with hospitals, universities and research centers that are focusing on validating products. We are not the kind of company that will presume a product works on its own."

Throughout his career at Matol, Bolduc has shown a commitment to the network marketing industry as well as the company he leads. Among his many other accomplishments, he has served as chairman of the Multi-Level Marketing International Association, and has helped several highly successful network marketing companies to get off the ground.

Likewise, Bolduc is quick to praise other industry executives such as Tupperware President Alan Kennedy and CEO Rick Goings. And he is liberal with his praise of companies like Amway, and even Matol competitor Bodywise.

Bolduc sees an almost unlimited future for the network marketing industry, albeit one that is different from both its past and present. "For every industry to keep moving, for it to evolve, you need start-ups," he says. "You need new blood, new ideas. Unfortunately start-ups are literally polluting the industry. Don't get me wrong, there are some fine start-ups. They are operating with standards; they are usually mentored by existing companies, or by a network of mentors. But others, all they want is to make a quick buck. I think that epidemic of start-ups is going to taper off in about a year or two" Bolduc predicts. "Where we now have thousands and thousands of companies, I think by the year 2000 there will again be about 100 companies that work in a serious way with governments and the various regulatory bodies. I think the 21st Century will see this industry go into a maturity cycle. The Wild West days of this industry are behind us. We're now in a building mode. We're in the process of building an industry that will be recognized by the general business community, and will take its right place in that community.

The companies that survive, Bolduc predicts, will be the ones that clearly define what they stand for and attract like-minded people committed to the company's goals. "Companies will," he says, "have to articulate what they stand for in such a way that it highlights their uniqueness and gives like-minded people something to rally around. The end result will be that people take ownership of their contribution and their participation in the company. They will have a sense of ownership."

Bolduc predicts that in this streamlined industry, companies will have to increasingly concentrate on educating distributors. "They have to know not only how to do something but why they are doing it," he says.

Bolduc has no doubt that Matol Botanical International Ltd. will be one of those companies that thrive in the 21st Century. And Matol will thrive in his opinion, largely because its distributors will continue to believe in the company's stated mission to "Impact World Health." He explains: "When I speak to distributors, I constantly tell them, 'don't get confused. It is still about impacting world health, one day at a time, one person at a time. It is still your contribution to Matol that fuels the company.'"

In other words, Bolduc inspires in Matol's distributors the same sense of passion and purpose that enabled Matol, despite having only one product, to become one of the stars of the network marketing industry.■

# Robin Stroll *Finds a Rewarding Life With Dorling Kindersley Children's Books*

*Jesse Hardman*

Thinking back to her childhood, Robin Stroll remembers life as a slower paced, more creative time. Forgoing the allure of television in the late 50s, her childhood was full of books, flowers, and animals. Her evenings were often spent with her parents and other siblings singing their favorite songs. She remarks that although her family did not have much money, they did have a lot of fun. Life can get away from us, however, filling our minutes, hours, days and weeks with so many jobs, commitments, appointments and other obligations, that we literally lose track of who we are and where we came from.

Stroll admits that somewhere along the way she too got caught up in the hustle and bustle of the career world. It is hard to fault her, though, as her path has been full of interesting and rewarding job experiences.

Having spent her whole life in California, Stroll chose to stay close to home when it came time for college. Growing up in Oakland, she ventured down Highway 1 to the University of San Diego, where she enrolled in an English Literature program. After spending four years developing her writing skills, she graduated. It was time to find out what she had learned and where she could apply her trade.

Her first stop was a newspaper in El Segundo, a town just south of Los Angeles. She arrived at the paper ready to write and begin a career as a reporter. Over the course of the next few years however, she would wear many hats. Her duties encompassed not only reporting but editing and photographing pictures as well. After a few fast paced years, Stroll decided to try something new.

Her next job found her working as a fund-raiser at Cal Tech, a highly regarded local college. Her specific project dealt with arms control.

Dealing with the Cold War confines of the 70s, her project brought members of the defense industry and the political science realm together to discuss the prevention of war. Her specific duties included writing various foundations and corporations seeking funding for the project.

She also wrote summaries of the research that was being collected. This included studying areas around the world that were potential hot spots for Soviet and U.S. aggression.

Moving out of the realm of the Cold War, she continued to use her fund-raising skills. In 1985 she began working for a special school in Altadina, California, that housed abused children. The school, always expanding its list of programs and services, kept Robin busy. She was in charge of locating new major donors who could help fund the progressive vision of the school. Some of the programs she helped get off the ground included one for deaf children who had been abused and a program which helped the students at her school learn how to re-enter society and function normally. Stroll really enjoyed the faculty and students at the school, so much so that she still keeps in touch with them and visits on occasion.

**Robin Stroll**

216

Taking a break from fund-raising, Stroll returned to concentrate on her writing. Over the course of the next few years she paid her dues as a technical writer. Some of her many clients included the oil industry, various computer companies and a health insurance company. Stroll found the writing she did and the community of writers she met while working these jobs very rewarding. She began to realize, however, that something was missing. Time was passing her by and she knew it. Her life was ready for a major change.

One day while attending a book fair on her lunch break, Stroll came across something that grabbed her attention. Browsing, she found a line of children's books published by Dorling Kindersley, a British marketing company. First marketed in 1993, these nonfiction books had an appealing nature to them. They were grounded in the idea that reality was just as entertaining and important a subject to children as make-believe. They proved this point by filling the pages with wonderful photographs of animals and other subjects. In Stroll's own words, "After just one look, I knew I had to have them." So, despite not having any children of her own, she bought some of the books, figuring she'd find someone to share them with.

This first encounter with the books was just the beginning. Soon she began to market the books part-time, cutting down on time spent with her writing jobs.

"To me, getting involved with these books was like buying

> **Life can get away from us, filling our minutes, hours, days and weeks with so many jobs, commitments, appointments and other obligations, that we literally lose track of who we are and where we came from.**

into some big company like AT&T in the beginning. It was the first time in my life where the timing seemed exactly right to do something like this." What Stroll began to realize was that not only did she believe in what these books could do for others, but also what marketing them could do for her. She had always wanted to make a good living while working for things she believed in, something she had already accomplished. In addition, however, she had wanted to balance these things with a more flexible schedule, one that allowed her to have a life outside of work.

Marketing these books has allowed her to set her own schedule. This does not mean she works less hours than before, only that now she can plan her work around her life. She has also begun to rekindle the creative fulfillment she felt as a child.

It is safe to say that Robin Stroll has, in a sense, completed one of her missions in life. She recently celebrated her 50th birthday this past September by quitting her part-time technical writing job. This move has allowed her to put her effort full-time into Dorling Kindersley's children's books and made her a very happy woman. "I was never looking for anything specific, just some peace of mind and a sense of humor. I now enjoy the funny things about life. I laugh a lot. I have time to discover the rich emotional elements of everyday life, and find happiness in my own back yard."

**Get Your Private, Free E-mail at http:// www.hotmail.com** ■

## In Nature, Nothing Retires

What, where, and how you do what you do is something well within your control, whether you're 20 or 70. It is never too late to find your passion, inject more variety into your daily round, and enjoy life. Nothing in nature retires. As a nation caught up in what Ken Dychtwald calls *The Age Wave,* more and more Americans can now expect to live longer, more productive lives.

As Break-It Thinkers join the age wave, they know that just because you're good at something doesn't mean that you have to do it for the rest of your life. People change. Times change. What you felt passionate about in one phase of your life may not be what turns you on 15 or 20 years later. It's important to gravitate toward those things that infuse your life with gusto, whether you are 28, 48 or 88.

# Make the Feds Your Next Customer

*Alan Rothman*

Dr. Robert Sullivan is an entrepreneur, author and consultant who has started numerous successful businesses on two continents. He frequently lectures on starting small businesses and entrepreneurialship and has appeared on CNBC's "Minding Your Business" and National Public Radio as a small business expert. Robert has spent some of his career in the corporate world and part in government, but his first love remains being involved in

> ## *The secret of selling to the government is to be knowledgeable about the process.*

activities that assist and energize the new entrepreneur. He also spent many years with the legendary Admiral Hyman Rickover and culminated his government career as a special assistant for information technology to the Assistant Secretary of the Navy for Research & Acquisition. His site, The Small Business Advisor, at http://www.isquare.com receives about 100,000 visitors per month and is in its third year. The site has been featured in numerous major publications such as *USA Today*, *The Wall Street Journal*, *Newsweek*,

*Entrepreneur* magazine and *Computer World*.

He is the author of *The Small Business Start-Up Guide* and *United States Government - New Customer!* According to Robert, the United States Government is the world's largest purchaser of goods and services to the tune of over $225 billion dollars annually. Knowledge is power and reviewing this interview will give you the initial tools and steps necessary in selling to the government so you get your piece of the pie.

**Alan**: Isn't it true that only large corporations can successfully sell to the government?

**Robert**: On the contrary, over 90% of all purchases made by the U.S. Government are less than $25,000. The really big contracts get the publicity, so the perception is that all the contracts are big ones.

**Alan**: Why should an entrepreneur consider the U.S. Government as a customer?

**Robert**: Because of size and volume. The U.S. Government is the largest customer in the world for supplies and services. You really should not ignore a customer like that!

**Alan**: Isn't the paperwork required in selling to the government so complex that the effort is not worth the reward?

**Robert**: The paperwork can be daunting, but only for the really big contracts. Many small businesses will only deal within the "small purchases" programs and for the

most part, the government simply issues your business a purchase order or uses a credit card just like any other customer!

**Alan**: Isn't it true that the government is such a large bureaucracy as a customer that it takes forever to get paid?

**Robert**: Once again, the only time this sort of information gets publicized is when a lot of money and a good story is involved. In fact, it is rare that the government does not pay within 30 days. And, if they pay later than 30 days, the law requires that you collect interest.

**Alan**: Are there times that being a small business can be a competitive advantage when dealing with the government?

**Robert**: The U.S. Small Business Administration (SBA) has a mandate to make sure small businesses obtain a certain percentage of everything the government buys. Because of this, nearly all government agencies have special small business programs that are designed to ensure this mandate is met. The SBA also operates electronic bulletin boards as well as a page on the Internet. Don't overlook them as a source of information and assistance.

**Alan**: Based on your background, training and experience, what is the best-kept secret on successfully selling to the government?

**Robert**: The secret of selling to the government is to be knowledgeable about the process.

**Alan**: What is the first step a person would want to take in selling a product or service to the government?

**Robert**: Determine the Standard Industrial Code (SIC) codes for your products or services. This code is used by many agencies when purchasing and you will need it when filling out various forms. SIC codes are listed in "The Standard Industrial Classification Manual" (700 pages) which is available at most larger libraries. Check the reference section. You can also purchase your own copy from the Government Printing Office for $29. You can reach the government office by calling them at (202) 512-1800.

**Alan**: What is a CAGE code and why is it important?

**Robert**: This is an alpha-numeric identifier assigned by the Defense Logistics Services Center and identifies your business. Many government purchasing activities use

> *You no longer have to register with every local procurement office to gain bid access to possible contracts of interest.*

CAGE numbers to identify the firms they do business with. This code is especially important if you want to sell to any of the Defense Agencies.

**Alan**: How do you go about obtaining this code?

**Robert**: You obtain a CAGE code by first contacting the agency with whom you are interested in doing business or an authorized Procurement Technical Assistance Center (PTAC) who will complete a

portion of Form "DD 2051." You then complete the form and submit it to:

**Defense Logistics Services Center**
ATTN: DLSC-FBA
Federal Center
74 North Washington
Battle Creek, MI 49017-3084

**Alan**: If someone needs assistance with additional forms or paperwork, what can they do?

**Robert**: They can visit or call the office of any government agency in their area and talk with the small business representative about selling to that respective agency. Simply review the U.S. Government section of your local telephone directory for numbers. You can also get copies from the General Services Administration Business Service Center in your area. Call (202) 708-5804 for the office nearest you. Also check with the SBA who can assist you with determining which agencies may be interested in your product or service. Call them at (800) 827-5722.

**Alan**: What is PASS and why is it important?

**Robert**: PASS, the Procurement Automated Source System, has been an important database for small businesses wishing to do business with the government. This program is being absorbed into a new program called "Pro-Net" and is administered by the SBA. The process is easy -- you simply register your business on line using the internet. visit Pro-Net at http://www.pro-net.sba.gov or go to the SBA site at http://www.sba.gov and click on pro-net.

**Alan**: Do you have any additional tips for minority-owned businesses?

**Robert**: Get listed in ABELS (Automated Business Enterprise Locator System), another important

database. Get an application by calling the Minority Business Development Agency at (202) 482-1958.

**Alan**: What is the significance of reviewing the Commerce Business Daily (CBD)?

**Robert**: You can review CBD for contract awards to determine sub-contracting opportunities and to check which agencies are purchasing your product or services. You may find copies of the CBD at most large libraries, or you may subscribe at a cost of $260/year by contacting the Government Printing Office at (202) 512-1800, or best of all, you may view the current issue for free on the Internet at: <http: //www.cos.gdb.org. But remember, the CBD only lists a very small percentage of what the government is buying.

**Alan**: What type of networking activities would you suggest in this field?

**Robert**: Most newspapers carry listings of companies that have won government contracts. Brainstorm and share ideas with local companies doing business with federal government agencies. You can also market directly to other contractors, state and local agencies that receive federal contracts. Find out who they are by reviewing the CBD. Additionally, your local SBA office may have lists of contacts.

**Alan**: Are there any additional tips you can share that would be of benefit to the small business person?

**Robert**: The Central Contractor Registry (CCR) provides a "single face" to a vendor for registering to do business with the government. The advantage of CCR is that your small business is on equal footing with the big guys. You no longer have to register with every local procurement office to gain bid access to possible

> *You can review CBD for contract awards to determine sub-contracting opportunities and to check which agencies are purchasing your product or services.*

contracts of interest. To register your company into the CCR, visit their website at <http://ccr.edi.disa.mil/ccr/>. Registration will require that you have a DUNS number. You may obtain a DUNS number from Dun & Bradstreet at (800)333-0505. This is a great free service.

**Alan**: Robert, I just want you to know that I was very impressed with the extensive information contained in your books, and highly recommend it to all readers of *Spare Time*. Do you have any closing comments?

**Robert**: My desire was to provide the best information possible for the small business person wishing to do business with the United States Government, the largest purchaser of goods and services in the world!

*Alan Rothman (arothman@fea.net) is an author, columnist, speaker, and consultant to the network marketing industry and the communications field. You can contact him by snail mail at 24401 Caswell Ct. Laguna Niguel, CA 92677. For info, call 714-362-9233 or leave a message at 800-593-9234. For those with AOL access, see my column under the keyword, Network Marketing, called Rothman's Secrets of MLM.*

*For "Power Networking: Why Enrich is for Everyone!" Visit http://www.hgionline.com and look under What's New? If you would like to participate and be part of our newly syndicated radio show, Creating Wealth from Home, make contact immediately as we are in production now.*■

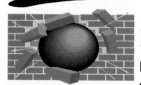

## Learn To Think Beyond The Fear

Fear prevents us from thinking clearly and creatively and causes most of the stress we experience. It is the greatest hindrance to successful risk taking and to performing our best under pressure. To keep ahead of change and to successfully confront the many challenges facing us, we need to learn how to overcome this insidious obstacle.

The good news about fear is that we have plenty of company. We all fear failing. Before taking a risk or tackling a challenging situation, *everyone* is afraid. Nobody lives without fear. In fact, if you tell me you have no fears, I will assume one of two things: Either you are playing it much too safe and not taking any risks, or you are totally out of touch with your feelings.

# Running on Empty?

# Fuel up at www.incite.net

Success in business requires more than a great idea. You've got to stay motivated, overcome rejection, develop your relational and communication skills, and stick with it.

We know you want to make your life count. That's why we developed Incite – a life-education resource on the Internet that aims to inspire and promote greatness in people.

Incite offers hundreds of workshops, books, audio and videotapes from categories such as leadership, biography, family, inspiration, worldview and personal development. In addition, you can subscribe free to "Daily Spark — Life Lessons from the World's Greatest Teachers," and get the boost you need to stick with it day in and day out.

Whether you're traveling across town, or traveling through life, you don't want to run out of fuel. Incite is a reservoir of resources you can tap week after week, month after month, that can help you down the road toward greatness.

**!ncite** ©

**Resources to Fuel Your Fire**

# Beverly Sassoon
## Introduces Common Sense Living to Network Marketing

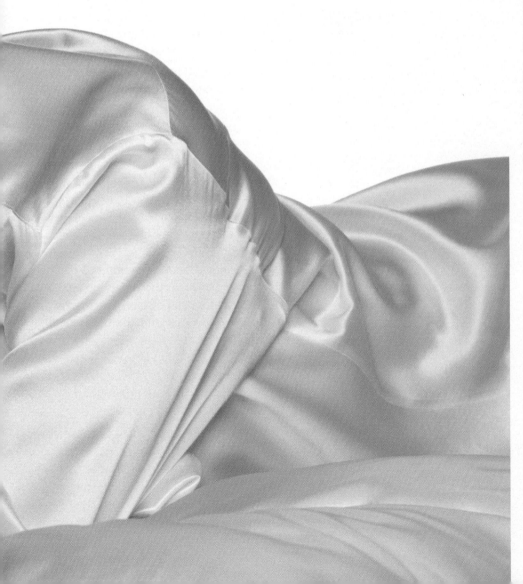

**"Beverly is the outgrowth of a total approach to living."**

## Fun... Talented... Smart and Tenacious

are the qualities that have made Beverly Sassoon popular among tough business executives, as well as best friends with her next door neighbors. Beverly is the ultimate baby boomer. She's the mother of four (and grandparent of one), a hard working executive, and is keenly interested in health care, wellness, and beauty issues.

Beverly's family background reads like a Beneton fashion ad. She's originally from Canada, with Irish, Scottish, and Polish roots. Vidal, her former husband, is from London, with Turkish and Russian heritage. Her son, Elan, attended school in Rio de Janeiro, and went on to marry a smart and talented Brazilian beauty from Sao Paolo. Her oldest daughter, Catya, is married to a musician from Zimbabwe. From that marriage, Beverly's uniquely named grandson, London, was born.

Beverly's common sense and uncommon business savvy, has always distinguished her as a unique executive capable of being in the right place at the right time...often!

With her diverse hands-on experience in product development, marketing, sales and corporate operations, it was her corporate skills, judgment and vision, which prompted her election to the Board of Directors of Vidal Sassoon. Additionally, for several years, she also served as their primary spokesperson.

Perceived by consumers as the embodiment of beauty, youth and vitality, Beverly Sassoon

has since written extensively on health and beauty issues in her published books and in articles for popular consumer magazines. Throughout her career she has built a trust with the health and beauty industry and has established an outstanding reputation with consumers around the world.

When direct response television took off, Beverly Sassoon was there. When home shopping (HSN and QVC) raced to its multi-million dollar success, Beverly Sassoon was one of its on-camera pioneers. She is now positioning her personality, knowledge, and powerful brand name in the right place -- network marketing -- to capitalize on the next chapter in contemporary retailing and global e-commerce.

Common sense living will be the theme of Beverly Sassoon International. She will introduce a line of common sense skin care, common sense nutrition, and several other lucrative and popular common sense product categories.

Beverly believes the common sense theme is particularly pertinent in light of the overwhelming nature of today's information highway and the constant bombardment of new product advertising. Common sense living will encourage people to strike a balance, avoid extremes and tap into their own inner wisdom when addressing health and beauty habits. This approach will appeal to baby boomers concerned with specific conditions that need treatment as well as the Generation X's who feel they, too, will one day have to treat age-related conditions and therefore want to examine prevention issues today. This is the reason its natural that her next focus would be to explore, develope and market a contemporary line of popular anti-aging products for the mass market.

Beverly is convinced that common sense living can touch upon our lives, our children's lives, their children's lives and even the lives of the important four-legged, furry family members. Ah hah...sounds like there may even be a common sense pet care line in the works.

Leveraging a globally recognized brand name, Beverly Sassoon International will debut its inaugural product line in the fall of '99, touting the dramatic anti-aging effects of its signature ingredient Coenzyme Q10, a breakthrough anti-oxidant that enhances cardiovascular circulation, significantly boosts the immune system, and has been successfully used to treat chronic aging diseases. Incorporating CoQ10 along with an exclusive blend of herbs, minerals, vitamins, amino acids, proteins and other enzymes will be the basis for the initial product line which includes an intensive bioenergetic night cream and nutrient day cream, a bioenergetic anti-aging serum for oily skin and another for dry skin, super cellular conductor ingestables, and a mental alertness energy drink.

Beverly believes that today's consumer is much different that in years gone by. She states, "I believe I am fairly representative of what is often called the aging population of today. I am a 53-year-old single woman. I also believe I have more years ahead of me than previous generations. The question is, what can I do to maximize my physical and emotional assets so I can live as stress free as possible and make healthy and wise decisions that allow me to live with energy, clarity and a purpose."

"There was a time when a woman my age was envisioned as old. She had allowed her skin to sag, her hair to gray, her waist to thicken and her gait to slow. Not so today...Today, men and women in their 40s, 50s and even 60s are energetic and vital. We still work, have romance in our lives and a bounce in our walk. We don't have to give in to the conditions that have historically attacked our minds and bodies. We can take action and benefit from advancing technology, medical updates, superior diagnostic tools, and effective products that can assist in interrupting the aging process."

Beverly claims she intends this next chapter of her life to be her biggest and best.

The success, profitability, motivation and encouragement of Beverly Sassoon distributors is the highest priority of her new universe. She's very family oriented and knows this next worldwide opportunity will capitalize on her already familiar family instincts.

Beverly encourages interested professionals to watch for the big announcement later in 1999. Beverly Sassoon International promises to be one of the smartest entries into network marketing in years...and why? Because it brings a dynamic product strategy, marketing savvy, a liberal compensation plan, and powerful, globally known brand names to those looking for a long-term stable success.

Hall of Famer Doris Wood, has stated that, "Persistence breaks down resistence." As Beverly looks over the past year she agrees and adds, "Our intention is to converge the best elements of multi-level distribution, home based shopping, personality-driven marketing and e-commerce into a newly structured international retailing entity." On her choice not to compete in the same product category with Vidal Sassoon, she is quick to respond with characteristic wit, "I'm staying out of his hair!"

*Beverly Sassoon International* corporate offices are located at: 501 Brickell Key Drive, Suite 505, Miami, FL 33131.∎

*A diplomat is a person who can tell you to go to hell in such a way that you actually look forward to the trip.*

Caskie Stinnett, quoted by Peter Potter, All About Success, 1988, "Tact"

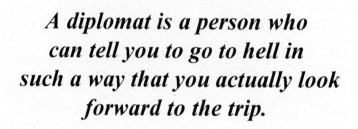

# Building a Competetive Advantage Through Strategic Alliances

*Lloyd Langdon*

**M**any of today's executives believe that costs for information services are rising too rapidly, that technology is changing too quickly and the customer is not getting their money's worth. These beliefs are fueling the corporate rush to build strategic alliances for outsourced solutions. The broad acceptance of outsourcing as a business tool is nothing more than the business megatrend of the 90's.

Since the industrial revolution, corporate America has been working under the model where the competitive edge of a company is measured by its size; a model where companies strive to own, control and directly manage all of their assets. More recently, companies are beginning to measure their competitive advantage based on how well they do and what they do. In other words, to use the current vernacular, how well do they perform in their 'core competency.' As a direct result of their efforts to concentrate on core competencies, American corporations have begun turning to outsourcing as a way of un-burdening themselves from tasks in which they lack expertise.

In industry studies conducted in 1996 by KPMG-Peat Marwick, Pitney Bowes Management Services, and the Outsourcing Institute, it was determined that 77 percent of the companies surveyed used some form of outsourcing. Furthermore, 40 percent of the dollars spent on outsourcing were spent on information technology.

**What is Outsourcing?** Outsourcing can be defined as "the contracting out of the provision of corporate support services."

**Why Outsourcing?**

**1) Cost reduction** - The overriding motivation to outsource for most companies is cost reduction. Studies indicate that savings gained primarily from economies of scale can be between 10 to 50 percent. These savings are made possible because the vendor of the outsourced service can spread the overhead associated to the provided service over many customers.

**2) Incremental increases in resources** - The resources available for the outsourced task are increased in small increments as opposed to stepped increments such as hiring a new employee or buying a new computer system.

**3) Access to technology** - Access to world class technology is more readily available through strategic partnerships with those who already have the technology you desire. Capital outlay can be reduced and conserved for other uses.

**4) Flexibility** - The commitment of capital to outsourcing varies directly with the need for the provided service. As the needs of the company grow or shrink, so do the expenses for the outsourced service.

**5) Freedom** - Freedom to focus on the core competencies of the company. Outsourcing lets the company focus on doing what they do best. Companies no longer get bogged in the mire of 'how to do' and are freed to focus on 'what to do.'

**6) Leverage** - Companies can leverage on the expertise of the service provider. The company gains competitive advantage immediately without going through the expense of development.

**7) Reengineering** - Companies gain competitive advantage as service providers reengineer their processes. The gain comes at no cost to the company.

**Key considerations when evaluating whether outsourcing is right for you are:**

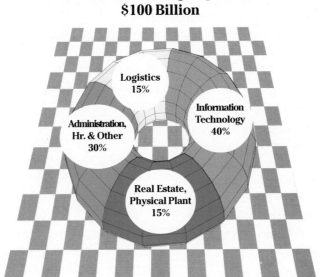

**1996 U.S. Outsourcing Expenditures: $100 Billion**

Logistics 15%

Information Technology 40%

Administration, Hr. & Other 30%

Real Estate, Physical Plant 15%

**A:** Will the use of the providers service provide a competitive or strategic advantage?

**B:** Does the outsourced service provide the organization with a component that differentiates the company in the marketplace?

**C:** Partners should be selected based on total capabilities, reputation and references; not price alone. Build a partnership that will provide opportunity for both parties to succeed.

**D:** Look for relationships that will bring the most value to your company instead of focusing on the lowest cost.

Outsourcing can enable organizations to succeed through increased concentration and focus in the areas which offer them the greatest competitive advantage, their core competency.

Jenkon International, the world leader in direct selling software, has its roots in outsourcing. In fact, Jenkon was initially established in 1978 as an outsource provider of information technology to direct selling companies. Having nearly twenty years experience in the industry as well as having supported over 800 direct selling companies, Jenkon has accumulated vast amounts of specialized knowledge that their customers routinely leverage competitive advantages from.

With the domination of the Internet as the preferred technology platform for the foreseeable future, Jenkon has reengineered their outsourcing services to include a hybrid product that allows their customers to gain the benefit of outsourcing their software needs without losing control of valuable information contained in the data from the outsourced solution. Jenkon now offers access to their world class direct selling software via the Internet.

Jenkon's Internet offering of their flagship product, Summit, can be configured to meet the needs of any direct selling company. Services provided can be as simple as the ability to enter representative applications and commissionable volumes to facilitate the bonus check process or a full-featured software solution, including accounts receivable, inventory, general ledger, auto system, EIS, customer service, order processing, warehouse management, international business solutions, etc...a complete custom tailored solution. Additionally, field sales representatives can be given access to the core business functions that they require to successfully build their organizations, such as order processing, downline inquiry, volume inquiry, etc. These are available through the representatives favorite web browser.

Finally, and perhaps the most exciting technology to reach direct selling companies this decade, is Jenkon's new PC based web-enabled productivity tool, NOW!. NOW!, aimed at helping the home-based entrepreneur build and manage their business. NOW! is a full-featured personal information manager with appointment calendar, task manager, and address & phone book systems. NOW! was developed by Jenkon in using an existing internationally renowned time management application as its basis. The software was enhanced to specifically address the needs of direct selling organizations. NOW! integrates with Jenkon's Summit product to give representatives full access to virtually all up-to-date information that pertains to their downline manager functions of the PIM. Representatives can place orders for products as well as enter new representative applications off-line. The information is uploaded to the corporate office next time they connect to the Internet.

Perhaps the most exciting benefit of this product is that the corporate office can insert tasks into the representatives task manager. The system can be configured to insert a set of scheduled tasks automatically each time a specified event occurs. Examples of events where this feature could be implemented include: a new recruit who has been added, or when a downline representative is promoted. The system can automatically insert into a representatives task list, a task telling her to contact the new recruit and welcome them aboard, contact the sponsor and offer congratulations etc. These are just a few examples of new technology that is available to Jenkons' outsourced and regular customers. For more information on these products, contact Jenkon International at (360) 256-4400.

Outsourcing is a bottom line driven alliance that integrates the core competencies of the outsourcing partners. One of the most startling examples of outsourcing at its best is Topsy Tail Company, with over $80 million in sales and three employees. The company is in reality a network of twenty carefully selected strategic alliances who handle everything from manufacturing, to servicing the retail outlets of the companies' hair care products.

Excellence, expertise and specialization are the keys to building a competitive advantage. To gain excellence and expertise, companies must specialize. Through specialization, companies lose the ability to provide excellence in areas that are not within their core competency, and thus the growth of outsourcing as one of the most popular solutions to this dilemma in today's business environment.■

# Inside Network Marketing

## Romantic Semantics; Deciphering MLM's Secret Language

*Leonard W. Clements*

**R**omantic: Imaginative, but impractical; not based on fact, imaginary.

**S**emantics: The study of meaning in language form with regard to its historical change.

These definitions courtesy of the American Heritage Dictionary. So, how does this apply to network marketing? Let us count the ways.

Network marketers have, over the last half century, evolved into some of the greatest spin doctors and word-smiths that our society has ever created. We've become masters at romancing our semantics. That is, we as an industry have created this wonderful, albeit misleading and illusionary way of stating facts. As paradoxical as that may sound, practically every line of every ad, and every sentence spoken at a typical opportunity meeting now contains some degree of evidence of this. To wit...

**"No, we don't accept credit cards...we're in the business of getting people out of debt, not further in debt!"**

I didn't make that one up. A prominent MLM company made this exclamation several years ago -- after burning through 22 Merchant Service providers that refused to accept their account. The proverbial lemonade out of lemons.

How about this classic: **"We are absolutely debt free!"** Translation: "No one will lend us money!" Now, understand. I'm sure there are many MLM companies who are debt free because they pay for everything with cash, and they can comfortably afford to do so. Good for them. But, how do you know? Simply proclaiming yourself debt free certainly implies your cash rich and financially prudent, or it could mean you can't initiate credit terms, or you've exploited so many of your vendors in the past they will only do business with you on a cash basis. The latter scenario would likely signal the death knell of the company. Yet, they could still claim, "We are absolutely debt free!" and they would be absolutely telling the truth. Another paradox. Dishonest honesty.

I've always loved this one: **"We're approaching momentum!"** Now, if we were to make the logical assumption that all MLM companies will eventually achieve some degree of fast growth if they stay in business long enough, practically any company could make this claim. But, what exactly is "momentum?" Is it 50% growth in one month? Is it 100% monthly growth over three months? One thousand percent in a week? Well, let's take a look at one recent situation. A 10-plus year old MLM company had never received more than 350 applications in a single day. That was their record. Then, one recent Thursday, out of nowhere, 800 applications swamped the home office. The next day, 1,300 more! Some of their distributors rode through MLMville yelling "Momentum is coming! Momentum is coming!" Was it? Mmm, well, sounds like it, doesn't it? But, let's take a peak behind the scenes. This company had a $295 enrollment package (I've changed the details here just slightly to protect the innocent). They had also just absorbed the distributor base of another MLM company. This new influx of distributors were given a grace period to re-enroll and have the $295 fee

229

> *Network marketers have, over the last half century, evolved into some of the greatest spin doctors and word-smiths that our society has ever created. We've become masters at romancing our semantics. That is, we as an industry have created this wonderful, albeit misleading and illusionary way of stating facts.*

waved. Guess when the deadline was? That's right. Five o'clock that Friday evening.

Pay no attention to that man behind the curtain.

Let's stay with this issue of "momentum" a bit longer. This is surely one of the most romanticized words in the MLMer vocabulary. What exactly is "approaching?" A common MLM myth that continues to go in and out of remission is that MLM companies hit momentum when they reach $50 million in annual sales. The truth is, one company out of thousands, over the last 53 years, went into momentum at that point. Not one before, not one since. But, for some reason, that's now the accepted benchmark by many MLM romantics. So, when

they boldly claim their company is going into momentum soon because they are **"approaching $50 million in annual sales,"** are they being truthful? It's hard not to be. If that company had sales last month of $10, and sales this month were $20, they are, in fact, "approaching" $50 million in annual sales.

**Rationalizing:** Lying with a clear conscience.

**That's the Clements Dictionary definition.**

The word games some companies play to avoid the multi-level marketing stigma are almost funny. Almost. The original title is a definition unto itself. Multi-level marketing: Multiple levels of people marketing. Pretty simple, isn't it? Yet there are companies out there that will deny ad nausea, even to the point of taking legal action, if you refer to them as a multi-level marketing operation – even though there are obviously multiple levels of people marketing there in. What's so absurd about this is that their entire case is based on nothing more than title changes. Their delineation from MLM is based solely on their making up a different group of words for things. I think I'll call the tires of my Mitsubishi "landing gear" and the body a "fuselage" and the cab a "cockpit" and the horizontal fin on my trunk a "wing" and then I can rightfully claim to be an airline pilot.

Here's a few other recent examples. I'll just run through them quickly.

**"We're listed with the Better Business Bureau!"** One of the most common ways a company get's "listed" with the BBB is by having complaints registered against it. A company chooses to be a member.

**("fill in the blank) has been**

**nominated for a Nobel Prize!"** I can nominate my cat for a Nobel Prize.

**("fill in the blank) has previously owned/operated two multi-million dollar network marketing companies!"** Mohammed Ali wanted to be a "four-time Heavy Weight Champion." To achieve this feat required that he lose at least three times. So, if so-and-so used to own and operate other MLM companies, what happened to them? They went out of business? They were shut down? The shareholders booted him out? He sold his interest and is now starting another MLM company in competition with his old company? The possibilities are myriad. None of them are good.

**"Our products are listed in the Physician's Desk Reference."** The PDR lists what you pay them to. The publisher "does not warrant or guarantee," nor have they performed "any independent analysis," nor are they "advocating the use of" any product found therein. That's straight from the forward of the 47th edition.

**"Our product is a $60 billion industry!"** In other words, you're trying to sell something everyone already possesses?

**"We don't sell lotions and potions!"** So, you're saying you've intentionally avoided the one product niche that the largest, most successful MLM companies and richest distributors are all involved in? That's a selling point?

**"No meetings!"** So, you're saying you don't offer what has been proven to be the single most effective enrollment and training method throughout MLM history? This is a benefit?

**"No selling!"** So, you're...lying?

**"Our infinity bonus pays 10% down to the first Platinum-With-Diamonds-In-It Director in the**

230

leg." Translation: "Our infinity bonus pays down a few more levels and then stops."

Mr. Webster and I have a very different definition of "infinity" than many MLM companies. I'm pretty sure infinity means doesn't stop.

Here's more illusionary benefits...

**"We allow you to enroll your spouse (or yourself) on your own first level!"** An illusionary benefit based on the illusion you're the only one that benefits. If everyone else has the same benefit, and they're all double-dipping too, then sure, you're get paid double — on half the volume!

**"No (or very small) monthly personal volume requirement!"** So, you create this big downline full of people all sitting around waiting for someone to order something. If you don't have to order very much, then they don't have to order much.

**"You can earn overrides on your own personal volume!"** This essentially amounts to a rebate. Problem is, it's really just a tax free loan to the company that you will pay income tax on twice! Think about it. You pay $10 of already taxed income for a bottle of vitamins. The company keeps it for a month, then pays you back $2 of your own money. They had free use of your money for a month, and Uncle Sam says that $2 is new income. You get double taxed — instead of just charging you $8 for the vitamins. The company benefits in two ways: Financially, and the creation of good will. The distributors actually think they're doing them a favor!

Here's my all-time favorite: **"We sell our service at slightly below cost**, but we make it up in volume." I think we should pause for a moment on that one.

Okay, let's continue.

**("fill in the company) was ten years in development!"** So, the founder thought about it for nine years, and spent the last year putting everything together?

**"We're in prelaunch!"** The birth of an MLM company is no different than the birth of a baby. You're never in "prebirth." Either you're born, or your not. Either your processing applications, shipping product, and cutting checks, or you're not. "Prelaunch" is nothing more than a marketing gimmick to entice the naive newcomer to MLM who still believes there is an inherent advantage to "getting in at the top." Some companies have romanced this illusion for literally years! I know one company that claimed they were in prelaunch in their third year of business!

**"Ground floor"** is abused in much the same manner. Some companies are now defining ground floor by the relatively small number of distributors they have, not their age. One such company recently claimed to be a "ground floor opportunity" even though they were over ten years old!

Statistics can be romanced as well. And when you couch them in well played semantics, the results can go from ridiculous to dangerous.

**"You can earn up to $90,000 per month, or more!"** Read this very real ad headline carefully. It essentially covers every number from zero to infinity. The ultimate Truth in Advertising.

**"Over 300,000 people have joined our company!"** This was also a true statement at the time. Of course, the ad forgot to mention that 230,000 had since quit. Note, it doesn't say they have 300,000, it says that's how many "have joined."

Along those same lines, several less-than-five-year-old MLM companies today are bragging about their distributor base of 500,000 plus. The catch is, they are counting how many sequential ID numbers they have given out throughout their history. Each could lose 50,000 reps next month, and gain 1,000 new ones, and that number will go up to 501,000.

**Hype:** To increase artificially.

> *"Prelaunch" is nothing more than a marketing gimmick to entice the naive newcomer to MLM who still believes there is an inherent advantage to "getting in at the top."*

And speaking of less-than-five-year-old companies, have you heard this one? **"Only 26 (29?, 32?, 36?) MLM companies have made it to their fifth anniversary."** The most ironic thing about this wholly incorrect claim (I have 79 such companies in my database), it was popularized by a leading distributor for a company that had not yet celebrated it's fifth anniversary. The intent here, obviously, was to scare prospects away from less-than-five-year-old companies. The reality is that the vast majority of MLM failures occur within the first two years. So, to suggest that the vast majority fail within the first five years would be an accurate statement, would it not? But then, so would "The vast majority of MLM companies fail within the first 20 years." Of course, you'd

231

only say that if you were involved in a 21-year-old company.

But the illogic of this scare-tactic propaganda goes even deeper. Even if the 26 company figure above were accurate, it still wouldn't really mean what it's intended to convey. Of all the MLM companies that have ever existed in the last 53 years, the vast majority launched this decade! Of course there are very few old MLM

> *...as cynical as I've become about this business, I still believe the "pros" (professionals) outnumber the "cons" (convicts). The desperate, aggressive, overzealous minority of MLMers out there just seem to be the one's that are always in our face. They stand out.*

companies. Using the same illogic, I can prove that the Model T Ford is better built and lasts longer than a Lexus. After all, of all the cars still on the road after 75 years of use, almost all are Model T's and not one is a Lexus.

This one drives me nuts: **"If you get four people who each get four, you can make $800 with just 20 people!"** These types of pitches will even be referred to as "conservative."

They are also assuming that every single distributor that you enroll will enroll four others, and that the bottom 16 will never quit even though they have no downline themselves. In fact no one ever quits, and every single distributor in your downline always orders each month.

**Conservative:** Moderate; cautious; restrained; erring towards the negative.

And what about those really low attrition rates we keep hearing about? Is a 6% attrition rate good? Sounds pretty good -- if they're talking about last year, or over the life of the company. Or, are they referring to yesterday? Or last week? We don't know. They never say. Wonder why.

Reorder rates can be manipulated in much the same way. More than one popular program has recently claimed a **"75% monthly reorder rate."** Okay, so 100 people order in January. Seventy five reorder in February. Then, 75% of them, or 56 people will reorder in March...and 42 in April...32 in May...24 in June...I think you see where this is going...and 12 months later you'll have no customers left – and still be able to make an honest claim to a 75% monthly reorder rate. Technically.

There was a company a few years ago that claimed 93% of all those surveyed had lost weight on their diet products. What wasn't revealed was that only those who had been on the product for at least six months were part of the survey. What I can't figure out is why the other 7% kept ordering!

"There are liars, damn liars, and statisticians." -- Mark Twain

The Aloe wars of the early 90s saw it's share of data romancing. One company said right on their 16 oz. bottle, "This bottle contains 100%

pure Aloe Vera." A competitor had the product assayed. It contained one ounce of pure Aloe Vera, and 15 oz. of water and flavoring. They sued, claiming false advertising. They lost. The bottle did indeed "contain 100% pure Aloe Vera." As well as water and flavoring.

Sales figures have seen more romance that a Harlequin novel. One popular company claimed sales in the hundreds of millions. Upon closer review, I found that almost half of their "sales" were the training packages they were charging their distributors, not the product they were in the business of selling. In fact, "sales" included administrative fees, shipping charges, marketing tools, and other such items. I guess a sale is a sale. Another company recently claimed a monthly sales figure of $8.5 million. Of course, they were quoting "retail" sales... and they have a 100% suggested markup...and an 8 oz. bottle of shampoo wholesaled for $12.50 ($25.00 suggested retail)... they have free distributor enrollment... so their products are probably never retailed, ever, so their actual sales were exactly half the number they were promoting.

There's an old saying, "If you torture the data long enough you can make it say anything." It seems it's also true that you can romance it into doing your bidding as well.

Do we, as an industry, tend to romance our incomes, just a little? For example, when someone says to you, "My income has reached $50,000 per month!" They forget to mention that a third came from a downline that was given to them as part of a sweetheart deal with the company, another third came from a past downline they moved over, and the other third came from the books and tapes they marketed to this prefab downline. Oh, and notice they didn't actually tell you they were making $50,000 right now; they clearly said their income "has reached" that level. That was in 1993. They're only making $5,000 now, and have $6,000 in monthly expenses. Unfortunately, I'm only exaggerating just a little.

I actually find it quite amusing when I hear these hucksters claim they were making some huge income in another MLM program, and they just "walked away" from it to join this hot, Earth

> **There's an old saying, "If you torture the data long enough you can make it say anything." It seems it's also true that you can romance it into doing your bidding as well.**

shaking, revolutionary new start-up deal. Obviously, there's always more to the story, such as, they sold their old downline, or their distributorship was terminated, or the company just filed Chapter 13. It's easy to walk away from a $50,000 check -- when it bounces. One "heavy hitter" called me recently to proclaim he'd just walked away from a $100,000 monthly income. True story. Even if his story were all true, you know why I'd never want to be enrolled by this guy? Because I wouldn't want an IDIOT for a sponsor! Or, someone who thought I was.

When my income gets to $100,000 per month, I'm going to brand my company's logo onto my forehead!

Please understand, I'm not suggesting every positive claim or impressive statistic about network marketing is bogus. In fact, as cynical as I've become about this business, I still believe the "pros" (professionals) outnumber the "cons" (convicts). The desperate, aggressive, overzealous minority of MLMers out there just seem to be the one's that are always in our face. They stand out.

Network marketing is good. Very good. There's no shortage of positive information out there. I'm just balancing the scale. This is the secret behind the trick. Take away the smoke and mirrors and the illusion loses it's ability to persuade.

Romance the truth. It's okay. Hype is powerless against it.

*Leonard Clements has concentrated his full-time efforts over the last eight years on researching and analyzing all aspects of network marketing. He is a professional speaker and trainer, and currently conducts Inside Network Marketing seminars throughout the U.S., Canada and Mexico. He is also the publisher of the "MarketWave Alert" letter, an MLM analysis and watchdog newsletter. Mr. Clements is the host of "Inside Network Marketing," a weekly live call-in radio show on KSCO 1080, and he is the author of the controversial book, "Inside Network Marketing," an objective, no-holds-barred, insider's look at the MLM industry. He is also the author of the best selling cassette tape "Case Closed! The Whole Truth About Network Marketing," which has been labeled "the best" generic recruiting tape by six MLM company presidents.*

*To receive additional information about MarketWave and its products, please call (800) 688-4766.* ∎

# Direct Sales & The Internet: A Perfect Marriage

*Sherri Mead*

The explosion of the Internet is poised to have a revolutionary impact on the direct sales industry. Accessibility to the Internet and the World Wide Web are bringing about momentous changes in how companies and distributors market their product and attract the attention of prospective clients and recruits. You may be asking yourself, "How exactly has this new medium become so popular?"

A brief history reveals the roots of the Internet, also known as the "Net," sprung from a project funded by the Department of Defense back in 1969. The goal was to connect four computers being used by contractors and universities that were involved in military funded research. During the 1980s, advances were incorporated by the National Science Foundation as they set out to connect five regionally located supercomputers. The academic community took advantage of the ability to exchange information related to research and education. Around 1994, several large corporations began to use the Internet for more commercial purposes. Before long, companies were posting their information on individual web sites. A web site is simply a location on a very large computer network called the Internet, and is a place to post an electronic brochure. Web sites are generally filled with text, audio, graphics and connections (also referred to as links) to other locations on the sites on the Internet.

The introduction of a browser (Netscape Navigator and Microsoft's Internet Explorer are the two most popular) provided a way for novices to navigate around the Internet and view the information being presented. Coming to the forefront also were Internet Service Providers (ISPs). These are organizations that provide users the ability to make a connection to the Internet (generally for a monthly fee). In addition to access, the user is able to receive electronic mail (e-mail) and to view information posted on the World Wide Web (WWW). Another way to connect to the Internet is through an online service (i.e. America Online and Compuserve), which gives access to chat rooms, searchable databases, bulletin boards, games and other proprietary services. The use, accessibility and popularity of the Internet is accelerating at a rapid pace. Today you will find most companies you do business with -- from your local church to the teenager that lives next door -- will have some type of presence on the World Wide Web.

Utilization of the Internet within the direct sales/multi-level marketing industry is coming about in three different areas. First of all, the corporation is posting a web site. The corporate web site is generally used to introduce the company and business opportunity and product line to the reader (the person that "surfed" to a particular location). Companies are able to take advantage of technology that allows them to change information displayed on their web site at very little cost. They are able to communicate company notices, meeting locations and times, announce new product availability, send a message from the president, attach a video and/or graphic images that promote the company product, etc. Options are limited only by the imagination of the web master! Information residing on the web site needs to be changed on a routing basis. One of the primary goals of a web site is to keep people coming back. Remember, with the advent of the web site, potential customers and/or distributors are able to find you.

The second way in which the Internet is being used is by independent distributor/consultant. Many home-based business builders have already captured a vision for the potential and are creating individual web sites. They are promoting their specific business opportunity or product and are giving the reader the ability to either sign up as a distributor and/or purchase product. It is certainly possible that the owner of the web site may end up sponsoring someone into the organization that they have never even met! The challenge to the independent distributor is how they take advantage of the advances in technology, while focusing on the very real person-to-person contact that makes this industry so successful. An additional challenge to the corporate office is the "policing" of individual web sites. Many companies are expanding their policies and procedures to address product claims and overall images that are being presented by the independent distributor.

234

The exciting news is that independent distributors have an advantage with access to prospects of different regions and social structures. The Internet has helped to remove barriers in the marketplace.

Having a presence on the web today is a benefit. As Internet popularity and accessibility increase, those without a web presence will be left behind. Today, the public at large are purchasing everything from flowers to airline tickets to cars. The Georgia Technical Institute shares the following statistics. There are an estimated 36 million users on the net. A sampling of 10,000 web users produced the following results. 68% of web users have purchased products and/or services over the web. 87% of users connect to the web on a daily basis. Over 80% consider e-mail and access to the web as indispensable technology. The most popular reason those surveyed give for connecting to the web is convenience of personal shopping and researching vendor/product information. Other surveys and industry estimates reveal that business transacted over the web had grown to 2.6 billion during 1996, and by the year 2001, will reach 200 billion. Electronic commerce is accelerating both in the number of web shoppers as well as the total amount that individuals are willing to spend over the Internet. For relatively new technology to have such a major impact in a short period of time is representative of how the Internet will impact society in the months and years to come.

The third, and perhaps most exciting way in which the Internet is being used, is to link the independent distributor with genealogy and sales information residing within the corporate database. This is accomplished via a link across the Internet in a real-time and online environment. Distributors can check on their current volumes, inquire on activity within their downline organization, enter new distributor applications, place sales orders, inquire on the shipping status of sales orders, view commission statements, e-mail downline members and much more --all independent of corporate personnel. Never before has the home-based person been given such sophisticated tools to operate their personal business. Once online with such technology, the independent distributor will represent only those companies offering real-time update and inquiry capability.

Direct sales companies choosing to take advantage of the opportunities offered via Internet will have a competitive advantage and attract more independent distributors. In a short time, however, companies will be expected to have systems in place to directly link the distributor with the corporate database. Certainly an upside to giving distributors access to information over the Internet can produce a reduction in overhead at the corporate office. Turning over entry of new distributors and sales orders to the distributor will reduce data entry personnel. Having access to sales order shipping status, downline reports and commission statement information will also reduce the number of customer service representatives required to answer such questions over the telephone.

The union of the Internet and direct sales industry has a promising and exciting future. Now is the time to investigate how you can incorporate and promote your business and product by taking advantage of the dynamic technology surrounding the Internet and the World Wide Web.

*Sheri Mead is Project Manager of NOW! Technologies for Jenkon International and member of DSA Internet Council.* ■

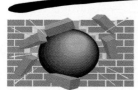

# Learn More From Mistakes Than From Failures

"Crisis can often have value," John Sculley says, "because it generates transformation...I have found that I always learn more from my mistakes, you aren't taking enough chances."

All of us have had occasion to learn more from our mistakes than our successes. This can be seen quite clearly in sports. In tennis, when a good player tries a new shot, say a backhand slice, and hits it into the net, he/she will go over the fundamentals to determine why he/she made the error. Then he/she will incorporate the necessary adjustments and take practice swings to cement the new learning. The next time he/she will hit it better. The correction has helped the player perfect the shot. Contrast this with players who don't take any risks. Satisfied to get the ball over the net, they play it safe, try nothing new, and their game doesn't improve.

The phenomenon is true in many areas. If you aren't making mistakes you aren't growing or learning. Or, as one chief executive says, "If you're not making mistakes, you're not doing anything worthwhile."

# Bruce Jenner Seeks Olympic Gold For Home-Based Entrepreneurs

In America's bicentennial year, Bruce Jenner captivated the world when breaking the alltime record by scoring 8,634 points in the decathlon at the Montreal Olympic Games. For this monumental achievement he earned the title of "The World's Greatest Athlete" and instantly became an American Hero. Since capturing the most celebrated event at the Olympic Games in 1976, Jenner has gone on to become a highly respected motivational speaker, sports commentator, entrepreneur, commercial spokesperson, television personality, actor, producer, author, and Vice Chairman of Longevity Network. He also serves on the Council of Champions for the Special Olympics and is an avid supporter of the Pediatric Aids Foundation.

Jenner's passion as a motivational speaker has gained him national acclaim. He is in demand from many Fortune 500 companies including Coca Cola, VISA, Anheuser Busch, MCI, Toyota, Kawasaki, and IBM Corporation. Corporate and community audiences alike remain enraptured by Jenner's unique story of self-inspired motivation and the tremendous opportunity for success that is afforded to all who live in America.

Jenner passionately emphasizes the industry of network marketing as the "opportunity avenue" of the next millennium. "Network marketing is entrepreneurship in a nutshell; pure and simple," he stated. "This industry is of the people, by the people and for the people. It is one of the few opportunities left in America for the average person with little or no investment savings," he maintains.

Jenner's quest to form a strategic alliance with a quality network marketing company came to fruition on July 3rd of 1997. He selected Longevity Network, a network marketing company based in Henderson, Nevada, as his infrastructure and "people" vehicle; a vehicle to help people who are willing to help themselves. Jenner, a rags-to-riches self-made millionaire, has a burning desire to give back to people everywhere who are struggling to find a way to improve their lives. The father of three chose Longevity Network because

*Shortly after his trajectory into the stratosphere for his monumental decathlon victory at the 1976 Olympics, Jenner's life was a rocky roller coaster ride for 14 years until his marriage to Kris in 1990. "Marrying Kris was without doubt, the turning point in my life."*

***The Jenner family (from left) Daughter Kendal being held by her mother, Kris, Bruce's daughter Khloe, and Kylie, nestled in the arms of her loving daddy***

of its "high-commitment to integrity, premium-quality product line and its family values corporate culture."

In a recent interview with Andy Robinson, this American icon discussed his childhood, athletic career and spelled out his vision for helping others pursue their dreams and achieve financial freedom:

**AR:** Countless millions around the globe are still familiar with your astounding success in the 1976 Olympic Games. What was it that got you started in athletics?

**Jenner:** Well, as a young child, I had to overcome the challenge of being dyslexic. I would sit in class terrified that the teacher would call on me to read aloud. My heart would start pounding and my hands were all sweaty. Reading the words on a page was like reading a billboard while doing the loop-the-loop on a roller coaster. I tried my best to guess which paragraph the teacher would call me on so I could prepare in advance. My total lack of self-confidence at that early age gave me the determination to become the very best at something, but I had to find my arena to play in. I found athletics to be my arena.

**AR:** Okay, so now we will fast forward to the Bruce Jenner "Post-Olympic-Gold" era. What was waiting for you after "The Games" in Montreal?

**Jenner:** What most people don't know is that my success after winning Olympic Gold in '76 was short-lived. I was thrown into a world that was totally unfamiliar and uncomfortable to me. I was surrounded by tele-prompters

as a TV sportscaster and I found myself suddenly thrown into a glass fishbowl as a celebrity and American hero. I was afraid! What I was hiding was that same mindset of

***His shining hour! Jenner, one arm around daughter Khloe and the other carrying the victory torch after his heart pounding miracle victory in Montreal***

237

Sports Illustrated

AUGUST 9, 1976   ONE DOLLAR

AWRRIGHT!

Bruce Jenner
Wins Big

USA
935

the nervous dyslexic schoolboy hiding from my teacher. After the Games I began quietly running away for nearly 14 years. In 1990, you would have found me living in a one-bedroom Los Angeles bungalow; my sink piled high with dirty dishes and my living room decorated with a dried-out Christmas tree. My main source of income was from public speaking jobs - at which I always wore my best attire - an out-of-style 1976 tuxedo. I was in trouble.

**AR:** This is a little known fact about Bruce Jenner. What was it that turned your life around 180 degrees in less than 10 years?

**Jenner:** Meeting my wife, Kris, was without a doubt the turning point in my life. We met on a blind date in 1990 and walked down the aisle five months later. Together, we have overcome the obstacles that used to keep me down and affect most of us. You know, problems of everyday life. Health problems, frustration in their jobs, difficulty in paying the bills and making ends meet. I was no different. I went through it all despite my fame and glory. I was fortunate to receive a second chance and I made good on that window of opportunity. I'm determined to do everything in my power to help others make good on their "second chance" for success. That's the very reason why I am so passionate about network marketing and the home-based business revolution.

*"Made it Ma --*
*Top of the World!"*

**AR:** What about network marketing appeals to you the most?

**Jenner:** The concept of people helping people achieve success. Network marketing has been around for over half a century. It's an industry that has experienced explosive growth for more than a decade in more than 44 countries with worldwide sales estimated at more than $100 billion. *Upline* magazine has called network marketing, "the peoples franchise." Most people don't know that the franchise concept - relied upon by thousands of fast food restaurants, video rental stores, and other successful businesses - was considered a scam by most Americans some forty years ago. Denounced by the media, franchising was even in danger of being outlawed by Congress. Today, the U.S. public buys and sells over one-third of the nations goods and services through franchises,

making it an almost $800 billion industry. I believe Network marketing is today where franchises were 30 or 40 years ago. It remains a largely misunderstood business, but we are working hard every day to help American's from all walks of life experience its vast potential.

**AR:** What kind of earning potential does an individual have with network marketing?

**Jenner:** According to *Entrepreneur* Magazine, the average home-based business posts annual revenues of $50,250 per year, and the top 20% of home-based businesses earn more than $75,000 per year. To put this into perspective, consider that the average person per capita income in the United States in 1997 was just $29,750.

**AR:** How many people across the country have been sold on the concept of working from home? ▶

**Jenner:** Well, studies show that a new home-based business is started every 11 seconds in the U.S. - that's 8,000 new businesses a day. In 1975, only 2.5 million people worked from their home. Today, 40 million people generate a portion of their income from a home-based business. With this tremendous growth, it's a certainty that these figures will dramatically increase. As a matter of fact, analysts predict in the very near future that nearly 50% of all households in America will support themselves at least in part from some form of home-based business.

**AR:** Those are very impressive numbers.

**Jenner:** Yea, but they could be bigger. According to the Market Wave Industry Newsletter, surveys indicate that about 85% of all Americans would like to own their own business, if they could. In other words, if all hurdles were removed, people would choose the option of being their own boss rather than working for someone else. But most people don't take action or the steps it takes to get involved and start their own business, generally because of four reasons. They believe that:

*The Moment of a Lifetime*

*Jenner addressing longevity distributors shortly after joining the Nevada-based network marketing company*

product categories in healthcare, fitness, nutritional supplements, apparel, and skin & hair care, all ensuring strict adherence to medical guidelines and current medical studies, Longevity proved a natural fit for us. Secondly, our relationship with Longevity's owners and management heads, Jim and Adi Song are dream team partners for me. Jim and Adi (Song) have built a solid corporate culture on trust, faith, integrity, and family values. I am extremely excited to combine our message with the Longevity products and financial vehicle.

**AR:** What is in the future for Longevity?

**Jenner:** Well, Longevity's five years in the industry have created a foundation which has enabled me to set forth a plan to accelerate the company's vision through both an electronic-media campaign as well as simply getting out there and shaking hands with the people. I simply help spread the word. I'm looking forward to changing home-based business in America by introducing thousands of people to network marketing — the last chance for the American dream to come true. Personal bankruptcies in America will hit over 1.2 million this year. Thousands of families need a way to make an extra $100, $300, $1,000 a month or more. Network marketing is an incredible way to do it for those who have the desire. Our message is clear: "Join us, dream big, and work hard."

1. It takes too much money; 2. It takes too much time; 3. It's too risky; 4. They don't know how.

Additionally, according to the Small Business Administration, nearly 9 out of 10 businesses fail in their first two years. No wonder people are afraid. This is why I want to show people -- people who want a second opportunity at success -- why I believe that network marketing eliminates these four obstacles.

**AR:** I understand that you have aligned yourself with Longevity Network. What was the attraction?

**Jenner:** Our first experience with Longevity was their incredible product line and we were ecstatic about the cutting-edge formulations they had to offer. With expanding

**AR:** Do you have any comments in closing?

**Jenner:** I would like all those who care about their future to have the potential to accomplish great things -- things that even they don't believe they can achieve. I want to encourage people to have a hope that makes sense and to awaken the champion within. The track stretches before you. Make each step of your life worthy of the greatness that lives deep inside. Always believe in the power of you and the overwhelming power of what people can do together as a team.

*For more information on **Bruce Jenner** or Longevity Network, please contact Andy Robinson at (702) 454-7000. E-mail, attn: Andy, mail@longevitynetwork.com.*∎

# SPECIAL REPORT

# GROWING GLOBAL

## The Worldwide Network Marketing Tidal Wave

*Ridgely Goldsborough*

One hundred and sixty thousand people per week join a network marketing company. That's 32,000 new people per day excluding weekends. And revenue: $150 billion dollars and growing at around 14% per year.

These are big numbers and they're only going to get bigger. Network marketing represents the largest global movement of people in the history of this planet. Nothing else even comes close. Housewives and lawyers, construction workers and accountants; people from all walks of life are gravitating at meteoric rates to the business of network marketing.

Low risk, high return, diversified income, great products are all terms often touted by professional networkers as benefits of the business. While all of those mentioned payoffs do in fact drive people into the industry, what keeps it growing at such an explosive rate is relationships: People helping people, building with people, serving people.

From its humble U.S. beginnings, network marketing now flourishes in 125 countries on all continents. Not surprisingly, the Far East is a hotbed for the industry.

In Japan, the number one market in the world, the Worldwide Federation of Direct Selling Associations (WFDSA) reports that 2 million distributors are responsible for sales of over $30 billion dollars per year. Considering that the WFDSA only includes figures of DSA (Direct Selling Association) member companies, the actual numbers are likely to be substantially higher. All of the companies that have to report earnings are posting record sales numbers. There seems to be no end in sight.

Amway Japan, for example, has nearly one million distributors. What's more, 70% of Amway's nearly $6 billion in total sales last year were generated in foreign markets. And Amway is not alone in American-based companies finding fertile soil offshore. Avon, the nation's largest direct seller of beauty products posted revenues of $5.2 billion in 1998 from their field force of nearly two million female representatives. A whopping 65 percent of Avon's sales were registered from 135 foreign ports, or a figure of $3.2 billion. The leader in percentage of overseas sales, however, is Tupperware, a 50-year-old company that serves more than 100 countries. The Orlando, Florida-based firm reportedly sold an astonishing 87 percent of its product line outside of the United States in 1998. Finally, Mary Kay currently counts representatives in 27 countries and this number will rise significantly as the Dallas, Texas headquartered firm looks to increase its penetration in underdeveloped world sites such as Africa, the Middle East, Eastern Europe, Russia, Latin America and Asia.

Taiwan and Korea are top ten markets; both approaching the $2 billion in sales marks. In fact, in Taiwan, one out of every 12 people in the country is a network marketer. Despite tight governmental restrictions, Korean network marketing companies continue to flourish. Dr. Charles King, founder of the University of Chicago's Network Marketing certification program, has been teaching one of the first international programs in Seoul, with an eye to expanding around the world shortly thereafter.

Although economic conditions keep the majority of Malaysia's wealth in the hands of a select few, over one million network marketers are on track to generate more than a billion dollars in product sales per year.

Thailand, one of the gateways to Southeast Asia, has a booming economy as well. With 14 million inhabitants

*In Japan, the number one market in the world, the Worldwide Federation of Direct Selling Associations (WFDSA) reports that 2 million distributors are responsible for sales of over $30 billion per year.*

▶

# Amway Targets Cyberspace With Quixtar

In an unprecedented move, Amway, the nation's largest direct selling company has targeted the Internet in what most analysts say will begin the launch of a new and highly successful venture for the 40-year-old Ada, Michigan-based firm. Welcome to Quixtar, Amway's new company that opened for business in September. Like Amway, it will sell hundreds of consumer products at volume discounts through its massive distributor base. In lock step, those distributors will earn commissions on their sales and bonuses from the sales of distributors they recruit.

That is where the comparative sidewalk ends. The one significant difference. Quixtar is the marketing equivalent of a new beginning. It will abandon any identification with Amway and seek to attract the under 30 market although it is anticipated that half of the company's current distributor base of 750,000 will eventually climb aboard Quixtar. "The word is change and everybody fears it," says Theodore Pritchett, an Amway distributor from Asheville, North Carolina. "Either we get on the Web and capitalize on the opportunity, or we let someone else get there first and we play catch-up," he reasoned.

Dave Rush, a retail consultant with Kurt Salmon Associated, also sees the move as a natural for Amway. "Externally, I see nothing but success here. If they can leverage their large sales force to drive more traffic to the Web, this will keep their administrative costs to a minimum while being a great marketing vehicle to drive sales. They key challenge in marketing on the Web is creating traffic to your site," Rush said. Ken Harris of Cannondale Associates feels the decision to go Internet points to a number of positives: "Quixtar won't be identified as an Amway company and this will help a great deal," Harris said. "Amway is seeking a new identity and with Quixtar, they have it. I believe Quixtar will be a $3 billion to $5 billion business in its first year."

With Quixtar, the company plans to spend much more on marketing. It has hired two ad agencies, Ogilvy & Mathers and Campbell-Ewald. TV commercials and billboards and print ads are being tested.

Amway sells 450 products under its brand. Its biggest sellers include Nutrilite vitamins, Artistry and Satinique skin care and cosmetics and cleansers. It also sells more than 10,000 brand name products from 1,500 companies including Firestone tires, Frito-Lay and MCI long distance service. *Excerpted from USA Today*

in Bangkok alone, it's easy to understand why network marketing companies are flocking to the capital city in droves.

China is the sleeping giant of them all, closely regulated and exploding, despite only a limited number of companies. Over one billion people emerging from communist rule and gently easing their way into capitalism represent a force of unimaginable magnitude. Currently, government restrictions make it difficult and expensive to set up shop on the mainland, although this is certain to change. The sheer product distribution lag is behind the rest of the modern world, particularly outside of the cities. Network marketing has the potential to fill the gap and companies are bidding ferociously for the privilege.

The land down under boasts MLM sales of more than $1.5 billion per year despite the expansiveness of the country. Australians travel long distances to share their business, driving five to seven hours to attend meetings and trainings.

With 400 million inhabitants and a number of strong economies, the European Economic Community (EEC) has four of the top markets and a host of up and comers. Germany, Italy and France have sales in excess of $3 billion per year and the United Kingdom sales exceed $1 billion. The formation of the EEC has contributed largely to the success of the industry. Throughout Europe, network marketers now move almost as freely as we do between states. This market opening has made it possible for companies to establish a hub or base of activities, which caters to the entire continent. Often, products are shipped from a central warehouse to multiple countries and order taking is similarly centralized.

The Netherlands has a well used company base due to its excellent transportation and telecommunications infrastructure. The European equivalent of our toll-free phone numbers are primarily based in the Netherlands, making this small country ideal for customer service and operator assisted services.

Perhaps most exciting in Europe is the former eastern bloc, where due to the lack of a conventional distribution structure, word-of-mouth advertising and personal delivery of products is thrusting network marketing to the forefront of product sales. Slightly over a year after Amway entered the market of Romania, over 1% of the population had joined the company - a truly staggering percentage. Slovenia, Poland, the Czech republic, Russia and Hungary are also growing at remarkable rates.

Nine hundred million dollars plus of products are sold across the plains of Spain, $300 million in the green hills of Austria, $200 million in the Swiss Alps and several hundred million more in the Scandinavian countries of Sweden, Norway and Finland.

The third largest market in the world is found in South America. Brazil, the largest country in the continent and the only one where Spanish is not the primary language, has almost one million distributors who generate over $4 billion in sales. In a land rich in untapped mineral deposits and other natural resources, the economy has yet to manifest its potential. Look for Brazil to become a major player in the future.

The rest of South America is made up of Spanish speaking countries where products are king. Product demonstrations and in-home meetings, usually conducted

The Netherlands has a well used company base due to its excellent transportation and telecommunications infrastructure. The European equivalent of our toll-free phone numbers are primarily based in the Netherlands, making this small country ideal for customer service and operator assisted services.

China is the sleeping giant of them all, closely regulated and exploding, despite only a limited number of companies. Over one billion people emerging from communist rule and gently easing their way into capitalism represent a force of unimaginable magnitude.

by women network marketers, are the cornerstone to the industry's growth. The Latin culture pay close attention to personal appearance, making personal care and nutrition products particularly easy to market. Argentina especially, is hugely successful with sales approaching a billion dollars annually.

Of all of the world's continents, Africa remains relatively untapped. The country of South Africa is the lone exception, with sales of $400 million. Stressed economic conditions in the rest of Africa have kept companies away. Still, the untouched natural resources are beginning to have an impact on some of the African countries, leading to greater available cash for product purchases. Couple that with a virtually non-existent product distribution infrastructure and the makings for network marketing success are in place.

One final future focus: India, where 80% of this huge country of more than 700 million people are "middle class," educated, entrepreneurial, hard working, plus, the majority speak English. India is the network marketing world's richest sleeping giant. The future will tell...

And speaking of future, here are a few parting thoughts. Everything runs in cycles. Only a short time ago, pioneers crossed the Western plains in covered wagons in search of freedom, riches and a better way of life . Now, we surf the net searching for the same thing.

A few years back, the shepherd exchanged wool for butter or tools with the farmer or the blacksmith. The same thing is happening again with network marketing.

Why wouldn't you buy your travel tickets from someone who buys nutritional products from you? Why wouldn't you have your long distance service with a representative who fills his or her personal care needs through your company?

In fact, tomorrow, when almost anything you need will be obtained through network marketing, why would you buy a single product from anybody that doesn't reciprocate? Okay, maybe that's a little exaggerated, but the point is well taken. We have started out bartering to support our needs and now we have come full circle. Network marketing is a relationship; a you-scratch-my-back-and-I'll-scratch-yours, mutual support business. Just like the old days. And it's rapidly becoming a tidal wave throughout the world.

*Ridgely Goldsborough is the chairman and publisher of NeTWORK MARKeTING LIFESTYLES magazine.* ∎

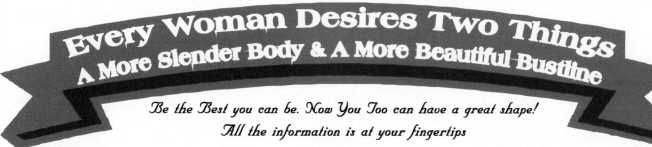

# Principles Of A Successful Compensation Plan

*Dan Jensen*

## Direct Selling Plans

### Party Plan

From one to several sales environment with the distributor arranging sales "parties" through a hostess. A distributor earns commissions on the inventory sold directly to retail customers in the party. Sales management is usually shallow. Distributors can often promote themselves to management through their recruiting and sales efforts, though higher levels of management are often appointed. The distributor recruits other agents and hostesses who hold parties and recruit retail customers. A hostess receives purchase credit for efforts based upon party success. Generally, there are several levels of management commissions; however, only a small percentage of total sales dollars is paid to management. High retail profits (35 to 50%) are common. Example: Tupperware.

### Traditional Direct Selling

One on one, the distributor sells directly to the consumer and earns commission on those sales. Management is limited and often appointed. Sponsoring is not aggressively pursued, except by sales management. Retail commissions are a large percentage of sale and are paid to the distributor/agent or retained in cash payment. Example: Rainbow Vacuum sales.

## Network Marketing/MLM Plans

### Australian or 2-up Plan

Based on a large commission on unlimited depth of a small amount of distributor's total group. Large scale recruiting is necessary to drive the program. The distributor gives up the first two of his/her recruits to their qualifying upline. This pass-up may move through an infinite number of levels. Typically, sales management positions are minimal. Volumes accumulate through unlimited depth, but limited width. Earnings are unlimited.

### Binary

Requires distributors to constantly assess their personal recruiting and sales management. Distributors activate Income Centers, then recruit distributors into each one. Income Centers can be considered a distributorship entity or business. Volume in each Income Center accumulates on each of its two legs (only two legs are allowed per Income Center -- a left and a right leg). Successful distributors in a Binary plan must constantly watch their downline to ensure volume up to a threshold where the maximum payment is made during a pay period. Volume accumulation starts again in the next period after maximum payment. Binary plans pay limited commission on unlimited levels of volume.

### Matrix

Similar to Uni-Level plan, except there is a limited number of distributors who can be placed on the first level. Recruits beyond the maximum number of first level positions allowed are automatically placed in other downline positions. Matrix plans often have maximum width and depth. When all positions in a distributor's downline matrix are filled (maximum width and depth is reached for all participants in a matrix), an additional matrix is started. Distributors earn unlimited commissions on limited levels of volume with minimal sales quotas. Example: Melaleuca Inc.

### Stair-Step/Breakaway

Characterized by distributors who are responsible for personal and group sales volumes. Volume is created by recruiting and retailing products. Various discounts or rebates are paid to group leaders. A group leader can be any distributor with one or more downline recruits. Once personal and group volumes are achieved, a distributor becomes a manager and "breaks away" from their upline manager. From that point, the new manager's group is no longer considered part of his/her upline manager's group, and is called "breakaway." Managers receive commissions on the group sales of their downline managers which often becomes the majority of their earnings. These plans pay unlimited commission on limited downline groups. This is the most common type of network marketing plan.

## Uni-Level

Often considered the most simple of compensations plans, Uni-Level pays commissions primarily based on the number of levels a recipient is from the original distributor purchasing product. Commissions are not based on title or rank achieved. By qualifying with a minimum sales requirement, distributors earn unlimited commissions on a limited number of levels of downline recruited distributors. Typically, there is no sales management position to achieve. Example: Kaire International, Inc.

# Introduction

A compensation plan that fails to motivate distributors can stagnate a company as fast as any other factor. While there are many factors that contribute to the success or failure of direct selling companies, the compensation plan is one of the biggest. There are many who ask what is the best compensation plan out there. Unfortunately, there is no answer; however, there are proven principles of success common to nearly all successful plans. What makes a compensation plan great? This article may help to identify the real success factors of a compensation plan.

## Golden Rules To Be Followed

Always provide incentive dollars for an expected behavior. Don't waste incentive dollars on behavior which provides little value to you or the distributor. Question each type of compensation and verify that it will provide the expected return on investment.

Leverage the principal of relationships. Most people recruit others they already know. They want to work with them. Be sure your plan builds on these relationships. A plan where a new recruit is trained or mentored by a person other than the sponsor usually results in poor recruitment and weak relationships.

### Recognition is as important as compensation

"Distributors will work for money but they will kill for a cause"— Jim Adams

### Five Successful Objectives

### 1. Sell Products to End Consumers

Retailing products to end consumers is key to moving products from garages to customers. Corporate failure is inevitable as people stop buying products which they do not (or cannot) sell.

Have a motivating retail/wholesale profit, a minimum of

25% discount from a retail 33% markup over wholesale. This retail profit is the basis on which people are motivated to retail products. Other motivations are usually artificial and will not withstand the test of time.

Have a realistic retail price, otherwise, people will not be able to sell to end consumers. Don't sell products whose wholesale price is really the market retail value and then add an artificial retail price.

Heavy emphasis on retailing from field leaders, training and market materials must be stressed.

Retailing products based on the hope of future rewards will never result in movement of a product to retail consumers. If distributors are selling products promoting the dream that the buyer will earn future commissions when they, in turn, sell the product to others, you will eventually be sitting on a "time bomb" of unhappy distributors with lots of inventory to sell in their garage. Companies that do this always fail. Proper retailing moves the product from distributor to end users in volumes justified by natural consumption.

### 2. Build Organizations

This is done by placing incentives on group volume building. Recruits must easily see that it is easier to have others do the selling to build their business besides their own selling. Recognition and reward should be built into the plan, especially for the new recruit. Most recruits are lost in the first 60 days because they lose confidence of succeeding in the long term. Rewarding them early keeps their interest and excitement.

Lack of rewards for new recruits results in sales leaders promoting "buy in" organization building. They pitch people that a "buy in" is an investment in their future. The new recruit has a greater inventory to keep them in longer but quickly becomes disillusioned. They are quick to complain to regulatory officers that "they were taken." Regulators are always on the watch for investment schemes of this nature. Rewarding people early is done by building a series of goals and rewards. As they reach each goal, they are recognized and compensated. It builds their confidence that they can achieve their future dreams.

This process builds the initial skills required to eventually become managers. Lack of early incentives builds ineffective field managers who do not have the skill to sell and recruit based on product viability.

## 3. Build Managers

Must follow the 'Build Organization' step, otherwise the field force will have many ineffective managers who do little to earn their compensation.

Managers are built by learning the basic skills of success for distributors, product retailing and recruiting. Once they learn these skills, they become managers as they teach others (those they recruit) to do the same. Successful managers learn the power of duplication.

Incentives are placed on group activities: Group Volume and Recruiting. Group Volume incentives usually rewards both selling and recruiting.

## 4. Build Sales Leaders

Incentives must exist to motivate and reward managers who build other managers. Avoid disincentives that penalize a manager when a new manager is created, otherwise managers work hard to suppress their own star performers from reaching their full potential for fear of losing significant compensation in the future.

Provide incentives which reward managers for several 'generations' of other downline managers so they will want to train their managers to build others as well.

Avoid making it too easy to become a sales leader. Distributors who don't know how to build or train other managers to succeed should not be entitled to become sales leaders. If they do, the field organization will be superficial and weak.

Remember that building strong sales leaders takes time, money and effort. Invest in training them to become effective sales leaders, to build effective managers, and to recruit product retailers and recruiters.

Provide incentives for your top performing sales leaders. Avoid having the plan quickly 'max out' otherwise, the top performers will wonder 'what's next' and you won't have an answer.

## 5. Retention

Retain people by helping them receive significant rewards for their time. You compete for their time and attention with many other opportunities and distractions. Make it worth their while early on.

As a distributor works the business, they build an 'equity investment' in their downline organization. They will continue to work the business if their downline continues to do the same. This is why a balanced emphasis on product retailing and recruiting is so important.

Distributors who build a downline are far more likely to continue to be active than those who do not.

If your product is consumable, use an "Auto Ship" program to build repeat business, both retail or preferred customer, and wholesale (to distributors).

Promote contests and competitions that can be won by everyone. Avoid the top ten contests where everybody loses except the top ten performers.

# Other Principles of a Successful Plan

Reasonable compensation percentages: Most compensation plans today pay between 30% and 50% to field distributors. If a company promotes a plan paying only 25% or so, they will have a hard time recruiting and keeping distributors unless other factors offset the competitive weakness. These factors might include how well the public accepts the product (telephone service or other common consumables) or intangible incentives which motivate distributors. In my opinion, real percentage payout should fall between 35% and 42%. Higher percentages are possible with high product margins. Theoretically, payout (the percentage the plan would pay if all commissions were paid out in every case) should not be more than 8% above actual to avoid disappointing distributors expecting more.

## Keep it simple:

Unfortunately, many plans are designed by and for MLM professionals. These plans often assume most people already understand terms and principles of MLM or can at least learn them quickly. This is most definitely not the case. While experience is essential when designing compensation plans, one must never forget that *ordinary people are the ones who must be motivated by it.* If new recruits are not motivated early, they quickly fall away. The more complex a plan becomes, the fewer people it will motivate. The plan needs to affect the heart of a distributor first, before it can affect his/her pocketbook.

## Avoid novelty or "fad" plans:

Changing a compensation plan is costly in terms of lost momentum and distributor commitment. When a distributor recruits another person, the compensation plan is often a significant part of the selling process. To change it later is, in essence, admitting that the original plan was not very good after all. Some people may perceive the change as a "bait and switch" tactic. By staying within more traditional plans, ones that have proven themselves over the years, a new MLM company can still be innovative, but are aware that if the plan goes out of fashion, you can count on it coming back a few years later. Stick to more traditional plans that won't need to be changed as new fads come and go.

## Don't put too much credence in the impact of your compensation plan:

Many entrepreneurs come to Jenkon convinced that they have the best possible compensation plan imaginable. When asked what product or service they will sell, they sometimes respond, *we are still looking for the right product*. Obviously, these well-intentioned people have focused on only one issue of starting their business, thinking that the compensation plan is the key to their future success. The facts however, are different. Many companies have gained great success despite poorly designed compensation plans. Put simply, the plan is only one part of the puzzle; it is not the whole part.

## Don't change it often:

Those that experiment with the compensation plan are asking for frustrated distributors to join other, more stable opportunities. Even good change can be traumatic. Be very reluctant to change the plan.

## Avoid recruiting "heavy hitters":

These very successful MLM professionals can bring tremendous short-term success but can also be a major cause for failure when they grow bored with your company and join another, often taking thousands of their downline with them. Wise companies always build slowly for the first few years until they have the critical mass to handle changes in business volumes. Don't design your compensation plan to focus on attracting these heavy hitters.

*Dan Jensen is founder of Jenkon International, Inc., a computer software firm specializing in the direct selling network marketing industry. Founded in 1978, and having served more than 600 industry clients, Jenkon has acquired an unequaled level of experience and knowledge about what makes companies successful in the industry. Many of Jenkon's clients have become industry leaders. Several industry leaders have come to Jenkon to utilize their advanced software technology, including Shaklee, Avon, etc. Most of Jenkon's clients start very small utilizing Jenkon's Summit V Business Management Software System in their smallest network marketing or direct selling company, from accurate and timely commission checks, to order processing, to managing downlines numbering in the hundreds of thousands. For many, Summit V has become the key to their success.* ■

# Life In The Fast Lane

Today's skills, knowledge, and products live fast, get old before their time, and die young. We are all being asked to learn, do and produce more with less money, fewer resources, and no time to spare. And this laser-fast pace of change will continue. "Mankind's cumulative knowledge has doubled in the last decade, and will double again every five years," says billion-dollar SPX Corporation CEO Robert D. Tuttle. "It is not an exaggeration to say that more scientific and technical advances will happen in the next year than happened in the *entire* decade of the 70s!"

"On a scale of 1 to 10, I would rate the changes that we have gone through since divestiture as a 4," an AT&T division vice president recently told a thousand of his beleaguered managers. "Using that same scale," he warned, "I see the changes coming at us an 8." His estimate may actually be too low! Change is happening faster than we can keep tabs on and threatens to "shake the foundations of the most secure American business," warned a recent study by the U.S. Congress's Office of Technology. No industry will escape, no one is exempt. Pardon the grammar, but if it "ain't broke" today, it will be tomorrow, Today's innovations are tomorrow's antiques.

# Hall of Fame
# 2000

How does one begin a selection process that will ultimately lead to the naming of inductees into our second annual Network Marketing/Direct Selling Hall of Fame? Once again we, as a company, stepped aside and assembled a knowledgeable and impartial panel to elect eight of the industries finest from a cast of over 100 nominees. For the hundreds of callers inquiring what role, if any, the Global Home Based Business Directory® staff played in the elective process, the answer is no role at all. Moreover, we never personally recommended a candidate(s) or attempted to influence the voting of an individual. Although a good many nominees failing to be inducted in our Class of 2000 would have proved extraordinary entrees, we nonetheless feel our panel deserves a high level of praise for unveiling what we strongly believe to be a stellar cast of honorees.

Our Hall of Fame selection is the only official ceremony of its type. The Global Home Based Business Directory® will provide our Hall of Fame members the recognition they so richly deserve and have unfortunately lacked due to the lack of a national voice in print.

Without further ado, it is our great pleasure to introduce our Class of 2000.

# Inductees

**Richard Brooke**

**Sandi Donaldson**

**Rex Maughan**

**Gary McDonald**

**Ruby Miller-Lyman**

**Forrest Shaklee**

**Mike Sheffield**

**Doris Wood**

Class of 2000

Class of 2000

**Richard Brooke** began his network marketing career in 1977 at age 22. He has been a full-time distributor and/or corporate executive since that time. His only prior work experience included a four-year career in a chicken processing plant upon graduation from high school.

**Richard Brooke**

After three years of failure (his third year's 1099 was $4,000), Brooke finally broke through, sponsoring first one, then several more superstars. He rose through 250,000 distributors to become the top field trainer, earning over $1 million to become the executive vice president of that company by the age of 30.

Brooke joined the Oxyfresh team as president and CEO in 1986. The company was insolvent with nearly $1 million of short-term debt and no cash, credit or assets. Sales had been declining monthly for over a year.

Oxyfresh began a methodical turnaround through aggressive financial management, stellar distributor service, new products, and a new culture of character and leadership development. Oxyfresh has set new sales records each year for the past 12 years. The company is debt-free and enjoys one of the finest reputations in the network marketing industry.

Twenty-five percent of the company's distributor force are doctors -- including dentists, chiropractors, physicians, naturopaths and veterinarians, who recommend Oxyfresh products to their patients. The most successful distributors are Roland and Virginia Fox, a retired Air Force couple from Spokane, Washington.

Brooke has served as a board member of the Multi-Level Marketing International Association, as well as the Ethics Committee of the Direct Selling Association. In March 1992, *SUCCESS*, a mainstream business magazine, was the first to feature MLM (in a positive light) in the industry's 52-year history. Out of 10 million network marketers, they chose Brooke for the cover and lead story.

In Brooke's latest book, "Mach II With Your Hair On Fire," he explains how he came to be on the cover. "In 1983, I purchased a mock-up of the cover of *SUCCESS* magazine with my picture on the cover. I framed it and hung it on my wall and I looked at it every day. My vision at that time was to be not only rich, but famous as well. I wanted something to prove to my friends and family that I really was cutting it. *SUCCESS* magazine seemed like the perfect proof."

And it was. Brooke and Oxyfresh have since been featured twice in *SUCCESS* magazine, as well as covered on a positive note in everything from the *San Francisco Chronicle*, to ABC's "20/20," NBC's "Today Show," CNBC, CNN, *Reader's Digest*, *Vogue*, *Allure* and *Income Opportunities* magazine.

Brooke is a featured speaker at the coveted Upline Master's Seminar, as well as a contributing editor to *Upline* magazine. He has co-authored the book, *The New Entrepreneurs...Business Visionaries for the 21st Century*, and has written the published book, *Mach II With Your Hair On Fire...The Art of Self- Motivation*.

Brooke has also created such breakthrough training programs as: *Value Based Prospecting, Listening Through Objections, The Four-Year Career Plan, Leadership as a Profession, and Vision and Self- Motivation*.

In addition, Richard and his wife, Rishon, conduct a series of six-day Visionary Leadership Retreats for the company's up-and-coming leaders. These retreats, limited to twelve individuals, provide hands-on development work in the areas of relationships, overcoming fear, vision, public speaking, leadership styles, listening and million-dollar business strategies.

"Oxyfresh has prospered because the company's leaders are passionately committed to providing the world with a new role model for network marketing; one where the highest ethical standards are expressed, and integrity, character development, a balanced lifestyle, and 'do the right thing' leadership replace greed, deception and questionable values," says Brooke.

# Hall of Fame

In an action as eloquent as her words, famed business consultant **Sandi Donaldson-Shenoha** has expanded her Moriah Marketing Group to better serve a significant segment of the network marketing and direct selling sector.

Called "Heaven's Downline™," it's a newsletter that, according to Sandi, will inform "the nucleus of Christians so considerable in our industry; those who will find our training message useful in achieving what is both honest and ethical -- in business as well as in everyday life."

"Effective consulting consists of strengthening mutual trust between companies and their distributors," she says. "People in the office may not understand the ups and downs of life in the field and trenches, while distributors must appreciate the complexity of the corporation." Thus her bottom line: "A skilled business consultant is a master troubleshooter; one who not only spots weaknesses, but also roots out causes and expedites the return to sound corporate health. Corrections are like remodeling a house. You need additions, upgrades, rearrangements, sometimes even removals and restarts that save companies thousands of dollars."

Sandi suggests being alert to even the most subtle signs of institutional malaise, declining morale in the office or field that reflects rescinding enthusiasm will show itself through falling sales and/or recruitment. She emphasizes: "We must understand that distributors go flat when their companies turn a deaf ear to them."

Sandi's credentials include a BS in sociology from Ohio State University, also a distinguished industry tenure starting as a director for Mary Kay Cosmetics, then a mint of experience as an executive employee of, and an advisor to such firms as Avon Products, Matol Botanical, Latasia Jewelry, QVC Network and myriads more.

Moriah's services run the gamut, from strategic planning and market development to training/recruitment and distributor services. Her versatility is apparent in such specialities as event management, incentive/award systems, even seminars/speech skills, bolstered by her participation in national speaker groups and her own "Power Talk" sessions.

Sandi recalls two soul-deep impacts upon her life. "The first was Mary Kay, the gatekeeper at my entry into direct selling. She helped improve my self-image by modeling what to value and nurturing a belief in myself, a key to the confidence that's carried me through." The second was life-changing surgery in late 1994. "While I was soon back to work as acting CEO of one of the MLM's largest international firms," she said, "the interval provided the luxury to ponder what to keep and what to let go, and the wonderful realization that what I needed was more balance in my life." That balance arrived precisely on November 3, 1995, when the slowed-down Sandi met Bill Shenoha. Not having been married for 18 years, she celebrated the occasion, by selecting the same date in 1998 for their nuptials. Thus came the new equilibrium.

Looking ahead at her perceived future of network marketing and direct selling, she invokes the parable of the stranger and two medieval stone masons:

"What are you building?" the traveler asks. "Oh, I'm just laying stone," answers the first mechanic. But when the kibitzer again asks the question, the second mason replies, "I'm building a cathedral."

To Sandi, this means that during the early days of MLM and related venues, pioneers were more or less laying stones--but without the solid visionary foundation that marks today's industry.

"In the early days," she said, "the 'high-touch' method of helping people prevailed, but the advent of 'high-tech' naturally inclined society to the automated, the impersonal, often even the brusque - people had literally lost touch in responding to others."

"But now" she added, "we must blend the high-tech with the high-touch, making MLM in the image of the cathedral that the second stone mason was building. It will never be a physical edifice, but it can, and soon should, be an ideal soaring more grandly from the bedrock values of honesty and trust among marketers."

Sandi Donaldson

252

# Hall of Fame

Rex Maughan

Though many in the world of network marketing have met **Rex Maughan**, anyone who has ever ventured into a business of any kind, given Maughan's track record, would indeed recognize him for what he is: a remarkably creative salesman who genuinely cares about his customers.

The founder of Forever Living Products International (FLP), a growing billion dollar world empire, Maughan focuses his thoughts and energy on bolstering healthy lifestyles and savings accounts alike.

Now in its 20th year, the Scottsdale, Arizona-based FLP consists of five million distributors in 65 countries. It experienced a $43 million jump in sales in 1997, totaling $1.255 billion for the year.

FLP has operations in Japan, Taiwan, Poland, Hong Kong, Malaysia, Great Britain, Philippines, Mexico, Argentina, Greece, and many others. This year, it is establishing offices in Africa, India, Scandinavia and other areas. At home in the United States, it has been named the No. 1 privately held business in Arizona the past three years by Arthur Anderson's ranking of top businesses.

"My goal is to help people in every country around the world to have better health and more money and time to enjoy it," says Maughan. "I believe the more money you have, the greater responsibility you have to help other people."

Indeed. A native of Soda Springs, Idaho, where he learned the value of hard work on his family's ranch, Maughan decided at a young age he wanted to be successful and he wanted to share the wealth.

Following graduation from Arizona State University, he worked several jobs before establishing himself in the Del Webb Corporation, where he served as vice president in charge of realty and management and recreational resorts. Though wildly successful by common standards, Maughan wanted more. The desire to expand worldwide and reach people of all income levels and backgrounds led him to the business of network marketing.

After carefully studying the potential of the business, focusing intently on compensation for all involved, Maughan decided it suited his aspirations perfectly. But first he needed a company philosophy and a distinctive product line.

He decided it was essential to establish a balanced distribution of compensation, making it realistic for everyone from corporate presidents to beginners to make a comfortable living without bearing an unreasonable workload.

"I arranged it so people could actually work where and when they want, make a good living, and have time to enjoy their lives," he says.

Maughan then set his sight on a previously untapped resource, Aloe Vera.

Thanks to careful research, he met a team of doctors who had invested the better part of two decades developing the stabilization of the plant, which supplies significant amounts of minerals, amino acids and vitamins, including B-12, a vitamin typically found only in animal products.

Maughan knew then his product would not only provide customers dietary supplements and other healthy products, the B-12 component would also offer vegetarians a unique vitamin resource.

"You can make all the money in the world, but if you don't have health, you won't enjoy it," he says. "That's why with Aloe Vera and other natural health products we knew we had the right mix."

# Hall of Fame

**Gary McDonald** has penned the title for his new book: "It started with Stanley." However, the 68-year-old pioneer in the direct selling industry doesn't have time to write it; he's too busy directing RACHAeL International, a health and beauty products company based in Orlando, Florida. Eventually, when he does write that book, McDonald has a wealth of experience to communicate to others.

Nearly 50 years ago, and as one of the founders of Tupperware Home Parties, Inc., McDonald was an early leader in innovative marketing techniques. Additionally, he went on to work with numerous leading marketers and their companies, such as Gillette, Inc., Colgate-Palmolive, Dayton Hudson, Schick Laboratories and more.

"In addition to the various marketing concepts, I want my book to include the warmth that does not exist in current marketing publications," McDonald stated. "I have known most of the top people in direct sales and network marketing. They are outgoing and giving. This is the side of the business I want to relate to others as well."

RACHAeL International, the company McDonald acquired nine years ago, keeps him extremely busy. The past two years has been devoted to transforming the direct sales business over to network marketing. He describes the company as "modest sized" with distributors in 46 states and several foreign countries. Despite this, McDonald was quoted as saying, "We have not yet experienced the real explosion we know network marketing will bring."

McDonald applies to RACHAeL the identical recipe he brought to Tupperware many years ago: "A product so good that people want to tell others about it," and a strong belief that "there is goodness in everyone." He also brings a love of learning and the ability to motivate people; qualities that won him the nickname, "Mr. Enthusiasm" within the direct selling industry.

**Gary McDonald**

While residing in Livonia, Michigan, at the young age of 20, McDonald had made his mark as a successful entrepreneur. Five years previously, he was selling Stanley Home Products (the title for his book). By age 16, he had become a Stanley manager, and the following year began selling for Tupperware. At the time, this new company was demonstrating its products in the retail marketplace. McDonald had another idea: To market the products through home parties. He was so successful he became one of the three founders of Tupperware Home Products, Inc.

In his 20 years with Tupperware, McDonald was instrumental in setting up the home party plan, developing all initial product and sales training materials, plus the implementation of a recruitment program that doubled the number of its sales force in less than two months.

McDonald went on to consult with several major companies before serving as vice president for Beeline Fashions, Inc., Tri-Chem, Inc., and Schick Laboratories. He also became active in the Direct Selling Association, serving twice as director and chairman of the board. Additionally, he helped in the development of a code of ethics for the direct selling industry. McDonald is proud of the fact he was the youngest person ever to be inducted into the DSA Hall of Fame.

As he now directs RACHAeL's conversion to network marketing, McDonald sees this as "the vehicle of the 21st century. Direct sales worked in the 50s, 60s and 70s" he says, "but time has now become so precious and people are less persuaded by typical advertising. Network marketing takes into account both of these realities."

McDonald has never faltered in his belief that there is goodness in all people. "If you're looking for the good" he states, "that's what you'll find. I look for an individual's strengths; what they do well. This is the part that enables them to grow, and sometimes, weaknesses just disappear."

Entrepreneur **Ruby Miller-Lyman** launched her colorful career with a direct selling company 47 years ago. Though she went on to create successful ventures in many fields, her passion was always to reach the pinnacle of success in the industry where she got her start. She is nearing that goal today as a top achiever and respected authority in network marketing, and as a distributor with a very large worldwide organization.

**Ruby Miller**

Ruby's energy and work ethic have always set her apart from the crowd. Raised on a farm in a family with ten children in Ogilvie, Minnesota, she worked in the local drugstore and meat market while pursuing a whirlwind of school activities as a cheerleader, drum major, athlete, choir member and Winter Carnival Queen.

After high school, Ruby moved to Minneapolis-St. Paul, and entered direct sales with a company called Radelle. Her original aim was to save money for college; however, she changed her goals after her rapid, early success. At age 18, she was able to pay cash for a new red and white Olds Delta 88; quite a feat in those days for a woman that age. At 19, she made a large down payment on her first new home. While on an all-expense paid trip to New York City, viewing the sights from the crown of the Statue of Liberty, she realized with excitement that her career was already underway, and that whatever she could conceive and believe, she could achieve. As for education, she committed herself to "becoming a master at my craft and staying on the cutting edge." Ruby says, "I've picked the best brains in the world."

Ruby later moved to Fargo, North Dakota, and worked as a model. She then made a typical entrepreneurial move and bought the modeling agency. From 1960 to 1980, Ruby launched many innovative ventures to help sell her MLM products, including becoming the owner of eight beauty salons. Through her salon business, Ruby spawned a health and weight management club called "The Trim-Away Club." Her passion to help others achieve their ideal goal weight came from being the largest of 10 children, weighing in at a hefty 13 pounds at birth. Ruby even journeyed to Shangri-La, the small remote principality of Hunza, high atop the Himalayan mountain range of 16,000 to 18,000 feet elevation. Her quest was to learn their excellent health secrets of youth and longevity, where the people live to be 100 to 130-years-old. Ruby featured many of her successful club members, who came from a five state area, on her "Woman 75" television show. In 1980, she took her weight management club concept to Nutri-Metics, a direct sales company, and moved to California. She then sold her businesses and went to work for Nutri-Metics as National Director for her club concept. After eight years, Ruby left Nutri-Metics and registered with Matol Botanical, returning to her first love, running her own home-based business. At Matol she met her husband, Ted Lyman, now her partner, traveling companion, soulmate and fellow adventurer.

Ruby sought always to master a changing industry as it moved from the early days of direct sales and party plan, to multi-level marketing, then network marketing. Working primarily for five major companies, she served on their executive boards and councils while learning everything she could about selling, recruiting, training, motivation and duplicating, keeping her on the cutting edge of the network marketing industry.

For the past three years, Ruby and Ted have dedicated themselves to Essentially Yours Industries, building a massive organization that spans the U.S. and many other countries. As one of EYI's leading trainers and newly appointed member to the EYI Executive Leadership Council, Ruby has worked alongside corporate to open Thailand, with many other countries now targeted. Their organization represents more than 20 percent of EYI's volume.

Ruby and Ted love their lifestyle, from their 30 second commute to their office to traveling the world for business and pleasure. They are committed to helping others achieve the goals of financial freedom, optimum health and time with their families. Their philosophy is to "live one day at a time and make it a masterpiece." One would be truly blessed to be a part of their winning team.

# Hall of Fame

**Dr. Forrest C. Shaklee, Sr.** came out of the heart of America. Born in 1894 on a farm in Carlisle, Iowa, he gave America his heart, his mind and a philosophy that still inspires the lives of millions. Through his philosophy, his life and the company he started, he changed lives, health, and the fortunes of people throughout the world.

**Forrest Shaklee**

Using the knowledge he gathered from a lifetime of studying the importance of nutrition in restoring and building health, Dr. Shaklee founded Shaklee Products in 1956 with his sons Forrest, Jr., and Raleigh, to produce and sell nutritional supplements. The company sales plan was firmly based on the Golden Rule and on Dr. Shaklee's philosophy of "Thoughtsmanship."

The direction of medicine after WWII had begun to shift from treating and curing disease toward health maintenance, a trend that continues today. Recognition of the importance of nutrition in good health had been recognized more clearly during this time, and nutrition was becoming a more scientific discipline. In this atmosphere the tiny nutritional supplements company took its first steps.

By 1958, the fledging company had 1,000 distributors in the field. The sales in 1962 were nearly equal to the sales of all previous years combined. That year, Shaklee Products moved to new headquarters in Hayward, California, and the company was incorporated. The product line included Herb-Lax® Laxative, Vita-Lea® Multivitamin and Multimineral Supplement, Liqui-Lea® Multivitamin with Iron Supplement and Instant Protein® Drink Mix. The company had also begun to diversify into household products and personal care products.

The corporation continued to grow. In 1970, the first Shaklee warehouse outside of Hayward was opened in Edina, Minnesota, and the company was shipping over five million pounds of product to more than 50,000 distributors throughout the nation.

Shaklee became a public corporation in 1973. Beginning in August 1977, its stock was traded on the New York Stock Exchange. During the same period, the company expanded its headquarters and entered international markets. Presently, Shaklee Corporation has operations in Canada, Mexico, Japan, Singapore, Malaysia and the Philippines.

Shaklee opened the world's largest nutritional products manufacturing facility in Norman, Oklahoma in 1979, and in 1980 moved its headquarters into the magnificent Shaklee Terraces in the heart of San Francisco's financial district. In 1982, Shaklee Corporation joined the prestigious ranks of the Fortune 500. Throughout all this impressive growth, the corporation remained guided by Dr. Shaklee's founding philosophy of the Golden Rule and harmony with nature.

Dr. Shaklee collected many personal honors in his career, including special recognition from the California Secretary of State. In 1975 he stepped down from his position as President and Chairman of the Board of Shaklee Corporation and accepted the position of Chairman Emeritus of Shaklee Corporation, a position he retained until his death in 1985 at the age of 91. In recognition of his many achievements, he is listed in the current editions of *Who's Who in the West, Who's Who in America, Who's Who in the World* and the *International Register of Profiles.*

Shaklee Corporation stands as a monument to the vision, the genius and the conviction of Dr. Shaklee. Through his vision he has enriched the lives and improved the health of thousands of people throughout the world. His philosophy of "Thoughtsmanship" is as valid and effective now as when it was first published. The corporation stands today as a living tribute to a visionary leader with an extraordinary philosophy.

# Hall of Fame

It is rare to find someone involved in MLM that doesn't know the name, **Mike Sheffield**. For nearly 30 years, his involvement in the industry has touched the lives of millions of MLM and also direct sales entrepreneurs. From independent distributor to corporate owner, product developer, to one of the leading U.S. and international management consultants, he has been at the forefront of every major industry advancement. His insight into "What's Hot and What's Not" link him with numerous multi-million dollar selling products. His ability to evaluate product, mission, and ideal marketing direction have earned him respect as the most prolific compensation plan designer in America.

**Mike Sheffield**

Sheffield began his life in rural Arkansas, the son of a high school teacher and grandson of an old-time traveling salesman. He has been teaching and selling ever since. It has been said that if you look under "Consultative Selling" in the dictionary, you will see Mike Sheffield's picture. An industry leader, Sheffield is co-founder and chairman of the MLMIA, the association for network marketing. This organization represents all network marketing companies, distributors, and industry suppliers worldwide. Uniquely qualified as a network marketing expert, Sheffield began his career as a successful distributor and later founded two successful network marketing companies with combined sales exceeding $30,000,000. With success in business spanning nearly 30 years, his background includes direct sales, multi-level marketing, product research and development, manufacturing, and consulting.

Sheffield is President of Sheffield Resource Network, a company recognized nationally as the leading MLM consulting firm and the preeminent expert on developing or sourcing many of the emerging new products finding their way into MLM. He has worked internationally, assisting in new product procurement and the necessary accompanying consulting assistance for MLM companies in Norway, England, Germany, Saudi Arabia, the Philippines, Australia, Canada, Mexico, Japan and China.

As a leading spokesperson for the MLM industry, Sheffield conducts seminars and lectures worldwide and has also been a frequent lecturer at various MLM conferences. He has to his credit numerous appearances on television and radio, having been a repeat guest as a new product expert analyst on Business Radio Network (BRN). He has also appeared as guest lecturer at the Schools of Business at Arizona State University, California Lutheran University and Anderson University. In addition, Sheffield has been a guest instructor on MLM compensation plans at the Graduate School of Business at the University of Illinois in Chicago. In 1998, he was selected to make a presentation on behalf of multi-level marketing at the Harvard Business School Association symposium. In 1998 and again in 1999, he organized and sponsored two of the industry's most important MLM events on the campus of the University of Texas at El Paso. Organizing for the Future I and II were successful academic conferences geared toward an intimate interaction of university business school faculty and MLM corporate executives to stimulate a better understanding and eventual classroom acceptance of MLM as an alternative method of product distribution.

Sheffield is one of the few Certified Professional Consultants to Management (CPCM) with specific emphasis on the network marketing industry. Certification is granted by the National Bureau of Professional Management Consultants. As a network marketing consultant, he has assisted in well over 300 company start-ups. His eight-hour MLM/network marketing training course for distributors, called "Putting the Pieces Together," has been released as a 16 audio cassette tape self-help course.

Sheffield now directs his attention to serving as chief consultant, new product advisor, developer, and resource agent for many prestigious companies including AOL Select, Home Shopping Network, The Fuller Brush Company and The Service Master Corporation.

# Hall of Fame

By 1985, **Doris Wood** had worked for nearly three decades in the network marketing industry. First as a distributor; part of several companies' corporate staff as director of training or vp of sales; owner of two MLM companies; speaker, writer and consultant. So she was in an ideal position to see that the industry lacked something important: a trade group that linked and represented everyone in the industry.

**Doris Wood**

"At that time, there were no organizations in the country for distributors, period," Wood recalls. "And there were none where suppliers, that we've always called support, had a vote, period. Moreover, there wasn't any organization where all three groups--corporate, support and distributors, were working together."

Thus Wood explains the rationale for establishing the Multi-Level Marketing International Association (MLMIA). By gathering three constituencies under one umbrella, Wood believed the MLMIA could provide support and serve as an advocate for the entire industry. For example, by educating regulators, consumers and insiders alike. Beginning in May 1985, she co-founded and served as the first President/Chairman of the Multi-Level Marketing International Association's Board of Directors.

Wood did not want to oversee the MLMIA's day-to-day operations. "It was not my goal to run the association," she says. "It was my goal to start it and make sure it continued and worked. I did not need to be in front." She never thought of herself as an administrator; she still doesn't. An administrator is exactly what Wood became. In January 1986, she took over as the MLMIA's Executive Director and ran the day-to-day operations. Since it was temporary, she continued to hold the other positions. She's held that position for almost 15 years--without pay. "I believe in what this association stands for," she says. The industry has benefited. Under Wood's leadership, the MLMIA has become a powerful voice. It's worked with regulators and legislators across the United States, filed friend-of-the-court briefs in legal cases and sponsored trade shows. Its training programs have helped raise ethical and professional standards. For distributors, MLMIA helps resolve disputes. It has helped many new companies get established.

In recognition of Wood's service, the MLMIA Board of Directors honored her several years ago with a good-natured roast and inducted her into the MLMIA Hall of Fame. Wood remains as busy as ever, with ambitious plans for the future. She continues to work as a consultant and speaker through The Wood International Group, or TWIG. (It's a pun. Remember her last name). The author of one widely read history of network marketing (We've Only Just Begun), she is working on several other books. She is also working on something else for the industry, her Internet web site, MLMRadio.com.

In the future, Wood hopes to expand the MLMIA's role internationally and establish a certification program to further raise the level of professionalism. Perhaps her most ambitious dream: establish a foundation to serve as the industry's historian/record keeper. Her own papers would be a good place to begin. "I haven't thrown away a scrap of paper that's come to me through multi-level marketing in 40 years," she says. And, her family can attest to that with three storage units, plus the garage almost full.

Wood has spoken on behalf of the industry throughout the United States and Canada, as well as Mexico, England, Norway, Hong Kong and Malaysia. She's worked as a consultant on six continents, and has been quoted or featured in every industry publication as well as main stream business magazines such as *Entrepreneur, Money* and *Success*. Wood is living proof that financial fortune doesn't always come hand-in-hand with respect and prominence. "Although I've never been adverse to money, it wasn't what motivated me," she admits. So what does motivate Doris Wood? "People," she says. "Helping, guiding and watching people be able to put their children through college or purchasing their own home. Seeing people have the freedom to become whatever they want to be. That's a lot of it--the freedom. And... I want to complete my mission, which is to *Strengthen MLM Around The World!*"

# Women of Distinction

Some refer to the Women of Distinction as a stepping stone to the coveted Hall of Fame, and while it's true all inductees would prove excellent candidates, their selection in this category represents a rare level of achievement. All award winners have overcome the many obstacles identified with network marketing/ direct selling and inexorably moved on to paramount levels of success, all the while giving back to the industry their time, effort and financial resources. That's really what it's all about. Success measured in terms of income alone will not reserve a table at the awards ceremony. Giving back of themselves to their downline, to the special people who provided assistance along their rough and rocky road to the top, these unselfish acts that grow in significance with each passing day and playing the role of the goodwill ambassador on behalf of the industry–your industry. This, and more, are characteristics of award winners.

# Inductees

Oi-Lin Chen
Jane Deuber
Connie Dugan
Janice Hymer
Carol Leclerc
Renata Lee
Adi Song
Sylvia Waiwaiole
Sabrina Wei

# Women of Distinction

**Oi-Lin Chen**, M.D., president of Sunrider International, was born in Hong Kong and moved to the United States with her husband, Tei Fu Chen, in 1974. The two of them founded Sunrider International in 1982 out of their home in Utah.

Since those humble beginnings, Sunrider International has grown to be a formidable global force in the multi-level marketing industry, with an expanding 300,000 square foot world headquarters located in Torrance, California. As president of a growing and highly respected herbal nutritional, personal care and beauty product manufacturer and distribution company, Oi-Lin is one of the few Asian women to command a position of such prominence.

Earning a medical degree from Kaoshiung Medical College in Taiwan in 1972, Oi-Lin served her residency in Pennsylvania and became a licensed medical doctor in the United States. Utilizing her knowledge of health and medicine, she played a primary role in the development of Kandesn, Sunrider's personal care and cosmetic line. Throughout the years, Oi-Lin has continued to develop and be in charge of quality control over Kandesn's growing line.

"The first 25 years of my life were spent on education. Our Chinese culture places a great deal of emphasis on schooling. I studied and attended medical school; that was where I met Tei Fu. When we married and started a family, I learned to juggle children, business and the practice of medicine," Oi-Lin states.

During her second 25 years of life, Oi-Lin has continued what she calls "the struggle to create, develop and build the best network marketing company in the world."

A mother of five, Oi-Lin explains, "I treat all Sunrider distributors as part of my extended family. Our goal is to give people everywhere the opportunity to live a healthier lifestyle, and in doing so, achieve financial independence. I believe Sunrider is a people business designed to help make dreams come true. Without dreams, there is really nothing to look forward to, work for or believe in."

With her scientific background, it comes as no surprise that Oi-Lin is hands-on throughout the formulation and manufacturing process of Sunrider's extensive product lines. Often seen in protective head and foot coverings, as well as a lab coat, she roams Sunrider's City of Industry manufacturing facilities and confers with technicians, scientists and researchers, as well as personally inspecting many of the production lines.

Oi-Lin says, "When I hear the owners of other health and beauty companies say they are committed to quality, I wonder how they can fulfill that commitment when they are not personally involved in researching and manufacturing their products! Our products are not diluted, because we do not depend on outsiders to give us so-called quality. We do 97% of our manufacturing and go through an expensive process of concentration which adds value and potency to our products."

Oi-Lin states that "in contrast, most companies sell products they have made by outside manufacturers. One company mixes, another bottles, and yet another packages and ships. At Sunrider, we do it all ourselves. Tei Fu and I come up with ideas for new products. We discuss them with our Advisory Boards--loyal and experienced distributors. We do research and development with our own staff formulators and scientists. We find the best ingredients from all over the world. We then mix, grind and concentrate the herbs for every product. Sunrider controls the entire process from beginning to end. Even our packaging is designed by our in-house creative staff."

Clearly a proud mother, Oi-Lin says, "Attend a Sunrider Grand Convention and you'll see my children work and perform on stage. Some like it more than others, but I give each of them the opportunity to learn our business. Their generation is the world's future."

# Women of Distinction

**Jane Deuber** rose to the forefront of network marketing on the dual tracks of academia and practical experience via prestigious Wittenberg University in her native Ohio. She then went on to California's rigorous Monterey Institute of International Studies, where she received an MBA, then by working in Taiwan with international trade companies.

Soon after returning from Asia, Jane searched for a business opportunity that would allow her to fulfill her lifelong dream of following in her father's footsteps as a successful entrepreneur. "I believe in the power of business ownership," explains Jane, "and network marketing allowed me to follow my dreams by owning my own business while empowering others to do the same."

Not content with simply joining one of the many network marketing companies in existence, Jane saw an opportunity to do what had never been done before: Create a company that combined the best of both party plan and multi-level marketing into one great program. After extensive research of nearly 20 companies, Jane and husband, Mario Villacres founded Latasia & Company in 1987. From the beginning, Jane realized that to ensure distributors short and long- term success, a company must offer two distinct product lines. "Our Expressions jewelry collection is at the heart of the program and is the key that opens the door for our consultants. Because it is an impulse product and easy to sell, distributors begin to profit as soon as they start their business. This early success builds confidence and reduces attrition common in the industry," Jane stated.

In addition to the jewelry, Jane saw the need for a product that would enable consultants to build repeat business for long-term residual income. To fill this need, she created the Perfect Balance Program, a unique product line of nutritional and personal care products that promote health and well-being through balanced living. Jane believes these are definitely changing the lives of the many people who use them.

Jane's keen understanding of what today's network marketers are looking for prompted her to borrow even more from the contrasted segments of the industry. "From party plan, we adopted the philosophies of the best support and training to help distributors through the challenges of building a home-based business." Explains Jane: "From network marketing we borrowed the extensive use of technology to build nationwide. With features such as fax-on-demand, weekly national conference calls and internet sites, we are able to give our consultants the support they need to build a thriving business." Latasia's impressive track record celebrates 11 years of consistent solid growth, and is evidence that distributors are hungry for an opportunity that encompasses the best of both worlds.

In July of 1997, Jane added yet another achievement to her resume when son Alexander was born! Jane's desire to spend more time with her son prompted her to make some important changes within Latasia. In January of 1999, Jane made the transition from CEO of Latasia to advisor to the new owners, Maria Baccari and Anthony Calendrelli. "Mario and I grew Latasia from a $5,000 investment in the third bedroom of our apartment, to a multi-million dollar enterprise. It was time for us to let go and allow Latasia to become all it is meant to be." In her new capacity as marketing consultant, Jane is able to continue shaping the future of Latasia, while allowing the new team of experts to take the company to new heights of success.

When asked what she feels she brings to the network marketing industry, Jane answered, "I have always believed that for a company to be successful it must provide more than a product and a plan. The network marketing successes of the 21st century will be instrumental in improving the quality of people's lives; not just provide an opportunity to earn additional income. Latasia has been a catalyst for this change, and will continue to set new standards in our industry. And for that, I will always be proud!"

261

# Women of Distinction

**Connie Dugan's** phenomenal success in network marketing began in 1990 with a stroke of pure luck. She and her family had recently moved from Boston, where they sold all their furniture, liquidated many investments and relocated to Hilton Head, South Carolina, in search of "a more enriching lifestyle and a great place to raise children." Along with her husband, who had also grown dissatisfied with the corporate world, they spent an entire year searching for a business to purchase. Despite their interest in several, none actually fit their needs. Dugan came across a classified ad for a home-based business that stated the earning potential was $10,000 a month. Though skeptical, she called for information. When the packet from Oxyfresh arrived, Dugan noticed one of the company's testimonials was from a former business associate. She called and peppered him with questions -- receiving in return, all positive answers.

Four years later, Dugan was one of Oxyfresh's top ten distributors. Now a Master Director, she also sits on the advisory board, acting as a liason between distributors and the company. However, it wasn't by sheer luck that she attained her position in such a short time. "By any standard, the home-based temp agency I ran in Boston was a success, but the company owned me," she recalls. She knew how to work hard -- too hard. "If I went on vacation and didn't answer the phone, I didn't make money."

From her good fortune with Oxyfresh, Dugan learned how to succeed in network marketing, following the principles of the man who became her mentor. "Your credibility," she says, "is everything." And just as she was helped, Dugan vowed to help others. "Call it fate, karma or whatever," Dugan says of her serendipitous discovery of the testimonial from a former business associate. "Doors open and we are introduced to opportunities when the time is appropriate." Her slogan is: "I will mentor millionaires the same way I was helped to create my business. I am passing the baton to help others do the same."

In eight years, 5,000 people have worked in her downline. With one dozen leader legs, most stretch along the East Coast from Florida to Maine.

Dugan spends the vast majority of her time working with distributors who are "on fire." She actually camps out with them for three or four days, getting to know them and to help design a plan that will get them going. "I don't cut people off, but I do throw them from the nest. You can't carry anyone over the finish line," she states.

Dugan believes that one of her gifts is the ability to stretch others beyond their personal limitations. The results are tangible; not only financial, but freeing up distributors to spend more time with their families; to enjoy their lives and give back to their community. Success changes how they see themselves. It empowers them.

Though Dugan's children are now teenagers, on most days she's there for them when they return from school -- just as she was when they were small. She has also done volunteer work in their schools, the community library, her church and the local hospital.

Now in her late forties, Dugan is earning an annual income in the high six figures. But she can't even imagine retirement. "It's doubtful whether I will ever stop networking, because I have something to pay back," she says. And it is Dugan's hope that those in her downline will also "share the gift and pass the baton."

# Women of Distinction

Integris co-founder, **Janice Hymer**, figured out early on in life how to combine the two ingredients that would make others happy and healthy, and in doing so, gave her personal joy and fulfillment.

### Janice Hymer

As a child growing up on a Texas cotton farm during the dust bowl years, Janice loved attending parties. At five years of age and dressed in a pretty organdy pinafore, her mother was braiding her hair for a party. Advising her, she stated, "Now Janice, remember, this is not your party." Because of her outgoing, take-charge personality, Janice would become the self-appointed party hostess, answering the door, taking the gifts and organizing the games. Her rationalization was that "somebody's got to do it!" That attitude carried her well into adulthood, greatly impacting her choice of careers.

Janice personally built a large catering company, overseeing in excess of 18,000 parties. Additionally, throughout this period she pursued a side interest in the health field. Janice had been fascinated by vitamins and nutrition since Adele Davis and Linus Pauling burst on the health forefront. From 1995 on, she has pursued this field aggressively; first as a hobby, then as a career in network marketing.

From the 1970s to the early 1980s, Janice was instrumental in helping build a family-run oil company into a publicly traded firm with over 200 employees. When the oil stock suddenly plummeted in early 1984, so did the family business. This devastation left them with huge debts. Janice's networking career, which began part-time in 1973, now became full-time. Her main objective was to pull her family completely out of debt.

Over the next 13 years, Janice was instrumental in building two large organizations. With her strong determination and tenacity, she not only propelled herself out of debt, but in the process, discovered a whole new aspect to her personality. She loved helping others become successful.

"In 1984, I couldn't imagine ever being as wealthy as I had been while involved in the family oil business. However, as I began pulling out of debt, I realized I was truly interested with achievement and loved helping others do so — even more than me. It's like giving birth to a child and seeing them graduate from Harvard," Janice said.

Always committed to cutting edge, scientifically based nutritional products, Janice helped found Integris in 1996. She sees an exciting future with the high impact of the Integris products, all of which truly and consistently make a difference. Her motivation is watching Integris unfold as a globally, life-changing force, both financially and physically. Within the large organization she has built at Integris, Janice is a mentor to hundreds. Indeed, the heart of Integris beats in Janice Hymer.

Many mentors along the way have taught Janice humility, longevity and giving. Her personal philosophy is to make memories every day and to realize how much impact we can have at any age or station in life; to always see the glass full; to go to sleep at night, knowing you did all you can do, and knowing you've done it all with fun, zest and dignity. Instead of thunderstorms, Janice sees rainbows; and instead of the philosophy of letting life happen, Janice makes life happen — for herself and others.

Janice resides in Castroville, Texas, with her childhood sweetheart and husband, Joe Hymer, M.D. They have sought the peace of a back-to-nature lifestyle as they live in their 150-year-old farmhouse on a quiet river. Her hobbies include golf, ballroom and Latin dancing, and is also an avid collector of Texas primitive antiques. She still enjoys parties and her networking provides numerous opportunities for Janice and Joe. Always committed to mentoring and motivating others, her many Integris trips are viewed as an opportunity to bond with leaders. Janice's natural warmth and Texas smile provide encouragement to all she comes in contact with. This is her key to success!

# Women of Distinction

With people as her passion, **Carrol Leclerc** can look past the current problems and prospects of multi-level marketing to the day when this presence in the global economy will be a portal through which the increasingly ethnically-diverse student generation can find its way into the world. A day when gaining hands-on experience in the basic commercial skills of accounting, some banking, reading and writing for commerce--even while honing our kids' people skills so essential in furthering the business relationship will become a reality.

As founder and president of the Multi-Level Marketing International Association (MLMIA), head of CLC Management Inc., and the organizer of three successful private MLM companies in her native Canada, Leclerc's concerns reflect her true commitment to direct marketing enterprise.

Like many in MLM, Carrol's first taste of success came via Amway. "I'd come from a nine to five job, modeling and various things," she recalls. "Amway taught me selling as 'duplication,' moving product as a second nature. I was so new I didn't know that most beginners didn't sponsor four or five people in a couple of days; 50 within the first month!"

Carrol fit right in when Mary Kay came to Canada. "I'd been teaching modeling in my own agency, but the new company was noted for teaching the whole range of opportunities. I went ahead and learned the inside secrets, becoming a sales director when the product was still relatively inexpensive."

Leaving because women were then bereft of decision-making power, Leclerc bought her own company, the first of several that has led to serving MLM clients in seven countries, with sales volumes from start-up to $300 million annually.

Early in that chapter of life, she found it convenient to employ a male lieutenant, given the executive world's then gender bias. However, she gained a measure of satisfaction when one of those men loudly announced to a masculine third party: "Hey! she's (Carrol) my boss."

Today, the suburban Vancouver, B.C.-based executive remains in the vanguard of network marketing, by speaking and writing voluminously as consultant and guru, plus a defining activity that exceeds national boundaries.

It's the championing of the global cause by informing consumers and corporate entities alike of the complexities of regulatory compliance. Her magnum opus is *The MLM Compendium of the Canadian Regulatory Compliance.* An indispensable tool for off-shore network marketing, based on Canada's strict regulatory infra structure.

"It's all to the good," says the dashing veteran of the enterprise; "Canada's rigorous compliance policies assure the highest level of consumer confidence, which ultimately encourages enhanced participation in network promotions."

MLM as a positive socializing force has also been in theme in Carrol's thought. "Here in Canada with our immense social diversity, MLM has helped both close ethnic enclaves because of its immediate financial rewards, and also the population at large by way of, say, the widened recognition of Asian medicinals and natural product applications."

Given to meaningful parables (as so many natural marketers are), Leclerc has one that tellingly illustrates the contrast between radical change and the societal erosion worked by time and repetition:

"I believe in the old-pebble-in-the-ocean example," she says. "Those ripples do affect other people, even if it is a long journey in getting to where we inevitably will go."

As a people-passionate person who has excelled at every level of the MLM industry--from a green-as-grass distributor (albeit a high-volume recruiter) to a chairperson of boards of directors--we must give heed to Carrol Leclerc, one who foresees the realities of our childrens' hopes to flourish (and compliance) no less than the sometimes illusory projections of things yet to come. "First things first," she says.

Carrol Leclerc

# Women of Distinction

A woman of high energy, resolute drive, a passionate love of independence, a strong sense of honesty and integrity, and an ability to lead others, **Renata Lee** has worked her way to success in the network marketing industry through sheer determination and a burning desire. After working full-time in the industry for ten years, Lee has developed three basic reasons why network marketing isn't for everyone. "First, if you don't like people, don't do network marketing, no matter how much money you think you're going to make. This is a people business! Second, if you don't like the telephone, don't do network marketing. This is a relationship business and you have to be willing to follow up, follow through, and spend time on the phone developing those relationships. And third, if you are not into personal growth, do not do network marketing. You will start to discover amazing things about yourself and grow in ways you never thought possible. So stop NOW if you do not want this to happen to you!"

Lee, who was raised in the Los Angeles area and spent her childhood summers in Montana climbing mountains with her father says, "You can't learn about network marketing from reading about it in a book. The only way to learn it is to do it. Or, as I tell people in my training sessions, 'The only way to it is through it.' I had many days where I felt like quitting, because when network marketing isn't working it can be miserable. But when it is working, it can be one of the most beautiful businesses there is. If you're willing to stray out of your comfort zone, and develop some persistence, tenacity, and a measure of patience, you will develop a business you never thought possible. The long-term rewards in the network marketing industry are extraordinary, financially and in every other way. I am a totally different individual today because I have grown so much, and I have developed long-term relationships that will be with me

forever!" Lee says she "fell into" network marketing while she was simultaneously managing the Mortgage Trading and Finance Department of Security Pacific Merchant Bank sixty hours a week and singing and dancing in a musical production called "Pepper Street," the longest running musical in L.A. She worked with nutritional products for her first seven years and did corporate training, becoming a regional seminar manager and reaching the top in all three companies she worked with. In her eighth year in the industry, she segued into a telecommunication company and had just over 42,000 people in her organization while also working as the first female corporate trainer brought on by that company. Eleven hundred people a week came into her organization while she also traveled the country doing corporate trainings. "My phone rang every thirty seconds for eighteen months. It was a remarkable experience! But you cannot build a network marketing business all alone. Without a team of people all believing in their product and working toward one common goal, 'leaders' such as myself cannot be successful. I have been blessed to have attracted other fabulous team builders who have become incredible leaders. It's an absolute delight seeing so many people with the potential of doing so well."

Recently, Lee worked for a company where her role filled a unique and fundamental need in the network marketing industry, that of a liaison between corporate and the field, acting as a "voice" for both sectors. "I came to understand what it takes to build a network marketing organization and what it takes to support it, how to merge corporate and the field into one voice. The communication gaps between the two create one of the greatest dichotomies of the industry and brings down many otherwise fine companies."

Renata Lee's present position is her biggest so far and attaches her to no particular company, but has to do with representation of the industry as a whole. "It is most important to me that network marketing be entirely legitimate," she concluded.

# Women of Distinction

Even as a child too young to envision the future, **Adrienne (Adi) Song** felt powerfully drawn to the idea of helping others.

"I dreamed of being a teacher," she said. "But that ambition has been more than realized here at Longevity Network, where my commitment is embodied in an enterprise that brings physical health and dependable financial wellness to millions of people worldwide."

Her career is a chapter straight out of the American Dream realized: A mother's family of Greek heritage that came to the U.S. to establish small-business roots in San Francisco; her dad's people, Washington state pioneers who published Spokane's first newspaper and established the city's landmark, Manito Park.

Song overcame her innate shyness early on by immersing herself in high school drama. Then, after classes at the University of Nevada, Las Vegas, she discovered the manifold satisfactions of helping others.

"I loved it when a close friend asked me to help start a free clinic in Los Angeles," she said, crediting the task of helping those less fortunate with raising her awareness of the health care industry.

Other directedness was rewarded when Adi returned to Las Vegas to help nurse her father during an extended illness, fate intervening when a friend suggested an interview with Jim Song. "He hired me and two years later we went on our first date. The rest is history."

Married and now in the same board room for 10 years, the Songs' commitment is distinguished among other nutritional firms for its medical-scientific advisory board, noted for introducing new life-enhancing products and guiding advanced research aimed at developing even new ones.

Adi Song, especially, has been the catalyst vital in inspiring a corporate culture based on family values, plus the integrity and fun that those virtues inspire. Distributor-wise, Longevity considers its pay plan the best and most cutting-edge in the industry. "We give all of our distributors a level playing field based on the best marketing plan and products. This allows people to grow on a personal and professional level, she says."

Consumers by the millions relate to the firm for its enduring ties with U.S. Olympic Decathlon Gold Medalist Bruce Jenner. Not only a celebrity endorser of products, he's also an entrepreneur who works in the trenches with the rest of the troops. Says Ms. Song: "Although a celebrity, he has the same sense of family and values that we have: A father, a loving husband and a very successful businessman; one who actually works in our network. Can anyone be more authentic than that?"

Looking to the new millennium and beyond, Song cites the bullish "Popcorn Report" of the marketing guru who foresaw the consumer trend of staying safe and sound at home while the whole retailing world came increasingly over the threshold via new information technologies.

"Like her," said Song, "I'm convinced we're still on the cutting edge of the revolution. Eventually, direct shopping will totally by-pass the retailer; no middleman or stops along the way. Ms. Popcorn also overlooked data that 95 percent of consumer-buying decisions are based on the personal recommendations of friends and associates."

Scanning the future, she is measuredly optimistic. While indicating that Longevity could be ready for global expansion, she cautions, "you must have strong roots at home before reaching out into other markets."

While crystal-balling the next millennium, she sees the Longevity Network solidifying its culture for the future benefits of not only its founding distributors, but also those trail-breakers' children and their childrens' children.

"I feel there's a global movement towards people helping people," she says. "What will heal our planet to create a better life is caring and helping each other."

You can bet your downline that this once-wistful little girl who did become both a teacher and a care-giver will be right on the cutting edge, as she has been at Longevity Network.

Once a harried mother who chose to wash dishes on the graveyard shift at Pan American Airways to keep her four young children together, **Sylvia M. Waiwaiole** today wears two distinguished hats: As North American executive field advisor for Matol Botanical International Ltd., and president-director of Matol Australasia Corp. Ltd. of New Zealand and Australia.

**Sylvia Waiwaiole**

Waiwaiole's roller-coaster route to success began in the bosom of her supportive family (she was the tenth of 11 children) on the Hawaiian island of Oahu. There, her faith was implanted by a devout mother and she received a private school education through the sacrifices of an older brother.

Flight kitchen chores occupied her in the mid 1960s, after a failed marriage and before she entered direct marketing by going house-to-house in a broken-down VW van, selling a multitude of products that included a patented "Sculptress" bra. The assignment kept her family together for a decade as she became the company's top sales producer and converted her communication skills into a deluxe Lincoln Continental, chests full of gems and a picture-book home in the Kailua area.

However, a low ebb followed: financial, physical and emotional. Her two sons abused substances, leading her to help fund the state's nationally-recognized "No Hope in Dope" drug prevention program, for which she was a nominee in Hawaii's 14th annual First Lady's Outstanding Volunteer Award.

That, plus her innate resilience, a deep faith in God and a bottle of Matol/Km, the firm's standby potassium compound, conspired in 1987 to turn things around, by joining the long-standing botanical company. "I had an incredible experience with the product," she said. "Plunging ahead again, I became one of the company's leading producers. My priorities were back in order: God, family and putting my energy where it would pay the most." Waiwaiole's tenacious determination helped put her among leading partners in the U.S. and Canada, and spilled over into the far-flung English-speaking nations of New Zealand, Australia and the United Kingdom where she's president-licensee and (her favorite title) Chief Marketing Officer of Matol Australasia. But there came a devastating discovery at the height of Matol's international expansion when she was diagnosed with breast cancer. Despite admitted anger and fear, she underwent surgery, endured six weeks of radiation and providentially confirmed that Matol products aided in her recovery.

"The day I was last radiated I flew to a Montreal leadership conference," she said. "Then and there I accepted the biblical lesson that we should rejoice in our sufferings because travail leads to perseverance, which in turn produces character and hope."

Almost anti-climactically, Sylvia's two doctors, Dr. Jesse Stoff, MD and Dr. Stanley Olsztyn, MD, treated her with a product, an immuno-modulator that help to support, and enhance the immune system. So effective were the results that she considered it in accord with Matol's mission of positively impacting the world's health and environment via products, services and programs that promote the quality of life and healthy living.

Convinced of its efficacy, Waiwaiole persisted for two years with Matol directors, even enlisting the aid of founder Robert Bolduc, in making it possible for the firm to become exclusive distributor of the product, now called Biomune OSF Plus.

"There's no other way it could have been done," she said. "It seems almost miraculous when you put your trust in God and totally accept the challenge."

Health restored, energy rejuvenated and even firmer in her faith, some see in Sylvia an almost biblical presence: About delivering Matol/Km to a Maori woman who lost one leg to surgical error and the other to diabetes, she said, "I held her, I wept with her. I read her some scripture, it made me realize how fortunate I am to have touched her life in some positive way."

# Women of Distinction

Life has a tendency to beat many of us down. The "Rat Race" of life pushes us into pigeon holes that stifle our will to succeed, and what dreams are left over, revolve around luck and lottery. **Sabrina Wei,** however, has never been one to rely on chance. She makes her own luck. As a go-getting entrepreneur who has worked her way to a seven-figure income while still in her twenties, Wei turned this attitude into a hard won reality. She has built her life, and her career, on the premise that each goal attained is one more rung up the ladder of life, leading toward the next, bigger challenge.

Sabrina Wei

Wei credits her high level of motivation and extraordinary accomplishments to the example that her parents provided all her life. Her mother and father emigrated from Taiwan and established themselves in Vancouver, Canada, as a teacher and chemist. Sabrina saw them constantly making sacrifices for herself and her younger brother, Lynden. She learned of discipline, dedication and diligence from their example, applying these qualities later to her own education and career goals.

However, a large portion of the credit belongs to Sabrina herself. Much of her success derives from her ability to throw off any self-imposed limitations. A shy student, Sabrina remembers being further isolated by the reality of an hour-long commute each way to and from school. This distance between her and her classmates created the perception that led her to being voted "Most Studious" in her high school graduating class. Once in university however, Sabrina decided to shed these limitations, joining several business and social clubs in a conscious effort to project a better, well-rounded image. After overcoming her initial hesitation, she ran for president of the Finance and Investment Club and won. This position gained her many invaluable business connections, both on campus and with financial leaders in the local community at a very young age. Wei's business career follows a similarly impressive course. She first put her accounting degree to good use as the youngest individual ever hired by what is now the prestigious CPA firm of Deloitte & Touche. However, she soon realized that even partner status would never allow her to meet the financial goals she had set for herself or create the time freedom that she ultimately was working for. So Sabrina took a calculated risk, and at the age of 20, launched a new career in network marketing that soon brought her the financial freedom she sought. It also allowed her to give back to her family after all of the support they'd given her. Of all the "perks" associated with her network marketing career, Sabrina values most the satisfaction of working closely and sharing the many benefits of her lifestyle with her family.

Her own company, Leading Minds International, Inc., was created to provide people from every background with the opportunity to achieve the same levels of success and personal growth as she experienced. A wide range of products and services (impact products, name brands, telecommunications and financial) guarantees everyone a "niche." Her lucrative compensation plan rewards weekly as well as monthly, reflecting her own experience as a distributor in recognition of the need for sustained levels of cash flow, as well as enthusiasm.

In Sabrina's mind, network marketing is the vehicle to take any individual along the road to financial freedom where they can pursue their long-term hopes and dreams. She believes it can take one there faster than the traditional "Plan A," but it is up to each individual to set up their ultimate destination and create a roadmap. By truly applying herself, letting go of the preconceived notions about herself and others, and with a willingness to take personal risks, Sabrina reached her goals well ahead of schedule. Working toward the next rung of her career and an extended vision for Leading Minds International, Wei illustrates that so long as a dreamer allows himself/herself to grow, there is no limit to what one can accomplish.

# Men of Distinction

We've often been asked if only distributors or representatives qualify for our Men of Distinction honors. While the majority of our inductees are highly successful distributors and representatives, this is not a prerequisite for admission into this very exclusive club. Nominees include company executives--even presidents, or those whose credentials are measured beyond financial success alone. Contributions to the industry, giving, sharing, unselfish acts and unsung commitments all figure prominently in the selection process. From a highly regarded list of 37 nominees, the following were chosen by our panel as the top of the mark. Certainly, controversy will abound; hundreds of respected successful distributors could make a strong case for their induction and our panel would be hard pressed to eliminate a good many of them. However, the verdict was rendered. Here then, is our winning class of 2000.

# Inductees

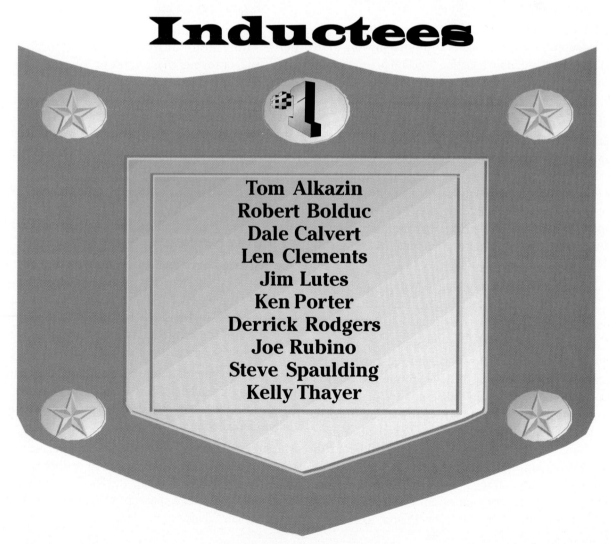

**Tom Alkazin**
**Robert Bolduc**
**Dale Calvert**
**Len Clements**
**Jim Lutes**
**Ken Porter**
**Derrick Rodgers**
**Joe Rubino**
**Steve Spaulding**
**Kelly Thayer**

# Men of Distinction

As one of the few Presidential Team leaders of New Vision International, **Tom Alkazin** offers a unique perspective on network marketing.

**Tom Alkazin**

"I was blessed," says this intense but soft-spoken 22-year veteran of the industry, "to have had company founder Ben Boreyko as a friend and coach; also for him giving Bethany Alkazin and I a chance as one of the 4,000 partners in the family's memorable rebound from the crushing bankruptcy of an earlier firm on the eve of Christmas, 1994."

Within the half year, New Vision was at $500,000 per month; doubling those revenues shortly after moving from Tulsa to Tempe, and now boasting 700,000 partners who generate $200 million annually and are squarely on target for hitting their $1 billion bullseye by the year 2000.

On the seven member board that counsels second-generation Boreyko leaders, BK (Benjamin Keith) and Jason, Alkazin commands industry ears. A native of La Jolla, California, and a resident of nearby Carlsbad, he's one of those who discovered early on that to be self-employed is invaluable in itself. Providentially, he opted in 1975 for an Amway distributorship while working full-time in computer science, his major at the University of San Francisco.

And all the better for that foresight. Within 18 months, deep cut-backs savaged that segment. But he wisely nurtured his MLM proceeds, seguing into layoff with more income than from his full-time job.

"Seeing massive layoffs first hand showed me just how devastating they can be. I'll never forget the trauma of those good people," said Alkazin. "It was the point of no return for me." While with Amway, he quickly became a diamond and found a jewel in his future wife. There, too, he could give his analytical bent full sway. "My premise emerged that there are four essential virtues in making a home office go. They are company, products, compensation, and system." He found a finely-tuned firm in New Vision: Zero debt, compound average monthly growth of 41.5 percent since 1995, unexcelled financial expertise, plus an ear constantly tuned to members of the team.

Product-wise it's also a winner; the innovator, maker and marketer of natural products designed to promote health and vitality. (Its Essential Minerals liquid sells a bottle every 10 seconds).

Compensation is unparalleled: Average monthly payout of 54.3 percent (maximum of 55 points), almost unheard of in an industry where the average is 40 to 43 percent. Cash disbursement to members in 1997 neared $129 million. Some individuals earned over $60,000 per month.

New Vision's system (some call it culture) is deliberately non-confrontational. It assumes that everyone entering the business has the ability to participate productively; not only those with prior MLM experience but also sincere people from any walk of life who can use an extra $300 to $400 a month. "This is the secret of our rapid growth," he said, "getting everyone who has the desire involved in the business. . . and just as soon as possible."

This too reflects the Alkazins' core belief. "We put relationship No. 1 in the business context. Genuine, reaching-out friendship to people at all levels. That leads them to care because they see that we truly care."

The Alkazins have two boys ages 12 and 15, and a daughter 8, all at a Christian school in which the couple is deeply immersed. Mom is a volunteer; Tom a school board member and basketball coach. "Faith and family take up most of our time, and in that order. We feel the results show the correctness of our path."

He foresees a shining future for the firm and its partners. Opening in Canada early in 1998, it looks south of the border in 1999; seemingly destined to becoming a billion dollar company by the year 2000.

Muses Tom Alkazin: "BK Boreyko's been driven by faith from the start, a conviction stated in his battle cry: 'We don't have a Plan B.' To that, the family and we partners have added, 'So let's make it go!' From that faith has come the confidence in our long-term stability."

He is the co-founder, chairman and C.E.O. of an ever-expanding corporation, recognized the world over for always being on the cutting edge.

**Robert Bolduc**

His creation, Matol Botanical International Ltd., has grown steadily since its inception in 1984, reaching the $250 million mark in sales its top year.

The distribution network he oversees, which includes more than 75,000 members, has brought to the world a top-quality line of lifestyle enhancement products, dietary supplements and vitamins, among others, which bring both repeat sales and word-of-mouth opportunities.

But more than the great wealth, more than the technological achievements or the growth milestones reached, **J. F. Robert Bolduc** (pronounced Balldoo) insists it is his genuine belief in the importance of his company's mission that continues to fuel his tremendous success. "I believe that a leader has to pick a lane, make choices," he says. "I did not start this company to make all the money; we started because of the belief level in our product. We believed it was absolutely foolproof."

"I am absolutely dedicated to the to law of the land in this company, which is, Give and Receive, the 48-year-old continues. "This is all about fellowship, which has to do with mentoring. This industry is based on sponsoring; that's the action, but it doesn't represent the philosophy.

"The real formula for success isn't magical; it's geared toward the responsibility of the leader to the individual, and the mentoring process. That all has to do with duplication, which only works if the master copy is worth duplicating."

Surprisingly, that translates into a rather simple, direct philosophy: Growth depends on the ability of the product and service to meet the needs of the client. And judging by Matol's success, its founder's work is not only being duplicated; it is satisfying customers' demands and distributors' needs.

Headquartered in Montreal, Quebec, Canada, Bolduc started his company with the unique product Matol/Km, a potassium mineral supplement. For the first seven years of its existence, Matol focused all of its efforts on that one product. Through perseverance, Matol/Km was marketed successfully, appealing to those seeking a healthier lifestyle. In fact, the flagship product has accounted for millions in sales.

"That caused us to be a phenomenon in the industry because we were recognized as a solid cooperative structure that was product driven," Bolduc says. "My own appreciation of Matol/Km came with the realization of its true potential. And I was given the opportunity to see its potential long before it was acknowledged as the 'Nobel Prize' product of the industry."

The success of Matol/Km eventually led to the development of several other products, including health cereals and snack bars, skin care lotion and a liquid nutritional supplement. In all, Matol's product line has earned the company a billion dollars in sales over the past 13 years, making it one of the most successful corporations of its size in the world. Still, Matol distributes only about a dozen products, preferring to focus on quality rather than sheer monetary income. Its official motto, which Bolduc is quick to point out, includes the phrase, "a serious nutrition company with a healthy attitude." That only works if the people who make the company believe it and keep their focus. And, of course, that has to be supported by their leader's sincerity

"To be successful, an organization must have people who believe," Bolduc says. "But there always has to be at least one person at the heart of the organization that believes in it no matter what — and that's my role.

"Matol is not something I do; it is something I am," he continues. "Our distributors carry the torch and I'm the keeper of the flame."

In doing just that, Bolduc always keeps at heart the wisdom of the late Mother Teresa, who once said, "We do no great things, only small things with great love."

"That's the perfect definition of success," Bolduc says. "You will find very few successful people who do not live by that quote. I know I do."

# Men of Distinction

**Dale Calvert** has finally realized a dream that began several years ago. With his perseverance and determination, he has made it to the top of the summit with New Image International, now serving as director of marketing. However, ambitious as he is, life wasn't always easy for Calvert...until New Image entered the scene.

Calvert was intent on moving out of their small, 600 square foot home. At times, this transition seemed like a dream. He had his heart set on living in the gated community of Mallard Point, a subdivision in Kentucky, consisting of large, stately homes. "I would drive out there at night in my beat-up Chevette and pull up to the gate, even though I knew I couldn't get in," Calvert recalls. But that never stopped him from visualizing he and his family would one day be a part of the community. A constant reminder they would someday live there, was a large picture in his makeshift office of the beautiful homes he longed to be a part of. This was the driving motivation that has brought him success with New Image, enabling he and his family to move into their new 4,000 square foot lakeside home at Mallard Point. However, Calvert had a tough road to hoe before making his dream come true.

Prior to New Image, he worked for two other network marketing companies. Additionally, he marketed a specialized health insurance product for persons who were self-employed. Times were often difficult. Just when he thought things were looking up, a financial reversal would occur. Even his credit cards had maxed out. "I even started looking back to when I once worked for IBM, wondering that if I had stayed there, I could have become a technician or department manager, but I couldn't see spending 40 years building a dream for someone else," Calvert said.

Calverts luck would change after New Image approached him to help implement a marketing plan for the company.

Dissatisfied with his current company, he thought he had nothing to lose.

Calverts wife, Stephanie, was at a loss for words when her husband initially told her he was leaving his then--current company to join New Image. However, so strong are their beliefs in the company, neither has ever looked back. With Calvert's marketing acumen, New Image associates are able to sell products directly to customers, which enables them to earn an income before sponsoring others. If an associate spends only a few hours each week sharing products with others, they are able to earn a few hundred dollars per month.

New Image was founded in January, 1994 by Ron Frederic, beginning with only 84 associates. At the end of the first year, sales reached $3.8 million. In 1997, New Image held their third national conference with 5,000 associates in attendance. With Calvert's help, sales had climbed to over $35 million.

"At some point, everyone's mother, brother, sister, aunt and uncle want to lose weight," Calvert stated. "I lost 16 pounds when I began taking New Image products, and when others saw what it did for me, they all wanted to buy the products."

Calvert is also proud of the fact he played an integral part in implementing New Image's training policy. "Most companies are not entirely focused on one method of teaching. This creates confusion with distributors. People don't know who to follow. New Image has unified its organization, separating us from the masses," Calvert said. He believes you should have one system and stick with it.

"We have been able to give others the freedom to do what they want, when they want. Building better lives for our associates and their families have always been a priority with New Image." Calvert concluded.

Realizing still another dream, Calvert and his family, including three daughters, are building yet a larger home consisting of 15,000 square feet on a 103 acre horse farm in central Kentucky. This is where he anticipates hosting many large company barbecues for the people that have enhanced his life to the fullest.

# Men of Distinction

**Leonard Clements** was born and raised in California, just north of San Francisco. He attended Sir Francis Drake High School ,where he graduated with honors while finishing in the top 10% in the nation in mathematics. After attending one year of college he decided to "take a semester off." Six years later he returned to earn his degree in Business Data Processing.

Len's MLM career began in 1979 with a health and nutrition company which, six months later (the same week that he gave notice at his job) went out of business. Len did get his job back, but that swift feeling of success had lit the entrepreneurial fire within him (or, as his one and only boss told him, made him "psychologically unemployable").

After a short stint with two other failed MLM companies, he decided to go the conventional route and opened a computer training facility in downtown San Francisco. After six profitable years of business (despite numerous thefts, car break-ins, a drug raid on an adjoining business, a suicide outside the front door, two drive-by shootings, and a major earthquake), he had enough of "The City." Len spent a full year doing his homework before reentering the MLM arena, and soon discovered that there was a ready and willing market for that same knowledge. He held his first *Facts & Myths Of MLM* seminar in his computer classroom in September of 1990. Those seminars were a success and soon became a twice monthly event, each time selling out the room. By popular demand of those seminar attendees, *MarketWave,* the newsletter, was born in January of 1991.

A prestigious business research and consulting firm in the area was investigating the idea of adding network marketing to their list of "low risk" business opportunities to offer their clients. Len was brought on board as their Senior Market Analyst, and within weeks a separate, entirely MLM-focused division was created called *MarketWave.* Later that year Len sold his computer business and purchased *MarketWave* outright.

*MarketWave* has remained an unaffiliated, objective information clearing house for the network marketing industry ever since. Len routinely puts in 50-60 hour work weeks writing his newsletter, providing telephone consulting, and conducting his Facts & Myths seminars (now called "Inside Secrets of Network Marketing") throughout the United States, Canada and Mexico. During this time, Len also authored the controversial book <u>Inside Network Marketing</u> (nationally published by Prima Publishing), an objective, no-holds-barred, insider's look at the MLM industry. He is also the author and producer of the best selling cassette tape, Case Closed! The Whole Truth About Network Marketing, which he designed specifically for skeptical or prejudice "outer circle" prospects.

In February of 1998, Len went on the air as host of the live talk radio program, Inside Network Marketing on KSCO, out of Santa Cruz. The show is currently being marketed for national syndication.

Len's *MarketWave* newsletter, which originally started out as just a part-time hobby, had grown into a full-time business serving over 1,800 clients in 14 countries. Deemed the "Consumer's Report" of multi-level marketing, *MarketWave* reviewed and rated MLM opportunities and exposed the various schemes and scams. The newsletter was sold in December of 1995 and renamed *Profit Now* (Profit Now discontinued publication in September of 1998). In January of 1999, Len resurrected his newsletter under the title *MarketWave Alert Letter*.

While there was a great deal of gratification working for the network marketing industry, Len realized that the residual income he sought was in the industry. He co-founded a team of well respected MLM leaders (including Corey Augenstein, publisher of MLM Insider) and returned to the field as a distributor.

Today, Len works exclusively as a distributor for Longevity Network and fully intends to continue his duties as one of the "watchdogs" of network marketing. Len currently resides in Fresno, California. He plans to move to either Henderson, North Virginia, or return to the Bay Area in the near future, but not San Francisco.

# Men of Distinction

At an early age, **Jim Lutes** came to the realization that the traditional nine to five routine was not for him. Fresh out of high school, he started his own business. It was at this time that he learned from his failures and also how to adjust his course. Back then, Jim would never have guessed he would one day be a top distributor for Integris International, not to mention the wealth he accumulated along the way.

"Living in San Diego afforded me the opportunity to be involved with many successful people who were working out of their home. I realized very early on that true success comes from within ones self," Jim said. It was at this point when Jim began a very serious training program in personal development. He read hundreds of books, attended every seminar he could and trained in hypnosis. Jim then opened a San Diego-based operation, teaching these strategies to various corporations around the country, as well as the general public. Having brought with him his own experience in personal development, combined with his business acumen, Jim's company grew very quickly. It was only a matter of time before he would be approached by a network marketing company. You might say he was the ideal prospect since he was wide open to the concept. Fortunately, he was approached by some people he highly respected and who had achieved a great deal of success, not only in networking, but other businesses as well. He was now ready to listen and see what they had to offer.

After only one year of involvement on a part-time basis, Jim made the decision to leave his own company and jump into networking full-time. "When I initially became involved in the industry, I noticed the people who were achieving great success were treating this business as they would any other. I also became aware of companies who would build based on nothing but hype," Jim stated. It was because of these observations that Jim became very cautious and selective where he would be investing his time, money and effort.

Late in 1996, Jim received a call from Larry Cantrell, president of Integris. Larry wanted to know how things were going with the company Jim was currently involved with. The timing couldn't have been better. "Even though I wanted to remain in the industry, I felt the company I was currently involved with was not aggressive enough for my taste," Jim stated. He wanted to be involved in a company who had large goals with an international vision.

Larry told Jim they were in the process of forming a company that had significant ties with the San Diego area. Additionally, the manufacturer was there, as well as the medical center which was owned by Dr. Kellas, chairman of the board for Integris. Jim had a high respect for Larry, so when he and Dr. Kellas planned a flight to San Diego for a meeting between the three of them, Jim was more than receptive to the idea. Jim stated, "I felt very fortunate on the day of the meeting. Everything I had been looking for in a company had been set before my very eyes."

The products Integris offered met the needs of the consumer, and were being used in a major clinic with very positive results. Everything was there and in its place: the capital, experience, mission and vision. Immediately Jim resigned from the company he was with, leaving behind the organization he had built and started from scratch with Integris. He readied himself for the 14 hour days and weekends, setting out to build another organization very quickly.

Despite the fact it's been slightly over two years, Jim has achieved an income level well into the six figures. He now spends part of his time working with other Integris leaders to put into motion an organized team within the company, with the intent of taking training and duplication to the next level. They are very excited about the company-wide team rollout, and are confident it will definitely set them apart in terms of support. "We are still a young company, and if you plan correctly, many other lives will be affected in a very positive way," Jim said.

When Jim is not working his business, he enjoys time with friends, vacationing, and taking a relaxing Harley ride up the coast of California. "The positive impact this industry can have on a person is incredible. I'm living proof of that. If you really want something and are willing to work hard to attain it, the opportunities are endles," Jim concluded.

# Men of Distinction

You don't have to be Superman to soar above the clouds and reach new heights. In fact, according to **Ken Porter**, it doesn't even require super skill or super talent. "It's called super commitment," Ken says. And that commitment has elevated him where he is today.

**Ken Porter**

Ken worked for years as a successful stockbroker, but his life was made up of 16-hour workdays. He thought he was doing what he had to do to earn an income and was planning to be a stockbroker for the rest of his life.

In 1992, a turnaround came when Ken and his wife, Carol, took a leap of faith and joined USANA. Although he had been successful in other network marketing companies in the past, this time he felt he had found a company he could build a future around. "Network marketing has always fascinated me," Ken says. "I was intrigued by the idea that an average person with limited capital and experience could work hard for a few years and create enough residual income to last a lifetime. I entered this industry to earn a great income, but have found that the real reward is not just the money, but the free time. Most people spend their entire lives giving up their precious time in an effort to earn only a small amount of money. Network marketing offers a far superior way to earn income and gives you the time to enjoy other pursuits in life. And best of all, those benefits are available to anyone who is teachable and is super committed to a better life."

Ken has reached the top level in USANA, becoming a Diamond Director in 1997, and is recognized as one of the top income earners in the company of over 100,000 distributors from around the world. With his sound understanding of network marketing, Ken spends much of his time training and teaching other distributors the principles that lead to financial independence. Ken is an avid industry advocate and through his years of experience, feels strongly that no other avenue or pursuit can come close to matching the quality of life that can be created through network marketing.

"The real essence of life is having the freedom of choice to spend time doing what you feel is important," he says. "We only live once and I enjoy the feelings I get when I help other people achieve their goals in life. If you're making a positive impact in the world and living the life of your dreams, what more could a person ask for?"

Ken encourages his fellow distributors and prospects to continually set high goals. "With a goal and a plan, regardless of the time, effort, or commitment it takes to reach that goal, and if you have a firm resolve and the right vehicle, then no obstacle or set of circumstances can stand in your way. Attaining the future of your dreams becomes only a matter of time."

"When we joined USANA, we didn't care how hard it would be," he adds. "We have worked more diligently at this than anything else in our lives. Before USANA, we weren't changing anyone's life, but now we are."

# Men of Distinction

Even in this modern day of communications, technology and transportation, there are multitudes of individuals who will never venture forth to discover the diversity of what life has to offer outside of the safe and comfortable surroundings of home. Although he had every reason to be such, **Derrick Rodgers** is not one of the "crowd!" Having spent the majority of his life in Kannapolis, North Carolina, Rodgers is steeped in a sense of community that will always keep him true to his roots. At first sight, one would not think he was the adventurous type. Rodgers, however, is a man of diversity and sees it as "the key to fulfilling life as it conditions a person to be flexible and resilient in the face of life's unexpected turns."

Rodgers is not one to be afraid of hard work. His father had instilled a hard and honest work ethic, along with an entrepreneurial spirit that allowed him to throw 100 percent of himself into every endeavor, no matter what it might be. His open attitude towards each new experience brought on the life skills that would later hold him in good stead.

After leaving Lee University in Cleveland, Tennessee, with a degree in business, Rodgers went home and joined his father in building a very successful property and life insurance agency. With a natural apptitude toward sales, marketing and management, he was instrumental in raising sales from $500,000 to $3,500,000, as well as expanding into multiple locations within three years. At the same time, Rodgers opened a premium finance company with his best friend which also flourished. With all this success, he was prudent enough to diversify into real estate, which has provided long-term, lucrative gains to his portfolio.

It was, however, in the insurance industry where Rodgers found a glimmer of what a residual income could do for a man and his life. Working hard today would build a portfolio of business that would pay out residuals in the future. But Rodgers eventually realized that insurance was not the complete answer. His strong Christian upbringing left him wanting to somehow help others. There was no way to split his time in helping others become successful in insurance, finance or real estate to the degree that he had himself.

Rodgers' first exposure to network marketing was through Amway, which was introduced to him by a friend. He immediately saw the benefits that network marketing had over traditional business and most importantly, he realized that he could build a team where everyone would be able to strive for the same success.

Cutting his network marketing teeth on Amway, Rodgers learned more about work ethic, preparation and time management, than everything that had come before. Most importantly however, were the opportunities that are available in the industry, such as compensation, management and vision. Every company has a different array of elements and Rodgers understood that he had to find the one that fit his own sense of *self*.

That search led him to the doors of International Heritage Incorporated during the summer of 1995. Confident that he had found his fit, he threw his entire support behind the start-up venture and was a major shareholder in the company. He served two terms on the board of directors, became a top five money earner and was a member of the Executive Council.

Rodgers thought he had found a home with International Heritage but soon learned that it was not to be a permanent part of his life. The company closed its doors in 1998. His vision and entrepreneurial spirit led him to become President and Co-founder of Leading Minds International, a Seattle-based company that is willing to step out and help set the pace of network marketing into the new millennium. He brings a philosophy of offering a system for lifestyle of the highest standard to its independent distributors in the spirit of partnership. Rodgers takes all diversity and life lessons that he has learned and goes forward, knowing that from humble beginnings mighty empires are built.

**Derrick Rodgers**

**Joe Rubino** was working as a dentist in the spring of 1991, so it's hardly surprising that he was introduced to network marketing through an oral hygiene kit. What's interesting is where some toothpaste, mouthwash and a topical gel took him.

Rubino's journey began when he saw an ad in a dentists' trade journal for alcohol-free mouth rinse, and a related business opportunity. Coincidentally, he had recently attended a seminar and heard a speaker present evidence linking cancer and alcohol, a common ingredient in mouthwash. Rubino and his dentist partner, Tom Ventullo, decided to try the rinse with a number of patients, some of whom had suffered for years from swollen, bleeding gums. The results, Rubino remembers, were impressive.

But he and Ventullo were still skeptical, so they gave the oral hygiene kit to several dentist friends. When they too reported excellent results, Rubino and Ventullo became Oxyfresh distributors. "We had no idea that it was going to take us where it did," Rubino says eight years later.

Along with their sponsor, Rubino and Ventullo have developed a comprehensive system designed to help distributors replicate their success, which they teach in network marketing courses throughout North America. Rubino also explains it in a recent book, *Secrets of Building a Million Dollar Network Marketing Organization from a Guy Who's Been There, Done That and Shows You How to Do It Too*. They have one of the most extensive internet sites in the industry, where they sell products, enroll new distributors and teach their system, Rubino says, without mailing a single piece of paper. He and Ventullo are national directors of Oxyfresh Worldwide and sit on the company's advisory board. Their organization includes 17,500 distributors located in every state and Canadian province.

Rubino, now in his early forties, has retired from dentistry. So has Ventullo. Though he won't divulge their annual income (it's company policy), Rubino does say they're making three times as much as they made in dentistry—and they had a million dollar a year practice (with, of course, far more overhead). In their best month, they made $62,000.

Rubino and his wife, who live in the Boston suburb of Boxford, Massachusetts, are building a home on 50 acres of wooded land. A second home in the White Mountains of New Hampshire, serves as a base for skiing and golf. They've traveled extensively throughout the United States and Asia, the Caribbean and Mexico. But that, Rubino insists, is a small part of the story.

Back when he was working as a dentist and dabbling in network marketing, Rubino says, he made a crucial realization. As a dentist, he was living what he calls "a life of shoulds." He *should* go to work every morning, he *should* see patients he didn't particularly like, *should* do procedures he didn't enjoy. "We really didn't own our lives," he says. "We were puppets in the game. Oxyfresh and network marketing allowed us to realize that we could design our lives; that we could spend our time with the people we wanted to spend time with, and could do the work we wanted to do."

That realization became a cornerstone of Rubino's approach to network marketing. "We believe your business will only grow as fast as you do," he explains. "Half of my book is about personal development."

What began with a dentist's quest for a safer mouthwash led Rubino to something much larger. "The products are important," he says, "because they form the basis of the opportunity. Without extraordinary products there would be no opportunity. But it's really not about products at all. The ability to contribute to people's lives is far more important than the finest mouthwash ever made. It's really about helping people design lives that work for them. We help them avoid the life of regrets that most people lead."

In Rubino's mind, this desire to help others is a key to success in network marketing. "If it's only about you, it serves to inspire no one else, and it's really a hollow victory," he claims. "We believe very strongly that by contributing to other people it will come back to you tenfold."

"Oxyfresh allowed me to be creative, and to live out what I consider to be my life purpose, which is to lead people and inspire others. Although as a dentist I was contributing to my patients, I realized I could impact the lives of many more people through network marketing. My vision is to impact 20 million people in the next 20 years through network marketing and Oxyfresh."

# Men of Distinction

For nearly a quarter century, **Steve Spaulding** has championed the network marketing industry through his uncompromising commitment to integrity and genuinely sharing the opportunity with others.

Spaulding has a particular affinity of seeing opportunities for people and helping them to see those possibilities for themselves.

Spaulding has been in network marketing since the industry was in its infancy. He first saw the potential of network marketing as a 21-year-old forklift operator at the Ragu Spaghetti Sauce plant. Spaulding knew what he wanted, but didn't know how to get there.

"In the beginning it was really just simple economics. I had figured out that it was impossible for me to work enough hours as a Teamster at the plant to get where I wanted to go. I didn't have any idea about all the other benefits that would come my way via a career in network marketing; I just wanted to find a system that paid enough money," he said.

Upon learning about a network marketing opportunity from Kurt Robb, Spaulding started to believe he had a contribution to make and that he would make a difference. That belief has carried him to the top of million dollar sales organizations, as well as top executive positions with multi-million dollar corporations. He realized that a fulfilling life would require satisfying, rewarding work; enjoying the fruits of that work; using your abilities, attributes and skills; optimizing your strengths; turning perceived weaknesses into strengths, and most of all, helping others acomplish all of these things.

Spaulding believes that the key to people championing this industry is through their own actions and dealing with people who possess integrity; it is taking your strengths and human potential and then optimizing them. The key is getting people into action. Do not confuse activity with accomplishment, but make sure their activity produces *results!* There is a no-nonsense, brass tacks, "here's how you do it" wisdom that Spaulding brings to the people he partners with; the people he supports; the people he is committed to. He does it openly and freely, allowing them to reap the benefits of this industry both personally and financially. "This is a business of working together, of being alive, of bringing the richness of what life can be about into being."

Spaulding is the co-founder of "Success By Design," the ten-year-old Scottsdale, Arizona, consulting firm that specializes in confidential analysis, leadership development and public relations for the direct selling and network marketing industries around the world.

"One of the most rewarding experiences I've had is being able to contribute to the network marketing movement on a global scale. Not only have I been able to see places with my family that most people only dream about, I've made friends all over the world. That is something that network marketing provides you can't put a dollar (or yen!) value on!"

Spaulding is an avid golfer, drawn to the sport by it's constant challenge and camaraderie. Sailboat racing, another of Spauldings' passions, promotes the teamwork, preparation, and courage that apply to daily living, especially in the working world. Spaulding believes that many of life's best lessons, for work as well as play, are learned through passion and enjoyment, not drudgery.

Spaulding is a sought-after coach, public speaker and trainer, and is an *upline* master. He has recently produced, with Hilton Johnson (MLM University founder), the wildly successful audio training series "Start, Right Now!" Inspired by John Milton Fogg, the program allows anyone to know "...exactly what to do from day one to succeed in network marketing!" So what benefit is the most valuable to people involved in network marketing? Spauldings' response is simple and candid. "Dreams come true!"

Steve, his wife, Susan, and son, A.J., reside in Scottsdale, Arizona.

# Men of Distinction

Kelly Thayer

When you mix a true entrepreneurial spirit with a little hunger, the results are usually phenomenal.

That's exactly what happened to **Kelly Thayer** back in 1980, as he sat on the edge of his bed and told his new wife of six months that he just lost his job. He was afraid of the future, but also determine to succeed. He decided this was the time to put an idea he had been working on into practice. With his unemployment check he bought a video camera and began recording everything from weddings to baseball games. Mountainland Productions, his first company, was born.

"Nothing worthwhile in life is easy," Thayer says. "You've got to work hard at what you want. You'll always face obstacles, and nothing will ever go the way you plan. So you can either complain and do nothing, or you can embrace your problems and turn them into opportunity. It's what we do with those challenges that separates us from success and failure."

Thayer's video recording service was immediately successful. However, it only took a few years to see the writing on the wall. People were buying video cameras to record their own events. His company was rapidly becoming obsolete.

For the next 16 years, Thayer dedicated his pioneering spirit to corporate clients in the network marketing industry. He knew that in order for the industry to grow, someone needed to create effective training and recruiting tools to empower the masses. In 1983, Thayer produced the first recruiting video for Sunrider, which helped catapult the network marketing company to international prominence.

This new direction brought tremendous growth. In the mid 1980s, Thayer's company had five employees. By 1990, it had 85 employees. And by 1991 it grew to 117. With in-house production, editing, duplication, creative marketing and packaging, the company--by now called Clear Image--was a full service marketing company for the network marketing industry.

Under his direction, the company produced and directed more than 700 films and videos for the direct selling and network marketing industry. Over the years, his work has garnered 17 of the respected Telly Awards for commercial film and video excellence. He has worked with clients such as Avon, Bodywise, Delta Airlines, Enviro-Tech, Herbalife, Jafra Cosmetics, Rexall Showcase International, Shaperite, and Tupperware.

More importantly, Thayer's programs have played a vital role in helping struggling companies. With his training and recruiting tools, many of these companies were able to pick themselves up from dismal performances to achieve record sales.

Thayer's success helping these companies didn't go unnoticed. In 1992, he was selected by *Inc.* Magazine, Ernst and Young, and Merril Lynch as the Service Entrepreneur of the Year for the Rocky Mountain Region. That same year, Thayer was also selected as the first Utah Valley Entrepreneur of the Year. In 1993, he was featured in the October Issue of *Entrepreneur* Magazine and on the November 1993 cover of *Inc.* Magazine.

Today, based on his vast experience and know-how, Thayer is considered by many to be the direct selling and network marketing industry's leading expert in marketing strategy and communications. His creative talent and proven track record make him one of the most sought after consultants in the industry.

"I've been blessed with good friends, great mentors, and a loving family," Thayer explains. "I've experienced good times and bad, and I've always learned from both. Life is full of opportunities. Take time to recognize what that opportunity is for you and go get it. The only person you can change is yourself."

Kelly enjoys being involved in the community and with his church. He currently serves his community on the CEDO Board, an incubator program for start-up companies. He loves skiing, golfing, and spending time with his wife, Kellie, and their five children.

# THE BEST

## Our Fortune 100 Gold Circle Members

A WORLDWIDE EXCLUSIVE

Fortune
100
Gold Circle

Never before in the history of the network marketing or direct selling industries have the very best companies in North America appeared under one cover -- until now. Following 16 months of exhaustive research, our staff and a panel of accredited industry analysts combined to select the best 100 companies based on a number of obvious criteria along with a special formula for the handful of new entries that are featured.

In most instances, our selection committee experienced no difficulty in choosing those companies whose exacting standards of excellence, integrity, longevity and success resulted in their automatic inclusion. For the remainder of inductees, a stringent set of guidelines was set forth. From a list of more than 50 candidates, those showcased met or exceeded our five part testing formula.

Conspicuous by their absence, are several leading companies that were selected, but were unable to meet our final deadlines.

Our ultimate goal in this painstaking undertaking is traced to one word -- credibility, and on that score we feel we have accomplished the seemingly impossible; that is to showcase the very best companies throughout the continent.

On a final note, all participating companies were assured that their full page profiles would be published unedited -- in their very own words. We have kept that promise and feel you, the reader, will be the prime benefactor of this decision.

# COMPANY PROFILE INDEX

21st Century Nutriceuticals ———————————————————— 283
Achievers Unlimited, Inc. ———————————————————— 284
AdvoCare International ———————————————————— 285
Aim International ———————————————————— 286
Alpine Industries ———————————————————— 287
American Communications Network ———————————————————— 288
American Longevity ———————————————————— 289
American Metalcraft Corporation ———————————————————— 290
Amway Corporation ———————————————————— 291
AVON ———————————————————— 292
BeautiControl ———————————————————— 293
Biometics International, Inc. ———————————————————— 294
BodyWise International ———————————————————— 295
CHARMELLE Inc. ———————————————————— 296
Colesce Couture ———————————————————— 297
Conklin Company, Inc. ———————————————————— 298
Direct Nutrition, Inc. ———————————————————— 299
Eagle Distributing Company ———————————————————— 300
Enrich International ———————————————————— 301
Envion International ———————————————————— 302
Enviro-Tech International ———————————————————— 303
Essentially Yours ———————————————————— 304
Eventus International ———————————————————— 305
Excel Communications, Inc. ———————————————————— 306
Forever Living Products International, Inc. ———————————————————— 307
FreeLife International ———————————————————— 308
Genisys International ———————————————————— 309
Gift Shows By Personal Creations ———————————————————— 310
Golden Neo-Life Diamite International ———————————————————— 311
Golden Pride International ———————————————————— 312
Herbalife International ———————————————————— 313
Homemakers Idea Company, The ———————————————————— 314
House of Lloyds Inc. ———————————————————— 315
I.D.E.A Concepts, Inc. ———————————————————— 316
Integris International ———————————————————— 317
Intelligent Nutrients, Inc. ———————————————————— 318
Jafra Cosmetics International ———————————————————— 319
Lady Remington Fashion Jewelry ———————————————————— 320
Latasia & Company ———————————————————— 321
Leading Minds International, Inc. ———————————————————— 322
Longevity Network, Ltd. ———————————————————— 323
Mannatech Inc. ———————————————————— 324
Market America ———————————————————— 325
Matol Botanical International, Ltd. ———————————————————— 326
Multiples at Home ———————————————————— 327
Natural Connections ———————————————————— 328

NaturesOwn — 329
Nature's Sunshine Products — 330
Nest Entertainment — 331
Network Action Company — 332
Neways International — 333
New Image International, Inc. — 334
New Vision International, Inc. — 335
NuCare — 336
Nutri-System Direct — 337
Nutrition For Life International — 338
Oxyfresh Worldwide, Inc. — 339
Pangea, Ltd. — 340
Petra Fashions, Inc. — 341
Pre-Paid Legal Services — 342
PriceNet U.S.A.com — 343
Princess House — 344
ProSTEP — 345
RACHAeL International — 346
Regal Ware, Inc. — 347
Reliv International — 348
Rena Ware International, Inc. — 349
Rexal Showcase International — 350
Right Solution, The — 351
RMC Group, Inc. — 352
Seaborne — 353
Shaklee Corporation — 354
ShapeRite — 355
Sportron International — 356
SportsNuts.com — 357
Starfire International — 358
Starlight International — 359
Sunrider International — 360
SupraLife — 361
Symmetry International — 362
TARRAH — 363
Tupperware — 364
Universal Sports Direct, Inc. — 365
USANA, Inc. — 366
Usborne Books At Home — 367
Viva America — 368
Viviane Woodard — 369
Wachters' Organic Sea Products — 370
Watkins Inc. — 371
West Bend Co., The — 372
Wicker Plus, Ltd. — 373
World Golf Corporation — 374
Young Living Essential Oils — 375

**LATE ENTRIES**
One World — 481
Rainforest Bio-Energetics — 482

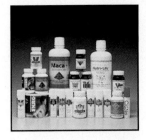

**_21st Century_**
nutriceuticals ™

21st Century Nutriceuticals is in the business of improving health and increasing wealth. All our actions are measured by our success in achieving these goals. We continually train, coach and inspire anyone with the desire to build teams. When you review our innovative signature product line and tremendous business opportunity, you will find 21st Century Nutriceuticals to be in the right place at the right time.

Our 25+ products are doctor-developed and scientifically researched, with our lead products containing trademarked and patented ingredients. Four of these innovative products specifically target major health concerns of our time: obesity, cardiovascular disease, smoking and aging.

Our lead product, the Maca Miracle Health Weight Management Program, is helping thousands of people successfully reduce stress, increase stamina, lose inches and assist weight loss. People who have never succeeded before with "Diet" programs are having amazing results with our all-natural, 100% effective Maca Miracle Health Weight Management Program. Wendy Higgins of Astoria, Oregon, is one of many who have reported remarkable results on the program: "I lost 60 pounds and over 42 inches with 21st Century Nutriceuticals. I've gone from a size 16 to a comfortable size seven. It's been exciting to experience such dramatic results from all-natural products. I feel healthy, energetic, terrific!" Incidentally, our 3-day Maca samples are producing one of the highest sponsoring success ratios ever in this industry. (Please review our fax-on-demand system to find out more about all our life-changing products available to you, ie: NutriYouth™ (HGH), Cardio-Safe™, CigNo™, NutriLife™, Rejoice™, Nutri-MEC™ and NutriSonic™).

When it comes to marketing and part-time people putting their precious and valuable time on the line in an effort to generate extra income, it is vitally important to succeed. At 21st Century Nutriceuticals, we will and must allow you the opportunity to reap the rewards of your efforts and time. As far as our company's compensation plan is concerned, with as few as 12 people on your team you could supplement your income $400 to $600 a month. Twenty team members could increase your earnings $800 to $1,000 a month. Forty two active team members pay $1,700 to $2,100 a month. Full-time business builders can be assured of the most lucrative residual income this industry can provide.

You have the freedom and opportunity to succeed, follow your dreams and put it all on the line. Your courage and personal strength will carry you day in and day out until you've reached optimum health and wealth. We will support you in these efforts. The starting point of success lies within your ability to take action. Please take a serious look at 21st Century Nutriceuticals' cause for prosperity. Browse the web, brochures, fax-on-demand, and all other extensions on **(888) 543-3873**.

Should you have any questions or need immediate assistance to place your order, call customer service at **(800) 638-7462**. We look forward to hearing from you soon. May we all achieve optimum health and wealth.

**21st Century Nutriceuticals, Spring Creek Place, Suite C2, Springville, UT 84663**
**Phone: (801) 489-7300, Fax: (801) 489-7377**

*Kathy Connelly*

# Achievers Unlimited, Inc.

Welcome to network marketing, the single most powerful distribution method in business today, offering the financial and personal freedom you dreamed of.

Welcome to Achievers Unlimited®, a risk-free opportunity that is making network marketing history. For three years in a row, industry experts have recognized Achievers as one of the best companies in the world for their excellence in: strong company management, leadership, integrity, superior products, pricing, lucrative compensation plan and support. Everything independent distributors need to achieve financial freedom.

These qualities become even more impressive when you hear the story of how Achievers began. In 1992, two innovative people, who as flight attendants for a major airline became tired of industry layoffs and an uncertain future, decided to start their own home-based business. Working out of their garage, with one single product and a genuine regard for people, created an empire. Today, Achievers has a full line of superior health care and nutritional supplements responsible for well over 200 million in consumer sales, simply by sharing great products that everyone needs.

Think about it! Do you live up to the high dietary standards set by the U.S. Department of Agriculture? Every day do you eat 3 to 5 servings of vegetables? Eat 3 to 5 servings of fruit? Exercise? Drink 6 to 8 glasses of water? Rarely eat red meat?

Don't feel bad. Very few do! Even if you are among the small population of Americans who eat right, it's not enough to ensure optimum health. That is why nutritional supplements are important for protecting as well as achieving optimal health. By adding supplements to your diet, fitness and sound stress reduction program, you are helping your body stay healthy. Fortunately, Achievers' line of natural nutritional supplements contains superior ingredients specially formulated to produce quality products that work down to the cellular level. We've combined the best of modern science and technology from the west with ancient herbal wisdom from the Far East. Our cutting-edge nutritional products are very affordable, in high demand and contain many wonderful gifts from nature, including phytoprotectors, probiotics, antioxidants, proanthocyanidins (OPCs) and patented chelated minerals.

Achievers phenomenal line of highly bioavailable nutritional supplements are scientifically designed for weight management, cellular health and well-being.

Whether you are looking to improve your health or your loved ones, considering a new career with unlimited earning potential, or just want to earn a little extra to cover your car or mortgage payments, Achievers has an exciting opportunity that can change your life.

We would love to offer you this same opportunity to become your own boss and to live the American dream, while improving your health.

**For more information or to order immediately using: Visa, MasterCard or Discover, call (800) 684-8856 today! Achievers Unlimited, Inc., 777 South Flagler Drive, West Tower, 9th Floor, West Palm Beach, FL 33401, Phone: (561) 835-3777, Fax: (561) 822-3080, Web site: www.achieversunltd.com**

*Charlie Ragus*

The AdvoCare story is one of an American dream come true. The story began with the dedication and commitment of one man...Charlie Ragus. His vision became reality through the belief and hard work of thousands.

Always aware of the importance of optimum nutrition, Charlie had a fervent desire to enhance peoples' lives by offering products which would help them achieve wellness.

At a worldwide symposium on nutrition and phytochemicals, Charlie encountered two scientists who shared his dream, Dr. Robert Hackman and Rich Scheckenbach. On discovering that their goals were parallel with his, Charlie asked the pair to develop products which would be on the leading edge of the nutritional frontier. This was the beginning of AdvoCare's Medical & Scientific Advisory Board.

With years of learning between them, Hackman and Scheckenbach poured their efforts into formulating products which would satisfy Charlie's demands; products which would be scientifically developed for maximum results.

Inaugurating his new company, Charlie chose the name AdvoCare in order to communicate his commitment to distributors: He would be an advocate who cared for them. Having been a distributor, he knew that only a company founded by a distributor specifically for distributors could succeed.

People tried the products, and the testimonials began pouring in: "I feel better than I have in years." "My energy level is unbelievable." "I've tried everything to lose weight, but nothing worked until I tried AdvoCare's product."

Founded in February 1993, the company has grown steadily. By 1998, AdvoCare had claimed its second annual award from S.M.U.'s Cox School of Business in recognition of its status as one of the fastest growing, privately held companies in the Dallas area.

Over the years, AdvoCare has continued to add some of the most eminent physicians and scientists to its Medical & Scientific Advisory Board--Nikolai Volkov, executive director of the Institute for Biomolecular Nutrition and former consultant to the Russian Olympic teams; Steve Watterson, Tennessee Oilers strength and rehabilitation coach and licensed researcher with the Drug Enforcement Administration; Dr. Harry Preuss, professor of medicine and pathology at Georgetown University Medical Center and president-elect of the American College of Nutrition, and Dr. Sidney Stohs, dean of the Creighton University School of Pharmacy and Allied Health Professions and professor of pharmacology at the university's School of Medicine.

Distributors have developed well-placed confidence in AdvoCare's Medical & Scientific Advisory Board, which boosts their eagerness to share the complete line of AdvoCare nutritional and weight management products.

AdvoCare's Sales Compensation Plan exemplifies the free enterprise system that makes America great. It has provided the opportunity for thousands of people with little experience or money to establish a successful business of their own.

People from all walks of life--from homemakers to business professionals--can participate and profit according to their goals and desires.

The AdvoCare free enterprise system is proof positive that dreams still come true.

**AdvoCare International, L.L.C., 1801 Royal Lane, Suite 1002, Dallas, TX 75234**
**Phone: (972) 910-9465, Fax: (972) 831-8830, E-mail: nhedrick@advocare.com**

**Ron Price**

## The AIM Companies

The AIM Companies have been using the simple strategy of providing the highest quality nutritional products and unmatched member service to build a dynamic, international group of companies.

In its first full year of business, AIM did $500,000 in sales. Today, AIM has grown into an international company with over 90,000 members worldwide and annual sales in excess of $50 million. It has expanded from a garage in Nampa, Idaho, to an international company with offices in Australia, Canada, Malaysia, New Zealand, Singapore, South Africa and Taiwan.

This success is based on quality products. AIM has a 25-plus product line, all backed by a money back guarantee. These products are geared to help maintain the health of the body systems. AIM Barleygreen™, AIM's flagship product, is the best selling green juice drink in the world. It holds this position not because of excessively aggressive distributors or misleading advertising, but because it is the best green juice there is. Backed by 25 years of research by scientists and doctors alike, AIM Barleygreen™ continues to win converts because of quality, not hype.

AIM also provides members with a wide range of high quality tools to educate others about health and nutrition. A 32-page monthly magazine provides much more than product news and congratulatory blurbs about members; it also contains extensive information on health and nutrition.

Two audio tape series provides members with interviews with alternative health luminaries: Lendon Smith, M.D., John Lee, M.D., Eugene S. Wagner, Ph.D., Barbara Reed Stitt, Ph.D., Nancy Appleton, Ph.D., and Alan Gaby, M.D. have all been heard on audio discussing important topics on health and nutrition. A quarterly video program provides similar information, but in a "videomagazine" format.

AIM's compensation plan, in the words of MLM consultant Ricky McPherson, "will be the hallmark in compensation plans that up-and-coming MLM companies will use as a standard for excellence."

AIM's compensation plan, titled the Ladder of Opportunity, provides a unique combination of stability and generosity. Based on the stairstep breakaway plan, the Ladder of Opportunity allows members to build both as deeply and as broadly as they desire and rewards them for that activity, as well as providing regular monthly commissions of up to 18 percent on the activities of members in your organization. AIM's compensation plan provides a lucrative bonus program that gives AIM members the opportunity to reap additional bonuses of up to 18 percent based on the activity of your group and breakaway directors.

Features of the Ladder of Opportunity include permanent titles, compression at all levels, low qualifications requirements, first-of-the-month promotions, free renewal with minimum purchase and a generous Leadership Bonus Program.

To make this dynamic compensation plan as "user friendly" as possible to members, AIM takes care of all commission payments, provides detailed commission statements, and maintains a top-of-the-line member database that allows members to check on their organizations activity through a toll-free computerized phone line, or through speaking directly with AIM's highly trained customer service representatives.

AIM International is the company for the twenty first century. A strong foundation based on a clear mission and values, past financial success, loyal members, top-rated and unique products and a top-notch compensation plan, all make AIM International the choice for the future. AIM is presenting you with the opportunity of a lifetime; the rest is up to you!

**AIM International, 3904 East Flamingo Avenue, Nampa, ID 83687**
**Phone: (208) 465-5116, Fax: (208) 463-2187, (800) 456-2462**

**William Converse**

Industries

**Michael Jackson**

In 1984, while William Converse was writing an engineering study for another company, he discovered the company's product didn't work. Converse developed his own ideas about how to make the device effective and offered the idea to the company, but they refused. Converse then developed his own technology further and produced the first ionizer units in his home laboratory.

Two years later, Converse received his first product endorsement from a source close to home--his wife. A migraine sufferer, Eva Converse found that her headaches disappeared when she was in the lab where the device was operating. Converse concluded that she had been reacting to dust in the air of their home and the ionizer was ridding the air of contaminants. The foundation for Alpine Industries was laid.

**ALPINE TODAY:** Alpine Industries is a multi-million dollar corporation that manufacturers, sells and distributes indoor environment products. Its hallmark product line of air purification systems addresses what the EPA calls the country's leading environmental health concern--indoor air pollution. In addition to being on the cutting edge of products for indoor environments, Alpine is one of the world's leading network marketing companies. It has been named "MLM Company of the Year" by *Bits 'n Pieces* magazine; was ranked number 17 in the list of "top direct selling companies" by *Wealth Building* and *Selling Power* magazines; was featured in *Success* magazine; and was ranked number 84 on the Inc. 500 list of America's Fastest Growing Companies.

Alpine's ionization-based, proprietary technology penetrates walls, doors and floors to sweep particulate matter from the air. The contamination isolated by this ionization process is then removed by low-levels of ozone. The result is clean, fresh air, much like what is found in the aftermath of summer thunderstorms. The effect is why Alpine products have been appropriately described as a "thunderstorm in a box."

Headquartered in Greeneville, Tenn., Alpine is led by entrepreneurs William Converse and Michael Jackson. To date, there are more than two million Alpine products in use around the world. Alpine employs more than 1,200 individuals and has over 250,000 dealers, of which 44 percent are active.

**UNIQUE NETWORK MARKETING:** Redefining the concept of network marketing, Alpine allows dealers to avoid risky conditions--like front-end loading, excess handling of the product and the need for up-front capital--that have plagued other multi-level sales businesses.

Alpine is committed to a network marketing plan with a strong emphasis on retail and recruiting that enables even entry-level sales representatives to make money from the very start. At Alpine, distributors generate sales commissions from the beginning; building a distributor network only adds to their business base and benefits. Men and women in Canada and the U.S. are earning $100,000 and much more during their first year of business with Alpine.

**PRODUCT LINES:** Alpine offers a vast product selection, including 21 different models of air purifiers, with its whole-house unit representing the bulk of sales. The major systems and related markets include: ▶ **Living Air:** Air systems for the home ▶ **Living Water:** Water purification system ▶ **Com Air:** Air systems for businesses ▶ **San Air:** Air systems for industry ▶ **Salon Air:** Air systems for beauty salons ▶ **Agri-Air:** Air systems for agriculture ▶ **Alive & Well:** Health and beauty consumable products.

**THE FUTURE:** The mid 1990s has witnessed rapid growth for Alpine. By the end of 1997, sales reached over $200 million, representing over a 2,700 percent growth in the last four years. To prepare for continued growth, Alpine is in the midst of constructing a $53 million corporate complex and manufacturing facility in Greeneville, Tenn.

**Alpine Industries, 310 T, Elmer Cox Drive, Greenville, TN 37745**
**Phone: (800) 989-2299, Fax: (423) 638-7561**

*Greg Provenzano*

ACN's mission is to provide an outstanding opportunity for individuals across the U.S. and Canada to gain more control in their lives...to have time, money and freedom to enjoy the things they love most...and to turn their dreams into reality.

ACN is a firmly established cooperative marketing company focused on helping consumers save more money on the telecommunications services they're already using, like long distance calling, paging and Internet services. ACN is a privately held, debt-free corporation with offices and distribution centers in Michigan and Ontario, Canada.

In just five years, ACN has helped hundreds of ordinary people achieve a level of personal and financial freedom that is extraordinary by anyone's measure; and literally thousands create lucrative part-time and full-time businesses of their own.

Since its creation in January 1993, ACN has quickly become one of the fastest growing companies in North America. From revenues of $2 million in its first year, ACN's annual revenues had skyrocketed to more than $100 million in 1997, and are projected to top $1 billion by the year 2000.

As a leader in marketing telecommunications, ACN takes full advantage of the largest and fastest growing industry in the world. With more that $600 billion in combined revenues today, telecommunications will easily become a trillion dollar industry. ACN utilizes cooperative marketing, by simply helping people they already know save money on services they already use every day. ACN representatives earn a portion of each new customer's bill every month for as long as the customer continues to use the service.

As great as the ACN opportunity is today, the future is even more exciting! As deregulation strikes local telephone utilities, ACN representatives have the opportunity to TRIPLE their earnings with their current customers. With the start of deregulation of electric and gas utilities, ACN representatives could see their current customer base paying them up to 10 times the income of long distance alone.

The key to ACN's remarkable business opportunity is the power of residual income. ACN representatives receive a percentage of their customers' monthly bills for as long as they continue to use the services--not just a one-time commission. Every time they develop a new customer or help an existing customer with an additional service, they give themselves a raise.

But that's just the beginning. As ACN representatives introduce others to the opportunity and their customers use ACN's services, the representatives' monthly residual income grows even faster. To make its compensation plan even more exciting, ACN offers additional incentives, including bonuses, expense allowances, vacations, and profit sharing.

ACN believes that regardless of how good the opportunity is, nothing is more important to a representative's success than its training system. Training is provided to representatives through a comprehensive video and audio system, which allows them to develop their skills and build their businesses at their own paces. ACN also offers a series of local, regional and national training events.

Like the hundreds of thousands of ACN representatives all across the U.S. and Canada, YOU have the power to change the course of your life forever. If there was ever a right place to be and a right time to be there, the place is ACN and the time is now. Opportunity's calling, and it's calling for you!

**ACN, PO Box 5000 Troy, MI USA 48007-5000**
**ACN Canada, 2660 Argentia Road, Mississauga, Ontario, Canada L5N 5V4**

*Joel Wallach*

Based in sunny San Diego, California, American Longevity was established in 1997 by Dr. Joel Wallach, and are committed to being your full service network marketing company for the new millennium, offering top-of-the-line nutritional, household and skin care products. Our Virgin Earth™ line of liquid minerals is the cornerstone to our product line.

American Longevity is a privately held company committed to being distributor friendly with a strong support staff, well built infrastructure, and a debt free balance sheet. All this adds up to a great company to be involved with. Additionally, Dr. Wallach insists that the company products be shipped fast and the commission checks "on time, every time." Usually, our products are shipped within 24 hours of being processed. Dr. Wallach has built a solid reputation in the network marketing industry. Many industry consultants such as Dave Stewart of MLM Consulting believe that Dr. Wallach's educational format will open a lot of eyes when it comes to nutrition and dietary supplements.

Dr. Wallach's innovative slant is derived from his background in veterinary medicine. Due to the lack of adequate health insurance, animal products such as meat and dairy are kept affordable by preventing and curing diseases with nutritional formulas in animal feed. When he began incorporating similar nutritional formulas with people, word soon was out that "if you're not happy with your doctor, see Dr. Wallach. He'll treat you like a dog, but you'll get better." Dr. Wallach is also famous as the author and narrator of the very popular Dead Doctors Don't Lie cassettes and nutritional books. Once you join the American Longevity family, you will participate in leads generated from Dr. Wallach's popular Dead Doctors Don't Lie syndicated radio talk show, as well as his powerful lecture series.

American Longevity has built its reputation on cutting edge nutritional products, fantastic growth, and a commitment to its associates. Our Stairway to Success Compensation Plan is among the best in the industry. This is one company where your business and residual income mean just that -- the best! Our first full year of operation we disbursed $5.3 million in commissions. If there were a simple description of American Longevity, it would be: Truth, justice and the American Longevity way, or in a word, AMERICANA!

Dr. Wallach's 30 years of nutritional and medical experience has given him insight on how he wants to see American Longevity develop in the far future. He realizes there are several network marketing companies who promise you the world; however, realistically, some companies only survive for a few years, leaving their distributors out in the cold.

Dr. Wallach cautions against this and makes it a point to tell potential associates that American Longevity is not a corporate profit machine. It is for this reason that Dr. Wallach has vowed to make American Longevity a family legacy for their associates; a legacy that can be passed from one generation to another. Truth, justice and the American Longevity way!

**Join the American Longevity team by contacting one of our independent associates,
or call our corporate office at: (800) 982-3198**

# American MetalCraft Corporation

AMC (Alfa Metalcraft Corporation) has been changing the quality of life since 1963 with its unique, patented, German-made 18/10 Stainless Steel Cookware. A leader in the field of nutrition for over 35 years and in over 36 countries, AMC is the largest manufacturer and seller of a unique "waterless, multi-cooking system."

Mr. Rene Stutz, U.S. CEO, sees a tremendous opportunity in the U.S. market. "Although AMC has had a small presence in the U.S., we are positioned to move aggressively into the cookware market. Our philosophy is: eat better--live better and based on the knowledge that proper nutrition is the key to a higher quality of life. To that end, we provide the cookware that enables anyone to cook without oil and without water, plus bake, brown, combine and serve. Our unique patented cookware retains all the natural vitamins and minerals in the food, making it more nutritious. In today's health conscious environment, there is no better product and we've been doing it and selling it for years!"

**AMC - The Company:** With international headquarters in Rotkreuz, Switzerland, and over 17,000 employees, AMC develops and manufacturers the cookware in AMC's own research facilities and manufacturing factories in Europe. In 1980, AMC founded the Alfa Institute--AMC's own research and development laboratory where nutritional scientists, home economists, dieticians and engineers, work together to design and develop products insuring AMC's innovative and technological leadership. In 1981, AMC founded the ISFE Foundation for the promotion of research and education in nutrition. The foundation supports researchers and scientists in the study of nutritional science and holds international symposiums where doctors, nutrition specialists, health organizations, scientists and business people join together to discuss current nutritional issues.

**AMC - Our Mission Statement to Customers:** To provide the world's best cookware for healthy, practical, economical and modern cooking. Guaranteed customer satisfaction with a lifetime warranty.

**AMC - The Opportunity:** AMC Cookware is sold through independent sales consultants directly to the customer. During in-home demonstrations, consultants prepare a sampling of highly nutritious and tasty food while showing guests how they can save on the cost of energy and spend less time in the kitchen. The materials, design and state-of-the-art technology of AMC cookware make it incomparable in today's market. There is other cookware on the market but none compare with AMC--Guaranteed! AMC is the "Rolls Royce" of cookware with a Lifetime Warranty.

We are looking for self-motivated people to join us in this ground floor opportunity. Part-time or full-time, we give you the training and resources to start your AMC career and make it as successful as you want it to be. We have a varied commission plan based on your personal sales, plus a percentage of the sales of any people you recruit and/or directly manage. There is no major investment, no inventory to stock, and no delivery of product. We provide financing and lay-a-way programs, plus free, no obligation gifts for the hostesses; and, of course, recognition and incentive programs for our sales leaders.

If you want to make money, make your own hours, like meeting people, interested in healthy cooking and nutrition, or learn more about AMC's products and cooking method, please write or call us today for more information.

**AMC Corporation, 595 Summer Street, Stamford, CT 06901**
**Phone: (203) 363-0331, Fax: (203) 363-0329, E-mail: amcusa@compuserve.com**
**Web site: www.amccookware.com**

With sales of $7 billion, affiliates in 49 countries on six continents, and a diverse product line from home and personal care products to vitamins and food supplements, Amway Corporation and its two publicly traded sister companies, Amway Asia Pacific Ltd. and Amway Japan Limited, make up one of the world's largest direct selling companies.

Under the leadership of Amway Chairman, Steve Van Andel and President Dick DeVos, who share the office of the Chief Executive, Amway today supports more than 3 million independent business owners. These distributors have embraced the Amway business opportunity and market a broad array of Amway products, plus many other name-brand products through its catalogs.

In the U.S., Amway offers more than 450 Amway brand products and thousands of famous brand products through its PERSONAL SHOPPERS® Catalog. Manufactured at Amway's World Headquarters, which now stretches for more than a mile on its original site in Ada, as well as at facilities in California, China, Korea and India, Amway products are respected for their high quality.

Amway has always been known for its complete home care line, including SA8® laundry products, its ARTISTRY® Skin Care and Shaded Cosmetics line, and its Nutrition and Wellness products, including NUTRILITE® vitamins and food supplements. Amway's home living line, including high-quality water and air treatment systems, provides Amway distributors additional opportunities to expand their businesses as do new co-branded products being introduced through unique arrangements with such companies as Rubbermaid and Waterford Crystal.

Amway's co-founders, Rich DeVos and Jay Van Andel, met when both were students at Grand Rapids Christian High School. While it was a business arrangement that brought the pair together, DeVos paid Van Andel a quarter each week for rides to and from school and it was their similar backgrounds, shared values and interest, and coinciding dreams for the future that made them fast friends. Early on, it was decided that one day they would start a company of their own.

DeVos and Van Andel founded Amway in 1959 in the basements of their homes, with a handful of distributors, a sales marketing plan that drew on a person-to-person marketing strategy, and single product--a biodegradable all purpose cleaner called L.O.C.

The new enterprise took on a life of its own, quickly outgrowing its tiny quarters and outpacing the most optimistic sales expectations of its founders. In 1960, the operation was moved to a small building on the corporation's current site in Ada, Michigan. In 1962, Amway became an international company when its first affiliate opened in Canada. By 1963, sales were 12 times the first year sales.

DeVos and Van Andel began expanding their international operations in earnest in the 1970s, adding affiliate markets in Australia, Europe and Asia. By the end of the 1980s, entrepreneurs supported by Amway were operating in 19 countries on five continents, marketing several hundred top-quality Amway products, plus many more name-brand products from its catalog programs.

The strong growth in the 1980s was surpassed by phenomenal expansion during the 1990s. In the early part of the decade, leadership of the corporation was transitioned from Rich and Jay to Dick and Steve. Since 1990, Amway's sales have tripled and the number of international affiliates it operates has more than doubled.

As Amway looks to the next millennium and beyond, it continues to strive to bring the Amway opportunity and the spirit of free enterprise to people everywhere. From Asia and Australia to Africa and the Americas, Amway is dedicated to providing an opportunity that allows individuals to achieve their goals through a business of their own.

**Amway Corporation, 7575 Fulton Street East, Ada, MI 49355, Phone: (616) 787-6000**

# AVON

Avon is the world's leading seller of beauty and related products, with $5.2 billion in annual revenues. Avon markets to women in 135 countries through 2.7 million independent sales representatives, including nearly one-half million in the United States. Avon product lines include such recognizable brands as Anew, Skin-So-Soft, Avon Color, Far Away, Rare Gold, Natural Millennia, Josie, Starring and Avon Skin Care, and the global master brand, Women of Earth. Avon is also one of the world's largest manufacturers of fashion jewelry, and markets an extensive line of apparel, gifts and collectibles.

Since 1885, 34 years prior to winning the right to vote, women have sold Avon across the United States. Avon's Women of Enterprise Awards program, created in 1987 in conjunction with the U.S. Small Business Administration, annually recognizes six women entrepreneurs for extraordinary business success.

It was the first "Avon Lady," Mrs. P.E.E. Albee of Winchester, New Hampshire, who pioneered the company's now famous direct selling concept, providing one of the first opportunities for American women to be financially independent at a time when their place was traditionally in the home. More than 40 million women worldwide (25 million in the U.S.) have sold Avon products since the company was founded 114 years ago. Additionally, their 100% money-back guarantee was instituted at this same time.

More beauty products carry the Avon brand name than any other in the world, and with the launch of Anew Perfecting Complex for Face in February 1992, Avon became the first major beauty company to introduce alpha hydroxy acid technology to millions of women.

In 1993, the company established the Avon Worldwide Fund for Women's Health, and to date, has raised $50 million for health-related problems of concern to women globally. Witness the Avon Breast Cancer Awareness Crusade, established in October 1993, which has raised more than $22 million in the U.S. in support of breast cancer education and access to early detection services.

**Avon Running:** Global Women's Circuit was launched in April 1998, and is a series of 10K races and 5K fitness walks that make fitness accessible to women of every age and ability, offering the only global circuit for women runners.

**Focusing on Diversity:** In September 1998, Avon was rated number one of the top public companies for executive women by *Working Woman* magazine; in October 1997, Avon was named one of *Working Mother's* magazines "100 Best Companies for Working Mothers" for the sixth time; in 1998, *Hispanic* magazine recognized Avon for providing outstanding opportunities for Hispanic employees. In addition, the company was cited as one of the "25 Best Places for Blacks to Work" by *Black Enterprise* magazine (February 1992).

**Reaching Consumers:** Each year, Avon prints over 600 million sales brochures in more than 12 languages. In the United States alone, the brochure is distributed every two weeks to nearly 16 million women. In 1997, Avon became the first major beauty brand to sell its products online through the website www.avon.com, and in December 1997, a consumer survey commissioned by *ComputerWorld* newspaper named www.avon.com the Best Site for *Holiday Shopping in Any Category.* In November 1998, Avon opened the *Avon Centre Spa, Salon and Store,* an elegant and spacious full-service spa and salon in the famed Trump Tower at Fifth Avenue and 57th Street in New York City. Nearly one-half of the women in the United States (48 million) rely on Avon and their beauty products. To reach today's busy women, 30% of Avon representatives sell in offices, factories, hospitals and schools -- wherever women work. Approximately 50% of American women have purchased from Avon in the last year; 90% have done so in their lifetime.

**More information on Avon and its products can be found on the company's website: www.avon.com**

*Jinger Heath*

*Richard Heath*

**BeautiControl consultants have it all!**

**Financial freedom, fun and flexibility!**

BeautiControl is an international direct sales wellness, skin care and cosmetics company that offers instant income potential, long-term financial freedom and the fun of selling the best products in the business! Founded by Jinger and Richard Heath in 1981, BeautiControl has been honored as a fast growth company by *BusinessWeek* and *Forbes,* and has consultants around the globe.

**Founders:** Richard Heath brings years of hands-on direct selling experience to work every day. He leads BeautiControl's international expansion efforts, manages all aspects of the business and the lucrative Career Plan, and keeps the company focused on supporting the dynamic success of our consultants. Jinger Heath develops our revolutionary products, and serves as BeautiControl's international spokesperson. She is regularly featured in the media along with BeautiControl products, and has appeared on the Oprah Winfrey Show, the View with Barbara Walters, and on CNN.

**Immediate income:** The Fast Track Star Bonus Plan speeds you into the fast lane of success. By following a simple, proven path to prosperity, you can generate immediate income and start earning immediately. You can earn up to $150 in direct commissions for every new consultant you sponsor. You can earn up to $210 in Star Bonuses for every new consultant on your team, and you can become a Certified Trainer and get paid for every person you train.

**Lucrative financial freedom:** With the BeautiControl Career Plan, you can make easy, part-time money, or build an executive level income and career. You earn lucrative commissions on the sales of everyone on your team. You can promote yourself anytime you want, based on your sales and recruiting success. Our top achievers regularly earn luxurious jewelry, exotic vacations, six-figure incomes and the use of new company cars.

**Revolutionary products:** The international renowned BeautiControl Research Institute is an independent, state-of-the-art research and testing facility under the leadership of Jinger Heath. Our products literally sell themselves.

**Dynamic skin repair and prevention duo:** Regeneration Gold and Cell Block-C provide an unbeatable defense against the ravages of sun, pollution, skin cancer, poor diet, stress and second-hand smoke. Together, they can help repair dangerous precancerous skin cell damage from sun, pollution and aging, and prevent future damage with antioxidant vitamin C free-radical fighters and daily broad spectrum SPF 20 protection.

Other major products include Skinlogics for women, comprehensive daily skin maintenance regimens uniquely customized to each client with our patented Skin Censors; Skin Strategies for men; the SlenderGenics weight management system, guaranteed to work or your money back; nutritional supplements targeted to your specific needs; a full line of color-coded glamour products to take the guesswork out of looking great; luxurious bath and body products; and unique problem-solvers.

**To learn more: BeautiControl offers six easy entry options, starting at just $39.95, to fit your needs. Contact your local BeautiControl consultant, call (800) BEAUTI-1 (232-8841) or visit www.beauticontrol.com**

# Biometics International, Inc.

Biometics International is an exceptional company specializing in providing advanced nutritional products. Founded in March 1993 with only 15 distributors, Biometics has experienced dramatic growth by successfully utilizing multi-level marketing. Today, there are thousands of distributors nationwide with more signing up every day!

The success of Biometics is due to a combination of phenomenal products, an exceptional income opportunity, and the results people receive from the products. Having sound business practices, exceptional corporate personnel, and the distributors themselves, has made Biometics an industry leader. The company has conscientiously positioned itself to be in the forefront of advanced nutritional technology to successfully lead the way into the next century.

At Biometics, our commitment is to provide the finest line of nutritional supplements available. We offer a compensation plan that is second to none and thus enhances the physical, financial and emotional well-being of our distributors and customers.

The nutritional approach used by Biometics is to provide products that are 100% safe and effective. The company utilizes only the highest quality of nutritional elements in formulating delicious, easy to take products in a liquid form--not the typical pill supplements taken by so many Americans.

For over five years, Biometics has helped thousands of people across the nation live happier, healthier lives. Based on these results, the company is confident that proper nutrition is essential to overall health--just ask someone who swears by the products! Biometics has spent time researching how amazing the body can be when given proper nutrition in a highly absorbable form such as the Emusol Micellization process used to formulate the products. When given the opportunity, the body may be able to correct many of the problems people experience simply by providing proper nutrition. Some research suggests that the side effects of improper nutrition and ineffective absorption is poor health and lack of energy.

The Biometics philosophy toward nutrition is very simple. Provide scientifically advanced formulations to enhance the body's natural metabolic process. Our products have been specifically formulated and exclusively manufactured using the patented Emusol Micellization process. This unique method enables the body to absorb essential fat-soluble nutrients with incredible speed and efficiency by converting them into a water-soluble form. The complex fat-soluble nutrients are broken down into very small particles called micelles that are traditionally difficult to absorb. This process makes the nutrients available to the body instantly. Biometics and the Emusol process guarantees that your body will always have the most effective nutrient delivery system available anywhere in the world.

Currently, Biometics has been experiencing phenomenal expansion. We have thrived in the network marketing industry for over five years and this can be attributed to the fact that we support our distributors. We are preparing them for the 21st century with the introduction of corporate supported distributor web sites, exclusive training sessions, leadership conferences, distributor recognition incentives, outstanding cash contest, as well as the release of new and exceptional products and programs. We will begin to teach a new, ground-breaking method of training that has people buzzing about Biometics across the country. This company is definitely on the path to eventually exceeding its predicted growth! At Biometics International, our commitment is to your future.

**Biometics International, Inc., 1170 Avendia Acaso, Camarillo, CA 93012**
**Phone: (805) 383-3535, Fax: (805) 383-3540**

*Tom T. Tierney*                                                                                                                    *Ray W. Grimm*

*"An environment where personal worth and growth are valued and encouraged is conducive to human empowerment."*
**- Thomas T. Tierney, Chairman, Body Wise International,** *21st Century Leadership***:** *Dialogues with 100 Top Leaders*

From its inception in 1989, Body Wise International has been acknowledged as a leader in nutrition, health and business. Recognized as "Newcomer of the Year" by the *Definitive Guide to Multi-Level Marketing* and one of *Entrepreneur* Magazine's "Top 500 Business Opportunities," Body Wise quickly established a reputation for quality; from the state-of-the-art manufacturing of its products to the lifestyle education of its consumers.

### Where Health and Wealth Go Hand in Hand
Body Wise is "a healthy way to do business." That's because Body Wise consultants make a positive impact by sharing their discovery of improved health with others and creating a substantial income in the process. They can literally reinvent their lives--whether that means earning extra income on top of what they are presently making or establishing a great new career with unlimited earning potential.

### Outstanding Compensation Plan
"For business builders--there isn't another plan in the industry that matches Body Wise."
Body Wise millionaire, Gary DeRitter.

The Body Wise compensation plan has been heralded as one of the finest in the network marketing industry. This program has celebrated new Body Wise millionaires every year since 1994--nearly 20 millionaires to date. One of the most rewarding programs ever designed, the Body Wise compensation plan's rebates are calculated on the basis of performance, ranging from four to 30 percent on Personal Group Volume. It pays up to ten generations on your organization--no infinite pay cut-offs or matching volumes. And, as if ten generations were not generous enough, Body Wise also offers special Leadership Development Bonuses to provide extra incentive as you build your organization.

### On-going Education and Support
Body Wise has created a simple, easy-to-learn system that will allow anyone to get on track very quickly. Once you learn this duplicatable process, you will be able to teach it to your consultants who will, in turn, use it to recruit others into the business as well. Not having to reinvent the wheel increases the likelihood of success dramatically!

In addition to the company's on-going lifestyle education, Body Wise continues to set precedence as one of the first network marketing companies in the world to offer an accredited, comprehensive nutritional education seminar designed for Wellness Practitioners, Practice Facilitators and their sponsors.

### A Company for Life!
Looking at all elements of the Body Wise opportunity--the company's solid nine-year history, its awards and accolades, science-based products, innovative Health Professionals' Program, an unparalleled consultant support and education, it is no wonder that Body Wise International continues to lead the way. We are a company for Life!

**Body Wise International, 24-hour Toll-Free Information Line: (800) 556-2405, Toll-Free Conference Calls: Tuesday/Thursday at 7, 8, 9 & 10 p.m., all time zones (800) 279-5849, Web site: http://www.bodywise.com**

# CHARMELLE

**Welcome to a world of beautiful jewelry...**

**Welcome to a world where dreams come true...**

**Welcome to the wonderful world of CHARMELLE!**

CHARMELLE's exclusive collection of European designed costume jewelry is both classical and timeless. The collection effortlessly combines the high-quality that you have come to expect from CHARMELLE with a wide range of interesting and exciting pieces for both women and men. The CHARMELLE collection is continuously updated with new designs that follow the latest European trends.

Each piece from the CHARMELLE collection has been finished by hand and thickly plated with gold, rhodium or silver. You can confidently wear the CHARMELLE collection knowing that all the pieces are nickel-free, with the exception of a few pieces that do not come into contact with the skin.

The CHARMELLE collection is only available through a network of independent consultants, who enjoy the benefits of running their own business, either full-time or part-time. They are also rewarded with numerous recognition awards and prizes. Recently, CHARMELLE has been sending successful consultants to exciting vacations in dream locations such as: Paris, London, Rome, Venice, Maui and Stockholm.

You too can become a CHARMELLE consultant and start your own business. Imagine...

▎▶ **More opportunities for financial independence**

▎▶ **More freedom to spend time with family and friends**

▎▶ **More flexibility to build your own business around your lifestyle**

▎▶ **More chances to enhance your social life and meet new people**

▎▶ **Extremely low start-up cost**

▎▶ **Rewarding and profitable compensation plan**

All this with a company that excels in service and support to its consultants. With an impeccable record of reliability and stability, CHARMELLE is a solid partner for all those ambitious people who want to start a successful home-based business. CHARMELLE is a proud member of the Direct Selling Association (DSA).

The market for costume jewelry is enormous and continuously growing. Why not benefit from it by joining CHARMELLE? You will be glad you did!

**CHARMELLE Inc., 101 Townsend Street, Suite 303, San Francisco, CA 94107**
**U.S.A., Phone: (415) 284-1684, Fax: (415) 284-1680, Toll-Free: (888) CHARMELLE**
**E-mail: acasuso@charmelle.com, Web site: www.charmelle.com**

# Colesce Couture®
## LINGERIE

*Stan Frederick*

**The Colesce Story:** Colesce is celebrating its 28th year of designing its extraordinary selection of lingerie and loungewear for today's woman. There are now more than 2,000 stocking items in our collection, over 30,000 independent consultants, and more than 15 million enthusiastic customers around the world. Our products are sold in Canada, England, Indonesia, Japan, Greece, Mexico, Russia, Spain, Thailand and Australia. Colesce is the trademark for the United States' oldest and largest designer and manufacturer of lingerie sold through home parties. A name with the sound of caress and in the spirit of the word coalesce, it was created to honor today's woman. Our logo is back-to-back "Cs" that form a butterfly; the universal symbol of change, growth and beauty; a reminder of our Colesce consultants who grow personally and professionally as they build their own lingerie business. Our mission is to enhance a woman's life and relationships by creating for her uniquely designed lingerie of the best value and finest quality in the world -- lingerie shown by certified consultants who explain the "language of lingerie" to help a woman communicate how she feels or how she wants to feel. Colesce...the lingeries that helps all of her relationships coalesce. Colesce lingerie is designed to wear and made to last. Every item is created by our design group so it's exclusively ours. We work hard to know how a woman lives, works and plays. Then we create pieces that she can wear for these occasions. We own and operate three manufacturing centers in the U.S. Our garments are sewn by highly trained seamstresses according to our exact specifications. Because we care, we hand inspect each garment before shipping. And we guarantee our products. It's so easy! Within 45 days of purchase, simply drop the item, along with the receipt, in the mail with our Customer Assistance Form stating what needs to be exchanged, and we'll take care of the rest.

Colesce is a member of the Direct Selling Association and the Direct Selling Education Foundation. We have been elected to its Board of Directors and subscribe to DSA's very stringent code of ethics. Our consultants carry the coveted Colesce ID Card that verifies their commitment to the highest level of personal conduct. Our company is a member of the Dallas Chamber of Commerce, Dallas Better Business Bureau and corporate support for the Kent Waldrep National Paralysis Foundation, American Cancer Society and the YMCA.

After a woman experiences the benefits of being the hostess of a Colesce fashion show, they often want to join the thousands of women who have decided to own their own Colesce business. They can begin as others have by paying a small registration fee. Then by holding a qualified Grand Opening, they receive a free fashion kit, valued at over $500. Training is arranged so that they are ready to hold their own fashion show in just a few days. Consultants can earn an average of $25 profit per hour. By holding two or three shows a week, they earn up to $900 a month on a part-time basis. Full-time career people can hold more shows and earn even more money. When they begin having fun, they can expand their business and move into management where first-level managers make $2,000 to $3,000 per month, while top-level managers can make in excess of $50,000 per year. The profits are just part of the fun and excitement of a career with Colesce. You will enjoy many rewards and benefits along the way, from brilliant diamonds to luxurious furs, world travel, shopping sprees at major department stores, cash bonuses and distinctive achievement awards. Register today and be in business tomorrow. No previous sales or fashion experience is required. You can begin now to achieve your financial goals.

**Colesce Courture, 9004 Ambassador Row, Dallas, TX 75247-4524**

**CONKLIN**®

*Judy Herbster*                                                                                           *Charles Herbster*

**Conklin is rich in success and spirit. Its inspirational beginning and ongoing professionalism offers individuals personal growth and financial rewards.**

Conklin Company Inc. is celebrating 30 years in the network marketing business as a diversified manufacturing company. At the core of the Conklin opportunity lie our quality products--more than 120 innovative solutions to meet the needs of the family, industrial agricultural and building markets.

All products have been developed within the company's own Research and Development Department, or have been developed at other institutions and brought to Conklin for marketing. Our strict quality controls and high specifications of the finest raw materials available provide representatives with excellent products to use and sell. Conklin products are sold in a variety of sizes, and we have an extremely loyal customer base. Conklin stands behind its proven products (many of which are industry leaders) and provides a satisfaction guarantee.

Conklin posts sales in excess of $33 million each year. We take pride in providing excellent service to the field. Corporate headquarters are located in Shakopee, Minnesota.

Distribution centers exist in Lincoln, Nebraska; Columbus, Ohio; Vancouver, Washington; and Fort Worth, Texas.

In the 1920s an innovative chemist and engineer by the name of Harry Conklin began dreaming of a future in which his products would enrich the lives of others. His commitment and faith resulted in the company's first products: cleaners, petroleum conditioners and lubricant additives. In 1969, his son expanded the business and opened the door to business ownership for thousands of entrepreneurs. The company is now owned by Charles and Judy Herbster who had each been successful field managers for Conklin. As a member of the Better Business Bureau of Minnesota for more than 25 years and a member of the Direct Selling Association, there is a strict adherence to a code of ethics by which Conklin does business. We provide service to over 20,000 Conklin independent representatives nationally.

A dedicated staff with years of experience and knowledge help representatives build their businesses. Brochures, video and audio tapes, demonstration and display materials and catalogs give your business a professional look. We provide business building information, voice mail, an information hot line, fax on request, a toll-free number for orders, monthly mailings, computer software to stay abreast of the activities of your organization, and a web site filled with current information on Conklin people, products and programs. We also provide fellowship through regional and national meetings and training programs, which guides representatives through every stage of their development.

At Conklin there are no sales quotas. You buy products at factory wholesale prices and resell them at suggested retail prices anywhere within the United States. You can realize growth rewards through product sales or sponsorship. Through our sound compensation plan, we provide incentives for sponsorship development and a volume discount program.

The Conklin Company is a successful and exciting growth oriented business. But even more importantly, it's an opportunity with distinct benefits for people in all walks of life to help themselves, their families and others succeed. It is a dream to be realized.

Full and part-time career opportunities are available.

**Conklin Company, Inc., 551 Valley Park Drive, PO Box 155, Shakopee, MN 55379**
**Phone: (800) 756-2475, Pam O'Brien, Communications Manager,**
**(612) 496-4223, Web site: www.conklin.com**

Direct Nutrition, Inc., sells a complete line of highly advanced anti-aging nutritional supplements. Direct Nutrition continually seeks to capture the latest in longevity supplements allowing consumers to achieve the highest possible quality of health and to extend the normal life expectancy.

Royce McCoy founded Direct Nutrition, Inc., in 1995 and is dedicated to setting new standards in the nutritional supplement and network marketing industry. Through years of experience, Royce's ability to develop a business into a tremendous success has been proven many times. His strong business background includes being president of an insurance brokerage firm, entrepreneurial owner of a chain of sporting goods stores, holding the honor of being claimed "Top Distributor" of several network marketing companies, and building organizations of over 20,000 people. In 1992, Royce served as chief executive officer and founder of the nation's fastest growing network marketing company. That company attracted more than 100,000 independent distributors, and realized more than 100 million dollars in revenue during its first two years. In recognition of his unique business finesse and marketing expertise, Royce was a finalist for the prestigious 1995 National "Entrepreneur of the Year" award sponsored by *Inc. Magazine*, Merrill Lynch, and Ernst and Young. His dedication to helping others achieve a healthier more productive life, along with helping them reach their financial goals, is what he considered his greatest accomplishment.

Direct Nutrition stands apart through its high quality line of nutritional supplements. It captures all the latest technology of the industry by developing products such as "The Original Formula," a nationally known weight loss product and Erriccson's "Coral Calcium," which is just breaking ground in the United States, but has been known for years worldwide for its phenomenal healing power. Direct Nutrition's products are supplied by only the top manufacturers and suppliers in the nation.

Direct Nutrition, Inc. is an international company with its headquarters in Dallas, Texas, and markets products not only in the U.S., but also in the Dominican Republic and Canada. Direct Nutrition is also a member of the prestigious Direct Selling Association (DSA). The Direct Nutrition mission is to provide the average individual the opportunity to establish a solid home-based business. Using a multi-level approach, Direct Nutrition offers its nationally based distributors and customers top quality nutritional products and a lucrative compensation plan. The corporate staff and leadership of Direct Nutrition have many years of experience in this industry. Their distributors are provided with the latest in innovative sales tools and strive to constantly educate them concerning the industry to keep them and Direct Nutrition on the cutting edge. Emphasis is also placed on communication via Direct Nutrition's intricate voicemail system, e-mail and access to their Internet web site. Direct Nutrition stands behind its policy of quality and integrity, thereby allowing the company's continued growth and retention level among its distributors.

Direct Nutrition's ultimate goal is to provide the best products and financial opportunity while incorporating ethical business practices and standards.

**Direct Nutrition, Inc., 10610 Metric Drive, Suite 121, Dallas, TX 74243**
**Phone: (214) 553-7733, Fax: (214) 553-7660**

# Eagle Distributing Company

*Michael Chapple*

**OUR MISSION** -- *To provide unlimited opportunity for growth to individuals as we all work together to make America a more fire safe place.* **GUIDING VALUES** -- *Respect For The Individual -- A Passion For Excellence -- An Obsession With Customer Service*

Eagle Distributing is made up of a group of people who are committed to our mission to provide unlimited opportunity for growth to individuals as we all work together to make America a more fire safe place. We believe that when each of us uses our God-given talents, following our company's guiding values of respect for the individual, a passion for excellence, and an obsession with customer service, we all win. Our most valuable treasure is the people who represent our company, and we treat them that way.

As to our mission, America has a very serious fire problem. In fact, *USA Today*, the nation's leading newspaper, has said that the United States of America has the worst fire death and injury record of all the industrialized nations of the world. Each year in our country we lose approximately 5,000 people to fire. Yes fire kills, but fire has its living victims too--those who grieve the loss of loved ones killed by fire, those who managed to get out alive (while others close to them may not have), those who are left homeless or jobless or impoverished because of fire. About half of these victims are children. Their scars, psychological as well as physical, often last a lifetime. Among the illnesses and injuries that require long hospitalization, few are as traumatic as serious burns. The frightening circumstances of the injury, the long isolation from family, the feeling of helplessness, the cosmetic operations that in many cases fall far short of expectations and the stigma of disfigurement, all contribute to a deep despondency that impairs recovery.

**QUESTION:** Where do we all feel the safest? **ANSWER:** Most people would say, "Right in my own home." Yes, 80% of fire deaths and injuries occur in the home. Most of these deaths and injuries occur between the hours of 10 PM and 6 AM while the occupants are asleep. This is especially shameful when you consider the fact that the educational information on home fire safety and the technology to put a stop to this, for the most part, is available. We have all heard the old saying, "an ounce of prevention is worth a pound of cure." When it comes to home fire safety, truer words were never spoken. That is why we developed our public awareness program on home fire safety and made it our business to do what we can to help make America a more fire safe place.

Our public awareness program on home fire safety puts a fence on the cliff rather than parking an ambulance down in the valley. Our program lasts about an hour. During our program, we leave a variety of home fire safety items with the family and explain how to best use them. Our program contains important information on how home fires can start and spread throughout a home. It also explains how to plan ahead with fire drills using Operation E.D.I.T.H. (Exit Drills In The Home).

After we have heightened the family's awareness to the ever-present danger of fire in the their home, we then do a demonstration of our Phoenix Systems 2100 residential fire detection system. With a well-presented program, approximately half of the families you visit will decide to have the Phoenix System installed in their home that night. The installation can be done on the spot by the security consultant. While installing the equipment, you or your partner can gather 15 to 20 customer referrals. The reason we are able to get so many referrals is because we have a PHOENIX SAVE-A-FAMILY PROGRAM.

We know we will only succeed in our mission to make America a more fire safe place by assuring your success. So we will be working just as hard as you to help you succeed. This business opportunity can provide you with excellent financial rewards, and because we save lives for a living, it will also provide you with great psychological rewards.

**E.D.C., Eagle Distributing Company, 7635 Main Street, Fishers, NY 14453**
**Phone: (716) 924-2150, Fax: (716) 924-0715**

# Enrich
# International

*Gary Holister*

Enrich International, the leader in nutritional supplements, is proud to be a part of one of the greatest industries in history. With a belief in changing the health of the world one person at a time, Enrich offers innovative products and educational programs that help people achieve improved health and financial independence.

Built on a foundation of vision, innovation and integrity, Enrich's roots reach back several decades. In 1972, Enrich founder Ken Brailsford and seven family members pooled their resources and collected $1,050 to start a business. Encapsulating cayenne pepper by hand and selling it to local grocery and health food stores, Ken began a legacy. He was the first in the industry to put herbs into capsules and has led the way ever since. To this day, Enrich is committed to developing and producing only the finest quality, natural products derived from the best ingredients available.

Enrich's top-quality products meet a special demand. Now more than ever, people are searching for natural alternatives that improve their health without the risk of side effects sometimes associated with synthetic products. New stories and studies about the wonder of natural products appear all over the world almost every day; the power of supplementation is finally becoming recognized.

In this ever-growing industry, Enrich is at an advantage. Four Ph.D.'s, who have accumulated more than 60 years of combined experience, lead its research and development team. This guarantees that Enrich formulates and offers only the finest nutritional supplements. Confident in the potency and efficacy of its products, Enrich backs each one with a money back satisfaction guarantee for every retail customer.

Enrich boast over 200 excellent natural supplements. The company houses its own manufacturing facility, which it developed and built complete with testing labs to ensure product quality. No other manufacturing plant in the industry matches its reputation for efficiency, quality and delivery.

Complementing its herbal supplements, Enrich offers an exclusive line of personal care products called E International*. This line, launched in 1997, features pure, dermatologist-tested botanicals that bring the same level of quality to the outside of the body that Enrich nutritional products bring to the inside. Enrich sees the launch of E international* as part of its continued commitment to the total health of the body.

Since the company's official inception in 1985, Enrich has enjoyed a history of growth. Between 1989 and 1993, sales increased by more than 2,300 percent. In 1996, *Inc. Magazine* named Enrich #65 on its list of fastest growing private companies in America, a move upward from rankings #92 and #444 in previous years. Enrich was also recognized as the sixth fastest growing company in Utah in 1996.

This commitment to continual growth is backed by the principles of service, quality and cutting-edge product development and has helped the Enrich opportunity spread around the globe. The company maintains offices in Canada, Malaysia, Brunei, Australia, New Zealand, and Trinidad, with numerous warehousing facilities throughout Russia and surrounding countries.

Enrich also offers a personal use program in Japan.

The Enrich ultimate compensation plan is the finest in the industry providing the perfect balance of earnings and growth incentives. This dynamic pay plan is ideal for beginners and experienced entrepreneurs alike. In addition to personal rebates and retail profits, distributors can enjoy a lifestyle leadership bonus and profit sharing program.

With a strong foundation in place and backed by quality products, Enrich offers the best opportunity in the world. The company looks forward to continuing to help all people attain total health, beauty, and financial independence.

**Enrich International, 748 North 1340 West, Orem, UT 84057**
**Phone: (801) 226-2600, Fax: (801) 226-8232, Web site: www.enrich.com**

*Matthew Freese*

## A message from founder Matthew J. Freese.

Envion is a company for dreams... and the people who make them come true. It is this dedication to transforming dreams into reality that makes Envion such an empowering force in the lives of thousands.

We're committed to providing you the best products to help meet today's challenging environment and lifestyles with health and vitality. For ages, people have searched for the "fountain of youth," with a goal of looking young and living a long life. This is what Total Body Wellness is all about, looking and feeling your best every day, at any age. It's a long-term, wellness "maintenance" program for your body based on protection, prevention, and caring for yourself right down to each cell. Total Body Wellness holds the key to living well and longer.

If you want to safely lose weight, experience increased energy, stay sharp and focused, and have healthy hair and radiant skin, Total Body Wellness will make a difference for you and your family. We guarantee your satisfaction 100 percent. When someone asks, "How are you?" we want you to say, "I feel great!" in every part of your life.

The best thing about Envion, is for the first time in 20-some years of being in the business, I'm directly in the business of truly helping people. Through our products, we can help people achieve Total Body Wellness. Through our business opportunity, people can help themselves financially.

There is tremendous personal growth happening to people in this company, and Envion offers a real sense of belongingness to our associates. The conventional corporate struggle to get to the top doesn't exist here at Envion. We are a team with a common focus and purpose. Our mission for life success is powerful and exciting, and through Envion, people can really make a difference in the world. Just imagine the possibilities!

Whatever your dreams, it's likely you can make them happen here. Whether it's to lose weight, enjoy better health, a bigger house, more free time with your family, or complete financial independence, I do hope you'll decide that your future is with Envion. Because after all...my dream is helping you live yours.

## Envion Time Line:

Envion premiers Programmed Nutrition products and business opportunity.

Presented with 1995 Company of the Year award from the Multi-Level Marketing International Association.

1995 Matt Freese featured in *Success* magazine cover story on network marketing professionals.

Envion becomes active member of Direct Selling Association in 1995.

1995 - Stanford Women's Swim Team with Coach Richard Quick wins PAC10 swim meets. Envion's products support their demanding nutritional needs.

1996 Atlantic Olympics, Olympic Coach Richard Quick's team comes away with 14 medals--five-time Gold Medalist Jenny Thompson says following a Zone favorable diet and using Envion products helps keep her focused.

Matt Freese is elected to the DSA Board of Directors in 1997.

1998 - Matt Freese and Envion introduced as a "Legend in the Making" at 1998 DSA Annual Convention.

1998 - Envion Diamonds Gary and Vicky Morgan address DSA Annual Convention.

Matt Freese elected to Board of Directors of the DSEFF in 1998.

1998 - Gold Directors, Ann and Steve Padover, featured in premier issue of *Network Marketing*.

**Envion International, 472 Amherst Street, Nashua, NH 03063-1204**
**Phone: (800) 436-8466, Fax: (800) 800-7873, Web site: www.envion.com**

*Rod Yanke*

A life-changing experience, a great idea and a desire to preserve the Earth's resources. That was the beginning of Enviro-Tech International, and it just might be the start of an exciting home-based career for you.

After a miraculous recovery from heart surgery, Rodney C. Yanke was determined to make a difference in the world. A successful businessman and entrepreneur, he founded the company in 1991 with a single product and a vision. The product was a waterless car wash; the vision was to change the lives of millions of people. That vision has remained the driving force behind Enviro-Tech's success, and as a publicly held corporation with a proven track record of high achievement, that vision becomes reality each and every day.

Yanke, now chairman of the board, innovated the waterless car wash category with DRI WASH 'n GUARD™ Waterless Car Wash featuring the exclusive PolyGuard-3™. DRI WASH 'n GUARD is a revolutionary new method of car care-a single product that in one step cleans, seals, polishes, and protects, without using a single drop of water. Dri Wash 'n Guard offers perhaps the most powerful product demonstration in network marketing. In just 30 seconds DRI WASH 'n GUARD sprayed directly onto a dirty vehicle will lift the dirt without scratching, polish and seal the surface. You can use it on trucks, vans, RVs, boats and even airplanes. In fact, the 20-Minute Detail Kit includes everything you need to completely detail a car in just 20 minutes.

We've modified the original PolyGuard formula, developing an entire line of DRI WASH 'n GUARD products that outperform everything else on the market *and* save billions of gallons of fresh water. Enviro-Tech International is making a difference.

Our waterless products for the home clean many household surfaces, including glass, mirrors, counter tops, tile, appliances, fabric, carpet, upholstery and more. We even have a product that allows you to wash your hands without using any water!

Three more product lines--Enviro-Tech Nutritionals™, INVE'™ Advanced Skin Care and BodyPruf personal care, feature exclusive formulations and proprietary technology, making them unlike anything else in the marketplace. All products in these lines contain Enviro-T™, our exclusive formula of pure, cold-processed aloe, Green Tea, and other herbs which enhance the effectiveness of our nutritional formulations and help to normalize skin and hair to a natural, healthy condition through our personal care products. Based on the finest European formulations available, our INVE' Advanced Skin Care offers a comprehensive regimen of exclusive skin care products and cosmetics that are effective and easy to use.

Unique and consumable products are essential, but are only part of Eviro-Tech's formula for your success. Our revolutionary, yet simple business plan enables you to share our exceptional products with family and friends without having to purchase a full-sized product first. And we have all the training and support material to help you get your home-based business going successfully.

**Enviro-Tech International can show you a new reality in home-based business. Let us help you change your life. Phone: (800) 711-9810**

# Essentially Yours

Essentially Yours Industries Corporation is a network marketing company. We market health maintenance products that provide the nutrition our bodies require to function at their optimum level. Our products work with the body to create a harmonious balance so that we remain (at-ease instead of dis-ease) healthy.

We started doing business in 1996 from our basements and garages. Since then we have grown to over 350,000 independent business associates. We are a company based on old-fashioned, honest ideals. Our mission is to create financial independence and alleviate debt one family at a time. EYI Corp., by example, has created a debt-free model for our associates to follow and we are grateful that many of them have adopted the same mission.

The name of the company, "Essentially Yours," tells all. We know it is the IBA who build this company--EYI is a result of their work. We are the stewards to serve and help them realize their dreams through this industry. Our goal is to provide a company that will give them the security of a long lasting and lucrative business opportunity.

The EYI products provide the essentials of life--air, food and water. The environment we live in has compromised each one of these elements and EYI Corp. products are meant to supplement the void in our nutrition created by environmentally compromised food.

In our quest to provide a long lasting and secure business opportunity, we formed a partnership with our manufacturer. This allowed us to have products exclusive to EYI and insure the highest quality of raw materials. Due to this relationship, we can rapidly respond to marketplace changes. Therefore, our associates can feel secure in building a long-term family business with Essentially Yours Industries Corp.

Our flagship products Calorad® and Definition™ are placed in one of the largest segments of the marketplace: weight loss and fitness. All of our products meet the criteria of new, old and only:

**NEW**--because of today's technology;

**OLD**--because ingredients have been tested and proven historically;

**ONLY**--because they are exclusive to EYI.

Due to the quality and performance of our products, we under promise and over deliver.

EYI Corp. has been blessed with a multitude of health care professionals who use and recommend our products. Our associates market to many retailers and you will find our products on the shelf of thousands of salons, health food stores, pharmacies, etc. We stand out in the industry in this area and again we are grateful for the wonderful products and the opportunity to change the economy one family at a time.

**Essentially Yours Corporation, #201-8322 - 130th Street, Surrey, B.C. V3W8J9, Canada**
**Phone: (604) 596-9766**
**E-mail: www@eyicom.com**

eventus.
International

*Richard Howard*                                                                                                    *Nolan Ryan*

Eventus International offers the world's most lucrative business opportunity in the booming $12 billion a year nutraceutical market. With the best compensation plan in existence, next generation nutraceuticals, corporate stability from its 18-year-old publicly traded founding company and cutting-edge electronic business support systems, Eventus International empowers its distributors, giving them the competitive edge in the global marketplace.

**Team Eventus:**
The Eventus world vision has attracted some of the greatest sports legends in history who enthusiastically endorse our industry leading products and an unprecedented ground-floor opportunity.

"Eventus is leading the world into the 21st century and I am honored to be a part of this revolutionary company."

**-Nolan Ryan, National Baseball Hall of Fame inductee with unprecedented 27-year major league pitching career.**

Other members of Team Eventus are: Nancy Lieberman-Cline, Women's Basketball Hall of Fame inductee and General Manager and coach of the WNBA's Detroit Shock. George Gervin, Basketball Hall of Fame inductee; Dallas Cowboys starting fullback Daryl "Moose" Johnson. Otis Birdsong, selected to the NBA All-Star Basketball team four times and Johnny Rodgers, Heisman Trophy winner.

**Cutting-edge formulas:**
Eventus innovation leads the multi-billion dollar nutraceutical revolution in preventative health, wellness and anti-aging products. With patented technologies, advanced ingredients and cutting-edge formulas that deliver real nutrition for building total health and wellness at the cellular level, Eventus products are world-firsts!

Eventus is the first and only company to offer a line of daily nutraceuticals customized by a person's specific heritage, with our exclusive **Heritage Gold™ Formulas**. Our groundbreaking **Veraloe Plus™** and **Veraloe Gold™** daily immune stimulation formulas are all-natural. Eventus world-first products also include the **LeanTrek™ Fat Loss System**, a unique combination of delicious meal replacement shakes and high-tech innovative activity tools for an effective weight loss/lean mass preservation program, and **AloeGest™**, a phytoestrogen and progesterone cream for women.

**Building your business empire:**
The earning potential of Eventus is explosive as our aggressive international expansion makes every person on the planet a potential customer. Built by distributors, for distributors, the Eventus compensation plan offers higher commissions and overrides and more bonuses than other network marketing plans. Distributors can enjoy immediate income, long-term prosperity with lucrative, sustainable downlines and multiple paychecks every month.

Distributors can choose from five easy entry options to join Eventus. The Fast Track Bonus Program provides large awards up-front for fast income through a coded bonus system. It is based on four legs for easy qualification but has unlimited width and pays on an unlimited number of levels. When distributors sign up their first four distributors and allow them to take advantage of the optional packages, everyone begins earning immediately.

**Get your piece of the e-commerce pie:**
Everything you need to rapidly grow your Eventus business is at your fingertips, electronically. Eventus literally links you to the new way of doing business in the new millennium. Through our interactive e-commerce web-based support tools, fax-on-demand, distributor phone services and 24-hour-a-day tech support, Eventus distributors have everything they need to stay on top, from virtual offices to personalized distributor web pages.

**To learn more about Eventus International, visit us at www.eventusonline.com,**
**or call: (800) 943-8085**

*Kenny Troutt*

Excel Communications, founded in 1988 by President, Chairman and CEO Kenny A. Troutt as a regional long distance re-seller, has catapulted from an unknown start-up company to become one of the largest long distance service providers in North America. At the time of its IPO in 1996, it was one of the youngest companies ever to be listed on the New York Stock Exchange. By 1997, Deloitte & Touche ranked Excel 44th among the country's fastest growing technology companies, noting the company's incredible 5,492% growth over just five years. Excel's innovative combination of business and multi-level marketing strategies were key to this tremendous growth.

"The foundation of Excel's success is relationship selling and personal attention to our customers," says Kenny Troutt. That "personal attention" was validated recently by participants in the J.D. Power and Associates Residential Long Distance Customer Satisfaction Survey. Excel ranked second in the more than $50 Billing category and tied for fourth in the less than $50--both increases from last year's ratings. J.D. Power and Associates noted that Excel now experiences "comparable overall satisfaction ratings to the leaders in each respective spending segment."

Excel acquired Telco Communications Group in October 1997, giving the company its own state-of-the-art switching network. This acquisition and migration yielded benefits with increased revenues of $489.4 million for the second quarter of 1998, compared to $330.6 million from the second quarter of 1997. In June, Excel announced a definitive agreement to merge with Montreal-based Teleglobe Inc. in a transaction valued at $US 7 billion. The combined company will become the fourth largest long distance carrier in North America. According to Troutt, Teleglobe's global network and licenses, combined with Excel's strong distribution channels, will create a global player that can market a host of products, including Internet access, calling cards, pre-paid calling cards and operator services. The new, more powerful company plans to extend its successful multi-level marketing approach into the G7 countries as their markets open to competition.

At the heart of Excel's success are its independent representatives (IRs). IRs begin their Excel business with a low initial investment, never need to purchase inventory and have the support of Excel's 3,000 customer service, network management, billing, and marketing employees. With low-cost entry, established products, strong corporate support and global reach, Excel has never been more attractive to entrepreneurs.

**For more information please visit Excel's web site at www.excel.com, or write to:**

**Excel Communications, Inc.**
**8750 North Central Expressway, Ste. 1500**
**Attn.: Public Relations**

# Forever Living Products

*Rex Maughan*

Forever Living Products International, Inc. (FLP) and its affiliates celebrated a 20th anniversary in 1998 looking better than ever with an expanding line of superior-quality products, substantial international growth and robust sales figures surpassing $1 billion annually. FLP produces and markets approximately 150 natural aloe vera-based and bee products including personal care items, nutritional health drinks, supplements and a variety of exceptional beauty products, all sold exclusively by distributors.

The 1998 launch of the Sonya Colour Collection has taken the appeal of the company to new heights, and distributors along with it! This elegant color cosmetics line rivals upscale department store brands, yet offers an exceptional value for women around the world who want to look their best.

FLP's international headquarters is located in Scottsdale, Arizona. The company operates in many of the global market's fastest growing industries: the health, beauty and nutritional products market and the home-based business or network marketing industry.

FLP continues to receive honors and recognition from leading companies and publications. Arthur Andersen's "*Arizona 100*" ranking named FLP as Arizona's largest privately held company for the past three years. A survey by *Inc. Magazine* ranked FLP as the sixth fastest-growing company in the country. In a similar article, *Venture* magazine ranked FLP as 28th among its top 100 fast-track companies.

The company also had the distinction of posting increased earnings every year for two decades, through two recessions, a widely fluctuating stock market and periods of high unemployment.

The popularity of drinking FLP's Aloe Vera Gel has helped catapult the company's sales to the top. The natural health drink consists of 100 percent pure, stabilized aloe vera gel that contains over 200 nutritional compounds including 20 minerals, 18 amino acids and 12 vitamins.

Founded by Rex Maughan, FLP currently has more than five million distributors worldwide, with products available in over 65 countries. Maughan and FLP are the world's largest growers, manufacturers and distributors of aloe vera, with more than 5,000 acres of aloe vera in the United States, Mexico and the Caribbean.

In addition to a generous marketing plan that gives distributors the opportunity to reach their highest goals, FLP also offers the chance to earn fabulous prizes ranging from international travel and special resort discounts to profit sharing incentives.

Since 1981, Forever Resorts has been providing the finest accommodations and unique vacation adventures to the traveling public and FLP distributors alike. With resorts and houseboats located in some of the most desirable locations in the United States, Forever Resorts offer active distributors special discounts and incentives as a reward for their efforts, a way to relax and give them yet another way to enjoy the fruits of their success.

International Super Rallies are held annually in the United States. Thousands of distributors from around the world flock to these high-energy events offering everything from sales training by internationally recognized sales trainers and motivational speakers to award ceremonies and banquets. Locales have included Phoenix, AZ, Washington, DC, Dallas, TX and Anaheim, CA.

As FLP continues upward on its progressive path, the growth and popularity of its ever-expanding product line and the enthusiasm of millions of distributors continue its steady advances. If you would like more information on how to enjoy the freedom of running your own independent home-based Forever business and achieve your highest goals, please call (800) 843-0422 today for more information!

**Forever Living Products International, Inc., 7501 East McCormick Parkway, Scottsdale, AZ 85250**
**Phone: (602) 998-8887**

**Raymond Faltinsky**

When FreeLife International Co-Founders, Ray Faltinsky and Kevin Fournier set out to establish a network marketing company that would set the standard for the entire industry, they left no stone unturned. Ray obtained his degree from Yale Law School, and he spent years performing groundbreaking research and writing a thesis on the network marketing industry before gaining first-hand experience himself. Kevin has a degree and an extensive background in business administration combined with many years of experience in network marketing.

Together they have formed exclusive relationships with Dr. Earl Mindell, the world's No. 1 nutritionist, father of the nutrition revolution and author of *Earl Mindell's Vitamin Bible,* as well as many other best-selling books; Linda Chae, the world's foremost expert in organic personal care products; and Eurovita International, the world's leading nutraceutical company. FreeLife's products, developed by these world renowned experts, simply cannot be duplicated by any other company.

Some of FreeLife's revolutionary products include: Trim4Life™, an all-natural, synergistically balanced weight management system that combines the best of what nature and science have to offer; Zinaxin™, a blockbuster nutraceutical based on a worldwide patented herbal extract that has been clinically proven to promote joint health; and Organic Essentials™, the world's first and only line of vegetable-based personal care products that contains 100 percent organically safe ingredients.

With its exclusive relationships and products, FreeLife is widely recognized as one of the fastest growing companies in the United States. Since its inception in March 1995, FreeLife has experienced exponential growth each quarter it has been in business.

FreeLife has been featured twice in the entrepreneurial magazine *Success* and is the youngest company ever to appear on the publication's cover; was featured extensively in Richard Poe's New York Times best-selling book "*The Wave 3 Way;*" is a member of the Direct Selling Association; was voted "Best Company of the Year" three years in a row (1995-1997) by the highly regarded publication *MLM Insider*; was voted "Company of the Year" for 1996 by *Profit Now Magazine,* and has received many other accolades from industry experts.

What sets FreeLife apart is that it is a mission-driven company built on a solid foundation of integrity and proprietary products. There are no special skills or education needed to succeed with FreeLife, only the desire to use the company's life-changing products, to share them with others and to develop leaders who do the same. FreeLife's low start-up cost makes it an affordable, accessible opportunity for everyone. The company's lucrative, 12-ways-to-earn compensation plan offers marketing executives the opportunity to earn short-term, mid-term and long-term residual income and to realize their financial dreams.

The mission of FreeLife is this: "To serve each other by promoting good health, well-being and the opportunity for an abundant life." These are not just words to Ray, Kevin and the other members of FreeLife's exceptional management team. They are the FreeLife way of life. There is no opportunity like the FreeLife opportunity. Make the call today that will enable you to enjoy the FreeLife.

**FreeLife International, 333 Quarry Road, Milford, CT 06460**
**Phone: (203) 882-7250, Fax: (203) 874-4982**

**An E-Commerce Company Offering Integrated Solutions For Positive Living**
*Today's Busy Lifestyle Creates Challenges.*
*Genisys Offers Immediate Solutions And Ultimately A Chance To Redefine Your Lifestyle!*

**Use Better Products And Services** - Genisys searches North America to assemble an ever growing section of products and services that promise to delight consumers. Many people use fine products today; however, our products must be at least as good or better, priced for value, and more natural whenever possible.

**A Focus To Family Wellness** - Wellness begins at the cellular level with affordable herbal supplementation. Natural personal care and cosmetics with fitness equipment will keep your family's health and appearance at its best. Add to that, biodegradable home care for the healthiest possible environment.

**Travel More, Spend Less** - Travel has proven a necessary part of maintaining mental wellness. Refresh yourself by taking a break from the "rat race." Discover new and exciting places while enjoying tremendous savings with our Discount Travel Programs.

**Shop Conveniently From Home** - After enrolling for free, Genisys consumers save time and money shopping by toll-free telephone or on the Internet @www.gtv.ca, with or without a credit card. In fact, for just a few hundred dollars, Websurfer Pro will convert your television into an Internet port. We are living the future of consumerism today!

**Earn Graduating Consumer Rewards** - Why pay a retailer's overhead and advertising costs when you could reward yourself instead? Imagine if through time, you could double the power of your purchasing dollar. Because it's free to enroll, the products are great and competitively priced, Consumer Rewards represent found benefits...
And **Support Charity** - An additional 25% of any product credits earned will be donated to charity.

**Develop A Home-Based Business** - By combining this wide appeal concept with referral marketing, participants may develop a residual profit centre, career, or even lifestyle income. We all have our dreams. If there was no downside and the possibility existed to earn your life back, would you invest a few hours a week until you arrive? Everyone is time challenged today. Stop spending time and start investing it! Together we could redefine your lifestyle with only a little time consistently invested. If not this, what? If not now, when?

**Good People, Good Philosophy** - Genisys participants are attracted to the idea of doing it better. As a result, we attract a better kind of person. You will enjoy support and experience personal development. Grow yourself, your income and have fun! What a concept!

**The Company** - Based in Calgary, Canada (currently expanding into the United States), Genisys promises a positive experience and a future full of opportunity with a focus to durability. We represent the future of consumerism and business offering our members a better, more healthy lifestyle and a more secure future.

**The Reality--Now And The Future** - For the network marketing industry to ever be considered mainstream, we believe the plan must reward people at each level of contribution and offer bigger pay developing smaller groups with retention as a key element. Technology will form an ever-expanding role in consumer interface, general communication, and enhanced access to critical information and education.

Get Ready World, The Future Of Network Marketing Has Arrived!

**Genisys International, #200, 3016-5 Ave. NE, Calgary, Alberta, Canada, T2A 6K4, Phone: (403) 777-9030, Fax: (403) 777-9042, E-mail: comm@gtv.ca--Please forward inquiries to Genisys or even better, find us online at: www.gtv.ca, click on Bio-Pages to choose a sponsor**

*Barbara Girson*

**MEMBER**
**DIRECT SELLING**
**ASSOCIATION**

Gift Shows by Personal Creations is a direct selling company, established in 1995, that features high-quality, unique personalized gifts. We are recognized for our wide product selection and fast turnaround time. We pride ourselves in offering excellent customer service and being an involved member of the Direct Selling Association. At present, we offer our home-based business opportunity throughout the United States and have aggressive plans for growth and expansion over the next three to five years, both domestically and abroad.

### How does Gift Shows by Personal Creations distribute our products?

We distribute our products to consumers through independent gift consultants, managers and directors. Our Gift Consultants market their own home-based business through a variety of methods, which include demonstrations or parties called "Gift Shows" and person-to-person selling. We also target markets such as corporate gifts, bridal and sports enthusiasts, to name a few.

### What types of gifts do we offer?

We offer time-saving, simple solutions for the perfect present. Whether a customer needs a gift for a birthday, wedding, anniversary, holiday, Bar/Bat Mitzvah, or Communion, they will have a choice. In essence, we have "Gifts For All Reasons, All Seasons™."

We use a variety of processes to personalize our products, such as: gold foil embossing, crystal and marble etching, four-color digital silk screening, computer-cut appliques, custom-framed prints, hand painting, laser printing and engraving. Most of our items are personalized in-house.

### Where are we located?

Our 75,000 square ft. manufacturing facility, warehouse and corporate office is located in Burr Ridge, Illinois. We staff 150 employees, which includes our own in-house graphics/catalog department and many talented artists and craftspeople.

### Why join our team?

#### ▶ Our Mission

Our mission is to help people express their feelings, celebrate life's special events and recognize achievements through our career, host and gift-purchasing opportunities.

#### ▶ Leadership

Barbara C. Girson, vice president, brings 19 years of direct selling industry experience to share with those interested in starting their own home-based business. She has been recognized nationally for helping others build a successful and profitable income. She has also been featured in *U.S.A. Today* and appeared on "CBS This Morning" for teaching others innovative approaches to use in reaching new customers. Barbara is a *summa cum laude* graduate from the University of Pittsburgh and has a B.S. in Education with an emphasis in business, marketing and distributive education.

### Benefits to Consultants

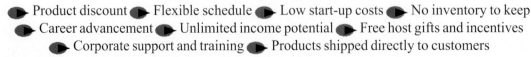

Product discount ◗ Flexible schedule ◗ Low start-up costs ◗ No inventory to keep
Career advancement ◗ Unlimited income potential ◗ Free host gifts and incentives
Corporate support and training ◗ Products shipped directly to customers

**Gift Shows by Personal Creations, 145 Tower Drive, Burr Ridge, IL 60521-9912**
**Phone: (800) 74-names, Web site: http://www.74names.com**

# GOLDEN NEO-LIFE DIAMITE
## INTERNATIONAL

*Jim Arnott*

In 1996, three international direct sales companies, Golden Products, Neo-Life Company and Diamite Corporation, came together to form GNLD. Each firm had established an excellent reputation for long-term success and consistent growth for 20 to 40 years. Today, united as one global force, GNLD has emerged as the most rapidly expanding network marketing opportunity in the world, with hundreds of thousands of distributors in 52 international markets!

Reflecting the true spirit of free enterprise, GNLD invites people from every background, age, gender, and educational level to open their own no-risk, low-investment, high-return GNLD business and discover the lifestyle of their dreams. Several long standing GNLD distributors have passed their home-based businesses down from generation to generation, keeping success in the family for four decades.

Every independent distributor is backed by GNLD's Global Business Support System, scientifically proven products, and a simple, highly profitable marketing plan that generously rewards volume consistency and leadership development. GNLD's extensive support system includes a popular fast-success program, first-class corporate literature, extended toll-free 800# service, and comprehensive, results-oriented training sessions.

Successful distributors are treated to substantial bonuses, exceptional travel opportunities, company-sponsored events in resort locales, workshops, retreats, and high-visibility recognition. Distributors are rewarded at every turn with certificates, prizes, prestigious jewelry, medals, feature stories in magazines, on videos, and more!

GNLD distributors merchandise superior whole-food nutritional supplements, unequaled herbal formulas, nature-based skin and personal care, earth-safe and effective home care, and NSF®-certified water enhancement systems. GNLD's more than 100 products represent the very best of nature and science, with leading-edge solutions that reflect the latest advances in research and technology.

Quality-conscious GNLD keeps a tight rein on product quality by researching, testing, and manufacturing its own nutritional supplements in company-owned facilities. The firm also holds a pharmaceutical manufacturing license, although not required by law. Product research and development is directed by GNLD's exclusive Scientific Advisory Board (SAB), a team of world-recognized scientists, led by premier toxicologist, Dr. Arthur Furst.

Health and nutritional product innovations include revolutionary **PhytoDefense**™, which delivers the phytonutrient power of six optimal servings from 25 different fruits and vegetables. Researchers from the government found that one component of PhytoDefense promotes healthy immune and antioxidant activity for healthy cellular tissue throughout the body.

A sampling of other fine products:

**Tre-en-en Grain Concentrates**®, with the vital lipids and sterols (missing from processed foods) that research shows promote enhanced nutrient utilization and efficient cellular function. Heart-healthy **NouriShake**®, an energy-boosting protein drink, provides all 22 amino acids the body needs to repair and replace cells. **Aloe Vera Plus**™, an anti-stress beverage that supports optimal energy and helps soothe and calm the digestive tract. Herbal products include **Masculine Herbal Complex** and **Feminine Herbal Complex**, which promote natural energetic balance and function. Skin Care products include **Vitamin E Therapy**, a clinical-intensity formula scientifically proven to boost the amount of vitamin E in skin *50 times,* for greater protection against skin-aging UV and oxidative damage. Home Care products include **Super 10**™ and **LDC**™, highly effective, concentrated and earth-safe formulas that replace cupboards full of specialty cleaners. Water Enhancement Systems include **Water Dome**®, a compact, NSF-certified filtering system that removes health hazards while providing ultra high quality drinking water at a fraction of the cost of bottled.

**GNLD, the World's Opportunity Company is making a positive difference in many lives! To find out more, Phone: (800) 432-5848 (U.S.), (905) 890-7120, (Canada)**

*Harry Hersey III*

Golden Pride International is more than just a company. It's the sharing of a dream--a dream made possible by free enterprise with a generous marketing plan designed for success.

Founded in 1983 by its President, Harry W. Hersey, Golden Pride International is a leader in the direct sales industry. GPI has been a member of the Direct Selling Association since 1983 and supports the Direct Selling Educational Foundation. President Hersey was recently elected Vice Chairman of the DSA Board of Directors, which ultimately leads to the position of Chairman of the Board.

The Company's 15-year history of expansion and growth is impressive. In 1989, Golden Pride purchased the 100-year-old W.T. Rawleigh health and home care company. In 1996, TARRAH, a skin care and cosmetics company, was also acquired. July 1998 brought about another exciting addition to the team. GPI formed a strategic alliance with Tony Little, America's #1 personal trainer. With Tony joining the team and his Eternal Energy Products, GPI now has the most energized nutritional spokesman in the world to take the company to unparalleled heights.

Golden Pride offers only the highest quality, synergistically blended, bio-available nutritional supplements. Each of Golden Pride's formulations has been synergistically balanced to create both a scientifically and nutritionally superior combination. The vast line of nutritional products includes heart-healthy formulations, nutrients, herbs, water filtration, weight loss, and more.

The W.T. Rawleigh line consists of traditional old-time remedies, flavorings and extracts, spices and seasonings, specialty foods, and household items. Some Rawleigh products even have the same formulations as when they were originally introduced back in 1889. Rawleigh has been a friend of the family for 110 years.

TARRAH skin care and cosmetics is the newest kid on the Golden Pride International block. The skin care products are formulated with an aloe vera and vitamin E base. They are enriched with botanicals and emollients to help balance and restore moisture to skin. The TARRAH glamour line is in a class of its own. The brilliant colors and enhancing tones are carefully blended and selected to offer the perfect complement to any skin tone.

The combination of Golden Pride's original focus on health supplements and nutritional products, along with the additional products from the Rawleigh and TARRAH companies, as well as Tony Little's Eternal Energy Products, gives GPI one of the most comprehensive product lines in North America. With nearly 500 different products to choose from, Golden Pride is a perfect fit for any home.

Golden Pride's mission statement is: To shape and protect the future of people's health and security through products nature provides. This mission has driven Golden Pride to develop a marketing pay plan that maximizes the independent distributors' earnings. The high paying and easy to understand marketing plan provides outstanding financial rewards for sharing the unsurpassed nutritional supplements, skin care, cosmetics, and home products.

A host of educational materials is available to all independent distributors. Golden Pride provides ongoing support through the use of numerous video tapes, audio cassettes, brochures, catalogs, and more. President Hersey and the executive staff also host frequent seminars across the U.S.A. and Canada to educate distributors and their guests on Golden Pride's superior products and unequaled opportunity.

This modern, family owned and operated company provides a refreshing distributor centered approach to business. An established, stable company in a growth mode makes GPI an ideal home for anyone interested in building a long-term business that will be there for their future.

**Golden Pride International, PO Box 21109, West Palm Beach, FL 33416-1109**
**Phone: (561) 640-5700, Fax: (561) 640-7333, Fax-on-Demand: (800) 640-3550, E-mail: gpride@flinet.com**

# HERBALIFE®

*Mark Hughes*

**Herbalife International; 18-year History of Premium-Quality Products** - Herbalife's retail sales of $1.5 billion in 1997 established the company as one of the largest and most successful direct selling organizations worldwide. Founded in 1980 by President and CEO Mark Hughes, Herbalife markets a growing base of premium-quality nutritional, weight management and personal care products in 38 countries across the globe. Herbalife products are available exclusively through its base of independent distributors.

As one of the pioneers of the nutritional movement nearly two decades ago, Herbalife products have earned a long-standing reputation for quality and effectiveness around the world. This favorable brand awareness enables Herbalife distributors to attract and retain a loyal and satisfied customer base. The company's healthy-lifestyle products are ideally suited for network marketing because consumers value the close personal contact and product knowledge Herbalife distributors provide.

**International Growth, New Products Enhance Distributor Opportunity** - Consistent with its dynamic growth strategies, Herbalife has continued to commence operations in new countries and introduce several innovative products each and every year. Global expansion efforts extended Herbalife's product availability to Indonesia and Turkey in 1998, raising the number of countries where it's products are marketed to 38.

1998 had also proven a record year for new product introductions, with more than 25 products launched in the first half alone. Herbalife greatly expanded its Personal Care offerings through the recent introduction of a full line of color cosmetics. Initially available in Russia, the high quality line for 1999, are now being introduced in many other markets.

These growth initiatives have led to an increasingly attractive and truly international business opportunity for independent distributors by enabling them to maximize their sales and business-building efforts.

**Financially Rewarding Marketing Plan** - Beyond excellent products and international growth opportunities, Herbalife offers one of the most financially rewarding marketing plans in the industry. The Herbalife plan compensates distributors for their product sales, as well as the sales of distributors within their downline organization, and permits them to purchase products at up to a 50 percent discount. The plan also includes a lucrative "President Team Bonus" pool, equivalent to one percent of Herbalife's total product retail sales, which is distributed to the highest achieving sales leaders once a year.

The company's business opportunity also uniquely enables distributors to operate, or sponsor other distributors, within any of the 38 countries where Herbalife products are approved for sale. Herblife is an active member of the Direct Selling Associations in 27 of these countries, including the United States, and all products come with a money-back guarantee in most markets.

**Outstanding Training and Support Services** - Herbalife distributors also benefit from outstanding distributor support programs, incentives and training opportunities that reward individual achievements and help distributors successfully build, manage and train their sales organizations. An increasing number of Herbalife's industry-leading distributor training, support and incentive programs include: regional training events, satellite TV training, all-expenses paid vacations to exotic locations and automatic reordering programs for monthly product shipments.

**The Time to Join is Now!** - With demand for healthy living products increasing rapidly across the globe, there has never been a better time to become a Herbalife distributor. Let the Herbalife International Business Opportunity help you achieve your goals today.

**For more information, please contact: Herbalife Distributor Relations, 1800 Century Park East, Los Angeles, CA 90067, Phone: (310) 410-9600, Web site: http://www.herbalife.com**

*Madolyn Johnson*

"Every year since the beginning, I've surprised my accountant with the amount of money I've made with The Homemaker's Idea Company®," says Carole Brown, now a Senior Executive Manager with the company. Over the past 15 years, Carole has grown to enjoy a consistent six-figure yearly income.

Since its creation 28 years ago, The Homemaker's Idea Company® has been beautifying homes and building people across the nation. Others like Carole have enjoyed the opportunity to sell the company's affordable and diverse product line of baskets and decorative home accessories while maintaining family priorities. With 80% of the products priced at $25.00 and under, customers can organize and decorate in any style they love at a reasonable price. A wide range of accessories, including linens, matching candles, and floral swags, complements an extensive variety of unique colors, shapes and exclusive basket designs.

Besides a remarkable product line, The Homemaker's Idea Company® offers its sales representatives the opportunity to make a substantial income. A strong ratio of representatives and managers earn incomes over $20,000 and those who love to decorate and organize feel completely at home with the company. A fully supportive organization with a culture of earning and sharing, the company provides its representatives incentives, recognition and opportunities to advance to managerial levels. In addition, the company serves as the distribution facility, eliminating the hassles of inventory, packing and deliveries.

Strong leadership and a steady growth pattern have earned the company widespread recognition. For the past three years, Founder and President, Madolyn Johnson, has been named an Entrepreneur of the Year finalist for the Illinois and Northern Indiana Region. In 1997, the Direct Selling Association awarded the company its prestigious "Vision for Tomorrow Award" for its commitment of time and resources with the charitable organization, "Christmas is April." Besides giving donations, the company has created teams of volunteers made up of representatives and home office staff that have helped "Christmas in April" rehabilitate the homes of low income families throughout the U.S. In just three years, the effort has grown from impacting 400 homes in 24 cities to 1,100 homes in 52 cities, spreading the company's mission of impacting lives one home at a time.

President Madolyn Johnson says, "I founded The Homemaker's Idea Company® so other women could have the choice of gaining the flexibility and extra income of their own business while building a family. The value of family and the belief that the home is the core of family life have created a common company focus. Everything revolves around the home...our products are designed **for** the home, sold **in** the home, **by** homemakers to other homemakers. Through our products and our people, we hope to make a difference and raise the level of dignity in the word homemaker."

Madolyn's own story is inspirational. After the birth of her first daughter, she chose not to return to her career in teaching but realized she wanted to be a stay-at-home mom with money. Her love for baskets and decorating led her to create her own business which grew into a party plan within just four months. Such rapid growth quickly depleted her teacher's retirement fund. With no assets or collateral for a bank loan, she shared her predicament with a friend and neighbor who quickly ran to her bedroom and pulled out a shoebox containing the money Madolyn needed. Instead of "starting on a shoelace," as the saying goes, the company was boosted by innovation and a shoebox! Now a multi-million dollar company, The Homemaker's Idea Company® continues to enrich lives and homes across the nation.

**The Homemaker's Idea Company, 1420 Thorndale Avenue, Elk Grove Village, IL 60007**
**Phone: (847) 860-5452, Fax: (847) 860-6647**

*Demi Lloyd*

## HOUSE *of* LLOYD
*Celebrating Life's Most Cherished Moments*

**Built to Last -** Since 1968, House of Lloyd has grown into one of the largest direct selling companies in the United States and we keep on growing! Thirty years ago, House of Lloyd was housed in a 850 square foot building. Over the next three decades, House of Lloyd grew to a total of two-and-a-half million square feet in three locations!

**So Much More Than a Job -** Harry Lloyd founded his company on the idea of providing opportunities for growth- -not only monetary, but personal, spiritual and professional growth as well. House of Lloyd is dedicated to providing a supportive environment in which thousands of individuals can achieve their aspirations, including world travel, career education, and lifelong friendships.

House of Lloyd's three product lines, Christmas Around the World®, Gifts by House of Lloyd®, and Cookin' the American Way®, offer a selection of merchandise designed to help people celebrate the cherished moments in their lives. Our sales associates take pride in knowing they are in the business of celebrating and creating sweet memories.

**Traveling the World -** Every year thousands of our sales associates across the country have remarkable travel experiences on House of Lloyd training meetings. These expense-paid adventures take House of Lloyd's sales associates and their guests to exciting destinations like Paris, Spain, Hawaii, Greece, Australia and Germany!

**Designed for Success -** To help ensure the success of its sales force, House of Lloyd offers an outstanding hostess program, free merchandise kit, leadership development and training, beautiful four-color catalogs and sales support materials, unlimited income and advancement potential, and a talented and enthusiastic support team.

**Spirit of Giving -** House of Lloyd believes in helping others. Our founder, Harry Lloyd, was very active in charity work and encouraged all his employees to help their fellow man, both in their own communities and in countries all over the world. The Harry J. Lloyd Charitable Trust was set up to continue Harry Lloyd's commitment to his religious faith, his family and the community. Every year substantial monetary donations are made to numerous organizations dedicated to spreading God's word. In addition, monetary donations are made to medical research programs. We're very proud to be a part of a company that reaches out to others in need. All our sales associates know that they too are an integral part in spreading hope and peace through the world.

**Continuing to Bring Joy and Meaning to Life -** On January 25,1997, after a long bout with cancer, Harry Lloyd passed away. It was Harry's wish that his daughter, Demi Lloyd, assume his responsibilities as chief executive officer of House of Lloyd.

Under Demi's direction, House of Lloyd launched its mission of bringing joy and meaning to life at its national sales meeting in February of 1998. House of Lloyd adopted its message, Celebrating Life's Most Cherished Moments™ to help drive its mission.

As a wife and a mother, Demi recognizes the demands on today's families in the workplace. In order to meet the need of many busy families and individuals, Demi directed the company to dedicate all its energy and resources to sharing all the wonderful opportunities it can offer women and men of all backgrounds and qualifications.

The continued success of House of Lloyd is inevitable. For when you take three product lines designed to enhance special times and add to it great opportunities for part-time and full-time income, world travel, an outstanding hostess program, and recognition of achievement, it all adds up to a company that's truly in the business of celebrating and creating sweet memories. And isn't that what life is all about!

**House of Lloyd Inc., 11901 Grandview Road, Grandview, MO 64030**
**Phone: (800) 733-2465, Fax: (816) 767-2177, Web site: www.houseoflloyd.com**

**Ken Hampshire**

**Steve Miles**

**I.D.E.A. Concepts** is the company that's pioneering an entirely new mode of business--directNET Marketing, the marriage of direct response advertising and NETwork Marketing.

Through 30-minute TV infomercials, radio programs, direct mail, best-selling books, and a wide range of other innovative strategies. I.D.E.A. Concepts generates tens of thousands of high-quality leads. "High-quality" because the vast majority are consumers who have already been sold a product.

These customer leads are then handed over to the company's distributor organization for ongoing follow-up. This hugely successful hybrid operation is revolutionizing the traditional network marketing business by removing the main obstacle encountered by most part-timers: how do I get new prospects?

The breakthrough directNet Marketing strategy is undoubtedly exciting, but it's only one of many attributes that sets I.D.E.A. Concepts apart from so many other companies.

Named as one of the top ten network marketing companies of 1998-1999 by the industry watchdog magazine "*Network Marketing Today* and *MLM Insider*," I.D.E.A. Concepts is no longer "the best kept secret in network marketing."

Founded by Ken Hampshire and Steve Miles in 1995, I.D.E.A. Concepts has developed a superior distributor support system run by a talented and experienced management team.

Free high-tech Internet access delivers full downline information at the press of a button and the ability to order and sponsor online 24 hours a day, plus a simple, duplicable audio-visual prospecting system provides a turnkey approach to recruiting new distributors.

Repeat sales are facilitated through state-of-the-art anti-aging and nutrition products, including the Syntra-5 lifepac, a veritable "health food store in the palm of your hand," a high potency stabilized liquid oxygen supplement, a weight management plan and the unique Genisys™ oxygenated skin care system.

I.D.E.A. Concepts' Independent Representatives are generously rewarded with a unilevel compensation plan that pays a staggering 60% on the three levels plus up to 10% infinity and 4% peak performance bonuses.

I.D.E.A. stands for:

**I**     **Inspiration**: The spark that ignites new ideas and ambition turning into action.

**D**     **Dedication**: Overcoming temporary setbacks and making a determined effort in the pursuit of

**E**     **Excellence**: The simple power of becoming "the best you dare to be."

**A**     **Achievement**: It's within the reach of every person and I.D.E.A. Concepts help you achieve the highest pinnacles of success.

The two hottest marketing methods of the 20th century, taken separately, are the engines that drive multi-billion dollar industries, direct response and network marketing. Imagine the potential of a far-sighted company that has the best of both and synergistically bonded them together. Imagine becoming part of the DirectNET explosion and join the I.D.E.A. team.

**I.D.E.A Concepts, Inc., 6021 S. Syracuse Way, #220, Englewood, CO 80111**
**Phone: (888) 921-6566, Fax: (303) 978-0891, Web Site: www.ideaconcepts.com**

*Larry Cantrell*

From its inception in January of 1997, Integris International quickly established itself in the network marketing industry as one company that was very serious about nutrition. Within the first year, the number of preferred customers and sales associates mushroomed to 30,000 and the company was operating in all 50 states, Guam and Puerto Rico. Industry leading experts attribute this remarkable success to the fact that Integris was able to penetrate the marketplace through direct mail, with unparalleled, science-based "showcase" products.

Co-founder, president and CEO, J. Larry Cantrell, offers this insight, "If there is one thing I have learned over the past decade in this industry, there is no substitute for experience. Therefore, for long-term success, I knew it was important to surround myself with a team of the most experienced and successful network marketing oriented professionals available. In all honesty, I would not trade my co-founder counterpart, Dr. Bill Kellas, our founding associates, management team and staff for any other team in this industry. It is also no coincidence that our slogan is "Serious Nutrition for Dynamic Health." From day one, it was our goal to develop an ever-expanding line of products that would clearly establish Integris as a global leader in nutrition. We have developed strategic alliance with the world's foremost manufacturers, leading research scientists and product formulators to accomplish this. These relationships give us access to the most current scientific studies and state-of-the-art products that pass the scrutiny of sports medicine authorities as well as domestic and international science organizations."

Already we have gone 2,000 feet below the sea to retrieve the purest and most bioavailable trace mineral source, and traveled around the world to unlock the secrets of a true superfood that contains antioxidants 6,000 times more effective than vitamin E. The science behind the Integris Diet System strongly suggests that it is the most technologically advanced weight loss system ever brought to the market. This synergistically blended four-product system contains proprietary ingredients and patented delivery systems that are exclusive only to Integris. As a company, we will spare no expense in order to provide the best that nutrition and science has to offer. We are especially pleased that UDA volleyball selected Integris as its official supplier of nutritional supplements. This is because we have products that will help people with their energy, stamina and performance.

The rare opportunity to market an array of truly effective, patented, one-of-a-kind, nutritional products, is attracting a host of health practitioners, veteran network marketers, as well as serious income opportunity seekers from virtually every walk of life. It is easy to see why the lucrative benefits of the Integris 74% maximum payout, compensation plan are also examined. This industry leading, unilevel plan pays out 54% with full compression, through six levels of sales volume and an additional 20% to leaders through generational overrides and bonuses. One of the most attractive aspects is that it only requires the development of three leadership "legs" in order to maximize the plan and potentially earn 3%, "non-blocking," to infinity override.

Combine all of this with the fact that the company has one of the most duplicable marketing systems available coupled with an outstanding company directed training program, and you truly have a "winning combination" worthy of anyone's serious consideration.

**Integris International, L.C.C., 8312 Sterling, Irvine, TX 75063**
**Phone: (972) 929-7307, Fax: (972) 929-3737, Web site: www.integriscorp.com**

# INTELLIGENT
# NUTRIENTS®

## CREATING WELL BEING

Intelligent Nutrients (IN) offers environmentally and nutritionally innovative lifestyle products and a lucrative business opportunity. IN opened its doors in October 1995 with the goal of creating a healthier world, and a mission *"to provide a healthy, eco-logical lifestyle with an economic business opportunity."*

Created by the founder of Aveda Corporation, the leader in plant-based hair, skin, make-up and Pure-Fume® products, Horst Rechelbacher created an opportunity to offer beauty and wellness from the inside out-intelligent.

Growing up in Austria with his mother who was an herbalist, Horst learned at an early age that plants have an innate power to heal. A consummate ecological entrepreneur, he built a way for people to utilize plants to create better health for themselves, the people around them and the planet--via network marketing. Individuals aren't the only ones who profit through IN's business opportunity. Service-based businesses such as salons, health clubs, massage associations and doctor's offices have also increased their bottom line as distributors of IN lifestyle products.

## FREEDOM TO GROW

IN lets you be in business for yourself--not by yourself. Distributors don't need a Ph.D in nutrition or be an expert in herbal supplements to begin changing their lifestyle for the better with IN. When distributors and customers need guidance, IN provides sales, distribution and ecological expertise.

We provide tools like a comprehensive information and communication service, weekly distributor conference calls for leadership development and training, automatic shipments for distributor convenience and Internet services for distributor training.

The IN plan combines our expertise and our distributors' experience. Whether it's long or short-term income, freedom to duplicate uplines as many times as a distributor wants, income rewards at all distributor levels, preferred customer options, product discounts, or the option of simply retailing the IN products, the IN plan has it.

## INTEGRITY

IN offers superior-quality nutritional supplements you can believe in. Our products unite ancient global wisdom with advanced science. They are crafted from innovative blends of essential vitamins, minerals and phytonutrients, and include certified organic, clinically-tested and ecologically-sound ingredients.

Everything IN does reflects an environmental commitment. IN products are grown by sustainable harvesting methods and are guaranteed to be free from pesticides, synthetic additives, artificial colors and dyes, preservatives and petrochemicals. They are non-irradiated and are not animal tested. Even eco-logical packaging, sales materials, and business practices minimize waste. IN is also affiliated with The Natural Step, a non-profit environmental education organization from Sweden, which works to build an ecologically and economically sustainable society. And IN celebrates every new distributor that joins us by planting a tree in their name.

Intelligent Nutrients provides you not only products, but a philosophy, not just another networking opportunity, but a set of values. We give distributors and customers a way to do well, feel well, and see green.

It's an idea whose time has come. Dozens of publications across the country and the world have featured IN's products and green business opportunity in their pages, including *Vouge, Mirabella, Allure, America Spa, and US News and World Report*. And interest is growing both at home and abroad.

**Intelligent Nutrients**--products and a company you can believe in.

**Intelligent Nutrients, Inc., 321 Lincoln Street NE, Minneapolis, MN 55413**
**Phone: (800) 311-5635, Web site: www.intelligentnutrients.com**

Westlake Village, California--Jafra Cosmetics International embraces new ownership. In partnership with Clayton, Dubilier & Rice, the Senior Management team at Jafra took the company private. Jafra's Partners in Success, Senior Management team, includes Ron Clark, chairman and chief executive, and Gonzalo Rubio, president and chief operating officer. Ron and Gonzalo together have over 60 years of experience with the leading companies in direct sales and cosmetics industry. Joining Ron and Gonzalo, Rip Mason brings expertise in his role as vice chairman and general counsel.

Ron's enthusiasm for Jafra began during the mid-80s when he served as U.S. president of Jafra Cosmetic International alongside co-founder Jan Day. For many years, he has held close the dream of returning to Jafra to carry the torch that Jan and Frank first ignited in August, 1956.

Never dreaming they would expand beyond Southern California, Jan and Frank Day launched Jafra Cosmetics from their Malibu home over forty years ago. The Days founded Jafra Cosmetics with a set of core values, top-quality products and a philosophy: a "sharing and caring" environment where a woman could build a career as an independent contractor, according to her own needs and at her own pace.

The first skin care class was held on August 6, 1956, and the word spread far and wide about the Jafra products, the concept and the opportunity.

The original product line consisted of nine skin care products and generated such interest during the 50s that Jafra classes were being held in homes in several states.

The 60s heralded a decade of milestones for Jafra--the opening of its own laboratory in Santa Monica; the development of a level for high achievers, the District Director program, and the creation of the Spanish Division.

By the 70s, Jafra had attracted the interest of growth-oriented companies and became a subsidiary of Gillette in 1973. Corporate offices were first established in Canoga Park and moved to Westlake Village in 1980. Jafra's unique selling proposition expanded internationally to South America, Europe and Mexico during this decade.

The 80s brought several enhancements to the product line and the program. Leadership conferences, incentive trips and new products all contributed to this explosive era and further extended Jafra's market share.

In 1998, Jafra welcomed new owners, Clayton Dubilier & Rice, as partners along with Senior Management. Clayton, Dubilier & Rice, (C.D.R.) has strong credentials with investments in 26 companies whose aggregate sales exceed $20 billion.

Jafra has maintained consistent growth over the past 42 years and has reached over $230 million worldwide. Over 255,000 Jafra consultants share Jafra products and the Jafra career opportunity worldwide.

Ron, Gonzalo and Rip, are dedicated to the success of Jafra. They reach out over the miles to share their commitment, extend the Jafra opportunity, and grow the Jafra family. Growth will continue with a focus on new markets, including expansion into Brazil and Poland. Additionally, Jafra will continue to offer state-of-the-art products, with a continuing and growing commitment to product research and development. For instance, in May 1998, Jafra launched improved sun care products containing Parsol 1789, providing protection from both UVA and UVB rays. Additionally, Jafra introduced sunless tanners for a sun-kissed look without time in the sun. Other product extensions include Jafra Clear Pore Clarifier and Clear Blemish Treatment containing Salicylic Acid for deep pore cleaning.

For Jafra Cosmetics International, this is the advent of another memorable, lively decade.

**Jafra Cosmetics International, 2451 Townsgate Road, Westlake Village, CA 91361**

*Victor Kiam*

*Lady* **REMINGTON** is doing business in the United States, United Kingdom, Puerto Rico, and Singapore, capitalizing on the growing interest and need for wardrobe and budget-stretching. *Lady* **REMINGTON** invented Versatility, a new concept demonstrated in Accessorizing Idea Shows by fashion advisors. The in-home or office seminar approach is rewarding to hostesses and the free, easy training, no investment, high income and flexible hours (plus free jewelry) has high appeal to people who want extra income, part or full-time opportunities, management careers or a way to job-test while still employed. The company has been in business for over 25 years. Contributing to their great success is a 100% Lifetime Exchange Guarantee and a strong working relationship with designers and manufacturers dedicated to innovation and quality. Beautiful catalogs, vacations, generous bonuses, and the fact that Accessorizing Idea Shows are fun to do and lead to high retention of managers.

## A Mission To Believe

Our Mission is to be the best fashion jewelry buying experience in the world. Today's educated consumers demand more than just a quality product, they demand quality service. The personal touch of a fashion advisor is the key to our mission. Through Accessorizing Shows, fashion advisors provide customers a convenient way to shop and show them how to stretch every dollar spent on accessories. This "added value" to our product, your personal service, combined with our Lifetime Replacement Guarantee, help us to become the best fashion jewelry buying experience in the world.

## Business Background

The purpose of this brief write-up is to furnish facts for business-oriented people who want information about the growth performance of a company offering opportunity to have their own recession-proof, high income business. In 1986, the company was acquired by Victor Kiam (the man who liked the razor so much he bought the company). *Lady* **REMINGTON** is an aggressive, stable, well-financed company with extensive plans for growth, domestically and internationally.

## Leadership And Growth

*Lady* **REMINGTON's** growth has been remarkable and the result is the envy of many in the direct sales and service industry. Ron Hacker, our president, Shirley Lewis, our executive vice president; and many other executives have been with *Lady* **REMINGTON** for 12 years or more. Those who have compared the income potential, marketing program, product, service, promotion activity, training and support, know why retention is so high. In all areas, *Lady* REMINGTON is highly competitive.

*Lady* **REMINGTON** is a member in excellent standing of the Direct Selling Association and abides by its Code of Ethics.

## Unusual Customer Service

We offer a toll free 800# to all *Lady* **REMINGTON** hostesses and customers to promptly service their questions or needs. In addition to a unique Lifetime Replacement Guarantee on all pieces in the *Lady* **REMINGTON** Jewelry Collection, the company gives a $5 (U.S.) Certificate if any item has to be returned. Pieces are replaced, not repaired and, if not available, a Gift Certificate for regular value of the returned piece is given regardless of the price paid. The *Lady* **REMINGTON** Save Plan has high appeal to customers who delight in learning how to stretch their wardrobes as well as their budget. And, the Hostess Program is extremely generous, too.

**Lady REMINGTON Fashion Jewelry, 818 Thorndale Ave., Bensenville, IL 60106-1102, Phone: (630) 860-3323, Fax: (630) 860-5634, E-Mail: info@ladyremingtonjewelry.com**
**Web site: http//www.ladyremingtonjewelry.com**

**Maria Baccari**

**Anthony Calandrelli**

Latasia & Company, founded in 1987, is changing the face of network marketing by offering distributors more than just products and a business opportunity; they offer an innovative approach to achieving financial independence while keeping their lives in balance.

For over 11 years, Latasia has helped women enhance their image and express their unique style with a line of high quality fashion jewelry. Now they have enhanced their business opportunity with the launching of the Perfect Balance Program in January of 1998. It encompasses 9 state-of-the-art nutritional and personal care products and a comprehensive approach to bringing health, well-being and balance into our lives. "We offer solutions to the most pressing issues of today," explains founder, Jane Deuber. "The need to reduced stress, improve health, increase self-esteem and live a more balanced life."

For over 11 years. Latasia has averaged 20% annual growth and enjoys a loyalty among distributors that is unique within the industry. Their long term success can be attributed to their commitment to quality, service and the success of their distributors. "This has not been a race to see how quickly we can build and then get out of the business," shared founder Mario Villacres. "Our intention is to build a company that makes a significant difference in the lives of our distributors."

Latasia's two product lines offer distributors the best of both worlds. The jewelry is an easy sale that generates immediate income and builds confidence while the Perfect Balance Program generates repeat sales of consumable products and build strong customer loyalty. What makes the Perfect Balance Program so effective is Latasia's Daily Balance Wheel. A simple and effective approach to maintaining balance and well-being. "There are three distinct daily eyeless that we all experience," Jane shares. "Our products are formulated to meet the changing needs of these cycles, for optimum physical and mental well-being. From Aromatherapy products that soothe the spirit, to nutritional products that energize and nourish the body, Latasia's Perfect Balance Program and products offer a simple formula for creating a happy, healthy life. By helping people make a shift in the way they live their lives each day, we inspire lasting change that builds strong customer loyalty."

Latasia has also piloted a unique fundraising program that enables distributors to work with local non-profit organizations to raise funds. Through the sale of their exclusive "Caring Pin," distributors give back to their community while building their business. "I believe every company should offer a philanthropic program." Explains Jane. "It's a win win for everyone!"

Latasia's marketing plan is designed to benefit distributors at every level. It features generous distributor discounts, immediate rebate bonuses, substantial overrides, personal and group volume bonuses, compressed level calculation, no breakaways and an infinity bonus that ensures long term income for leaders. When a distributor makes an immediate profit through the sale of products and sponsoring, they gain confidence and practical experience that will carry them to the next level of leadership.

As Latasia approaches the next millennium, they will continue their commitment to quality, integrity and service, while continuing to meet the changing needs of society. The future belongs to companies who do more than move products, but inspire a "lifestyle" shift that leads to lasting success and personal well-being.

**Latasia & Company, 225 Lighthouse Ave., Monterey, CA 93940**
**Phone: (800) 873-3075, Fax: (831) 646-0230, E-mail: latasia@latasia.com**

LEADING*minds*™
INTERNATIONAL
*An Environment for Forward Thinking People*

*Sabrina Wei*

*Derrick Rodgers*

Sabrina Wei and Derrick Rodgers have a huge task ahead of themselves, establishing a company in an industry that is evolving constantly at break-neck speed. Network marketing has come to be recognized as an efficient and profitable method of moving products. The industry has grown and society has learned to embrace it as the trend towards the 21st century. Technology has given rise to new compensation plans that allow fairer treatment of a distributor's efforts. Behold the birth of a new concept in network marketing. Leading Minds International represents the best that modern day networking, technology and products have to offer. It is time to make a difference.

Leading Minds is steeped in the belief that products must be high impact, value based and perform as promised. They must be products that people would want to consume, with or without an attached opportunity.

Their product portfolio is geared towards today's society, starting with an "Age Defiance" line that is designed to help people feel good and look younger; high quality exclusive nutritional supplements; skin care; salon quality hair/body care as well as other high impact products, and telecommunications with long distance service; cellular phones and Internet access; fine collectibles that are some of the most prestigious name brands around the world, as well as financial services that create wealth, and establish security.

In addition to all this, there needs to be an up-front, weekly compensation plan that rewards the distributor today to the degree that he/she can make a living, coupled with a monthly compensation plan that creates a long term residual income from the repeat sales of high impact, value based products.

What does it take to put together an opportunity like this? Professional parties, technology consultants, product formulators and exclusive vendors, outsourced fulfillment, marketing and imaging team, and financial strength that come together based upon the vision and the abilities of the people at the helm. Both Derrick and Sabrina have an ample supply of both. With a successful background in insurance and real estate development, Derrick has served on the board of directors and became a top money earner with a $200 million network marketing company. Sabrina has been with a recognized, top three, world renowned accounting firm, runs her own investment consulting business out of Hong Kong and Taiwan, and has been to the very top of two network marketing companies. They have both taken everything they learned from Corporate America, as well as over 20 years of combined network marketing experience in order to create Leading Minds International.

Very few start-ups show as much potential as Leading Minds International has. "No company can become a world class contender unless it takes on a team building concept," she says. "Because we are willing to be honest with ourselves, we know our strengths and weaknesses. This way we are able to target what areas we need enhanced as a company and go out and find the best to take us to the top."

A veritable who's who of industry insiders are participating in the formation and start-up of this fledgling company. A company that promises to have sound management, incredible products and a sizzling compensation plan all leads toward that line "If you build it, they will come." And that's exactly what they are doing. LMI also has a leadership program that edifies the field leaders and allows them to share in company profits.

"Give me a place to stand and I can move the world!" Leading Minds International is the new kid on the network marketing block and they are definitely taking a stand to make a difference.

**Leading Minds International, Inc., Washington Technical Center, 923 Powell Avenue SW, Renton, WA 98055 Phone: (425) 793-9225, (888) 275-4LMI, Fax: (425) 793-9555**

## LONGEVITY NETWORK, LTD.
*Creating Health, Wealth & Happiness for the World™*

*Adi Song*

Welcome. Our passion punches no time clock. The size of our ideas will blow your mind. Our culture is based on family values. We'll do whatever it takes. Welcome to Longevity in health. Welcome to Longevity in business. Welcome to Longevity Network.

Longevity Network launched its marketing and sales campaign in the spring of 1994. For nearly four years prior to that launch, the CEO/President team of Longevity, Jim and Adi Song, passionately put their hearts, minds, and souls into building the core of Longevity's business--its incredible broad spectrum product line. They worked with some of the world's best nutritional, health, skin, body and hair care professionals to develop cutting-edge products with the mission of bringing results and positive changes to millions of consumers worldwide. Knowing full well that without great products there would be no repeated sales volume and thus, no fruits of business Longevity for the people who would make life-changing decisions to share in the Longevity cause for *Creating Health, Wealth & Happiness for the World™*.

Next, Jim and Adi Song created a business infrastructure that all of its independent entrepreneurs could utilize and depend on. They created a corporate culture based on family values so that people everywhere would be supported and have fun as Longevity entrepreneurs. They created this infrastructure for their distributors in the very same way that they nurture their family through constant love, understanding, positive thinking, caring, generosity, education and humanity.

Longevity is a member of the Henderson Chamber of Commerce, the Better Business Bureau and the Direct Selling Association. Longevity has also been featured in *Success* magazine, the best selling book *Wave 3: Way to Building Your Downline*, was voted "Best Company of the Year" four years in a row (1995-1998) by the highly regarded publication *MLM Insider*, and was named 1997 Company of the Year by *Profit Now Magazine*.

Jim and Adi Song are perfectly clear that there are five elements that make up a great home-based business income opportunity. From each element there must be consistent high quality standards in order for the independent entrepreneurial distributor force to enjoy prosperity and longevity. These are:

### 1. THE MANAGEMENT 2. THE PRODUCT LINE
### 3. THE PAY PLAN 4. THE SUPPORT SYSTEMS
### 5. THE "MAGIC"

Longevity Network is proud to be acknowledged by many well-recognized experts as a company which has been painstakingly built and continues to enhance and improve all five elements. Longevity's reputation is that of a company whose character has always represented consistent integrity, values, morals, ethics, and continued education. This distinction is ever-growing and touching the hearts of tens of thousands of people who have joined the Longevity cause--respected people who spread the word about Longevity to the people they know and meet.

**Longevity Network, Ltd., 5 Longevity Drive, Henderson, NV 89014 U.S.A.**
**Phone: (702) 454-7000, Fax: (702) 435-4786**

Mannatech Inc. is a well established network marketing company based in Coppell, Texas, blazing new trails in glyconutritionals, while changing the way people think about health care and wellness. It's an exciting place to be with a highly motivated team of more than 450,000 independent associates and proprietary products backed by scientific validation. Mannatech™ is well positioned to become a dominant force in the multi-billion dollar health and nutrition industry.

Utilizing one of today's most effective distribution system--network marketing--Mannatech is led by a strong, experienced management team committed to building a successful international company, and an award-winning scientific team dedicated to continued innovative research and development. Complementing these elements is a proven marketing plan. In November 1998, the company marked the beginning of its international expansion by opening operations in Australia.

Research and development of carbohydrate-based products is what puts Mannatech at the forefront of nutritional supplement companies in a projected multi-billion dollar industry. Rather than attempting to develop synthetic carbohydrates as drug companies are doing, Mannatech has developed naturally-occurring, plant-derived, carbohydrate-based products.

Mannatech's products are designed to use nutrients working through normal physiology to maintain optimal health through improved nutrition. The foundation of all Mannatech products is centered on the use of Ambrotose® complex. This patent-pending complex was developed by Mannatech researchers and is available only through the company. It is utilized as a stand-alone dietary support product, as a key ingredient in combination with other beneficial food components, and is the primary component in a unique line of skin care products.

In 1996, the American Naturopathic Medical Association (ANMA) presented its highest scientific honor of recognition to Bill McAnnalley, Ph.D., research pharmacologist, and H. Reg McDaniel, MD, pathologist for the development of Ambrotose® complex, and the subsequent application for patent. ANMA is the largest association for natural health care practitioners in the United States.

Whether you are a world-class athlete, a weekend warrior or just someone who wants to enjoy optimal health, Mannatech's exclusive products can enhance your life. Mannatech believes that health conscious people should be rewarded, not penalized, for their approach to health. The company has contracted with International Benefits Association (IBA) to offer four MannaCare health plans to provide the small business owner or entrepreneur with the benefit of alternative care, plus traditional coverage at affordable prices.

Mannatech can also help provide the extra income you've been looking for and the independence you've dreamed about. Mannatech's innovative compensation plan is so generous it has been rated among the best in the business by the trade publication *MLM Insider*. Even if your goal is simply to supplement your income, there's a place in Mannatech for you.

The company is committed to seeing their independent associates succeed. That's why they've put an array of effective business building tools and information at their disposal. You don't have to be a super salesman or research scientist--Mannatech has the expertise and shares it with associates. Among the proven, effective tools the company offers are: ◆International Cell-Talk LIVE Recruiting Calls **(800) 820-6004** or **(800) 626-9374** 9:30 pm (CT) on Tuesday and 7:30 pm (CT) on Thursday - Spanish: 8:00 pm (CT) on Wednesday at **(800) 261-3209**
◆24-hour Training Modules **(615) 733-0025** ◆24-hour Toll-Free Information Line **(800) 832-0797**
◆Fax-on-Demand Scientific Review **(972) 304-9405**
◆MECS (Mannatech Education & Communication System) **(888) 867-4180**
◆Physicians' conference call for registered health care professionals

324

*James Ridinger*

Many people are now owning a business and working for themselves, to reach a higher standard of living, enhanced quality of life and peace of mind afforded by real financial security. However, owning a business often involves enormous risk and large capital outlays--intimidating obstacles for most people. Unfortunately, opportunities such as franchises are not within practical reach of the average person, and many home-based businesses offer little or no chance to achieve a professional income level. For these challenges, Market America presents the solution.

It is Market America's mission to provide the highest quality market-driven products to consumers through its unique UnFranchise® system, designed for the average person to succeed. Market America provides individuals with a proven business plan, tools, products and systems to achieve their desired levels of financial success. The company has identified the significant challenges of risk and large capital outlays that face people and manufacturers, crafting this resolution into this country's most powerful home-based business opportunity.

Market America is a debt-free, publicly traded product brokerage company based in Greensboro, North Carolina. The company was founded in 1992 by President and CEO, James "JR" Ridinger, who had previously served for over 22 years as a sales representative, consultant and executive in the direct sales industry. Ridinger's vision was to develop a program to address challenges facing direct sales companies, products, marketing plans and independent contractors, thereby creating a system where companies and individuals can flourish.

The embodiment of this vision is Market America's business development plan, the UnFranchise® system, which combines the best attributes of franchising and network marketing while eliminating the weaknesses of each. This plan is similar to a franchise, offering a proven business plan, management and marketing tools, training, and systemization, along with an organized structure for business growth. However, it is called the UnFranchise® because there are no franchise fees or ongoing royalties to pay, nor are their any territorial limits on Market America UnFranchise® owners as to where they may operate a business.

It is through this system that Market America has maintained a distributor retention rate continually exceeding industry standards. The company also leads the industry with optimal commission payouts, standardized training and refined tools for business growth. Today, Market America is a thriving, multinational company with a growing distributor base and projected annualized sales exceeding $124 million.

The hub of the company's product brokerage is **Market America's Mall Without Walls.** This virtual Mall makes available a wide variety of high quality, market-driven products and services for sale and distribution by UnFranchise owners.

Central to product retailing is Market America's **Preferred Customer Program**. This program helps develop one-to-one relationships between distributors and their best customers through collecting information to better serve these customers. The results are loyal customers with long-term buying habits, better customer service and more profits for distributors.

To promote distributor success, Market America has developed accessible, standardized distributor training through **The National Meeting, Training, and Seminar System (NMTSS)**, a comprehensive business training and support network of meetings and events throughout North America. Distributor participation is overwhelming, illustrated by Market America's Annual International Convention, which in 1998 brought over 15,000 in attendance.

Market America's **Management Performance Compensation Plan (MPCP)** is unique and powerful, developed to reward UnFranchise owners for retail sales and helping others succeed through solid management and supervision.

**Market America, 7605 Business Park Drive, Greensboro, NC 27409**
**Phone: (336) 605-0040, Fax: (336) 605-0041**

**Robert Bolduc**

Matol Botanical International Ltd. is a growing international company co-founded in 1984 by J.F. Robert Bolduc, Matol's Co-Founder, Chairman & Chief Executive Officer. Headquartered in Montreal, Quebec, Canada, Matol offers health and nutrition products through its 300,000 worldwide members.

Matol has accumulated over $1 billion in sales worldwide since its inception and has sold over 26 million bottles of Km™, its flagship liquid nutritional product. Matol has operations in 11 countries on five continents which includes the U.S., Canada, Mexico, United Kingdom, Indonesia, Thailand, Nigeria, Taiwan, Singapore, New Zealand and Australia.

Matol's corporate mission is to 'Impact World Health' and nobody supports this concept more than the CEO, J.F. Robert Bolduc. "Even though being financially successful is important, there is nothing more rewarding than positively affecting someone's life," says Bolduc. "When I read letters from our distributors that say how one of our products helped them or someone they love, it really makes me feel that we have helped make a difference in someone's life."

This 'corporate culture' is endemic to all of Matol's people from the newest distributor to the Matol corporate executives and staff. This is what makes Matol such a special company in the network marketing industry. The sense of belonging to a 'family' while realizing your dreams attracts a lot of people. "Everyone wants to make money but they also want to feel that they are part of something special," says Bolduc. Matol's success is due in large part to their culture and philosophy of 'Give and Receive.'

Bolduc says their success is also due to Matol's willingness to ensure the integrity of their products, people and programs. A firm commitment to quality made Matol, and specifically Km™, the success of the industry. Now, along with the Biomune OSF™ product line, he intends to catapult Matol and its distributors to the 'Tip of the top of the industry.'

The corporate culture and commitment to excellence has attracted both seasoned distributors and experienced industry executives who see the potential of Matol. They feel confident that Matol is not some fly by night company but a 'serious nutrition company with a healthy attitude; around for decades to come. Bolduc says, "Matol is the oldest new company in the industry which is demonstrated by the enthusiasm of the home office staff."

No one exemplifies this more than Matol's Vice President of Marketing, Dan McCormick, who has earned over $7 million in the network marketing industry as a distributor. His expertise and experience are a vital part of Matol's future success. "Who better to lead the marketing division than someone who has been there," Bolduc says. "He knows exactly what a distributor wants and needs to be successful. His experience is priceless and he has the integrity needed for this position."

Not only is Matol committed to quality people but to quality products. Their state-of-the-art manufacturing and bottling plant, quality control lab, research and development facility, received an award at the First International Congress on Homeopathy & Alternative Medicine for 'The Laboratory which contributed the most to the Research and Development of Efficient Products.' Matol never launches a product unless it meets their high quality standards and passes all of their rigorous quality control tests.

The full story behind Matol's success begins with Karl Jurak, who developed the Km™ formula way back in 1922. J.F. Robert Bolduc believes that the past is important to their success and he has written a book chronicling the company's history which pays tribute to everyone involved with Matol's success over the years. As the sleeve reads, "*Matol Moments* is one book with many stories. From one man's personal vision, to the treasured memories of the countless people that shared in a dream, Matol moments is a journey of discovery--and the journey has just begun."

**Matol Botanical International, Ltd., 1111 - 46e Avenue, Lachine, Quebec Canada  H8T 3C5**

*Katherine Gardner*

Throughout the mid 1980s, Multiples fashion knits were available globally in department stores, military exchanges and boutiques. By 1990, it became apparent that single working parents and dual career households had become common, and the traditional 9 to 5 work schedule inhibited the achievement of quality family life. This situation and Kate's love of helping women flourish and grow, led to the decision to sell Multiples through the Home Show "Party Plan" forum. This innovative response to changing lifestyle needs of women has become a successful solution for women seeking the flexibility a home-based business offers.

For Kate, Multiples At Home is an extension of her personal and professional mission to motivate, stimulate and grow the collective wisdom of women.

In 1999, Multiples At Home celebrates ten years as a direct selling company. Over these years, the consistent commitment to offer style, quality and "cutting-edge" fashion in affordable, easy-care garments has been the product foundation. Multiples is proud to fill a dynamic market niche and is backed by one of the nation's leading apparel designer manufacturers, Jerell, Inc. This relationship allows Multiples the opportunity and resources to adapt as fashions change.

Multiples is a compatible collection of versatile knit styles, including pants, tops, skirts, jackets and styling accessories. Also available are figure-flattering garments for plus and petite women. The "original" Multiples product line provided an opportunity for each garment to be styled in "Multiple" ways. Although this opportunity to create magic through styling remains inherent to the product line, Multiples fashions have grown far beyond this initial concept. Today, Multiples include garments designed for career, casual and evening wear. Many styles adapt easily to women experiencing weight fluctuation, and also, fashionable maternity wear.

Across the nation, women have also discovered how easily Multiples travel. Just roll them up! A simple carry-on bag is all that is required for a week-long trip! The secret to packing light is seven easy-fitting styles that create 20 terrific looks, This amazing 7 = 20 styling progression is detailed in step-by-step sketches and a comprehensive set of styling cards. An additional proud feature of Multiples is the "made in the USA" label. The high performance fabric used to manufacture Multiples is milled in the Carolinas of 50 percent premium California combed cotton and 50 percent pill-free polyester. The combination of fabric for the 21st century and the Multiples Basic Color palette includes: black, white, ivory, navy, bluebonnet, red and jade. Additional fashion collections are introduced each season offering new color trends in solids, prints, stripes, patterns and specialty fabrics.

The opportunity to sell Multiples is available to women across the country. There are no educational or employment requirements. The women who represent Multiples receive the title of fashion consultant and are trained to provide customer convenience and service through small Home Fashion Shows. The incentive for a customer to hostess a fashion show is her opportunity to receive garments FREE and HALF PRICE. The incentive for a fashion consultant to demonstrate Multiples is the immediate income she earns with each sale.

There is no ceiling on income for Multiples fashion consultants. Every consultant has a sponsor who helps her design a business plan to meet her income goals. In addition to the extraordinary opportunity to earn 25% to 40% sales commission, consultants may also build a career in field management.

The number of Multiples fashion consultants are growing from coast to coast. Call today and find out how to get started.

Multiples At Home is a proud member of the Direct Selling Association.

**Multiples At Home, 1431 Regal Row, Dallas, TX 75247, Phone: (800) 727-8875, E-mail: mltplsusa@aol.com**

*Marina Buckley*

Network marketing uses the principal of word-of-mouth advertising. Product information is shared through personal endorsements and the independent distributor replaces the traditional middlemen. Distributors earn money through their retail sales and commissions based on the sales volume of others they have recruited to their organization. You care about your health and would like to earn income. What do you do next? Follow our duplicable program and achieve the success you work for! Natural Connections distributors can earn Fast Start, Infinity and Generation Override bonuses in addition to commissions seven levels deep!

You can make a difference; a better, healthier life for yourself and others. Natural Connections, Inc. (NCI) products, services and business opportunity are designed to be of great value to you.

Practicing physicians have seen first-hand what a fantastic difference Natural Connections comprehensive health promoting nutritional vitamins can make and we invite you to discover for yourself what our safe, scientifically advanced formulas can do for your health.

Medical leaders in cultures around the world have been asked for their guidance in helping maintain and restore health, joining the best of tried and true old world knowledge with new research and clinical studies. Natural Connections brings you the finest vitamins and formulas available, including unique patented ingredients and exclusive, proprietary combinations of herbs and nutrients. Physicians, biochemists and other scientists have designed these synergistic blends from years of research and development.

People everywhere are looking for cures or treatments of their conditions, diseases or symptoms and many simply want to live healthier, longer lives. You can help your body be at its best with a Natural Connections nutritional program of modern non-prescription vitamin, mineral, herb and enzyme formulations. Designed with your needs in mind, product examples include: longevity, heart disease and cancer risk, high cholesterol, high triglycerides, weight loss, prostate conditions and cancer, lungs, heart, joints, memory, kidneys, skin, muscles, bones, artery, sports, men, women, girls, boys, adults and children. You can take advantage of our online computer data search and reference capabilities, detailed product information and pictures, links and featured American and international health and medical news and order through our secured checkout.

Our Founder and Medical Director, Richard E. Buckley, MD, has spent many years researching the effects of nutritional supplementation. Through extensive research and world travel to ancient healing centers and rain forests, Dr. Buckley has seen first-hand the strong benefits of plants, minerals, enzymes, vitamins and other nutritional substances. His conclusions resulted in our line of products based on clinical studies and traditional wisdom. The introduction of nutritional formulations to a medical practice in 1993 met with such overwhelming success and patient benefit that this became the genisys for Natural Connections.

Please see distributor brochure for more opportunity information and our product catalogue and product brochure for more information on the full Natural Connections line of products including: Memory Max (with Ginkgo biloba), Heart Smart (with Coenzyme Q-10), Prostate Specific (with Saw Palmetto), Joint Specific (with glucosamine), Winter Formula (with Echinacea and OPC-85), Rahab Special, Executive Stress, Women's Special, Weight-Less and many more. Join Natural Connections in providing information and quality products for those who want to take an active part in their health and well-being and earn extra income!

**Natural Connections, 301 West Harford Street, Milford, PA 18337 USA**
**Corporate Offices, Phone: (570) 296-2020, Phone Orders: (800) 297-7341, Fax Orders: (570) 296-4767**
**Web site: http://naturalconnections.com**

# NATURE'S OWN

*Magnus Ahlen*

**The Company and the Vision** - Nature'sOwn is an international network marketing organization that, through the sharing of the Scandinavian vision of health, aims to improve the quality of life for their distributors and customers by developing and offering the best business opportunity and products available.

**The Business Opportunity** - Nature'sOwn offers a genuine business opportunity that can provide both personal freedom and financial independence. As a distributor in Nature'sOwn, you earn income through your own and your downline's sales of products. There is also a company bonus program that has a generous payout. Distributors have the opportunity to expand their earning potential by introducing others to the business and thereby making their downlines grow larger.

**The Marketing Plan** - The proven binary marketing plan makes it easy to start your Nature'sOwn business, full or part-time. There is a good chance to earn a fair income with as little as 5 to 10 hours work per week. The marketing plan is very easy to understand and there is no breakaway. Your downline will be yours forever.

**Education & Training** - Nature'sOwn has designed a comprehensive educational program to provide all distributors with marketing training and a thorough understanding of the products and their qualities. The company runs several training camps each year, under the management of both corporate trainers and distributors.

**The Products** - Nature'sOwn's goal is to be a leader in developing and selling the best weight management, nutritional, sport nutritional and personal care products. The company has created product groups in all these areas with the purpose to make you both look and feel good. Of course the products are environmentally friendly. They are also only possible to buy through Nature'sOwn's distributors.

**The Founders** - The owners of Nature'sOwn, Magnus Ahlen and Lars Murback, have been involved in international business for almost 25 years. Together they have recruited, educated and established distributors in different parts of the world. They started Nature'sOwn in 1993, and the company is now one of the leading network marketing companies in Scandinavia. In the USA, Nature'sOwn is in its establishing phase, which means that new American distributors can get a very high position in a stable and sound company. The U.S. headquarter's is located in Stratford, Connecticut.

**Research and Development** - Research and development is conducted in Sweden under the supervision of Dr. Ernst Nystrom, MD, the world renowned Endocrinologist. Dr. Nystrom is affiliated with the University Hospital in Gothenburg, Sweden. He is also the chairman of the Product Advisory Board. This knowledgeable group of specialists have the responsibility of assuring that Nature'sOwn's products are always at the forefront of research and that the products conform to the laws and regulations in each country of established distribution.

**The Business Ethics** - Nature'sOwn is a member of the Direct Selling Association and complies with the DSA Code of Ethics in every country where the company operates; at present eight with more soon to come.

**Nature'sOwn, 400 Long Beach Boulevard, Stratford, CT 06497**
**Phone: (800) 400-9868, or (203) 380-8900, Fax: (203) 380-1780**
**Web site: www.naturesownusa.com, E-mail: email@naturesownusa.com**

**Daniel Howells**

Nature's Sunshine Products, a direct selling company, manufactures and markets tableted and encapsulated herbal products, high quality natural vitamins, food supplements, skin care and other complementary products. It has marketing operations in the U.S., Brazil, Colombia, Mexico, Japan, South Korea, Canada, Venezuela, the United Kingdom, El Salvador, Guatemala, Costa Rica, Peru, Panama, Argentina, Ecuador, Honduras and Nicaragua. The company also has exclusive distribution agreements with selected companies in Australia, New Zealand, Malaysia and Norway.

In the Untied States, we are witnessing a veritable revolution in health care. Mounting costs of medical care and a more knowledgeable populace are promoting more and more individuals to take an active role in their own well-being. An often quoted study in the *The New England Journal of Medicine* notes that one in three Americans have used alternative therapy, with herbal supplements being one of the most popular.

The company distributes its products to consumers through an independent sales force comprised of managers and distributors. During the past three years, the growth rate of active distributors has increased significantly over that which was experienced in the past. The accelerated growth rate is primarily due to the continued expansion into new international markets in Latin America as well as Asia. Due to the increased awareness of the benefits of herbs, vitamins and supplements, new customers having a desire to purchase the products at wholesale cost instead of at retail cost sign up as distributors of the company. Distributors acquire not only specific product information but essential tips in the start-up of their business through extensive educational programs, which include, regional meetings, conventions, publications and videos. With this knowledge, they can help guide their customers to the right herbal product with an expertise and assurance generally unavailable in most retail outlets.

For the year ended 1997, the company achieved its eleventh straight year of record sales revenue and net income. In addition, the company completed the year with record levels of sales managers and distributors.

Nature's Sunshine has committed itself to manufacturing and distributing only the finest quality products in the natural health market. All raw materials that arrive at Nature's Sunshine for production are meticulously tested for optimum strength and purity. During the production process, continual checks are made to ensure against contamination of any kind. The company takes great pride in maintaining and operating its facilities in a manner that not only meets but exceeds industry standards for quality. While a strong market brings the challenge of increased competition, Nature's Sunshine is confident this product quality will keep us a leader in the herbal products market as it has for over 26 years.

Last year, 38 new product formulations were introduced. Among the new offerings were Ultimate Echinacea, two new diet formulations and a new line of personal care products. During NSP's most recent National Convention held in New Orleans, Louisiana, in August 1998, a new weight loss program and line of pure essential oils were introduced, bringing our product line total to well over 500.

Nature's Sunshine currently has 682,000 square feet of production, warehousing and office facilities and employs approximately 1,000 people. It is the dedication of Nature's Sunshine's people--both the employees and the independent sales force--that maintains its leading position in the marketplace. Every facet of the company's growth is based upon the solid foundation of qualified, motivated long-term employees and distributors who have the vision to see the company successfully into the 21st century.

**Nature's Sunshine Products, 75 East 1700 South, Provo, UT 84606**
**Phone: (801) 342-4300**

# Nest Entertainment

Organized in 1992, Nest Entertainment is the parent of a host of companies in the entertainment industry. Nest is dedicated to creating, producing, marketing and distributing the highest quality in-home family entertainment that reinforces moral values and builds character. Nest is moving forward rapidly to become the premier family entertainment company by the year 2000.

Nest products primarily are sold directly to customers through independent distributors via in-home demonstrations called Showcases and Yello Dyno® Power Houses. The demonstrations provide an environment where potential customers can view the products with their children and gain confidence in the value of the products before purchasing. Someone becomes a distributor by purchasing a $99 starter kit. There is no inventory requirement because all product purchases are shipped directly to the customer by Nest. Nest products also are sold through catalog sales, telemarketing and television infomercials as well as a few outside organizations and ministries.

Just as a nest is a safe haven for the young, Nest Entertainment strives to nurture and protect young children by producing fun, entertaining products that teach and strengthen positive ideals in children. Nest has four major product lines. It is the premier producer and distributor of the highly acclaimed, award-winning animated Bible story video series for the family that have been seen all over the world: *The Animated Stories from the New Testament*™ and *The Animated Stories from the Bible*™. Each video story is developed to be nondenominational and is reviewed at each stage of the production process by an Independent Advisory Board of recognized theologians whose sole responsibility is to ensure scriptural accuracy.

Nest's third product line is the *Animated Hero Classics*® series, which features stories about such heroes as George Washington, Abraham Lincoln, Thomas Edison, Florence Nightingale, Louis Pasteur, Pocahontas, Harriet Tubman and others.

Each animated video is designed to be an interactive learning experience and opens the door for life-enriching family discussions. Each comes with an activity book that helps children internalize the experience through games, puzzles, drawings and questions-and-answer exercises. Supplemental audio tapes and music videos also extend children's involvement with the stories.

The fourth product line features Yello Dyno, the kids' safety champion, who helps parents teach children how to protect themselves from dangerous people and situations. Product packs combine the power of videos, music and workbook activities to give children Yello Dyno's confidence-building way to safety.

Former Walt Disney Productions® director Richard Rich heads up the team at Rich Animation Studios in Burbank, California, a Nest subsidiary, which creates the high-quality animated stories for Nest Entertainment. Rich was instrumental in directing such beloved animated features as *The Rescuers, The Fox and the Hound, The Adventures of Winnie the Pooh,* and Nest's first full-length feature film, *The Swan Princess*™. Currently the studio is developing an animated theatrical feature from the award-winning production *The King and I.*

Nest Entertainment's management team, composed of experienced industry leaders from the direct selling and home video industries, is led by President and CEO Doug Martin, who was most recently vice chairman of Primerica Financial Services and president of Tupperware North America.

**Nest corporate headquarters is located at 6100 Colwell Blvd., Irving, TX 75039**
**For information about becoming an independent Nest distributor please call Toll-Free, (888) 454-3709**

**NETWORK ACTION COMPANY**

**How to organize yourself automatically and succeed faster**

New and experienced distributors have discovered a new and exciting way to get to their money goals faster. It's a simple, low-tech paper and pencil solution specially designed for network marketers called the **Business Builder Action Pack**. Distributors in the trenches, on the frontline, swear by the **Business Builder** because it works!

**How this amazing proven solution can make you rich**

The **Business Builder** helps people to systematically learn the business and keeps them organized. The best part is it's a proven template for action that makes it easy for you to know exactly what you need to do next to grow your business! That's why the **Business Builder** is the secret weapon of new and experienced distributors in more than 45 companies including everything from Prepaid Legal, Amway, Herbalife, NSA, Mary Kay, and dozens more.

How does it work? The **Business Builder** works because it helps you schedule your work and operate your business without confusion. It also lets you sit down and show someone exactly how to do their business step-by-step. This makes a tremendous difference in getting people to take action and stay in the business so that both you and they can profit.

The **Business Builder** is much more than a proven way to organize and operate your entire business out of one binder. It's so complete and easy to use that it comes with all the information and encouragement you or anyone in your organization, of any capacity or experience, needs to know to succeed in this business and make the most of their opportunity!

**Here's how to build a strong network marketing business**

First, treat your business like it's a goldmine!

That means work your business systematically, day-by-day. Dig actively like all successful business people do. Use the **Business Builder** to automatically learn and practice all the right business-like habits fast. Also encourage the people you sign up to do the same so that they can get a bigger commission check from the start and reach their income goals faster.

When your team uses the **Business Builder** to work step-by-step, everyone up and down the line is happier and automatically gets more done in less time. Communication and goal setting improves. Productivity goes up! Paychecks get bigger overnight!

**The key to getting to your money goals the easy way**

You can't succeed at anything without organizing your work. You can't build a house or write a book without scheduling the work in writing and doing it day-by-day to get the job done right. In short, you can't make a cake, plan a party, or build a business without writing down and scheduling what you're going to do, then taking action to do it.

The **Business Builder** is the missing ingredient in network marketing. It's the key to your long-term success because without it most people you sign up will quit before they figure out how to organize and operate their businesses this proven easy way. The **Business Builder** gives everyone in your organization a practical way to reach their income goals by getting more done in less time without stress, and without confusion or frustration.

**To hear distributors tell why they use the Business Builder call (512) 374-4701 or you can visit our Web site: www.networkaction.com. Or to order the Business Builder now call (800) 870-8034 Order with confidence. Includes a 30 day, try-it-out, write-in-it, Money Back Guarantee**

*Dee Mower*

*Tom Mower*

Neways International distributes healthy alternative and personal care products in fifty different countries. Located in Salem, Utah, it is a debt-free, privately held company headed by founders Tom and Dee Mower. It is firmly rooted in Tom's realization over ten years ago that many of the ingredients used in traditional cosmetics and personal care products were inferior and possibly dangerous. From an education in chemistry, experience in chemical production and distribution, and an abiding interest in herbology, Tom also knew that these potentially harmful or carcinogenic ingredients were commonly used "by everyone" because they were cheap, easily diluted, and universally available--a woefully inadequate recipe for producing personal care products. Believing that better alternatives could be found, Tom developed the philosophy of "researching the research" to formulate top-quality products other companies believed too difficult and too expensive to produce and distribute. He and his professional team of biochemists and leading herbalists in the United States, New Zealand and China, continually pour over thousands of studies and reports generated by the scientific community every year.

Neways' ten product lines are free from potentially carcinogenic or otherwise harmful ingredients, providing consumers with safe products for health, beauty and living. These lines include nutritional health supplements, skin care, hair care, personal hygiene, body contouring, nail care and dental care products, as well as cosmetics, household cleansers, and automotive performance additives. Neways and the Neways products were featured as future thinking and future caring products by CBS television and numerous other media in 1998.

Standing by these products are some of the world's top athletes, trainers and coaches. Believers in the Neways Opportunity and wide range of nutritional supplements and personal care products, 1996 Greco-Roman Wrestling Silver Medalist Matt Ghaffari, 1992 Decathlon Gold Medalist Robert Zmelik, and 1996 Olympic Women's Gymnastics Coach Bela Karolyi, all tout the efficacy of Neways products. Underpinning the diverse lines of safe Neways products is the strength and versatility of Neways itself. The corporate headquarters and primary manufacturing facilities located in Salem, Utah, are among the largest of their kind in the United States, and its manufacturing facility in Auckland, New Zealand, is the third largest maker of cosmetics and personal care products in the Southern hemisphere. Expanding its worldwide ability to produce and distribute its own products, Neways also maintains a production facility on the Volga River in Volgograd, Russia.

With assets totaling over $150 million in 1,400,000 square feet of offices, warehouses and manufacturing facilities, Neways currently has a presence in nearly 40 countries. Neways' worldwide sales topped $144 million in 1996 and $200 million in 1997, with over $300 million in sales for 1998. Neways is one of the fastest growing nutritional and personal care companies in the world, boasting approximate growth rates of 10 to 25 percent per month, thanks to its revolutionary products, debt-free status, and generous compensation plan. The Neways Multi-plex/Affinity Compensation Plan combines a dynamic, hybrid unilevel system with a powerful stairstep-breakaway plan laced with rapid, deep-paying infinity bonuses, meeting the immediate needs of beginners while rewarding the long term efforts of established leaders. The Multiplex Program is designed to reward new and developing distributors with a "quick check" for their beginning efforts. The Affinity Marketing Program, focused on large, fully developed downlines, is the "wealth-building" compensation program for network leaders. As an incentive to leaders who qualify through success, the Neways Car Bonus Program will make car payments up to a limit (beyond standard commissions) on any distributor car purchase.

With effective products, a stable international corporation, and a generous compensation plan, Neways continues to offer network marketers an outstanding vehicle for attaining a healthier lifestyle and achieving financial success.

**Neways International, 150 East 400 North, PO Box 651, Salem, UT 84653**
**Phone: (801) 423-7260, Fax: (801) 423-2350, Web site: www.neways.com**

*Ron Frederic*

*Dale Calvert*

Every once in awhile, a very unique network marketing company comes along with leadership that really understands what it takes to succeed in our industry. Its success has nothing to do with what kinds of products it sells. It has nothing to do with whether the company's compensation plan is a forced matrix, a breakaway plan, or a binary. It also doesn't matter much how high a percentage the company pays back to the distributors. Most MLM companies end up paying close to the same percentage in commissions, bonuses and incentives.

So what does influence a company's ultimate success? One key ingredient is building its people. After all, what is a network marketing company? It is a living, breathing organization of people. When a company that understands this comes along, it is wise to get out of its way.

NII is just such a company! This Georgetown, Kentucky-based company has leadership that really grasps and applies this principle. Ron Frederic and Dale Calvert, the corporate leadership of NII, not only understand this principle but also are building their company with this primary concept in mind. The company's slogan is, "Dedicated to Improving Your Image and Lifestyle." This is not a ploy to generate interest in the company--it is the underlying philosophy behind every decision made at the corporate level.

Ron Frederic, owner and NII president, was a key principal in building four successful corporations by the time he was 30. After divesting his stock in those companies, he semi-retired and spent the next 18 years in the ministry. Then, in 1990, Frederic started seeking another business. It was then he discovered network marketing and began investigating the concept. Frederic liked the fact that if a distributor built an organization correctly, it would pay that distributor for the remainder of his/her life.

After spending two years with another company and achieving the top level, Frederic struck out on his own. But not before he met a young man, Dale Calvert. For the last 15 years, Calvert has been involved in network marketing/direct sales. He has taught others what he's learned. He has written several training manuals and produced hundreds of audio/videotapes on the subject. When you talk to him, the recurring theme you'd encounter is that to construct a large organization, you must first build people. They, in turn, will build business.

Most network marketers think that to develop financial independence they must become professional salespeople. While it's true that a product must be moved, Calvert teaches that salespeople don't move products--leadership does! Developing leadership has been the focus from the beginning. Most people enter the network marketing industry with the skills, attitudes and leadership abilities to fail. Calvert designed support and training systems that help the average person develop the skills necessary for those who are now enjoying the success provided by the NII opportunity. The leadership concept is definitely working. The unified, duplicable training system Calvert devised has become NII's backbone to success. Nine out of ten distributors following the system report making money their very first week.

**New Image International, Inc., PO Box 1038, Georgetown, KY 40324**
**Phone: (502) 867-1895, Fax: (502) 863-5640, Web site: http://www.newimageint.com**

New Vision® International, Inc., a network marketing company, was incorporated by the Boreyko family in December 1994. It was established in honor of their late mother, Dottie Boreyko, who taught her family to "dream big dreams because small dreams had no magic." The founders, father Ben, and his children, Lynne, Karen, BK and Jason Boreyko, established the company with the purpose of creating a distributor friendly organization that would provide a positive growth environment for its members and employees. Based in Tempe, Arizona, New Vision distributes nutritional supplements and personal care products.

The Boreyko family has over twenty years experience in the network marketing industry and a track record that includes generating more than $200 million in sales for other network companies. The success they have already enjoyed laid the ground work for developing a business plan that included what they perceived to be the optimal tools for success: superior products, strong leadership, world class customer service and a fast, lucrative marketing plan. The central idea was to offer "the ultimate vehicle for the person who dares to dream."

New Vision International opened its doors in March of 1995 with a clear mission statement: "To enrich the quality of people's lives." Within six months the company's revenues grew to $500,000 per month, while remaining debt-free. Last year, the company generated almost $200 million in revenue. New Vision has successfully integrated the traditional concept of network marketing into a business that leverages the concept of distributor-based marketing with the added tools and technology to facilitate rapid sales of nutritional, weight management and personal care products. Its distributor compensation plan is unequaled in the industry. Currently there are over 700,000 New Vision independent distributors nationwide. In a *Success* magazine article featuring the Boreyko brothers, Jason commented that people in network marketing tend to move from company to company looking for a home. According to BK, New Vision believes its members have found a home in a company with a top pay plan and the right products for today's consumer. Driven by the public's demand for excellence in dietary supplements, New Vision offers a wide range of products. Every product is formulated to the highest level of quality through the use of cutting edge technologies that extract and deliver the rarest and best ingredients available in the market today. The star product is Essential Minerals. Essential Minerals is 100 percent plant source minerals, totally dissolved in an ionic state. These plant source minerals have been proven by a leading independent laboratory to contain approximately 65 major and trace minerals. Other products include nutritional supplements, sports supplements for individuals with a more intense level of activity, 40-30-30 Zone nutrition products and personal care products.

It seems the combination of destiny, luck and timing brought five surviving family members together in the network marketing environment, and allowed them to become successful. The Boreyko siblings know that a lifetime of exposure to the network marketing industry has given them a solid foundation and first hand knowledge of what it takes to be the best in this field. The Boreyko's formed New Vision with the triple cornerstone of "Honesty, Integrity and Loyalty." They propelled these standards into an unprecedented rise to prominence as the nation's leading interactive nutritional marketing and distribution company. Today, the Boreyko children lead the way for thousands of people who dare to "Dream Big Dreams."

New Vision International is located in Tempe, Arizona. It employs approximately 250 people and distributes more than 30 nutritional, personal care and weight management products through a network of approximately 700,000 independent distributors nationwide. Customer product orders are filled through a 75,000 square foot automated distribution facility which has the capacity to utilize more than 1,000 employees and fill 28,000 orders per day.

**New Vision, 1920 East Broadway, Tempe, AZ 85282**
**Phone: (602) 927-8650, Fax: (602) 927-8665, Web site: nviworld.com**

*Dr. Lynn Myers*

Dr. Lynn Myers is widely regarded as one of the country's foremost experts on nutritional supplements and has appeared on *CNN Headline News* and *ESPN's One on One Sports*. Dr. Myers served as Chief Pathologist and has taught at the University of Texas Medical School.

## Chewtrition™--Huge Market Demand

Lynn Myers, MD, became convinced that good nutrition is the key to a longer, healthier life. He developed Chewtrition, a new delivery system that allows important nutrients to be quickly and easily absorbed into the body. Chewtrition uses one of our favorite products, chewing gum, to help our body absorb more of what we need faster. It's a fun and effective way to get nutrients into your system. Chewtrition is changing the way millions of Americans get their nutrition and you can be on the forefront of this revolution.

## Chew Gum and Increase Energy

Creatine Chewtrition works to boost energy levels. Chew two pieces right before exercise or during work for sustained energy.  Here's what people say about Creatine Chewtrition:

"We give Chewtrition during pre-game and again at half-time and our guys really see a boost of energy. Last year we won four games in the fourth quarter and I believe the gum helped us win those games."
*Mike Grant, Head Strength Coach, Mississippi State University*

"I use Chewtrition every day as do many of my clients. We have all experienced significant increases in strength, endurance and body leanness. This, plus the efficiency, cost and convenience of Chewtrition make if far superior to all other creatine delivery systems."
*Dan Bales, Certified Personal Instructor*

## Chew Gum and Lose Weight

Ignite Chewtrition™  works to control your appetite and increases the burning of fat. Chew Ignite 15 minutes before meals or snacking to control food cravings. Here's what people say about Ignite:

"For the past fifteen years I've specialized in helping people lose weight. I've seen hundreds of diet products come and go. None, in my opinion, compare to Ignite. My patients have seen terrific results--they're eating less and are able to control their food cravings. Plus, Ignite contains only natural ingredients and no stimulants."
*Michael Steelman, MD, Weight Loss Specialist*

"I've tried dozens of diets but saw very little results. Ignite Chewtrition takes away my food cravings. Sometimes I even have to remember to eat. I've lost more than thirty pounds in thirty days."
*Jerry McCall, Radio DJ*

## Getting Started is Simple

NuCare has a professional marketing staff ready to help you build your business. You don't have to worry with meetings, product orders and service. All you do is refer people to the toll-free number. It's really that simple!

NuCare is a member of the Direct Selling Association

**Call today for free information: (888) 682-2731,  or visit our  Web site: nucare.com or creatinegum.com**

*Your Direct Source
For Health & Wellness*

***Bryan Haverson***

Nutri/System, a nationally recognized weight loss industry leader that has been helping millions of people lose weight successfully for over 27 years, has shifted its focus to the direct sales arena. Once an exclusively center-based business, Nutri/System first opened its retail weight loss centers in 1971. Recognizing the need for more convenient and affordable services, corporate Nutri/System shifted its primary method of distribution from retail to direct sales in March of 1998. This new direct sales company, Nutri/System Direct, exceeded $1M in sales within six months of its inception.

Nutri/System Direct's entry and emergence in the direct selling industry marks a very significant event in the history of direct sales. Why? Because Nutri/System has national name recognition, superior products, and a 27-year proven track record of having successfully served over 10 million customers. Nutri/System's history of weight loss success and expertise lends instant credibility to your business--the kind of credibility that most new companies could never even hope to achieve. And when you add the fact that over $200 million dollars in advertising spending has occurred over the past 27 years to build name recognition--well, it's very impressive!

Nutri/System Direct offers customers the same, proven Nutri/System Weight Loss Program in a more comfortable, convenient, and affordable manner. Nutri/System foods, vitamins, minerals, and herbal supplements are shipped directly to your customers' home or office, so there's no need for embarrassing and time consuming, center visits. Best of all, there are no program fees; customers pay only for the food they order. A weekly Nutri/System Direct food package costs only $49.95 per week (plus shipping/tax) and includes 7 breakfast, 7 lunch, and 7 dinner entrees, and 7 snack/desserts. Customers choose their favorite selections from a variety of delicious, low-fat, portion-controlled entrees and desserts. A Nutri/System Direct representative meets with customers, either in person or over the phone, to explain the program, answer any questions, and provide encouragement and support on an ongoing basis.

Nutri/System Direct also offers an exciting new business opportunity with very low start-up costs and tremendous potential. It's an incredible opportunity for anyone who wants to take advantage of a convenient, affordable, and effective weight loss method with 27 years of proven success and an exciting financial opportunity to earn income by owning your own part-time or full-time business. By helping others live a healthier lifestyle, Nutri/System Direct representatives develop a sense of value, satisfaction, and positive well being. Currently, there are nearly 1,000 Nutri/System Direct representatives nationwide--and the number is growing every day!

**Nutri/System Direct, L.L.C. 202 Welsh Road, Horsham, PA 19044**
**Phone: (215) 706-5300, Fax-on-Demand: (512) 505-6875**
**HYPERLINK http://www.nutrisystemdirect.com, http://www.nutrisystemdirect.com**

*David Bertrand*

Nutrition For Life International, a direct selling company established in 1984, develops and distributes nutritionals, antioxidants, homeopathics, herbs, filtration systems, weight-loss and natural skin care products that are sold directly through a network of 96,000 independent distributors throughout the world. It has marketing operations in the U.S., Canada, the United Kingdom, Netherlands and the Philippines. The company is dedicated to developing unmatched nutritional and health care products coupled with an exceptional business opportunity.

Nutrition For Life is certainly benefiting from the strong growth of the nutritional supplement and natural personal care markets. According to a leading industry publication, *Nutrition Business Journal*, sales of herbal remedies, including ginseng, ginko biloba, and other botanicals will reach $4.3 billion at year end. The company has been able to capitalize on this growing trend by developing superior products and marketing them through an ever-expanding distributor base.

A concentrated focus on product research, innovation and quality enables Nutrition For Life to develop products that satisfy diverse and changing consumer needs. With every product, the company seeks to combine the best of science and nature. Since the company's beginning, it has offered an extensive line of herbs, homeopathics and natural skin care, long before it was popular to do so. In recent years, the company has developed nutritional products that utilize powerful whole food concentrates, antioxidants and phytonutirents. In 1997, the company was the first among its competitors to introduce a complete line of soy foods called Heartful Gourmets, an assortment of 17 delicious meat-free main courses. This commitment to provide reliable, high-quality, consumer-focused products and services uniquely positions Nutrition For Life to be a strong leader in this growing industry. Nutrition For Life will continue to lead the way, pioneering new paths for healthier lives.

Although products play a crucial role in the company's growth, it is the people who have propelled Nutrition For life to the forefront. The company's generous, leadership-based compensation plan enables distributors to pursue their financial goals and improve their quality of life through Nutrition For Life. In fact, Nutrition For Life has succeeded in part by remaining at the leading edge of distributor compensation, a plan that is leadership driven. Those who succeed in establishing strong networks move more products and make more money. The company's seamless, global compensation plan gives independent distributors the opportunity to build worldwide sales networks. Management enjoys knowing that it offers one of the strongest business opportunities available, along with the most generous compensation program in the industry. The company recently introduced a unique executive right away option that now allows distributors to sign onto the program for $199, as well as a generous House Payment Bonus Program which entitles the company's highest achievers to receive free mortgage payments.

Nutrition For Life continues to modify and update its programs to ensure its competitiveness and solidify its stronghold in the industry.

**For more information on Nutrition For Life International visit our Web site: http://nutritionforlife.com**

*Richard Brooke*

## What do you want in a network marketing company?

**A Ground-Floor Opportunity** - Oxyfresh Worldwide, Inc. is a ground-floor opportunity with a proven track record. Not many ground-floor opportunities can claim 15 years of success.

**A Company With Integrity** - Oxyfresh has created a new standard in network marketing--a culture of personal empowerment and leadership development. Leading industry trade journals such as *Upline* magazine, *Entrepreneur* magazine, *Business Opportunity* magazine, and the premier issue of *Network Marketing* magazine continue to recognize us. Our distributors and products have been positively featured in the national media through television, newspapers, and magazines, such as *SUCCESS* magazine, *Reader's Digest*, CNN, and ABC News, just to name a few.

Oxyfresh is a long-standing member of the Direct Selling Association and the Multi-Level Marketing International Association. Our president and CEO, Richard Brooke, serves on the Ethics Committee of the DSA and has been nominated to serve on the DSA's Board of Directors.

**Products That you Believe in** - Oxyfresh products are unsurpassed in quality and effectiveness. Thousands of health professionals use and recommend them; thousands more Oxyfresh distributors build successful businesses with the help of them.

We offer something for all walks of life: leading edge oral health care products; unsurpassed nutritional supplements; nontoxic, safe, and effective pet care; environmentally friendly home and personal care products, award-winning skin and hair care, and innovative and effective air purification. Oxyfresh products reflect a commitment to long-term excellence and maintain a competitive edge in the network marketing arena.

**An Opportunity to Grow, as a Person and as a Leader** - Oxyfresh is renowned for its character and leadership development programs. At Richard and Rishon Brooke's Six-Day Visionary Leadership Retreats, Oxyfresh distributors are pampered to the full extent of the word. They are challenged with physical and mental tasks. They define and refine their leadership skills. And they create friendships that last a lifetime.

At National Leadership Conferences, Regional Meetings, One-Day Schools, and Home Meetings, Oxyfresh distributors are empowered. They learn about the business. They learn about themselves.

**A Company That is Ethical** - Oxyfresh is committed to maintaining a distributor culture whereby each distributor honors the values and protects the business of fellow distributors, which supports the Oxyfresh image. Through a culture of cooperation, the diverse, yet like-minded people of Oxyfresh instill a new perception of honesty, integrity, and opportunity--a standard for the entire network marketing industry.

**A Company That Has a Future** - In 1986, Richard Brooke took over the corporate operations of Oxyfresh and the company has experienced growth and success ever since. That success is the result of the efforts of independent distributors, a dedicated corporate team, and an experienced Advisory Board.

At Oxyfresh, we are committed to a Code of Ethics and Cultural Commitments. We have experienced over a decade of record growth and we're still growing. We have a passion for helping people develop their finances, their character, and their leadership.

At Oxyfresh, you can experience unlimited growth and success. You have the potential and Oxyfresh is the vehicle to help you attain personal and financial freedom. Let Oxyfresh help you make a difference in your life and your future!

**Oxyfresh Worldwide, Inc., 12928 East Indiana Avenue, Spokane, WA  99216**
**Phone: (509) 924-4999, Fax: (509) 924-5285**

*Ronald Mahan*

**A revolution in business**...an adventure in life! Headquartered in suburban Atlanta, Pangea offers superior nutritional and sensory skin care products--products that "make you look better, feel younger and live longer." Pangea capitalizes on today's cutting edge breakthrough in science. Our vision is to create the best business opportunity in the world, bar none. That is, an opportunity so interesting, so daring, so fresh, so engaging, so human, so well-focused as to products and opportunity that, at one and the same time, it builds a quality reputation for the future as it allows us to share success in the present.

**Pangea is a division of Fuisz Technologies, Ltd.,** a company that develops proprietary technologies for a wide range of drug delivery, nutraceutical and food applications. Pangea is the marketing arm of Fuisz. The Pangea/Fuisz Network benefits from over 120 employed researchers and scientists on staff who are engaged in the development of high-tech, new-millennium products. The company also benefits from research facilities and offices located in Chantilly, Virginia and Atlanta, Georgia, as well as international locations in Ireland, France, Italy and Germany. Pangea/Fuisza is setting the pace in scientists, patents, and technology. Pangea and Fuisz are developing the most dynamic and innovative products in the world. With over 60 patents in its technology and over 50 patents pending, Fuisz Technology knows that to develop miracle products you need miracle technology.

**Shared Success**™ is the way Pangea runs its business and the way its business partners--Pangea distributors--run theirs. This philosophy is based on values and principles being as important as products and profits. Ron Mahan, President of Pangea, states: "It empowers us, as individuals and as organizations, to achieve optimum success by linking our well-being to the well-being of our partners, the well-being of our customers, the well-being of our community, and the well-being of our world."

**The company has a major focus on E-Commerce which is the wave of the future**. E-Commerce means there is a focus on making all purchases electronically with the major emphasis on Internet Buying. Pangea/Fuisz is committed to developing the largest on-line drugstore/superstore on the Internet. It's called Rx Drugstore. Here, people from all over the world can roam our Internet drugstore aisles stocked with everything from health and beauty aids to herbs and vitamins, diapers and baby formula to laundry detergent and cleaning products or light hardware items. Rx Drugstore features over 1,000 products including OTC drugs. You can purchase everyday products like Tide® or Tylenol®, toothbrushes, toothpaste, shaving cream or roll-on-deodorant while seated comfortably in front of your computer. Hundreds of new everyday products are being added every month. Shopping at Rx Drugstore is easy, it's quick, it's convenient. Pangea/Fuisz is working to help you simplify your life. Rx Drugstore offers competitive prices and the convenience of having your order shipped to your front door.

**Internet shopping** is the wave of the future! Pangea offers an opportunity with a credible company that offers products you already use every day. No one loses--everyone wins. Don't waste a minute--call the number below.

**Pangea, Ltd., 995-D Mansell Road, Roswell, GA 30076**
**Phone: (770) 998-9181, Fax: (770) 998-9159**

*Ingrid Hodges*

Petra Fashions was established in 1979, and has since become the fastest growing party plan company in the nation, specializing in the direct sale of designer lingerie and sleepwear all priced under $40! Petra carries everything from elegant full-length gowns, to cotton blend boxer shorts and robes, in sizes that range from small to 5X. Each garment is manufactured in the United States, exclusively for Petra Fashions.

As an independent sales representative with Petra Fashions, there is absolutely no limit to what you can earn! It all depends on how often you choose to work, and how much merchandise you sell. For example, if you hold a show with guest purchases of $300, you will earn a $75 profit. And, since the average show usually lasts about 2 1/2 hours, your hourly wage would be approximately $30. This means that if you hold just two shows per week with average sales of $300 or more, your monthly profit would be over $600. In addition, Petra's Platinum Key Club Program allows you to earn a monthly bonus of 20% of your profits!

Petra encourages you to succeed by offering special incentives, such as bonus cash, beautiful jewelry and exotic trips. Plus, your achievements are continuously recognized in the company newsletter, *In the Spotlight*, as well as other special publications that are distributed nationwide. With Petra, your hard work is truly appreciated.

Advancement opportunities are always possible with Petra. By simply sharing the Petra Opportunity with others, you can self-promote to a higher level. And, once you start climbing Petra's "Management Ladder of Success," you will become eligible for additional monthly bonuses, as well as your very own car allowance.

As a member of the Petra Family, you will be in business for yourself, but not by yourself. Your director will make sure that you receive the necessary training to build a strong, successful business. Plus Petra's home office sends out a bi-weekly newsletter that contains the latest company promotions, sales contest and recognition.

Petra guarantees that you'll love your job as much as you will love the great income that goes along with it. You will meet a variety of new people, play games at your shows, and present a line of merchandise that is geared toward making people feel good about themselves. What other job offers all that?

As an independent sales representative with Petra, you will be supported by the best Hostess Program in the industry (on average, hostesses earn hundreds in free lingerie), as well as by advertising nationally in *Woman's Day* and *Family Circle* magazines. In fact, Petra's beautiful designer garments for women, men and children practically sell themselves, so you'll find it easy to achieve high show profits. Petra makes it easy for you in other ways, too, because you'll never have to worry about sales quotas, assigned territories, or costly inventory maintenance.

With Petra Fashions, you'll enjoy the best of both worlds. Petra offers you the opportunity to build your very own business while working at a pace that suits your lifestyle. Think about it. In addition to earning an outstanding income, you will also have the freedom to schedule your work around your family and personal activities. It's an ideal situation!

**For more information about the Petra Opportunity to book a show call (800)-PETRA-4-U--(800) 738-7248**
**Petra Fashions, Inc., 35 Cherry Hill Drive, Danvers, MA 01923**
**Phone: (978) 777-5853, Fax: (978) 774-6721**
**E-mail: petra@petra4u.com, Web site: www.petra4u.com**

# Pre-Paid Legal Services

"Justice For All"

**Harland Stonecipher**

Pre-Paid Legal Services, Inc. has been providing affordable legal services to America's middle-income families since 1972. In addition, this publicly held company also provides a means of improving one's lifestyle and financial outlook.

There is a real need for our Pre-Paid Legal membership. Surveys and statistics tell us that on any given day, 52 percent of middle income Americans have some type of legal problems. Our products give them access to top quality lawyers and law firms at a reasonable cost. The need for such a product as the Pre-Paid Legal membership and its affordable price, combined with one of the best distribution systems in America, are the reasons our company will continue to grow rapidly for many years to come.

We also give you the chance to be in business for yourself, but not by yourself. Unlike some network marketing companies, PPL requires no inventory, delivery or collections, and start-up costs are low. Most importantly, we offer unlimited income potential and long-term residual income opportunities. And our Fast $tart To $uccess program gives you the chance to advance up the commission structure at a more rapid pace. It's a win-win situation for all involved. No sales experience is needed. Our associates are comprised of people from all walks of life--like former corporate presidents, teachers, hairdressers, secretaries, police officers, real state agents, and ministers. This truly is the opportunity of a lifetime!

Our goal is to give every American--not just the wealthy, equal access to the legal system. "Unfortunately the Justice System does not work that way. The most implacable barrier to equitable distribution of justice in the United States is economics. Too many Americans just cannot afford much justice" (excerpt from the American Bar Journal, August 1994). PPL utilizes a system of Provider Law Firms, giving our members direct access to this select group of highly qualified attorneys. Because PPL contracts directly with the law firms, we are their biggest clients; therefore, our members are also their biggest clients.

While more and more people are finding Pre-Paid Legal as the answer to their legal needs, the market is still vastly untouched. It is a huge market--a multi-billion dollar market which encompasses 80 percent of the population. And in 1997, we added 283,723 new members, which was a four percent increase over the new memberships added in 1996.

The growing need for affordable legal services was the focus of much media attention in 1997, and Pre-Paid Legal has been called a "sign of the times" for this litigious society we live in. A sampling of the growing number of publications taking notice of our company and sharing our story with their readers includes: *Home Office Computing*, January 1997 - *Wall Street Journal*, September 18, 1997 - *Washington Business Times*, March 24, 1997 - *Fortune*, September 29, 1997 - *Black Enterprise Magazine*, July 1997 - *Success* Magazine, July/August 1997 - *Success* Magazine, October 1997 - *Forbes*, November 3, 1997, and *Home Office Computing*, September 1997

Our company was also featured in the publication *Wall Street's Picks for 1998* with a review by Michael DiCarlo of DFS Advisors. Pre-Paid Legal was in good company among other selected stocks for 1998, including Chrysler, Dell Computer, McDonald's and Wells Fargo.

As awareness of our services continues to climb, so does our commitment to our members and our associates. After 25 years, we continue to focus solely on the goal of providing quality, affordable legal services to America's families and a marketing plan that levels the playing field.

**To learn more about Pre-Paid Legal Services, visit our Web site at: www.pplsi.com**

# PriceNet USA.com

PriceNet USA.com is a solid and stable Internet company. Incorporated in October 1997 and located in Newport Beach, California, it is well financed and also a publicly held company listed on the NASDAQ stock exchange. The symbol is PUSA. This company has positioned itself as a dominant force in the Internet home shopping industry, and has recently acquired several well established businesses in order to enhance their position. PriceNet has proprietary e-commerce technology, a data base of merchandising content, trained sales force and a host of unique, high-tech state-of-the art consumer communications products and telecommunication services.

Ron Touchard has been in the network marketing industry for over 18 years on a full-time basis. Not only has he earned a handsome income, his success has also been well documented. He has been featured on the cover of several home-based business magazines and is the master distributor for PriceNet USA.com. Additionally, he is a member of the board of directors and chairman of the Advisory Council. PriceNet USA.com is the perfect Internet home-based business opportunity, enabling all who join to have their own personalized e-commerce shopping mall, along with your photo. With five million products from manufacturers such as Sony, Panasonic, RCA, GE, Kodak, Canon, Nikon, CTX, TwinLab, Whirlpool, Maytag, Sub-Zero, Pioneer, Bose, Fuji, Epson and Casio, to name just a few, you have your own access code and personalized web site address in which to advertise free shopping cards you pass along, directing others to your mall on the Internet. Additionally, we offer a designer outlet with literally dozens of name brands and approximately 30,000 toys for children, plus many more categories and thousands of products. When others purchase from you, your income is immediate, and in turn, you may also sell this mall for additional income.

Comparable to having a franchise, this is the most lucrative business opportunity in America because everyone knows the Internet is the future and that there is a tremendous amount of money to be made. For only $495 dollars you get your own Internet business with five million products, all on your own customized mall. There is absolutely no cost for warehousing, employees, and best of all, no overhead! By the end of 1998, there were over three and one-half million web sites on the Internet, which made it difficult to locate various products. Branding will be the key, people need to know where to go and the addresses they will go to shop will be PriceNetusa.com, Others will find it much easier to locate the products they wish to purchase. PriceNet and its suppliers have agreed to their unique distribution, enabling them to offer thousands of products at extremely low prices, all without the normal advertising costs. Anyone from around the world can shop your mall, 24 hours a day, 365 days a year. Their exposure is worldwide and covers a significant and growing customer base. What if you, as the average person, had the opportunity to join PriceNet to begin building your business on either a part-time or full-time basis, all the while earning stock options in the company? This is an opportunity you can't afford to pass up. PriceNet has designed their program so that anyone, regardless of background, education or prior business experience are able to earn a sizeable income in a very short period of time.

Every eleven seconds someone joins the quiet revolution and begins working at home. You don't need a computer to run your business because we have acquired, and are making available to you and your customers, a new TV Internet Access Box that is positioned on top of your television, hooking you to the Internet without a computer.

With PriceNet's simple turnkey business, small initial investment and incredibly low monthly overhead, this is the network marketing opportunity for the new millennium.

**For information on PriceNetusa.com contact: Ron Touchard, 2785 Pacific Coast Hwy.,
Suite E-307, Torrance, CA 90505
Phone: (310) 782-1458, Fax: (310) 782-7078
E-mail: RTouchard@msn.com, or Ron@pricenetusa.com**

# PRINCESS HOUSE®
## *easy living with style*

**A Smart Career Opportunity** -- Since 1963, Princess House has been providing outstanding part-time and full-time earning and advancement opportunities to people across the United States. Today, nearly 15,000 independent sales consultants have realized their dream of owning their own business by supplying unique home enhancement products via in-home parties.

Each consultant provides the customer with creative do-it-yourself ideas that literally show busy people how to "turn their house into a home" by creating special family gatherings, decorating accents and unique gifts. The success of our "home consultants" in providing unique personalized service is best measured by consistent growth in sales, with more than $10 million in purchases made last year.

**A Tradition of Product Excellence** -- Starting in a small rural Massachusetts community in 1963, Princess House was originally a handful of people dedicated to quality and craftsmanship. Today, in West Virginia, our artisans still use traditional glass-blowing techniques to create our family of hand-blown crystal. We have sought out the finest craftspeople from around the world to manufacture our cookware, bakeware, lead crystal figurines, stoneware and porcelain.

**A Million Fans --** More than one million people will host or attend a Princess House home party this year, drawn by the attraction of a personalized shopping experience that is entertaining, educational and life enhancing. Our Hostess Plan of free and discounted merchandise is one of the most rewarding in the industry. Monthly customer specials offer the extra value today's consumers are looking for. A monthly "Easy Ideas" theme packs consultant presentations with tips, techniques and recipes that offer new and simple ways to make life at home extra special. Our customers also enjoy convenient gift express service and a half-priced replacement policy.

**A Mission of Caring & Sharing --** Over the years, hundreds of thousands of people have benefited from the Princess House earning opportunity. It has changed thousands of lives by enabling people to earn good money immediately ($20 to $25 per hour), while learning the skills necessary to build and develop their Princess House business, thereby creating unlimited long-term opportunity.

**Fast Facts**

- Princess House was established over 35 years ago by entrepreneur Charles Collis.

- Since the early 90s, Princess House has experienced an annual growth rate of more than 15%.

- With Princess House, our consultants begin earning money at their home parties immediately, with average earnings of $20 to $25 per hour for each party.

- Princess House has created more than thirty millionaires, and countless others among our independent contractors have earned hundreds of thousands of dollars.

- We are very proud of our Spanish speaking consultants and organizers, one of the fastest growing segments of our business.

- Our exclusive collections include products for casual living, home entertainment, gift-giving, decorating and cooking/serving.

- Princess House owns and operates the largest hand-blown glass facility in the United States located in Weston, West Virginia, and operates a state-of-the-art distribution center in Rural Hall, North Carolina.

**Princess House, 470 Miles Standish Blvd., Taunton, MA 02780, Phone: (800) 622-0039, Fax: (508) 823-5182**
**E-mail: custsvc.princesshouse.com, Web site: www.princesshouse.com**

# ProSTEP, Inc.

*Kevin Lehmann*

Since its inception in 1994, ProSTEP has rapidly become the largest and most trusted lead generation, training and support company in the network marketing industry. More MLM distributors rely on them as a one-stop shop for their network marketing needs than every other lead generation company combined. ProSTEP believes that network marketers must have four critical components to succeed in business today:

**A Never-ending Source of Pre-qualified Prospects.** ProSTEP sets the standard as the only company to generate tens of thousands of direct response, pre-qualified prospects every month utilizing a creative combination of electronic, print and direct mail.

**Progressive, Cutting-edge Training in Sales and Marketing.** ProSTEP members receive progressive training and support with a focus on "hi-tech" recruiting techniques that are balanced with "hi-touch" communication skills. ProSTEP believes that proper training is vital to your success in network marketing. These tools include: the ProPak Training Kit, the ProSTEP Training Tape Library, Quarterly Prospective Magazines, Monthly Audio Newsletters, Weekly Interactive Training Calls, 24-Hour Fax Brochure, and a Toll-Free Presentation Line.

**The Latest, Most Innovative Communications.** Communication is the very pulse of network marketing. ProSTEP recognizes this critical need and not only provides you with the latest innovative communications technology, they also teach you how to use and apply it to your business-building efforts. ProSTEP has a variety of communications tools designed to maximize your efforts, to include: Free voice mail and fax-on-demand services, an 8.9 cent rate long distance service, and free personalized conference calling.

The Internet has become the true communications tool of the 90s and will become ever more vital in the new millennium. ProSTEP's new Internet division gives your business the web presence you need. With service that includes web hosting, web and graphics design services and classified and banner advertising.

**Immediate Cash Flow to Offset Start-up Costs and Sustain Momentum.** ProSTEP understands how crucial it is to generate immediate and sufficient cash flow to survive in network marketing. In fact, ProSTEP is a pioneer in reversing the trend of the network marketing industry by paying the highest commissions on the very first level. This puts money in your pocket when you need it the most--at the beginning. That's why they've devised a powerful yet simple compensation plan that pays you three different ways: Quick Pay Commissions that range from $100 to $400 for each member you enroll, Override Commissions that can earn you $3,000 to $12,000 per month with only 130 members in your first three levels, and Infinity Bonus Commissions that can earn you up to $20 on every member below your first level. These four critical components have been part of ProSTEP from the very beginning, but they have gotten even better with the addition of new and improved promotional materials, training tools, compensation plans, and membership levels.

ProSTEP's recent expansion reflects their continued commitment to helping network marketers plan, implement and manage their business at its most effective level, according to Kevin Lehmann, president and CEO of ProSTEP, Inc. "Our members have come to expect the expertise and capabilities that ProSTEP provides to assist them in the set-up and expansion of their network marketing business. We will continue to exceed their expectations with strategic services and benefits which will add significant value to their ProSTEP Membership and improve their network marketing skills."

**For more information about the exciting opportunities with ProSTEP, call our toll-free ProSTEP presentation line at: (800) 784-0093, download our informative Fax Brochure at: (850) 654-8999**

**visit us online at http://www.prostepinc.com**
345

**Gary McDonald**

RACHAeL International is a company built on exceptional health and beauty products with an incredibly generous plan by people who have experience in direct marketing which has won them international awards in the direct selling and general business community.

**PRODUCTS** - RACHAeL's complete line of aloe-based all-natural skin care and body care products are without equal. Their famous "half face" test challenges all to do half of their face with RACHAeL skin care and the other half with any other product at any price and to see the "RACHAeL difference." Invariably, RACHAeL is picked as "best by far."

RACHAeL's line of Glamour Color emphasizes the importance of the right color harmony with all products coded to the right color for each person: "Cool," "Warm" or "Universal."

Silk-N-Sheen Hair Care Products with all-natural ingredients emphasize aloe and jojoba. They are so concentrated, they provide the perfect "simple answer" to luxurious, healthy, manageable hair.

The natural answer to health and overcoming physical problems is provided with the Biophynutrient line of health care nutritional products. Formulas unique, and powerfully effective, provide endless testimonials of restored health, happiness and vigor.

These products are so effective that people tell others about them because of their enthusiastic response to the results they obtain.

This is the key to network marketing--products so good you want to tell the world about them.

**PLAN** - With the RACHAeL Plan, you are paid very generously for doing that sharing, With discounts, bonuses and commissions and "infinity" payments, which assure that residual income. And you start that cash flow with an *investment* of only $20 for the Business Kit/manual, audio tapes, video tapes, sample products and literature.

The plan includes an "automobile plan" and special "retirement" or "college tuition" accounts, as well as company paid health care, as you make your six or even seven figure income.

**PEOPLE** - President and Chairman of the Board of RACHAeL International, Gary McDonald, has led not just companies to success, but also the Direct Selling Industry. One of the founders of Tupperware Home Parties, Inc., he served as Executive Vice President of Tupperware and Tupperware International. He was instrumental in bringing the entire direct selling industry into the limelight of positive public recognition. He was twice chairman of the board of the Direct Selling Association, bringing about the "Code of Ethics" for the direct selling industry.

Gary was the youngest person ever to receive the association's highest honor--induction into the DSA "Hall of Fame." This honor has been accorded to fewer than 50 people in the association's nearly 100 years of existence.

The board of directors includes Vernon and Lavon Dragt who have been in direct selling for nearly 40 years. They built the biggest Tupperware distributorship in the world. They developed and promoted from their distributorship the greatest number of successful distributorships of anyone in Tupperware ever!

Their international recognition includes receiving the Religious Heritage of America Award for Business and Professionals. Other awardee's include, Dr. and Mrs. Norman Vincent Peale, Mr. and Mrs. Paul Harvey and President Ronald Reagan, to name a few.

**RACHAeL International, 1706 East Semoran Blvd., Apopka, FL 32703, Phone: (888) 617-7170, Fax: (407) 814-0217, Web site: www.rachaelinternational.com, E-mail: rachael4@ix.netcom.com**

# REGAL.

*Jeffrey Reigle*

The Regal success story began in 1945, when James O. Reigleand and several close associates purchased the Kewaskum Aluminum Company. The plant, which was doing military work, was immediately retooled to produce stainless steel sauce pans to be sold through direct sales. From this humble, two-pan product line, Regal has grown to become the largest, privately held housewares company in the United States. The company is a major supplier to the direct selling industry and its products are sold in more than 100 countries worldwide. In addition, Regal has been a member of the Direct Selling Association since 1953.

Regal is separated into two divisions; a retail division: in which products are sold through retail stores; and the direct sales division, in which premium, high quality products are manufactured, marketed and sold. The original, two-pan cookware line has evolved into complete product lines of superior rangetop cooking systems. They are made of multi-layered stainless steel or high quality aluminum and are exclusively for direct sellers. An impressive assortment of kitchen appliances, healthy cooking accessories and sophisticated water and air filtration systems complements the high quality cookware offerings.

Regal supports its direct sales-exclusive products with an innovative program of marketing services, promotion assistance and recruiting support. Its well planned conventions and seminars are designed and organized to be educational, motivational, entertaining and mutually beneficial.

Today, Regal is led by Jeffrey Reigle, grandson of the founder, and a team of experienced, dedicated professionals. Regal management realized that forming partnerships and strategic alliances with other companies are the keys to success in the 21st century--much more beneficial than the traditional vendor, customer relationship.

Through its strategic partnerships, Regal is able to coordinate early project development and share in design, quality and manufacturing information with its partners. Costs are reduced, new technology is more accessible, inventory control is improved and communications are streamlined for both partners. Consequently, Regal is able to manufacture better quality products more efficiently and less expensively.

Regal recognized the importance of forming partnerships and strategic alliances many years ago. We have developed many of these relationships with several established and professional companies in the industry, including two companies for more than 40 years.

Although Regal has enjoyed a reputation of being a leader in the direct sales business for more than 50 years, we didn't think it was time to rest on our laurels. With the 21st century almost upon us, we're working hard to develop new, state-of-the-art products and forming new partnerships and strategic alliances. We're looking forward to a bright future.

**Regal Ware, Inc., 1675 Reigle Drive, Kewaskum, WI 53040**
**Phone: (414) 626-2121, Fax: (414) 626-8565, Website; www.regalware.com**

*Robert Montgomery*

Founded in 1988 by the successful entrepreneur, Robert L. Montgomery, Reliv boasts an impeccable reputation both on Wall Street and within the network marketing industry. Throughout its 10+ year history, this innovative food science company has gained renown for the integrity of its products, its compensation plan and its management team.

Reliv's achiever in the industry was recently honored with the election of President and CEO, Robert Montgomery, to the Direct Selling Association's (DSA) board of directors. Montgomery was also selected to the DSA's Direct Selling Education Foundation committee as well as the prestigious Chairman's Council, which consists of 12 CEO's from the industry's most revered companies.

The company is publicly traded on the NASDAQ exchange and maintains its world headquarters in Chesterfield, MO. Recently, Reliv underwent a $4 million building expansion, allowing the company to house corporate offices, research and development, and manufacturing operations under one roof, thus ensuring strict control over product quality and responsiveness to the needs of customers and distributors.

**Proven Products** - Reliv products have brought better health and new hope to thousands of people worldwide. From the original Reliv Classic® nutritional supplement, which provides a full days balanced nutrition in a single serving, to our latest developments in soy-based meals and supplements, Reliv remains committed to providing customers with delicious, easy-to-use products that bring life-changing results.

Recent product introductions have focused on the functional foods area which provides food solutions to many of the chronic health issues facing us today. A prime example of Reliv's innovation in the functional food arena is Reliv Arthaffect® nutritional supplement, which combines the best of ancient herbal wisdom with cutting-edge technology. The key ingredient, patented Arthred®, was proven to promote healthy joint function through $10 million in clinical trials. Reliv currently holds four U.S. patents for its products and is a member of the prestigious Functional Foods for Health Institute.

The complete product line encompasses high quality powdered nutritional supplements, weight management products, sport drinks, nutritional bars, high fiber/antioxidant formulations, gourmet style soy-based meals and skin care.

**Lucrative Compensation** - Reliv counts several millionaires among its distributors, as well as a large contingent of part-timers who are earning substantial profits. Distributors earn income via retail and wholesale profits, bonuses, overrides and additional incentives paid to top leaders through the Reliv Ambassador Program.

Bonuses and overrides are based on retail volume. Retail profits range from 25% to 45% based on increasing group volume. Wholesale profits range from 5% to 20% on the volume of personally sponsored downline distributors.

**International Opportunities** - Reliv is currently sold in the United States, Canada, Mexico, Australia, New Zealand and the United Kingdom. The company continues to pursue expansion into key markets around the globe.

**The Reliv Mission: Nourish Our World**

Reliv's number one goal is to improve the health and well-being of people everywhere. Through the distribution of leading edge nutritional products and charitable gifts made through the company's Kalogris Foundation, Reliv is committed to the worldwide fight against hunger.

**Reliv International, PO Box 405, Chesterfield, MO 63005-0405**
**Phone: (314) 537-9822, Fax: (314) 537-9753, Orders: (800) 735-4887, Web site: www.reliv.com**

*Russ Zylstra*

**Our Mission: Rena Ware...leading the global market with a commitment to excellence in health and nutrition products for the home environment, while providing you with the opportunity and the support to build your own business and enjoy personal, professional and financial success.**

## Company History

Rena Ware International, Inc. is dedicated to helping people worldwide achieve healthier lifestyles through high quality cookware, specialty accessories, entertainment products and water filtration systems.

Now more than ever, people are striving to improve their health and environment. Rena Ware provides consumers with innovative products to improve the food and water they consume.

Founded in Washington state in 1941 by Fred "Pop" Zylstra, a Dutch immigrant, Rena Ware has seen many changes through three generations of Zylstra family leadership. Fred Zylstra's son, O.W. "Bill" Zylstra, worked closely with his father to develop the nucleus of the company. During the 1970s and 1980s, Bill's son, Russ Zylstra, now chief executive officer and president, widened Rena Ware's product line to include water filtration systems and other products that promote healthier lifestyles.

Rena Ware's international headquarters is located in Redmond, Washington.

## Sales Force

Rena Ware products are distributed on five continents by dedicated, knowledgeable and professional consultants. Rena Ware's direct selling method embodies the "personal approach." Products are presented in the customer's home during an appointment made at the customer's convenience.

Rena Ware offers its consultants the opportunity to be in charge of their careers while enjoying strong support from the company as they work towards success. Unlike many direct selling organizations, Rena Ware does not require consultants to purchase inventory or make a financial investment to get started. The company provides training, presentation materials, and professional lead acquisition programs. Once consultants are established, they have many opportunities to advance within the company, as well as to earn exciting prizes and travel opportunities. Rena Ware consultants enjoy unlimited growth and earnings along with the unparalleled satisfaction that comes from helping others to better their lives.

Rena Ware has been a member of the Direct Selling Association since 1955.

## Product Line

Rena Ware products include a full line of high-quality stainless steel "waterless" cookware; VIVA, a gourmet stainless steel cookware line; a variety of specialty accessories and entertainment products; and a line of water filtration systems. All Rena Ware products share a common purpose: helping people achieve healthier lifestyles through the food and water they consume.

**Rena Ware International, Inc., PO Box 97050, Redmond, WA 98073-9750**

*Dave Schofield*

Rexall Showcase International® (RSI) manufacturers and markets unique, high-quality products that can truly make a difference in people's lives by impacting the way they look and feel. Based on science, RSI's exclusive products range from nutritional supplements and homeopathic medicines to personal care products and advanced water filters. These products are greatly consumable and appeal to a broad consumer base. RSI also provides an outstanding opportunity for individuals to fulfill their dreams of time freedom and financial independence by becoming independent distributors.

**Build Your Business With RSI** - The company's distributors enjoy one of the best compensation plans in the industry, a low start-up cost and, if qualified, stock option and stock purchase plans. Distributors also can take advantage of ample training and networking opportunities through local meetings, regional programs, national events, a voice-mail system and a business-building system already in place.

There is tremendous opportunity throughout the United States for distributors to build a successful and sustaining business. RSI's opportunity also extends to Hong Kong, Taiwan, South Korea and Mexico. The company will continue to open in other countries as one of its long-term growth initiatives designed to bolster the success of the company and its distributors.

**Cutting-Edge Products** - Experts agree that key to a company's success is powerful products. That is why RSI continually expands its line of exclusive, scientifically based products that address major health concerns. In order to give its distributors a competitive edge, the company seeks breakthrough ingredients for which it can obtain exclusive distribution rights within the industry and develop proprietary formulas.

**Phenomenal Growth** - RSI has achieved phenomenal growth since its inception in 1990, and consumer demand for its unique products has driven up sales an average of 50 percent per year for the past five years. In fiscal year 1998, which ended August 31, RSI sales increased 51 percent, reaching an all-time high of approximately $160 million.

**Solid Corporate Support** - Adding to RSI's strength, its parent company, Rexall Sundown, Inc., is a multi-million dollar corporation, a member of the prestigious Nasdaq-100, has no long-term debt and is growing rapidly. RSI distributors benefit from an established infrastructure, vast manufacturing capabilities, one of the highest quality levels in the nutritional supplement industry and solid corporate support. Further, the Rexall family of companies--with its licensed pharmacists, nutritionists, other professionals and consultants, is dedicated to new product research and development.

**A Time-Honored Name** - For almost 100 years, Rexall has stood for quality and trust in consumers' minds. Products manufactured at its state-of-the-art plants are subject to extremely stringent quality control programs. In fact, Rexall has earned high scores from one of the most prestigious independent quality audit firms in the health-product manufacturing industry. This firm, Shuster Laboratories, Inc., has repeatedly evaluated the company against the applicable Good Manufacturing Practices established by the FDA. Rexall Sundown's scores are consistently the highest quality control scores Shuster awards to nutrional supplement manufacturers. This level of excellence ensures that when distributors share RSI products with consumers, they are offering a powerful line they can be proud to represent.

**To learn more about RSI or its business opportunity, write to: Rexall Showcase International, 853 Broken Sound Parkway NW, Boca Raton, FL 33487**
**Phone: (561) 994-2090, Web site: www.rexallshowcase.com**

# The Right Solution

*Flo Ternes*                                                                                    *Rick Bailey*

The Right Solution is a distributor of life-enhancing products. It has a unique entrepreneurial, multi-level (network marketing) marketing system. Currently in its 5th year of business, Rick Bailey purchased it in January of 1995 and serves as president/CEO. In 1990, he became involved in the multi-level/direct selling business and was able to understand the business from the perspective of a distributor/team member. He firmly believes that our employees are our greatest asset and portray the image of the company. Rick has focused most of his energy in 1999 on expansion, acquisitions, new product development, corporate image, and financing.

**Flo Ternes** has 29 years in senior management. He was in the airline industry and finished his career as City Vice President at Continental Airlines. He became president of NutriCology in April 1997, and left to join TRS in January of 1998 as chief operations officer. We believe there are six areas that relate to success. These are as follows: 1. Company must maintain honor and trust --2. Quality products that work --3. Fair and equitable compensation plan --4. Continue worldwide search for new products and technology --5. Receptive to change --6. Everyone is equal in our drive towards success.

Our health and nutritional products are divided into five categories:

**Health Pack:** Fortress Plus, Armor Guard, RFV 29, Mineral Magic Colloidal Minerals, Buffered Vitamins C, Vita-Greens, OxygenPlus.

**Immune Pack:** BodyGuard with Lactoferrin, Myco--Enhance Mushrooms, Cytolog

**Heart Pack:** Smart Heart Fiber Drink, Smart Heart Herbal Tablets, Smart Heart Metabolic Formula

**Weight Loss Pack:** Body Trim 1, Body Trim 2, Body Trim 3, (herbal Detox Tea), Lite Solution, Cellution

**Specialized Products:** Organic Germanium, Modified Citrus Pectin, Ymotion Wild Yam Cream for Women, Wild Yam Lotion for Men, Arthred, PR10, Prozaplex, Stabilium, DHA, Calcium Elenolate, Oxygen Plus, Herbal Detox Tea.

We will be introducing an educational package that includes business and personal development in the first quarter of 1999, which allows team members to not only benefit from the educational materials, but earn additional commissions on sales.

We currently have more than 30,000 team members and 12,000 are in Japan. The unique compensation plan has established our company as a leader in the industry. Our unique compensation plan has the following characteristics:

1. No time limit on commissions.

2. No limits on working with the downline. The compensation plan is a binary with a unilevel touch, meaning that only two people, one on the left and on the right, are on the first level of each distributor.

The network develops downward instead of across. Commissions are based on the group wholesale volume of each "side" of the distributor. All volumes flow up the network without limits as to the number of levels involved. Bonus money is paid weekly and effective immediately.

3. Placement is user-friendly and flexible.

**Vision:** Our five-year business plan includes expansion into Philippines, Hong Kong and Australia. We see exciting high growth opportunity for all team members, employees, and its shareholders.

**"The Right Solution" our name says it all!**
**Anyone interested in joining our team please give us a call at: (800) 315-9877**

### The Monroes

Rose Marie and Pete Monroe have developed a philosophy that has successfully worked for their family and their business; that is, to keep their priorities in order...faith first, family second, and career third.

Their success is grounded in these priorities and the belief that everyone deserves the best in life and more importantly, that you can have it. Life-long dreams becoming realities have become the standard, and not the exception, for the Monroes and for thousands of others who have joined them on the journey of success.

It is a philosophy that encourages the idea that every person is somebody important, a "VIP," a leader, and that you can make a difference for yourself, your family, and your fellow man.

Today, through RMC, the Monroes are developing a worldwide network of people with a common cause to assist their fellow man for the benefit of all mankind and to turn your personal dreams into realities.

"Help yourself by offering a hand to help someone else" is a proven fact in RMC. RMC and the Monroes view every individual as a leader who can be successful by offering others the opportunity to be a leader.

For those in RMC, it is simple: to be happy, motivated, prosperous and successful. Just follow the RMC philosophy by maintaining the right priorities in your life and by helping someone else through the RMC program to become happy, motivated, prosperous and successful.

The Monroe's business history is rich with success with over one quarter billion dollars in skin care and cosmetic sales as direct marketers. Late in 1993 and throughout 1994, the Monroes organized RMC Group Inc. as part of their marketing effort to expand the product line and financial opportunity. In 1995, that expansion included the introduction of the Body Management System program and nutritional supplements.

In 1996, RMC's management team began to implement a network marketing concept to expand the company's customer base. In July 1998, the company launched the RMC IMPACT PROGRAM to continue to grow into the 21st century. The RMC OPPORTUNITY has the potential for anyone who is willing to work, the opportunity to earn a solid income, build independence, achieve personal dreams, and live the lifestyle they choose as the "Chairman of the Board" of their own company!

The RMC product line has met consumer needs who have used the products. RMC has created results-driven products that lead to success in network marketing. A person who uses the products soon recognizes the results, and often shares the products with people they know.

The products originated in 1982 with Rose Marie Monroe, Creator of the Rose Marie Collection and Dr. William Wellman, co-creator. The most carefully selected ingredients from 1982 are still used today in the personal care, men's care and skin care products. Now, with over 60 world class products, RMC customers reach all around the world with health and nutrition, wellness programs, anti-aging programs, telecommunications, Internet and so much more.

One distinct difference that RMC offers all distributors is the opportunity to double or triple their income with only a small network of other distributors in their network. With this one distinct difference and the ability to start earning commissions as a customer of the RMC products, RMC feels that this is the way the RMC network continues to expand with career oriented network marketers.

We invite you to take a closer look at a family dream of free enterprise that has turned into a multi-million dollar reality.

**RMC Group, Inc., 2969 Interstate Street, Charlotte, NC 28208**
**Phone: (800) 888-673-3741, Fax: (800) 280-0762, E-mail: mmonroe@rmcgroup.com**

# S·E·A·B·O·R·N·E®

Seaborne is the industry leader in chitin-based dietary supplements. Founded in 1994, Seaborne is the U.S. division of Japan Health Summit, Inc., which has annual sales of approximately a half billion dollars and dominates the Japanese chitin dietary supplement industry.

Seaborne is successful because of its strong heritage, quality products and a rewarding career opportunity. It is a debt-free company headquartered in the international city of Atlanta, Georgia. The corporate office, set on 20 acres, is equipped with a state-of-the art marketing, bottling and distribution facility; a 24-hour automated information system, and a multilingual staff. Seaborne is active in organizations such as the Direct Selling Association and the Council for Responsible Nutrition.

The centerpiece of Seaborne's products is a functional food called Chitin. Based on $60 million of research by the Japanese government, Chitin has been appreciated for over 20 years for its health benefits. Naturally found in the shells of crustaceans such as crab, shrimp or lobster, Chitin is an "adaptogen" which research indicates will enable the body to more effectively deal with stress factors. In Japan, Chitin is the choice dietary supplement of over 10,000 physicians.

Seaborne dietary supplements are a blend of ingredients that are safe, natural and highly effective. Using the finest quality Chitin, Chitosan, Chitin and Chitosan Oligosaccharides made exclusively from crab shell and imported from Japan, Seaborne products are unique because they contain the full spectrum of Chitin. Combining this functional ingredient with phyto-nutrients, antioxidants and whole foods provide distributors and users exclusive products found nowhere else in the world!

Seaborne currently has two product groups. The first is their advanced nutritional products, EssentialSea Max and EssentialGold. Each combines Chitin and its derivatives with other powerful nutrients such as lecithin, vitamins C&E, garlic, and beta-carotene. The synergy derived from this potent mix gives you a "supper food" unparalleled in the world. The second group is a Weight Control and Health Optimizing System containing 4 products: EssentialSea Slim, EssentialSea Phyto-Blend, EssentialSea Vitalizer and EssentialSea Smoothie. These products make up the newest member of the Seaborne family combining chitin, phyto-nutrients, soy isoflavones, vitamins and minerals.

Seaborne also offers a simple, rewarding and flexible earnings opportunity. This genuine opportunity offers ongoing corporate support, no risk and an unlimited sales territory. When sharing these unique, competitively priced products, you can earn a discount up to 55 percent, overrides up to 25 percent and a monthly $700 Cash Bonus on the sales activity of your organization. So whether you are looking to sell a few products at retail, start a part-time career or find the opportunity of a lifetime, Seaborne's program is designed to fit your personality, business style and personal goals!

**For those interested in this fascinating opportunity, please contact Ken Womack, V.P. of Sales. Seaborne, a division of Japan Health Summit, Inc., 6200 Windward Parkway, Alpharetta, GA 30005**
**Phone: (770) 663-6692, Fax: (770) 663-6701**
**Web site: www.seaborne.com, E-mail: info@seaborne.com**

*James Whittam*

Dr. Forrest C. Shaklee, Sr. (1894-1985) was a man ahead of his time. He believed that the health of the environment is entwined with the health of every person who inhabits it. In 1956, he began a family venture with the idea of manufacturing products in harmony with nature. The enterprise rapidly became a New York Stock Exchange-listed *Fortune 500* company.

Now, more than four decades later, Shaklee Corporation is a well-established and respected health industry leader, investing over $180 million in breakthrough scientific research and new product innovations. A global company, Shaklee has distributors and consumers in the United States, Canada, Japan, Malaysia, Mexico and the Philippines. Over the years, the company has paid the individuals who have built independent Shaklee businesses throughout the world more than $3 billion of income.

Shaklee manufacturers its own nutritional products--a complex and expensive undertaking, but one that guarantees quality control and product formulations that meet Shaklee's exacting standards. The Norman, Oklahoma Manufacturing Center is a state-of-the-art showcase of leading-edge pharmaceutical quality processing and production. In an average month the plant produces more than one million pounds of Shaklee products for the national market. Shaklee's three U.S. customer satisfaction centers process and ship more than 40,000 cases of product daily.

At research centers in California, a total of over 126,000 square feet is devoted to research and development work and scientists use advanced testing and quality control methods in product testing and development. Though Shaklee performs as many as 63,000 laboratory tests for quality on nutritional products and their ingredients in a single year, the company conducts no animal testing.

New nutritional product concepts and product research studies are evaluated and conducted by independent research scientists at leading universities. In the past decade alone, Shaklee is responsible for more than eighty research abstracts and articles published in major scientific journals throughout the world. Shaklee's Scientific Advisory Board, a group of nationally recognized physicians and scientists, provides expertise in nutrition, biochemistry, cardiovascular health and sports medicine.

Shaklee provides the nutritional expertise that makes the winning difference in many history making accomplishments, including: Voyager, the first nonstop, non-refuled flight around the world; The Daedalus Project, setting the world record for human-powered flight: 72 miles between the Greek islands of Crete and Santorini; four Mount Everest expeditions, including the first American to reach the top without supplemental oxygen; the International Arctic Project, the first international explorer team to successfully cross the Arctic Ocean; and Team Shaklee, a top amateur cycling team with riders who have set ten world records and which sent six riders to the 1996 Olympics.

With a Shaklee business opportunity, all the pieces are in place to offer a rewarding career with unlimited potential for growth. In addition to cash earnings, Shaklee Sales Leaders can qualify to drive a Bonus Car in as little as three months. Qualifying sales leaders are rewarded with a variety of national and international convention travel to exclusive locations such as San Francisco, Hawaii, Geneva, Rome and Barcelona.

Many people first become interested in Shaklee by using the products. They become Preferred Members and buy at a discount. Many more want to learn how to stay financially and physically healthy throughout life with their own Shaklee business.

**Shaklee Corporation, 444 Market Street, San Francisco, CA 94111**
**Phone: (800) SHAKLEE, or (415) 954-3000, Fax: (415) 954-2412, Web site: www.shaklee.com**

**Dr. Whittam, president and chief executive officer of Shaklee Corporation, succumbed to lung cancer on April 15, 1999, at the age of 49. He is survived by his wife, Sibylle, daughter Lauren, and sons Christopher and Alexandre.**

## Mission Statement:

ShapeRite's mission is to be your family's trusted partner in your home-based business through unparalleled business opportunities, time-honored family values, and acclaimed natural products.

## Where we came from:

In 1989, the Martin Family founded ShapeRite in Salt Lake City, Utah. The Martins began with only a handful of nutritional products, based on the science of standardized herbs and guaranteed potency. They decided to sell these dynamic products through network marketing.

## Where we've been:

ShapeRite expanded from $1 million in revenue and five employees in 1991, to approximately $50 million and 80 employees in 1995. Anticipating future growth in 1997, an 80,000 square foot facility, comprised of approximately 20,000 square feet of office space and 60,000 square feet of warehouse and manufacturing space was purchased.

## Where we are now:

As we approach the 21st century, our vision begins with naming the product. Each ShapeRite product label clearly states the body system it is intended to support, or the overall benefit you can expect to gain. Cardio for the heart, Immune for the immune system, Inner Sun for nervousness, anxiety, stress, etc. We start with three levels of support: **Foundation Support** - an overall wellness concept, one that treats both the body and the mind. **System Support** - with the proper standardized herbal blends, we make products that work when you take them and produce the desired effects. **Specific Support** - each product in the ShapeRite line features at least one Standardized, Guaranteed Potency which also includes the synergistic catalysts and co-factors of the whole herb that targets a specific system and produces the core benefit.

Through the highest compensation, the simplest plan, easy advancement, immediate earnings, recognition and awards, and ongoing distributor support, the ShapeRite opportunity is one of the most lucrative in the industry.

## Where we are going:

Excited about the future, ShapeRite intends to be an industry leader in both nutritional and personal care products. As we continue to expand our product line, we also continue to incorporate the most effective and beneficial botanical combinations found from technological advances around the globe.

In addition to being dedicated to innovative product design, ShapeRite ensures the success of our employee and distributors by teaching business, financial, and leadership skills and by providing meaningful recognition of achievement. We believe this vision for the future will set us apart as an industry leader. Our business is continuously rededicated through research and service to provide a business that mutually benefits everyone involved. Move with ShapeRite as we move to our next level and into the next millennia.

**ShapeRite, 9850 South 300 West, Sandy, UT 84070**
**Phone: (801) 562-3600, Fax: (801) 562-3611, Web site: www.shaperite.com**

**Keith Harding**

Sportron International is a company on the move that has taken a commanding presence in the network marketing industry since its inception in 1992. The founders, Dr. Alan Tomlinson and Mr. Keith Harding, have a combined 50 years experience in direct sales. Both Dr. Tomlinson and Mr. Harding are recognized worldwide as knowledgeable speakers, superior leaders, and dedicated businessmen with a credible and ethical background history. They are equally dedicated to the mission of the company and its distributors that states, "To enable all people to improve their economic well-being and enhance their quality of life."

Sportron thrives on the development of state-of-the-art nutritional products based on a "systems approach" pioneered by Dr. Tomlinson that targets each system of the body with a technologically advanced formula. Sportron is bound by a commitment to provide innovative products for the new millennium. Sportron places great pride in its products and its prosperity. For example, the flagship products Ultragard and Turbo are reaching people across the nation with great excitement, helping them feel and look better than ever before. Sportron is recognized as the undisputed leader in the nutrition industry.

Sporton is poised for explosive growth. In fact, *Selling Power* magazine named Sportron as one of the top 300 largest sales forces in the United States and the 27th largest growing network marketing company in the world. Sportron is established in nine countries throughout the world including South Africa and Canada.

Sportron boasts an incredible benefits package for its distributors which includes free weekly training and conference call participation, a 24-hour communication network, a downline information service on-line, a dynamic company web page, personalized distributor web pages, a discounted long distance program, discounted travel rates, and the ability to contribute to the Kim Michelle Cancer Fund for children at no charge. The opportunity is unlimited and the compensation plan is beyond compare.

Sportron offers no sign-up fee or inventory requirements, bonuses up to $50,000, car bonuses, performance bonuses, and a unique roll-up and back-up order feature that can enable anyone to earn up to 300% more than similar plans. Weekly and monthly payments on enrollments and personal purchases make it possible for new associates to easily start earning money within their first week.

Sportron believes that the secret to success is simplicity. When a program is so simple that anyone can do it, then it can be easily duplicated, and duplicity is the key to exponential growth. Sportron's Success System has been designed with the fudamentals of tested and proven methods that ensure the potential for each and every associate to easily start earning money within their first week.

**For more information on Sportron International, please call: (972) 509-1234, E-mail: marketing@sportron.net, or look up our web page at: www.sportron.net, or write to: Sportron International, Attn.: Kevin Harding, 2901 Summit Ave., Suite 300, Plano, TX 75074**

*Ken Forrest*

## History

In 1996, Kenneth (Ken) Forrest had a dream to create the world's ultimate sports club. Since that time, Ken has assembled a top-flight management team and elite Board of Directors specializing in media, sporting goods, e-commerce, direct sales, and corporate finance and law, to bring to market a world-class online sports community. Today, SportsNuts.com is the world's largest Internet-based sports club and host to the world's largest online e-sports mall. In April of 1999, SportsNut.com became publicly traded company (SPNT).

## The Internet

The continually updated website located at **www.SportsNuts.com** offers everything for sports fans and participants, including sports scores, stats, news and highlights. The Community or "Club" environment includes many features to bring together sports fans in fun and exciting ways such as prizes, trivia, contests, fantasy sports, exclusive events and tournaments, and much more, including a huge E-Sports Mall and full service Internet access through SportsNut.com ISP. Electronic commerce will grow from $8 billion in 1998 to $250 billion in 2005, and fifty percent of the $2 trillion in retail sales will shift to the Internet within 10 years. ISP subscribers are getting online at a rate of 60 new customers per minute around the world. SportsNuts.com is uniquely positioned to take advantage of these trends.

## Sports Industry Meets Direct Selling

The sports, outdoors and fitness industries represent a stable growing market exceeding $200 billion annually. SportsNuts.com is the largest online sports "club" and the first company of its kind to simultaneously use the Internet, media advertising, and network marketing to sell sports, outdoors and fitness products/services to its worldwide members called "Fans." SportsNuts.com's aggressive growth curve reflects the fervent passion for sports demonstrated by people around the world, and capitalizes on the power of sports as an engine for bringing these enthusiasts together.

## The Business of Sports

SportsNuts.com provides its players (independent distributors) with the opportunity to capitalize on the exploding Internet and sports industries in the simplest way possible. Independent players maintain no inventory, make no deliveries or collections, have no employees, and enjoy great tax benefits. Players "Get Paid to Play" by receiving commissions on SportsNuts.com product and service sales, VIP Fan membership sales, Fast Break Bonuses, ISP sales, E-Sports Mall sales and much more.

## World Class Player Support Services

To meet the needs of thousands of players building successful businesses, SportsNut.com has put together an extensive and efficient Player Support System. This system includes not only timely and accurate corporate support, but also tools that empower players to support themselves and each other via our Online Player Support Web site, including online real-time information 24 hours a day.

**Main address: SportsNuts.com, Inc., 10421 South 400 West, Suite 550, Salt Lake City, UT 84095**
**Shipping Address: SportsNuts.com, Inc., 754 North 1890 West, Provo, UT 84601**
**Phone: (801) 816-2500, Fax: (801) 816-2599**
**Web site: www.SportsNuts.com, E-mail: corpinfo@sportsnuts.com**

Starfire International has everything you are looking for in a business opportunity. The company is very stable and secure and has operated completely debt-free since September 1993, enabling 90 percent of all profits to return to the distributor force.

Starfire believes in paying members generously for their efforts at helping to grow and build the business. If you have done the most, you will earn the most, no matter when you joined the company, or who your sponsor may be. This is possible because the structure is not MLM. We call it Multi-Dimensional Marketing (MDM), and it puts you on a level playing field with the heavy hitter and first-timer alike. At Starfire, everyone joins one sales organization instead of building their own dowline. You get to tap into the existing organization and simply by earning points for such things as introducing others, you can pass those who are less personally sponsored and earn commission from all those below you. If you have the most points, you tap into sales from every active member and earn the top commission!

Starfire offers an incredible opportunity with a low, one-time, lifetime membership fee of $30. For this $30, you will receive a kit with a video to get you started, a monthly newsletter to keep you updated on the company and breakthroughs in health, as well as monthly activity reports so you don't have to worry about any of the paperwork. The start-up cost is low as well, with immediate compensation for introducing just one to two active members allowing you to break even in your new business right away, earning $75, the monthly minimum order. Paychecks are sent out every month and have always been sent on time and in full. At least 25 percent of all members are earning checks and our retention rate is 99%.

Starfire's growing line of over 60 cutting-edge products will surely allow you to experience improved health while you create your fortune choosing which ones to sell to others. Products include Ericsson's Preventive Medical Group Alka-Mine Coral-Calcium from Okinawa, which creates antioxidant water loaded with ionic trace minerals. This reverse aging water helps to balance the body's pH for better health and costs less than bottled water. Although we are one of five companies to offer Coral-Calcium in the U.S., we are definitely the best! If you are already purchasing a coral, make sure it is Ericsso's. Starfire also offers eight exclusive Energetic Solutions, which are homeopathically prepared complexes that help to increase energy, boost stamina, relieve allergies, PMS symptoms and food allergies, stimulate the digestive system, enhance utilization of vitamins and minerals, and re-energize your body on the cellular level. Star Gold is our exclusive and very complete multi-vitamin mineral supplement with over 100 nutrients in a special energizing base! Our exclusive heart support formula, Elation! has everything to help keep your blood flowing. Other top quality products are MSM (organic sulphur), Chitosan (fat sucking fiber), Pycnogenol (antioxidant), Gingko (memory enhancer), Mild Silver Protein (colloidal silver), DHEA (the mother hormone), Organic Green Papaya Bars (delicious and nutritious) and many more including, pure water filters, microwater units, soaps, rebounders, natural lighting and a whole host of environmentally friendly products. Starfire is also the only wholesaler for the ChildLife line of children's health supplements including a bifidus flora, essential fatty acids, vitamin C, multi-vitamin/mineral, Echinacea and more. All of these taste good with no sugar!

Starfire's innovative founders, Dr. Glen Swartwout, director of research and development, and Mr. John Moylan, director of marketing, are proud to offer you the opportunity to change your life and enhance your health.

**You can reach us at: 900 Leilani Street, Hilo, HI 96720, Phone: (888) 889-7882, Fax: (800) 249-5991, E-mail: starfire@aloha.net, Web site: http://www.star-base.net, two minute message (within the continental U.S.): (800) 935-5171, ext. 3068, Fax-on-Demand: (704) 904-1818, doc 417.**

*Steve Goldberg*

As a successful Hollywood producer for over 25 years, Steven Goldberg knows what it takes to make a production a real winner. Whether it's a television series, a concert tour, or a major motion picture, it takes a lot of hard work, determination and a never-ending supply of creative talent and marketable product. And that's exactly what you'll find at Starlight International.

## Products That Work

Starlight's success is a direct result of our long-term focus on the efficacy, credibility and marketability of a select group of products designed to meet the health and beauty needs of today's lifestyles. Our Products Research Council is comprised of leading members of the international alternative and complimentary health community. Under their guidance, our growing line of formulations offer real and lasting benefits to consumers who notice the improvements to their health, not in weeks or months, but often in a matter of hours or days. And that impressive impact on hundreds of thousands of retail customers insures repeat and re-order business for our independent distributors month after month, year after year.

## Sales Techniques That Work

Our commitment to our independent distributors involves more than just an innovative product line. We have also developed a simple, easy to follow, duplicable plan for retailing and recruiting. This proven sales method includes award winning packaging, retail customer samples, and highly effective sales materials guaranteed to generate interest. And all of this is backed up by state-of-the-art training, communication and support technologies, including our free Fax-on-Demand and Electronic Voice Messaging Systems which provide 24-hours-a-day, 7-days-a-week access to the information, ordering and training systems needed to build a successful downline organization.

## Results That Are Indisputable

These are just some of the reasons why Starlight has enjoyed such explosive growth since its founding in October of 1993. What began as one product distributed by a handful of independent distributors has grown, as of 1/1/99, to nearly 20 products being sold by over 80,000 distributors in all 50 states plus Puerto Rico and several US possessions. From a concept to $140 million in wholesales in just five years speaks volumes about Starlight's rock solid foundation.

## The Future Is Bright

Starlight remains a wonderful opportunity for anyone whose visions of the future includes building his/her own business while enjoying all the recognition and financial rewards of one of the industry's most competitive marketing and compensation programs. From car allowances to international world-class travel incentives, nobody else does it in Starlight style.

**To learn more about Starlight International, its products and business opportunity, write to us at 80 Garden Court, Suite 100, Monterey, CA 93940, or send us a fax at (831) 373-0500, or visit our Web site at: www.starlightonline.com**

*Oi-Lin Chen*

Truly a unique company, Sunrider conceptualizes, researches, develops, manufactures, produces, packages and distributes each of its vast range of products. Currently operating in more than 27 countries, Sunrider® was founded in 1982 by owners, Drs. Tei Fu and Oi-Lin Chen, each of whom has merged a scientific background with an entrepreneurial spirit and an understanding of the best of eastern and western cultures.

**The Best of the East and West** -- Combining traditional Chinese philosophy and concepts with modern western technology, Dr. Tei Fu Chen developed Sunriders' highly concentrated line of herbal foods and beverages based on the Philosophy of Regeneration, with its emphasis on the balance between Yin and Yang (the negative and positive forces of nature) and the five elements: water, wood, fire, metal and earth.

Sunrider® is also renowned for its superb skin care, personal care and cosmetic lines under the Kandesn® brand. Kandesn® also encompasses the exclusive Oi-Lin® line of health and beauty products, formulated with cutting-edge skin care technology and premium natural ingredients culled from around the world.

The latest product line launched by Sunrider® is SunSmile®, featuring a wide array of items for oral hygiene and household cleaning, as well as a revolutionary Fruit & Vegetable Rinse. As with all of Sunrider's herbal foods and beverages, Kandesn® and SunSmile® products are researched, developed and manufactured exclusively in facilities that are wholly owned and controlled by Sunrider®.

**Self-Owned Manufacturing Facilities** -- Known globally for its stringent quality control systems, Sunrider® owns manufacturing plants in the City of Industry, California; Tianjin, China; Huang Pu, China; Taichung, Taiwan; and Singapore. In addition, one of the two City of Industry facilities boasts three on-site laboratories--Microbiology, Chemistry, and Research and Development--which ensure up-to-date development at all times.

**Outstanding Research & Development** -- Unique in its owner expertise and control of products from concept to final packaging, Sunrider® also grows, tests, harvests and concentrates the herbs which go into its exclusive formulations. In their unending search for exceptional herbal combinations, the Chens have established and maintained botanical gardens where more than 100 varieties of herbs are charted from seed to germination to mature plant. Specialists determine which parts of each plant are most beneficial and only those are used in Sunrider® formulations.

In August of 1998, Sunrider® President, Dr. Oi-Lin Chen, personally orchestrated the grand opening of the U.S.A. Sunrider Botanical Garden. Herbs are grown in a 1,200 square foot greenhouse as well as outdoors in custom-crafted boxes. Located on the northern acre of Sunrider's 300,000 square foot World Headquarters in Torrance, California, the Botanical Garden is also a cultural monument.

**Business Opportunity** -- The Sunrider® marketing plan is based on equal opportunity and has proven to be successful for distributors in different economics around the world. In fact, the Sunrider® business opportunity has proven to be recession-proof in country after country.

Distributors, depending upon rank, earn increasing bonuses, rebates and incentives, including a remarkable Auto/ Home Fund which pays for a new vehicle or home. There are also travel incentives which give distributors the opportunity to earn free trips to Sunrider® conventions and seminars.

**Continued Growth and Expansion** -- Always looking ahead, the Chens continue to lead Sunrider® towards new horizons. They constantly reinvest in the company and personally train and develop distributors into independent business people through seminars and creative marketing tools. Now is the ideal time for people to embrace the Sunrider Opportunity for a Lifetime™.

**Sunrider International, 1625 Abalone Avenue, Torrance, CA 90501**
**Phone: (310) 781-8096, Fax: (310) 222-9271/2, Web site: www.sunrider.com**

*Bryan Noar*

SupraLife is a fast-emerging leader in the formulation, manufacturing and marketing of unique and innovative preventive health, weight management, sports and fitness and personal care products. Launched in San Diego, California, in 1991, and previously known as Soaring Eagle, SupraLife has grown impressively over the past seven years. With a beefed-up infrastructure and enhanced compensation plan now in place, SupraLife is well poised for explosive growth. Successful international launches have already taken place in the United Kingdom and Holland, and future expansion plans include several other exciting markets.

SupraLife has built its success around a line of unique breakthrough products that use organic liquid trace minerals as their base. The flagship products, Total Toddy and Ultra Body Toddy, contain carefully balanced ratios of more than 90 different vitamins, minerals, amino acids, antioxidants and phytochemicals. They are thought to be the world's most complete full spectrum liquids and can be taken straight or mixed in juice. Consumer loyalty is astounding. First, because the products really work and second, because they are generally more convenient and more economical than handfuls of pills.

SupraLife also offers a wide range of specialized products on the forefront of an emerging field known as Integrated Nutrition. By simply adding the appropriate Super Nutrient, Biotic Code or Slim-Slim products to one's regular full spectrum Toddy regimen, powerful customized Integrated Nutrition programs can be developed to fit virtually any nutritional need. A few favorites in this line are AllerForce for allergies, Flex-Flow for joints, SugarEze for glucose metabolism, and Sports Toddy, a powerful performance drink used by former Olympians Steve Scott and John Howard. All formulas contain time-tested ingredients backed by clinical studies, and all are proprietary.

SupraLife products are distributed exclusively through a recently enhanced hybrid unilevel/breakaway multi-level compensation plan that rewards distributors fairly as well as generously. Activity is accurately tracked using a Jenkon Summit V global computer system. The marketing and training materials are first class, especially the extremely impressive 'business-in-a-briefcase' Distributor Kit (included in the $49 sign-up fee). The company also offers comprehensive administrative support, regular live training seminars conducted by corporate executives and outside experts, and weekly conference calls. In addition, the corporate team closely monitors the ongoing needs of the field through an active Distributor Advisory Board.

The management team is dynamic, creative, and has solid business experience. SupraLife's vision-driven President, Bryan Noar, is a licensed CPA with more than 10 years of successful network marketing experience both in the field and in the office. After becoming a top distributor with one of the world's leading network marketing companies he turned his attention to MLM consulting before jumping back into the corporate side of things and achieving a strong reputation for success. Marketing & Sales is headed up by Mike Lewis, an internationally known 'heavyweight' with almost 15 years of MLM experience and a reputation for getting results fast. V.P. Operations & Finance, Steve Leisenring, is a licensed CPA who spent several years with Arthur Andersen & Co. before joining SupraLife.

But what really sets SupraLife apart is the FREE nutritional counseling, technical support and education available to SupraLife distributors and preferred customers through the internationally recognized Institute of Nutritional Science. This service alone is worth many times the sign-up fee!

Given SupraLife's proven track record and exceptionally strong product line, coupled with the strong worldwide trend towards healthier living, the opportunity for anyone who is interested in becoming a SupraLife distributor is nothing short of spectacular!

**SupraLife, PO Box 261280, San Diego, CA 92196-1280**
**Phone: (619) 653-6520, Fax: (619) 271-8375, E-mail: marketing@toddy.com, Web site: www.toddy.com**

**Rudy Revak**

# SYMMETRY

Well-known and respected in the industry of direct selling, Mr. Rudy Revak has started an exciting company offering some of the most technologically advanced nutritional and personal care products available in the marketplace today. Symmetry International, now nearly 100,000 distributors strong, was launched in May of 1995 and has already achieved nearly $100,000 million in sales in nine countries worldwide.

Capitalizing on his nearly three decades of experience in the industry, Mr. Revak created in Symmetry the first cellular marketing system ever to be seen in direct selling. Having seen for himself the best components of the various plans that exist in companies throughout the world, Mr. Revak designed this cellular marketing structure to be the most progressive opportunity known to direct sellers. Weekly commissions and lucrative monthly bonuses are just two of the many unique aspects.

After amassing one of the most knowledgeable and experienced sales and marketing teams in the business, Mr. Revak combined this innovative marketing system with revolutionary products which offer the most advanced technology in nutrition today. The product line offers the most leading edge technology in nutrition, botanical nutraceutical, sports nutrition and skin care science and continues to expand as new discoveries are made. With teams of researchers working behind the scenes, Mr. Revak has and will continue to show his commitment to providing the absolute latest in nutrition and health care products to people around the world.

With both the lucrative business opportunity and state-of-the art products available to them, thousands of distributors around the United States, Canada, the Caribbean, the Philippines, Mexico (and soon, the Pacific Rim and Eupore) are sharing in Mr. Revak's vision to build the largest and most respected company ever seen in the industry, while at the same time offering people from all walks of life a real chance to reach some of their greatest goals and dreams.

"My goal is to have Symmetry become one of the most respected direct-to-consumer companies in the world," says Mr. Revak. "This will be accomplished by following our mission to enrich people's lives for a better tomorrow, physically, mentally, personally and financially."

Already featured in such top national publications as *Success* magazine and *Working at Home*, Rudy Revak is also an active member of the Direct Selling Association and has recently been named to the board of directors of the Direct Selling Education Foundation, or DSEF, which plays a critical role in providing a positive landscape in which direct selling companies are able to thrive. Mr. Revak will be assisting in the DSEF's efforts to serve the public interest with education, information and research, thereby encouraging greater public awareness and acceptance of direct selling in the global marketplace.

Symmetry is also partnered with the World Federation of Direct Selling Associations, or WFDSA. The WFDSA has established the World Codes of Conduct which all members must abide by in order for the industry to maintain the highest ethical standards and credibility so vital to its continued growth.

**For more about Symmetry International, 420 South Hillview Drive, Milpitas, CA 95035**
**Phone: (800) Symmetry or (408) 942-7700, Web site: www.symmetry.3000.com**

# TARRAH

In December of 1996, TARRAH, formerly known as LadyLove Skin Care, became part of the Golden Pride International family.

**The Company** - Founded in 1983 by its President, Harry W. Hersey, Golden Pride International is a leader in the direct sales industry. GPI has been a member of the Direct Selling Association since 1983 and its 15-year history of expansion and growth is impressive. After six years of tremendous growth in the health supplement and nutritional products industry, the company acquired the 100-year-old W.T. Rawleigh Company. In 1996, the 24-year-old LadyLove Skin Care Company was purchased and was expanded into Canada in 1998. In July of that same year, a strategic alliance was formed with Tony Little, America's #1 personal trainer--GPI now has the most energized nutritional spokesman in the world to help take the company to unparalleled heights.

**The Mission** - TARRAH's mission is: 1) to offer quality skin care and beauty products with personalized service and convenience to customers and, 2) to create a career opportunity that allows TARRAH consultants to grow personally, professionally and financially.

**The Product** - TARRAH's skin care and body care products are formulated with an aloe vera and vitamin E base. They are enriched with botanicals and emollients to help balance and restore moisture to the skin. The cosmetics line is in a class of its own, with brilliant colors and enhancing tones which are carefully blended and selected to offer the perfect complement to any skin tone. Golden Pride offers the highest quality, synergistically blended, bio-available nutritional supplements. The vast line includes heart-healthy formulations, nutrients, herbs, water filtration, weight loss, and more. The W.T. Rawleigh line consists of traditional old-time remedies, flavorings and extracts, spices and seasonings, specialty foods, and household items. The combination of Golden Pride's original focus on health supplements and nutritional products, along with the additional products from the Rawleigh and TARRAH companies and Tony Little's Eternal Energy line gives GPI one of the most comprehensive product lines in North America. With nearly 500 different products to choose from, Golden Pride is a perfect fit for any home.

**The Program** - TARRAH's marketing plan is designed to maximize the independent consultants' earnings. The high paying, easy to understand plan provides outstanding financial rewards for sharing the products and the management opportunities with others. A host of educational materials is available to all independent consultants through the use of brochures, catalogues, audio and videotapes and more. The management team also hosts meetings and seminars to support and educate the consultant staff.

**The People** - Our President, Harry W. Hersey, has many years of experience in the direct selling industry, ranging from being an independent distributor to being a part of the executive management team for several direct selling companies. He is a highly respected, creative and innovative leader in the industry and was recently elected vice chairman of the DSA Board of Directors, which ultimately leads to the position of chairman of the board.

Leslie Campbell, executive vice president and chief operating officer, has had domestic and international experience in all facets of the direct selling industry and has served on committees for the DSA and DSEF.

TARRAH provides a refreshing consultant-centered approach to business in an established, stable company in a growth mode. TARRAH is the ideal place for anyone interested in building a long-term business that will be there for his or her future.

**Golden Pride International, PO Box 21109, West Palm Beach, FL 33416-1109**
**Phone: (561) 640-5700, Fax: (561) 640-7333, Fax-on-Demand: (800) 640-3550, E-mail: gpride@flinet.com**

Tupperware is one of the world's leading direct selling companies with nearly one million independent consultants selling Tupperware's premium food storage containers, serving-ware, microwave cookware and children's toys in more than 100 countries. For over 50 years, Tupperware has been making it all possible in homes around the world--providing high quality products, rewarding careers, good times and long lasting memories to three generations.

> "Each day I become prouder to be a part of the Tuperware family. Tupperware is truly a heart company -- one filled with caring people who are dedicated to helping you achieve your dreams. Whatever you want to be is what Tupperware wants for you."
>
> **Betty Palm, President, Tupperware U.S.A.**

### The Party

A Tupperware party is starting every 2.2 seconds somewhere in the world. Today's Tupperware parties provide much more than just an opportunity to purchase Tupperware® products. They are fun! Tupperware parties provide possibilities to socialize, laugh, learn, and build friendships and memories that will last a lifetime.

### The Product

Tupperware is known for innovative products and premium quality. The Tupperware® brand is one of the most loved and trusted names in housewares. In addition to the high praise Tupperware receives in homes around the world, the graceful design and functionality of Tupperware® products have been recognized and acquired by a number of the world's art museums and industrial design collections, and have won design awards in the United States, Europe and Japan.

### The Possibilities

The Tupperware culture of caring and sharing offers a flexible career to meet the many needs of today's women. A career with Tupperware means that you will have time for all the things you treasure most, while working at home according to your own schedule. The many rewards of a Tupperware career include the opportunity to earn part-time to executive and personal encouragement.

**Tupperware:** Making it all possible!

**For more information, please contact Tupperware at PO Box 2353, Orlando, FL 32802**
**Customer Services: (800) 858-7221**
**Web site: www.Tupperware.com**

*Beth Ann McFadyen*

Universal Sports Direct, Inc. (USD) is the first network marketing company that pays its representatives to love sports! USD markets licensed sports products, collectibles, memorabilia and sports lifestyle products through direct sales from their catalog. The fact that almost everyone, worldwide, loves sports and their unique position as the first multi-level marketing company to bring a variety of sports products to the marketplace has resulted in phenomenal growth.

Swainson Hawke, founder and chairman of the board started the company in 1997, in Atlanta, Georgia, with a small, twelve page catalog and only a handful of independent representatives. Less than one year later, USD had released its third catalog with 80 pages of innovative and diversified products. Currently, over 5,000 representatives nationwide distribute catalogs and sell products. This explosive growth can be attributed to two factors: USD's exciting product line and the Team Marketing concept.

The sale of sports products represented hundreds of billions of dollars last year. The sales of licensed sports products alone (those that are licensed to sell by such organizations as the NFL, MLB, NBA, NCAA, and NHL) jumped 70 percent from 1990 to 1996. These figures do not take into account NASCAR, which is the number one watched sport in the U.S. and other licensed sports products. Whether it is a cap with a favorite college team, a key chain boasting a champion car, or an autographed baseball card, everyone loves to be associated with a winner! Sales are successful largely due to the fact that the customers are not limited to the products from their local area, as found in most retail outlets or other catalogs. Typically, sports fans remain true to their favorite teams, no matter where they live. So if you are a true blue Cardinals fan or a graduate from Ohio State now living in Miami, there are loads of products available to you! Most products are available in multiple sports, teams and players. You choose your favorites!

USD promotes a winning lifestyle as well. Swainson Hawke's vision provides a holistic approach to enjoy life. Therefore, USD offers many consumable products such as "Power Punch" for better nutrition and "Triple Play" for weight loss. The catalog even includes a personal spa system for relaxing after a stimulating workout. Some of the outstanding products in USD's catalogs are exclusive to the company and can only be purchased from Universal Sports Direct. This will allow USD to increase its name recognition in the marketplace as more new products are added with the Universal Sports Direct "Exclusive" Logo. Our Product Development Department is skilled in finding fun and exciting products for our representatives and customers.

The Corporate Management Team, led by Beth Ann McFadyen, co-founder and president, wanted to offer a marketing plan that would truly give every independent representative a chance to win. The Team Marketing concept was developed so that each team member has the opportunity to develop a successful business and to earn an unlimited income, not just from his or her own efforts, but also when they aided in another's success. The compensation plan allows for immediate weekly bonuses and monthly income, while long-term income may be built as team sales continue and increase. In addition, representatives have the option of training for a "Coaches" position, enabling them to earn income as they train new representatives themselves.

The Management Team provides support for the field sales force through training classes, videos, fax-on-demand, fax blasts, a nationwide voice mail system and the most innovative management tools available. At Universal Sports Direct, Inc. "Where Everyone Wins" every independent representative is given an opportunity to be "PAID TO LOVE SPORTS, AND A LOT MORE!"

**Universal Sports Direct, 15555 Oakbrook Drive, Suite 175, Norcross, GA 30093**
**Phone: (770) 825-0706, Fax: (770) 849-0745**

**Dallin Larsen**

## Industry leader

In one of the fastest growing industries in the world today, USANA is leading the way in the quest for improved health and wellness through optimized nutrition. Established in 1992, this science-based nutrition company has become one of America's fastest growing corporations due to its superior product line, considered to be the best in the industry, and its innovative network marketing program that amply rewards both the average and the ambitious distributor.

For two consecutive years *MLM Insider* magazine has named USANA one of the ten best companies in network marketing and the company also received the Distributors Choice award as the top network marketing company for 1997 and 1998. USANA is financially strong and publicly traded on NASDAQ (symbol: USNA).

## The key to health is prevention

Founder Myron Wentz, Ph.D., is a pioneer in cell-culture technology. In the early 1970s, he founded Gull Laboratories, which soon became the world's leading producer of commercially available diagnostic test kits for viral diseases. In the 1990s Dr. Wentz's focus shifted from disease detection to disease prevention. He and other scientists were finding that our environment, lifestyle, and diet factors were continually eroding our health. One of the most significant research findings was the value of antioxidants in countering the negative effects of free radicals in the human body. In an effort to find and make available to the health-conscious consumer the best antioxidants, vitamin and mineral formulas, and other nutritionals, Dr. Wentz founded USANA, Inc.

Today, USANA's products provide optimal cell-level nutrition, fiber, and antioxidant protection for our bodies. Dr. Wentz is applying the same level of scientific expertise, technical brilliance, and dedication he employed in pioneering viral diagnostics to create breakthrough approaches to nutritional wellness.

## Lucrative marketing plan

While USANA's products provide tremendous health benefits, its business opportunity can be highly rewarding as well. The innovative business plan is more evenly distributed than traditional multi-level marketing programs and is fair to everyone involved. Financial success can be achieved by sponsoring as few as two distributors into an organization. The cellular compensation plan is a binary system in which distributors build balanced left and right side downline organizations for the purpose of selling USANA products.

## Continued growth

With current operations in the United States, Canada, the Caribbean, Australia, New Zealand, and the United Kingdom, USANA has developed a strong distributor base throughout the world. Each year, as a result of USANA's dynamic growth and expansion strategies, new countries are added to the USANA family.

USANA continues to develop new products, but only after exhaustive research is performed and specific health benefits and claims are proven to the satisfaction of USANA's team of expert scientists. Each formula is thoroughly tested and adjusted during the development phase until maximum bioavailability and effectiveness can be guaranteed.

## True health and true wealth

Just as true health means more than the absence of disease, true wealth goes beyond the mere accumulation of money. It is that powerful feeling of freedom and independence that provides immense personal and professional satisfaction. At USANA, we are proud to offer our distributors an opportunity to achieve both true health and true wealth.

**Lee & Mary Deehaute**

Welcome to the wonderful world of Usborne Books. You are embarking on a journey representing the finest books and educational materials on the market today. Our number one priority is the family. We provide an opportunity for a flexible work schedule thus allowing for a balance between your family and your business. The fact that the product is for children also makes this opportunity enticing because you can involve your children and therefore make it a family business. "Our mission is to provide all children access to the best quality books published!" UBAH believes that children should have every opportunity available to them. One of the basics is a good education.

Usborne Books At Home is a network marketing system. Direct selling provides a natural setting for marketing the books. Customers can see the benefits for their children and receive recommendations based on their needs. It is an informal sales approach. Just open the book!

The five ways that you can market Usborne Books are home shows, direct sales, book fairs, fund raisers, and school and library sales. This is an opportunity for someone who wants to work for him or herself, either part-time for extra income, or full-time, building financial security.

We offer a product that is unsurpassed in the quality of illustrations and material content. We now have over 900 titles and add new titles each January and July. Our products are the most affordable in the direct selling industry, which enhances your opportunity to build a business.

Usborne Books are designed graphically to draw the students in, to make them want to learn the material and to help them retain that knowledge. The magic of Usborne Books is that they make both reading and learning fun and do not create a boring or intimidating experience. Peter Usborne set out to break down a child's resistance to reading and learning at home. These books are so well organized that children absorb and recall much of the vast amount of information presented.

Usborne Books are fascinating, lavishly illustrated books written with humor, surprise and drama. They incorporate activities and puzzles to challenge a child's observation and intelligence. Their superb printing quality and exceptionally well produced graphics, high ratio of pictures to text, short magazine-like format and unique detail set Usborne Books apart from anything yet produced. There is a wide range of subjects covering hobbies, science, nature, parent's guides and more. Usborne Books truly appeals to all ages, infants to adults, with prices to suit everyone. The books are printed on acid-free paper, so the pages will last forever, if taken care of properly.

Our home office staff is dedicated to providing excellent support for your needs through information access, product selection and order fulfillment.

Educational Development Corporation, the parent company of Usborne Books At Home, has been recognized by publications including *Forbes* and *Business Week* as being among the fastest growing companies in the nation. Also, UBAH was recently featured in *Wealth Building Magazine* as one of "142 Proven Direct Sales Firms" and was also featured in "*Better Parenting*," a nationally aired television program. We are very proud of Usborne Books At Home and what has been accomplished and we look forward to your involvement in the continued success of our marketing program. For exciting details on this wonderful opportunity call the number below.

**Usborne Books At Home, Phone: (800) 611-1655**

**Dave Watson**

VIVA America is one of the world's premier high-tech nutritional health care providers. By putting the emphasis on scientific research, VIVA has capitalized on its competitive edge and has quickly become a front-runner in the emerging nutraceutical industry. In the nutritional supplement business, quality counts. Each year VIVA America spends millions of Research and Development dollars on innovative nutraceuticals, which are nutritional supplements with pharmaceutical applications.

Using proprietary technologies and patented scientific processes, this cutting-edge company had developed a number of breakthrough products clinically proven to be safe and effective. Results of these rigorous clinical studies have been published in esteemed peer-reviewed medical journals. VIVA America continues to invest in R&D as well as clinical trials at major U.S. universities to ensure we continue to set the standard for safety and efficacy.

VIVA America is an exceptional company in part because it is vertically integrated. Not all nutritional supplements are created equal. In fact, studies prove many of them don't contain what the label says. VIVA strictly monitors and controls all aspects of their product production including the farms on which fruits and vegetables are grown, raw materials, product formulation, manufacturing, packaging, quality control, and distribution.

VIVA America's world headquarters is in Costa Mesa, California. VIVA operates a multi-million dollar, 105,000 square foot, FDA-licensed, pharmaceutical grade manufacturing facility. It is home to an organic chemistry lab, analytical lab, microbiology lab, R&D, cosmetic and botanical research labs. It also contains several quality control centers. VIVA is committed to excellence in every aspect of the company's operation.

VIVA America is owned by David Fan who not only has a science background, but also a Master's Degree in Business. As an investment banker, he helped bring a major nutritional network marketing company public in the 1970s and established his interest in the nutritional and network marketing industries. His science and business background allowed him to clearly understand the value of network marketing as a highly effective global distribution channel. Fan has invested in the best, acquiring the state-of-the-art manufacturing facility, investing heavily in research and technology, and surrounding himself with experts in all aspects of nutritional research.

The scientific facilities are headed by Dr. Simon Hsia, one of the world's leading nutritional research scientists. Prior to joining VIVA in 1991, Dr. Hsia was the Senior Staff Scientist for the worlds largest nutritional networking marketing company. Dr. Hsia works closely with a staff of 20 scientists, five of whom are Ph.D.'s. VIVA has many affiliations with major medical teaching universities that conduct ongoing clinical studies specifically on our products.

Because VIVA has taken the time to assemble the best facilities, laboratories, scientists, and staff, the company's success has spread internationally. VIVA has a strong presence in Taiwan, Malaysia, Indonesia, Hong Kong, Singapore, Brunci, and the Philippines. There are about 75,000 VIVA distributors internationally.

After proving itself around the world, the company has positioned itself for a strong focus on the U.S. market and is prepared for explosive growth in 1999. Consumers have repeatedly demonstrated their interest in quality nutritional supplements. VIVA's nutritional supplements deliver all the benefits you desire backed by the high quality consumers demand. We guarantee each VIVA supplement delivers the precise, standard recommended dosage of each ingredient.

VIVA offers an incredible business opportunity to achieve financial freedom. Plus it has all the benefits of a home-based business; flexible hours, low overhead and freedom. With the help and support of this progressive, dynamic company, you can take advantage of these opportunities to improve your lifestyle and watch your bank account grow. VIVA is offering that chance to build your own business for the new millennium.

**VIVA America, 1239 Victoria Street, Costa Mesa, CA 92627, Phone: (949) 645-6100**

**Work At Home
Personal Prosperity
305 Hahani Street #122
Kailua, Hawaii 96734**

"Dad, you promised
to go to this game!"

**What are two things every parent needs more of?**

# What does every parent need more of?

## T I M E and M O N E Y !

## Is There a Solution?

*"Mom, why can't we afford a pet?"*

- Would you like to be able to spend more time with your family?
- Would you like to work at something you actually enjoy doing?
- Would you like to have money for family vacations you've always dreamed of?

**If this sounds like where you want to be, Send in this postcard for your free booklet on how to increase your time & money!**

Name: _____

Address: _____

City/State/Zip: _____

Phone: _____ Email: _____

# Viviane Woodard

**Innovation--Glamour--Opportunity.** With 40 years experience in the exciting world of skin care and cosmetics, Viviane Woodard has been often imitated but never equaled. In 1958, the research chemists of Viviane Woodard perfected a truly extraordinary moisturizing process called vita-moisturization to add moisture to the skin and hold it there to quench beauty's thirst for moisture scientifically. Just as in nature, it is moisture that sustains all that is new and beautiful. Remove the moisture from a smooth plum and it shrivels into a wrinkled prune. A beautiful rose fades and becomes brittle when deprived of its moisture. The same principle applies to the skin. Woodard was one of the first to offer skin care based on water, not oils, and the company's reputation for cutting edge technology and superior products has grown ever since.

From its earliest days, the company was associated with the Hollywood film industry, endorsed by the Hollywood Society of Makeup Artist and the products used by many leading ladies of the silver screen. But these were not the only women who were stars with Viviane Woodard. From the beginning, the products were offered direct to the public through independent beauty advisors, thousands of whom built successful careers teaching women the techniques of skin care and makeup application.

The secret of success in any business is to find a need and fill it. As true today as 40 years ago, Woodard continues to answer the many needs of people with its superior products and beauty advice and instruction. This much needed and appreciated service of personalized makeup instruction teaches women how to choose the beauty products best for them and how to apply them.

Woodard views its mission as "bringing beauty and opportunity for personal growth and success into the lives of others." It's a business of helping people create a desired image for themselves and developing or enhancing a lifestyle. For some, it may mean an opportunity to turn extra time into extra money and for others, maybe a dream of a whole new career.

Its beauty advisors need only a desire to learn and earn!

Today, the opportunity in Woodard is stronger than ever with a generous marketing plan, support and tools. It's adaptable to individuals and community needs. It offers "choice" in how a person affiliates (a $49.95 kit includes a $49.95 re-saleable skin care set and immediate investment return) and how they build their business. Its sales programs are simple and direct, whether by sampling, individual or group lessons, mail and telephone repeat business--based on one common principle "to serve and educate." It fills different needs for different people, all of whom are important, worthwhile and meaningful.

Woodard's beauty advisors enjoy strong customer loyalty and high repeat sales. Its product line built on the strength of its effective and result-oriented skin care products also includes makeup, glamour, bath and body, fragrance and specialty gift items for the entire family. Woodard's products are manufactured in its own facility under the watchful eye of experienced research and production professionals.

It's a company built on a tradition and history with its focus on the future.

**For more information, contact the corporate office: Phone: (818) 989-5818, or (800) 423-3600**
**Fax: (818) 904-3316**
**E-mail: viviane@earthlink.net or visit our Web site: http://www.woodard.com**

# Wachters' Organic Sea Products

**Background:** Founded in 1932 by visionary scientist, Dr. Joseph V. Wachter, Sr., whose mission was to bring the benefits of sea plants to humankind. Wachters' Organic Sea Products (Wachters') manufactures and distributes health, nutrition and personal care products in over 26 countries. With an extensive product line of 150 products, divided into nine product divisions, Wachters' has consumable products to meet everyone's needs, from multi-vitamin/mineral combinations to environmental products. That means repeat business from the masses.

**The Company:** Wachters' is headquartered in the San Francisco Bay area, for distribution throughout the U.S. The company also has offices in Calgary, Alberta, for distribution throughout Canada; and, Manila, the Philippines, for distribution throughout Southeast Asia. Wachters' is debt-free, owns its manufacturing facility, which is FDA approved, and in compliance with a number of government agencies, including: U.S. Food & Drug Administration, State Food and Drug, Department of Agriculture, Federal Trade Commission, et al. Wachters' has total control over its product quality, and follows GMP, Good Manufacturing Practices. Besides utilizing the highest grade, natural ingredients, Wachters' products contain no preservatives, artificial colorings, artificial flavorings, sugar, starch, or animal products. Wachters' products are also certified "Kosher-Parve," as a result of passing stringent testing of its ingredients, facilities and equipment.

**The Products:** Wachters' has been the pioneer in the health/nutrition industry, with its Exclusive Blend of Sea Vegetation™--a unique combination of organic compounds, comprising up to 15 different species of the highest quality sea vegetation from around the world, which is included in the base of each of its products, and serves as a synergistic activator (spark plug), of the other ingredients, thereby enhancing their effectiveness. Wachters' team of nutritional scientists combined this Exclusive Blend™, with well-founded Chinese and Ayruvedic remedies of the past, and leading edge technology of the future, to assure that their "all-natural" products are without equal--anywhere!

**The Opportunity:** Wachters' provides a uniquely incredible marketing opportunity. Throughout its incredible 67-year history, it has maintained relationships with its dedicated, long-term distributors (ranging from 5 to 40 years, and more), who have earned substantial income from their Wachters' business--businesses which have allowed them to travel the world, live an excellent lifestyle, retire without worry, and provide them with an asset that they can bequest to their children, grandchildren and their grandchildren's children.

**The Compensation Plan:** Wachters' compensation plan is one of the most lucrative in the industry, with a 67.5% payout, based on retail. The best news is that Wachters' distributors have achieved financial freedom, while helping millions of people throughout the world change their lives by improving their health and well-being through the use of Wachters' superior products--all the while gaining financial freedom. These factors set the Wachters' opportunity apart from any other in the industry today! Additionally, the company's nine product divisions provide for the opportunity to market a variety of consumable products that work, while maintaining consistent volumes and increasing profits and bonuses.

**Summary:** With the longest operating history in the industry, Wachters' is dedicated to their mission of "Spreading Good Nutrition Around the World." The company cares about its people. Its customers and distributors have dramatic testimonials about the benefits of the products, which covers a 10 to 40 year time span, and the impact they have had on so many lives. Contact Wachters' today and see how your life can change!

**Wachters' Organic Sea Products, 360 Shaw Road, South San Francisco, CA 94084, Phone: (650) 588-9567, Fax: (650) 875-1626, E-mail: wachterosp@aol.com, Web site: www.wachters.com, Principals: Carrie Jean Minnucciani and Victor P. Republicano, Jr.**

# "Enhancing lives one person at a time"

More than 80,000 Watkins associates based in North America, Puerto Rico and New Zealand, offer Watkins quality products and business opportunity to their customers. It is through this unique networking opportunity that thousands of people have been able to achieve their dreams. Watkins is unique in the network marketing industry. Minimum purchases or inventories are not required. Associates may earn anywhere from a few hundred dollars a month to hundreds of thousands of dollars a year. All associates experience unequaled customer service support from Watkins, the first network marketing company.

Watkins Incorporated was founded in 1868 by J.R. Watkins. Since that time, the company has been committed to providing products to make you feel better, live longer and preserve the well-being of our planet. Watkins offers gourmet food, health and nutrition products, personal care and home care items, all geared toward healthier living. These quality products are currently offered in the United States, Canada, Puerto Rico and New Zealand.

Located in Winona, Minnesota, Watkins corporate headquarters employs more than 425 people. The corporate office building was designed by famous Prairie-school architect George Washington Maher, and completed in 1911. It is one of the most unique and beautiful office buildings in the world, adorned with Italian tile mosaics and Tiffany glass. Watkins also has a state-of-the-art distribution center in Winona along with warehouse facilities in Winnipeg, Manitoba and Winona.

When J.R. Watkins sold his first bottle of liniment to a neighbor in rural Minnesota, and then enlisted others to do the same, he founded "network marketing." This first product called "Red Liniment," was a natural healer, made with capsicum from the red pepper plant and camphor from the camphor tree, an Asian evergreen. J.R. Watkins mixed the ingredients in his own laboratory. By the time of his death in 1911, he had more than 2,500 individuals marketing Watkins products. The company still markets Red Liniment today.

The long, rich heritage of the Watkins company is built on quality products, unrivaled customer service, and recognition by its peers as an innovative leader. It was J.R. Watkins who originated the idea of putting a customer satisfaction "trial mark" on his bottles, creating the first money-back guarantee.

Watkins was a family business when it was established in 1868, and it remains so today under the comprehensive guidance of the Irwin Jacobs family. In 1978, Watkins was purchased by Jacobs, who rose from modest beginnings to the Forbes 400 list of wealthiest Americans. His son Mark is the company's president. Father and son work together toward the Watkins vision for the future that Jacobs first conceived when he purchased the company. They are dedicated to helping other entrepreneurs achieve success through their independent Watkins home-based businesses.

**Watkins Incorporated**
**150 Liberty Street, Winona, MN 55987-9070**
**Phone: (507) 457-3300**
**Web site: www.watkins-inc.com**

# The West Bend Company

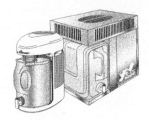

The West Bend Company is a major manufacture of water distillers and high quality stainless steel cookware for direct to the home sales and premium/incentive use in the direct selling industry. The company is also known worldwide as a top ranked small electrical appliance manufacturer for retail distribution channels.

West Bend began in 1911, when seven men formed The West Bend Aluminum Company to produce aluminum pie plates, pans, ladles and cups. The first manufacturing facility was an old button factory positioned on the west bend of the Milwaukee River. By 1920, the company had developed the "waterless cooker" making West Bend a household word.

Presently, Thomas W. Kieckhafer is president of the company which employs approximately 1,200 people at its 1.5 million square foot facility in West Bend, Wisconsin. The company has been implementing world-class manufacturing principles to maintain quality and reduce waste since the early 1980s.

West Bend Water Systems was created in 1989 to meet the growing worldwide demand for quality water purification products. The West Bend Company purchased an established water distiller manufacturer in St. Catharines, Ontario, acquiring the proven technology that is the foundation of West Bend Water System's success in the industry. A worldwide leader in water distillation products for the home, West Bend Water Systems manufactures the only distillers bearing the Water Quality Association's Gold Seal for performance and quality. Product flexibility and distributor support have made West Bend Water Systems a favorite of direct selling organizations the world over. The products can be built to conform with any voltage and power cord requirement. New product development has been ongoing, resulting in the development of a plastic countertop distiller, the first and only one of its kind made in the U.S.A.

The Premiere Cookware Division is involved in producing some of the highest quality cookware on the market. Throughout the world, families have learned to cook the "minimum moisture" way with West Bend cookware. Our direct-to-the-home selling technique allows the cookware representative to teach consumers how to prepare food using less grease, less water and less salt than traditional cooking methods for a healthier diet. The West Bend manufacturing credo is "Team Effort Achieves Manufacturing Excellence," or TEAM Excellence. This philosophy focuses on employee involvement to increase productivity, reduce set-up time and scrap, and reduce the cost of producing the product. Techniques used include cellular manufacturing, quick change tooling, cross trained employees, computers, quality controls, SPC type data collection, and alternative pay plans to improve manufacturing.

West Bend's commitment to supplying the direct selling industry can best be summed up in the company Mission Statement: At the West Bend Company, customers are the reason we exist. Our mission is to provide products and services that exceed our customer's expectations. We are committed to Total Quality and Just-In-Time operating philosophies and implementing change to achieve this goal. To this end, we will:

▶Empower people ▶Provide educational opportunities

▶Create partnerships with our customers, both internal and external, as well as our suppliers

▶Continuously improve ▶Eliminate waste

**The West Bend Company, 400 W. Washington Street, West Bend, WI 53095, Web site: www.westbend.com, West Bend Water Systems Division, Phone: (414) 334-6908, Fax: (414) 334-6964, E-mail: water@westbend.com, Premiere Cookware Division, Phone: (414) 334-6896, Fax: (414) 334-6964, E-mail: cookware@westbend.com**

*Helen Aiken*

We all have dreamed of having extra money. I know that I did, and that is why I started my own home-based business in 1981. As a wife and mother of four, I wanted to help increase our income, but I also wanted to spend time with my family. I was looking for the perfect situation...I wanted to earn extra money, but I wanted to select hours to fit my schedule, and to work with people. This type of business helped me find the balance I needed and since founding **Wicker Plus, Ltd**. I've been able to offer that same opportunity to many others. This is also a business that helps build a lot of self-esteem not only for the many women involved directly in our business but also their families...their children. It's a chance for all of us to make a difference in the lives of those we care about most.

As a business owner I learned "hands on" every phase of our business, from the actual selling, to the packing of orders, to the buying trips--sometimes overseas. Even today, it is important to me to be a very involved business owner. I can still be found at times in one of our warehouses, personally overseeing the quality, packing and shipping of our merchandise. I attend as many meetings, workshops, and events as I can. After all, this is a business that is as much about people as it is about products!

**Wicker Plus, Ltd.** wants to "be there" for each and every one of our sales consultants and directors, whether they are interested in earning a few extra dollars or have in mind a career level income. We currently have over 500 active sales consultants, selling our product throughout the continental United States. We want them to have the time and flexibility to enjoy their families, travel, or indulge in whatever other dreams they may have. It's their business--we want to help them make it happen! Enthusiasm and a responsible attitude are the key! Everyone has their own individual level, but it seems that the higher the level of enthusiasm a person possesses the higher the level of success that will follow!

**Next, we offer our Mission Statement:** Our mission is to be the best, do the best and offer the most to those interested in balancing a fulfilling home life with personal and financial career benefits, and to their customers who want more welcoming, more attractive, and more organized homes.

**As for our opportunity:** We are a very well established company, but we still have a lot of room for much more growth. With the advent of more attention being placed on home and family, our product line is definitely "in the right place at the right time!"

**As how we may differ:** We appreciate our hostesses tremendously! They are the lifeblood of our business so we reward them with a "can't be beat" generous Hostess Program! Treating our hostesses well has in turn made it easier for our consultants to also be successful! We appreciate our sales consultants and directors too. One way we show that appreciation is by way of our annual Trip Promotion! We've taken our people to the Bahamas, Cancun, Hawaii, Cruises... and we've had a great time!

**We offer a vast array of home decorating accessories:** Wicker baskets, wood framed prints, stoneware, florals, lace, wooden shelves and accessories. We also offer merchandise in a variety of styles--country, contemporary, rustic, Victorian, southwestern, and more! And, with the versatility of our product line we are able to re-merchandise many of the items to give them several different looks! And, our prices are very affordable! And, our merchandise makes wonderful gifts for many, many occasions! So, when you put all these Wicker Plus, "Pluses" together, you can see that we appeal to a very large market of people!

**Wicker Plus, Ltd., N112W14600 Mequon Road, Germantown, WI 53022**
**Phone: (414) 255-7377**

World Golf Corporation®, a nationally recognized home-based golf business opportunity, is the industry standard in combining a passion for the game of golf with a part-time or full-time income opportunity.

World Golf Corporation's executive leadership showcases top-tier businessmen and women with managerial, operational, IT systems and marketing backgrounds who drive the World Gold Corporation opportunity to the top of the network marketing industry, while positioning the corporation as the premier gold network marketing company in the world.

World Golf Corporation offers the chance to purchase high quality golf products and golfing services at wholesale prices while earning commission and playing more golf. Our products and services include top-of-the-line titanium woods, forged and cast irons, competitive sets of wedges, putters, golf bags and travel bags, the World Golf Tour Series golf balls, the World Golf Tour™ and Players Club™.

### FILA® Brand Golf Equipment

World Golf Corporation is a wholly owned subsidiary of Renaissance Golf Products, Inc.®, a publicly traded company (symbol OTC:BB FGLF). Renaissance holds a license from FILA® Sport S.p.A. to market golf products in various parts of the world bearing the FILA® trademark. The FILA® brand products line is extensive and very well established, offering FILA® brand golf equipment such as FILA® brand golf clubs, golf bags and golf accessories. World Golf Corporation is committed to providing high quality merchandise at reasonable prices in order to build a strong and profitable business for all of its distributor members and tournament players.

### Ball Program

No matter what your playing level or ball preference may be, we have a ball that suits the needs of every golfer. World Golf Corporation has the exclusive marketing rights to a series of golf balls that in scientific objective testing have proven to fly further, spin better and cost less than competitive brands. Our Grand Tour Series balls stacked up against the competition in an article found in the February 1999 *Golf Digest* magazine as premium "golf balls designed for obtaining ultimate distance and control." In addition, we have two types of tour balata golf balls, and golf balls made of two, three, and four piece construction to meet the highest standards of even the most demanding golfer.

### The World Golf Tour™

World Golf Corporation offers exciting golf tournament series aimed at providing well organized, enjoyable and competitive golf tournaments to golfers of every skill level. The World Golf Tour facilitates honest, "sandbagger-resistant" and affordable competition on a national scale. With tens of thousands of rounds of golf played in World Golf Tournaments each year, our World Golf Tour Computerized Golf Scoring System™ (patent pending), allows our players the opportunity to compete against other golfers in a fair and honest environment. Come join us at our next World Golf Tour event. The schedule of tournaments is found on our web site at www.worldgolftour.com/worldtour/schedule.html.

### The World Golf Tour Players Club™

The World Golf Tour Players Club was established to provide a foundation for the creation of income through the sport of golf. Players Club members operate their own home-based golf businesses which allow for tax deductions on many golf-related expenses. Players Club membership provides enhanced tour member privileges, including VIP treatment at corporate events and Players Club Only receptions and award banquets. Join the World Golf Tour Players Club and be a part of the elite mobile country club for the passionate golfer.

**World Golf Corporation, 12187 South Business Park Drive, Suite 100, Draper, UT 84020**
**Phone: (801) 924-6000, Web site: www.worldgolftour.com**

## YOUNG LIVING ESSENTIALS OILS OFFERS ANCIENT
## REMEDIES FOR A HEALTHY MODERN LIFESTYLE
Company Owns and Operates One of the World's Largest Organic Herb Farms
for the Production of Therapeutic-grade Essential Oils.

PAYSON, UT: One company is on the cutting edge in developing solutions to combat health concerns brought about by stress, poor dietary habits, pollution and age: Young Living Essential Oils. The oldest company in North America to specialize in the cultivation of organic herbs for essential oils and dietary supplements, it is the first to combine essential oils with a line of advanced herbal and vitamin formulas. Young Living's essential oils, dietary supplements and personal care products are internationally known for their exceptional quality, cutting-edge formulations and safe ingredients.

With thousands of acres of farmland in Idaho, Utah and France, the company attempts to control every phase of its herb cultivation and essential oil distillation. Experts carefully monitor each step of the process, from seed selection to herb cultivation and distillation. No pesticides, fungicides, herbicides or chemical fertilizers are used. All plants are grown according to exacting standards set down by its Founder and President, Dr. D. Gary Young.

Dr. Daniel Pcnoel, M.D., an international authority on essential oils, states, "I found Young Living's Essential Oils to be top quality, definitely deserving the term 'therapeutic grade.' Young Living is a North American leader in producing and properly marketing the highest grade of essential oils."

Moreover, Young Living subjects its essential oils to one of the most rigorous quality control programs in the industry. Every batch of essential oils is quarantined, inspected and sent to independent laboratories for analysis by state-of-the-art, high-resolution gas chromatography, mass spectroscopy and infrared spectra analysis.

Dr. Gary Young, a world-renowned researcher and educator in the field of holistic health care, founded Young Living almost a decade ago. Dr. Young has spent the last 25 years in search of natural ways to improve overall health and wellness through both modern and ancient science.

Young Living has developed essential oils and blends to strengthen the body's most important systems. Products have been scientifically designed to focus on the glandular, cardiovascular, digestive, skeletal, muscular, nervous, respiratory and immune systems as well as skin, hair and oral hygiene. The company is one of the few manufacturers to market a line of pure personal care products free of potentially harmful synthetic ingredients.

With over 120,000 distributors and $30 million in sales in the United States and Canada alone, Young Living Essential Oil's reputation for manufacturing the finest holistic products has earned them worldwide recognition.

The acclaimed producer, director and actor, Steven Seagal--an expert in herbs and oils, states, "Young Living has a line of products that is very rare and that does not exist anywhere else in the world. Gary Young has sought out some of the greatest minds on earth and produces the purest essence of oils that I have ever seen."

One of the world's most respected authorities on fitness, Dr. Robert Delmonteque, also praises Young Living's products. Trainer of the original seven astronauts and a syndicated columnist on fitness for over 300 newspapers, he put it succinctly, "Young Living has made a startling difference in my life."

**Young Living Essential Oils, 250 South Main Payson, UT 84651**
**Phone: (801) 465-5400, Fax: (801) 465-5424, Order Entry: (801) 763-9963**
**Web site: www@youngliving.com**

# This Page Has
# No Business In
# This Directory
## It Belongs In TheMail
## Don't Delay!
## Start Your Future Today

**Please send me my collector's copy of the
2000 Global Home Based Business Directory**®

~~$39.95~~ **Now only $29.95**

Add $6.00 Shipping & Handling (Minnesota residents add 6.5% sales tax)

(all sales final)

**PAYMENT**

**MONEY
ORDER**

Name_____

Address_____

City/State/Zip_____

Phone_____Fax_____

Credit Card#_____Exp. Date_____

Signature_____

**Send To: Marketing Solutions, Inc.
HC 6, Box 58A
Aitkin, MN 56432
Phone: (800) 496-0277, Fax: (218) 927-4613**

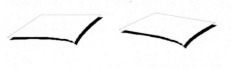

# A PUBLIC SERVICE FOR OUR READERS

# Consumer Information Center

## EVERYTHING From A to Z

### Relax; your life has just become easier

Following one year of exhaustive study and research, our editorial staff has compiled the most comprehensive compilation of consumer information ever published under one cover. You'll find every conceivable organization, agency, bureau, club, association, service group and committee in this prodigious 100 plus page public service volume. From listings ranging from Better Business Bureaus, employment, housing, women's rights and charitable organizations, to social services, retirement, civil rights, physically and mentally challenged and foster grandparents, this invaluable one stop source will save you time and money and eliminate the frustration and anxiety of locating that one, or more, special program club or association you won't find anywhere else. There's more; much more. How about information on the fish and wildlife services, volunteer associations, venture capitalists and SBA Microloans. Hold on! SBA Microloans? That's right. This program was founded for those seeking loans from $100 to $25,000.

All entries include complete addresses, phone numbers and applicable information in this three section compendium. No more searching in a dozen directories or making endless phone calls for those impossible to locate numbers. They're all here in an easy to find alphabetized table of contents. Your life has just become a little less complicated.

# Contents (2)

**Page 445 - U.S.**
**Page 476 - Canada**
*Know your rights!*

## U.S.

Attorney Generals----------------------380
Better Business Bureaus-------------385
Chambers of Commerce---------------395
Small Business Administrations------400
SBA Microloans-------------------------403
Secretaries of State------------------410
Venture Capitalists--------------------411
Employment-----------------------------416
Environment/Ecology-----------------419
Housing----------------------------------426
Human/Civil Rights-------------------427
Marriage/Divorce---------------------430
Physically/Mentally Challenged------432
Retirement------------------------------436
Service Clubs---------------------------437
Veterans---------------------------------439
U.S. Voluntary Service
Organizations--------------------------440
Women's Rights------------------------445
Youth-------------------------------------447

**Page 400**
*U.S. SBA's*

**Page 439 - U.S.**
**Page 474 - Canada**

*Veterans
Associations*

**Page 419 - U.S.**
**Page 462 - Canada**
*Help protect our land*

**Page 432 - U.S.**
**Page 467 - Canada**

*Physically
challenged
no more*

**VOLUNTEERS NEEDED**

**Page 440**

**Page 436 - U.S.**
**Page 469 - Canada**
*No more rocking chairs
for retirees*

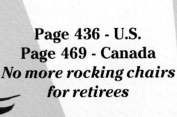

## Canada

Business Bureaus----------------------451
Chambers of Commerce---------------453
Charitable Organizations-------------456
Environment/Ecology-----------------462
Human/Civil Rights-------------------465
Physically/Mentally Challenged------467
Retirement------------------------------469
Social Organizations------------------470
Social Services------------------------471
Veterans---------------------------------474
Women's Rights------------------------476
Youth-------------------------------------477

**Page 447 - U.S.**
**Page 477 - Canada**
*Harvest time
for the young*

**Page 403**
*Need a loan?*

# Attorney Generals

**Alabama**
Honorable William H. (Bill) Pryor Jr.
Office of the Attorney General
State House
11 South Union Street
Montgomery, AL 36130
Phone: (334) 242-7300

**Alaska**
Honorable Bruce M. Botelho
Attorney General of Alaska
PO Box 110300
Diamond Courthouse
Juneau, AK 9981-0300
Phone: (907) 465-3600

**American Samoa**
Honorable Albert Mailo
Attorney General of American Samoa
PO Box 7
Pago Pago, AS 96799
Phone: (684) 633-4163

**Arizona**
Honorable Grant Woods
Attorney General of Arizona
Office of the Attorney General
1275 West Washington Street
Phoenix, AZ 85007
Phone: (602) 542-4266

**Arkansas**
Honorable Winston Bryant
Attorney General of Arkansas
200 Tower Building
323 Center Street
Little Rock, AR 72201-2610
Phone: (501) 682-2007

**California**
Honorable Daniel E. Lungren
Attorney General of California
1300 L Street, Suite 1740
Sacramento, CA 95814
Phone: (916) 324-5437

**Colorado**
Honorable Gale A. Norton
Attorney General of Colorado
Department of Law
1525 Sherman Street
Denver, CO 80203
Phone: (303) 866-3052

**Connecticut**
Honorable Richard Blumenthal
Attorney General of Connecticut
55 Elm Street
Hartford, CT 06141-0120
Phone: (860) 566-2026

**Delaware**
Honorable M. Jane Brady
Attorney General of Delaware
Carvel State Office Building
820 North French Street
Wilmington, DE 19801
Phone: (302) 577-3838

**District of Columbia**
Honorable Charles F.C. Ruff
District of Columbia Corporation Counsel
441 4th Street NW
Washington, DC 20001
Phone: (202) 727-6248

**Florida**
Honorable Robert A. Butterworth
Attorney General of Florida
Office of the Attorney General
The Capitol, PL 01
Tallahassee, FL 32399-1050
Phone: (904) 487-1963

**Georgia**
Honorable Michael J. Bowers
Attorney General of Georgia
40 Capitol Square SW
Atlanta, GA 30334-1300
Phone: (404) 656-4585

## Guam

Honorable Calvin E. Holloway
Attorney General of Guam
Judicial Center Building
120 West O'Brien Drive
Agana, GU 96910
Phone: (671) 475-3324

## Hawaii

Honorable Margery S. Bronster
Attorney General of Hawaii
425 Queen Street
Honolulu, HI 96813
Phone: (808) 586-1282

## Idaho

Honorable Alan G. Lance
Attorney General of Idaho
Statehouse
Boise, ID 83720-1000
Phone: (208) 334-2400

## Illinois

Honorable Jim Ryan
Attorney General of Illinois
State of Illinois Center
100 West Randolph Street
Phone: (312) 814-4714

## Indiana

Honorable Jeff Modisett
Attorney General of Indiana
Indiana Government Center South
Fifth Floor
402 West Washington Street
Indianapolis, IN 46204
Phone: (317) 233-4386

## Iowa

Honorable Tom Miller
Attorney General of Iowa
Hoover State Office Building
Des Moines, IA 50319
Phone: (515) 281-3053

## Kansas

Honorable Carla J. Stovall
Attorney General of Kansas
Judicial Building
301 West Tenth Street
Topeka, KS 66612-1597
Phone: (913) 296-2215

## Kentucky

Honorable Albert Benjamin Chandler III
Attorney General of Kentucky
State Capitol, Room 116
Phone: (502) 564-7600

## Louisiana

Honorable Richard P. Leyoub
Attorney General of Louisiana
Department of Justice
PO Box 94095
Baton Rouge, LA 70804-4095
Phone: (504) 342-7013

## Maine

Honorable Andrew Ketterer
Attorney General of Maine
State House Station Six
Augusta, ME 04333
Phone: (207) 626-8800

## Maryland

Honorable J. Joseph Curran, Jr.
Attorney General of Maryland
200 Saint Paul Place
Baltimore, MD 21202-2202
Phone: (410) 576-6300

## Massachusetts

Honorable Scott Harshbarger
Attorney General of Massachusetts
One Ashburton Place
Boston, MA 02108-1698
Phone: (617) 727-2200

## Michigan

Honorable Frank J. Kelley
Attorney General of Michigan
PO Box 30212
525 West Ottawa Street
Lansing, MI 48909-0212
Phone: (517) 373-1110

## Minnesota

Honorable Mike Hatch
Attorney General of Minnesota
State Capitol, Suite 102

St. Paul, MN 55155
Phone: (651) 296-3353

**Mississippi**
Honorable Mike Moore
Attorney General of Mississippi
Department of Justice
PO Box 220
Jackson, MS 39205-0220
Phone: (601) 359-3692

**Missouri**
Honorable Jeremiah W. (Jay) Nixon
Attorney General of Missouri
Supreme Court Building
207 West High Street
Jefferson City, MO 65101
Phone: (314) 751-3321

**Montana**
Honorable Joseph P. Mazurek
Attorney General of Montana
Justice Building
215 North Sanders
Helena, MT 59620-1401
Phone: (406) 471-2682

**Nebraska**
Honorable Don Stenberg
Attorney General of Nebraska
State Capitol
PO Box 98920
Lincoln, NE 68509-8920
Phone: (402) 471-2682

**Nevada**
Honorable Frankie Sue Del Papa
Attorney General of Nevada
Old Supreme Court Building
198 South Carson
Carson City, NV 89710
Phone: (702) 687-4170

**New Hampshire**
Honorable Jeffrey R. Howard
Attorney General of New Hampshire
State House Annex
25 Capitol Street
Concord, NH 03301-6397
Phone: (603) 271-365

**New Jersey**
Honorable Peter Verniero
Attorney General of New Jersey
Richard J. Hughes Justice Complex
25 Market Street, CN 080
Trenton, NJ 08625
Phone: (609) 292-4976

**New Mexico**
Honorable Tom Udall
Attorney General of New Mexico
PO Drawer 1508
Santa Fe, NM 87504-1508
Phone: (505) 827-6000

**New York**
Honorable Dennis C. Vacco
Attorney General of New York
Department of Law - The Capitol
2nd Floor
Albany, NY 12224
Phone: (518) 474-7330

**North Carolina**
Attorney General of North Carolina
Department of Justice
PO Box 629
Raleigh, NC 27602-0629
Phone: (919) 733-3377

**North Dakota**
Attorney General of North Dakota
State Capitol
600 East Blvd.
Bismarck, ND 58505-0040
Phone: (701) 328-2210

**N. Mariana Islands**
Honorable Robert B. Dunlap II
Acting Attorney General of the
Northern Mariana Islands
Administration Building
Salpan, MP 96950
Phone: (670) 664-2341

**Ohio**
Honorable Betty D. Montgomery
Attorney General of Ohio
State Office Tower
30 East Broad Street

Columbus, OH 43266-0410
Phone: (614) 466-3376

**Oklahoma**
Honorable Drew Edmondson
Attorney General of Oklahoma
State Capitol
2300 North Lincoln Blvd., Room 112
Oklahoma City, OK 73105
Phone: (405) 521-3921

**Oregon**
Honorable Hardy Myers
Attorney General of Oregon
Justice Building
1162 Court Street NE
Salem, OR 97310
Phone: (503) 378-6002

**Pennsylvania**
Honorable Michael Fisher
Attorney General of Pennsylvania
Strawberry Square
Harrisburg, PA 17120
Phone: (717) 787-3391

**Puerto Rico**
Honorable Jose Fuentes - Agostini
Attorney General of Puerto Rico
PO Box 192
San Juan, PR 00902-0192
Phone: (809) 721-7700

**Rhode Island**
Honorable Jeffrey B. Pine
Attorney General of Rhode Island
150 South Main Street
Providence, RI 02903
Phone: (401) 274- 4400

**South Carolina**
Honorable Charles Molony Condon
Attorney General of South Carolina
Rembert C. Dennis Office Building
PO Box 11549
Columbia, SC 29211-1549
Phone: (803) 734-3970

**South Dakota**
Honorable Mark Barnett

Attorney General of South Dakota
500 East Capitol
Pierre, SD 57501-5070
Phone: (605) 773-3215

**Tennessee**
Honorable Charles W. Burson
Attorney General of Tennessee
Office of the Attorney General
500 Charlotte Avenue
Nashville, TN 37243
Phone: (615) 741-6467

**Texas**
Honorable Dan Morales
Attorney General of Texas
Capitol Station
PO Box 12548
Austin, TX 78711-2548
Phone: (512) 463-2191

**Utah**
Honorable Jan Graham
Attorney General of Utah
State Capitol, Room 236
Salt Lake City, UT 84114-0810
Phone: (801) 538-1326

**Vermont**
Honorable Wallace J. Malley
Acting Attorney General of Vermont
109 State Street
Montpelier, VT 05609-1001
Phone: (802) 828-3171

**Virginia**
Honorable James S. Gilmore III
Attorney General of Virginia
900 East Main Street
Richmond, VA 23219
Phone: (804) 786-2071

**Virgin Islands**
Honorable Julio A. Brady
Attorney General of the Virgin Islands
Department of Justice
G.E.R.S. Complex
48B-50C Kronprinsdens Gade
St. Thomas, VI 00802
Phone: (809) 774-5666

**Washington**
Honorable Christine O. Gregoire
Attorney General of Washington
PO Box 40100
1125 Washington Street SE
Olympia, WA 98504-0100
Phone: (360) 753-6200

**West Virginia**
Honorable Darrel V. McGraw, Jr.
Attorney General of West Virginia
State Capitol
Charleston, WV 25305
Phone: (304) 558-2021

**Wisconsin**
Honorable James E. Doyle
Attorney General of Wisconsin
State Capitol Building
PO Box 7857, Suite 114 East
Madison, WI 53707-7857
Phone: (608) 266-1221

**Wyoming**
Honorable William U. Hill
Attorney General of Wyoming
State Capitol Building
Cheyenne, WY 82002
Phone: (307) 777-7841

# Better Business Bureaus

**Better Business Bureaus** (BBBs) are nonprofit organizations supported primarily by local business members. The focus of BBB activities is to promote an ethical marketplace by encouraging honest advertising and selling practices, and by providing alternative dispute resolution. BBBs offer a variety of consumer services. For example, they provide consumer education materials; answer consumer questions; provide information about a business, particularly whether or not there are unanswered or unsettled complaints or other marketplace problems; help resolve buyer/seller complaints against a business; including mediation and arbitration services; and provide information about charities and other organizations that are seeking public donations.

BBBs usually request that a complaint be submitted in writing so that an accurate record exists of the dispute. The BBB will then take up the complaint with the company involved. If the complaint cannot be satisfactorily resolved through communication with the business, the BBB may offer an alternative dispute settlement process, such as mediation or arbitration. BBBs do not judge or rate individual products or brands, handle employer/employee wage disputes or give legal advice.

If you need help with a consumer question or complaint, call your local BBB to ask about its services. Those bureaus that provide information via 1-900 telephone numbers charge $3.80 for the first 4 minutes, $.95 per minute thereafter, with a maximum charge of $9.50. Some numbers require a major credit card to access information and charge a flat fee of $3.80. Or you can contact the BBB online at www.bbb.org for consumer fraud and scam alerts, and information about BBB programs, services and locations.

BBB*OnLine* provides Internet users an easy way to verify the legitimacy of online businesses. Companies carrying the BBB*OnLine* seal have been checked out by the BBB, and agree to resolve customer concerns regarding goods or services promoted online. Visit www.bbbonline.org for a list of participating companies, complete program standards and more.

The Council of Better Business Bureaus, the umbrella organization for the BBBs, can assist with complaints about the truthfulness and accuracy of national advertising claims, including children's advertising; provide reports on national soliciting charities; and help to settle disputes with automobile manufacturers through the BBB AUTO LINE program.

In addition to the BBBs listed below, there are 16 BBBs in Canada. These addresses can be obtained in the Canadian section of this book.

## Council

**Council of Better Business Bureaus, Inc.**
4200 Wilson Blvd.
**Arlington**, VA 22203
Phone: (703) 276-0100
Fax: (703) 525-8277

## Bureaus

**Alabama**
1210 South 20th Street

PO Box 55268
**Birmingham**, AL 35205
Phone: (205) 558-2222,
(800) 834-5274 (in AL)
Fax: (205) 538-2239

1528 Peachtree Lane, Suite 1
**Cullman**, AL 35057
Phone: (205) 558-2222,
(800) 824-5274 (in AL)
Fax: (205) 538-2239

118 Woodburn
**Dothan**, AL 36305
Phone: (334) 794-0492,
(800) 824-5274 (in AL)
Fax: (334) 794-0659

205 South Seminary Street, Suite 114
**Florence**, AL 35630
Phone: (205) 740-8223

107 Lincoln Street, NE
PO Box 36804
**Huntsville**, AL 35801
Phone: (205) 533-1640
Fax: (205) 533-1177

100 North Royal Street
PO Box 2008 (36652-2008)
**Mobile**, AL 36602-3295
Phone: (334) 433-5494
Fax: (334) 438-3191

## Alaska

2805 Bering Street, Suite 5
PO Box 93550
**Anchorage**, AK 99503-3819
Phone: (907) 562-0704
Fax: (907) 562-4061

PO Box 74675
**Fairbanks**, AK 99707
Phone: (907) 451-0222
Fax: (907) 451-0228

## Arizona

4428 North 12th Street
**Phoenix**, AZ 85014-4585
Phone: (900) 225-5222
(602) 264-1721

3620 North 1st Ave., Suite 136
**Tucson**, AZ 85719
Phone: (520) 888-5353
Fax: (520) 888-6262

## Arkansas

1415 South University
**Little Rock**, AR 72204-2605
Phone: (501) 664-7274
Fax: (501) 664-0024

## California

705 18th Street
PO Box 1311 (93302-1311)
**Bakersfield**, CA 93301
Phone: (805) 322-2074
Fax: (805) 322-8318

315 North La Cadena
PO Box 970 (92324-0814)
**Colton**, CA 92324
Phone: (900) 225-5222
Fax: (909) 825-6246

6101 Ball Road, Suite 309
**Cypress**, CA 90630-3966
Phone: (900) 225-5222
(909) 426-0813
Fax: (714) 527-3208

2519 West Shaw, #106
**Fresno**, CA 93711
Phone: (209) 222-8111
Fax: (209) 228-6518

3727 West Sixth Street, Suite 607
**Los Angeles**, CA 90020
Phone: (900) 225-5222,
(909) 426-0813
Fax: (213) 251-9984

510 16th Street, Suite 550
**Oakland**, CA 94612-1584
Phone: (510) 238-1000
Fax: (510) 238-1018

400 S Street
**Sacramento**, CA 95814-6997
Phone: (916) 443-6843
Fax: (916) 443-0376

5050 Murphy Canyon Road, Suite 110
**San Diego**, CA 92123
Phone: (619) 496-2131
Fax: (619) 496-2141

1530 Meridian Ave., Suite 100
**San Jose**, CA 95125
Phone: (408) 445-3000
Fax: (408) 265-4528

400 South El Camino Real, Suite 350
PO Box 294
**San Mateo**, CA 94401-0294
Phone: (650) 696-1240
Fax: (650) 696-1250

213 Santa Barbara Street
PO Box 129 (93102-0129)
**Santa Barbara**, CA 93102
Phone: (805) 963-8657
Fax: (805) 963-8556

11 South San Joaquin Street, Suite 803
**Stockton**, CA 95202-3202
Phone: (209) 948-4880
Fax: (209) 465-6302

## Colorado
3022 North El Paso (80907-5454)
PO Box 7970
**Colorado Springs**, CO 80933-7970
Phone: (719) 636-1155
Fax: (719) 636-5078

1780 South Bellaire, Suite 700
**Denver**, CO 80222-4350
Phone: (303) 758-2100
Fax: (303) 758-8321

1730 South College Ave., Suite 303
**Fort Collins**, CO 80525-1073
Phone: (970) 484-1348,
(800) 571-0371 (in WY)
Fax: (970) 221-1239

119 West 6th Street, Suite 203
**Pueblo**, CO 81003-3119
Phone: (719) 542-6464
Fax: (719) 542-5229

## Connecticut
Parkside Building
821 North Main Street
**Wallingford**, CT 06492-2420
Phone: (203) 269-2700
Fax: (203) 269-3124

## Delaware
1010 Concord Ave., Suite 101

**Wilmington**, DE 19808-5532
Phone: (302) 594-9200
Fax: (302) 594-1052

## District of Columbia
1012 14th Street, NW, 9th Floor
**Washington**, DC 20005-3406
Phone: (202) 393-8000
Fax: (202) 393-1198

## Florida
5830 142nd Ave. North, Suite B (34620)
PO Box 7950
**Clearwater**, FL 33758-7950
Phone: (813) 535-5522 (Pinellas County),
(800) 525-1447 (in FL)
Fax: (813) 530-5863

7820 Arlington Expressway, #147
**Jacksonville**, FL 32211
Phone: (904) 721-2288
Fax: (904) 721-7373

921 East Gadsden (32501)
PO Box 1511
**Pensacola**, FL 32597-1511
Phone: (850) 429-0222
Fax: (850) 429-0006

1950 SE Port St. Lucie Blvd., Suite 211
**Port St. Lucie**, FL 34952-5579
Phone: (561) 870-2010
Fax: (561) 337-2083

580 Village Blvd., Suite 340
**West Palm Beach**, FL 33409-1904
Phone: (561) 686-2200
Fax: (561) 686-2775

1011 North Wymore Road, Suite 204
**Winter Park**, FL 32789-1736
Phone: (407) 621-3300,
(800) 275-6614 (in FL)
Fax: (407) 629-5167

## Georgia
101 1/2 South Jackson, Suite 2
PO Box 808 (31702)
**Albany**, GA 31701

Phone: (912) 883-0744
Fax: (912) 438-8222

PO Box 2707
**Atlanta**, GA 30301
Phone: (404) 688-4910
Fax: (404) 688-8901

301 7th Street (30901)
PO Box 2087
**Augusta**, GA 30903-2085
Phone: (706) 722-1574
Fax: (706) 724-0969

208 13th Street
PO Box 2587 (31902-2587)
**Columbus**, GA 31901-2137
Phone: (706) 324-0712
Fax: (706) 324-2181

277 Martin Luther King Blvd., Suite 102
**Macon**, GA 31201-3476
Phone: (912) 742-7999
Fax: (912) 742-8191

6606 Abercorn Street, Suite 108-C
**Savannah**, GA 31405
Phone: (912) 354-7521
Fax: (912) 354-5068

## Hawaii
First Hawaiian Tower
1132 Bishop Street, 15th Floor
**Honolulu**, HI 98613-2822
Phone: (808) 536-6956
Fax: (808) 523-2335

## Idaho
1333 West Jefferson
**Boise**, ID 83702-5320
Phone: (208) 342-4649
Fax: (208) 342-5116

1575 South Blvd.
**Idaho Falls**, ID 83404-5926
Phone: (208) 523-9754
Fax: (208) 524-6190

## Illinois
330 North Wabash Ave., Suite 2006
**Chicago**, IL 60611
Phone: (312) 832-0500
Fax: (312) 832-9985

3024 West Lake, Suite 200
**Peoria**, IL 61615-3770
Phone: (309) 688-3741
Fax: (309) 681-7290

810 East State Street, 3rd Floor
**Rockford**, IL 61104-1101
Phone: (815) 963-2222
Fax: (815) 963-0329

## Indiana
722 West Bristol Street, Suite H-2
PO Box 405 (46514-2988)
**Elkhart**, IN 46515-0405
Phone: (219) 262-8996
Fax: (219) 266-2026

4004 Morgan Ave., Suite 201
**Evansville**, IN 47715-2265
Phone: (812) 473-0202
Fax: (812) 473-3080

1203 Webster Street
**Forte Wayne**, IN 46802-3493
Phone: (219) 423-4433
Fax: (219) 423-3301

22 East Washington Street, Suite 200
Victoria Center
**Indianapolis**, IN 46204-3584
Phone: (317) 488-2222
Fax: (317) 488-2224

6111 Harrison Street, Suite 101
**Merriville**, IN 46410
Phone: (219) 980-1511
(219) 769-8053,
(800) 637-2118 (in IN)
Fax: (219) 554-2123

207 Dixie Way North, Suite 130
**South Bend**, IN 46637-3360
Phone: (219) 277-9121
Fax: (219) 273-6666

## Iowa

852 Middle Road, Suite 290
**Bettendorf**, IA 52722-4100
Phone: (319) 355-6344
Fax: (319) 355-0306

505 5th Ave., Suite 950
**Des Moines**, IA 50309-2375
Phone: (515) 243-8137,
(800) 202-1600 (in IA)
Fax: (515) 243-2227

505 6th Street, Suite 417
**Sioux City**, IA 51101
Phone: (712) 252-4501
Fax: (712) 252-0285

## Kansas

501 Southeast Jefferson, Suite 24
**Topeka**, KS 66607-1190
Phone: (785) 232-0454
Fax: (785) 232-9677

328 Laura
PO Box 11707 (67201)
**Wichita**, KS 67211
Phone: (316) 263-3146
Fax: (316) 263-3063

## Kentucky

410 West Vine Street, Suite 340
**Lexington**, KY 40507-1629
Phone: (606) 259-1008,
(800) 866-6668 (in KY)
Fax: (606) 259-1639

844 South Fourth Street
**Louisville**, KY 40203-2186
Phone: (502) 583-6546,
(800) 388-2222 (in KY)
Fax: (502) 589-9490

## Louisiana

1605 Murray Street, Suite 117
**Alexandria**, LA 71301-6875
Phone: (318) 473-4494
Fax: (318) 473-8906

2055 Wooddale Blvd.
**Baton Rouge**, LA 70806-1546
Phone: (504) 926-3010
Fax: (504) 924-8040

3008 Park Ave., Suite 204
**Houma**, LA 70364
Phone: (504) 868-3456,
(800) 259-9766 (in LA)
Fax: (504) 876-7664

100 Huggins Road
**Lafayette**, LA 70506
Phone: (318) 981-3497
Fax: (318) 981-7559

3941-L Ryan Street
PO Box 7314
**Lake Charles**, LA 70606-7314
Phone: (318) 478-6253
Fax: (318) 474-8981

141 Desiard Street, Suite 808
**Monroe**, LA 71201-7380
Phone: (318) 387-4600
Fax: (318) 361-0461

1539 Jackson Ave., Suite 400
**New Orleans**, LA 70130-5843
Phone: (504) 581-6222
Fax: (504) 524-9110

3612 Youree Drive
**Shreveport**, LA 71105
Phone: (318) 861-6417,
(800) 372-4222 (in LA)
Fax: (318) 861-6426

## Maine

812 Stevens Ave.
**Portland**, ME 04013-2648
Phone: (207) 878-2715
Fax: (207) 797-5818

## Maryland

2100 Huntingdon Ave.
**Baltimore**, MD 21211-3215
Phone: (900) 225-5222
Fax: (410) 347-3936

## Massachusetts
20 Park Plaza, Suite 820
**Boston**, MA 02116-4344
Phone: (617) 426-9000
Fax: (617) 426-7813

293 Bridge Street, Suite 320
**Springfield**, MA 01103-1402
Phone: (413) 734-3114
Fax: (413) 734-2006

32 Franklin Street
PO Box 16555
**Worcester**, MA 01608-1900
Phone: (508) 755-2548
Fax: (508) 754-4158

## Michigan
40 Pearl NW, Suite 354
**Grand Rapids**, MI 49503
Phone: (616) 774-8236
Fax: (616) 774-2014

30555 Southfield Road, Suite 200
**Southfield**, MI 48076-7751
Phone: (248) 644-9100
Fax: (248) 644-5026

## Minnesota
2706 Gannon Road
**St. Paul**, MN 55116-2600
Phone: (612) 699-1111,
(800) 699-7665
Fax: (612) 699-8285

## Mississippi
4500 155 North, Suite 287
PO Box 12745
**Jackson**, MS 39236-2745
Phone: (601) 987-8282,
(800) 987-8280 (in MS)
Fax: (601) 987-8285

## Missouri
306 East 12th Street, Suite 1024
**Kansas City**, MO 64106-2418
Phone: (816) 421-7800
Fax: (816) 472-5442

205 Park Central East, Suite 509
**Springfield**, MO 65806-1326
Phone: (417) 862-4222
Fax: (417) 869-5544

12 Sunnen Drive, Suite 121
**St. Louis**, MO 63143
Phone: (314) 645-3300
Fax: (314) 645-2666

## Nebraska
3633 O Street, Suite 1
**Lincoln**, NE 68510-1670
Phone: (402) 476-5855
Fax: (402) 476-8221

2237 North 91st Plaza
**Omaha**, NE 68134-6022
Phone: (402) 391-7612
Fax: (402) 391-7535

## Nevada
PO Box 44108
**Las Vegas**, NV 89116-2108
Phone: (702) 320-4500
Fax: (702) 320-4560

991 Bible Way
PO Box 21269
**Reno**, NV 89515-1269
Phone: (702) 322-0657,
(888) 350-4222
Fax: (702) 322-8163

## New Hampshire
410 South Main Street, Suite 3
**Concord**, NH 03301-3483
Phone: (603) 224-1991
Fax: (603) 228-9035

## New Jersey
400 Lanidex Plaza
**Parsippany**, NH 07054-2797
Phone: (973) 581-1313
Fax: (973) 581-7022

1721 Route 37 East
**Toms River**, NJ 08753-8239
Phone: (732) 270-5577
Fax: (732) 270-6739

1700 Whitehorse-Hamilton Square, Suite D-5
**Trenton**, NJ 08690-3596
Phone: (609) 588-0808
Fax: (609) 588-0546

16 Maple Ave.
PO Box 303
**Westmont**, NJ 08108-0303
Phone: (609) 854-8467
Fax: (609) 854-1130

## New Mexico

2625 Pennsylvania, NE, Suite 2050
**Albuquerque**, NM 87110-3657
Phone: (505) 346-0110,
(800) 873-2224 (in NM)
Fax: (505) 346-2696

308 North Locke
**Farmington**, NM 87401-5855
Phone: (505) 326-6501
Fax: (505) 327-7731

201 North Church, Suite 330
**Las Cruces**, NM 88001-3548
Phone: (505) 524-3130
Fax: (505) 524-9624

## New York

346 Delaware Ave.
**Buffalo**, NY 14202-1899
Phone: (716) 856-7180
Fax: (716) 856-7287

266 Main Street
**Farmingdale**, NY 11735-2618
Phone: (900) 225-5222
Fax: (212) 533-6200

257 Park Ave. South
**New York**, NY 10010-7384
Phone: (900) 225-5222,
(212) 533-6200
Fax: (212) 477-4912

Learbury Centre
401 North Salina Street
**Syracuse**, NY 13203
Phone: (900) 225-5222
Fax: (315) 479-5754

30 Glenn Street
**White Plains**, NY 10603-3213
Phone: (900) 225-5222
Fax: (212) 533-6200

## North Carolina

1200 BB & T Building
**Asheville**, NC 28801-3418
Phone: (704) 253-2392
Fax: (704) 252-5039

5200 Park Road, Suite 202
**Charlotte**, NC 28209-3650
Phone: (704) 527-0012
Fax: (704) 525-7624

3608 West Friendly Ave.
**Greensboro**, NC 27410-4895
Phone: (336) 852-4240
Fax: (336) 852-7540

3125 Poplarwood Court, Suite 308
**Raleigh**, NC 27604-1080
Phone: (919) 872-9240
Fax: (919) 954-0622

PO Box 69
**Sherrils Ford**, NC 28673-0069
Phone: (828) 478-5622
Fax: (828) 478-5462

500 West 5th Street, Suite 202
**Winston-Salem**, NC 27101-2728
Phone: (336) 725-8384
Fax: (336) 777-3727

## Ohio

222 West Market Street
**Akron**, OH 44303-2111
Phone: (330) 253-4590
Fax: (330) 253-6249

1434 Cleveland Ave., NW (44703)
PO Box 8017
**Canton**, OH 44711-8017
Phone: (330) 454-9401
Fax: (330) 456-8957

898 Walnut Street
**Cincinnati**, OH 45202-2097
Phone: (513) 421-3015
Fax: (513) 621-0907

2217 East 9th Street, Suite 200
**Cleveland**, OH 44115-1299
Phone: (216) 241-7678
Fax: (216) 861-6365

1335 Dublin Road, #30-A
**Columbus**, OH 43215-1000
Phone: (614) 486-6336
Fax: (614) 486-6631

40 West Fourth Street, Suite 1250
**Dayton**, OH 45402-1830
Phone: (937) 222-5825,
(800)776-5301 (in OH)
Fax: (973) 222-3338

219 North McDonel (45801)
PO Box 269
**Lima**, OH 45802-0269
Phone: (419) 223-7010
Fax: (419) 229-2029

3103 Exec. Parkway, Suite 200
**Toledo**, OH 43606-1310
Phone: (419) 531-3116,
Toll free: (800) 743-4222 (OH
and MI)
Fax: (419) 587-6001

25 Market Street
PO Box 1495
**Youngstown**, OH 44501-1495
Phone: (330) 744-3111
Fax: (330) 744-7336

## Oklahoma
17 South Dewey Ave.
**Oklahoma City**, OK 73102-2400
Phone: (405) 239-6081
Fax: (405) 235-5891

6711 South Yale, Suite 230
**Tulsa**, OK 74136-3327
Phone: (918) 492-1266
Fax: (918) 492-1276

## Oregon
333 SW Fifth Ave., Suite 300
**Portland**, OR 97204
Phone: (503) 226-3981
Fax: (503) 226-8200

## Pennsylvania
528 North New Street
**Bethlehem**, PA 18018-5789
Phone: (610) 866-8780
Fax: (610) 868-8668

29 East King Street, Suite 322
**Lancaster**, PA 17602-2852
Phone: (900) 255-5222,
(215) 448-3870
Fax: (717) 291-3241

1608 Walnut Street, Suite 6
**Philadelphia**, PA 19103
Phone: (900) 225-5222,
(215) 893-3870
Fax: (215) 893-9312

300 6th Ave., Suite 100-UL
**Pittsburgh**, PA 15222-2511
Phone: (412) 456-2700
Fax: (412) 456-2739

The Connell Building, Suite 407
129 North Washington Ave. (18503-2204)
PO Box 993
**Scranton**, PA 18501-0993
Phone: (717) 342-9129
Fax: (717) 342-1282

## Puerto Rico
PO Box 363488
**San Juan**, PR 00936-3488
Phone: (787) 756-5400 (8:30 am-4:30 pm)
Fax: (787) 758-0095

Rhode Island
120 Lavan Street
**Warwick**, RI 02888-1071
Phone: (401) 785-1212
Fax: (401) 785-3061

## South Carolina

2330 Devine Street (29205)
PO Box 8326
**Columbia**, SC 29202-8326
Phone: (803) 254-2525
Fax: (803) 779-3117

307-B Falls Street
**Greensville**, SC 29601-2829
Phone: (864) 242-5052
Fax: (864) 271-9802

1601 North Oak Street, Suite 101
**Myrtle Beach**, SC 29577-1601
Phone: (843) 626-6881
Fax: (843) 626-7455

## Tennessee

PO Box 1178 TCA
**Blountville**, TN 37617-1178
Phone: (423) 325-6616
Fax: (423) 325-6621

1010 Market Street, Suite 200
**Chattanooga**, TN 37402-2614
Phone: (423) 266-6144
Fax: (423) 267-1924

2633 Kingston Pike, Suite 2 (37919)
PO Box 10327
**Knoxville**, TN 37939-0327
Phone: (423) 522-2552
Fax: (423) 637-8042

6525 Quail Hollow, Suite 410 (38120)
PO Box 17039
**Memphis**, TN 38187-0036
Phone: (901) 759-1300
Fax: (901) 757-2997

414 Union Street, Suite 1830
PO Box 198436
**Nashville**, TN 37219-8436
Phone: (615) 242-4BBB
Fax: (615) 254-8356

## Texas

3300 South 14th Street, Suite 307
**Abilene**, TX 79605-5052

Phone: (915) 691-1533
Fax: (915) 691-0309

724 South Polk (79101)
PO Box 1905
**Amarillo**, TX 79105-1905
Phone: (806) 379-6222
Fax: (806) 379-8206

2101 South IH35, Suite 302
**Austin**, TX 78741-3854
Phone: (512) 445-2911
Fax: (512) 445-2096

PO Box 2988
**Beaumont**, TX 77701-2988
Phone: (409) 835-5348
Fax: (409) 838-6858

PO Box 3868
**Bryan**, TX 77802-4413
Phone: (409) 260-2222
Fax: (409) 846-0276

216 Park Ave.
**Corpus Christi**, TX 78401
Phone: (512) 887-4949
Fax: (512) 887-4931

2001 Bryan Street, Suite 850
**Dallas**, TX 75201-3093
Phone: (900) 225-5222,
(214) 740-0348
Fax: (214) 740-0321

Northwest Plaza, Suite 1101
**El Paso**, TX 79901
Phone: (915) 577-0191
Fax: (915) 577-0209

1612 Summit Ave., Suite 260
**Fort Worth**, TX 76102-5978
Phone: (817) 332-7585
Fax: (817) 882-0566

5225 Katy Freeway, Suite 500
**Houston**, TX 77007
Phone: (900) 225-5222
(713) 867-4946, (713) 867-4944 (Spanish)
Fax: (713) 867-4947

916 Main Street, Suite 800
**Lubbock**, TX 79401-3410
Phone: (806) 763-0459
Fax: (806) 744-9748

10100 Country Road, 118 West
PO Box 60206
**Midland**, TX 79711-0206
Phone: (915) 563-1880
Fax: (915) 561-9435

3121 Exec. Drive (76904)
PO Box 3366
**San Angelo**, TX 76902-3366
Phone: (915) 949-2989
Fax: (915) 949-3514

1800 Northeast Loop 410, Suite 400
**San Antonio**, TX 78217-5296
Phone: (210) 828-9441
Fax: (210) 828-3101

3600 Old Bullard Road, #103-A (75701)
PO Box 6652
**Tyler**, TX 75711-6652
Phone: (903) 581-5704,
(800) 443-0131 (in TX)
Fax: (903) 534-8644

2210 Washington Ave.
**Waco**, TX 76701-1019
Phone: (254) 755-7772
Fax: (254) 755-7774

609 International Blvd. (78596)
PO Box 69
**Weslaco**, TX 78599-0069
Phone: (956) 968-3678
Fax: (956) 968-7638

4245 Kemp Blvd., Suite 900
**Wichita Falls**, TX 76308-2830
Phone: (817) 691-1172
Fax: (817) 691-1174

## Utah
1588 South Main Street
**Salt Lake City**, UT 84115-5382
Phone: (801) 487-4656
Fax: (801) 485-9397

## Vermont
(Contact Boston office)
(800) 4BBB-811

## Virginia
586 Virginia Drive
**Norfolk**, VA 23505
Phone: (757) 531-1300
Fax: (757) 531-1388

701 East Franklin, Suite 712
**Richmond**, VA 23219
Phone: (804) 648-0016
Fax: (804) 648-3115

31 West Campbell Ave.
**Roanoke**, VA 24011-1301
Phone: (540) 342-3455
Fax: (540) 345-2289

## Washington
1401 North Union, #105
**Kennewick**, WA 99336-3819
Phone: (509) 783-0892
Fax: (509) 783-2893

4800 South 188th Street, Suite 222 (98188)
PO Box 68926
**Sea Tac**, WA 98168-0926
Phone: (206) 431-2222
Fax: (206) 431-2211

508 West 6th Ave., Suite 401
**Spokane**, WA 99204-2730
Phone: (509) 455-4200
Fax: (509) 838-1079

32 North 3rd Street, Suite 410
PO Box 1584
**Yakima**, WA 98901
Phone: (509) 248-1326
Fax: (509) 248-8026

## Wisconsin
740 North Plankinton Ave.
**Milwaukee**, WI 53203-2478
Phone: (414) 273-1600
Fax: (414) 224-0081

# Chambers of Commerce

## Alabama
Business Council of Alabama
PO Box 76
Montgomery, AL 36101-0076
Phone: (334) 834-6000, Fax: (334) 262-7371

## Alaska
Alaska Chamber of Commerce
217 2nd Street, #201
Juneau, AK 99801
Phone: (907) 586-2323, Fax: (907) 463-5515

## Arizona
Arizona Chamber of Commerce
1221 East Osborn Road, #100
Phoenix, AZ 85014
Phone: (602) 248-9172, Fax: (602) 265-1262

## Arkansas
Arkansas Chamber of Commerce
410 South Cross, PO Box 3645
Little Rock, AR 72203-3645
Phone: (501) 374-9225, Fax: (501) 372-2722

## California
California Chamber of Commerce
1201 K Street, 12th Floor, PO Box 1736
Sacramento, CA 95812-1736
Phone: (916) 444-6685, Fax: (916) 444-6685

## Colorado
Colorado Association of Commerce
1776 Lincoln Street, #1200
Denver, CO 80203-1029
Phone: (303) 831-7411, Fax: (303) 860-1439

## Connecticut
Connecticut Business and Industry Assn.
370 Asylum Street
Hartford, CT 06103-2022
Phone: (203) 244-1900, Fax: (203) 278-8562

## Delaware
Delaware Chamber of Commerce
1201 North Orange Street, PO Box 671
Wilmington, DE 19899-0671
Phone: (302) 655-7221, Fax: (302) 654-0691

## District of Columbia
District of Columbia Chamber of Commerce
1301 Pennsylvania Ave. NW, #309
Washington, DC 20004
Phone: (202) 347-3537, Fax: (202) 347-3537

## Florida
Florida Chamber of Commerce
136 South Bronough Street, PO Box 11309
Tallahassee, FL 32302-3309
Phone: (904) 425-1200, Fax: (904) 425-1260

## Georgia
Georgia Chamber of Commerce
233 Peachtree Street, #200
Atlanta, GA 30303-1504
Phone: (404) 223-2264, Fax: (404) 223-2290

## Hawaii
Hawaii Chamber of Commerce
1132 Bishop Street
Honolulu, HI 96813-2830
Phone: (800) 545-4300, Fax: (808) 545-4309

## Idaho
Boise Area Chamber of Commerce
300 North 6th, PO Box 2368
Boise, ID 83701
Phone: (208) 344-5515, Fax: (208) 344-5849

## Illinois
Illinois Chamber of Commerce
311 South Wacker Drive, #1500
Chicago, IL 60606-6619
Phone: (312) 938-7100, Fax: (312) 983-7101

## Indiana
Indiana Chamber of Commerce
One North Capitol Ave., #200
Indianapolis, IN 46204-2248
Phone: (317) 264-3110, Fax: (317) 264-6855

## Iowa
Iowa Dept. of Economic Development
200 East Grand
Des Moines, IA 50309
Phone: (515) 242-4700, Fax: (515) 242-4749

**Kansas**
Kansas Chamber of Commerce
835 SW Topeka Blvd.
Topeka, KS 66612-1671
Phone: (913) 357-6321, Fax: (913) 357-4732

**Kentucky**
Chamber of Commerce
464 Chenault Road, PO Box 817
Frankfort, KY 40602-0817
Phone: (502) 695-4700, Fax: (502) 695-6824

**Louisiana**
Louisiana Association of Business
3113 Valley Creek Drive, PO Box 80258
Baton Rouge, LA 70898-0258
Phone: (504) 928-5388, Fax: (504) 929-6054

**Maine**
Maine Chamber of Commerce
126 Sewall Street
Augusta, ME 04330
Phone: (207) 623-4568, Fax: (207) 622-7723

**Maryland**
Maryland Chamber of Commerce
60 West Street, #100
Annapolis, MD 21401-2458
Phone: (410) 269-0642, Fax: (410) 269-5247

**Massachusetts**
Great Boston Chamber of Commerce
One Beacon Street, 4$^{th}$ Floor
Boston, MA 02108-3114
Phone: (617) 227-4500, Fax: (617) 227-7505

**Michigan**
Michigan Chamber of Commerce
600 South Walnut Street
Lansing, MI 48933-2200
Phone: (517) 371-2100, Fax: (517) 371-7224

**Minnesota**
Minnesota Chamber of Commerce
30 East 7$^{th}$ Street, #1700
Saint Paul, MN 55101
Phone: (651) 292-4650, Fax: (651) 292-4656

**Mississippi**
Mississippi Economic Council

PO Box 23276
Jackson, MS 39225-3276
Phone: (601) 969-0022, Fax: (601) 353-0247

**Missouri**
Missouri Chamber of Commerce
428 East Capitol Ave., PO Box 149
Jefferson City, MO 65102
Phone: (314) 634-3511, Fax: (314) 634-8855

**Montana**
Montana Chamber of Commerce
2030 11$^{th}$ Ave., PO Box 1730
Helena, MT 59601
Phone: (406) 442-2405, Fax: (406) 442-2409

**Nebraska**
Nebraska Chamber of Commerce
PO Box 95128
Lincoln, NE 68509
Phone: (402) 474-4422, Fax: (402) 474-2510

**Nevada**
Nevada Chamber of Commerce
PO Box 43499
Reno, NV 89505
Phone: (702) 686-3030, Fax: (702) 686-3038

**New Hampshire**
New Hampshire Business Association
122 North Main
Concord, NH 03301
Phone: (603) 224-5388, Fax: (603) 224-2872

**New Jersey**
New Jersey Chamber of Commerce
50 West State Street, #1310
Trenton, NJ 08608
Phone: (609) 989-7888, Fax: (609) 989-9696

**New Mexico**
Association of Commerce
2309 Renard Place SE, #402
Albuquerque, NM 87106-4259
Phone: (505) 842-0644, Fax: (505) 842-0734

**New York**
Coney Island Chamber of Commerce
1015 Surf Ave.
Brooklyn , NY 11224
Phone: (718) 875-1000, Fax: (718) 237- 4274

## North Carolina

North Carolina Citizens for Business
225 Hillsborough Street, PO Box 2508
Raleigh, NC 27602
Phone: (919) 828-0758, Fax: (919) 821-4992

## North Dakota

Greater North Dakota Association
2000 Schafer Street, PO Box 2639
Bismark, ND 58502
Phone: (701) 222-0929, Fax: (701) 222-1611

## Ohio

Ohio Chamber of Commerce
35 East Gay Street, 2nd Floor
Columbus, OH 43215-3181
Phone: (614) 228-4201, Fax: (614) 228-6403

## Oklahoma

Oklahoma Chamber of Commerce
330 NE 10th Street
Oklahoma City, OK 73104-3200
Phone: (405) 235-3669, Fax: (405) 235-3670

## Oregon

Albany Chamber of Commerce
435 West First Ave., PO Box 548
Albany, OR 97321
Phone: (503) 926-1527, Fax: (503) 926-7064

## Pennsylvania

Pennsylvania Chamber of Business
417 Walnut Street
Harrisburg, PA 17101
Phone: (717) 255-3252, Fax: (717) 255-3298

## Rhode Island

North Central Chamber of Commerce
PO Box 3861
Centredale, RI 02911
Phone: (401) 273-1310, Fax: (401) 273-2570

## South Carolina

South Carolina Chamber of Commerce
1201 Main Street, #1810
Columbia, SC 29201-3254
Phone: (803) 799-4601, Fax: (803) 779-6043

## South Dakota

Commerce Association of South Dakota
PO Box 190

Pierre, SD 5750-0190
Phone: (605) 224-6161

## Tennessee

Chattanooga Area Chamber of Commerce
1001 Market Street
Chattanooga, TN 37402
Phone: (615) 756-2121, Fax: (615) 267-7242

## Texas

Texas Chamber of Commerce
400 West 15th, #910
Austin, TX 78701-1647
Phone: (512) 472-1594, Fax: (512) 320-0280

## Utah

Utah Chamber of Commerce
PO Box 310
West Jordan, UT 84084-0310
Phone: (801) 569-5151, Fax: (801) 565-8978

## Vermont

Vermont Chamber of Commerce
PO Box 37
Montpelier, VT 05601
Phone: (802) 223-3443, Fax: (802) 229-4581

## Virginia

Virginia Chamber of Commerce
9 South Fifth Street
Richmond, VA 23219
Phone: (804) 644-1607, Fax: (804) 738-0903

## Washington

Association of Washington Business
1414 South Cherry, PO Box 658
Olympia, WA 98507-0658
Phone: (360) 943-1600, Fax: (360) 943-5811

## West Virginia

West Virginia Chamber of Commerce
PO Box 2789
Charleston, WV 25330
Phone: (304) 342-1115, Fax: (304) 342-1130

## Wisconsin

Wisconsin Manufactures and Commerce
501 East Washington Ave., PO Box 352
Madison, WI 53701-0352
Phone: (608) 258-3400, Fax: (608) 258-3413

**Wyoming**
Casper Chamber of Commerce
500 North Center Street, PO Box 399
Casper, WY 82602
Phone: (307) 234-5311, Fax: (307) 265-2643

# Small Business Administrations

**Alabama**
Birmingham SBA District Office
2121 8th Ave. North, #200
Birmingham, AL 55403
Phone: (205) 731-1344

**Alaska**
SBA District Office
222 West 8th, Room 67
Anchorage, AK 99513
Phone: (907) 271-4022

**Arizona**
SBA District Office
2828 North Central Ave., #800
Phoenix, AZ 85004
Phone: (602) 640-2316

**Arkansas**
SBA District Office
2120 Riverfront Drive, #100
Little Rock, AR 72202
Phone: (501) 324-5871

**California**
SBA District Office Administration
2719 North Air Drive, Suite 200
Fresno, CA 93727
Phone: (209) 487-5791

**Colorado**
SBA District Office
721 19th Street
Denver, CO 80202
Phone: (303) 844-3984

**Connecticut**
Hartford SBA District Office
330 Main Street, 2nd Floor
Hartford, CT 06106
Phone: (860) 240-4700

**Delaware**
Delaware Economic Development Office
824 Market Street, 2nd Floor
Wilmington, DE 19801
Phone: (302) 573-6294

**District of Columbia**
Economic Development Administration
1110 Vermont Ave. NW, Suite 900
Washington, DC 20005
Phone: (202) 606-4000

**Florida**
SBA Miami District Office
1320 South Dixie Hwy., Suite 301
Coral Gables, FL 33146
Phone: (305) 536-5521

**Georgia**
SBA District Office
1720 Peachtree Road NW, 6th Floor
Atlanta, GA 30309
Phone: (404) 347-2441

**Guam**
238 Archbishop F.C. Flores Street, Room 508
Agana, GU 96901
Phone: (671) 472-7277

**Hawaii**
Honolulu SBA
300 Ala Moana Blvd.
Honolulu, HI 96850
Phone: (808) 541-2990

**Illinois**
SBA Regional Office
511 West Capital Ave., Suite 302
Springfield, IL 62704
Phone: (217) 492-4416

**Indiana**
SBA District Office
429 North Pennsylvania Street, #100
Indianapolis, IN 46204
Phone: (317) 226-7272

**Iowa**
U.S. Small Business Association
The Lattner Building, 215 4th Ave. SE
Cedar Rapids, IA 52401
Phone: (319) 362-6405

## Kansas
100 East English Street, Suite 510
Wichita, KS 67202
Phone: (316) 269-6616

## Kentucky
SBA SCORE
600 Martin Luther King Hwy., #188
Louisville, KY 40202
Phone: (502) 582-5971

## Louisiana
SBA District Office
365 Canal Street, #2250
New Orleans, LA 70130
Phone: (504) 589-6685

## Maine
SBA  District Office
40 Western Ave.
Augusta, ME 04330
Phone: (207) 622-8378

## Maryland
SBA District Office
10 South Howard Street, 6th Floor
Baltimore, MD 21201
Phone: (410) 962-4392

## Massachusetts
SBA District Office
10 Causeway Street, Room 265
Boston, MA 02222
Phone: (617) 565-5590

## Michigan
SBA District Office
477 Michigan, Room 515
Detroit, MI 48226
Phone: (313) 226-6075

## Minnesota
SBA District Office
100 North 6th Street, #610C
Minneapolis, MN 55403
Phone: (612) 370-2324

## Mississippi
SBA District Office
101 Capitol Center Street,  #400
Jackson, MS 39201
Phone: (601) 965-4378

## Missouri
SBA District Office
323 West 8th Street, #501
Kansas City, MO 64105
Phone: (816) 374-6708

## Montana
SBA District Office
301 South Park, Room 334
Helena, MT 59626
Phone: (406) 441-1081

## Nebraska
Rural Economic and Community Development
11145 Mill Valley Road
Omaha, NE 68154
Phone: (402) 221-4691

## Nevada
SBA District Office
301 East Steward Street, Room 301
Las Vegas, NV 89125
Phone: (702) 388-6611

## New Hampshire
U.S. Dept. of Commerce
143 North Main Street
Concord, NH 03301
Phone: (603) 225-1400

## New Jersey
Federal Business Center
Two Gateway Center, 4th Floor
Newark, NJ 07102
Phone: (973) 645-2434

## New Mexico
State of New Mexico Economic Development
526 Silver Ave. SW, Suite 312
Albuquerque, NM 87102
Phone: (505) 766-1870

## New York
SBA Regional Office
26 Federal Plaza, Room 3100
New York, NY 10278
Phone: (212) 264-4354

## North Carolina
U.S. Small Business Administration

200 North College Street, #A2015
Charlotte, NC 28202
Phone: (704) 344-6563

## North Dakota
SBA District Office
667 2nd Ave. North, Room 219
Phone: (701) 239-5131

## Ohio
SBA District Office
11 Superior Ave., Suite 630
Cleveland, OH 44114
Phone: (216) 522-4180

## Oklahoma
SBA District Office
210 West Park Ave., #1300
Oklahoma City, OK 73102
Phone: (405) 231-5521

## Oregon
SBA Portland District Office
1514 SW 5th, Suite 1050
Portland, OR 97201
Phone: (503) 326-2682

## Pennsylvania
SBA Regional Office
100 Chestnut Street, Suite 108
Harrisburg, PA 17101
Phone: (717) 782-3840

## Rhode Island
SBA District Office
380 Westminster Mall
Providence, RI 02903
Phone: (401) 528-4561

## South Carolina
U.S. SBA
1835 Assembly Street, Room 358, PO Box 2786
Columbia, SC 29202
Phone: (803) 765-5377

## South Dakota
SBA District Office
110 South Phillips Ave., #200
Sioux Falls, SD 57102
Phone: (605) 330-4231

## Tennessee
SBA District Office

50 Vantage Way, #201
Nashville, TN 37228
Phone: (615) 736-5881

## Texas
SBA Regional Office
8625 King George Drive, Building C
Dallas, TX 75235
Phone: (214) 767-7633

## Utah
SBA District Office
125 South State Street, Room 2237
Salt Lake City, UT 84138
Phone: (801) 524-5804

## Vermont
SBA District Office
87 State Street, Room 205
Montpelier, VT 05602
Phone: (802) 828-4422

## Virginia
SBA District Office
1504 Santa Rosa Road
Richmond, VA 23229
Phone: (804) 771-2400

## Washington
U.S. SBA REGIONAL Office
Park Place Building, 17th Floor
Seattle, WA 98101
Phone: (206) 553-7310

## West Virginia
SBA District Office
168 West Main Street, 6th Floor
Clarksburg, WV 26301
Phone: (304) 623-5631

## Wisconsin
Department of Development
212 East Washington Ave., Room 213
Madison, WI 53703
Phone: (608) 264-5261

## Wyoming
SBA District Office
Federal Bldg., 100 East B Street, #4001
Casper, WY 82601
Phone: (307) 261-6500

# SBA Microloans

The U.S. Small Business Administration's Microloan Program was developed for those times when just a small loan can make the real difference between success and failure. Under this program, loans range from less than $100 to a maximum of $25,000. SBA has made these funds available to nonprofit organizations for the purpose of lending to small business and they can also provide intense management and technical assistance. A microloan must be repaid on the shortest term possible--no longer than six years, depending on the earnings of the business. The interest rates on these loans will be competitive and based on the cost of money to the intermediary lender. This program is currently available in 44 states. To learn which nonprofit organizations in your area offer this program, call the Small Business Answer Desk at (800) 8-ASK-SBA, or contact U.S. Small Business Administration (SBA), 409 Third Street SW, Suite 8300, Washington, DC 20416, (202) 205-6490.

## Lenders

### Alabama

Elmore Community Action Committee, Inc.
Contact: Marion D. Dunlap
1011 West Tallassee
PO Box Drawer H
Wetumpka, AL 36092
Phone: (334) 567-4361

### Alaska

Community Enterprise Development
Contact: Perry R. Eaton
1577 C Street Plaza
Anchorage, AK 99501
Phone: (907) 274-5400

### Arizona

Chicanos Por La Causa, Inc.
Contact: Pete Garcia
1112 East Buckeye Road
Phoenix, AZ 85034
Phone: (602) 257-0700

### Arkansas

Arkansas Enterprise Group
Contact: Brian Kelley
605 Main Street, Suite 203
Arkadelphia, AR 71923
Phone: (501) 246-9739

White River Planning and Development
Contact: Van C. Thomas
1652 White Drive

PO Box 2396
Batesville, AR 72503
Phone: (501) 793-5233

### California

Arcata Economic Development Corporation
Contact: Kathleen E. Moxon
100 Ericson Court, Suite 100
Arcata, CA 95521
Phone: (707) 822-4616

Coalition for Women's Economic Development
Contact: Mary Riddle
315 West Ninth Street
Los Angeles, CA 90015
Phone: (213) 489-4995

Valley Rural Development Corporation
Contact: Michael E. Foley
3417 West Shaw, Suite 100
Fresno, CA 93711
Phone: (209) 271-9030

### Colorado

Greater Denver Local Development Corporation
Contact: Cecilia H. Prinster
1981 Blake Street, Suite 406
PO Box 2135
Denver, CO 80206
Phone: (303) 296-9535

Region 10 LEAP, Inc.
Contact: Stan Broome

PO Box 849
Montrose, CO 81402
Phone: (303) 249-2436

## Connecticut
New Haven Community Investment Corp.
Contact: Salvatore J. Brancati, Jr.
809 Chapel Street, 2nd Floor
New Haven, CT 06510
Phone: (203) 776-6172

## Delaware
Wilmington Economic Development Corp.
Contact: Edwin H. Nutter, Jr.
605-A Market Street Mall
Wilmington, DE 19801
Phone: (302) 571-9088

## District of Columbia
ARCH Development Corporation
Contact: Duane Gautier
1227 Good Hope Road
Washington, DC 20020
Phone: (202) 889-5023

H Street Development Corporation
Contact: William J. Barrow
611 H Street NE
Washington, DC 20002
Phone: (202) 544-8353

## Florida
Community Equity Investments Inc.
Contact: Daniel R. Horvath
302 North Barcelona Street
Pensacola, FL 32501
Phone: (904) 444-2234

United Gainsville Community
Development Corporation, Inc.
Contact: Vian M. Cockerham
214 West University Ave., Suite D
PO Box 2518
Gainsville, FL 32501

## Georgia
Fulton County Development Corporation
Contact: Maurice S. Coakley
10 Park Place South, Suite 305

Atlanta, GA 30303
Phone: (404) 659-5955

Small Business Assistance Corporation
Contact: Tony O'Reily
31 West Congress Street, Suite 100
Savannah, GA 31401
Phone: (912) 232-4700

## Hawaii
The Immigrant Center
Contact: Patricia Brandt
720 North King Street
Honolulu, HI 96817
Phone: (808) 845-3918

## Idaho
Panhandle Area Council
Contact: Jim Deffenbaugh
11100 Airport Drive
Hayden, ID 83835-9743
Phone: (208) 772-0584

## Illinois
Greater Sterling Development Corporation
Contact: Reid Nolte
1741 Industrial Drive
Sterling, IL 61081
Phone: (815) 625-5255

Illinois Development Finance Authority
Contact: Philip S. Howe
5310 Sears Tower
Chicago, IL 60606
Phone: (312) 793-5586

## Indiana
Eastside Community Investments Inc.
Contact: Dennis J. West
26 North Arsenal Ave.
Indianapolis, IN 46201
Phone: (317) 637-7300

Metro Small Business Assistance Corporation
Contact: Debra A. Lutz
1 NW Martin Luther King Jr. Blvd.
Evansville, IN 47708-1869
Phone: (812) 426-5857

## Iowa

Siouxland Economic Development Corporation
Contact: Kenneth A. Beekley
400 Orpheum Electric Building
PO Box 447
Sioux City, IA 51102
Phone: (712) 279-6286

## Kansas

South Central Kansas Economic
Development District, Inc.
151 North Volutsia
Wichita, KS 67214
Phone: (316) 683-4422

Center for Business Innovations, Inc.
Contact: Robert J. Sherwood
4747 Troost Avenue
Kansas City, MO 64110
Phone: (816) 561-8567

## Kentucky

Kentucky Highlands Investment Corporation
Contact: Jerry A. Rickett
362 Old Whitley Road
London, KY 40741
Phone: (606) 864-5175

## Louisiana

Greater Jennings Chamber of Commerce
Contact: Jerry Arceneaux
414 Cary Ave.
Jennings, LA 70546
Phone: (318) 824-0933

## Maine

Coastal Enterprises, Inc.
Contact: Ronald L. Phillips
PO Box 268
Wiscasset, ME 04578
Phone: (207) 882-7552

Northern Maine Regional Planning Committee
Contact: Robert P. Clark
2 South Main Street
PO Box 779
Caribou, ME 04736
Phone: (207) 498-8736

## Maryland

Council for Equal Business Opportunity, Inc.
Contact: Michael Gaines
800 North Charles Street
Baltimore, MD 21201
Phone: (410) 576-2326

## Massachusettes

Economic Development Industrial Corporation of Lynn
Contact: Peter M. DeVeau
37 Central Square, 3rd Floor
Lynn, MA 01901
Phone: (617) 592-2361

Jobs for Fall River
Contact: Paul L. Vigeant
One Government Center
Fall River, MA 02722
Phone: (508) 324-2620

Western Massachusettes Enterprise Fund
Contact: Christopher Sikes
324 Wells Street
Greenfield, MA 01301
Phone: (413) 774-7204

## Michigan

Ann Arbor Community Development Corporation
Contact: Michelle Richards Vasquez
2008 Hogback Road
Ann Arbor, MI 48105
Phone: (313) 677-1400

Detroit Economic Growth Corporation
Contact: Robert W. Spencer
150 West Jefferson, Suite 1500
Detroit, MI 48226
Phone: (313) 963-2940

Northern Economic Initiatives Corporation
Contact: Bobby J. Wells
1009 West Ridge Street
Marquette, MI 49855
Phone: (906) 228-5571

## Minnesota

Northeast Entrepreneur Fund, Inc.
Contact: Mary Mathews
820 Ninth Street North

Virginia, MN 55792
Phone: (218) 749-4191

Minneapolis Consortium of Community Developers
Contact: Karen Reid
1808 Riverside Ave.
Minneapolis, MN 55454-1035
Phone: (612) 338-8729

Northwest Minnesota Initiative Fund
722 Paul Bunyan Drive NW
Bemidji, MN 56601
Phone: (218) 759-2057

## Mississippi
Delta Foundation
Contact: Harry J. Bowie
819 Main Street
Greenville, MS 38701
Phone: (601) 335-5291

Friends of Children of Mississippi, Inc.
Contact: Marvin Hogan
4880 McWillie Circle
Jackson, MS 39206
Phone: (601) 362-1541

## Montana
Capital Opportunities/District lX Human
Resource Development Council, Inc.
Contact: Jeffrey Rupp
321 East Main Street, Suite 300
Bozeman, MT 59715
Phone: (406) 587-4486

Women's Opportunity and Resource Development, Inc.
Contact: Kelly Rosenleaf
127 North Higgins Ave.
Missoula, MT 59802
Phone: (406) 543-3550

## Nebraska
Rural Enterprise Assistance Project
Contact: Don Ralston
PO Box 406
Walthill, NE 68067
Phone: (402) 846-5428

West Central Nebraska Development District, Inc.
Contact: Ronald J. Radil

710 North Spruce Street
PO Box 599
Ogailala, NE 69153
Phone: (308) 284-6077

## Nevada
none

## New Hampshire
Institute for Cooperative Community
Contact: Don Mason
2500 North River Road
Manchester, NH 03106
Phone: (603) 644-3103

## New Jersey
Trenton Business Assistance Corporation
Contact: James Harveson
319 East State Street
Trenton, NJ 08608-1856
Phone: (609) 989-3509

Union County Economic Development Corporation
Contact: Maureen Tinen
1085 Morris Ave., Suite 531
Union, NJ 07083
Phone: (908) 527-1166

Jersey City Economic Development Corporation
Contact: Thomas D. Ahearn
601 Pavonia Ave.
Jersey City, NJ 07306
Phone: (201) 420-7755

## New Mexico
Women's Economic Self Sufficiency Team
Contact: Agnes Noonan
414 Silver South West
Albuquerque, NM 87102-3239
Phone: (505) 848-4760

## New York
Adirondack Economic Development Corporation
Contact: Ernest Hohmeyer
Trudeau Road
PO Box 747
Saranac Lake, NY 12983
Phone: (518) 891-5523

Hudson Development Corporation
Contact: Lynda S. Davidson
444 Warren Street
Hudson, NY 12534
Phone: (518) 828-3373

Manhattan Borough Development Corporation
Contact: Patricia Swann
15 Park Row, Suite 510
New York, NY 10038
Phone: (212) 791-3660

## North Carolina
Self-Help Ventures Fund
Contact: Robert Schall
413 East Chapel Hill Street
Durham, NC 27701
Phone: (919) 956-8526

## North Dakota
Lakes Agassiz Regional Council
Contact: Irvin D. Rustad
417 Main Ave.
Fargo, ND 58103
Phone: (701) 239-8526

## Ohio
Enterprise Development Corporation
Contact: Karen A. Patton
900 East State Street
Athens, OH 45701
Phone: (614) 592-1188

Columbus Countrywide Development Corporation
Contact: Mark Barbash
941 Chatham Lane, Suite 207
Columbus, OH 43221
Phone: (614) 645-6171

Hamilton County Development Corporation
Contact: David K. Main
1776 Mentor Ave.
Cincinnati, OH 43221
Phone: (513) 632-8292

Women's Entrepreneurial Growth
Contact: Susan Hale
58 West Center Street
Akron, OH 45212

## Oklahoma
Rural Enterprises, Inc.
Contact: Sherry Harlin
422 Cessna Street
Durant, OK 74701
Phone: (405) 924-5094

Tulsa Economic Development Corporation
Contact: Frank F. McCrady III
130 North Greenwood Ave., Suite C
Tulsa, OK 74120
Phone: (918) 585-8332

## Oregon
Cascades West Financial Services, Inc.
Contact; Deborah L. Wright
408 SW Monroe Street
Corvallis, OR 97333
Phone: (503) 757-6854

## Pennsylvania
The Ben Franklin Technology Center
of Southeastern Pennsylvania
Contact: Phillip A. Singerman
3624 Market Street
Philadelphia, PA 19104-2615
Phone: (215) 382-0380

York County Industrial Development Corporation
Contact: David B. Carver
One Market Way East
York, PA 17401
Phone: (717) 846-8879

## South Carolina
Charleston Citywide Local Development Corporation
Contact: Sharon Brennan
496 King Street
Charleston, SC 29403
Phone: (803) 724-3796

Santee Lynches Regional Development Corporation
Contact: James T. Darby, Jr.
115 North Harvin Street
Sumter, SC 29151-1837
Phone: (803) 775-7381

## South Dakota
NE South Dakota Energy Conservation Corporation

Contact: Arnold Petersen
414 Third Ave.
Sisseton, SD 57262
Phone: (605) 698-7654

**Tennessee**
South Central Tennessee Development District
Contact: Joe Max Williams
815 South Main Street
PO Box 1346
Columbia, TN 38402
Phone: (615) 318-2040

**Texas**
Business Resource Center Incubator
Contact: Curtis Cleveland
4601 North 19th Street
Waco, TX 76708
Phone: (817) 754-8898

Southern Dallas Development Corporation
Contact: Jim Reid
1402 Corinth, Suite 1150
Dallas, TX 78205
Phone: (214) 428-7332

**Utah**
Utah Technology Finance Corporation
Contact: Todd Clark
177 East 100 South
Salt Lake City, UT 84111
Phone: (801) 364-4346

**Vermont**
Economic Development Council
of Northern Vermont, Inc.
Contact: Connie Stanley-Little
155 Lake Street
St. Albans, VT 054787
Phone: (802) 524-4546

Northern Community Investments Corporation
Contact: Carl J. Garbelotti
20 Main Street
St. Johnsbury, VT 05819
Phone: (802) 748-5101

**Virginia**
Ethiopian Community Development Council, Inc.

Contact: Tsehaye Teferra
1038 South Highland Street
Arlington, VA 22204
Phone: (703) 685-0510

Business Development Centre, Inc.
Contact: Karen Mauch
147 Mill Ridge Road
Lynchburg, VA 24502
Phone: (804) 582-6100

People Incorporated of Southwest Virginia
Contact: Robert G. Goldsmith
988 West Main Street
Abingdon, VA 24210
Phone: (703) 628-9188

**Washington**
Snohomish County Private Industry Council
Contact: Emily Duncan
917 134th Street SW, Suite A-10
Everett, WA 98204
Phone: (206) 743-9669

Tri-Cities Enterprise Association
Contact: Dallas E. Breamer
2000 Logston Blvd.
Richland, WA 99352
Phone: (509) 375-3268

**West Virginia**
Ohio Valley Industrial and Business
Development Corporation
Contact: Terry Burkhart
12th and Chapline Streets
Wheeling, WV 26003
Phone: (304) 232-7722

**Wisconsin**
Advocap, Inc.
Contact: Richard Schlimm
19 West First Street
PO Box 1108
Fond du Lac, WI 54936
Phone: (414) 922-7760

Impact Seven, Inc.
Contact: William Bay
100 Digital Drive

Clear Lake, WI 54005
Phone: (715) 263-2532

Northwest Side Community Development Corporation
Contact: Howard Snyder
5174 North Hopkins Ave.
Milwaukee, WI 53208
Phone: (414) 462-5509

Women's Business Initiative Corporation
Contact: Becky Pileggi
3112 West Highland Blvd.
Milwaukee, WI 53208
Phone: (414) 933-3231

# Secretary of State

| | | | |
|---|---|---|---|
| Alabama | (205) 262-7210 | New Hampshire | (603) 271-3242 |
| Alaska | (907) 465-3520 | New Jersey | (609) 984-1900 |
| Arizona | (602) 542-4285 | New Mexico | (505) 827-3601 |
| Arkansas | (501) 682-1010 | New York | (518) 474-4750 |
| California | (916) 445-6371 | North Carolina | (919) 733-4201 |
| Colorado | (303) 894-2200 | North Dakota | (701) 224-2900 |
| Connecticut | (203) 566-7143 | Ohio | (614) 466-2530 |
| Delaware | (302) 736-4111 | Oklahoma | (405) 521-3911 |
| Florida | (904) 487-6000 | Oregon | (503) 378-4139 |
| Georgia | (404) 656-2881 | Pennsylvania | (717) 787-7630 |
| Hawaii | (808) 518-2517 | Rhode Island | (401) 227-2357 |
| Idaho | (208) 334-2300 | South Carolina | (803) 734-2158 |
| Illinois | (217) 782-2201 | South Dakota | (605) 773-3537 |
| Indiana | (317) 232-6531 | Tennessee | (615) 741-2816 |
| Iowa | (515)281-5864 | Texas | (512) 463-5701 |
| Kansas | (913) 296-2236 | Utah | (801) 538-1040 |
| Kentucky | (502) 564-3490 | Vermont | (802) 828-2363 |
| Louisiana | (504) 342-4857 | Virginia | (804) 786-2441 |
| Maine | (207) 289-3501 | Washington | (206) 753-7121 |
| Maryland | (301) 974-5521 | West Virginia | (304) 345-4000 |
| Massachusetts | (617) 727-9180 | Wisconsin | (608) 266-8888 |
| Michigan | (517) 373-2510 | Wyoming | (307) 777-7378 |
| Minnesota | (612) 296-2079 | District of Columbia | (202) 727-6306 |
| Mississippi | (601) 359-1350 | American Samoa | (684) 633-4116 |
| Missouri | (314) 751-2379 | Guam | (671) 472-8931 |
| Montana | (406) 444-2034 | Puerto Rico | (809) 723-4344 |
| Nebraska | (402) 471-2254 | U.S. Virgin Islands | (809) 773-6449 |
| Nevada | (702) 885-5203 | | |

# Venture Capital

With federal and state money getting harder to come by, and banks experiencing serious problems of their own that restrict their willingness to loan money, anyone interested in starting a business or expanding an existing one may do well to look into venture capital. Venture capitalists are willing to invest in a new or growing business venture for a percentage of the equity. Below is a listing of some of the associations, government agencies, and businesses that have information available on venture capital.

In addition, there are venture capital clubs throughout the country where entrepreneurs have a chance to present their ideas to potential investors and learn about the process of finding funds for ventures that might be long on innovative ideas for a business, but short on proven track records.

**Alabama**
(AL, LA, MO, TX)
Birmingham Venture Club
PO Box 10127
Birmingham, AL 35202
Contact: Patricia Fox
Phone: (205) 323-5461, Fax: (205) 250-7669

Mobile Venture Club
451 Government Street
Mobile, AL 36652
Contact: Walter Underwood
Phone: (205) 433-6951, Fax: (205) 431-8608

**Alaska**
Alaska Pacific Venture Club
405 West 27th Ave.
Anchorage, AK 99503
Phone: (907) 563-3993, Fax: (907) 279-9319

**Arizona**
Arizona Ventures
2419 North Black Canyon Highway
Phoenix, AZ 85009
Contact: Merritt Chamberlain
Phone: (602) 254-8560, Fax: (602) 254-9650

**Arkansas**
Venture Resources Inc.
100 South Main Street
Little Rock, AR 72201
Phone: (501) 375-2004, Fax: (501) 375-8317

**California**
(CA, OR, WA)
Orange Coast Venture Group

23011 Moulton Parkway, Suite F2
Laguna Hills, CA 92653
Contact: Renee Wagoner
Phone: (714) 855-0652, Fax: (714) 859-1707

(CA, OR, WA)
Orange County Venture Group
PO Box 2011
Laguna Hills, CA 92654
Contact: Gregory Beck
Phone: (714) 855-0652, Fax: (714) 380-1128

(CA, OR, WA)
Community Entrepreneurs Organization
PO Box 2781
San Rafael, CA 94912
Contact: Dr. Robert Crandall
Phone: (415) 435-4461

San Diego Venture Group
750 B Street, Suite 2400
San Diego, CA 92101
Phone: (619) 595-0284, Fax: (619) 231-8055

**Colorado**
Rockies Venture Club, Inc.
4950 East Evans, Suite 115
Denver, CO 80222
Contact: Matia Lester
Phone: (303) 831-4174

**Connecticut**
(CT, MA, MI, NJ, NY, IN, OH, PA, DC)
Connecticut Venture Capital Fund
200 Fisher Drive
Avon, CT 06001

Contact: Sam McKay
Phone: (203) 677-0183, Fax: (203) 676-0405

## District of Columbia
Baltimore-Washington Venture Group
Michael Dingman Center
College Park, MD 20742-7215
Contact: Mark Feuerberg
Phone: (301) 405-2144, Fax: (301) 314-9152

## Florida
(FL, GA, TN, KY)
Gold Coast Venture Capital Club
5820 North Federal, Suite A-2
Boca Raton, FL 33478
Phone: (407) 997-6594, Fax: (407) 997-6347

Gold Coast Venture Capital Club
11401-A, West Palmetto Park Road
Boca Raton, FL 33428
Contact: Mike Donnelly
Phone: (407) 488-4505, Fax: (407) 487-4483

(FL, GA, TN, KY)
Florida Venture Group
2838 Kansas Street
Oviedo, FL 32765
Contact: Maryjim King
Phone: (407) 365-5374, Fax: (407) 365-5374

## Hawaii
Hawaii Venture Capital Association
2800 Woodlawn Drive, Suite 280
Honolulu, HI 96822
Phone: (808) 526-1277, Fax: (808) 524-2775

## Idaho
Rocky Mountain Venture Group
2300 North Yellowstone, Suite E
Idaho Falls, ID 83402
Contact: Dennis Cheney
Phone: (208) 526-9557, Fax: 208) 526-0953

Treasure Valley Venture Capital Forum
Boise State University College of Business
1910 University Drive
Boise, ID 83725
Phone: (208) 385-1640

## Iowa
Iowa City Development
ICAD Group
PO Box 2567
Iowa City, IA 52244
Contact: Marty Kelley
Phone: (319) 354-3939, Fax: (319) 338-9958

## Illinois
Madison Dearborn Partners
70 West Madison, Suite 1330
Chicago, IL 60602
Phone: (312) 732-5400, Fax: (312) 732-4098

## Indiana
Venture Club of Indiana
PO Box 40872
Indianapolis, IN 46240-0872
Phone: (317) 253-1244, Fax: (317) 253-1244

## Kentucky
Kentucky Investment Capital Network
Capital Plaza Tower, 23rd Floor
Frankfort, KY 40601
Phone: (502) 564-7140, Fax: (502) 564-3256

Mountain Ventures Inc.
PO Box 1738
London, KY 40743
Phone: (606) 864-5175, Fax: (502) 564-3256

## Louisiana
(AL, LA, MO, TX)
Louisana Seed Capital Corporation
339 Florida Street, Suite 525
Baton Rouge, LA 70801
Contact: Kevin Couhig
Phone: (504) 383-1508, Fax: (504) 383-1513

(AL, LA, MO, TX)
Greater New Orleans Venture Capital Club
301 Camp Street
New Orleans, LA 70130
Contact: Judy Houston
Phone: (800) 949-7890, Fax: 504) 527-6950

## Maryland
Mid Atlantic Venture Association
9690 Deereco Road, Suite 800

Timonium, MD 21093
Contact: Maryanne Gray
Phone: (410) 560- 2000, Fax: (410) 560-1910

## Massachusetts
Venture Capital Fund of New England
160 Federal Street, 23rd Floor
Boston, MA 02110
Phone: (617) 439-4646, Fax: (617) 439-4652

## Michigan
(CT, MA, MI, NJ, NY, IN, OH, PA, DC)
Southeastern Venture Capital
The Meyering Corporation
206 30 Harper Ave., Suite 103
Harper Woods, MI 48225
Contact: Carl Meyering
Phone: (313) 886-2331

(CT, MA, MI, NJ, NY, IN, OH, PA, DC)
New Enterprise Forum
211 East Herron, Suite 1
Ann Arbor, MI 48104
Contact: Barb Sprague
Phone: (313) 665-4433

## Minnesota
The Entrepreneurs Network
1433 Utica Ave. South, Suite 70-3
Minneapolis, MN 55416
Phone: (612) 542-0682

St. Paul Venture Capital
8500 Normandale Lake Blvd., Suite 1940
Bloomington, MN 55437
Phone: (612) 830-7475, Fax: (612) 830-7475

## Mississippi
Magnolia Venture Capital Corporation
PO Box 2749
Jackson, MS 39207
Phone: (601) 352-5201, Fax: (601) 355-1804

## Missouri
Venture Group Inc.
233 West 47th Street
Kansas City, MO 64112
Phone: (816) 531-5585, Fax: 816) 531-8818

Missouri Innovation Center
5650 A South Sinclair Road
Columbia, MO 65203
Phone: (314) 446-3100, Fax: (314) 446-3106

## Montana
(CO, MT, UT, NM, ID, AZ)
Montana Private Capital Network
7783 Valley View Road
Poulson, MT 59860
Contact: Jon Marchi
Phone: (406) 883-5470, Fax: (406) 883-5470

## Nebraska
(IL, IA, NE, MN, WI, SD, ND, KS)
Grand Island Industrial Foundation
309 West 2nd Street, PO Box 1486
Grand Island, NE 68802-1486
Contact: Andrew G. Baird
Phone: (308) 382-1154, Fax: (308) 382-1154

## New Jersey
(CT, MA, MI, NJ, NY, IN, OH, PA, DC)
Venture Association of New Jersey, Inc.
177 Madison Ave., CN 1982
Morriston, NJ 07960
Contact: Amy or Jay Trien
Phone: (201) 267-4200, Fax: (201) 984-9634

## New York
(CT, MA, MI, NJ, NY, IN, OH, PA, DC)
Long Island Venture Group
Long Island University
Room 309, North Blvd.
Brookville, NY 11548
Contact: Carol Caracappa
Phone: (516) 299-3017, Fax: (516) 299-2786

(CT, MA, MI, NJ, NY, IN, OH, PA, DC)
New York Venture Group
605 Madison Ave., Suite 300
New York, NY 10022-1901
Contact: Burt Alimansky
Phone: (212) 832-7300, Fax: (212) 832-7338

(CT, MA, MI, NJ, NY, IN, ON, PA, DC)
Westchester Venture Capital Network
222 Mamaroneck Ave.
White Plains, NY 10605
Phone: (914) 948-2110, Fax: (914) 948-0122

## Ohio

(CT, MA, MI, NJ, NY, IN, OH, PA, DC)
Columbus Investment Interest Group
37 North High Street
Columbus, OH 43215
Contact: Diane Essex
Phone: (614) 225-6087, Fax: (614) 469-8250

(CT, MA, MI, NJ, NY, IN, OH, PA, DC)
Ohio Venture Association, Inc.
1127 Euclid Ave., Suite 343
Cleveland, OH 44115
Contact: Joan McCarthy
Phone: (216) 566-8884, Fax: (216) 696-2582

## Oklahoma

Oklahoma Venture Forum
101 North Broadway, PO Box 26788
Oklahoma City, OK 73126-0788
Contact: Steve Thomas
Phone: (405) 636-9736, Fax: (405) 270-1090

## Oregon

Northwest Capital Network
PO Box 6650
Portland, OR 97228-6650
Contact: Dawn Lewis
Phone: (503) 282-6273, Fax: (503) 282-2976

Oregon Enterprise Forum
2611 Southwest Third Ave., Suite 200
Portland, OR 97201
Contact: Carl Flipper
Phone: (503) 222-2270, Fax: (503) 241-0827

Portland Venture Group
PO Box 2341
Lake Oswego, OR 97035
Contact: Glen Smith
Phone: (503) 697-5907, Fax: (503) 241-0827

## Pennsylvania

CT, MA, MI, NJ, NY, IN, OH, PA, DC0
Dekaware Valley Venture Group
1234 Market Street, Suite 1800
Philadelphia, PA 19107
Contact: Carolyn Keim
Phone: (215) 972-3960, Fax: (215) 972-3900

Enterprise Venture Capital
Corporation of Pennsylvania
111 Market Street
Johnstown, PA 15901
Phone: (814) 535-7597, Fax: (814) 535-8677

## South Dakota

Dakota Ventures Inc.
PO Box 8194
Rapid City, SD 57709
Contact: Don Frankenfeld
Phone: (605) 348-8441, Fax: (605) 348-8452

## Tennessee

(FL, GA, TN, KY)
Mid-South Venture Group
5180 Park Ave., Suite 310
Memphis, TN 38119
Contact: William Richey
Phone: (901) 761-3084, Fax: (901) 685-5282

Tennessee Venture Capital Network
7 Cope Administration Building
Murfreesboro, TN 37132
Contact: Richard Prince
Phone: (615) 898-2100

## Texas

(AL, LA MO, TX)
Houston Venture Capital Association
1221 McKinney, Suite 2400
Houston, TX 77010
Contact: Lynn Gentry
Phone: (713) 750-1500, Fax: (713) 750-1501

Texas Venture Capital Network
8920 Business Park Drive, Suite 275
Austin, TX 78759
Phone: (512) 794-9398, Fax: (512) 794-0448

Capital Southwest Venture Corporation
12900 Preston Road, Suite 700
Dallas, TX 75230
Phone: (214) 233-8242, Fax: (214) 233-7362

## Utah

(CO, MT, UT, NM, ID, AZ)
Mountain West Venture Group
48 Market Street, #200

Salt Lake City, UT 84101
Contact: Robert Springmeyer
Phone: (801) 364-5300

Utah Ventures
419 Wakara Way, Suite 206
Salt Lake City, UT 84108
Phone: (801) 583-5922, Fax: (801) 583-4105

## Vermont
Vermont Venture Network
PO Box 5839
Burlington, VT 05402
Phone: (802) 658-7830, Fax: (802) 658-0978

## Virginia
Richmond Venture Capital Club
9101 Midlothian, Suite 900
Richmond, VA 23235
Contact: Sally Cook
Phone: (804) 560-7000

## Washington
(CA, OR, WA)
Northwest Venture Group
PO Box 21693
Seattle, WA 98111
Phone: (206) 746-1973

## West Virginia
Enterprise Venture Capital Company
PO Box 460
Summerville, WV 26651
Contact: William Bright
Phone: (304) 872-3000, Fax: (304) 872-3040

## Wisconsin
Wisconsin Venture Network

823 North Second Street, Suite 605
Milwaukee, WI 53203
Phone: (414) 278-7070

## International Clubs
Puerto Rico Venture Capital Club
PO Box 2284
Hato Rey, PR, 00919
Contact: Danol Morales
Phone: (809) 787-9040

Johannesburg Venture Capital Club
162 Anderson Street
PO Box 261425
EXCOM 2023 RSA
Johannesburg, South Africa, 2001
Contact: Graham Rosenthal

Cape Town Venture Capital Association
12th Floor, Shell House
Capetown, South Africa, 8001
Contact: Colin Hultzer

## Canadian Clubs
Edmonton Chamber of Commerce
600 10123 99th Street
Edmonton, Alberta Canada, T5J 3G9
Contact: Ace Cetinski
Phone: (403) 464-3560

Venture Capital/Entrepreneurship
Club of Montreal, Inc.
1670 Sherbrooke Street
East Montreal (Quebec) Canada, H2L 1M5
Contact: Claude Belanger
Phone: (514) 526-9490

# Employment

## American Association of Working People (AAWP)

4435 Waterfront Drive, Suite 101, PO Box 4949, Glen Allen, VA 23058-4949, Contact: W.C. Williams III, Chairman and CEO, Phone: (804) 527-1905, Fax: (804) 747-5316

Seeks to address the special interests and needs of working Americans and their families. Conducts research, educational, and charitable programs; provides children's services.

## Career Planning and Adult Development Network (CPADN)

4965 Sierra Road, San Jose, CA 95132, Contact: Richard L. Knowdell, Executive Director, Phone: (408) 559-4946, Fax: (408) 559-8211

Counselors, trainers, consultants, therapists, educators, personnel specialists, and graduate students who work in business, educational, religious, and governmental organizations, and focus on career planning and adult development issues. Seeks to: establish a link between professionals working with adults in a variety of settings.

## Center for Economic Options

601 Delaware Ave., Charleston, WV 25302, Contact: Pam Curry, Exec. Director, Phone: (304) 345-1298

Seeks to improve the economic position and quality of life for women, expecially low income and minority women.

## Employment Support Center (ESC)

711 8th Street NW, Washington, DC 20001-3747

Trains individuals to lead support groups for job seekers. Operates a job bank for employment assistance; helps people learn to network for job contacts, provides technical assistance to employment support self-help groups.

## Employment and Training Service Center (ETSC)

950 Upshur Street NW, Suite 200, Washington, DC 20011-5620, Contact: Brenda Y. Boykins

Jointly administered by the U.S. Department of Labor and the U.S. Department of Health and Human Services. Seeks employment of welfare recipients (16 and older) in unsubsidized jobs, utilizing employment related programs whenever possible, to supplement ETSC-funded activities.

## Federation Employment and Guidance Service (FEGS)

114 5th Ave., 11th Floor, New York, NY 10011, Contact: Alfred P. Miller, Exec. Vice President, Phone: (212) 366-8400, Fax: (212) 366-8490

Voluntary, nonsectarian community human service agency. Serves more than 50,000 persons anually in over 117 locations with individual and group career development services, including psychological testing, job placement, and vocational rehabilitation as well as mental health, residential, developmental, clinical, and youth services. Provides programs in economic development and criminal justice.

## Formerly Employed Mothers at the Leading Edge (FEMALE)

PO Box 31, Elmhurst, IL 60126, Contact: Debbie Sawicki, Director, Phone: (630) 941-3553, Fax: (630) 941-3551

Women who have left the paid work force to raise their children at home. Promotes respect and recognition for at-home mothering as a valid life option. Works to educate and motivate business and government to address the needs of families by conducting letter writing campaigns and drawing media attention to work/family issues. Advocates improved and expanded childcare options; mandated family leave policies; family sensitive work options such as part-time, flex-time, and job-sharing; childcare and tax legislation that does not discriminate against parents who choose to forego paid employment in order to care for their children; and child-friendly public places (stores, restaurants, etc.). Provides opportunties for networking among members in order to ease the transition from paid employment to at-home motherhood.

## Green Thumb (GT)

2000 North 14th Street, Suite 800, Arlington, VA 22201, Contact: Andrea J. Wooten, President, Phone: (703) 522-7272, Fax: (703) 522-0141

Provides job placement services, training, and part-time community service employment for unemployed persons 55 years of age or older, having income at or near poverty income level.

## Homeworkers Organized for More Employment (HOME)

PO Box 10, Orland, ME 04472, Contact: Lucy Poulin, Exec. Director, Phone: (207) 469-7961, Fax: (207) 469-1023

Individuals who produce home crafts for income. Primary purpose is to provide supplemental income for low- income families through sale of their crafts through HOME's retail, catalog, and wholesale departments. Conducts education classes, craft fair and craft shows.

## Human Resources Development Institute (HRDI)

1101 14th Street NW, Suite 320, Washington, DC 20005, Contact: Lynn Meyers, Exec. Director, Phone: (202) 638-3912, Fax: (202) 783-6536

Serves as an employment and training arm of the AFL-CIO. Works to assure full labor participation in employment and training programs funded under the Job Training Partnership Act. Assists in developinig JTPA programs for dislocated and economically disadvantaged workers and provides technical services in support of labor-operated programs. Offers job search and placement services for disabled persons and early intervention and return-to-work services for recently disabled union members.

## Industry-Labor Council

National Center for Disability Services, 201 I.U. Willets Road, Albertson, NY 11507-1599, Contact: Gary Kishanuk, Manager, Phone: (516) 747-6323, Fax: (516) 747-2046

Corporations (190) and labor unions (8) committed to improving employment opportunities for persons with disabilities. Acts as consultant and technical assistant on matters concerning employment of persons with disabilities; provides a clearinghouse for information on topics such as the Americans With Disabilities Act, accessibility, out-reach and recruiting, reasonable accommodation, legislation, and disability management; encourages discussion of critical issues. Offers in-house training programs and audio/visual training packages; conducts research projects. Refers industry and labor to recruiting sources nationwide that in turn refer disabled applicants; operates placement service; makes available children's services.

## Jobs for America's Graduates (JAG)

1729 King Street, Suite 200, Alexandria, VA 22314, Contact: Adrienne R. Smith, Phone: (703) 684-9479, Fax: (703) 684-9489

Participants are state education programs, high schools, vocational centers and community colleges. Develops statewide school-to-work transition programs and establishes local boards to ensure that states properly implement the models. Operates dropout prevention program.

## Jobs for the Future (JFF)

1 Bowdoin Square, Boston, MA 02114, Contact: Arthur H. White, Chariman, Phone: (617) 742-5995, Fax: (617) 742-5767

Seeks to integrate quality education and work oportunities. Offers technical assistance and training to educators, executives, and policy makers. Conducts research and disseminates results on trends in learning among students and employees.

## National Association of Older Worker Employment Services (NAOWES)

409 3rd Street SW, Suite 200, Washington, DC 20024, Contact: A.E. (Sonny) Marks, Program Operations Director, Phone: (202) 479-1200, Fax: (202) 479-0735

A constituent unit of The National Council on the Aging. Works to ensure that all individuals, regardless of age, are allowed to use their skills and talents as productive and contributing members of the workforce. Through promotion of adequate funding and coordination among federally funded programs, and through other initiatives targeted to meeting thc needs of the growing older worker pool, it helps to ensure that older workers are provided access to professional services throughout the country.

## National Employment Counseling Association (NECA)

5999 Stevenson Ave., Alexandria, VA 22304, Contact: John L. Jaco, Exec. Director, Phone: (703) 823-9800, Fax: (703) 823-0252

A division of the American Counseling Association. Those engaged in employment counsleing, counselor education, research, administration or supervision in business and industry, colleges and universities, and federal and state government; students. Offers professional leadership and development services; provides opportunities for professional growth through workshops and special projects.

## Opportunities Industrialization Centers of America (OICA)

1415 North Broad Street, Philadelphia, PA 19122, Contact: Art Taylor, CEO & President, Phone: (215) 236-4500, Fax: (215) 236-7480

Network of employment and training programs. Serves disadvantaged and underskilled Americans of all races. Seeks to develop the "whole person" and enables individuals to become self-sufficient, productive workers.

## Options

225 South 15th Street, Suite 1635, Philadelphia, PA 19102-3916, Contact: Lesley Mallow Wendell, Exec. Director, Phone: (215) 735-2202, Fax: (215) 735-8097

Career advising and human resource consulting service. Provides consulting and training programs on the changing workforce and workplace. Offers counseling on career issues such as job searches, career changes and career management. Provides consultation in the areas of managing change, career management, mentoring, effective communication, outplacement, managing diversity, and spouse employment assistance.

## Vocational Foundation, Inc. (VFI)

902 Broadway, 15th Floor, New York, NY 10010, Contact: Rebecca Taylor, Exec. Director, Phone: (212) 777-0700, Fax: (212) 673-8975

A free voluntary vocational training, guidance, and job placement service for economically and educationally disadvantaged young people (ages 16 to 21) who are referred by other accredited public and voluntary agencies in New York City. Seeks to aid high school dropouts and young people with correctional and drug abuse histories. Works to provide access to job training and employment options to women. Supports self-employed women and small business owners by offering training and technical assistance and information. Advocates women's legal right to employment, training, education, and credit. Seeks to inform the public on economic issues related to women.

## Womens Disabled Businesspersons Association (WDBA)

5850 Hardy Ave., No. 112, Suite 207, San Diego, CA 92115, Contact: Urban Miyares, President, Phone: (619) 586-1199, Fax: (619) 578-0637

Persons with disabilities, corporations, organizations, government agencies, and interested individuals. Works to help disabled entrepreneurs and professionals maximize their potential in the business world. Encourages the participation and performance of the disabled in the workforce.

# Environment/Ecology

## American Forests
910 17th Street NW, No. 600, Washington, DC 20006, Contact: Deborah Gangloff, Exec. Director, Phone: (202) 955-4500, (800) 368-5748, Fax: (602) 955-4588
A citizens' conservation organization working to advance the intelligent management and use of forest, soil, water, wildlife, and all other natural resources. Promotes public appreciation of natural resources and the part they play in the social, recreational, and economic life of the U.S.

## American Oceans Campaign
725 Arizona Ave., Suite 102, Santa Monica, CA 90401, Contact: Robert H. Sulnick, Exec. Director, Phone: (310) 576-6162, (800) 8-OCEAN-0, Fax: (310) 576-6170
Safeguards the vitaly of the oceans and coastal waters. Committed to scientific information in advocating for sound public policy; developing partnerships with all entities interested in protecting the environment. Seeks to ensure healthy sources of food and coastal recreation as well as to protect the ocean's grandeur for future generations.

## Americans Rivers
1025 Vermont Ave. NW, Suite 720, Washington, DC 20005, Contact: Rebecca R. Wodder, President, Phone: (202) 347-9224, (800) 296-6900, Fax: (202) 347-9240
A public interest group working to preserve and restore America's river systems; fosters a river stewardship ethic. Focuses on types of river protection methods.

## American Wildlands
40 East Main, Suite 2, Bozeman, MT 59715, Contact: D. Dan Chandler, Phone: (406) 586-8175, (303) 649-1211, Fax: (406) 586-8242
Dedicated to conserving the nation's wildland resources. Promotes the protection and responsible management of wildland resources, including wilderness, watersheds, wetlands, free-flowing rivers, fisheries, forests, rangelands, and wildlife; works to identify and investigate wilderness areas, wild and scenic rivers, and other natural areas needing protection; conducts scientific and economic research of wildland resources, making findings available to the public. Sponsors programs, forums, and institutes on proper land and water management on publicly owned lands. Conducts Timber Management Policy Reform and Sustainable Forestry Program which seeks reform on national forest policy and Corridors of Life, a scientific prospect to identify and protect habitat linkages in the Northern Rockies. Promotes proper use of earth, soil, water, plant, animal, and atmospheric resources; studies the interrelationship between man and wildland resources, assists citizens through technical assistance programs.

## Association of State Wetland Managers
PO Box 269, Berne, NY 12023-9746, Contact: Jon Kusler, Exec. Director, Phone: (518) 872-1804, Fax: (518) 872-2171
Professional and other interested individuals who are involved in wetland management. Seeks to: promote and improve protection and management of U.S. wetlands; fosters cooperation among government agencies and integration of public, private, and academic protection programs. Encourages the exchange and dissemination of information and ideas between members; identifies, coordinates, and conducts research concerning wetland protection needs and techniques. Works to improve public knowledge and awareness of the field. Provides technical assistance in areas such as regulations, management, acquisition, assessment, litigation, and land-use incentives.

## America The Beautiful-Fund
1511 K Street NW, Suite 611, Washington, DC 20005, Contact: Nanine Bilski, President, Phone: (202) 638-1649, (202) 638-1687, (800) 522-3557
Offers recognition, technical support, and small seeds grants to private citizens and community groups to initiate new local action projects that improve the quality of the environment. Projects affects environmental design, land preservation, green plantings, civic arts, and historical and cultural preservation, through citizens' volunteer services.

## Center for Holistic Management
1010 Tijeras Ave. NW, Albuquerque, NM 87102, Contact: Shannon Horst, Exec. Director, Phone: (505) 842-5252, Fax: (505) 843-7900
Seeks to improve the human environment and quality of life through Holistic Resource Management. Objectives are to: produce stable environments with sound watersheds; restore profitability to agriculture; reestablish seriously damaged riparian (streamside) areas; prevent waste of financial resources by governments, international agencies, and private individuals due to poor resource management; educators in Holistic Resource Management.

## Center for Marine Conservation (CMC)

725 DeSales Street NW, Suite 600, Washington, DC 20036, Contact: Roger E. McManus, President, Phone: (202) 429-5609, Fax: (202) 872-0619

Dedicated to the conservation and protection of the marine wildlife and their habitats. Promotes public awarness and education. Advocates correct management of marine resources and promotes conservation of endangered species and their habitats. Seeks to insure that human activities will not lead to the extinction of these species. Activities have included beach cleanups resulting in new state programs to reduce marine debris in the Gulf of Mexico and the establishment of sanctuary for critically endangered humpback whales in the Caribbean. Conducts programs in fisheries, conservation, species recovery, habitat conservation, and pollution prevention. Operates the Marine Debris Information Office. Also works to prevent accidental entaglement and drowning of marine animals in debris and fishing gear and has repeatedly thwarted efforts to increase international trade in sea turtle products.

## Coastal Conservation Association (CCA)

4801 Woodway, Suite 220 West, Houston, TX 77056, Contact: Walter W. Fondren lll, Phone: (713) 626-4234, Fax: (713) 626-5852

Organizations, corporations and individuals interested in conserving the natural resources of U.S. saltwater coastal areas. Seeks to advance the protection and conservation of all marine life. Operates GCCA/John Wilson Hatchery near Corpus Christi, Texas, to bolster the redfish population in the Gulf of Mexico. Lobbies state governments to enact legislation favorable to conservation and sport fishing. Conducts seminars regarding current topics in marine conservation; bestows awards; maintains New Tide youth program. Contributes funds for marine ecological research.

## Conservation International (CI)

2501 M Street., NW, Suite 200, Washington , DC 20037, Contact: Peter Seligmann, President, Phone: (202) 429-5660, Fax: (202) 887-5188

Corporations and individuals in 15 countries interested in environmental protection and conservation. Cooperates with governments and other organizations to help all nations develop the ability to sustain biological diversity and the ecosystem that support life on earth while addressing basic economic and social needs. Has sponsored an agreement whereby a portion of Bolivia's debt to United States banks was forgiven in exchange for Bolivia's promise to protect a part of the Amazon rainforest; other project sites include Costa Rica and Mexico. Promotes scientific understanding through research programs; encourages and facilitates ecosystem management and conservation-based development. Conducts public outreach programs; assists in formulation and implementation of policy. Maintains small library.

## Charles A. and Anne Morrow Lindbergh Foundation

708 South 3rd Street, Suite 110, Minneapolis, MN 55415-1141, Contact: Reeve Lindbergh, President, Phone: (612) 338-1703, Fax: (612) 338-6826

Perpetuates the partnership of aviators Charles A. Lindbergh (1902-1974) and Ann Morrow Lindbergh and promotes their vision of balance between technological advancement and environmental preservation. Conducts educational programs. Awards research grants.

## Conservation Technology Information Center ( CTIC)

c/o Jim Mitchel, 1220 Porter Drive, Room 170, West Lafayette, IN 47906-1383, Contact: John Hebblethwaite, Phone: (765) 494-9555, Fax: (765) 494-5969

Promotes environmentally and acibinucally responsible decision making by farmers through dissemination of information. Serves as a clearinghouse on natural resource management, agricultural techniques, and other environmental initiatives; facilitates communication between agricultural companies, farmers, governmental, agricultural organizations and media.

## EarthSave International

620 Distillery Commons, Louisville, KY 40206-1922, Contact: Patricia Carney, Exec. Director

EarthSave promotes food choices that are healthy for the planet. We educate, inspire and empower people to take positive action for all life on earth.

## Earth Day 2000

11965 Venice Blvd., No. 408, Los Angeles, CA 90066, Contact: Caroline Harwood, Director, Phone: (310) 397-5270, (800) 727-8619, Fax: (310) 391-0053

Individuals interested in the environment. Campaigns for truth on environmental claims on labeling and in advertising. Reports on products and services that are good for the environment. Conducts research and educational programs. Offers guidebooks and curriculum for teachers, students, and activists interested in environmental programming.

## Earth Island Institute (EII)

300 Broadway, Suite 28, San Francisco, CA 94133, Contact: David R. Brower, Chairman, Phone: (415) 788-3666, Fax: (415) 788-7324

Individuals working to coordinate environmental and wildlife protection projects. Seeks to develop innovative projects for the conservation, preservation and restoration of the global environment; promotes ecologically and socially sound development. Sponsors Brower Fund to provide funding for environmental and peace projects; supports the Urban Habitat Program, which develops multicultural urban environmental leadership; administers International Marine Mammal Projects, which works to protect whales and dolphins through the prevention of the slaughter of dolphins caught in tuna nets.

## Environmental Defence Fund (EDF)

257 Park Ave., South, New York, NY 10010, Contact: Fred D. Krupp, Exec. Director, Phone: (212) 505-2100, (800) 684-3322, Fax: (212) 505-2375

Links science, law, economics, and engineering to create innovative and economically viable solutions to environmental problems. Four areas of focus include protecting and restoring biodiversity (with an emphasis on rivers and watersheds); stabilizing climate by developing policies to reduce dependence on fossil fuels; reducing risks to human health from exposure to toxic chemicals; and protecting oceans from pollution and overfishing.

## Forest Trust (FT)

PO Box 519, Santa Fe, NM 87504-0519, Contact: Henry H. Carey, Director, Phone: (505) 983-8992, Fax: (505) 986-0798

Dedicated to the protection of America's forest. Works to protect the integrity of the forest ecosystem and improve the lives of people in rural communities. Challenges traditional forest management philosophies and provides resource protection strategies to grassroots environmental organizations, rural communities, and public agencies. Provides lands stewardship services to owners of private lands of significant conservation value.

## Friends of the Earth (FOE)

1025 Vermont Ave. NW, Suite 300, Washington, DC 20005, Contact: Brent Blackwelder, President, Phone: (202) 783-7400, Fax: (202) 783-0444

Dedicated to protecting the planet from environmental disaster; preserving biological and ethic diversity; empowers citizens to have an effective voice in environmental decisions; promotes use of tax dollars to protect the environment; other interests include ground water and ozone protection, toxic waste cleanup, and reforming the world bank and sustainable development which addresses the need to reduce over-consumption in the U.S.

## Global Response

PO Box 7490, Boulder, CO 80306-7490, Contact: Paula Palmer, Executive Director, Phone: (303) 444-0306, Fax: (303) 449-9794

Individuals concerned with ecology and the environment. Responds to environmental emergencies around the world by writing letters. Alerts members to environmental threats; recommends actions; provides names and addresses of corporations or governments responsible.

## Global Warming International Center (GWIC)

22 West 381 75th Street, Naperville, IL 60565-9245, Contact: Dr. Sinyan Shen, Director, Phone: (630) 910-1551, Fax: (630) 910-1561

Ministerial agencies and industrial corporations. Concerned with impacts and effects of global warming. Provides a focus for government, the private sector, and academia to share information on global warming internationally. Coordinates training for personnel dealing with environmental issues, energy planning, and natural resource management through the Institute for World Resource Research. Established the Global Warming Index and the Extreme Event Index for international standardization.

## Greenpeace U.S.A. (GPUSA)

1436 U Street NW, Washington, DC 20009, Contact: Barbara Dudley, Exec. Director, Phone: (202) 462-1177, Fax: (202) 462-4507

Conservationists who believe that verbal protest against threats to environmental quality are not adequate. Initiates active, though nonviolent, measures to aid endangered species such as placing boats between harpoonists and whales and placing themselves bodily between hunters and seal pups. Monitors conditions of environmental concern including the greenhouse effect, radioactive and toxic waste dumping, and a comprehensive test ban for nuclear weapons. Conducts research and lobbying efforts and media campaigns.

## Greenhouse Crisis Foundation (GCF)

1660 L Street NW, Suite 216, Washington, DC 20036, Contact: Jeremy Rifkin, President, Phone: (202) 466-2823, Fax: (202) 466-2823

Seeks to stimulate global awareness of the greenhouse effect caused by an increase in atmospheric gases from industrial pollution; these gases have formed a chemical shield around the earth, resulting in global warming and related atmospheric problems, such as ozone depletion and acid rain. Maintains the Greenhouse Crisis Education Campaign, a program to advise individuals about what they can do to address the crisis. Sponsors events to develop international communication on the greenhouse effect such as International Local Government Network, which addresses how to implement changes in urban energy use, transportation, recycling, and urban reforestation; Global Greenhouse Network, comprised of environmental organizations, wilderness preservation groups, and individuals from the entertainment community offering recommendations to urban global warming.

## Interfaith Council for the Protection of Animals and Nature (ICPAN)

3691 Tuxedo Road, NW, Atlanta, GA 30305, Contact: Lewis G. Regenstein, Director, Phone: (404) 814-1371

Individuals of all religious faith who share an interest in conservation of natural resources and environmental protection. Works to make religious leaders, institutions, and the public aware of humanity's "moral and spiritual obligation," as emphasized in the Bible and many religious teachings, to protect animals and the natural environment. Conducts educational campaigns including lectures and slide shows.

## International Association of Fish and Wildlife Agencies (IAFWA)

444 N. Capitol Street NW, Suite 544, Washington, DC 20001, Contact: R. Max Peterson, Exec. Vice President, Phone: ( 202) 624-7890, Fax: (202) 624-7891

Educates the public about the economic importance of conserving natural resources and managing wildlife property as a source of recreation and a food supply; supports better conservation legislation, administration, and enforcement.

## Kinds for Clean Environment (Kinds FACE)

PO Box 158254, Nashville, TN 37215, Contact: Trish Poe, Exec. Director, Phone: (615) 331-7381, (800) 952-3223, Fax: (615) 333-9879

Children, parents, teachers, and others working to improve the environment. Focus is on children organizations and implementing ideas and programs on their own, supported and assisted by parents and teachers (membership free to children). Provides children's services and educational programs. Operates Environmental Resource Center. Provides bi-monthly newsletter.

## National Audubon Society (NAS)

700 Broadway, New York, NY 10003, Contact: John Flicker, President, Phone: (212) 979-3000, Fax: (212) 353-0377

Works to conserve and restore natural ecosystems, focusing on birds and other wildlife for the benefit of humanity and the earth's biological diversity.

## National Forest Foundation (NFF)

1099 14th Street NW, Suite 5600-W, Washington, DC 20005, Contact: Terry Austin, Acting President, Phone: (202) 501-2473, (202) 216-9750, Fax: (202) 219-6585

Supports the U.S. Forest Service in its management of the 191 million acres of public land entrusted to its care and activities that support multiple use and cooperative forestry. Its mission is to "help care for the Nation's Forests and build a better future for America." Programs focus on forest conservation, recreation, wildlife and fisheries, forest protection, and education.

## National Wildlife Federation (NWF)

8925 Leesburg Pike, Vienna, VA 22184, Contact: Mark Van Putten, President, Phone: (703) 790-4000

Nation's largest member-supported conservation group, with over four million members and supporters. Federation of state and territorial affiliates, associate members and individual conservationist-contributors. Seeks to educate, inspire and assist individuals and organizations of diverse cultures to conserve wildlife and other natural resources and to protect the earth's environment in order to achieve a peaceful, equitable and sustainable future. Encourages the intelligent management of the life-sustaining resources of the earth and promotes greater appreciation of wild places, wildlife and the natural resources shared by all. Publishes educational materials and conservation periodicals. Conducts a variety of conservation advocacy and education programs, including Conservation Summits, NatureLink, National Wildlife Week and the Backyard Wildlife Habitat Program. Produces nationally distributed multimedia programming on conservation topics and issues, ranging from IMAX films to television specials and series.

## Natural Resources Defense Council (NRDC)

40 West 20th Street, New York, NY 10011, Contact: John H. Adams, Exec. Director, Phone: (212) 727-2700, Fax: (212) 727-1773

Lawyers, scientists, public health specialists, and transportation, energy, land use, and economic planners. Dedicated to the wise management of natural resource through research, public education, and the development of public policies. Concerns include land use, coastal protection, air and water pollution, nuclear safety and energy production, toxic substances, and protection of wilderness and wildlife. Works to increase public understanding of the means by which law may be used to protect resources; engages in litigation that may set widely applicable precedents or preserve natural resources. Monitors federal departments and regulatory agencies concerned with the environment to ensure that public interest is considered. Conducts several research projects.

## Nature Conservacy (TNC)

1815 North Lynn Street, Arlington, VA 22209, Contact: John C. Sawhill, President, Phone: (703) 841-5300, Fax: (703) 841-1283

Dedicated to the preservation of biological diversity through land and water protection of natural areas. Identifies ecologically significant lands and protects them through gift, purchase, or cooperative management agreements with government or private agencies, voluntary arrangements with private landowners, and cost-saving methods of protection. Provides long-term stewardship for 1,600 conservancy-owned preserves and makes most conservancy lands available for non- destructive use on request by educational and scientific organizations.

## National Registry of Environmental Professionals (NREP)

PO Box 2068, Glenview, IL 60025, Contact: Richard A. Young, Exec. Director, Phone: (847) 724-6631, (847) 724-4223

Certifies auditors, property assessors, lending analysts, indoor air quality specialists, hazardous and chemical material managers, ISO 14000 program administrators, environmental managers, engineers, technologists, scientists, and technicians. Promotes legal and professional recognition through professional registration credentialing. Offers accreditation. Provides lists of qualified environmental professionals to governmental agencies. Sponsors workshops through 30 official test center universities.

## National Tree Society

PO Box 10808, Bakersfield, CA 93389, Contact: Gregory W. Davis, President, Phone: (805) 589-6912, (800) SAY-TREE, Fax: (805) 589-7135

Interested individuals organized to preserve the earth's biosphere by planting and caring for trees. Seeks to raise public understanding of the need for trees and the role they play in maintaining a healthy environment; works to acquire forest and other lands to ensure the continued growth of trees on such lands; establishes nurseries to supply the trees needed to "replace the millions destroyed annually and to offset man's ever increasing use of combustion." Offers training in the planting and caring of trees; fosters research; is developing a specialized library focusing on the bio-sphere. Maintains and promotes the National Tree Fund, which provides financial support to plant and care for trees.

## Rainforest Action Network (RAN)

221 Pine Street, Suite 500, San Francisco, CA 94104, Contact: Mr. Randall Hayes, President, Phone: (800) 989-RAIN

Seeks to preserve the world's rainforest through activism on issues including the logging and importation of tropical timber, cattle ranching in rainforest, the activities of international development banks, and the rights of indigenous rainforest people. Sponsors letter writing campaigns, boycotts, and demonstrations; conducts grass roots organizing in the U.S., buildings coalitions, and collaborates with other environmental, scientific, and grass roots groups; facilitates communication among U.S., and Third World organizers. Works to educate the public about the effects of tropical hardwood logging; promotes ecologically sound plantations to restore degraded land. Conducts research; sponsors media outreach projects; compiles statistics. Provides free information for school teachers and students.

## Rainforest Alliance (RA)

650 Bleecker Street, New York, NY 10012, Contact: Daniel Katz, Exec. Director, Phone: (212) 677 1900, (888) MY-EARTH, Fax: (212) 677-2187

Works for conservation of tropical forests for the benefit of global community. Develops and promotes economically viable and socially desirable alternatives to the destruction of tropical forests, and endangered, biologically diverse natural resources. Educates and researches the social and natural sciences; develops cooperative partnerships with businesses, governments and local people.

## Student Conservation Association (SCA, Inc.)

PO Box 550, 689 River Road, Charlestown, NH 03603-0550, Contact: Valerie J. Shand, Acting President, Phone: (603) 543-1700, Fax: (603) 543-1828

Individuals, foundations corporations and groups who support the association's programs. In cooperation with the National Park Service, the U.S. Forest Service, and other federal, state, local, and private agencies which manage public lands and natural resources, the association offers educational programs for high school and college students and other adults to assist with the stewardship of national parks, forests, and other resource areas. High school participants build and repair structures and trails, and carry out ecological restoration work. College students and other adults assist professionals with wildlife research, wilderness management, environmental education, archaelogical surveys, and other tasks. Conducts educational and vocational programs providing jobs skills training, work experience, and exposure to career options in natural resource fields. Operates AmeriCorps programs for Corporation for National Service.

## Sierra Club (SC)

85 2nd Street, 2nd Floor, San Francisco, CA 94105 3459, Contact: Carl Pope, Exec. Director, Phone: (415) 977-5500, Fax: (415) 977-5799

Individuals concerned with nature and its interrelationship to human beings. Promotes protection and conservation of the natural resources of the U.S. and the world; educates others about the need to preserve and restore the quality of the environment and the integrity of those ecosystems. Works on urgent campaigns to save threatened areas; is concerned with problems of wilderness, forestry, clean air, coastal protection, energy conservation, population, international development lending, and land use. Attempts to influence public policy at all governmental levels through legislative, administrative, legal, and electoral means. Schedules wilderness outings, talks, and film exhibits.

## Sierra Student Coalition (SSC)

145 Waterman Street, 1st Floor, Providence, RI 02906, Phone: (401) 861-6012, (888) JOIN-SSC, Fax: (401) 861-6241

Students interested in ecology and environmetal protection.

Activist program of the Sierra Club. Serves as a network of students-run grass roots environmental organizations. Develops and implements strategies for grass roots environmental action, local issues campaigns, and social justice initiatives. Provides information, resources, and assistance to local organizations. Conducts leadership training programs; sponsors charitable activities; makes available children's services.

## Scenic America (SA)

21 Dupont Circle NW, Washington, DC 20036, Contact: Meg Maguire, President, Phone: (202) 833-4300, Fax: (202) 833-4304

Coalition of individuals and organizations interested in preserving and enhancing America's scenic beauty; affiliates organizations at the local and state level. Works with individuals, government agencies, planning and zoning commissions of local governments, and citizen, business, state and national groups. Promotes billboard and sign control; provides legal and technical assistance on sign control; preservation of scenic byways, and aesthetic regulation to municipalities and citizen's groups. Provides advice to communities wishing to develop effective sign control and scenic preservation strategies. Maintains speakers' bureau; compiles statistics; conducts seminars.

## Student Environmetal Action Coalition

PO Box 31909, Philadelphia, PA 19104-1909, Contact: Peter Chowla, Interim Project Director

Students and student organizations; interested others. Seeks to empower students working for environmental justice. Serves as a clearinghouse on students environmental and social justice issues. Coordinates national and regional activities.

## United States Tourist Council (USTC)

Drawer 1875, Washington, DC 20013-1875, Contact: Dr. Stanford West, Exec. Director, Phone: (301) 565-5155

Conservation-concerned individuals who travel; institution and industries that supply goods and services to the traveler. Objectives are to achieve: historic and scenic preservation; wilderness and roadside development; ecology through sound planning and education; support of scientific studies of natural wilderness areas.

## Waterfowl U.S.A (WUSA)

Box 50, Waterfowl Bldg., Edgefield, SC 29824, Contact: Roger White, President, Phone: (803) 637-5767, Fax: (803) 637-6983

Hunters, conservationists, and others dedicated to raising money for developing, preserving, restoring, and maintaining waterfowl habitats in the U.S. Seeks to: publicize the needs of waterfowl; develop state and local wetland projects; improve waterfowl resting areas, wood duck nest boxes, and planting areas that feed migrating and resident waterfowl; establish public shooting areas. Conducts wood duck research. Cooperates with other waterfowl groups.

## Wildlife Conservation Society
2300 Southern Bldg., Bronx NY 10460, Contact: William Conway, President, Phone: (718) 220-5100, Fax: (212) 220-7114

Supporters of international species survival strategies and habitat/ecosystem conservation projects. Operates Bronx Zoo, Aquarium for Wildlife Conservation, and three other wildlife centers in New York. Publishes and disseminates environmental education curricula to nationwide school audience, including extensive teacher training programs. Conducts baseline, field studies, provides professional training of foreign field of biologists, and prepares recommendations for parks and protected area management. Maintains an office in Nairobi, Kenya.

## Wolf Heaven International
3111 Offut Lake Road, Tenino, WA 98589 Contact: J.D. Kendall, General Manager, Phone: (360) 264-4695, (800) 448-9653, Fax: (360) 264-4639

Individuals interested in the conservation and understanding of wolfs and wolf populations. Seeks to educate the public and increase awareness of the need for conservation. Provides presentations to school, civic, and outreach programs. Encourages research.

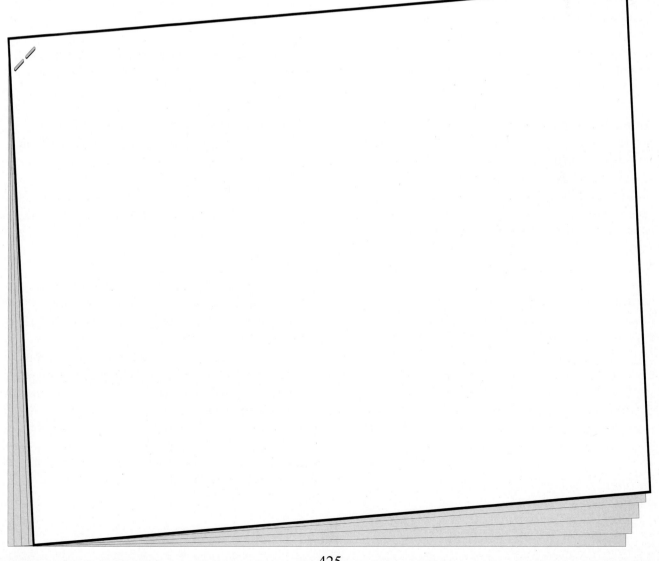

# Housing

## Christmas in April
1536 Sixteenth Street, NW, Washington, DC 20036-1402, Contact: Claudia Rizzo, Phone: (202) 483-9583, (800) 4RE-HAB9, Fax: (202) 483-9081

Local grass roots volunteer organizations. Promotes availability of adequate and affordable housing to low-income individuals. Cooperates with local communities to conduct rehabilitation of housing, particularly for elderly and handicapped individuals.

## Cooperative Housing Foundation (CHF)
8300 Colesville Road, Suite 420, Silver Spring, MD 20910, Contact: Michael E. Doyle, President & CEO, Phone: (301) 587-4700, Fax: (301) 587-2626

Leaders in housing cooperative, labor, business and civic organizations who are interested in improving the quality of housing and communities, especially for persons of modest income. Provides private sector assistance directed at economic development, settlements and planning. Sponsors the development of cooperative and self-help housing.

## Habitat for Humanity International (HFHI)
121 Habitat Street, Americus, GA 31709-3498, Phone: (912) 924-6935, Fax: (912) 924-6541

Works in partnership with people in need throughout the world to build shelter that is sold to them at no profit through no interest loans. Funds, building materials and labor are donated by individuals, churches, corporations and other organizations who share the goal of eliminating substandard housing in the world.

## National Affordable Housing Network
PO Box 3706, Butte, MT 59702, Contact: Barbara Miller, Exec. Director, Phone: (406) 782-8145, Fax: (406) 782-5168

Conducts research and demonstration projects to design safe, comfortable, affordable housing for disadvantaged families. Utilizes the collective experience of staff members to design and build homes that require less energy, water, and natural resources.

## National Association of Housing Cooperatives (NAHC)
1614 King Street, Alexandria, VA 22314, Contact: Herbert

J. Cooper-Levy, Exec. Director, Phone: (703) 549-5201, Fax: (703) 549-5204

Nonprofit housing cooperatives controlled by member-owners and representing about 1,000,000 families. Sets standard; promotes development of housing cooperatives through research, education, and forums. Aids individuals and groups interested in forming housing cooperatives to find sources for technical advice and assistance. Covers topics such as management, energy conservation, board-member relations, development of community facilities, conversion from rental to cooperative home ownership, and community relations.

## National Foundation for Affordable Housing Solutions (NFAHS)
11200 Rockville Pike, Suite 220, Rockville, MD 20852, Contact: Martin C. Schwartzberg, President, Phone: (301) 998-0498, Fax: (301) 998-0420

Works to: preserve existing affordable housing; create new housing opportunities; link social services to housing programs in poor communities.

## National Homeowners Association (NHA)
PO Box 221225, Chantilly, VA 20153, Contact: John L. Weidlein, President, Phone: (703) 581-1515, Fax: (703) 581-1234

Promotes a political and economic climate favorable to American home owners; provides legislative/regulatory liason. Conducts political, educational and consumer programs.

## National Housing Conference (NHC)
815 15th Street NW, Suite 538, Washington, DC 20005, Contact: Robert J. Reid, Exec. Director, Phone: (202) 393-5772, Fax: (202) 393-5656

Housing authority officials, community development specialists, builders, bankers, lawyers, accountants, owners, residents, insurers, architects and planners, religious organizations, labor groups and national housing and housing related organizations. Mobilizes support for effective programs in housing and community development as well as affordable and accessible housing for all Americans.

# Human/Civil Rights

## A. Philip Randolph Educational Fund (APREF)
1444 Eye Street NW, No. 300, Washington, DC 20005, Contact: Norman Hill, President, Phone: (202) 289-2774, Fax: (202) 289-5289

Seeks to: eliminate prejudice and discrimination from all areas of life; educate individuals and groups on their rights and responsibilities; defend human and civil rights; assist in the employment and education of the underprivileged; combat community deterioration, delinquency and crime.

## Amnesty International of the U.S.A. (AIUSA)
322 8th Ave., New York, NY 10001, Contact: William F. Schulz, Exec. Director, Phone: (212) 807-8400, (800) AMNESTY, Fax: (212) 627-1451

Works impartially for the release of men, women and children detained anywhere for their conscientiously held beliefs, color, ethnic origin, sex, religion, or language, provided they have neither used nor advocated violence. Opposes torture, "disappearances," and executions without reservation and advocates fair and prompt trials for all political prisoners. Has consultative status with the United Nations and the Council of Europe.

## American Civil Liberties Union (ACLU)
132 West 43rd Street, New York, NY 10036, Contact: Ira Glasser, Exec. Director, Phone: (212) 944-9800, Fax: (212) 869-9065

Champions the rights set forth in the Bill of Rights of the U.S. Constitution: freedom of speech, press, assembly and religion; due process of law and fair trial; equality before the law regardless of race, color, sexual orientation, national origin, political opinion, or religious belief. Activities include litigation, advocacy and public education.

## American Civil Liberties Union Foundation (ACLUF)
125 Broad Street, 18th Floor, New York, NY 10004, Contact: Ira Glasser, Exec. Director, Phone: (212) 549-2500, Fax: (212) 549-2646

Established as the tax-exempt arm of the American Civil Liberties Union. Purposes are legal defense, research, and public education on behalf of civil liberties including freedom of speech, press, and other First Amendment rights. Sponsors projects on topics such as children's rights, capital punishment, censorship, women's rights, immigration, prisoners' rights, national security, voting rights and equal employment opportunity.

## Americans for Religious Liberty (ARL)
PO Box 6656, Silver Spring, MD 20916, Contact: Edd Doerr, Exec. Director, Phone: (301) 598-2447, Fax: (301) 438-8428

Individuals dedicated to preserving religious, intellectual, and personal freedom, the constitutional principle of separation of church and state, democratic secular public education, reproductive rights, and the Jeffersonian-Madisonian ideal of a pluristic secular democracy. ARL was founded to counter attacks on church/state separation by sectarian special interests.

## Anti-Repression Resource Team (ARRT)
Contact: Ken Lawrence, Director, Phone: (814) 237-3095

Combats all forms of political repression including: police violence and misconduct; Ku Klux Klan and Nazi terrorism; spying and covert action by secret police and intelligence agencies.

## Center for Concern (CC)
3700 13th Street NE, Washington, DC 20017, Contact: James E. Hug, Exec. Director, Phone: (202) 635-2757, Fax: (202) 832-9494

People working with grass roots and international networks to show the connections between global and local justice. Promotes social analysis, theological reflection, policy advocacy, research, and public education on global and local issues such as poverty, underemployment, unemployment, hunger, women's rights, economic justice and social development.

## Citizens Committee for the Right to Keep and Bear Arms (CCRKBA)
Liberty Park, 12500 NE 10th Place, Bellevue, WA 98005, Contact: Ken Jacobson, Exec. Director, Phone: (206) 454-4911, Fax: (206) 451-3959

Citizens interested in defending the Second Amendment; more than 150 members of Congress serve on the advisory board. Conducts educational and political activities, and in-depth studies on gun legislation.

## Congressional Friends of Human Rights Monitors (CFHRM)
House of Representatives, 1432 Longworth Buildings, Washington, DC 20515, Contact: Robert Zachritz, Exec. Officer, Phone: (202) 225-6465

A coalition of members of the U.S. House and Senate. Promotes human rights on an international level. Writes letters on behalf of individuals who monitor human rights violations and victims worldwide.

## Congressional Human Rights Caucus (CHRC)

U.S. Congress, Office of Representative, John Porter, 2373 Rayburn H.O.B., Washington, DC 20514, Contact: Alexandra Arriaga, Coordinator

Bipartisan congressional members organization of the House of Representatives concerned with human right abuses around the world. Coordinates efforts of the members of Congress to end these abuses and to secure freedom from religious, ethnic, cultural, or political persecution for all people. Provides information on specific human rights cases; sponsors forums; serves as a congressional liason with human rights organizations.

## Death With Dignity Education Center (DDEC)

520 South El Camino Real, Suite 710, San Mateo, CA 94401-0816, Contact: Charlotte P. Ross, Exec. Director, Phone: (415) 344-6489, Fax: (415) 344-8100

Diverse group of people who believe in an inherent right to make their own choices regarding their health care and end-of-life decisions. Informs and educates the public about physicians aid-in-dying so that they can make informed decisions regarding issues related to end-of-life choices.

## Department of Civil Rights, AFL-CIO

815 16th Street NW, Washington, DC 20006, Contact: Richard Womack, Director, Phone: (202) 637-5270, Fax: (202) 508-6903

Serves as official liaison with women's and civil rights organizations and government agencies working in the field of equal opportunity; helps to implement state and federal laws and policies; aids affiliates in the development of affirmative programs to expand opportunities for minorities and women; prepares and disseminates special materials on civil rights; speaks at union and civil rights institutes, conferences and conventions.

## First Amendment Foundation

1313 West 8th Street, Suite 313, Los Angeles, CA 90017, Contact: Frank Wilkinson, Exec. Director, Phone: (213) 484-6661, Fax: (213) 484-0266

Seeks to protect the rights of free expression for individuals and organizations. Disseminated educational information on the first amendment.

## Freedom to Advertise Coalition (FAC)

2550 M Street NW, Suite 500, Washington, DC 20037, Contact: Penny Farthing, Phone: (202) 457-6313, Fax: (202) 457-6315

United to protect the rights of advertisers. Works to protect the rights of commercial free speech as guaranteed by the constitution.

## Human Rights Advocates International (HRAI)

341 Madison Ave., 20th Floor, New York, NY 10017, Contact: Sanford Mevorah, Exec. Director, Phone: (212) 986-5555

Protects and promotes human rights by coordinating and providing legal services, constitutional law resources, counseling and investigations of alleged human rights violations.

## International Women's Rights Action Watch (IWRAW)

University of Minnesota, Humphrey Institute of Public Affairs, 301 19th Ave. South, Minneapolis, MN 55455, Contact: Marsha Freeman, Director, Phone: (612) 625-5094, Fax: (612) 624-0068

Resource and communication center for an international network of over 4,000 individuals and groups concerned with implementation of the Convention of the Elimination of Discrimination Against Women (CEDAW). Works closely with non-governmental organizations in developing countries and with the CEDAW secretariat and the members of the CEDAW committee.

## Judge David L. Bazelon Center for Mental Health Law

1101 15th Street NW, Suite 1212, Washington, DC 20005, Contact: Chris Koyanagi, Exec. Director, Phone: (202) 467-5730, Fax: (202) 223-0409

Purpose is to clarify, establish, and enforce the legal rights of people with mental and developmental disabilities. Provides technical assistance and training to lawyers, consumer groups, providers of mental health and supported housing services, and policymakers at federal, state and local levels.

## National Association for the Advancement of Colored People (NAACP)

4805 Mt. Hope Drive, Baltimore, MD 21215, Contact: Kwasie Mfume, President, Phone: (410) 358-8900, Fax: (410) 358-3818

Persons "of all races and religions" who believe in the

objectives and methods of the NAACP. To achieve equal rights through the democratic process and eliminate racial prejudice by removing racial discrimination in housing, employment, voting, schools, the courts, transportation, recreation, prisons, and business enterprise. Offers referral services, tutorials, job referrals and day care.

## National Association to Protect Individual Rights
5015 Gadsen, Fairfax, VA 22032-3411, Contact: Karen Morison, President, Phone: (703) 425-5347
Conducts research on issues including information privacy and government budgeting. Provides information to public officials, members, interested individuals and the press.

## National Urban League (NUL)
120 Wall Street, New York, NY 10021, Contact: Hugh Price, CEO & President, Phone: (212) 310-9000, Fax: (212) 344-5332
Voluntary nonpartisan community service agency of civic, professional, business, labor, and religious leaders with a staff of trained social workers and other professionals. Aims to eliminate racial segregation and discrimination in the United States and to achieve parity for blacks and other minorities in every phase of American life. Works to eliminate institutional racism and to provide direct service to minorities in the areas of employment, housing, education, social welfare, health, family planning, mental retardation, law and consumer affairs, youth and student affairs, labor affairs, veterans' affairs, and community and minority business development.

## Puebla Institute (PI)
1319 18th Street NW, Washington, DC 20036, Contact: Nina Shea, President, Phone: (202) 296-5101, Fax: (212) 296-5078
Nonpartisan, lay Catholic human rights organization concerned with human and religious rights around the world. Fosters public awareness of religious repression; works to help religious activists secure their freedom and pressures for the resolution of human rights abuses.

## Second Amendment Foundation (SAF)
James Madison Building, 12500 NE 10th Place, Bellevue, WA 98005, Contact: Joseph P. Tartaro, President, Phone: (206) 454-7012, (800) 426-4302, Fax: (206) 451-3959
Individuals dedicated to promoting a better understanding of "your constitutional right to privately own and possess firearms." Compiles statistics.

## Sons of Liberty (SL)
PO Box 503, Brisbane, CA 94005, Contact: Joseph W. Kerska, President, Phone : (415) 468-2402
Politically conservative individuals seeking to defend the U.S. Constitution. Concentrates efforts on the right to keep and bear arms; opposes gun control, including restrictions on semi-automatic weapons. Maintains that mandatory gun registration precedes confiscation, which infringes upon individual freedom. Claims that less than one percent of registered guns are used for illegal purposes, therefore gun control would constitute harassment of 99% of gun owners.

## Support Coalition International
PO Box 11284, Eugene, OR 97440-3484, Contact: Janet Foner, Coordinator, Phone: (541) 345-9106
Coalition of human rights, support, and advocacy groups. Works to expose and stop psychiatric human rights violations such as involuntary drugging and excessive use of electroshock. Supports emotional support as an alternative to psychiatric coercion.

## Trade Union Leadership Council (TULC)
8670 Grand River Ave., Detroit, MI 48204, Contact: Larry K. Lewis, President, Phone: (313) 894-0303, Fax: (313) 894-0311
Primarily black trade unionists in Michigan, but membership is open to anyone. Seeks to eradicate injustices perpetrated upon people because of race, religion, sex, or national origin. Seeks increased leadership and job opportunities for blacks.

## Workers' Defense League (WDL)
275 7th Ave., New York, NY 10001, Phone: (212) 627-1931, Fax: (212) 627-4628
Labor-oriented human rights organization. Provides counseling to workers on employment related problems via telephone. Conducts educational campaigns to defend and advance workers' rights.

# Marriage/Divorce

## America's Society of Separated and Divorced Men (ASSDM)

575 Keep Street, Elgin, IL 60120, Contact: Richard Templeton, President, Phone: (708) 695-2200

Separated and divorced men. Works to assist men "in fighting the divorce racket." Dedicated to the elimination of unreasonable alimony, child support, custody and property settlement awards. Devoted to establishing respect for marriage in the courts, and to upholding the rights of fathers to their children. Educates the public about divorce customs and practices.

## Association for Couples in Marriage Enrichment (ACME)

PO Box 10596, Winston-Salem, NC 27108, Contact: David and Sarah Catron, Exec. Directors, Phone: (910) 724-1526, (800) 634-8325, Fax: (910) 721-4746

Married couples united to promote and support effective community services to foster successful marriages; improve public acceptance and understanding of marriage as a relationship capable of fostering personal growth and mutual fulfillment; educate and assist married couples in seeking growth and enrichment in their marriages. Conducts marriage enrichment retreats and growth groups, marital communication training courses, enrichment programs, and basic and advanced training workshops.

## Children's Rights Council (CRC)

220 Eye Street NE, Suite 140, Washington, DC 20002-4362, Contact: David L. Levy, President, Phone: (202) 547-6227, (800) 787-KIDS, Fax: (202) 546-4272

Promotes strengthened families through education and advocacy. Works to achieve divorce and custody reforms, and to minimize hostilities between parents involved in marital disputes. Favors shared parenting, education, mediation, access enforcement, emotional and financial child support, family formation, family preservation, and school-based programs for children at risk.

## National Marriage Encounter (NME)

4704 Jamerson Place, Orlando, FL 32807, Contact: Chuck and Sandy Ogg, Phone: (407) 282-8120, (800) 828-3351, Fax: (407) 282-8120

Offers weekend retreat programs organized by married couples and a member of the clergy. Retreats are aimed at encouraging communication between married partners and emphasizing personal and religious growth.

If you can read this, you are close to the lowest CPM in the nation!
Call today for details...

**(800) 496-0277**

# Physically/Mentally Challenged

**Academic Language Therapy Association (ALTA)**
4020 McEwen Road, Suite 105, Dallas, TX 75244-5019,
Phone: (972) 233-9107, Fax: (972) 490-4219
Seeks to establish, maintain, and promote high standards
of education, practice and conduct for the profession of
academic language therapy. Provides services for children
and adults who have problems with reading, writing and
spelling. Conducts educational programs; provides referral
services; sponsors annual spelling bee.

**Accent on Information**
PO Box 700, Bloomington, IL 61702, Contact: Betty
Garee, Editor, Phone: (309) 378-2961, Fax: (309)
378-4420
A computerized retrieval system designed to help disabled
persons live more effective lives by offering access to
information on problems, subjects of concern, and
products and services available to the handicapped.
Established by Accent on Living, Inc., a publisher of
magazines and books for the handicapped. Sponsors
exhibition booth that travels nationwide to related exhibits
two to three times per year.

**Advocates for Communication Technology
for Deaf/Blind People (ACT)**
PO Box 652, Columbia, MD 21045, Contact: Sheryl
Cooper, President, Phone: (410) 381-3377
Seeks to enhance the quality of communication for deaf
and blind people through improved technology. Provides
communication technology to persons unable to afford it.

**American Association of
People with Disabilities (AAPD)**
1819 H Street NW, Suite 330, Washington, DC 20006,
Phone: (202) 457-8168, (800) 840-8844, Fax: (202)
457-0473
People with disabilities in America. Represents citizens
with disabilities working together for common goals.
Designed to bring about unity, leadership and impact by
being advised and managed by people with disabilities
for people with disabilities.

**American Disability Association**
2201 Sixth Ave. South, Birmingham, AL 35233, Contact:
William J. Freeman, President, Phone: (205) 323-3030,
Fax: (205) 251-7417

Serves as a support group for individuals with disabilities.
Provides exchange of information on disability issues.
Makes available children's services, educational and
research programs, and charitable services.

**Assistance Dogs of America**
8806 State Route 64, Swanton, OH 43558, Contact:
Dino Brownson, President, Phone: (419) 825-3622,
(800) 841-2254
Individuals, corporations, civic and fraternal organizations,
and dog and kennel clubs. Provides specially trained dogs
to persons with mobility impairments, multiple physical
disabilities, or terminal illness for the specific purpose of
increased independence.

**Beach Center on Families and Disability**
3111 Haworth Hall, Lawrence, KS 66045, Contact: Ann
Turnbull, Phone: (913) 864-7600, Fax: (913) 864-7605
Works to provide families with the resources and skills
needed to help their children with disabilities to reach
their full potential. Conduct research on empowering
adolescents and parents of children with disabilities,
efficacy of parent to parent support, family support policy,
friendships, family-centered care, child abuse, and
neglect, and the role of fathers. Informs the public of
research results through a doctoral program, training
services and technical assistance.

**Center on Human Policy**
805 South Crouse Ave., Syracuse, NY 13244-2280,
Contact: Steven Taylor, Ph.D., Director, Phone: (315) 443-
3851, (800) 894-0826, Fax: (315) 443-4338
Consumers and students; parents of persons with
disabilities; human services administrators and staff
members; professionals in psychology, special education,
rehabilitation, sociology, law, social work, and planning.
Goal is to promote the integration of persons with severe
disabilities into the mainstream of society. Disseminates
information to families, human services professionals, and
others on laws, regulations and programs affecting
children and adults with disabilities.

**Challenged Conquistadors**
SAU Box 750, Magnolia, AR 71753, Contact: Shaun
Best, Phone: (501) 235-4558, (800) 501-0139, Fax:
(501) 235-4800

Works to increase self preservation, reduce dependency, and eradicate negative stereotypes, myths, and stigmas. Targets active, positive, challenged role models to show others that success is obtainable. Reinforces individual empowerment and capabilities to reveal the talents inherent in all challenged individuals and reap rewards as opposed to the "stagnation and destruction that many social programs had achieved." Offers educational and research programs.

## Council for Learning Disabilities (CLD)

PO Box 40303, Overland Park, KS 66204, Contact: Kirsten McBride, Exec. Secretary, Phone: (913) 493-8755, Fax: (913) 492-2546
Professionals interested in the study of learning disabilities. Works to promote the education and general welfare of individuals having specific learning disabilities by: improving teacher preparation programs.

## Dateable International

35 Wisconsin Circle, Chevy Chase, MD 20815, Contact: Robert S. Watson, MSW, Phone: (301) 656-8723, Fax: (301) 657-4327
Purpose is to bring together persons with disabilities for love and friendship. Provides individual counseling and support network.

## Direct Link for the Disabled

PO Box 1464, Solvang, CA 93464-1464, Contact: Linda Lee Hary, Phone: (805) 688-1603, Fax: (805) 686-5285
Information resource and referral service linking local, state, and national resources for all disabilities, health conditions, and rare disorders. Provides free information and easy access to more than 12,000 organizations for individuals and families.

## Disability Rights Education
## and Defense Fund (DREDF)

2212 6th Street, Berkeley, CA 94710, Contact: Arlene Mayerson, Directing Attorney, Phone: (510) 644-2555, Fax: (501) 841-8645
Dedicated to the principle that people with disabilities have the right to lead full and integrated lives, with the freedom of choice and dignity. Seeks to educate the public and policy-makers in order to further the civil rights and liberties of people with disabilities. Educational activiites include: training state and local government officials, attorneys, and judges on disability rights compliance requirements such as the Americans with Disability Act.

## Dole Foundation for Employment
## of People with Disabilities

1819 H Street, Suite 340, Washington, DC 20006-3603, Contact: Paul G. Hearne, President, Phone: (202) 457-0318, Fax: (202) 457-0473
Promotes the employment of people with disabilities. Bestows grants to organizations that conduct innovative job training and placement programs.

## Goodwill Industries International (GII)

9200 Wisconsin Ave., Bethesda, MD 20814, Contact: Fred Grandy, President & CEO, Phone: (301) 530-6500, Fax: (301) 530-1516
Federation of Goodwill Industries organizations across North America and the world are concerned primarily with providing employment, training, evaluation, counseling, placement, and job training, and other vocational rehabilitation services and opportunities for individual growth for people with disabilities and other special needs. Member Goodwill Industries organizations collect donated goods and sell them in Goodwill retail stores as a means of providing employment and generating income.

## Goodwill Industries Volunteer Services (GIVS)

9200 Wisconsin Ave., Bethesda, MD 20814, Contact: Joy Cony, President, Phone: (301) 530-6500, Fax: (301) 530-1516
Persons interested in volunteer work in programs serving people with disabilities. Supports the efforts of national local Goodwill Industries International, Inc. programs through volunteer services.

## Job Accommodation Network (JAN)

West Virginia University, PO Box 6080, Morgantown, WV, 26506, Contact: Barbara T. Judy, Project Manager, Phone: (304) 293-7186, (800) 526-7234, Fax: (304) 293-5407
International information and referral service for employers, rehabilitation and social service counselors, and person with disabilities. Offers information and counseling service to employers interested in learning how to hire, retain, or promote disabled persons.

## Learning Disabilities Association of America

4156 Library Road, Pittsburgh, PA 15234, Contact: Jean Petersen, Exec. Director, Phone: (412) 341-1515, Fax: (412) 344-0224
Parents of children with learning disabilities; interested professionals. Works to "advance the education and general well-being of children with adequate intelligence who have

learning disabilities arising form perceptual, conceptual, or subtle coordinative problems, sometimes accompainied by behavior difficulties."

## Learning How (LH)

PO Box 35481, Charlotte, NC 28235, Contact: Cheryl Shore, Managing Director, Phone: (704) 376-4735, Fax: (704) 376-4738

Works with the physically disabled community by providing the opportunity to be independent through mentoring, training, and employment programs, and by educating the community at large through information, referral, and networking.

## Mainstream

3 Bethesda Metro Center, Suite 830, Bethesda, MD 20814, Contact: Patricia M. Jackson, Exec. Director, Phone: (301) 654-2400, (800) 661-8239, Fax: (301) 654-2403

Offers services and products to increase employment opportunities for people with disabilities. Assists companies and organizations in their efforts to "mainstream" people with disabilities into employment. Operates Mainstream Disability Employment Network, which makes referrals to placement services around the country.

## Mobility International U.S.A. (MIUSA)

PO Box 10767, Eugene, OR 97440, Contact: Susan Sygall, Exec. Director, Phone (541) 343-1284, Fax: (541) 343-6812

Disabled persons, organizations serving the disabled, exchange programs, and libraries. Advocates international, educational and recreational travel exchange programs that accommodate disabled persons. Provides information for people participating in international educational exchanges. Organizes international exchange programs for the non-disabled and disabled.

## National Association of the
## Physically Handicapped (NAPH)

Bethesda Scarlet Oaks, No. GA4440 Lafayette Ave., Cincinnati, OH 45220-1000, Contact: Helen Lee Roudebush, Administrative Assistant, Phone: (513) 961-8040, Fax: (517) 792-7549

Physically handicapped persons; associate members are nonhandicapped. Seeks to advance the social, economic, and physical welfare of the physically handicapped. Promotes involvement of the physically handicapped in the planning and administration of all programs in their interest.

## National Center for Disability Services (NCDS)

201 I.U. Willets Road, Albertson, NY 11507, Contact: Dr. Edmund Cortez, President, Phone: (516) 747-5400, Fax: (516) 746-3298

Serves as a center providing educational, vocational, rehabilitation, and research opportunties for persons with disabilities. Work is conducted through the following: Abilities Health and Rehabilitation Services, a New York State licensed diagnostic and treatment center which offers comprehensive outpatient programs in physical therapy, occupational therapy, speech therapy, and psychological services; Career and Employment Institute, which evaluates, trains, and counsels more than 600 adults with disabilities each year, with the goal of productive competitive employment; Henry Viscardi School, which conducts early childhood, elementary, and secondary programs, as well as adult and continuing education programs; Research and Training Institute, which conducts research on education, employment, and career development of persons with disabilities, and hold seminars and workshops for rehabilitation service professionals.

## National Center for Learning Disabilities (NCLD)

381 Park Ave. South, Suite 1401, New York, NY 10016, Contact: Bonnie Kessler, Exec. Director, Phone: (212) 545-7510, Fax: (212) 545-9665

Promotes increased public awareness of learning disabilities. Makes available resources and provides referrals to volunteers, parents and professionals working with the learning disabled; develops and replicates programs for the learning disabled; NCLD also makes its services and publications available to U.S. citizens living overseas. Provides children's services.

## National Information Center for Children
## and Youth with Disabilities (NICHCY)

PO Box 1492, Washington, DC 20013, Contact: Suzanne Ripley, Director, Phone: (202) 884-8200, (800) 695-0285, Fax: (202) 884-8441

Provides information to assist parents, educators, care-givers, advocates, and others in helping children and youth with disabilities participate as fully as possible in school, at home, and in the community. Provides personal responses to specific questions, referrals to other organizations/sources of help, prepared infomation packets, and technical assistance to parent and professional groups.

## Progress

480 Craighead Street, Suite 201, PO Box 41005, Nashville, TN 37204, Contact: Bonnie Sanders, Assistant Exec. Director, Phone: (615) 297-3344, Fax: (615) 297-5312

Dedicated to enhancing the image of people who have disabilities and encouraging their full participation in community life. Provides support and services for developmentally disabled people. Operates group homes and residential treatment and training program for at-risk adolescent males with disabilities. Offers assistance with transportation, meal preparation, medical needs, finances and personal hygiene needs.

## Siblings for Significant Change (SSC)

105 East 22nd Street, 7th Floor, New York, NY 10010, Contact: Gerri Zatlow, Director, Phone: (212) 420-0776, (800) 841-8251, Fax: (212) 420-0433

Siblings of disabled individuals; parents, educators, social workers, medical professionals, and researchers interested in siblings of disabled individuals. Provides peer support, legal assistance, and psychological counseling to siblings of the handicapped. Coordinates social activities for families with handicapped members and works on projects and audiovisual programs designed to increase national awareness of the difficulties faced by families of disabled individuals.

# Retirement

## American Association of Retired Persons (AARP)

601 East Street NW, Washington, DC 20049, Contact: Horace B. Deets, Exec. Director, Phone: (202) 434-3377, Fax: (202) 434-2320

Persons 50 years of age or older, working or retired. Seeks to improve every aspect of living for older people. Has targeted four areas of immediate concern: Health care, women's initiative, worker equity, and minority affairs. Provides group health insurance program, discounts on auto rental and hotel rates, and a specially designed and priced motoring plan. Sponsors community service programs on crime prevention, defensive driving, and tax aid. Offers special services to retired teachers through National Retired Teacher Association, division of AARP. Sponsors mail order pharmacy services. Maintains 20,000 volume library.

## American Association of Retirement Communities (AARC)

2020 Pennsylvania Ave., Suite 902, Washington, DC 20006, Contact: Rick Smyre, Chairman, Phone: (800) 517-3847

Works to promote retirement as an industry. Assist local officials in developing strategies to attract retirees to communities. Provides information about the retirement market and educates local officials on the economic benefits of retirees to a community. Facilitates planning for growth and the increased demand for services which accompany increased retiree population.

## Association of Retired Americans (ARA)

9102 North Meridian Street, Suite 405, Indianapolis, IN 46260, Contact: Earl E. Heath, President, Phone: (317) 571-6888, (800) 806-6160, Fax: (317) 571-6895

Senior Americans, age 45 or more interested in enhancing their lives through group benefits. Purpose is to offer a program of high quality, low-cost benefits and services to members. Services available through ARA are: discounts on prescriptions, eyeglasses and hearing aids; low interest credit cards; discounts on lodging, car rental, tours, cruises and airfare; insurance benefits including emergency air medical transportation. Assists governmental bodies and agencies with the development of programs and legislation which benefit and promote the well-being of mature Americans.

## Institute for Retired Professionals (IRP)

New School for Social Responsibility, 66 West 12th Street, New York, NY 10011, Contact: Michael I. Markowitz, Director, Phone: (212) 229-5683, Fax: (212) 691-7172

Retired professionals including doctors, lawyers, dentists, teachers, business executives, artists and others. Purpose is to provide an intense learning program in which members are both teachers and students, utilizing the experience and talents of members while meeting their needs and interests. Conducts over 60 peer-learning groups. Aids colleges in forming peer-learning programs.

## International Society for Retirement Planning (ISRP)

833 Market Street, Suite 511, San Francisco, CA 94103-1824, Contact: Julie Dudley, Director, Phone: (415) 974-9631, (800) 537-9728, Fax: (415) 974-0300

Personnel directors, financial planners, and consultants; business, union, and government organizations. Acts as a clearinghouse on common methods, techniques, materials, devices, and content used in pre-retirement counseling and planning programs. Holds presentations on topics including women and retirement, spirituality, financial planning, and second careers.

## Active 20-30 Association of U.S./Canada

915 L Street. 1000, Sacramento, CA 95814-3705, Contact: Karen L. Roberts, Exec. Director, Phone: (916) 447-3217, (800) 547-2030, Fax: (916) 442-0223

Business and professional men and women between the leadership academy, and Social Security Reform Town Hall Meeting. Maintains Hall of Fame exhibit hall and museum.

# Service Clubs

**Active 20-30 Association of U.S./Canada**
915 L Street 1000, Sacramento, CA 95814-3705, Contact: Karen L. Roberts, Exec. Director, Phone: (916) 447-3217, (800) 547-2030, Fax: (916) 442-0223
Business and professional men and women between the ages of 20 and 40 interested in citizenship, fellowship, and community betterment.

**AMBUCS**
PO Box 5127, High Point, NC 27262, Contact: J. Joseph Copeland, Exec. Director, Phone: (910) 869-2166, Fax: (910) 887-8451
Local service club. Dedicated to creating opportunities for independence for people with disabilities. Each chapter also adopts a major civic project to coincide with mission statement.

**Circle K International**
3636 Woodview Trace, Indianapolis, IN 46268-3196, Contact: Lisa F. Baize, Administration, Phone: (317) 875-8755, ( 800) 547-2647, Fax: (317) 879-0204
College students worldwide interested in serving others and developing friendships and leadership skills. Provide an opportunity for responsible student action in meeting the needs of the campus and community.

**Junior Chamber International**
400 University Drive, Coral Gables, FL 33134, Contact: Benny L. Ellerbe, Secretary General, Phone: (305) 446-7608, Fax: (305) 442-0041
National Jaycee organization representing 400,000 individuals between the ages of 18 and 40 dedicated to the principles of leadership training through community development; conducts charitable programs; sponsors competitions. Maintains program information library.

**Junior Optimist Clubs**
4494 Lindell Blvd., St. Louis, MO 63108, Contact: Teri Flotron, Program Manager, Phone: (314) 871-6000, Fax: (314) 371-6006
Boys and girls in grades 6 through 9 throughout North America. Sponsored by Optimist International and local Optimist Clubs in North America. Fosters adult/youth relationships. Conducts community-serving and citizenship-building activities.

**Junior Optimist Octagon International**
6494 Lindell Blvd., St. Louis, MO 63108, Phone: (314) 371-6000, Fax: (314) 371-6006
Boys and girls in grades 7 through 12 throughout North America. Sponsored by Optimist Clubs in North America. Fosters adult/youth relationships. Conducts community service and citizenship building activities. Compiles statistics.

**Key Club International**
3636 Woodview Trace, Indianapolis, IN 46268, Contact: Leslie A. Murphy, Admin., Phone: (317) 875-8755, Fax: (317) 879-0204
Clubs for secondary school students interested in service for others, good citizenship, and leadership training. Sponsored by Kiwanis International.

**Kiwanis International**
3636 Woodview Trace, Indianapolis, IN 46268, Contact: A.G. Terry Shaffer, International Secretary, Phone: (317) 875-8755, (800) 549-2647, Fax: (317) 879-0204
Local clubs representing business and professional individuals in 78 countries and geographic regions. Seeks to: provide assistance to the young and elderly; develop community facilities; foster international understanding and goodwill. Sponsors Young Children: Priority One, a service program to benefit children up to age five. Sponsors Key Club International for high school students, Circle K International for college students, and Builders Club for junior high school students.

**The Links**
1200 Massachusetts Ave. NW, Washington, DC 20005-4501, Contact: Bonnie C. Mann, Phone: (202) 842-8686, Fax: (202) 842-4020
Organization of women committed to the community through educational, cultural and civic activities. Provides enrichment experiences for those who are educationally disadvantaged and culturally deprived, and support for talented individuals. Sponsors charitable activities and a National Grant-In-Aid Program.

**Lions Clubs International**
300 22nd Street, Oak Brooks, IL 60523, Contact: Mark C. Lukas, Exec. Administrator, Phone: (630) 571-5466, Fax: (630) 571-8890

Local clubs representing business and professional men and women in 180 countries and geographic areas. Provides community service in order to increase international understanding and cooperation. Fosters awareness of environmental, social, and health related problems. Activities include: Blindness prevention; work with the deaf; drug awareness programs; international youth camp programs; youth exchange. Maintains Leo Clubs (for young adults), and the Lions Club International Foundation for sight conservation and work with the blind.

### National Assistance League

5627 Fernwood Ave., Los Angeles, CA 90028, Contact: Virginia Tobias, President, Phone: (213) 469-5897, Fax: (213) 469-6069

"To act as a friend at any and all times to men, women and children in need of care, guidance and assistance, spiritually, materially and physically." Each chapter controls and administers at least one self-sustaining philanthropic project. Projects include boy's clubs, children's theatre guilds, clothing centers, day nurseries, dental centers, family services, geriatric programs, girls' clubs, centers for the hearing, visually, and speech-impaired, homemakers service, hospital equipment bank, toy loans, volunteer bureaus, wellbaby clinics, and youth employment service.

### National Association of Junior Auxiliaries

PO Box 1873, Greensville, MS 38702-1873, Contact: Norma N. DeLong, Exec. Director, Phone: (601) 332-3000, Fax: (601) 332-3076

Women over 21 years of age. Encourages women to become active and constructive participants in their communities, assume responsible leadership in meeting community problems, render charitable services which are beneficial to the general public, and cooperate with other organizations performing similar services. Offers children's services.

### National Exchange Club

3050 Central Ave., Toledo, OH 43606-1700, Contact: David A. Nershi, Exec. Vice President, Phone: (419) 535-3232, (800) 924-2646, Fax: (419) 535-1989

Business and professional men's and women's service clubs involved in child abuse prevention, crime prevention, good citizenship, youth and community service. Sponsors Americanism, Youth and Community Service projects including the Freedom Shrine, "One Nation Under God," National Crime Prevention Week.

### NGA

1007 B Street Road, Southampton, PA 18966, Contact: Maryanna Trembath, Exec. Director, Phone: (215) 322-5759

Contributors of new clothing, household linens and basic personal care items distributed locally to those in need, through recognized community organizations and agencies which register with our national organization and agree to give our gifts to needy people.

### Optimist International

4494 Lindell Blvd., St. Louis, MO 63108, Contact: Stephen P. Lawson, Exec. Director, Phone: (314) 371-6000, Fax: (314) 371-6006

Service clubs dedicated to youth and community service. Motto is "Friend of Youth." Sponsors oratorical contest and substance abuse prevention programs.

### Sertoma International

1912 East Meyer Blvd., Kansas City, MO 64132-1174, Contact: Trip Gore, Exec. Director, Phone: (816) 333-8300, (800) 593-5646, Fax: (816) 333-4320

Civic service club of business and professional men and women in Canada, Mexico, and the United States. Motto is to render "service to mankind" (phrase from which group's name is derived).

### U.S. Junior Chamber of Commerce

PO Box 7, 4 West 21st Street, Tulsa, OK 74102-0007, Contact: Tim Jackson, CMP, Exec. Vice President, Phone: (918) 584-2481, Fax: (918) 582-7736

Civic service organization of young people, ages 21 to 39, dedicated to providing leadership training for its members through service programs. Annually selects nation's Ten Outstanding Young Americans, Four Outstanding Young Farmers, and Ten Healthy American Fitness Leaders; administers International BB Gun Match and shooting education program and anti-youth smoking program.

# Veterans

## American Military Retirees Association (AMRA)

426 US Oval, Suite 1200, Plattsburgh, NY 12903, Contact: Col. David G. Fitz, President, Phone: (518) 563-9479, (800) 424-2969, Fax: (518) 563-9479

Persons honorably retired for length of service or disability from all branches and grades of the armed forces and their widows or widowers; persons still on active duty. Goals: to maintain "COLA" Program; authorization for CHAMPUS for all military/VA medical facilities. Works to support or oppose legislation in the best interests of members and to protect the earned privileges and benefits of military retirees. Testifies before Congress on legislation affecting members. Offers supplemental health insurance.

## Black Veterans for Social Justice (BVSJ)

686 Fulton Street, Brooklyn, NY 11217, Contact: Mr. Mashariki, President, Phone: (718) 935-1116, Fax: (718) 935-1629

Black Veterans of the military services. To aid black veterans in obtaining information concerning their rights, ways to upgrade a less-than-honorable discharge, and Veterans Administration benefits due them and their families. Seeks to prohibit discrimination against black veterans. Provides educational programs; facilitates veterans' sharing of skills acquired while in service.

## Ladies Auxiliary to the Veterans of Foreign Wars of the United States (LAVFWUS)

406 West 34th Street, Kansas City, MO 64111, Contact: Margaret Bergeron, Secretary of Treasure, Phone: (816) 561-8655, Fax: (816) 931-4753

Wives, widows, mothers, stepmothers, grandmothers, daughters, foster daughters, stepdaughters, granddaughters, sisters, half-sisters, step-sisters, and foster-sisters to persons eligible for membership in the VFW. Conducts voluntary hospital and rehabilitation work and sponsors various patriotic, Americanism, and youth activities.

## Regular Veterans Association of the United States (RVA)

5200 Wilkinson Blvd., Charlotte, NC 28208-5450, Contact: Archie L. Hargett, Phone: (704) 394-6104, Fax: (704) 391-9998

Active, retired, disabled, and honorable discharged members of the Armed Forces of the United States who served in peace or war. Provides assistance to veterans, widows, and family members in obtaining government benefits. Sponsors service programs through the Veterans Administration; conducts welfare programs to assist disabled and needy veterans.

## The Retired Enlisted Association (TREA)

1111 South Abilene Court, Aurora, CO 80012, Contact: John Muench, Exec. Director, Phone: (303) 752-0660, (800) 338-9337, Fax: (303) 752-0835

Retirees who have served in the military as enlisted persons; medically retired persons. Associate members are enlisted persons who have been on active duty for at least 10 years; widows/widowers of retired enlisted persons. Supports the rights and benefits of retired enlisted persons and their families. Lobbies at national, state, and local levels.

## Veterans of Foreign Wars of the United States (VFW)

406 West 34th Street, Kansas City, MO 64111, Contact: Larry Rivers, Phone: (816) 756-3390, Fax: (816) 968-1157

Overseas veterans of the Spanish American War, World Wars I and II, the Korean and Vietnam wars, the Persian Gulf War, Grenada, Panama, and Lebanon in which an overseas campaign medal was received. Seeks to: insure the national security through maximum military strength; speed the rehabilitation of the nation's disabled and needy veterans; assist the widows, orphans, and dependents of disabled and needy veterans; promote Americanism through education in patriotism and constructive service to the communities in which we live.

# U.S. Voluntary Service Organizations

**Working overseas is not the only way to gain community development experience. In many areas of the U.S. people face conditions of poverty similar to those found in the Third World. Voluntary service in the U.S. can offer a low-cost opportunity for building solid credentials towards a career in community development.**

## Abya Yala Fund

PO Box 28386, Oakland, CA 94604, Phone: (510) 763-6553

Abya Yala is an organization providing resources and technical training to indigenous people from South and Central America and Mexico. The group works to help indigenous people address development issues in their communities in a way that is culturally appropriate and environmentally sustainable. Interns will work at the Oakland office on research, administration, fund-raising, event coordination, and translation. Plans for opening regional offices in Central and South America will open opportunities for overseas volunteer work, preferably interns who speak Spanish, Portuguese, or an indigenous language.

## Acorn

117 Harrison, #200, Chicago, IL 60605, Phone: (312) 939-7488

ACORN (Association of Organizations for Reform Now) is a neighborhood-based, multi-racial membership organization of low-income families working to gain power within institutions that affect their everyday lives. Volunteers work as grassroots organizers throughout the U.S. They receive a salary and must commit to 1 year of service. A working knowledge of Spanish and previous organizing experience are preferred, but not required.

## AmeriCorps*VISTA

Corporation for National Service AmeriCorp Programs 1201 New York Avenue, Washington, DC 20525, Phone: (800) 942-2677

For more than 30 years, AmeriCorps*VISTA members have been serving disadvantaged communities. The program increases the capability of people to improve their lives. Members of AmeriCorps*VISTA work and live in the communities they serve, creating programs that can continue after they complete their service. Members must be at least 18 years old, and there is no upper age limit.

## Bike-Aid

Overseas Development Network (ODN), 333 Valencia Street, Suite 330, San Francisco, CA 94103, Phone: (415) 431-4480, (800) RIDE-808

Bike-Aid is an educational and fund-raising project of the Overseas Development Network (ODN), a national student-based organization which addresses the global problems of poverty and injustice by raising money for small-scale, self-help community development projects in both the U.S. and the Third World. ODN also organizes educational events in the U.S. Each summer six Bike-Aid teams of 20 cyclists set off from Seattle, Portland, San Francisco, Montreal and Chapel Hill, NC to bike across the country, finally joining together in Washington, D.C. Along the way cyclists meet with community activists in homeless shelters, farmers' cooperatives, environmental action groups and Native American communities. Bike-Aid participants both educate people about the work of ODN and learn about the issues facing the communities they visit.

## Center for Third World Organizing

1218 East 21st Street, Oakland, CA 94606, Phone: (510) 533-7583, Fax: (510) 533-0923

Center for Third Organizing (CTWO) is a research and training center working on issues affecting Third World communities in the U.S. Their summer apprenticeship program is for young people of color who are involved in work for social change. Each summer this 3-month program trains people, primarily college students, in the techniques of community organizing. Volunteers for this program receive housing and a stipend. Other internships are sometimes available, including research and writing for the center newsletter.

## Citizen Action

1730 Rhode Island Avenue NW, #403, Washington, D.C. 20036, Phone: (202) 775-1580

Citizen Action is a national membership organization of

people working for social changes. There are over 32 state affiliate offices throughout the country. Volunteers work as field organizers and fund-raisers around issues such as health care, the environment, foreign policy, energy, and insurance reform. Excellent verbal communication and good interpersonal skills, as well as commitment to progressive issues are required. Placements vary from 6 months to a year. Stipends are negotiable.

## Committee for Health Rights In the Americas

474 Valencia Street, Suite 120, San Francisco, CA 94103 Phone: (415) 431-7760, Fax: (415) 431-7768
Committee for Health Rights In the Americas (CHRIA) is a nonprofit humanitarian organization working in support of health rights across borders. CHRIA works on behalf of immigrant and refugee health rights and has projects in El Salvador, Nicaragua, Guatemala, and Mexico. Spanish-speaking mental health professionals are needed to staff the Centro Ignacio Martin-Baro in Berkeley, California, a volunteer mental health clinic primarily for Central American refugees. CHRIA administers the Training Exchange, a project which sends health care professionals who are fluent in Spanish to Central America to help develop primary care training programs in medical schools, nursing schools, and other health care institutions. CHRIA takes delegations to Central America and Mexico for technical exchange, medical aid, and documentation of health rights.

## East Coast Migrant Health Project, Inc.

1234 Massachusetts Ave. NW, #C-1017, Washington, D.C. 20005, Phone: (202) 347-7377, Fax: (202) 347-6385
The East Coast Migrant Health Project Inc., (ECMHP) directs its energies toward the empowerment of migratory and seasonal farm workers and their families through the provisions of health care, outreach services, preventative health education, and group networking. ECMHP places staff with health providers along the U.S. East Coast to ensure that services are available and accessible to migrant/seasonal farm workers. Volunteers are health professionals of all levels, as well as social workers and others interested in providing outreach services. There is a particular need for nurse practitioners, community and public health nurses, licensed practical nurses, and other professionals with specialty certificates. The project also recruits people in allied health fields, such as social workers, nutritionists, health educators, psychologists, and community service workers. Geographic mobility and possession of a car with adequate insurance is a must.

Staff receive a competitive salary and benefits. The minimum length of commitment is one year. Language skills in Spanish or Creole are helpful.

## Fish and Wildlife Service

U.S. Fish and Wildlife Service
4401 North Fairfax Drive, Arlington, VA 22203, Phone: (703) 358-2009
Would you like to spend some time banding birds at a national wildlife refuge, feeding fish at a national fish hatchery, or doing research in a laboratory? Then consider volunteering with the U.S. Fish and Wildlife Service. There are no age requirements; however, anyone under 18 must have written parental approval. Young people under 16 years of age are encouraged to volunteer as part of a supervised group, such as a Boy Scout troop, Girl Scout troop, or 4H Club. Contact one of the U.S. Fish and Wildlife regional offices for possible volunteer programs in your area.

## Forest Service Volunteers

Public Affairs Office U.S. Department of Agriculture
PO Box 96090, Washington, DC 20090-6090, Phone: (202) 205-1760
The Forest Service has a volunteer program for almost everyone--retirees, professionals, housewives, students, teenagers. Typical jobs include working with specialists in resource protection and management, cooperative forestry, or research. You may also work at a Visitor Information Center by conducting natural history walks.

## Foster Grandparents Program

Corporation for National Service
National Senior Service Corps
121 New York Ave. NW, Washington, DC 2525, Phone: (800) 833-3722
Since 1965, the Foster Grandarents Program has provided valuable aid to children and youth with exceptional needs. Foster Grandparents serve 20 hours a week in sckools, hospitals, drug treatment centers, correctional institutions, and Head Start and day care centers--helping children who have been abused or neglected, mentoring troubled teenagers and young mothers, and caring for premature infants and children with physical disabilities.

## Health Research Volunteers

Normal Volunteer Program Clinical Center
Quarter 15 D-2, 4 West Drive, Bethesda, MD 20892, Phone: (301) 496-4763

Many of the research programs at National Institutes of Health require normal volunteers who can provide clinicians with indices of normal body functions. There is a small compensation for their participation.

## Higher Education
Corporation for National Service
Learn and Serve programs
12201 New York Ave. NW, Washington, DC 20525, Phone: (202) 606-5000
Learn and Serve America: Higher Education helps create and strengthen community service and service learning initiatives at colleges and universities, which involve a wide array of students and organizations working together to address community needs. Grants also support technical assistance for expanding the field of service learning.

## Institute of Cultural Affairs (ICA)
4220 North 25th Street, Phoenix, AZ 85016, Phone: (602) 955-4811, (800) 742-4032, Fax: (602) 954-0563, Phone: (312) 769-6363 or ICA-West, 1504 25th Ave., Seattle, WA 98122, Phone: (206) 323-2100
The Institute of Cultural Affairs (ICA) is a non-profit research, training, and demonstration group concerned with developing leadership capacities and global awareness. The Phoenix office of ICA needs interns and volunteers for office work, community development, educational research, and graphics production. The Chicago office offers a 3-week training course for those interested in human development, team building and strategic planning along with service career exploration. In Seattle, volunteers can work on "Rite of Passage Journeys" for youths and other community development projects. For information on ICA projects, contact the office nearest you.

## Los Ninos
287 "G" Street, Chula Vista, CA 91910, Phone: (619) 426-9110, Fax: (619) 426-6664
Los Ninos provides long-term community development programs along the U.S./Mexico border in the areas of agriculture and nutrition. Programs are designed to promote self-reliance and social awareness. Long-term projects are carried out by interns serving 1-year placements. They receive room, board, and a $50 per month stipend. Summer, weekend, and week long programs are also offered to U.S. participants who want to learn more about development along the U.S./Mexico border.

## Lutheran Volunteer Corps
1226 Vermont Ave. NW, Washington D.C. 20005, Phone: (202) 387-3222
Lutheran Volunteer Corps volunteers work through agencies in a number of areas including direct service, public policy, advocacy, community organizing, and education. Placements are in Baltimore, MD; Wilmington, DE; Washington, D.C.; Chicago, IL; Milwaukee, WI; Minneapolis/St. Paul, MN; Seattle and Tacoma, WA. Volunteers live communally with 3 to 7 other volunteers. Travel, room and board, medical coverage, and daily work-related transportation expenses are covered. The program is open to people from all faith perspectives.

## Mennonite Voluntary Service
722 Main Street, PO Box 347, Newton KS 67114-0347, Phone: (316) 283-5100
Mennonite Voluntary Service (MVS) helps meet the needs of poor and disadvantaged people in the U.S. and Canada. Volunteer placements range from staffing food banks and emergency assistance centers to working with migrant farm workers. Social work, community organization, housing rehabilitation, and education skills are in particular demand. Initial terms of 2 years are strongly encouraged, though some assignments are available for 1 year. Spanish is helpful or required for some positions. Volunteers must be Christians and at least 18-years-old. All expenses are covered by MVS.

## National Civilian Community Corp.
Corporation for National Service
1201 New York Ave. NW, Washington, DC 20525, Phone: (800) 942-2677
A full-time residential service program, AmeriCorps NCCC (the National Civilian Community Corps) combines the best practices of civilian service with the best aspects of military service, including leadership and team building. Men and women, ages 18-24, serve full-time and are based at one of four AmeriCorpsNCCC campuses, in Petty Point, MD, Charleston, SC, Denver, CO, and San Diego, CA.

## National Park Service
Office of Interpretation
National Park Service
18th and C Streets NW, Washington DC 20240, Phone: (202) 523-0582
The National Park Service provides many opportunities for volunteers to help at their many parks and historic sites. Contact the National Park Service nearest you.

## Passionist Lay Missioners

5700 North Harlem Ave., Chicago, IL 60631-2342, Phone: (312) 631-6336, Fax: (312) 631-8059

Passionist Lay Missioners are volunteers who seek to address immediate and systemic problems of poverty by working with economically disadvantaged and disenfranchised people in Chicago, Detroit, and Cincinnati. Positions begin in August and last for 1 year or more and include social workers, youth workers, advocates for the homeless, teachers and teacher's aides, emergency intervention workers, community organizers, peace and justice advocates, prisoners' rights advocates, child care workers, counselors, domestic violence workers, clerical workers, care givers for the elderly, legal aides, and more. Volunteers live in community in low income, inner-city neighborhoods. They live a simple lifestyle and explore connections between work, community, faith and social justice. Volunteers pay for their own transportation to the orientation in August. Room and board, health insurance, monthly stipend of $100 and transportation during the year are provided. Applicants must be 21-years-old, with some college education or practical work experience, and be willing to engage in spiritual reflection.

## Peace Brigades International
## North America Project

1233 Harvard Square Station, Cambridge, MA 02238, Phone: (617) 491-4226

Peace Brigades International has recently formed a North America Project (NAP) based on the model of work done by PBI in Central America and Sri Lanka. The goal is to help bring about a just resolution of conflict without resorting to violence. The initial focus of NAP is the struggle for justice by Native Americans, but the project is not necessarily limited to this area. PBI forms international teams of volunteers who will seek the most appropriate ways to support non-violent struggle for justice in each situation. Some ways might include training for local people doing human rights watches, observing, accompanying people who might be threatened for their social activism, peace education, and developing a network of people who will respond with letters, faxes, and phone calls to appropriate authorities in cases of urgency. NAP volunteers may also be formed into on-call "Ready Response Brigades," that will be ready to respond in a crisis situation on short notice. Volunteers must speak English, be at least 25-years-old, and attend a 2 week PBI training.

## Peace Corps Volunteers

Office of Private Sector Relations

1990 K. Street NW, Room 8400, Washington, DC 20526, Phone: (202) 606-3406

Here is your chance to travel to a distant land to offer a much needed helping hand. The Peace Corps' purpose is to promote world peace and friendship. Volunteers serve for two years, living among the people with whom they work. Volunteers are expected to become a part of the community. Projects are designed to match the skills of the volunteers to help solve specific development problems.

## Proyecto Libertad

113 North 1st Street, Harlingen, TX 78550, Phone: (210) 425-9552, Fax: (210) 425-8249

Proyecto Libertad (PL) is a legal office on the Texas/Mexico border representing Central American Refugees. PL provides legal services, help in applying for political asylum, and advocacy for Central Americans (including minors) in detention. PL also raises bond money and contacts relatives. On a systemic level, PL participates in federal litigation to protect refugee rights. Volunteers work on all aspects of the program. Volunteers must speak Spanish and be sensitive to multi-cultural differences. A car is extremely useful. Volunteers cover their expenses, but some assistance may be available.

## Retired Business Executives

Service Corps of Retired Executives
(SCORE) Naional SCORE Office
409 Third Street NW, Washington, DC 20240, Phone: (800) 634-0245

Retired Business Executives volunteer their time and services to help small business solve their operating and management problems. Assigned SCORE counselors visit the owners in the place of business to analyze the problems and offer guidance. In addition to learning more about the SCORE program by calling the toll-free number, also refer to your local telephone directory to contact the community-based SCORE center.

## Retired and Senior Volunteer Program

National Senior Service Corps
1201 New York Ave. NW, Washington, DC 20525, Phone: (800) 833-3722

One of the largest volunteer efforts in the nation, the Retired and Senior Volunteer Program (RSVP) matches local problems with older Americans who are willing to help. RSVP members choose how and where they want to serve, and determine how many hours a week they can serve. They organize neighborhood watch programs, tutor teenagers, renovate homes, teach English to immigrants, program computers, help people recover from natural disasters--whatever their skills and interest lead them to.

## Senior Companion Program
National Senior Service Corps
1201 New York Ave. NW, Washington, DC 20525, Phone: (800) 833-3722
Providing assistance and friendship to seniors who have difficulties with daily living tasks, members of the Senior Companion Program help other seniors retain their dignity and independence. In their 20 hours of service each week, Senior Companions help clients with chores such as paying bills, buying groceries, and finding transportation to medical appointments. Senior Companions receive training in topics such as Alzheimer's Disease, stroke, diabetes, and mental health, and alert doctors and family members of potential health problems.

## Sioux YMCAs
PO Box 218, Dupree, SD 57623, Phone: (605) 365-5232, Fax: (605) 365-5230
Volunteers of college age or older serve for two months during the summer as camp staff at Leslie Marrowbone Memorial YMCA Camp, working with eight to 14-year-old Sioux children. Also needed are community work volunteers to live in small, isolated Lakota communities to support various youth and family projects. These placements are for nine months through Americorps. Other community volunteer positions are available. Volunteers must have camp or community work skills, and be flexible and able to share their own cultures, as well as relate to others. The YMCA can help with room and board.

## Teach for America
20 Exchange Place, 8th Floor, New York, NY 10005, Mailing address: PO Box 5114, New York, NY 10185, Phone: (800) 832-1230, (212) 425-9347
Teach for America is a national teacher corps of individuals from all ethnic backgrounds and academic majors. Corps members work for a minimum of 2 years as full-time, salaried teachers in urban and rural under-resourced public schools. The summer prior to entering the classroom, participants attend an intensive training institute. The program is intended for recent college graduates who are interested in making a difference and having an immediate impact.

## United Farm Workers
PO Box 62, La Paz, Keene, CA 98122, Phone: (805) 822-5571
United Farm Workers (UFW) works for justice for farm workers and safe food for consumers. Volunteers spend 1 year or more in rural or urban areas, organizing farm workers and consumers. Opportunities are also available in computer-related and administrative capacities. Volunteers receive room and board and a small stipend.

## Ursuline Companions in Mission
College Center Room 155, New Rochelle, NY 10805, Phone: (914) 654-5270, (914) 576-6774
Volunteers are sent to inner-city and rural work sites in the U.S. to provide education, social work, health care, pastoral ministry, and outreach to the elderly. Volunteers must be 21 years or older and possess skills compatible with needs of specific ministries. Placements are for summer or for year-round.

## Veterans Voluntary Service
Veterans Administration Medical Center
Refer to your local telephone directory for the nearest VA medical center. Many opportunities exist for volunteers to help veterans.

# Womens Rights

## Clearinghouse on Women's Issues
PO Box 70603, Friendship Heights, MD 20813, Contact: Ruth G. Nadel, President, Phone: (202) 362-3789, Fax: (202) 362-3789

Nonpartisan clearinghouse for national, regional, state, and local women's and civil rights organizations. Purpose is to exchange and disseminate educational information and materials on issues related to discrimination on the basis of race, sex, age, or marital status, with particular emphasis on public policies affecting the economic and educational status of women.

## Feminist Majority Foundation
1600 Wilson Blvd., Suite 801, Arlington, VA 22209, Contact: Eleanor Smeal, President, Phone: (703) 522-2214, Fax: (703) 522-2219

Seeks to encourage women to fill leadership positions in business, education, media, law, medicine, and government. Sponsors Feminization of Power Campaign, which provides a vehicle for achieving FMF'S goals and promotes a national feminist agenda; conducts national campus campaign; makes available internship programs.

## International Black Women's Congress
1081 Bergen Street, Newark, NJ 07112, Contact: Dr. La Francis Rodgers-Rose, President, Phone: (201) 926-0570, Fax: (201) 926-0818

Women of African ancestry; interested individuals. Objective is to unite members for mutual support and socioeconomic development through: annual networking tours to Africa; establishing support groups; assisting women in starting their own businesses; assisting members in developing resumes and other educational needs; offering to answer or discuss individual questions and concerns. Conducts educational, research, and charitable programs; compiles statistics. Operates speaker's bureau and rites of passage programs for girls and adult women.

## National Federation of Business and Professional Women's Clubs
2012 Massachusetts Ave. NW, Washington, DC 20036, Contact: Cynthia Gady, Acting Exec. Director, Phone: (202) 293-1100, Fax: (202) 861-0298

Men and women of every age, religion, political party, and socioeconomic background. Works to achieve equity for all women in the workplace through advocacy, education, and information. Provides professional development, networking, and career advancement opportunities for working women. Sponsors a grass roots action team to influence elected officials on issues concerning women. Sponsors National Business Women's Week during the third week of October.

## 9 To 5 National Association of Working Women
231 West Wisconsin Ave., Suite 900, Milwaukee, WI 53203, Contact: Ellen Bravo, Exec. Director, Phone: (216) 566-9308, (414) 274-0925, Fax: (414) 272-2870

Women office workers. Seeks to build a national network of local office worker chapters that strives to gain better pay, proper use of office automation, opportunities for advancement, elimination of sex and race discrimination, and improved working conditions for women office workers. Works to introduce legislation or regulations at state level to protect video display terminal operators. Produces studies and research in areas such as reproductive hazards of Video Display Terminals (VDTs), automation's effect on clerical employment, family and medical leaves, and stress. Conducts annual summer school for working women.

## Women's Action Alliance
370 Lexington Ave., Suite 603, New York, NY 10017, Contact: Karel R. Amaranth, Exec. Director, Phone: (212) 532-8330, Fax: (212) 779-2846

The alliance is dedicated to realizing the vision of self-determination for women. Committed to creating, testing, and implementing innovative program models to affect positive change in the lives of women and girls, particularly those who are underserved. Program models address issues of self-esteem, equity in education and in the workplace, health (including substance abuse, AIDS, child and maternal care, and breast cancer), domestic violence, and sexual harassment. Provides individuals, community organizations, women's centers, and schools with information, strategies, and technical assistance. Advocates on behalf of women before the media, government, and the business and research communities.

## Theos Foundation
322 Blvd. of the Allies, Suite 105, Pittsburgh, PA 15222-1919, Contact: Pat Saloga, Phone: (412) 471-7779, Fax: (412) 471-7782

Established to aid and assist in the planning and development of practical and educational programs for the widowed in the U.S. and Canada. Conducts periodic educational programs on a specific topic pertaining to grief. Name of the group is derived from the initial letter of the motto, "They Help Each Other Spiritually."

## Widowed Persons Service

601 East Street NW, Washington, DC 20049, Contact: Ann Studner, Sr. Programming Specialist, Phone: (202) 434-2260, Fax: (202) 434-6474

A program of the American Association of Retired Persons. National outreach group of volunteers of all ages, widowed for at least 18 months, who listen to and support new widows and widowers in adjusting to widowhood. Volunteers are trained in listening, support, and finding appropriate referrals when necessary.

## Feminist Center for Human Growth and Development

300 East 75th Street, Suite 26-D, New York, NY 10021, Contact: Charlotte Schwab, Ph.D., Exec. Director, Phone: (212) 717-5234

An educational organization that provides resources, information, and referral support system for people who need personal or career counseling. Goal is to formulate a "new theory of personality development that will help to free women and men from the social, political and cultural limitations that now form the basis of existing psychological theories." Conducts nonsexist and feminist lectures, panels, and counseling. Sponsors participatory and experiential workshops and groups on such topics as relationships, self-identity, self-steem, goalsetting, risk taking, networking, assertiveness, and positive communication. Offers a nonsexist therapy training program for human resources personnel and others interested in counseling women and men.

## International Network for Women in Enterprise and Trade

601 East Street NW, Washington, DC 20049, Contact: Ann Marie Carl, Phone: (703) 413-4111, Fax: (703) 414-4117

Promotes accessibility of information and other resources for businesswomen. Establishes women's libraries and clearinghouses; facilitates development of coalitions and networks among businesswomen.

## National Women's Mailing List

PO Box 68, Jenner, CA 95450, Contact: Jill Lippitt, Director, Phone: (707) 632-5763, Fax: (707) 632-5589

A project of the Women's Information Exchange. Seeks to utilize information technology to facilitate outreach, communication networking, and resource-sharing among women. Individual women and women's organizations are able to sign up to receive mail in a variety of interest areas, such as politics, health, sports, women's culture, and spirituality. Names and addresses from this data bank are sorted according to geography, demography, organizations conducting mailings of interest to women.

## The Nurturing Network

200 Clocktower Place, Suite 200A, PO Box 223099, Carmel, CA 93922-3099, Contact: Mary Cunningham Agee, Exec. Director, Phone: (800) TNN-4MOM

A nationwide network of volunteers who provide practical support for college and working women facing unplanned pregnancies. Members offer counseling, medical services, nurturing homes, employment, and assistance with financial and educational issues. Makes available referrals for legal assistance, adoption, and support services for over 8,000 mothers and their children.

## Older Women's League

666 11th Street NW, Suite 700, Washington, DC 20001, Contact: Deborah Briceland-Betts, Exec. Director, Phone: (202) 783-6686, Fax: (202) 638-2356

Middle-aged and older women; persons of any age who support issues of concern to mid-life and older women. Primary issues include access to health care insurance, support to family caregivers, reform of Social Security, access to jobs and pensions for older women, effects of budget cuts on women, and maintaining self-sufficiency throughout life. Operates speakers' bureau; prepares educational materials; compiles statistics.

# Youth

## Center on Children and the Law

750 15th Street NW, 9th Floor., Washington, DC 20005-1009, Contact: Howard Davidson, Director, Phone: (202) 662-1720, Fax: (202) 662-1755

Information clearinghouse that provides attorneys with technical assistance, legal advice, and training in the area of children's legal rights. Disseminates information on foster care, termination of parental rights, child abuse reporting, and other children's legal issues. Seeks to influence legislation affecting children's rights; trains state child welfare agency personnel. Conducts legal research on the evolution of children's rights in the U.S. Operated by the Young Lawyer's Division of the American Bar Association.

## American Coalition for Abuse Awareness (ACAA)

PO Box 27958, 1858 Park Road NW, 2nd Floor, Washington, DC 20038-7959, Contact: Sherry Quirk, President, Phone: (202) 462-4688, Fax: (202) 462-4689

Works to champion the rights of victims and survivors of childhood sexual abuse. Promotes enactment of federal and state legislation establishing the right of a child to be free from sexual victimization and appropriate protection to ensure that it extends or eliminates the statutes of limitation relating to civil lawsuits brought by adult survivors of childhood sexual abuse. Works to increase public and media awareness of the sexual abuse issue; seeks to establish a comprehensive network of legal professionals dedicated to advancing the rights of survivors of childhood sexual abuse.

## American Human Association Children's Division (AHA)

63 Inverness Drive East, Englewood, CO 80112-5117, Contact: Karen Farestad, Ph.D., Director, Phone: (303) 792- 9900, (800) 227-4645, Fax: (303) 792-3333

Individuals and agencies who seek to protect children from neglect and abuse. Works to insure effective and responsive community child protective services. Provides comprehensive in-service training for professionals, including social workers, physicians, teachers, and law enforcement personnel. Offers evaluation and technical assistance to community and state child protective programs. Conducts ongoing research into the nature and course of child maltreatment. Advocates national and state legislation and policy to protect children.

## American Professional Society on the Abuse of Children (APSAC)

407 S. Dearborn Street, Suite 1300, Chicago, IL 60605, Contact: Delores J. Brooks MS, Exec. Director, Phone: (312) 554-0166, Fax: (312) 554-0919

Phychologists, social workers, physicians, attorneys, nurses, law enforcement personnel, child protective services and mental health workers, administrators, researchers, and allied disciplines in the field of child abuse and neglect. Mission is to ensure that everyone affected by child maltreatment receives the best possible professional response, by promoting effective interdisciplinary approaches to the identification, intervention, treatment, and prevention of child abuse and neglect. Aims to advance professional education by offering interdisciplinary national training programs; works to improve coordination among professional guidelines; encourages research in all fields of child maltreatment; disseminates research to professionals; provides guidance, support, and encouragement for professionals; and educates legislators, the public, and the media about the complex issues of child maltreatment.

## Black Community Crusade for Children (BCCC)

25 East Street NW, Washington, DC 20001, Contact: Barbara Kelly-Sease, Director, Phone: (202) 628-8787, Fax: ( 202) 662-3580

African-American clergy educators, policy makers, and community leaders. Seeks to ensure that "no child is left behind, and that every child has a Healthy Start , a Head Start, a Fair Start, a Safe Start, and a Moral Start in life, with the support of caring parents and nurturing communities." Works to mobilize the Black community on behalf of Black children. Conducts programs in areas including: community buildings; spritual, character, and leadership development; intergenerational mentoring; interracial and interethnic communication; interdisciplinary networking; training. Organizes Freedom Schools which provide meals and economic and cultural enrichment programs in African-American communities. Operates Students Leadership Network for children (SLNC); maintains farm once owned by African-American author Alex Haley.

## Boys and Girls Clubs of America

1230 West Peachtree Street NW, Atlanta, GA 30309,

Contact: Roxanne Spillet, President, Phone: (404) 815-5700, (800) 854-CLUB, Fax: (404) 815-5757

Young development organization offering services to more than 2 million disadvantaged youth. Promotes the health, social, educational, vocational, and character development of youth. Clubs known as the "Positive Place for Kids," conduct a variety of guidance activities every afternoon and evening. Current programs emphasizes drug and alcohol prevention, delinquency intervention, health and fitness, career exploration, educational enhancement, and leadership development.

## Camp Fire Boys and Girls

4601 Madison Ave., Kansas City, MO 64112-1278, Contact: Stewart Smith, Exec., Director & CEO, Phone: (816) 756-1950, Fax: (816) 756-0258

Girls and boys up to 21 years of age. Provides, through a program of informal education, opportunities for youth to realize their potential and to function effectively as responsible, caring, and self-directed individuals. Seeks to improve conditions in society that affect youth. Activities focus on small group learning by doing, developing a positive self-image, responsibility and creativity, gaining decision-making and planning skills, and learning to appreciate, care about, and work with others. Each local council is also encouraged to provide informal educational opportunities through self-reliance training, child care, camps, and club programs.

## Catholic Guardian Society (CGS)

1011 1st Ave., New York, NY 10022, Contact: John J. Frein, Exec. Director, Phone: (212) 371-1000, Fax: (212) 371-1512

Cares for dependent, neglected, abused, and delinquent children. Operates group homes, foster homes, agency-operated boarding homes, and adoption services. Operates intermediate care facilities for profoundly retarded or developmentally disabled children and adults. Provides medical, mental health, and respite care. Offers a foster home program for HIV infected children.

## Child Abuse Listening and Mediation (CALM)

PO Box 90754, Santa Barbara, CA 93190-0754, Contact: Anna Kokotovic, Exec. Director, Phone: (805) 965-2376, Fax: (805) 963-6707

Social Service program to prevent and treat child sexual abuse, physical abuse, and emotional abuse, and offer early intervention for stressed families. Objective is to reach parents who feel that they cannot cope with their problems and frustrations and who may be in danger of taking out their feelings against their children. Offers referrals to other organization and resources. Provides short and long-term counseling regarding parent-child problems. CALM's volunteers are available to go into the home as family aides, to act as "compassionate listeners and friendly neighbors" and help in situation of crisis. Provides emergency child care for parents under stress. Maintains speakers' bureau and resource library. Conducts program of public information and education and an in-school education program for students, parents, and teachers on prevention and recognition of child maltreatment. Other services include: individual, marital, and family counseling for high risk families and families involved in physical, emotional, or sexual abuse and neglect; support treatment groups for parents of sexualy abused children, for adults who were molested as children, and for children sexually abused within the family; parent support groups focusing on parent education and child development and improving parent/child interaction. Conducts weekly Parental Support Groups (one bilingual). Offers counseling groups for adult offenders legally ordered to seek counseling.

## Families, 4-H, and Nutrition

United States Department of Agriculture, Cooperative State Research Education and Extension Service, Washington, DC 20250-2225, Contact: Alma C. Hobbs, Deputy Admin., Phone: (202) 720-2908, (202) 720-6059, Fax: (202) 690-2469

Youth, Primarily nine to 19-years-old, in rural and urban areas of 3,150 counties in the United States; the District of Columbia; Puerto Rico; Guam; Virgin Islands; American Samoa; Micronesia; and Northern Marianas. Serves as a young education program of the Cooperative Extension System. Volunteer adult and junior leaders guide the program with the help of the U.S. Department of Agriculture and participating governments. Assists youths in acquiring knowledge, developing life skills, and forming attitudes that will enable them to become a self-directing, contributing members of society.

## International Child Resource Institute (ICRI)

1581 Le Roy Ave., Berkeley, CA 94708-1941, Contact: Ken Jaffe, Exec. Director

Individuals interested in issues regarding day care for children, including maternal and child health, child abuse prevention, neglect, and other children's issues. Organizations and companies that furnish or are engaged in child care. Implements model projects to gather information on techniques and practices involved in innovative forms of care and child health. Provides technical assistance to individuals, corporations, and government agencies that wish to establish and maintain child care centers and other children's programs. Serves as a clearinghouse for information on children's issues. Maintains offices in Brazil, Ethiopia, Kenya, and Malaysia.

## National Center for Missing and Exploited Children (NCMEC)
2101 Wilson Blvd., Suite 550, Arlington, VA 22201, Contact: Ernest E. Allen, President, Phone: (703) 235-3900, (800) 843-5678, Fax: (703) 235-4067
To aid parents and law enforcement agencies in preventing child exploitation and in locating missing children. Serves as a national clearinghouse of information of effective state and federal legislation directed at the protection of children. Provides technical assistance to individuals, parents, groups, agencies, and state and local government involved in locating and returning children in cases of child exploitation.

## National Child Labor Committee
1501 Broadway, Suite 1111, New York, NY 10036, Contact: Jeffrey Newman, Exec. Director, Phone: (212) 840-1801, Fax: (212) 768-0963
Parent organization of National Committee on Employment of Youth and National Committee on the Education of Migrant Children. Provides direct and technical assistance to programs on youth-related issues, particularly education, job training, and employment.

## National Committee to Prevent Child Abuse
332 South Michigan Ave., Suite 1600, Chicago, IL 60604-4357, Contact: A. Sidney Johnson III, Exec. Director, Phone: (312) 663-3520, Fax: (312) 939-8962
Serves as a national advocate to prevent the neglect and physical, sexual, and emotional abuse of children. Facilitates communication about program activities, public policy, and research related to the prevention of child abuse. Fosters greater cooperation between existing and developing resources in the area of prevention. Operates the National Center on Child Abuse Prevention Research. Conducts annual national media campaigns and child abuse prevention programs. Provides training and technical assistance.

## National Council of Young Men's Christian Associations of the United States of America
A volunteer movement characterized by local program control designed to meet the community needs of people of all ages, races, religions, abilities, and incomes. Focus is on nuturing the healthy development of children, promoting positive behavior in teens, and strengthening families. Provides group activities, facilities for physical and health education and training, youth sports activities, aquatics instruction, camping, parent-child programs, child care, and counseling. Works to address a diversity of social issues through innovative programs in juvenile justice, international exchange and education, job training, relief work, and environmental action. Each YMCA functions independently to meet the needs of the community it serves. Maintains placement service and hall of fame. Compiles statistics. A member of World Alliance of Young Men's Christian Associations.

## One Child At A Time (AIA)
4040 Crabapple Lake Court, Roswell, GA 30076-4253, Contact: Jodie R. Darragh, Director, Phone: (770) 552-0415, Fax: (770) 552-0129
Adopting families and relatives' parent groups; concerned citizens. Objectives are to promote international understanding through service to children and those in need; to facilitate the international adoption procedure when it is in the best interests of the child. Provides medical supplies, medical escorting services, overseas family assistance, overseas vocational training assistance, and adoption placement. The group was instrumental in the passage of the Amerasian Bill, passed Oct. 22, 1982. Works with children worldwide, but most frequently in Africa, Korea, India, Vietnam, Russia, Ukraine, Thailand, Romania, and Central and South America. Is currently seeking sponsors for Amerasians aged 18 and over. Maintains Americans for International Aid and Adoption, which serves in the adoption placement of children overseas and assists in the collection and distribution of funds. Serves as an information clearinghouse; keeps Americans informed of the plight of Amerasians.

## Pride
3125 East Lake Street, Minneapolis, MN 55406, Contact: Kristin Berg, Coordinator, Phone: (612) 728-2065, Fax: (612) 728-2616
A program of family and children's service of the Minneapolis Metro Area. Works to help women and teenage girls who have been used in prostitution, while promoting societal change to stop the perpetuation of commercial sexual exploitation. Services include: PRIDE groups, information and referral, transitional housing, TeenPRIDE for girls advocacy services, court intervention, 24-hour crisis line, child care, crisis intervention, and

individual support. Conducts community education and public speaking on the issues of prostitution and working with survivors.

## Project Cuddle (PC)

2 Venture Plaza, Suite 380, Irvine, CA 92618, Contact: Debbe Magnusen, Exec. Officer, Phone: (714) 432-9681, Fax: (714) 545-6866

Seeks to improve the lives of drug-exposed babies and abused children. Educates those interested in adopting drug-exposed babies. Supplies stuffed toys to children being brought to protective custody by police officers.

## Variety Club International (VCI)

350 5th Ave., Suite 1119, New York, NY 10118, Contact: Mrs. Rosalie Sochinski, Exec. Director, Phone: (212) 695-3818, Fax: (212) 695-3857

Entertainment and leisure-related industries. Sponsors programs to raise funds for children's camp.

## Village of Childhelp (VC)

PO Box 247, 14700 Manzanita Park Road, Beaumont, CA 92223, Contact: Thomas N. Alexander, Admin., Phone: (909) 845-3155, Fax: (909) 845-8412

A project of Childhelp U.S.A. Residential Program designed exclusively for abused children and their families.

# Canadian Business Bureaus

**Assn. of Atlantic Women Business Owners/ Assn. des femmes entrepreneures de l'Atlantique**
Penny Mosher, President
Lynda Beckett, Exec. Director
1819 Granville Street, Suite 304
Halifax, NS B3J 1X8
Phone: (902) 422-2828, (880) 858- 6461
Fax: (902) 422-9711

**Black Business and Professional Assn.**
Sandra Whiting, President
675 King Street West, Suite 203
Toronto, ON M5V 1M9
Phone: (416) 504-4097, Fax: (416) 504-7343

**British Columbia Human Resources Management Association**
Mary Wallace Poole, Exec. Director
Suite 704, 1130 West Pender Street
Vancouver, BC V6E 4A4
Phone: (604) 684-7228, Fax: (604) 684-3225

**Business Council of B.C.**
Jerry L. Lampert, President/CEO
Suite 810, 1050 West Pender Street
Vancouver, BC V6E 3S7
Phone: (604) 684-3384, Fax: (604) 684-7957

**The Business Development Centre**
Juanne Hemsol, Gen. Manager
1801 Eglinton Ave. West, Suite 214
Toronto, ON M6E 2H8
Phone: (416) 789-2485, Fax: (416) 789-0365

**Canadian Arbitration, Conciliation and Amicable Composition Centre Inc.**
Prof. Paul J. Davidson, President
c/o Department of Law
1125 Colonel By Drive
Carleton University
Ottawa, ON K1S 5B6
Phone: (613) 230-0155, Fax: (613) 230-1249

**Canadian Assn. for Home Based Business/Assoc. canadienne des enterprise a domicil**
Ann Wells, Exec. Director
1200 East Prince of Wales Drive
Ottawa, ON K2C 1M9
Phone: (613) 724-7964, Fax: (613) 724-4795

**Canadian Council for International Business**
Delta Office Tower
350 Sparks Street, Suite 501
Ottawa, ON K1R 7S8
Phone: (613) 230-5462, Fax: (613) 230-7087

**Canadian Council of Better Business Bureaus**
Allan G. Searle, President
#368, 7330 Fisher Street SE
Calgary, AB T2H 2H8
Phone: (403) 531-8686, Fax: (403) 531-8697

**MAJOR CENTRES:**

**BBB of Calgary & Southern Alberta**
Norman H. Haines, President
Suite 350, 7330 Fisher Street SE
Calgary, AB T2H 2H8
Phone: (403) 258-2920, Fax: (403) 640-2514

**BBB of Central & Northern Alberta**
P. Ross Bradford, President
514 Capital Place, 9707-110th Street
Edmonton, AB T5K 2L9
Phone: (403) 488-4094, Fax: (403) 482-1150

**BBB of Mainland of British Columbia**
Carol E. Tulk
Suite 404, 788 Beatty Street
Vancouver, BC V6B 2M1
Phone: (604) 682-2711

**BBB of Montreal Inc.**
Robert Tremblay, President
2055, rue Peel, bur. 460
Montreal, QC H3A 1V4
Phone: (514) 286-1236

## BBB of Newfoundland & Labrador

Mel Strong, Gen. Manager
360 Topsail Road
St. John's, NF A1E 2B6
Phone: (709) 364-2222

## BBB of Nova Scotia

Lou Gannon, Jr.
1888 Brunswick Street, Suite 601
Halifax, NS B3J 3J8
Phone: (902) 422-6581, Fax: (902) 429-6457

## BBB of Mid-Western Ontario Inc.

Patricia J. Tallman, President
354 Charles Street East
Kitchener, ON N2G 4L5
Phone: (519) 579-3080

## BBB of Western Ontario

Janet B. Delaney, President
Box 2153, London, ON N6A 4E3
Phone: (519) 673-3222

## BBB of Ottawa-Hull Inc.

Leslie King, Exec. Director
130 Albert Street, Suite 603
Ottawa, ON K1P 5G4
Phone: (613) 237-4856

## BBB of Saskatchewan

Eileen McLeod, Exec. Director
Suite 302, 2080 Broad Street
Regina, SK S4P 1Y3
Phone: (306) 352-7601

## BBB of Metropolitan Toronto

Peter Lalonde, President
St. Johns Road, Suite 501
Toronto, ON M6P 4C7
Phone: (416) 766-5744 (admin.), (416) 766-3222
Fax: (416) 766-1970

## BBB of Vancouver Island

Susan Brice, Managing Director
#201, 1005 Langley Street
Victoria, BC V8W 1V7
Phone: (250) 386- 6348, Fax: (250) 386-2367

## BBB of Windsor & District

Joseph L. Amort, Gen. Manager
500 Riverside Drive West
Windsor, ON N9A 5K6
Phone: (519) 258-7222, Fax: (519) 258-1156

## Canadian Organization of Small Business

Donald Eastcott, Man. Director/Corp. Secretary
Box 11246
Edmonton, AB T5K 3J5
Phone: (403) 423-2672, Fax: (403) 423-2751

## Canadian Professional Sales Assn.

Terry Ruffell, President
145 Wellington Street West, # 310
Toronto, ON M5J 1H8
Phone: (416) 408-2685, (888) 267-CPSA,
Fax: (416) 408-2684

## Institute of Certified Management Consultants of Manitoba

Stuart McKelvie, President
Barbara Campbell, Exec. Director
1315 Pembina Hwy, Box 23041
Winnipeg, MB R3T 2B6
Phone: (204) 488-4507, Fax: (204) 489-1749

## The Institute of Corporate Directors

Andre J. Galipeault, President
55 Street Clair Ave. West, Suite 255
Toronto, ON M4V 2Y7
Phone: (416) 944- 8282, Fax: (416) 967-6320

## Ontario Business Advisory Council

James G. Carnegie, Exec. Director
2345 Yonge Street, Suite 808
Toronto, ON M4P 2E5
Phone: (416) 482-0985, Fax: (416) 482-5879

## Small Business Network Inc.

R. Starr, Director
360A Newkirk Road
Richmond Hill, ON L4C 3G7

# Chambers of Commerce

**Abbotsford Chamber of Commerce**
Leona Klingspon, Manager
2462 McCallun Road
Abbotsford, BC V2S 3P9
Phone: (604) 859-9651, Fax: (604) 850-6880

**Alberta Chamber of Commerce**
Norman S. Leach, Exec. Director
2105 T-D Tower, Edmonton Centre
Edmonton, AB T5J 2Z1
Phone: (403) 425-4180, Fax: (403) 429-1061

**Atlantic Providence Chamber of Commerce**
Paul Daigle, President/CEO
236 St. George Street, Suite 110
Moncton, NB E1C 1W1
Phone: (506) 857-3980, Fax: (506) 859-6131

**The Board of Trade of Metropolitan Toronto/World Trade Centre Toronto**
Elyse Allen, Gen. Manager
One First Canadian Place, Box 60
Toronto, ON M5X 1C1
Phone: (416) 366-6811, Fax: (416) 366-6840

**British Columbia Chamber of Commerce**
700 W. Pender Street, Suite 1607
Vancouver, BC V6C 1G8
Phone: (604) 683-0700, Fax: (604) 683-0416

**British Columbia 4-H Provincial Council**
Collen Lepik, Exec. Director
844 Windbreak Street
Kamloops, BC V2B 5P1
Phone: (250) 376-0373, Fax: (250) 554-2723

**Canada-Israel Chamber of Commerce**
48 St. Clair Ave. West, # 1100
Toronto, ON M4V 2Z2
Phone: (416) 410-7273

**Canada-Pakistan Business Council**
Anwar (Andy) Merchant, President
2 Forest Laneway, Suite 2103
North York, ON M2N 5X7
Phone: (416) 590-0929, Fax: (416) 590-0945

**Canada Romania Business Council**
c/o DEPAG
Deposit Agency of Canada Inc.
67 Yonge Street, # 1402
Toronto, ON M5E 1J8
Phone: (416) 364-4112, Fax: (416) 364-4074

**The Calgary Chamber of Commerce**
Glenn L. Tibbles, Managing Director/COO
517 South Centre Street
Calgary, AB T2G 2C4
Phone: (403) 750-0400, Fax: (403) 266-3413

**The Canadian Chamber of Commerce**
Tim Reid, President
Michelle Banning, Media Relations
Delta Office Tower
350 Spark Street, Suite 501
Ottawa, ON K1R 7S8
Phone: (613) 238-4000, Fax: (613) 238-7643

**Regional Offices:**
**Toronto Office:**
Sharon Glover, Sr. Vice President
(Corporate Affairs and Membership)
Eleanor McMahon, Communications
BCE Place, 181 Bay Street, Box 818
Toronto, ON M5J 2T3
Phone: (416) 868-6415, Fax: (514) 868-0189

**Quebec:**
W.G. Browne, Manager
1080, cote du Beaver Hall, bur. 715
Montreal, QC H2Z 1T2
Phone: (514) 866-4334, Fax: (514) 866-7296

**Chamber of Commerce Executives of Canada**
Linda Robert, Sec.Treasurer
55 Metcalfe Street, Suite 1160
Ottawa, ON K1P 6N4
Phone: (613) 238-4000, Fax: (613) 238-7643

**La Chambre de commerce du Montreal metropolitain/Board of Trade of Metropolitan Montreal**
Luc Lacharite, Vice President

5 Place Ville-Marie, Niveau Plaza, bur. 12500
Montreal, QC H3B 4Y2
Phone: (514) 844-4000, Fax: (514) 871-1255

## Chambre de commerce du Quebec

Michel Audet, President
500 Place d'Armes, bur. 3030
Montreal, QC H2Y 2W2
Phone: (514) 844-9571, Fax: (514) 844-0226

## Chambre de commerce et d'industrie du Quebec metropolitain/Board of Trade and Industry of Metropolitan Quebec

Alain Kirouac, Directeur General
17 rue St-Louis, QC G1R 3Y8
Phone: (418) 692-3853, Fax: (418) 694-2286

## Chambre de commerce francaise au Canada

Pierre Lapointe, President
360, rue Street-Francois-Xavier
Montreal, QC H2Y 2S8
Phone: (514) 281-1246, Fax: (514) 289-9594

## Edmonton Chamber of Commerce

Martin D. Salloum, General Manager
Suite 600, 10123-99th Street
Edmonton, AB T5J 3G9
Phone: (403) 426-4620, Fax: (403) 424-7946

## Greater Kingston District Chamber of Commerce

Gail Logan, Gen. Manager
209 Wellington Street
Kingston, ON K7K 2Y6
Phone: (613) 548-4453, Fax: (613) 548-4743

## Greater Victoria Chamber of Commerce

Glenn Terrell, CEO
525 Fort Street
Victoria, BC V8W 1E8
Phone: (250) 383-7191, Fax: (250) 385-3552

## Manitoba Chamber of Commerce

Lance Norman, Exec. Vice-President
167 Lombard Ave., Suite 167
Winnipeg, MB R3B 0V6
Phone: (204) 942-2561, Fax: (204) 942-2227

## Metropolitan Halifax Chamber of Commerce

Valerie Payn, Gen. Manager
PO Box 8990, Halifax, NS B3K 5M6
Phone: (902) 468-7111, Fax: (902) 468-7333

## New Brunswick Chamber of Commerce

Rhona Levine-Ruben, Chairman
Federal Business Development Bank
570 Queen Street
Fredericton, NB E3B 5B4
Phone: (506) 452-3025, Fax: (506) 452-2416

## Newfoundland Ocean Industries Assn.

Ruth Graham, Exec. Director
Atlantic Place, 215 Water Street, Suite 602
Box 44
St. John's, NF A1C 6C9
Phone: (709) 753-8123, Fax: (709) 753-6010

## Offshore Technologies Assn. of Nova Scotia

Tina Battcock, Business Manager
World Trade and Convention Centre
1800 Argyle Street, Suite 813
Halifax, NS B3J 3N8
Phone: (902) 425-4774, Fax: (902) 422-2332

## Ontario Chamber of Commerce

Ian Cunningham, Exec. Director
2345 Yonge Street, Suite 808
Toronto, ON M4P 2E5
Phone: (416) 482-5222, Fax: (416) 482-5879

## Ottawa-Carleton Board of Trade

Kim Kelly, Gen. Manager
350 Albert Street, Suite 1710, Box 13
Ottawa, ON K1R 1A4
Phone: (613) 236-3631, ext. 26, Fax: (613) 236-7498

## Regina Chamber of Commerce

Deanna Dalla-Vicenza, Exec. Director
2145 Albert Street, Regina, SK S4P 2V1
Phone: (306) 757-4658, Fax: (306)757-4668

## Saint John Board of Trade

Darryl Goyetche, Gen. Manager
40 King Street, Box 6037
Saint John, NB E2L 4R5
Phone: (506) 634-8111, Fax: (506) 632-2008

**St. John's Board of Trade**
D. Gail Ryan, Finance Manager
5127  Street, John's, NF A1C 5V5
Phone: (709) 726-2961, Fax: (709) 726-2003

**Saskatoon Chamber of Commerce**
Dwight Percy, Exec. Director
345 South 3rd Ave.
Saskatoon, SK S7K 1M6
Phone: (306) 244-2151, Fax: (306) 244-8366

**Sudbury and District Chamber of Commerce**
Debbi M. Nicholson, Exec. Director
166 Douglas Street West
Sudbury, ON P3E 1G1
Phone: (705) 673-7133, Fax: (705) 673-2944

**Swiss Canadian Chamber of Commerce**
**(Ontario) Inc.**
Alfred Mettler, Exec. Office
6795 Steeles Ave. West
Etobicoke, ON M9V 4R 9
Phone: (416) 741-2256, Fax: (416) 741-0140

**Vancouver Board of Trade**
Suite 400, 999 Canada Place
Vancouver, BC V6C 3C1
Phone: (604) 681-2111, Fax: (604) 681-0437

**Winnipeg Chamber of Commerce**
Shelley Morris, President
167 Lombard Ave.,  Street 500
Winnipeg, MB R3B 3E5
Phone: (204) 944-8484, Fax: (204) 944-8492

**Yellowknife Chamber of Commerce**
Cheryl Best, Exec. Director
Suite 6, 4897-49th Street
Yellowknife,  NT X1A 3T5
Phone: (867) 920-4944, Fax: (867) 920-4640

# Charitable Organizations

**AboutFace**
Anna Pileggi, Exec. Director
99 Crowns Lane, 4th Floor
Toronto, ON M5R 3P4
Phone: (416) 944-3223, (800) 665-3223
Fax: (416) 944-2488

**Associated Medical Services, Inc.**
Mrs. M. Wildridge, Corporate Secretary
14 Prince Arthur Ave., Suite 101
Toronto, ON M5R 1A9
Phone: (416) 924-3368, Fax: (416) 323-3338

**Bible League of Canada**
Rev. D.J. Tigchelaar, Exec. Director
3067 Mainway Drive, Box 5037
Burlington, ON L7R 3Y8
Phone: (416) 319-9500, (800) 363-9673
Fax: (416) 319-0484

**The Birks Family Foundation**
Mr. G. Drummond Birks, Exec. Director
606 rue Cathcart, bur. 534
Montreal, QC H3B 1K9
Phone: (514) 397-2567, Fax: (514) 397-1121

**Birthright International**
Mary Berney, Co-President
777 Coxwell Ave.
Toronto, ON M4C 3C6
Phone: (416) 469-4789, (800) 550-4900 (24hrs.), Fax:
(416) 469-1772

**British Columbia Women's Institute**
Jan Marshall, Office Administrator
20510 Fraser Hwy.
Langley, BC V34 4G2
Phone: (604) 533-6564, Fax: (604) 533-6564

**Calgary Safety Council**
Shelina Wardrope, President/Gen. Manager
24-28th Ave. SW
Calgary, AB T2S 2Y1
Phone: (403) 290-0446

**Canada Peace Park Assn.**
Roy Cadwell, Chairman
Lester B. Pearson Peace Park, R.R. 3
Tweed, ON K0K 3J0
Phone: (613) 478-6337

**Canadian Assn. of Food Banks**
Julia Bass, Exec. Director
530 Lakeshore Blvd. West
Toronto, ON M5V 1A5
Phone: (416) 203-9241, Fax: (416) 203-9244

**Canadian Foodgrains Bank**
Trish Jordan, Communications Coordinator
#400, 280 Smith Street, Box 767
Winnipeg, MB R3C 2L4
Phone: (204) 944-1993, (800) 665-0377
Fax: (204) 943-2597

**Canadian Friends of Peace Now**
Frank Guttman, Simon Rosenblum, Presidents
Mintzy Clement, Office Administrator
300 John Street, Box 87631
Thornhill, ON L3T 7R4
Phone: (905) 764-3997, Fax: (905) 764-3408

**Canadian Give the Gift of Literacy Foundation**
Sharon English, Coordinator
35 Spadina Road
Toronto, ON M5R 2S9
Phone: (416) 975-9366, Fax: (416) 975-1839

**Canadian Hard of Hearing Association/Association des malentendants canadiens**
Fred Clark, President
2435 Holly Lane, Suite 205
Ottawa, ON K1V 7P2
Phone: (613) 526-1584, TDD: (613) 526-2692
Fax: (613) 526-4718

**Canadian Progress Charitable Foundation**
Molly Trussler, Exec. Director
2395 Bayview Ave.

North York, ON M2L 1A2
Phone: (416) 446-1830, Fax: (416) 446-6857

## Canadian Women's Foundation
Chandra Budhu, President
Beverly Wybrow, Exec. Director
Shannon Doherty, Director of Development
133 Richmond Street West, Suite 504
Toronto, ON M5H 2L3
Phone: (416) 365-1444, Fax: (416) 365-1745

## CARE Canada
A. John Watson, Exec. Director
Box 9000, 6 Antares Drive
Ottawa, ON K1G 4X6
Phone: (613) 228-5600, Fax: ( 613) 226-5777

## Catholic Church Extension Society of Canada
Rev. Timothy Coughlan, President
1155 Yonge Street,  #201
Toronto, ON M4T 1W2
Phone: (416) 934-3424, Fax: (416) 934-3425

## Cheshire Homes Foundation (Canada) Inc.
Bob Webber, Exec. Director
40 Orchard View Blvd., Suite 215
Toronto, ON M4R 1B9
Phone: (416) 487-0443, Fax: (416) 487-0624

## Child Find British Columbia Inc.
Richard Achtem, Chairman
Suite 202, 724 Powell Street
Vancouver, BC V6A 1H6
Phone: (604) 251-3463, (800) 387-7962
Fax: (604) 255-9968

## Child Find Manitoba, Inc.
Myrna Driedger, Exec. Director
#1110, 405 Broadway
Winnipeg, MB R3C 3L6
Phone: (204) 945- 5735, Fax: (204) 948-2461

## Christian Aid Mission
James S. Eagles, President
201 Stanton Street
Fort Erie, ON L2A 3N8
Phone: (905) 871-1773, Fax: (905) 871-5165

## Christian Children's Fund of Canada
Mary Lynne Stewart,
Development Director
1027 McNicoll Ave.
Scarborough, ON M1W 3X2
Phone: (416) 495-1174, Fax: (416) 495-9395

## Christian Reform World Relief Commitee of Canada
Wayne DeJong, Director
3475 Mainway, Box 5070
Burlington, ON L7R 3Y8
Phone: (905) 336-2920, Fax: (905) 336-8344

## Coalition of National Voluntary Organizations/ Organisations nationales volontaires
Al Hatton, Exec. Director
396 Cooper Street, #420
Ottawa, ON K2P 2H7
Phone: (613) 238-1591, Fax: (613) 238-5257

## Coast Foundation Society
Darrel Burnham, Exec. Director
293 East 11th Ave.
Vancouver, BC V5T 2C4
Phone: (604) 872-3502/03, Fax: (604) 879-2363

## Daily Bread Food Bank Foundation of Toronto
Susan Cox, Exec. Director
530 Lakeshore Blvd.
Toronto, ON M5V 1A5
Phone: (416) 203-0050, Fax: (416) 203-0049

## Development Services International of Canada
Elinor Ratcliffe, Director
875 Speedsville Road, Box 3190
Cambridge, ON N3H 4S8
Phone: (519) 653-3275, Fax: (519) 653-1337

## Donner Canadian Foundation
Allan Gotlieb, Chairman
8 Price Arthur Ave., 3rd., Floor
Toronto, ON M5R 1A9
Phone: (416) 920- 6400

## The Eaton Foundation
Mr. P.J. Wilson, Chairman

250 Yonge Street
Toronto, ON M5B 1C8
Phone: (416) 343-3500, Fax: (416) 343-3526

## Canadian Federation of Junior Leagues
Diana Johnson, Chairman
154 Oxford Street
Winnipeg, MB R3M 3J5
Phone: (204) 487-1155, Fax: (204) 487-0403

## The Gairdner Foundation
Bill Gairdner, Chairman
255 Yorkland Blvd., Suite 220
Willowdale, ON M2J 1S3
Phone: (416) 493-3101, Fax: (416) 493-8158

## H. G. Bertram Foundation
(restricted to charitable organizations in the Hamilton/
Dundas area)
Michael H. Brown, Sr., Trust Officer
Royal Trust, 4th Floor
Box 7500, Stn. A
Toronto, ON M5W 1P9
Phone: (416) 955-5065, Fax: (416) 955-5091

## The Hamber Foundation
D. Woods, Secretary
c/o Canada Trust
4 Bentall Centre, Box 49390
Vancouver, BC V7X 1P3
Phone: (604) 641-4700, Fax: (604) 641-4769

## Help the Aged (Canada)
Pierre Barbeau, Exec. Director
5th Ave., #99
Ottawa, ON K1S 5K4
Phone: (613) 232-0727, Fax: (613) 232-7625

## The Hospital for Sick Children Foundation
Dianne Lister, President
555 University Ave., Suite 1725
Toronto, ON M5G 1X8
Phone: (416) 813-6166, Fax: (416) 813-5024

## In-Definite Arts
Gene R. Neel, Exec. Director
7140-C Fairmount Drive SE
Calgary, AB T2H 0X4
Phone: (403) 253-3174, Fax: (403) 255-2234

## International Child Care
Dana Osbum, National Director
2476 Argentia Road, Suite 113
Mississauga, ON L5N 6M1
Fax: (905) 821-6319

## Laidlaw Foundation
Nathan H. Gilbert, Exec. Director
365 Bloor Street East, Suite 2000
Toronto, ON M4W 3L4
Phone: (416) 964-3614, Fax: (416) 975-1428

## Learning Enrichment Foundation
Eunice Grayson, Exec. Director
116 Industry Street
Toronto, ON M6M 4L8
Phone: (416) 769-0830, Fax: (416) 769- 9912

## Missing Children Society Canada
Rhonda Morgan, Chair
Suite 219, 3501-23rd Street NE
Calgary, AB T2E 6V8
Phone: (403) 291-0705, (800) 661-6100
Fax: (403) 291-9728

## Partners in Rural Development
Bruce Moore, Exec. Director
323 Chapel Street
Ottawa, ON K1N 7Z2
Phone: (613) 237-0180, Fax: (613) 237-5969

## Plenty Canada
Lawrence McDermott, CEO
R.R. 3, Lanark
ON K0G 1K0
Phone: (613) 278-2215, Fax: (613) 278-2416

## The Salvation Army
Lt. Col. C. Moore, Treasurer
2 Overlea Blvd.
Toronto, ON M4H 1P4
Phone: (416) 425-2111, Fax: (416) 422-6189

## Save the Children-Canada/Aide
## a l'enfance-Canada
4141 Yonge Street, Suite 300
Toronto, ON M2P 2A8
Phone: (416) 221-5501, Fax: (416) 221-8214

**ShareLife**
Marilyn Burns, Communications Director
1155 Yonge Street,
Toronto, ON M4T 1W2
Phone: (416) 934-3411,Toll-free (800) 263-2595,
Fax: (416) 934-3412

**UNICEF Canada**
Azim Kassam, Controller
443 Mount Pleasant Road
Toronto, ON M4S 2L8
Phone: (416) 482-4444, Fax: (416) 482-8035

**Provincial Offices:**

**UNICEF Alberta**
Pam Crosby, Provincial Director
1022-17th Ave. SW
Calgary, AB T2T 0A5
Phone: (403) 245-0323, Fax: (403) 228-3881

**UNICEF British Columbia**
Shirley Kepper, Provincial Director
536 West Broadway
Vancouver, BC V5Z 1E9
Phone: (604) 874-3666, Fax: (604) 874-5411

**UNICEF Manitoba**
Bonnie Lafolla, Office Manager
160 Stafford Street
Winnipeg, MB R3M 2V8
Phone: (204) 477-4600, Fax: (204) 477-4040

**UNICEF New Brunswick**
Elizabeth Beveridge, Office Manager
51 Canterbury Street
Saint John, NB E2L 2C6
Phone: (506) 634-1911, Fax: (506) 652-7583

**UNICEF Newfoundland**
Deborah Glassman, Provincial Director
354 Water Street, 2nd Floor
Mailing Address:
Box 28045 Avalon Mall RPO
St. John's, NF A1B 4J8
Phone: (709) 726-2430, Fax: (709) 722-0223

**UNICEF Nova Scotia**
Jocelyn Boyd, Provincial Director

1491 Carlton Street
Halifax, NS B3H 3B8
Phone: (902) 422-6000, Fax: (902) 425-3002

**UNICEF Ontario**
Jaqueline Bradshaw, Provincial Director
33 Eglinton Ave. East
Toronto, ON M4P 1L7
Phone: (416) 487-4153, Fax: (416) 487-8875

**UNICEF Prince Edward Island**
Winston Cheverie, Chairman
Box 294
Charlottetown, PE C1A 7K4
Phone: (902) 894-8771, Fax: (902) 894-8771

**UNICEF Quebec**
Marquis Giguere, Provincial Director
4474, rue St-Denis
Montreal, QC H2J 2L1
Phone: (514) 288-5134, Fax: (514) 288-7243

**UNICEF Saskatchewan**
Sandra Grismer, Office Manager
Suite 314, 220-3rd Ave. South
Saskatoon, SK S7K 1M1
Phone: (306) 242-4922, Fax: (306) 652-7105

**United Way/Centraide Canada**
David Armour, President
56 Sparks Street, Suite 404
Ottawa, ON K1P 5A9
Phone: (613) 236-7041, Fax: (613) 236-3087

**United Way of Greater Toronto**
Dr. Ann Golden, President
26 Wellington Street East, 11th Floor
Toronto, ON M5E 1W9
Phone: (416) 777-2001, Fax: (416) 777-0962

**United Way of Greater Victoria**
Maureen Duncan, Exec. Director
1144 Fort Street
Victoria, BC V8V 3K8
Phone: (250) 385-6708, Fax: (250) 385-6712

**United Way of the Alberta Capital Region**
Anne Smith, President
10020-10th Street

Edmonton, AB T5J 1K6
Phone: (403) 990-1000, Fax: (403) 990-1919

**United Way of the Lower Mainland**
Ron Dumouchelle, CEO
4543 Canada Way
Burnaby, BC V5G 4T4
Phone: (604) 294-8929, Fax: (604) 293-0020

**United Way of Winnipeg**
Jo Wright, Director Resource Dev.
5 Donald Street, 3rd Floor
Winnipeg, MB R3L 2T4
Phone: (204) 477-5360, Fax: (204) 453-6198

**Vision Institute of Canada**
Dr. M.J. Samek, Exec. Director
16 York Mills Road, Suite110
North York, ON M2P 2E5
Phone: (416) 224-2273, Fax: (416) 224-9234

**World Vision Canada**
Dave Toycen, President
6630 Turner Valley Road
Mississauga, ON L5N 2S4
Phone: (905) 821-3030,  Fax: (905) 821-1356

**21st Century Science & Technology Fdn.**
Milson Macleod, President
Box 1657
Edmonton, AB T5J 2N9
Phone: (403) 462-5118, Fax: (403) 463-7311

# REACH MILLIONS OF READERS

## FREE Publicity

## FREE Publicity

FOR ALL

NETWORK MARKETING AND DIRECT SELLING COMPANIES

SEND US YOUR

PRESS RELEASES, NEWS ARTICLES, NEW PRODUCT ANNOUNCEMENTS, SPECIAL EVENTS, CONFERENCES, CHANGE OF ADDRESS, AND ALL OTHER PUBLIC INFORMATION YOU WANT PUBLISHED IN THE

# THE GLOBAL HOME BASED BUSINESS DIRECTORY

Please Send Correspondence to:

Marketing Solutions, Inc., 27442 Burgstaler Road, Aitkin, MN 56431

Attention: Publicity Department

 *Check Us Out!*

Visit Our Web Site: ghbbd.com for ordering information and current news about our Global Home Based Business Directory and the many web sites and newstand locations where our directory can be purchased. For volume discount orders or personalized promotion projects, please call (800) 496-0277.

## Several Web Sites Where Our GHBBD Can Be Purchased

amazon.com

barnesandnoble.com

borders.com

2 millionbooks.com

booksnow.com

chapters.ca

buy.com

BookLand

# Environment/Ecology

**Air and Waste Management Association**
Michael Schroeder, Chair
21-10405 Jasper Ave., Suite 149
Edmonton, AB T5J 3S2
Phone: (403) 263-7113, Fax: (403) 263-7116

**Alberta Wilderness Association**
Dianne Pachal, Conservation Director
Station D, Box 6398
Calgary, AB T2P 2E1
Phone: (403) 283-2025, Fax: (403) 270-2743

**All About Us Canada Inc.**
Seymour Trieger, Exec. Director
RR 6, Yellow Point Road
Ladysmith, BC V0R 2E0
Phone: (250) 722-3349, Fax: (250) 722-3359

**Amalgamated Conservation Society**
Wayne Zaccarelli, Secretary-Treasurer
Box 8741
Victoria, BC V8W 3S3
Phone: (250) 382-8502

**Association for the Protection
of Fur-Bearing Animals**
Michelle Clausius, Exec. Director
2235 Commercial Drive
Vancouver, BC V5N 4B6
Phone: (604) 255-0411, Fax: (604) 255-1491

**Association of Municipal Recycling**
Linda Varangu, Exec. Director
25 Douglas Street
Guelph, ON N1H 2S7
Phone: (519) 823-1990, Fax: (519) 823-0084

**British Columbia Environmental Network**
Anne-Marie Sleeman, Exec. Director
1672 East 10th Ave.
Vancouver, BC V5N 1X5
Phone: (604) 879-2279, Fax: (604) 879-2272

**British Columbia Water & Waste Association**
Catherine Gibson, Exec. Director
341 North Road, Suite 236

Coquitlam, BC V3K 3V8
Phone: (604) 936-4982, Fax: (604) 931-3880

**Calgary Ecological Centre Society**
Trevor Borden, President
Kensington Postal Outlet, Box 61171
Calgary, AB T2N 4S6
Phone: (403) 263-8228

**Canada Earthsave Society**
Justis Raynier, President
1093 West Broadway, Suite 103
Vancouver, BC V6H 1E2
Phone: (604) 731-5885, Fax: (604) 731-5805

**Canadian Earth Energy Association**
Bill Eggertson, Exec. Director
130 Slater Street, Suite 605
Ottawa, ON K1P 6E2
Phone: (613) 230-2332, Fax: (613) 237-1480

**Canadian Environment Industry Association**
Ronald V. Portelli, President
350 Sparks Street, Suite 208
Ottawa, ON K1R 7S8
Phone: (613) 236-6222, Fax: (613) 236-6850

**Canadian Nature Federation**
Julie Gelfand, Exec. Director
1 Nicholas Street, Suite 520
Ottawa, ON K1N 7B7
Phone: (613) 562-3447, Fax: (613) 562-3371

**Canadian Parks and Wilderness Society**
Mary Granskou, Exec. Director
401 Richmond Street West, Suite 380
Toronto, ON M5V 3A8
Phone: (416) 979-2720, Fax: (416) 979-3155

**Chapters:**

**Calgary/Banff**
Ann Lemorande
319-10th Ave. SW, Suite 306
Calgary, AB T2R 0A5
Phone: (403) 232-6686, Fax: (403) 232-6988

**British Columbia**
Sabine Jessen, Exec. Director
611-207 West Hastings Street
Vancouver, BC V6B 1H7
Phone: (604) 685-7445, Fax: (604) 685-6449

**Edmonton**
Sam Gunsch
8210-109th Street, Box 52031
Edmonton, AB T6G 2T5
Phone: (403) 433-9302, Fax: (403) 433-9305

**Manitoba**
Roger Turenne, Chairperson
Box 344
Winnipeg, MB R3C 2H6
Phone: (204) 237-5947, Fax: (204) 237-5947

**Nova Scotia**
Colin Stewart, Chairperson
73 Chadwick Street
Dartmouth, NS B2Y 2M2
Phone: (902) 466-7168

**Ottawa Valley**
Jean Langlois, Chairperson
Station D, Box 3072
Ottawa, ON K1P 6H6
Phone: (613) 730-2797, Fax: (613) 730-0005

**Wildlands League**
Tim Gray, Exec. Director
401 Richmond Street West, Suite 380
Toronto, ON M5V 3A8
Phone: (416) 971-9453, Fax: (416) 979-3155

**Canadian Wildflower Society**
Shirley Wiggans, Business Secretary
4981 Hwy 7 East, Unit 12A, Box 228
Markham, ON L3R 1N1
Phone: (905) 294-9075, Fax: (416) 466-6428

**Citizens Network on Waste Management**
John Jackson, Coordinator
17 Major Street
Kitchener, ON N2H 4R1
Phone: (519) 744-7503, Fax: (519) 744-1546

**The Clean Nova Scotia Foundation**
Meinhard Doelle, Exec. Director
Central, Box 2528
Halifax, NS B3J 3N5
Phone: (902) 420-3474, Fax: (902) 424-5334

**Conservation and Development Association of Saskatchewan**
Karen Grayson, Secretary-Manager
Box 116
Nipawin, SK S0E 1E0
Phone: (306) 862-3380, Fax: (306) 862-3380

**Conservation Council of New Brunswick**
David Coon, Policy Director
180 Saint John Street
Fredericton, NB E3B 4A9
Phone: (506) 458-8747, Fax: (506) 458-1047

**The Conservation Council of Ontario**
Doug Petry, President
3 Church Street, Suite 400
Toronto, ON M5E 1M2
Phone: (416) 410-6637, Fax: (416) 863-6755

**Conservation International Canada**
Sandy Wiseman, Chairman
1415 Bathurst Street, Suite 202
Toronto, ON M5R 3H8
Phone: (416) 535-4966, Fax: (416) 535-3065

**Conservation Ontario**
Jim Anderson, Gen. Manager
120 Bayview Parkway, Box 11
Newmarket, ON L3Y 4W3
Phone: (905) 895-0716, Fax: (905) 895-0751

**Earthroots**
Sarah Winterton, Director
401 Richmond Street West, Suite 410
Toronto, ON M5V 3A8
Phone: (416) 599-0152, Fax: (416) 340-2429

**Ecology Action Centre**
1568 Argyle Street, Suite 31
Halifax, NS B3J 2B3
Phone: (902) 429-2202, Fax: (902) 422-6410

**Evergreen Foundation**
Geoffrey Cape, Exec. Director
355 Adelaide Street West, Suite 5A
Toronto, ON M5V 1S2
Phone: (416) 596-1495, Fax: (416) 596-1443

**Federation of Alberta Naturalists**
Jorden Johnston, President
Box 1472
Edmonton, AB T5J 2N5
Phone: (403) 453-8629, Fax: (403) 453-8553

**Federation of British Columbia Naturalists**
Leslie-Ann Drummond, Administration Officer
1367 West Broadway, Suite 321
Vancouver, BC V6H 4A9
Phone: (604) 737-3057, Fax: (604) 738-7175

**Federation of Ontario Naturalists**
John Lounds, Exec. Director
355 Lesmill Road
Don Mills, ON M3B 2W8
Phone: (416) 444-8419, Fax: (416) 444-9866

**Greenpeace Canada**
Jeanne Moffat, Exec. Director
185 Spadina Ave., Suite 600
Toronto, ON M5T 2C6
Phone: (416) 597-8408, Fax: (416) 597-8422

**Is Five Foundation**
Tom Scanlan, Director
400 Mt. Pleasant Road, Suite 4
Toronto, ON M4S 2L6
Phone: (416) 480-2408, Fax: (416) 480-2546

**Lifeforce Foundation**
Box 3117
Vancouver, BC V6B 3X6
Phone: (604) 669-HOPE, Fax: (604) 669-HOPE

**Manitoba Eco Network**
Anne Lindsey, Exec. Director
70 Albert Street, #2
Winnipeg, MB R3B 1E7
Phone: (204) 947-6511, Fax: (204) 947-6514

**The Nature Conservatory of Canada**
Sheri-Lynn Armstrong
110 Eglinton Ave. West, Suite 400
Toronto, ON M4R 1A3
Phone: (416) 932-3202, Fax: (416) 932-3208

**Manitoba Naturalists Society**
Herta Gudauskas, Exec. Director
63 Albert Street, Suite 401
Winnipeg, MB R3B 1G4
Phone: (204) 943-9029, Fax: (204) 943-9029

**Nature Saskatchewan**
Curt Schroeder, Exec. Director
1860 Lorne Street, Room 206
Regina, SK S4P 2L7
Phone: (306) 780-9273, Fax: (306) 780-9263

**New Brunswick Federation of Naturalists**
Frank Longstaff, President
277 Douglas Ave.
Saint John, NB E2K 1E5
Phone: (506) 832-9087, Fax: (506) 832-3848

**Niagra Peninsula Hawkwatch**
Mike Street, President
73 Hatton Drive
Ancaster, ON L9G 2H5
Phone: (905) 648-3737

**Ontario Environment Network**
Cecillia Fernandez, Coordinator
25 Douglas Street
Guelph, ON N1H 2S7
Phone: (519) 837-2565, Fax: (519) 837-8113

**Ottawa Field Naturalists' Club**
W.J. Cody, Business Manager
Box 35069
Ottawa, ON K1Z 1A2
Phone: (613) 722-3050

**Pollution Probe**
Ken Oglivie, Exec. Director
12 Madison Ave.
Toronto, ON M5R 2S1
Phone: (416) 926-1907, Fax: (416) 926-1601

**Prince Edward Island Wildlife Federation**
Dawna Gillis, President
Box 753
Charlottetown, PE C1A 7L9
Phone: (902) 887-2155

**Use these handy postpaid cards to start your very own home-based business now !**

## BUSINESS REPLY MAIL
FIRST-CLASS MAIL PERMIT NO. 2 AITKIN, MN

POSTAGE WILL BE PAID BY ADDRESSEE

MARKETING  SOLUTIONS
HC  6  BOX  58A
AITKIN  MN  56431-9901

## BUSINESS REPLY MAIL
FIRST-CLASS MAIL PERMIT NO. 2 AITKIN, MN

POSTAGE WILL BE PAID BY ADDRESSEE

MARKETING  SOLUTIONS
HC  6  BOX  58A
AITKIN  MN  56431-9901

## BUSINESS REPLY MAIL
FIRST-CLASS MAIL PERMIT NO. 2 AITKIN, MN

POSTAGE WILL BE PAID BY ADDRESSEE

MARKETING  SOLUTIONS
HC  6  BOX  58A
AITKIN  MN  56431-9901

Use
these
handy
postpaid
cards
to start
your
very own
home-
based
business
now !

# Human/Civil Rights

**Action Group Against Harrassment & Discrimination in the Workplace**
Bronwen Williams, President
49 Montpetit Street
L'Original, ON K0B 1K0
Phone: (613) 632-9828, Fax: (613) 632-9828

**Alberta Civil Liberties Association**
George Blochert, President
2500 University Drive NW
Calgary, AB T2N 1N4
Phone: (403) 543-6323, Fax: (403) 543-6322

**Alliance For Life**
Michelle Blanchette, Exec. Director
B1-90 Garry Street
Winnipeg, MB R3C 4H1
Phone: (204) 942-4772, Fax: (204) 943-9283

**Amnesty International, Canadian Section**
Roger Clark, Secretary General
214 Montreal Road, Suite 401
Vanier, ON K1L 1A4
Phone: (613) 744-7667, Fax: (613) 462-4114

**B.C. Civil Liberties Association**
John Westwood, Exec. Director
815 West Hastings Street, Suite 425
Vancouver, BC V6C 1B4
Phone: (604) 687-2919, Fax: (604) 687-3045

**B'nai Brith Canada**
Frank Dimant, Exec. Vice President
15 Hove Street, Suite 200
Downsview, ON M3H 4Y8
Phone: (416) 633-6224, Fax: (416) 630-2159

**Canadian Abortion Rights Action League Inc.**
344 Bloor Street West, Suite 306
Toronto, ON M5S 3A7
Phone: (416) 961-1507, Fax: (416) 961-5771

**Canadian Association of Statutory Human Rights Agencies**
Council of Human Rights

Parliament Buildings
Victoria, BC V8V 1X4
Phone: (250) 387-3710, Fax: (250) 387-3643

**Canadian Centre For Victims of Torture**
Mulugeta Abai, Exec. Director
194 Jarvis Street, 2nd Floor
Toronto, ON M5B 2B7
Phone: (416) 363-1066, Fax: (416) 363-2122

**Canadian Civil Liberties Association**
D.S. McLaughlin, Director of Education
229 Yonge Street, Suite 403
Toronto, ON M5B 1N9

**Canadian Human Rights Foundation**
Ruth Selwyn, Exec. Director
1425, Blvd.
Montreal, QC H3G 1T7
Phone: (514) 954-0382, Fax: (514) 954-0659

**Member Associations:**

**Newfoundland-Labrador Human Rights Association**
Jerry Vink, Exec. Director
155 Water Street, Box 6203
St. John's, NF A1C 6J9
Phone: (709) 754-0690, Fax: (709) 754-0690

**Civil Liberties Association- National Capital Region**
Jack MacKinnon, President
2190 Tawney Road
Ottawa, ON K1G 1C5
Phone: (613) 733-6640, Fax: (613) 733-6640

**La Lique des droits et LIBERTES**
Lucie Lemonde, Presidente
4416, boul. Saint-Laurent
Montreal, QC H2W 1Z7
Phone: (514) 849-7717, Fax: (514) 849-6717

**Saskatchewan Association on Human Rights**
Barbara Dedi
39 Springstein Ave.

Regina, SK S4R 7J4
Phone: (306) 949-0787, Fax: (306) 949-0787

**Canadians For Responsible Government**
John Kroeker, President
Station E, Box 4111
Ottawa, ON K1S 5B1
Phone: (613) 733-7414

**Christians Concerned for Racial Equality**
Wesley H. Wakefield, Chairman
Station A, Box 223
Vancouver, BC V6C 2M3
Phone: (250) 498-3895

**Citizens for Public Justice**
Harry J. Kits, Exec. Director
229 College Street, Suite 311
Toronto, ON M5T 1R4
Phone: (416) 979-2443, Fax: (416) 979-2458

**Coalition For Equality**
Roger Samson, Gail Tricco, Co-Chairs
Box 18000
St. John's, NF A1C 6C2
Phone: (709) 753-2202, Fax: (709) 753-4110

**Conscience Canada**
Kate Penner, Coordinator
Central PO Box 8601
Victoria, BC V8W 3S2
Phone: (250) 384-5532, Fax: (250) 382-8378

**Croation Committee for Human Rights**
Dr. J.S. Gamulin, President
1174 Clarkson Road North
Mississauga, ON L5J 2W2
Phone: (905) 823-9567, Fax: (905) 823-4393

**Human Concern International**
A Nazir, Chairman
Station C, Box 3984
Ottawa, ON K1Y 4P2
Phone: (613) 742-5948, Fax: (613) 742-7733

**Human Life International**
Theresa Bell, Exec. Director
Station V, Box 7400
Vanier, ON K1L 8E4
Phone: (613) 745-9405, Fax: (613) 745-9868

**Human Rights Institute of Canada**
Dr. Marguerite, President
246 Queen Street, Suite 303
Ottawa, ON K1P 5E4
Phone: (613) 232-2920, Fax: (613) 232-3735

**League for Human Rights of B'nai Brith**
Dr. Karen Mock, National Director
15 Hove Street, Suite 210
Toronto, ON M3H 4Y8
Phone: (416) 633-6227, Fax: (416) 630-2159

**Regional Offices:**
**National Office**
Dr. Karen Mock, National Director
15 Hove Street, Suite 210
Toronto, ON M3H 4Y8
Phone: (416) 633-6227, Fax: (416) 630-2159

**Eastern Region**
Robert Libman, Regional Director
6900 boul. Decarie, bur. 219
Montreal, QC H3X 2T8
Phone: (514) 733-5377, Fax: (514) 342-9632

**Manitoba Association for Rights and Liberties**
177 Lombard Ave., Suite 502
Winnipeg, MB R38 0W5
Phone: (204) 947-0213, Fax: (204) 956-0976

**Mid-West Region**
Sophie Tapper, Regional Director
123 Doncaster Street, Suite C403
Winnipeg, MB R3N 2B2
Phone: (204) 487-9623, Fax: (204) 487-9648

**Ontario Coalition for Abortion Clinics**
Michelle Robidoux, Organizer
Station P, Box 753
Toronto, ON M5S 2Z1
Phone: (416) 969-8463

**Right to Life Association of Toronto**
June Scandiffio, President
120 Eglinton Ave., Suite 700
Toronto, ON M4P 1E2
Phone: (416) 483-7869, Fax: (416) 483-7052

# Physically/Mentally Challenged

**Accessible Housing Society**
Dianne Nickel, Exec. Director
2003-14th Street NW, Suite 103
Calgary AB T2M 3N4
Phone: (403) 282-1872, Fax: (403) 284-0304

**Action League of Physically Handicapped Adults**
Michelle Robert-Cronin, Access Services Coordinator
1940 Oxford Street East, Suite 8
London, ON N5V 4L8
Phone: (519) 457-3070, Fax: (519) 457-3069

**Autism Society Ontario**
Joan Cuipak, Exec. Director
1 Greensboro Drive
Toronto, ON M9W 1C8
Phone: (416) 512-9880, Fax: (416) 512-8026

**The Bob Rumball Centre for the Deaf**
Shirley Cassel, Programs Director
2395 Bayview Ave.
North York, ON M2L 1A2
Phone: (416) 449-9651, Fax: (416) 449-8881

**The B.C. Lions Society
for Children with Disabilities**
Foundation for Children with Disabilities
177 West 7th Ave., #300
Vancouver, BC V5Y 1K5
Phone: (604) 873-1865, Fax: (604) 873-0166

**BC Rehabilitation Society**
William Fraser, President/CEO
G.F. Strong Ctr., 4255 Laurel Street
Vancouver, BC V5Z 2G9
Phone: (604) 734-1313, Fax: (604) 737-6359

**Calgary Action Group of the Disabled**
Mary Lee Phipps, Manager
426-8th Ave. SE
Calgary AB T2G 0L7
Phone: (403) 262-5400, Fax: (403) 262-3004

**Calgary Residential Services Society**
Sheila Gibson, Exec. Director

3410 Spruce Drive SW
Calgary, AB T3C 3A4
Phone: (403) 246-4450, Fax: (403) 246-4530

**Canadian Association for Community Living**
Diane Richler, Exec. Vice President
Kinsmen Bldg., York University, 4700 Keele Street
North York, ON M3J 1P3
Phone: (416) 661-9611, Fax: (416) 661-5701

**Canadian Association of the Deaf**
James Roots, Exec. Director
2435 Holly Lane, Suite 205
Ottawa, ON KIV 7P2
Phone: (613) 526-4785, Fax: (613) 526-4718

**Canadian Hearing Society**
David Allen, Exec. Director
271 Spadian Road
Toronto, ON M5R 2V3
Phone: (416) 964-9595, Fax: (416) 928-2506

**Canadian Paraplegic Association**
Eric Boyd, Managing Director
1101 Prince of Wales Drive, Suite 320
Ottawa, ON K2C 3W7
Phone: (613) 723-1033, Fax: (613) 723-1060

**Canine Vision Canada**
Ron Brown, Exec. Director
Box 907
Oakville, ON L6J 5E8
Phone: (905) 842-2891, Fax: (905) 842-3373

**The Cerebral Palsy Foundation (Grotto)**
Charles Sinclair, Exec. Secretary
324 Scarborough Road
Toronto, ON M4E 3M8
Phone: (416) 699-6297

**Christian Blind Mission International**
Art Brooker, National Director
Box 800
Stouffville, ON LA4 7Z9
Phone: (905) 640-6464, Fax: (905) 640-4332

## Community Involvement of the Disabled
Willena Cook, President
295 George Street, Suite 304
Sydney, NS B1P 1J7
Phone: (902) 564-9817, Fax: (902) 564-5758

## Connect Society
Colleen Robinson, Exec. Director/CEO
11342-127th Street
Edmonton, AB T5M 0T8
Phone: (403) 454-9581, Fax: (403) 447-5820

## Council of Canadians with Disabilities
Mr. Laurie Beachell, National Coordinator
294 Portage Ave., Suite 926
Winnipeg, MB R3C 0B9
Phone: (204) 947-0303, Fax: (204) 942-4625

## Deaf Youth Canada
Joseph McLaughlin, Chairperson
5455 Rumble Street
Burnaby, BC V5J 2B7
Phone: (604) 664-8560, Fax: (403) 664-8561

## Disability Information Services of Canada
Diana Brent, Project Coordinator
501-18th Ave. SW, Suite 304
Calgary, AB T2S 0C7
Phone: (403) 229-2177, Fax: (403) 229-1878

## Disabled Peoples' International
Lucy Wong-Hernandez, Exec. Director
101-7 Evergreen Place
Winnipeg, MB R3L 2T3
Phone: (204) 287-8010, Fax: (204) 453-1367

## Easter Seal Ability Council, South Office
Susan law, South Regional Administrator
811 Manning Road NE
Calgary, AB T2E 7L4
Phone: (403) 235-5662, Fax: (403) 248-1716

## Easter Seals/March of Dimes
William A. Hoch, Exec. Director
90 Eglinton Ave. East, Suite 511
Toronto, ON M4P 2Y3
Phone: (416) 932-8382, Fax: (416) 932-9844

## Handicapped Action Group, Inc.
Allan Buchan
1201 Jasper Drive, Suite A
Thunder Bay, ON P7B 6R2
Phone: (807) 343-0414, Fax: (807) 344-6140

## Hearing Ear Dogs of Canada
Ron Brown, Exec. Director
Box 907
Oakville, ON L6J 5E8
Phone: (905) 842-7344, Fax: (905) 842-3373

## Independence Plus Inc.
Brenda Seely, Exec. Director
66 Waterloo Street, Suite 125
Saint John, NB E2L 3P4
Phone: (506) 648-9148, Fax: (506) 648-3423

## Intervention Manitoba Inc.
Cheryl Ramey, Program Director
307 Devon Ave.
Winnipeg, MB R2G 0C4
Phone: (204) 338-1617, Fax: (204) 339-6193

## Kinsmen Rehabilitation Foundation of B.C.
Andy Danyliu, CEO
999 West Broadway, Suite 300
Vancouver, BC V5Z 4R1
Phone: (604) 736-8841, Fax: (604) 738-0015

## Manitoba League of Persons With Disabilities
David Martin, Provincal Coordinator
294 Portage Ave., Suite 200
Winnipeg, MB R3C 0B9
Phone: (204) 943-6099, Fax: (204) 942-3146

## Ontario March of Dimes
Andria Spindel, Exec. Director
10 Overlea Blvd.
Toronto, ON M4H 1A4
Phone: (416) 425-3463, Fax: (416) 425-1920

## Persons United for Self-Help Central
Marilyn Ferrel, Coordinator
79 Court Street North
Thunder Bay, ON P7A 4T7
Phone: (807) 345-3400

# Retirement

## Alberta Council on Aging
Christine Lawrence, Exec. Director
#1740, 10130-103rd Street
Edmonton, AB T5J 3N9
Phone: (403) 423-7781, Fax: (403) 425-9246

## Assn. of Adult Day Support Programs
Barbara J. McKernan, Exec. Director
10023-115th Street
Edmonton, AB T5K 1S9
Phone: (403) 454-9107, Fax: (403) 482-3696

## Calgary Seniors' Resource Society
Theresa Robertson, Administrator
807 6th Street SE, Box 716
Calgary, AB T2G 4V8
Phone: (403) 266-6200, Fax: (403) 269-5183

## Canadian Assn. of Retired Persons
Murray Morgenthau, Exec. Director
27 Queen Street East, Suite 1304
Toronto, ON M5C 2M6
Phone: (416) 363-8748, Fax: (416) 363-8747

## Canadian Pensioners Concerned Inc.
### National Board:
Bruce Mutch, President
51 Bond Street
Toronto, ON M5B 1X1
Phone: (416) 368-5222

### Provincial Divisions:

### Alberta
Roy Swift, President
11622-74th Ave. NW
Edmonton, AB T6G 0G2
Phone: (403) 434-3302

### Nova Scotia
Joan Lay, President
7071 Bayers Road, #302
Halifax, NS B3L 2C2
Phone: (902) 455-7684, Fax: (902) 455-1825

### Ontario
Mae Harman, President
51 Bond Street
Toronto, ON M5B 1X1
Phone: (416) 368-5222, Fax: (416) 486-1528

## Chats-Community Home Assistance to Seniors
Deborah Egan, Exec. Director
628 Davis Drive, Suite 200
Newmarket, ON L3Y 8P8
Phone: (905) 898-3967, ext. 317, Fax: (905) 898-3626

## Meals Here and There Inc.
Gloria Greff
310 Danforth Ave.
Toronto, ON M4K 1K5
Phone: (416) 466-0587, Fax: (416) 252-5770

## National Pensioners and Senior Citizens Federation
Edith Johnston, Secretary
3033 Lake Shore Blvd. West
Toronto, ON M8V 1K5
Phone: (416) 251-7042, Fax: (416) 252-5770

## Older Adult Centres Assn. of Ontario
Anita Machin, Admin. Services Manager
1185 Eglinton Ave. East, Suite 604
North York, ON M3C 3C6
Phone: (416) 426-7038, Fax: (416) 426-7388

## Ontario Assn. of Non-Profit Homes and Services for Seniors (O.A.N.H.S.S.)
Michael Klejman, Exec. Director
7050 Weston Road, 7th Floor, Suite 700
Woodbridge, ON L4L 8G7
Phone: (905) 851-8821, Fax: (905) 851-0744

## Retirement Plus
Barbara Buckspan, Manager
344 Bloor Street West, Room 207
Toronto, ON M5S 3A7
Phone: (416) 961-6888, Fax: (416) 961-6859

# Social Organizations

## Association of Canadian Clubs
Barbara E. Crowder, National Director
237 Nepean Street
Ottawa, ON K2P 0B7
Phone: (613) 236-8288, Fax: (613) 236-8299

## Canadian Progress Club
Molly Trussler, Exec. Director
2395 Bayview Ave.
North York, ON M2L 1A2
Phone: (416) 446-1830, Fax: (416) 446-6857

## The Empire Club of Canada
Royal York Hotel, Convention Mezzanine
100 Front Street West
Toronto, ON M5J 1E3
Phone: (416) 364-2878

## Knights of Columbus
## Canadian Provincial Offices:

### Manitoba State Council
410 De Salaberry Ave., Suite 201
Winnipeg, MB R2L 0Y7
Phone: (204) 663-8022, Fax: (204) 669-7947

### Saskatchewan State Council
Bob Schlosser, Administration Secretary
639 Main Street
Saskatoon, SK S7H 0J8
Phone: (306) 665-7858, Fax: (306) 665-1245

## The Rotary Club
## Chapters:

### Charlottetown
John Scales, President
Box 608
Charlottetown, PE C1A 2S4
Phone: (902) 566-4444

### Edmonton
Virginia Nascimento, Exec. Secretary
10111 Bellamy Hill NW
Edmonton, AB T5J 1N7
Phone: (403) 429-3256, Fax: (403) 426-4355

### Fredericton
Ray Wilson, President
Box 301
Fredericton, NB E3A 5B6
Phone: (506) 454-4461

### Montreal
1 Place du Canada
Montreal, QC H3B 4C9
Phone: (514) 861-6385, Fax: (514) 861-6386

### Regina
W.L. Whelan
Box 164
Regina, SK S4P 2Z6
Phone: (306) 584-0056, Fax: (306) 584-0056

### St. John's
Box 1794
St. John's, NF A1C 2Z6
Phone: (709) 781-4010, Fax: (709) 781-4010

### Toronto
Eunice Doucette, Exec. Director
Royal York Hotel, 100 Front Street West
Toronto, ON M5J 1E4
Phone: (416) 363-0604, Fax: (416) 363-0686

### Whitehorse
1203 Spruce Street
Whitehorse, YT Y1A 4G4
Phone: (867) 633-5479, Fax: (867) 633-4935

### Winnipeg
J. Snider, Rotary Manager
350 St. Mary Ave.
Winnipeg, MB R3C 3J2
Phone: (204) 942-2058, Fax: (204) 942-6654

# Social Services

**Action for Social Change**
Pamela Cross
20 Chestnut Street
Kingston, ON K7K 3X3
Phone: (613) 544-2382

**Alcohol & Drug Concerns, Inc.**
Karl Burden, CEO
4500 Sheppard Ave. East, Unit H
Agincourt, ON M1S 3R6
Phone: (416) 293-3400, Fax: (416) 293-1142

**Alcoholics Anonymous-Central
Service Committee**
Box 3133H
Halifax, NS B3K 5Z1
Phone: (902) 461-1119

**Big Brothers of Canada**
Michael McKnight, Exec. Director
5230 South Service Road
Burlington, ON L7L 5K2
Phone: (905) 639-0461, Fax: (905) 639-0124

**Regional Associations:**

**Big Brothers and Sisters - Atlantic Region**
Betty Hitchcock, Resource Coordinator
29 Bedell Ave.
St. John, NB E2K 2C1
Phone: (506) 648-9794, Fax: (506) 648-9794

**Big Brothers of B.C. and Affiliate Big Sisters**
George Alliston, Regional Exec. Director
Unit 371, 800-15355 24th Ave.
Surrey, BC V4A 2H9
Phone: (604) 878-1037, Fax: (604) 536-5717

**Big Brothers of Ontario**
Laurie LeBlanc, Regional Exec. Director
5230 South Service Road
Burlington, ON L7L 5K2
Phone: (905) 639-0461, Fax: (905) 639-0124

**Big Brothers of Metropolitan Toronto**
Barbara Hickey, Exec. Director

1320 Yonge Street
Toronto, ON M4T 1X2
Phone: (416) 925-8981, Fax: (416) 925-4671

**Big Brothers and Sisters of Saint John**
Lauri Flood, Exec. Director
66 Waterloo Street
St. John, NB E2L 3P4
Phone: (506) 635-1145, Fax: (506) 633-7781

**Big Brothers of Greater Vancouver**
Gordon Therriault, Exec. Director
1193 Kingsway Street, Suite 102
Vancouver, BC V5V 3C9
Phone: (604) 876-2447, Fax: (604) 876-2446

**Big Brothers Association of Winnipeg, Inc.**
Karen Fonseth, Exec. Director
177 Lombard Ave., #803
Winnipeg, MB R3B 0W5
Phone: (204) 988-9200, Fax: (204) 988-9208

**Big Sisters Association of Ontario**
Madeline Bergin, Exec. Director
2750 Dufferin Street
Toronto, ON M6B 3R4
Phone: (416) 789-7859, Fax: (416) 789-7850

**Canadian Association of Elizabeth Fry Societies**
Kim Pate, Exec. Director
151 Slater Street, Suite 701
Ottawa, ON K1P 5H3
Phone: (613) 238-2422, Fax: (613) 232-7130

**Member Associations:**

**The Elizabeth Fry Society of Calgary**
Deborah Bartlett, Michelle Clarke
1009-7th Ave. SW, Room 204
Calgary, AB T2P 1A8
Phone: (403) 294-0737, Fax: (403) 262-0285

**Elizabeth Fry Society of Cape Bretos**
Darlene MacEachern, Exec. Director
106 Townsend Street
Sydney, NS B1P 5E1
Phone: (902) 539-6165, Fax: (902) 539-0290

**The Elizabeth Fry Society of Edmonton**
Carol Hutchings, Exec. Director
10523-100th Ave.
Edmonton, AB T5J 0A8
Phone: (403) 421-1175, Fax: (403) 425-8089

**The Elizabeth Fry Society of Kingston**
Trish Crawford, Exec. Director
308 Wellington Street
Kingston, ON K7K 7A8
Phone: (613) 544-1744, Fax: (613) 544-0676

**Elizabeth Fry Society of Mainland Nova Scotia**
2830 Agricola Street, #100
Halifax, NS B3K 4E4
Phone: (902) 454-5041, Fax: (902) 420-2873

**The Elizabeth Fry Society of Manitoba**
Carol Thiessen, Exec. Director
773 Selkirk Ave.
Winnipeg, MB R3W 2N5
Phone: (204) 589-7335, Fax: (204) 589-7338

**Elizabeth Fry Society of New Brunswick**
Jean Steeves, President
39 McDougall Ave.
Moncton, NB E1C 6B1
Phone: (506) 789-7077, Fax: (506) 853-7582

**Canadian Citizenship Federation**
Read E. Brook, Exec. Secretary
396 Cooper Street, Suite 402
Ottawa, ON K2P 2H7
Phone: (613) 235-1467, Fax: (613) 235-3233

**Capital Families Association**
Marjorie Schmidt, President
555 Goldstream Ave.
Victoria, BC V9B 2W4
Phone: (250) 478-1122, Fax: (250) 478-9199

**Edmonton John Howard Society**
Maureen Collins, Exec. Director
10526 Jaser Ave., Suite 301
Edmonton, AB T5J 1Z7
Phone: (403) 428-7590, Fax: (403) 425-1549

**Child Welfare League of Canada**
Sandra G. Scarth, Exec. Director

180 Argyle Ave.
Ottawa, ON K2P 1B7
Phone: (613) 235-4412, Fax: (613) 788-5075

**The Family Centre of Northern Alberta**
Rod Rode, Exec. Director
9912-106th Street
Edmonton, ON M5B 1Z8
Phone: (403) 423-2831, Fax: (403) 426-4918

**Family Service Association of Metropolitan Toronto**
Paul Zarnke, Exec. Director
355 Church Street
Toronto, ON M5B 1Z8
Phone: (416) 595-9230, Fax: (416) 595-0242

**Family Service Bureau**
Corinne Bokitch, Exec. Director
2020 Halifax Street
Regina, SK S4P 1T7
Phone: (306) 757-6675, Fax: (306) 757-0133

**Family Service Canada**
Margaret Fietz, President/CEO
220 Laurier Ave. West, Suite 600
Ottawa, ON K1P 5Z9
Phone: (613) 230-9960, Fax: (613) 230-5884

**Family Service Centre of Ottawa-Carleton**
Rosemary Hegge, Administration Manager
119 Ross Ave.
Ottawa, ON K1Y 0N6
Phone: (613) 725-3601, Fax: (613) 725-5651

**Family Service Ontario**
Dr. Hugh Drouin, Exec. Director
1243 Islington Ave., Suite 802
Toronto, ON M8X 1Y9
Phone: (416) 231-6003, Fax: (416) 231-2405

**Goodwill Industries of Toronto**
Jim Dreiling, President
234 Adelaide East
Toronto, ON M5A 1M9
Phone: (416) 362-4711, Fax: (416) 362-0720

**Lions Clubs International, Multiple District A**
155 Beaver Creek Road East, Unit 9

Richmond Hill, ON L4B 2N1
Phone: (905) 771-6400, Fax: (905) 771-6692

## Lookout Emergency Aid Society
Karen O'Shannacery, Exec. Director
429 Alexander Street
Vancouver, BC V6A 1C6
Phone: (604) 255-0340, Fax: (604) 255-0790

## Christian Volunteers in Corrections
Waldy Klassen, Exec. Director
2825A Clearbrook Road
Clearbrook, BC V2T 2Z3
Phone: (604) 859-3215, Fax: (604) 859-1216

## Parent Finders Incororated-Toronto
Holly Kramer, President
Station F, Box 1008
Toronto, ON M4T 2T7
Phone: (416) 465-8434

## Parent Finders of Canada
Joan E. Vanstone, National Director
3998 Bayridge Ave.
West Vancouver, BC V3V 3J5
Phone: (604) 926-1096, Fax: (604) 926-2037

## Parents Against Drugs
Diane Buhler, Exec. Director
7 Hawksdale Road
North York, ON M3K 1W3
Phone: (416) 395-4970, Fax: (416) 395-4972

## People Against Impaired Driving
Donna Christensen, President
10005-84th Street
Edmonton, AB T6A 3P8
Phone: (403) 462-2426, Fax: (403) 462-2596

## Personal Growth Foundation
David Michaels, Marketing Consultant
51st Street, Box 37057, Lynwood
Edmonton, AB T5R 5Y2
Phone: (403) 434-4834

## SOS Children's Villages Canada
Carol Faulkner, National Director
130 Albert Street, Suite 1203
Ottawa, ON K1P 5G4
Phone: (613) 232-3309

## Saskatchewan Association for Community Living
Karen Rongve, Exec. Director
3031 Louise Street
Saskatoon, SK S7J 3L1
Phone: (306) 955-3344, Fax: (306) 373-3070

## Saskatoon Crisis Intervention Services
Bob Sims, Exec. Director
1410-20th Street West
Saskatoon, SK S7M 0Z4
Phone: (306) 933-6200, Fax: (306) 664-1974

## Second Harvest Food Support Committee
Zoe Cormack Jones, Exec. Director
444 Yonge Street
Toronto, ON M5B 2H4
Phone: (416) 408-2594, Fax: (416) 408-2598

## Silent Voice Canada, Inc.
Beverly Pageau, Exec. Director
699 Coxwell Ave.
Toronto, ON M4C 3C1
Phone: (416) 463-1104, Fax: (416) 778-1876

## Survivors of Suicide Support Programs
Anne Cole, Health Promotion Coordinator
349A George Street North, Suite 301
Peterborough, ON K9H 3P9
Phone: (705) 748-6711, Fax: (705) 748-2577

## Toronto Association of Neighbourhood Services
Barbara Volk, President
29 Summerhill Gardens
Toronto, ON M4T 1B3
Phone: (416) 924-8262, Fax: (416) 924-2722

## Urban Alliance of Race Relations
Antoni Shelton, Exec. Director
675 King Street West, Suite 202
Toronto, ON M5V 1M9
Phone: (416) 7033-6607, Fax: (416) 703-4415

## Visiting Homemakers Association
David A. Wright, Exec. Director
170 Merton Street
Toronto, ON M4S 1A1
Phone: (416) 489-2500, Fax: (416) 489-7533

# Veterans

## The Army Cadet League of Canada
C.J. Devaney, Exec. Director
305 Rideau Street
Ottawa, ON K1N 9E5
Phone: (613) 991-4348, Fax: (613) 990-8701

## Regional Offices:

## Ontario
Peter B. Kristjansen, Exec. Director
4900 Yonge Street, Suite 600
North York, ON M2N 6B7
Phone: (416) 952-4531, Fax: (416) 952-4533

## Quebec
Rejean Larise, General Manager
Ed. 22, C.P. 1000
Courcelette, QC G0A 4Z0
Phone: (418) 844-5000, Fax: (418) 844-2133

## Army, Navy and Air Force Veterans in Canada
Ian D. Inrig, Dominion Secretary Treasurer
6 Beechwood Ave., Suite 2
Vanier, ON K1L 8B4
Phone: (613) 744-0222, Fax: (613) 744-0208

## Provincial Headquarters:

## Alberta
J.R. Brooks, Secretary Treasurer
755 Lake Twintree Court SE
Calgary, AB T2J 2W2
Phone: (403) 278-5853, Fax: (403) 271-4942

## British Columbia
Mary Mcleod, Secretary Treasurer
951 East 8th Ave., #200
Vancouver, BC V5T 4L2
Phone: (604) 874-8105, Fax: (604) 874-0633

## Manitoba
K.A. Eccles, Secretary Treasurer
275 Garry Street
Winnipeg, MB R3C 1H9
Phone: (204) 943-6166, Fax: (204) 943-6166

## Nova Scotia Command
Reid Moore, Secretary
87 Rendell Drive
Bras D'Or, NS B0C 1B0
Phone: (902) 544-1018, Fax: (902) 544-1018

## Ontario
Ken S. Barnett Secretary Treasurer
408 Royal York Road
Toronto, ON M8Y 2R5
Phone: (416) 259-4145, Fax: (416) 259-1677

## Quebec
Roger Chabot
15837, rue Bellerive
Montreal, QC H1A 5A6
Phone: (514) 642-5309, Fax: (514) 640-2088

## Saskatchewan
E. Gillette, Secretary Treasurer
359 North 1st Ave.
Saskatoon, SK S7K 1X5
Phone: (306) 652-3171, Fax: (306) 653-4760

## Canadian Corps Association
S.W. Heesaker, Secretary
201 Niagara Street
Toronto, ON M5V 1C9
Phone: (604) 681-9207, Fax: (604) 681-9864

## Canadian Corps of Commissionaires
100 Gloucester Street, Suite 201
Ottawa, ON K2P 0A4
Phone: (613) 236-4936, Fax: (613) 563-8508

## Royal Canadian Military Institute
Norbert Luth, General Manager
426 University Ave.
Toronto, ON M5G 1S9
Phone: (416) 597-0286, Fax: (416) 597-6919

## Veterans Against Nuclear Arms
David Morgan, National Chairman
240 Holyrood Road
North Vancouver, BC V7N 2R5
Phone: (604) 985-7147, Fax: (604) 985-1260

# Volume Discount Orders

**Direct Selling**
**NETWORK MARKETING**
Companies · Distributors
Marketing Solutions
Ask us About Our
Volume Discount Program

*Ideal For Promotion, Recruiting, Marketing,*
*Premium Incentives, or a High Profit Center*

**Call Toll Free**
**(800) 496-0277**

# Womens Rights

**Aboriginal Womens Council of Saskatchewan**
Teresa Woods, Council Member
118-12th Street East, #101
Prince Albert, SK S6V 1B6
Phone: (306) 763-6005, Fax: (306) 922-6034

**Action Travil des femmes**
Ginette Bernier
4706, rue Wellington
Verdun, QC H4G 1X3
Phone: (514) 768-7233, Fax: (514) 768-8697

**Alberta Council of Women's Shelters**
Arlene Chapman, Provincial Coordinator
9912-106th Street, #34
Edmonton, AB T5K 1C5

**Calgary Women's Emergency Shelter**
Karen A. Blase, Exec. Director
Edmonton Trail NE, Box 52051
Calgary, AB T2E 8K9
Phone: (403) 290-1552, Fax (403) 237-7728

**Canadian Association of Sexual Assault Centres**
77 East 20th Street
Vancouver, BC V5V 1L7
Phone: (604) 872-8212, Fax: (604) 876-8450

**Central Alberta Women's Emergency Shelter Society**
Mary Boyd, Exec. Director
Box 561
Red Deer, AB T4N 5G1
Phone: (403) 346-5643, Fax: (403) 341-3510

**Education Wife Assault**
Tiffany Veinot
427 Bloor Street West, Box 7
Toronto, ON M5S 1X7
Phone: (416) 968-3422, Fax: (416) 968-3425

**National Council of Women of Canada**
Julie Johnston, Exec. Assistant
270 MacLaren Street, Suite 33
Ottawa, ON K2P 0M3
Phone: (613) 232-5025, Fax: (613) 232-8419

**New Brunswick Women's Institute**
Stella Quarterman, Office Administrator
65 Brunswick Street, Room 251
Fredericton, NB E3B 1G5
Phone: (506) 454-0798, Fax: (506) 458-2606

**The Ontario Coalition of Rape Crisis Centres**
George Sabourin, Exec. Director
355 Wilson Ave.
Timmins, ON P4N 2T7
Phone: (705) 268-8381, Fax: (705) 268-3332

**Prince Edward Island Right to Life Association**
Vincent McIntyre, President
Box 1988
Charlottetown, PE C1A 7N7
Phone: (902) 894-5473, Fax: (902) 892-2424

**Saskatchewan Women's Institute**
Beth Ratzlaff, Administration Coordinator
117 Science Place
Saskatoon, SK S7N 5C8
Phone: (306) 966-5566, Fax: (306) 966-8717

**Support to Single Parents, Inc.**
Nancy J. Hartling, Exec. Director
154 Queen Street
Moncton, NB E1C 1K8
Phone: (506) 858-1303, Fax: (506) 855-4116

**Vancouver Status of Women**
877 East Hastings Street, #309
Vancouver, BC V6A 3Y1
Phone: (604) 255-5511, Fax: (604) 255-5511

**Womanpower Inc.**
Darlene Labadie, Coordinator
171 Queens Ave., Suite 604
London, ON N6A 1C1
Phone: (519) 438-1782, Fax: (519) 438-7904

**Women in Transition Inc.**
Rita Kohli, Exec. Director
900 Dufferin Street, Box 24029
Toronto, ON M6H 4H6
Phone: (416) 533-3428, Fax: (416) 539-9338

# Youth

**Adoption Council of Canada**
Elspeth Ross, Information Coordinator
Box 8442, Stn. T
Ottawa, ON K1G 3H8
Phone: (613) 235-1566, Fax: (613) 788-5075

**Alberta Block Parent Assn.**
Linda Maciocha, Secretary
166 Greenwood Drive
Spruce Grove, AB T7X 1Y7
Phone: (403) 960-9331

**Alliance for Children**
Kealy Wilkinson, Exec. Director
60 St. Claire Ave. East, Suite 1032
Toronto, ON M4 T 1N5
Phone: (416) 515-0466

**B.C. Parents in Crisis Society**
Julie Norton, Exec. Director
Suite 620, 1155 West Pender Street
Vancouver, BC V6E 2P4
Phone: (604) 669-1616, (800) 665-6880 (in B.C.)
Fax: (604) 669-1636

**Block Parent Program Inc.**
Marianne MacBride, Chairman
83 Sherwood Forest Drive
Marham, ON L3P 1P9
Phone: (800) 563-277

**Boys and Girls Club of Alberta**
John Mulka, Exec. Director
11759 Groat Road
Edmonton, AB T5M 3K6
Phone: (403) 453-8656

**Boys and Girls Clubs of British Columbia**
Keith Pattinson, Regional Director
7595 Victoria Drive
Vancouver, BC V5P 3Z6
Phone: (604) 321-5621, Fax: (604) 321-5941

**Boys and Girls Clubs of Canada**
7100 Woodbine Ave., Suite 405

Markham, ON L3R 5G2
Phone: (905) 477-7272, Fax: (905) 477-2056

**Boys and Girls Clubs of Greater Vancouver**
Richard L. Ryan, Exec. Director
2875 St. George
Vancouver, BC V5T 3R8
Phone: (604) 879-6554, Fax: (604) 879-6525

**Boys and Girls Clubs of New Brunswick**
Linda M. Stephenson, Exec. Director
440 Wilsey Road, Suite 205
Federicton, NB E3B 7G5
Phone: (506) 444-0815, Fax: (506) 444-0817

**Boys and Girls Clubs of
New Foundland and Labrador**
Jackie Pollard, Provincial Coordinator
810 Pleasantville, Box 8700
St. John's, NF A1B 4J6
Phone: (709) 722-5556, Fax: (709) 722-5576

**Boys and Girls Clubs of Ontario**
Marion Price, Exec. Director
346 Main Street East
Hamilton, ON L8N 1J1
Phone: (905) 521-4441, Fax: (905) 521-3062

**Canadian 4-H Council/Foundation**
Mike Nowosad, Exec. Director
1690 Woodward Drive, Suite 208
Ottawa, ON K2C 3R8
Phone: (613) 723-4444, Fax: (613) 723-0745

**Canadian Assn. for Young Children/Assoc.
canadienne pour les jeunes enfants**
Gloria McLaren, Office Manager
5417 Rannock Ave.
Winnipeg, MB R3R 0N3
Phone: (204) 831-1658

**Canadian Child Care Federation/Federation
cdnne des services de garde a l'enfance**
Dianne Bascombe, Exec. Director
30 Rosemount Ave., Suite 100

Ottawa, ON K1Y 1P4
Phone: (613) 729-5289, (800) 858-1412
Fax: (613) 729-3159

## Canadian Council for Exceptional Children
Jean Ganley, Admin. Assistant
101 Politek Court, #36
Gloucester, ON K1J 9J2
Phone: (613) 747-9226

## Canadian Foundation for the Love of Children
Edmonton Centre
1524 Midland Walyn Tower
Edmonton, AB T5J 2Z2
Phone: (403) 448-1752, Fax: (403) 441-9893

## Canadian Foundation for Children, Youth & the Law
720 Spadina Ave., #405
Toronto, ON M5S 2T9
Phone: (416) 920-1633, Fax: (416) 920-5855

## Canadian Friends of Boys Town Jerusalem
Denise Gold, Director
2788 Bathurst Street, Suite 200
Toronto, ON M6B 3A3
Phone: (416) 789-7241, Fax: (416) 789-1090

## Canadian Junior Chamber
James Bradfield, President
701 Rossland Road East, Suite 834
Whitby, ON L1N 9K3
Phone: (905) 948-0048, Fax: (613) 666-5434

## Canadian Young Judaea
Risa Epstein-Gamliel, Exec. Director
788 Marlee Ave.
Toronto, ON M6B 3K1
Phone: (416) 781-5156, Fax: (416) 787-3100

## Canadian Youth Foundation
Lucie Bohac Konrad, Exec. Director
215 Cooper Street, 3rd Floor
Ottawa, ON K2P 0G2
Phone: 613) 231-6474

## 4-H Foundation of Alberta
Jerry Hall, Chairman
Box 550

Edmonton, AB T5J 2K8
Phone: (403) 427-2541, Fax: (403) 422-7755

## Child Care Advocacy Association of Canada
Jocelyne Tougas, Exec. Director
323 Chapel Street
Ottawa, ON K1N 7Z2
Phone: (613) 594-3196, Fax: (613) 594-9375

## Child Find Alberta Society
Eric R. Sommerfeldt, Exec. Director
424-10th Street NW, Suite 101
Calgary, AB T2N 1V9
Phone: (403) 270-3463, Fax: (403) 270-8355

## Child Find Canada
Robert N. Morris, Past President
710 Dorval Drive, Suite 508
Oakville, ON L6K 3V7
Phone: (905) 845- 3463, Fax: (905) 845-9621

## Child Find New Brunswick
Keith Ross, Exec. Director
210 Brunswick Street
Fredericton, NB E3B 1G9
Phone: ( 506) 459-7250, Fax:  (506) 459-8742

## Child Find (Ontario) Inc.
Jackie Cutmore, Exec. Director
710 Dorval Drive, Suite  210
Oakville, ON L6K 3V7
Phone: (905) 842-5353, (800) 387-7962

## Child Find PEI  Inc.
Mary Scott, President
Box 1092
Charlottetown, PE C1A 7M4
Phone: (902) 368-1678, Fax: (902) 368-1389

## Child Find Saskatchewan Inc.
Phyllis Hallatt, President
1002 Arlington Ave., #41
Saskatoon, SK S7H 2X7
Phone: (306) 955-0070, (800) 513-FIND (3463) (in Saskatchewan), Fax: (306) 373-1311

## Girls Guides of Canada
Christine A. Featherstone, Exec. Director
50 Merton Street

Toronto, ON M4S 1A3
Phone: (416) 487-5281, Fax: (416) 487-5570

## Hostelling International-Canada

Gratton Sheely, National Director
205 Catherine Street, Suite 400
Ottawa, ON K2P 1C3
Phone: (613) 237-7884, Fax: (613) 237-7868

## Provincial Offices:

### Northern Alberta

Catherine Wilde, Marketing Manager
10926-88th Ave.
Edmonton, AB T6G 0Z1
Phone: (403) 432-7798, Fax: (403) 433-7781

### Southern Alberta

Jim Zackowski, Exec. Director
1414 Kensington Road NW, Suite 203
Calgary, AB T2N 3P9
Phone: (403) 283-5551, Fax: (403) 283-6503

### British Columbia

John Hopkins, Exec. Director
134 Abbott Street, #402
Vancouver, BC V6B 2K4
Phone: (604) 684-7111, Fax: (604) 684-7181

### Great Lakes

Joel Marier, Exec. Director
209 Church Street
Toronto, ON M5B 1Y7
Phone: (416) 363-0697, Fax: (416) 368-6499

### Manitoba

Owen Desnoyers, Exec. Director
194-A Sherbrook Street
Winnipeg, MB R3C 2B6
Phone: (204) 784-1131, Fax: (204) 784-1133

### Nova Scotia

Robert Semple, Exec. Director
5516 Spring Garden Road, Box 3010 South
Halifax, NS B3J 3G6
Phone: (902) 425-5450, Fax: (902) 425-5606

### Ontario East

75 Nicholas Street
Ottawa, ON K1N 7B9
Phone: (613) 235-2595, Fax: (613) 235-9202

### Quebec

Claude Coude
4545, av. Pierre-De-Coubertin
Montreal, QC H1V 3R2
Phone: (514) 252-3117, Fax: (514) 252-3119

### Saskatchewan

Lianne Gusway, Exec. Director
2014-14th Ave.
Regina, SK S4P 0X5
Phone: (306) 791-8160, Fax: (306) 721-2667

## JMJ Children's Fund of Canada Inc./Caisse canadienne JMJ de l'enfance

M.J. Ferrari, President
20 Marlborough Ave.
Ottawa, ON K1N 8E7
Phone: (613) 232-9829, Fax: (613) 232-9829

## Junior Achievement of British Columbia

Carole Simpson, President
475 West Georgia Street, Suite 110
Vancouver, BC V6B 4M9
Phone: (604) 688-3887, Fax: (604) 689-5299

## Junior Achievement of Canada

George Habib, President/CEO
1 Westside Drive
Toronto, ON M9C 1B2
Phone: (416) 622-4602, Fax: (416) 622-6821

## Junior Achievement of Manitoba Inc.

Joan Lawless, Exec. Director
5-266A Linwood Street
Winnipeg, MB R3J 2C6
Phone: (204) 956-6080, Fax: (204) 831-5284

## Kids Help Foundation

Rhoda Payne, Managing Director
439 University Ave., Street 300
Toronto, ON M5G 1Y8
Phone: (416) 586-5437, Fax: (416) 586-0651

## Manitoba Child Care Assn. Inc.

Dorothy Dudek, Exec. Director
364 McGregor Street
Winnipeg, MB R2W 4X3
Phone: (204) 586-8587, Fax: (204) 589-5613

**National CGIT Association**
Susan Rogers, National Coordinator
195 The West Mall, Suite 414
Etobicoke, ON M9L 5K1
Phone: (416) 622-3979, Fax: (416) 622-3979

**Manitoba & NW Ontario CGIT Association**
Mrs. J. Instance, Chairperson
11-131 Tyndall Ave.
Winnipeg, MB R2X 0Z3
Phone: (204) 633-6480

**Maritime Regional CGIT Committee**
Joan Cho, Chairperson
35 Main Street
St. Stephen, NB E3L 1Z3
Phone: (506) 466-1013

**Ontario CGIT Association**
Joanne Wood, President
310 Danforth Ave.
Toronto, ON M4K 1N6
Phone: (416) 465-5726, Fax: (416) 465-5726

**New Directions for Children,
Youth and Families**
Dr. Linda J. Trigg, Exec. Director
777 Portage Ave., Suite  400
Winnipeg, MB R3G ON3
Phone: (204) 786-7051, Fax: (204) 774-6468

**Ontario Assn. of Children's Aid  Societies**
Mary McConville, Exec. Director
75 Front Street East, 2nd Floor
Toronto, ON M5E 1V9
Phone: (416) 366-8115, Fax: (416) 366-8317

**Ontario Coalition for Better Child Care**
Kerry McCuaig, Exec. Director
500A Bloor Street West, 2nd Floor
Toronto, ON M5S 1Y8
Phone: (416) 538-0628, Fax: (416) 538-6737

**Quebec Council of Parent
Participation Pre-Schools**
Jedy Tuck, Co-ordonnatrice
20551, ch.Lakeshore
Baie d'Urfe, QC H9X 1R3
Phone: (514) 457-3291

**Saskatchewan Foster Families Assn.**
Pat Peters, Program Administrator
2347 Broad Street
Regina, SK S4P 1Y9
Phone: (306) 565-2880, Fax: (306) 347-8268

**Society for Emotional Development in
Children/La societe d'aide au developement
affectif de l'enfant**
S. John Diamond, President
1122, rue St-Catherine, ouest
Montreal, QC H3B 1H4
Phone: (514) 861-1527, Fax: (514) 935-7898

**Step-By-Step Child Development Society**
Juanita Hagman, Exec. Director
508 Clarke Road, Suite 101F
Coquitlam, BC V3J 3X2
Phone: (604) 939-7436, Fax: (604) 939-2997

**Wayne Holbrook**

OneWorldOnline.com is much more than just an innovative company. It is a powerful, timely concept dedicated to empowering individuals with an unparalleled business opportunity for long-term success. Founded in 1998, OneWorldOnline.com has worked to harness the power of Internet technology to create a global community that will revolutionize commerce through the collective power of individuals such as yourself.

OneWorldOnline.com is the answer the world has been waiting for; it's the future in a new light! A full solution e-commerce company dedicated to providing a vast array of value driven Internet products to develop your new business or enhance an existing one. OneWorldOnline.com, a publicly traded company, has assembled and committed the necessary resources to create one of the world's finest management and technology teams. Through the creation of full solution e-commerce web sites, customized to specific industries, we allow professionals and individuals to compete with and gain market share in an ever-growing competitive world, at a fraction of the cost.

Through the use of cutting-edge technological advances, OneWorldOnline.com offers its members hundreds, if not thousands, of life enhancing opportunities, from the convenience of shopping online for products and services, to accessing cultural, and educational sites exclusive to OneWorldOnline.com.

OneWorldOnline.com is successfully launching the type of global community that will lead us into the 21st century. Just imagine a worldwide community where you can access an exclusive:

* **Shopping Network** with thousands of name-brand and proprietary products * **Virtual Library** with hundreds of titles from the classics. * **Video Arcade** with the latest electronic games for the entire family * **Discount Travel Agency** offering discounted fares and group pricing on air travel, hotels, cruises, car rentals and packaged tours * **Online Banking** offering its members a full-range of services from car loans to mortgages, as well as checking and saving accounts and credit cards * **Personal Reminder Service** to ensure that no important occasion is ever missed again, whether a school play or an anniversary, or an early morning meeting in Cleveland * **One World Online Internet Radio Channel** * **Online Auction** to help you stretch your dollar while buying that special item you've been looking for * **Online Horoscopes** * **Online Movie Reviews** * **Online Classifieds** bringing buyers and sellers together instantly around the globe * **One World Online News Room** * **Chat Rooms** in which to meet your OneWorldOnline.com neighbors * **OneWorldOnline.com Internet Service Provider** for home or business * **And much, much more........**

The Internet business revolution that the world has been talking about for years is finally here. For the first time ever, OneWorldOnline.com makes it possible for anyone--even those who have just recently been introduced to the Internet to become successful entrepreneurs in the multi-billion dollar world of electronic commerce (e-commerce).

E-commerce buying and selling products and services over the Internet is projected to reach over $100 billion in 1999 and more than double to $250 billion in 2005. Microsoft, IBM, AT&T, Apple, Intel, Netscape and dozens of other corporate giants are currently laying the groundwork and jockeying for position to get their share of this exciting new marketplace. How can you get yours? Simply join the OneWorldOnline.com community as a member and find out more about the world of e-commerce.

**For further information about OneWorld's home-based business opportunities, write: 4778 North 300 West, Suite 200, Provo, UT 84604, or call (801) 852-3540**

# Rainforest Bio-Energetics

**Enjoy the Abundant Health and Financial Freedom You Dream of While Saving the Rainforest**

**Unique Proprietary Products.** Rainforest Bio-Energetics® is the source of these healthful botanical herbs from the Amazon Rainforest. The products work. You'll never have to worry about "me too" competition. Founder and President, John Easterling, began his relationship with the Rainforest and the indigenous people more than 21 years ago. Nutrient rich plants are wildcrafted, collected and graded in the Rainforest. These formulas are not available anywhere else. A 4,000 acre company-owned natural reserve is maintained in the Amazon Basin.

**"Cookie Cutter" Recruiting Tools.** The company supports you with powerful tools and a step-by-step program that is tested and proven. Our magalog, sales letters, ads, audio and video tapes, card decks and Internet pages are unequaled in the industry. All materials are prepared under the direction of legendary marketing genius, Ted Nicholas.

**Established and Solid Parent Company.** Rainforest Bio-Energetics® has been in business for more than nine years. Most network marketing companies fail during the critical first five years.

**Award Winning Company.** Rainforest Bio-Energetics® has been selected by *MLM Insider/Network Marketing Today* as "One of the 12 Best Companies in MLM" from over 3,000 companies examined.

**Growth Industry.** Become part of one of the world's fastest growing industries currently enjoying sales of $11 billion dollars annually, and growing by $1.5 billion a year. The time is now for herbal health solutions. And more people than ever want to own their own business.

**Easy-to-Understand Profit Plan.** You don't need to be a math whiz to understand our lucrative compensation program, Earn Immediate income and lifetime residual income. Our plan goes 5 levels deep plus Infinity Bonuses, Weekly Quick Start! Bonuses, profit sharing and Rainforest trips.

**Well Managed Organization.** The company's officers, directors and management have vast experience and a proven track record of success.

**No Experience Necessary.** You will be taught everything you need to know to be successful. The ongoing leadership program includes a training manual and other printed materials, the Rainforest newsletter, seminars and company gatherings featuring the best trainers in the field.

**Doctors' Endorsements.** For the first three years of Rainforest Bio-Energetics® existence, its herbal products were made available only through doctors. These physicians are from countries throughout the world.

**Direct Public Stock Offering.** Associates may purchase shares in the company's stock offering directly from the company, commission free. This is another way associates can profit from our growth.

**Enjoy Better Health.** And help improve the health of others. Nothing is more rewarding and satisfying.

**Help Save the Rainforest.** The Amazon Rainforest is a rapidly vanishing global resource. Widely known as the "lungs of our planet," we must save it for ourselves, our children and our grandchildren--all of mankind. Every time you purchase or move a bottle of product in commerce, you are helping. A full 10% of the company's profit goes back into the Rainforest and to the indigenous people.

Rainforest Bio-Energetics® is about people. It's about health. It's about financial opportunity. Its about fun. It's about saving the Rainforest. It's about time!

I urge you to take the first step toward an abundant, healthy life. I'm certain you'll be glad you did.

**Rainforest Bio-Energetics, 1002 Jupiter Park Lane, Jupiter, FL 33458**
**Phone: (800) 835-0850, Fax: (561) 575-7935, Web site: www.rainforestbio.com**

# ADVERTISING INDEX

| | |
|---|---|
| Achieve Your Dreams | 87 |
| Amway Corporation | VII, 49, 91,149,161 |
| Australasia Corporation | 77 |
| BeautiControl Cosmetics | V, 117 |
| Essentially Yours | 83, 245 |
| Eventus International | III, 101 |
| FreeLife International | 177 |
| Global Partners | 35, 133 |
| Home Business Journal | 65 |
| IDEA Concepts | 11, 69 |
| Integris International | 61, Inside Front Cover |
| Internet Mall | 1, 2 |
| IV Group, Inc., The | 157, 377 |
| Leading Minds International | 25, 123 |
| LeadMaster Corporation | 213 |
| Mannatech | 193 |
| Market Wave, Inc. | 141 |
| Matol Botanical International, Ltd. | 3, 105,145, 163, Inside Back Cover |
| Moss & Phillips | 243 |
| Network Action Company | 95, 114, 115, 116 |
| New Image International | XI, 23, 59, 103 |
| One World Online.com | 167 |
| Oxyfresh | IX |
| Personal Prosperity Hawaii, Inc. | 135, 195, 199 |
| Peter McGugan Productions | 165 |
| Pre-Paid Legal Services | 102, 103 |
| PRICE NET U.S.A. Inc . | 113 |
| Ransom Hill Press | 19 |
| Signature Media Services | 201, 221 |
| Startouch International | 171 |
| Sunrider International | 127 |
| Universal Sports Direct | 233 |
| VHS Direct | 41, 137, 155 |
| Watkins, Inc. | 121 |

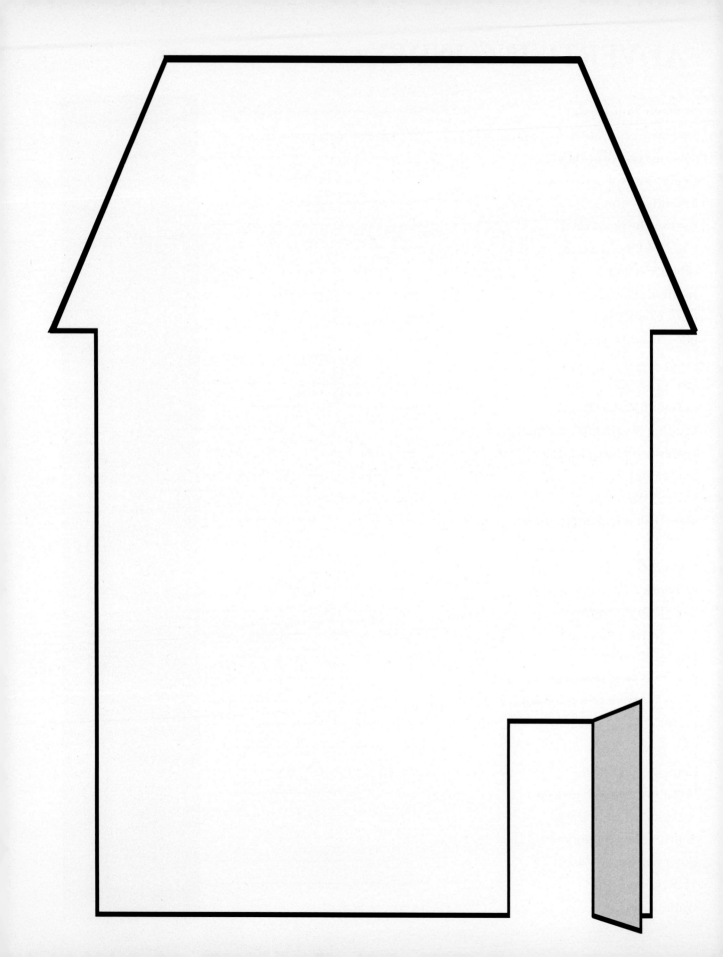